Most Comprehensive Origins of Clic

ISBN **978-1-935786-41-2**

Printed in the United States of America

St. Clair Publications
P. O. Box 726
Mc Minnville, TN 37111-0726

http://stclairpublications.com

MOST COMPREHENSIVE ORIGINS OF CLICHÉS, PROVERBS AND FIGURATIVE EXPRESSIONS

CLICHÉS , OLD SAYINGS, PROVERBS, IDIOMS, AXIOMS, SIMILES, METAPHORIC EXPRESSIONS, COMMON SHORT RHYMES, CATCH PHRASES AND CURIOUS WORDS IN THE ENGLISH LANGUAGE

WITH DEFINITIONS AND EARLY CITATIONS

Stanley J. St. Clair

Edited by S. John St. Clair

StCP

Cover Design

Kent Grey-Hesselbein Design Studio
www.kghdesignstudio.com

the dictionary of
Vulgar Tongue
Francis Gross

Author's Introduction

When I first released this Original Volume of *Most Comprehensive Origins of Cliches, Proverbs and Figurative Expressions*, I felt that it was my '*final effort* at producing a work containing the majority of the common figurative English phrases in use within my lifetime—both those of previous volumes, many of which have been revised and improved and hundreds more.' In fact, these were the very words in the introduction prior to this last revision in October 2018.

When I had began researching for my original cliché origin books, meant to be humorous, I discovered that much of the information already in print, even by major publishers, and even more so online, is incomplete, often undocumented, or in some cases, *inaccurate*. Also, none of the major publications carry detailed early citations, as I have included herein.

In combing through ancient works of this type, novels, and periodicals, as well as modern volumes of etymology and phrase origins and definitions, I have found more than ever, that every tongue on earth is ever-evolving, and that we often take for granted the words and expressions that have become as natural to us and the breath we breathe.

As this Original Volume became more popular, I realized that it contained only a fraction of the expressions that are in our vocabulary, and thus, my work continued, and a second volume was published, now a third and truly last volume is being released in November 2018. This is being followed by an index book to tie the series together.

In this massive work I am not only including the time-worn sayings and clichés which we have so freely inserted into our vocabularies over the past several decades in America, the U.K. (a few are decidedly British), Australia and other countries where English is spoken in a fair capacity, but I am utilizing more fresh phrases which are coming of age as I am typing these words. Another innovative feature is a proverb which I am introducing to 'test the waters.' I am coining it and you will have to read the book to discover it.

Since my mother was a school teacher once included in '*Who's Who in North Carolina Education*' who would remove printed works from the shelves and systematically edit the typos as she read, writing and editing just came to be engrained into my makeup. When I gave up art (something which I dearly love, and for which I received early recognition) as 'not my strongest talent,' I adopted writing and have found its pursuit irresistible. Words have become my paint and the computer, my brush. It is my fondest hope that this book will become a standard-bearer for future authoritative reference. It includes clichés, old sayings, metaphoric idioms, axioms, proverbs, similes, curious words, and a few common short rhymes and acronyms. The smaller type, wider margins, and enlarged pages as well as the removal of personal references, condensing some earlier entries and omitting illustrations, enabled me to cram much more into this one. Since my degree is in Religious Education, rather than English, I have expended many thousands of hours in self-education and research. While coming to understand etymology and practical lexicography as they apply to expressions in order to be effective and knowledgeable in this realm, I have strayed to the extent of being more in-depth in the explanations than an average dictionary. It has been my objective to always burst myths about phrase origins when applicable. Even with all of this massive effort, which has literally taken years, there is no possible way to include all English phrases in any single volume.

This volume was first revised in March 2014 by reformatting and adding seventy-five plus additional or totally rewritten phrases which I considered important to our modern culture, and briefly shortened a few of the original entries, thereby increasing the text insignificantly. New entries are identified with an asterisk (*). Rewritten enhancements are indicated by two asterisks (**).

In March 2015 I did a bit more formatting, adding an additional twenty-three entries noted with three asterisks (***), while making other minor changes.

More revisions were made in 2018, and the present revision in 2020. I have added no new entries since 2015, but have enhanced many of the originals, and made it more congruent. I added new information which later became available on certain entries in later volumes. The index book has also been revised to reflect the 2020 changes.

Note: quotations from books, periodicals, etc. herein are printed as in the original document; spelling and punctuations will reflect the period, country of publication, and authors' misspellings when applicable.

Definitions

Acronym – a word formed from the initial letters or groups of letters of words in a set phrase or series of words

Aphorism - a tersely phrased statement of a truth or opinion; an adage

Axiom – a self-evident truth that requires no proof

Cliché - a trite, stereotyped expression; a sentence or a phrase usually expressing a popular or common thought or idea that has lost originality, ingenuity and impact by long overuse

Corruptive derivative - This is a newly coined phrase in this book (obviously not the 'proverb' mentioned in the introduction) which is a combination of corruption and derivative. A corruption of a word is a misspelling or change which later becomes an accepted word. A derivative is a new word or phrase derived from the same original base word, often from another language. Therefore, a corruptive derivative, as used in this book, is a newly formed phrase based on previously accepted words which, though deemed incorrect, became an accepted expression.

Curious words and catch-phrases – expressions which are often used, whether as a single word or a phrase, which seem strange as to their exact origin or meaning and need clarification

Earliest known citation– as used herein means earliest dated printed reference found during extensive research for this dictionary.

Etymology – the derivation of a word

Idiom - an expression, the meaning of which is not predictable from the usual definitions of its constituent elements or from the general grammatical rules of a language, and that is not a constituent of a larger expression of like characteristics

Metaphoric phrase – a cliché or expression which applies in a broader sense to a comparison or resemblance of a literal image to a figurative one; an idiom

Metonymic adage – aka 'metonymy' is a figure of speech used in rhetoric in which a thing or concept is not called by its own name, but by the name of something intimately associated with that thing or concept.

Practical Lexicography - the craft of compiling dictionaries

Proverb - a short popular saying, usually of unknown and ancient origin, that expresses effectively some commonplace truth or useful thought; adage

Simile – A figure of speech in which two unlike things are explicitly compared

Old saying – a phrase of obscure origin which has become a part of popular jargon

A

Above and beyond the call of duty***

This expression was coined to refer to public servants such as police officers, firefighters, and soldiers. It means that a person has done a lot more than expected and preformed acts of heroism or bravery in the effort to save lives or serve his or her fellow man in such a great way to be worthy of special recognition.

The earliest verifiable citation of the phrase is in the *Calendar of the Royal College of Surgeons of England*, 1874:

> "In order that the Medal of Honor may be awarded, officers or enlisted men must perform in action deeds of most distinguished personal bravery or self-sacrifice ***above and beyond the call of duty*** so conspicuous as clearly to distinguish them..."

Absence makes the heart grow fonder

The heart of this proverb has been present in culture since the days of the Roman Empire near the turn of the last age. The poet Sextus Propertius gave the world the earliest form of this saying in his work, *Elegies*. Properly translated to modern English, it read:

> "Always toward absent lovers love's tide stronger flows."

The Pocket Magazine of Classics and Polite Literature, in 1832, printed a contemporary version attributed to a Miss Strickland.

> "'Tis **absence**, however, that **makes the heart grow fonder**."

The proverb can be deemed to mean that the lack of anything can make the desire for it grow more intense.

Accidents will happen

This simple proverb has been with us since the mid-19th century. The first known citation is in John Muller's *A treatise containing the practical part of fortification*, published in 1755:

> "But, notwithstanding all human precautions that can be taken, yet **accidents will happen**."

In today's vernacular it has been largely replaced by a vulgar saying, 'S**t happens.' It meant that in spite of the best efforts of mankind to prevent unexpected disasters, many are sure to occur.

The most well-known version of this thought was sent down to us by beloved British novelist, Charles Dickens, in *The personal history of David Copperfield* in 1850.

> "'My dear friend Copperfield' said Mr. Micawber, '**accidents will occur** in the best-regulated families; and in families not regulated by that pervading influence which sanctifies while it enhances the - a - I would say, in short, by the influence of Woman, in the lofty character of Wife, they may be expected with confidence, and must be borne with philosophy.'"

Robert Burns and later John Steinbeck capitalized on the idea with the line, 'The best laid plans of mice and men often go awry' (see).

accident waiting to happen, An

This idiom has been around a lot longer than Billy Brag's song by this title from his Folk Album, *Don't Try This at Home*. Since the 1970s, in a literal sense it is meant to draw attention to something that needs to be repaired, removed or replaced before a serious tragedy occurs unnecessarily. In a figurative sense, it applies to persons who are certain to cause trouble and need to change their tactics before someone gets hurt, especially emotionally. Related phrases are 'a disaster waiting to happen' and 'a time bomb waiting to go off.'

Achilles heel

This idiom means a weak or vulnerable spot or a disadvantage of which others may be unaware.

It is derived from Achilles, the hero of Homer's *Iliad*, who was the son of King Peleus, and the sea goddess, Thetis, who was the great-grandson of the Greek god, Zeus. Because his mother had dipped him in the river Styx as a baby, Achilles was fearless as a warrior in battle, thus thought to be invincible. However, according to the story, she had held him by the heel, failing to get it wet. The heel, consequently, was a vulnerable spot. Apollo learned of this secret and whispered it to Paris, who deliberately shot an arrow into his heel, killing him.

Acid test

Even before the beginning of the California gold rush, prospectors and dealers alike needed a sure way to distinguish pyrite and base metal from the genuine article. A test was developed, originally in the late 18th century, with only nitric acid which was able to dissolve other metals more redily than gold. Later acid tests used a mixture of nitric and hydrochloric acids.

Standing or passing the acid test quickly came to mean holding up under extreme conditions. The earliest known citation of a figurative use of this phrase is from the Wisconsin paper *The Columbia Reporter*, November, 1845:

"Twenty-four years of service demonstrates his ability to stand the **acid test**, as Gibson's Soap Polish has done for over thirty years."

In the 1960s hippy community, the 'acid test' in a punned context determined whether LSD users could cope with the psychological demands of taking the drug. This is cited in Maurer and Vogel's *Narcotics and Narcotic Addiction*, 1967:

"A common phrase amongst users is 'can you pass the **acid test**?'"

Across the board

Early examples of this phrase include ones related to the playing of card games, but in the context of the cliché, it was used to mean 'encompassing all aspects,' and early on referred to 'across the board wagers' marked up by bookmakers on odds in horse races. It was when equal amounts were bet on the same contestant to win, place or show in a particular event.

It seems to have been coined in America, the earliest example being from *The Atlanta Constitution*, in November 1901:

"Cousin Jess won the steeplechase after a hard drive in the stretch, lowering the best previous time of 4-09 by seven seconds. Dr. Einus in the fourth race, a 100 to 1 shot, heavily played **across the board**, ran second."

Across the board now means including all classes or categories in any prospective.

Across the pond

From evidence at hand, this common expression was coined during or just after World War I by the U.S. Military, and refers either to the U.K. or Europe, the U.S. or Canada, depending upon which side the speaker is on, as 'the pond' is a nickname for the North Atlantic Ocean. The earliest known references in print are from 1919. *One in Twelfth U.S. Infantry*, 1798—1919:

"Outside of a few cases of 'flu' the men of the Regiment arrived at Camp Mills in good shape and had soon forgotten their experiences of the past eight days, looking forward to the preparation for and the big trip **across the pond**."

Another that year is from *Alabama's Own in France* by William Henry Amerine. Chapter Ten is titled: ***Across "the Pond" at Last***.

As an idiom, it did not gain popularity, however, until the 1970s. One early example is from *Outlaws of America: The Underground Press and its Content*, 1972, by Roger Lewis:

"Across the Pond

"The Alternative Press in Britain

"Although American papers have had a marked influence upon their British counterparts, the differences between them are quite distinct."

Actions speak louder than words

The meaning is very overt. What people actually do gives more credence to their true intent than the words they mouth. In this form, it originated in the United States and has been around for many decades. The basis has been with humanity much longer.

The 16th-century French writer, Michel de Montaigne, who is generally credited with inventing the essay, stated, "Saying is one thing, doing is another."

Even before this, St. Francis of Assisi, who embodied this principle, is credited with saying, "Preach the gospel at all times. Use words if necessary."

Add(s) fuel to the fire*** (See: Fan the flames)

Add insult to injury

This cliché is ancient. The Roman Phaedrus, (some of his work credited to Aesop) who lived in the time of Christ (15 B.C. – 50 A.D.), wrote a fable about a bald man and a fly. The fly bit the head of the bald man, who tried to kill it with a heavy blow. The fly then said in a sneering tone, "You want to avenge an insect's sting with death; what will you do to yourself, who have **added insult to injury**?" It was first recorded in English in 1748.

Adding insult to injury is making an already bad situation even worse.

Against all odds

This positive affirmation idiom has been around since at least the 19th century. It was the title of a book by F.W. Currey printed as a serial in *The Dublin University Magazine* in 1875 and 1876.

Since the late 1960s it has been in the titles of hundreds of books, articles, a movie in 1984, starring Jeff Bridges and Rachael Ward, Columbia Pictures and a soundtrack song by Phil Collins. It has also been used by many authors, and means that success may be achieved in spite of adversity when believed so.

Age before beauty

When wishing to flatter young ladies, gentlemen have utilized this phrase over the last two-plus centuries, though sometimes in jest. It is uncertain who coined it, but it was in use in the Victorian era, as is evidenced by its inclusion in an article in the Illinois newspaper, the *Decatur Republican,* in 1869.

Later it was recorded as a supposed quote from playwright / politician Claire Boothe Brokow, then with *Vanity Fair*, later known as Claire Boothe Luce. She reportedly said it somewhat sarcastically to legendary New York writer Dorothy Parker while holding a door open for her in a hotel lobby in the 1930s. Parker snapped back. Luce later denied it, but Parker, it seems, stuck to it. A London periodical gave the story on September 16, 1938 not mentioning Luce by name.

13

On October 14th the same year, the *Hartford Courant* printed the following in the celebrity gossip column of Sheilah Graham:

> *Dorothy Parker tells me of the last time she encountered Playwright Clare Boothe. The two ladies were trying to get out of a doorway at the same time. Clare drew back and cracked, "**Age before beauty**, Miss Parker." As Dotty swept out, she turned to the other guests and said. "Pearls before swine."*

Though it originated in England, this incident greatly helped to popularize it.

Air one's dirty laundry (in public)*

This old idiom means to reveal someone's scandalous and embarrassing secrets. It is sometimes attributed to Napoleon. In French it is *Il faut laver son linge sale en famille.* The translation refers to airing it in public. Napoleon, however, used a reverse version of the expression in a more restricted setting regarding one's family. "One needs to wash one's dirty laundry with family around."

The earliest verifiable printed example of a form of this metaphor in English is found in *The African Abroad* by William Henry Ferris, 1913, on page 396, regarding attempts by some to discredit Booker T. Washington:

> "He likes to discover and reveal defects in his leaders. He likes to wash **his dirty linen** and **air his** petty grievances in public."

All dressed up with no place to go

This common saying has a variety of meanings, all somewhat connected. It can infer that a person is working hard, but has no plan or goal. It can also mean that someone is expecting something to happen that just isn't going to materialize. Or, it could, and does mean in certain cases, something a bit more literal: a person looks good, but doesn't have anywhere to show off his or her new clothes, etc.

The phrase was coined in America, and has been around for many years. It was popular in the 1960s and '70s and is still used today.

All hell broke loose*

This figure of speech means a mêlée erupted as a result of a tense situation. The term, per se, developed under Christianity, but has its roots in pre-Christian

14

Anglo-Nordic religion, in which the word hell derived from the goddess, Hel, who ruled over the underworld, or hell. The word is linguistically consistent in all Germanic languages including Gothic. Angol-Nordic mythology speaks of hell breaking open as a part of Ragnarok, the apocalypse of the gods and the reshaping of the world. Christianity added the idea of demons, but did not originate it. In both Greek and Anglo-Nordic mythology, hell literally broke up and its contents poured onto the earth, causing chaos and devastation.

John Dryden (1631-1700) used what may have been the premier figurative citation in *Dramatic Works,* written about 1672:

"Verily, I think **all Hell's broke loose** among you."

All in the same boat

A 1944 World War II movie, *Lifeboat,* starring Tallulah Bankhead, contained this phrase, but is not its origin. This phrase has been around since the age of Ancient Greece, and has been used figuratively for centuries.

In 1862, Artemus Ward also used this in *The Draft in Baldwinsville.*

"We are **all in the same boat.**"

It means that when we realize someone else is in the same circumstances as we, the best alternative is cooperation on reaching a solution to the common challenges.

All one can say grace over*

This old folksy Americanism was first found printed in *Folk Sayings from Indiana* by Paul Brewster of the University of Missouri, included in *American Speech*, December, 1939 published by Duke University Press.

"**All I can say Grace over**—All I can find the time for."

All over the map***

This modern cliché refers to a person's being unclear in his or her thinking and scattered in beliefs or going off on tangents. A great example is from *A Call to Account* by Chris Hajek, 2003, Dundurn Press, Canada, page 223:

"It's *all over the map*. It makes no sense. There's no coherence to it."

All roads lead to Rome

The ancient system of highways in Rome radiated like spokes from the center of the city. Hence, all roads literally led to Rome in the surrounding area. By the 12th century this saying was already being used.

In time it has figuratively come to mean that there are many ways to reach the same outcome or destination. It is like 'there is more than one way to skin a cat' (see).

All's fair in love and war

This cliché means just what it implies—that love and war are the only two instances in which standard rules of fair play do not apply. It is used as leverage when someone is so much at odds with another person as to lose all sense of care about how their differences are to be resolved.

The origin of this saying goes back to Renaissance English poet and playwright John Lyly's popular book, *Euphues the Anatomy of Wit* (1578). The actual quote was, "The rules of **fair** play do not apply **in love and war**."

All sizzle and no steak

The clear meaning of this and other such proverbial phrases is that anyone can talk the talk, but to prove oneself one must walk the walk. How about 'put your money where your mouth is'? (See) Similar sayings also include 'all bark and no bite,' 'all foam and no beer,' 'all smoke and no fire,' 'all icing and no cake' and 'all talk and no cider' (see) or action. This one became popular in the late-20th century. One example is from a 1999 article in the *International Journal of Nonprofit and Voluntary Sector Marketing,* Volume 4, Issue 2. It was called "Nonprofit community increasing nervousness about Year 2000," by Gary M. Grobman, and downplayed the likely effect of 'the Y2K bug.'

> "Y2K may be the equivalent of the Kohotek comet—**all sizzle and no steak**."

Grobman, it turned out, was correct.

All's well that ends well

Many likely believe that the Shakespearian play by this title was the origin of this well-known cliché, but not so. Another of our favorites from John Heywood, who included it in *A dialogue conteinyng the nomber in effect of all the prouerbes in the Englishe tongue*, in 1546:

> "Lovers live by love, ye as larkes live by leekes
> Saied this Ales, muche more then halfe in mockage.
> Tushe (quoth mine aunte) these lovers in dotage
> Thinke the ground beare them not, but wed of corage
> They must in all haste, though a leafe of borage
> Might by all the substance that they can fell.
> Well aunt (quoth Ales) **all is well that endes well**."

Shakespeare was well acquainted with Heywood's work and wrote *All's Well That Ends Well* less than 50 years later, in 1601. It's not only used as the title of the play, but line also appears in the text.

> **"All's well that ends well**; still the fine's the crown;
> Whate'er the course, the end is the renown."

All talk and no cider

Also, 'all talk and no action' means about the same as 'much ado about nothing.' This colloquial Americanism dates from the turn of the 19th century. There is a popular story explaining its origin about a party supposedly organized for the purpose of sharing a barrel of superior cider.

Apparently when the subject of politics was introduced and talked about, it supplanted pleasure and drinking as the focal point of the party. Disappointed guests left the gathering mumbling, "**All talk and no cider**."

It has been around since before 1891 when it was listed on page 114 in *Slang and its Analogues Past and Present, Volume II* by John Stephen Farmer and William Ernest Henley.

Whatever the origin, this and similar clichés have been utilized for centuries around the world to express disdain over those who loquaciously make empty promises and leave responsibility to others sitting on the sidelines while polishing their own egos.

All that glitters is not gold

The Merchant of Venice is the origin. The original was actually 'glisters' rather than glitters, but the rest was intact as penned by Shakespeare in 1586. The reference reads:

> **"All that glitters is not gold**;
> Often have you heard that told:"

This has come to symbolize the constant struggle of humanity to seek for prosperity, and in so doing, often 'grab at straws' (see) which appear to be ways to 'get rich quick.' Just because something looks good doesn't mean that it is—usually it is quite the opposite.

All the bells and whistles

This term means a top of the line product with the full complement of accessories. The phrase was used in a literal sense as early as the 18th century, particularly in regard to warnings or promotional events. It began to be used figuratively during the 1960s. The earliest known *verifiable* reference is in an ad for a car in a Madison, Wisconsin newspaper, *The Capitol Times* in June, 1971 for a car:

> "'69 Riviera: One owner and driven very few miles, with **all the bells and whistles**, $3695"

Examples soon began to be in use for all sorts of products, including computers. There is no definitive reason why this term evolved to mean what it does, however many feel that it may have been inspired by a fairground calliope or theater organ. Just as likely, it could have been the locomotive with its steam whistle and bells, which was used as an example in the decades before the phrase began to be cited in a metaphoric sense. The following is from *Fifteen Decisive Events in California History,* by Rockwell Dennis Hunt, page 50, 1959:

> "Sacramento had ample reason to celebrate. Thirty assembled locomotives led the grand choir composed of **all the bells and whistles** of the city in what was described as 'one prolonged demonstration of joy.'"

All the buzz

This cliché originated in the late 20th century in America, and means 'excitement' or 'trend.' Something causing a 'buzz' is getting a lot of attention from the masses of people or in a given locale.

18

All the rage

The word 'rage' originated in Middle English (1250-1300) and is from the late Latin, *rabia*, a form of the earlier *rabiēs* meaning madness from which we get the name of the disease for which dogs are vaccinated. But in this common idiom, it means something quite dissimilar: wildly popular or the latest style, implying that it may be a passing fad. 'Rage' here expresses a passion. Today, though, this phrase is still in use, 'the thing' might resonate this meaning more commonly among the younger generation.

The phrase was used in a literal sense by Homer in *The Iliad* (circa 8th century B.C. as translated by Pope between 1715 and 1720) in Book XXII:

"While cast to **all the rage** of hostile power."

The root of the current figurative meaning was introduced in a 1795 comedy play, performed at the Theater Royal, Covent Garden in London written by Frederick Reynolds titled *The Rage*. The first lines of the Prologue were as follows:

"E'en the last pulse of ebbing life be o're,
When the eye turns towards his native shore,
This thought be ev'n the parting pang assuage
That there—Humanity is still ***The Rage.***"

Sometimes the word rave is incorrectly substituted for rage. The term gained much popularity from the 1920s to the 1960s.

All things come to he who waits

Like 'all that glitters in not gold,' this proverb is also very old, and may be a takeoff on a biblical verse from *Isaiah 40:31*.

"But they that wait upon the Lord shall renew their strength…"

Though she did not likely originate the saying, it was used by Violet Fane (1843-1905) in her poem *Tout vient a qui sait attendre.*

"'Ah, **all things come to those who wait**,'
(I say these words to make me glad),
But something answers soft and sad,
'They come, but often come too late.'"

All tied up in knots, tie the knot

The first one is akin to 'butterflies in my stomach' (see). A knot, in this sense, is defined as any cluster or small group of things, and when people get 'bumfuzzled' (see) about a situation their gastric juices get jumbled in their stomach and they can become physically ill.

Though these are different clichés they are listed together because of the use of 'knot,' and the fact that there could be some connection. The word knot itself is from the Middle English from the Old English cnotte, and *The Legend of St. Katherine*, circa 1225, used the Middle English word 'cnotte' to mean the tie of the bond of wedlock.

"Swa ye cnotte is icnut bituhhen unc tweien."

It's hardly recognizable as English, as it seems a bit Scandinavian to Germanic. Now marriage gets a lot of folks all 'in a tizzy' (see). But the meaning stuck and it continued to be used in various books through the ages.

Francis Grose, in *The Dictionary of the Vulgar Tongue,* 1811, which enjoyed several editions, and today is foreign to our way of thinking on most terms, listed the 'knot tied with the tongue' referring to marriage.

"He has **tied a knot** with his tongue, that he cannot untie with his teeth: i.e. he is married."

All tied up in knots came to mean nervous and irritable. A variation is also included herein under 'don't get your panties in a wad (or knickers in a knot).'

All work and no play made Jack a dull boy*

This is a very old proverb pointing to the fact that everyone needs time for recreation, no matter how important his or her position may be. It was first printed in James Howell's *Proverbs* in 1659.

All your eggs in one basket

There is some debate among researchers as to which came first with this saying, Mark Twain, or Andrew Carnegie. The two were certainly contemporaries. Twain seems likely, who used it in 1894 in *Pudd'nhead Wilson's Calendar,* in chapter fifteen:

"Put **all your eggs in the one basket** and—watch that basket."

Carnegie used the phrase in an essay titled, *How to Succeed at Life,* but this was from *The Pittsburg Bulletin,* 19 December 1903, and printed by *The New York Tribune* even later. In the biography *Andrew Carnegie* by Joseph Frazier Wall (University of Pittsburg Press, 1989, page 197), he stated that the phrase was 'later borrowed by Twain.' There seems to be no evidence that Carnegie said it first.

Almighty dollar

This popular expression for the American unit of currency originated in Washington Irving's *The Creole Village.* The sketch was first published in the November, 1836 issue of *Knickerbocker Magazine.* It then appeared in 1855 as part of *Wolfer's Roost and Other Papers,* and was based on Irving's memories of a steamboat voyage which he had taken in Louisiana. Apparently impressed by the small, isolated riverbank communities, he wrote: "The **almighty dollar,** that great object of universal devotion throughout our land, seems to have no genuine devotees in these peculiar villages; and unless some of its missionaries penetrate there, and erect banking houses and other pious shrines, there is no knowing how long the inhabitants may remain in their present state of contented poverty."

Almost nearly, but not quite hardly*

Though these words could be broken down and picked apart, this redundant, comical saying is simply for emphasis on something which may be thought to be true or perfect, but in reality comes up short of expectations. It is used primarily in rural America, and caught on in Southern Appalachia. Though it may have been around earlier, this exact phraseology does not seem to appear in print before 1984 when Bill Nunn utilized it in his self-help *Column Book,* on page 109, regarding an I.Q of "149-almost-genius."

A clear, verifiable example was cited by Pete Stamper on page 159 in *It All Happened in Renfro Valley* in 1999:

"Buck was a fine vocalist who had **almost nearly, but not quite hardly,** made it as a recording artist a couple of times before coming to the Valley."

Renfro Valley, on I-75 in the Daniel Boone National Forrest in Kentucky, is widely known for its Country Blue Grass music, comedy and Barn Dance show, begun in the 1930s.

Always a bridesmaid, never a bride

This phrase—meaning often a candidate for something, but never selected—goes back to the 19th century. *Godey's Lady's Book and Magazine*, February, 1871 had what appears to be the first variant reference:

"Three times a bridesmaid, never a bride."

It then appeared in Ellen M. Ingraham's *Bond and Free: A Tale of the South,* 1882, this way:

"Always a maiden, never a wife."

Here 'maiden' meant 'bridal attendant.'

Am I my brother's keeper?

This well-used cliché is from the *Bible, Genesis 4:9, KJV*. When Cain killed his brother Abel, God asked him where his brother was. He replied flippantly, **"Am I my brother's keeper?"**

This came to be used as a denial of responsibility for anyone other than the person speaking, and often is reversed to express the need for all people to feel a call for the protection of our fellow man.

Anger is only one letter short of danger

This axiom is a quote sometimes attributed to former first lady Eleanor Roosevelt. Actually, it is from author Elliott Larson, but he may not have been the first to say it. Anger is our mind's way of reacting to perceived wrongs. However, what can be good, can also be very destructive. Anger is such a problem for some people that anger management classes have become a viable way to control it.

Another day, another dollar

The most likely genesis of this cliché is that it originated from the days when sailors were paid by the day. The average pay in the late 19th century was about a dollar a day in the U.S. Later it was used in a figurative sense by the working class to stress the need to work every day in order 'to make ends meet' (see).

This idea has caught on in the music industry. A popular country single by this title was written and recorded by Wynn Stewart in 1962 which was used in 2010 by Volkswagen in an ad for the Jetta. It starts out, and repeats throughout:

"**Another day another dollar** daylight comes I'm on my way;
"**Another day another dollar** workin' my whole life away."

Then, twenty years later, a British post-punk group, Gang of Four, recorded a song by this name released by Warner Brothers Records in 1982.

Ten years after that, another song by this title was released by Allison Krause. The chorus is:

"**Another day another dollar**,
That's what I'm working for today.
Another day another dollar,
Sure can't buy my blues away."

Ants in one's pants*

To have ants in one's pants means to be excessively jittery or anxious. It was coined by the 1930s. Some attribute it to U.S. Army General Hugh S. Johnson who headed the National Recovery Mission in 1933 to 1934. It is certain that he made it popular. The earliest verifiable printed citation is from the *Princeton Alumni Weekly*, May 19, 1939, where is appears in a joking fashion about an alumnus, Jack Plants, and his wife, Loranah St. Clair Plants on their twenty-fifth anniversary:

"It seems only yesterday we were going around the campus singing that old Chaucerian ballad— Rocky Plants' Got **Ants In His Pants**."

It was used by American humorist, H. Allen Smith in his book, *Life in a Putty Knife Factory*:

"She dilates her nostrils a lot, the way Valentino used to do it in the silent movies to indicate that he had **ants in his pants**."

The term antsy, popular in the 1960s likely derived from this saying.

Any job worth doing is worth doing well

A number of Internet sites attribute the coining of this proverb to Dave Vanderbeck of Yardville, New Jersey in 1850.

Actually, this is an old proverb dating back to at least the 18th century. The Earl of Chesterfield, in a letter to his son in October 1746 wrote the following:

> "Care and application are necessary… In truth, **whatever is worth doing at all is worth doing well**."
> [1746 Chesterfield *Letter* 9 Oct. (Published 1932) III. 783]

Since it is an axiom, the meaning is clear. Later it was used by other authors, including H.G. Wells in *Bealby* in 1915:

> "'**If a thing's worth doing at all**,' said the professor, '**it's worth doing well**.'"

Any port in a storm***

This very old metaphor means that when one is faced by a situation for which no desired solution is available, it is better to accept any help offered, and that any solution is better than nothing. It was derived from the fact that in olden days when ships sailed, storms came up unexpectedly and the captains would frantically search for any safe port in which to anchor the ship until the storm passed. It is said to have been used in this respect as early as the mid-18th century. By the 19th century it was being cited in a number of publications.

In 1821 the expression was used in the Waverly Novels, *Kenilworth the Pirate* by Sir Walter Raleigh.

> "'For,' said he, 'second thoughts ire best; and as this Scottishman's howf lies right under yonr lee, why, take *any port in a storm*.'"

As early as June 1855 it was called an "old proverb" in the *Knickerbacker* or *New York Monthly Magazine*

> "…but it so happened that about one o'clock at night, or rather morning, he brought up at my tent, and, acting upon the old proverb —- perhaps it is not a. proverb, only a saying —-of '*any port in a storm*,' he pitched in, without as much as saying, …"

Any way you slice it*

This American-coined idiomatic expression means 'in whatever manner you consider this,' or 'there's no other way to look at this.' This was derived from a previous saying, popularized by Carl Sandburg in *The People, Yes*, 1936. But it was not the original with him.

"No matter how thick or how thin **you slice it** it's still baloney."

We find the following in the magazine, *Game Breeder and Sportsman,* Volume 36:

> "Such, for instance, is the sage statement popularized by the American public within recent years, concerning the Bologna sausage: 'No matter how thin **you slice it**, it's still boloney!'"

Then in 1941, in *Public Utilities Fortnightly*, a closer version appeared:

> "We are in a war. **Slice it any way you** please and we are still in a war."

In 1945, *Hearst's International Combined with Cosmopolitan* published the present phrase:

> "Now, **any way you slice it**, the funeral director's profit comes from the sale of what the trade calls 'merchandise.' It is quite true that he is paid — as well he should be — for his skill and knowledge, his personal services, and the overhead..."

apple a day keeps the doctor away, An

Reference to this was initially found in a Welsh folk proverb."Eat an apple on going to bed, and you'll keep the doctor from eating his bread." The phrase was first coined as we know it in the U.S. in 1913 by Elizabeth Wright in *Rustic Speech and Folk-lore.*

> "Ait a happle avore gwain to bed, An' you'll make the doctor beg his bread; or as the more popular version runs: **An apple a day Keeps the doctor away**."

apple doesn't fall far from the tree, The

This is also used with 'acorn' rather than apple, but the meaning is the same: usually a notation to the fact that children frequently exhibit traits similar to those of their parents. Related clichés are, 'a chip off the old block' (see) and 'like father, like son.' There are a number of references which have been used for hundreds of years around the globe. Probably the earliest is from the 16th century German: *der Apfel fellt nicht gerne weit vom Baume.*

The American philosopher Ralph Waldo Emerson apparently was the first to use a form of it in English in a letter in 1839, when he wrote that 'the apple never falls far from the stem.' But here Emerson meant it in a different sense—to describe that tug on the heart strings, which often brings us back to our childhood home.

A century later, however, the saying appeared in its current form and connotation in *Body, Boots, and Britches* by H. W. Thompson.

Apple of one's eye

This idiom comes from the *Bible*. In *Psalm 17:8* the psalmist asks God 'keep me as **the apple of your eye**.' It means the center of thoughts; one to be loved and appreciated.

Arm candy*

This modern slang Americanism refers to a young attractive person who accompanies an older person to social events. The term came into usage in the 1990s. An early example, which serves to define it, is from Harold Stanley French's self-published book, *You Can Be a Hoot: To the Man Over 50, Over 60, Over 70*, 1999, page 246:

> "A wealthy man can obtain the services of '**arm candy**', a tall, gorgeous, slender, great looking model-type young woman to grace his arm at public functions where he is seen and, hopefully noticed and admired for his success..."

Armed to the teeth

This started as one of several phrases with 'to the teeth,' a version of 'up to here' (see) meaning completely, as in I've had it up to here. The first known citation of 'armed to the teeth' was in a speech in 1841 by British statesman, Richard Cobden, who, while talking on the national defense budget said, "Is there any reason why we should be **armed to the teeth**?"

As all get out*

Meaning, 'to an extreme degree,' this saying crept into American English slang in the 19th century, first used a bit differently in *Legends of a Log Cabin*, by Chandler Robbins Gilman, 1835, page 198:

"Squire and Ma'am wouldn't have no objections; but Sally wouldn't look at him in the courtin' line, and no wonder, the doctor was forty if he was a day, and about as good looking **as 'get out;'** any how, Sally would n't have nothin' to say to him."

This form may also be found in *Charcoal Sketches* by Joseph C. Neal in 1838:

"We look as elegant and beautiful **as get-out**."

Note: both had to do with a person's looks.

Then, in May 1864, *The Ladies' Repository* has what could be the first printed reference to the current phrase in an article by Mrs. Caroline Soule titled 'A Soldier of the Republic':

"If I'd come home and told her he was a captain. or colonel, or even first lieutenant, I'll bet she'd had a high old time over it; but because he's had sense enough to go into the ranks, she's huffy as — **as all get out;** and he slammed the front door after him."

As a man sows, so shall he reap

This is from the *Bible* in *Galatians 6:7*, "Be not deceived, God is not mocked, for whatsoever a man soweth, that shall he also reap." (*KJV*) It was passed down from the essence of *Proverbs 22:8*, "He who sows wickedness reaps trouble, and the rod of his fury will be destroyed," (*NIV*) and accented by a lesson taught by Jesus in *Matthew 13*, known as the parable of the sower.

The entire point being made is that whenever we treat others badly, it will 'come back to haunt us' (see), and when we ignore the basic laws, both natural and physical, we will suffer the consequences.

ASAP

Originally U.S. Army slang, this acronym came into use in about 1955 as a short form of 'as soon as possible.' It was intended to mean that what was being demanded of a soldier needed to be carried out without delay. A medical equivalent term would be 'stat,' a shortening of the Latin, *statim*, meaning immediately. Especially since the 1990s, it has been in common use by the masses. This term has been adapted by several organizations.

As a twig is bent, so grows the tree

We owe the receipt of this proverb to none other than Alexander Pope, who wrote in his exhaustive letter to the Right Honorable Richard Lord Viscount Cobham, titled *Epistle to Cobham* in 1734:

"'Tis education forms the common mind,
Just **as the twig is bent, the tree's inclined**."

The proverb came to mean that the way a person is reared and educated will determine his or her future.

As broke as a convict

Similes have been around for hundreds of years. 'Back in the day' (see) convicts often had no visitors and less money. When this was coined, likely in the late 19th to early 20th century, the biggest part of prisoners owned nothing but 'the clothes on their back.' To express deprivation, no other comparison could 'hit the nail on the head' (see) better than this one.

The word 'convict' is from the Latin, *convictus*, the past participle of *convincere*, from which we also get 'convince' and originated in Middle English between 1350 and 1400.

As cool as a cucumber

One of hundreds of English similes, this one dates back to the 18th century. It was first recorded in John Gay's *New Song on New Similes* in 1732:

"I...**cool as a cucumber** could see The rest of womanhood."

Here, cool means calm and collected rather than cool to the touch. If someone is 'cool as a cucumber' it means that they can face the most reprehensible situation without worrying if their deodorant will hold out.

As dry as a bone / dust / a powder house

All of these similes have been in use since at least the mid-20th century to express something totally void of moisture. A powder house, used to store gunpowder, of necessity was kept extremely moisture free to prevent making the powder useless (See 'keep your powder dry'). An article in a Texas publication, *The Frontier Times Magazine*, in May 1948, included the following line:

"The Attoyac and Angelina rivers were both **dry as a powder house**, and the thirsty cattle had made trails in the bed of the streams."

As dumb as (or dumber than) a box of rocks

This is a metaphorical colloquialism which came into Southern American culture in the early 1990s and gained popularity nationwide through the past twenty years. An early example is from *Westward!* by Dana Fuller Ross, 1992:

"You're **dumb as a box of rocks**," Peggy said, but she was talking to Lulie's back. The girl had already drifted off.

As easy as pie

This simile obviously isn't talking about baking a pie. It was coined in 19th century America, when it referred to the ease of eating a tasty pastry. The task was related to pleasant times when family was gathered for festive occasions. There are a number of examples, not all in the self-same phraseology. In fact, the first known printed reference is to a variant of this, 'nice as pie,' in 1855, in an article titled *Which, Right or Left?*

"For nearly a week afterwards, the domestics observed significantly to each other, that Miss Isabella was **as nice as pie**."

Mark Twain used pie in this sense several times in *The Adventures of Huckleberry Finn*, published in 1884. Here is one of those examples:

"You're always **as polite as pie** to them."

The earliest known printing of 'as easy as pie,' per se, appeared in the Rhode Island newspaper, *The Newport Mercury* in June 1887, in a comical story about two New Yorkers who were down on their luck.

"You see veuever I goes I take mit me a silverspoon or knife or some things an' I gets two or three dollars for them. It's **as easy as pie**. Vy don't you try it?"

As every school boy knows

This pre-notation is used as a put-down to someone whom the speaker (or writer) is implying should be aware of the facts being stated. It seems to have been in use earlier, but was popularized by and is often accredited to Lord Thomas Babington Macaulay, who wrote in his essay *On Lord Clive* in 1840:

"**Every schoolboy knows** who imprisoned Montezuma, and who strangled Atahualpa."

As fast (or quick) as greased lightning

This one is a bit easier to find its root. Lightning is fast enough, and has been a symbol of speed for hundreds of years. It can be referenced from the seventeenth century. Thomas Comber used 'quick as lightning' in the litany, *A Companion to the Temple*, in 1676:

"Now if the Attendants be bright as the Sun, **quick as Lightning**, and powerful as Thunder; what is He that is their Lord?"

The earliest references to 'greased lightning' are from the early 19th century. For one, the British Lincolnshire newspaper, *The Boston, Lincoln, Louth & Spalding Herald*, published an article in January, 1833, including the following line:

"He spoke **as quick as 'greased lightning'**."

Adding the word 'greased' makes it seem even more unbeatable as a simile.

As fine as frog's hair

This Americanism means someone feels fantastic! We find a citation of it back as far as 1865 in C. Davis's *Diary*:

"I have a better flow of spirits this morning, and, in fact, feel **as fine as frog's hair**, as Potso used to say."

Note he says 'Potso *used to say*,' indicating that the phrase had already been around awhile. Obviously, frogs are hairless, and this simile points to the fact that someone feels so fine that there is no feeling quite like it.

As flat as a flitter / fritter

A fritter is an archaic name for a flat cake cooked in a frying pan containing fruit. In the Americn South, the saying is more often 'flat as a flitter.' This has been in use by the Scotch-Irish in the Appalachians since at least the early 20th century, and was likely a mispronunciation of fritter. Using this simile means something is excessively flat. Also, 'flat as a pancake' is used in some locales.

As fresh as a daisy

This idiom originated in England in the late 1700s, and means alert, full of energy and always ready to go. 'Daisy' comes from the Old English, 'Day's eye.' The flower was given this name from the assumption in the old days that a daisy was never tired, because it closes up at night and opens anew each morning, representing sleep. Thus, its pedals were always fresh-looking.

Fresh as a Daisy is the title of a 1969-'70 pop song by Emitt Rhodes.

As good as gold

In this phrase, good doesn't mean what it normally does. It refers to someone or something that is well behaved, such as a child who has remembered his or her manners with someone the child is unaccustomed to being with.

Banknotes, which Americans know as bills, weren't considered to be money. They were promissory notes, like IOUs. Gold or silver, as referred to in the *Bible*, were the real money. This had the intrinsic value. In the U.K., banknotes still include printed messages to this end. The One Pound carries the inscription, *"For the Gov.' and Comp. of the Bank of England"* which is undersigned by the Chief Cashier of the Bank of England.

'As good as gold' meant that something was genuine and to be accepted just like the real currency.

The first recorded use of this figuratively was in 1845, in Thomas Hood's poem, *The Lost Heir.*

"Sitting **as good as gold** in the glitter."

The present-day meaning has evolved through the years.

As happy as a lark

This simile was in circulation in the English language as early as the late 18th and early 19th centuries. Though other such terms such as 'happy as a clam' (mid-19th century) and 'happy as a dead pig in the sunshine' (from the Deep South), have entered the speech of various segments of our American population, 'happy as a lark' seems to have been of the longest endurance and widest usage.

31

As happy as a lark is derived from the cheerful song of this beautiful and common songbird. One example is from the New York publication, *Puck, Volume 10,* Issue 103, 1882:

> "On, on we went, and I began to feel **as happy as a lark**, when what do you suppose happened?"

As honest as the day is long

Though the length of days definitely varies in different seasons and in diverse parts of the world, this phrase is intended to mean honest beyond reproach.

It was coined by American philosopher and author, Henry David Thoreau (1817-1862), in *Life without Principle.*

> "Such is the labor which the American Congress exists to protect,-honest, manly toil,-**honest as the day is long**,-that makes his bread taste sweet, and keeps society sweet,-which all men respect and have consecrated; one of the sacred band, doing the needful but irksome drudgery."

Ask me no questions and I'll tell you no lies

This well-known phrase is from Irish playwright Oliver Goldsmith (1728-1774) and was coined in the 18th century in a poem.

It is used when folks want someone to refrain from being inquisitive.

Ask Me No Questions, I'll Tell You No Lies became the title of a song by Jo Stafford in 1950; the British band, the Bangles scored in *Austin Powers, the Spy Who Shagged Me* with *Ask Me No Questions and I'll Tell You No Lies* in 2000.

As lost as last year's Easter eggs

This is apparently a very new simile started by an Internet answer forum, along with 'as lost as a puppy dog on a cold rainy morning.' As a rule last year's Easter eggs would be lost indeed—more like non-existent.

As nervous as a cat on a hot tin roof

This simile has become the epitome of jittery and paranoid. It was actually coined as a result playwright Tennessee Williams 1955 hit Broadway play, *A Cat on a Hot Tin Roof.*

As nervous as a long-tailed cat in a room full of rocking chairs

This is a simile for being extremely touchy and jumpy at the least thing. A cat with a long tail would be watching carefully to make sure a rocker didn't come down on its tail. Cats often twich their tails when they feel that something may be threatening them. The earliest sources attribute this to Tennessee Ernie Ford, as this one from *The Antique Automobile*, 1955:

> "Tennessee Ernie Ford says that driving on the freeways makes him **as nervous as a long-tailed cat in a room full** of people sitting in **rocking-chairs.**"

As old as Methuselah

This is another phrase of biblical origin. Methuselah was recorded in *Genesis 5:21-27* as the son of Enoch, and was said to have lived to the ripe old age of 969—the oldest man in the *Bible.*

'As old as Methuselah' has come to be used as a comical term applied to someone who is considerably more aged than the speaker.

As pale / white as a ghost /sheet

The earliest citation of this saying dates from the 1600s. The word ghost is of Germanic origin before 900 AD. When a person is very scared, or sometimes in sickness, the blood drains from their face, leaving them appearing very pale. Since the whitest things in those days were sheets, (spirits were also viewed as white) the simile was a natural one to coin.

As plain as the nose on one's face

Something that is as plain as the nose on your face can't be denied. This commonly used cliché has been around since at least the sixteenth century, and is attributed to Francis Rabelais (1495-1553), and comes from *Works, the*

Author's Prologue of the Fifth Book. The actual quote is, "**Plain as the nose in a man's face.**"

As pleased as punch / As proud as punch

This simile derived from the old British puppet named Mr. Punch, who took his name from the 16th-century Italian puppet, Polichinello or *Punchinellio* used in the *Commedia dell'arte.* British beaches featured 'Punch and Judy' shows which declined during the last half of the 20th century because of the idea that they were 'politically incorrect' (see).

The expression 'As pleased as punch' didn't come into play, however, until the late 18th century. The earliest known reference in print is from *The Baviad and Maeviad* by William Gifford, 1797:

> "Oh! how my fingers itch to pull thy nose! **As pleased as Punch**, I'd hold it in my gripe."

The capitalization of Punch gives away its origin. After the phrase was coined, 'as proud as Punch' also became popular, as evidenced by Charles Dickens in *David Copperfield,* 1850:

> "I am **as proud as Punch** to think that I once had the honour of being connected with your family."

As pure as the driven snow

The concept of white as a symbol of purity goes all the way back to the fifteenth century as was expressed by John Lydgate in his *Henry VI's Triumphal Entry into London,* circa 1435:

> "Alle cladde in white, in tokne off clennesse, Lyche pure virgynes."

More directly relating to the root of the simile, there were several Shakespearean references to snow as a symbol of purity. For example, in *Macbeth,* 1605, we find:

> "MALCOMB:
> "Black Macbeth will seem **as pure as snow**."

Then in *The Winter's Tale,* 1611:

"AUTOLYCUS:
"Lawn **as white as driven snow.**"

As rare as hen's teeth

Also 'as scarce as hen's teeth,' and 'scarcer than hen's teeth,' this phrase is used to mean that something is non-existent. Chickens, on the whole, don't possess teeth at all, and digest their food by first collecting it in their craw, a sack which gradually releases the food to their 'second stomach,' called a gizzard, which serves as a grinder of a sort.

However, it was reported in *Science Daily* on February 26, 2006, that scientists have discovered a breed of chicken called Talpid that actually has a complete set of choppers. The team of researchers is based in the Universities of Manchester and Wisconsin and has developed a process which can induce growth of teeth in normal chickens.

The actual origin this simile, however, is very obscure, but it goes back to at least the mid-19th century and likely earlier. *The Richard H. Adams, Jr. papers,* U.S. Civil War records of 1862, has a notation at the bottom, "Records of the 5th Cavalry are **as rare as hen's teeth**." This seems to be the earliest reference in print.

As slow as molasses (in January)

Molasses is the slowest pouring of sweet syrupy substances eaten by human kind. And January is traditionally the dead of winter. Over the years this has been used, with the one about the snail, to describe the ultimate creep.

But history tells us that there was at least one exception to this. On January 15th, 1919, slightly after noon, a flood of molasses rushed through Boston. It was one of those winters when the temperature there had climbed to an unseasonably warm 46 degrees Fahrenheit. A gigantic 2,320,000 gallon tank of molasses burst, causing its contents to sweep through the streets in a 30-foot wall resulting in death and destruction. I guess that proves that nothing is always true and too much sweet stuff can be fatal.

As snug as a bug in a rug

This rhyming metaphor did not come into being in the 1950s, as some may believe. It first appeared in print in 1769. But the meaning of this curious saying as it was in the 18th century was also quite different than today. 'Snug' was then used to mean, 'neat, trim and well prepared,' specifically as it referred to ships of the day. It had been so defined since at least the lattersixteenth century.

Before bugs were insects, they were ghosts or spirits. In 1535, the *Cloverdale Bible* uses it in this fashion in *Psalms 91:5*:

> "So yt thou shalt not nede to be afrayed for eny bugges by night, ner for arowe that flyeth by daye."

By 1642, however, bug also meant 'beetle' or something like it, as seen in Daniel Rogers' *Naaman the Syrian*.

> "Gods rare workmanship in the Ant, the poorest bugge that creeps."

As noted in the beginning of this entry, the first known printed reference to 'as snug as a bug in a rug' was in 1769. It is in David Garrick's writings about Shakespeare called *Garrick's vagary, or, England run mad*; with particulars of the Strafford Jubilee.

> "If she [a rich widow] has the mopus's [coins or money], I'll have her, **as snug as a bug in a rug**."

The word 'rug' here, is a Tudor word with the same source as the word 'rag.' But then, rugs were not on the floor, but were thick woolen bed covers, what might today be blankets. So a 'bug in a rug' would have been happy and snug, indeed.

As stiff as a poker / board

Poker was the first application of the stiff analogy. A poker is an iron rod used to stoke fires and move logs in fireplaces. Both pokers and boards are unbendable and fit the bill. Stiff as a poker was in use earlier, but first recorded by Thomas De Quincy. One printing is from *Autobiographical Sketches 1790-1803*, page 453, 1863.

> "...he astonished his whole household by suddenly standing bolt upright **as stiff as a poker**; his sister remarking to the young gentleman that he (the visitor) was in luck that evening..."

As sure as night follows day

This simile, intended to express the utmost certainty, has been used since at least the mid-19th century when it appeared in the *Calcutta Review* from the University there.

By the end of the century it was being used in books and magazines such as *McCalls* in 1897:

> "No woman should suffer her scalp to remain In that condition one minute, for **as sure as night follows day**, sooner or later she will find the doors of society closed against her. Ladies especially are subject to scalp diseases..."

As sure as you were born

This one has also been with us since the early-to-mid 1800s. An early example comes from Thomas Haliburton in *The Clockmaker*, 1841:

> "Now, says I, there's another bit of advice I'll give you free gratis for nothin',—never buy a horse on the dealer's judgment, or he will cheat you he can; never buy him on your own, or you will cheat yourself **as sure as you are born**."

It became a favorite saying of Charles Dickens and was used in a number of his novels.

As the crow flies

This universal comparison was coined in the U.K. and has been long used in Scotland to denote the shortest route, likely because of the presence of many crows there. The choice of a crow, other than for this reason, seems inappropriate, since their flight patterns are not notable for their straightness, and they frequently fly in long arcs in search of food.

The first known printed citation is from the *London Review of English and Foreign Literature* by W. Kenrick, 1767.

> "The Spaniard, if on foot, always travels **as the crow flies**, which the openness and dryness of the country permits; neither rivers nor the steepest mountains stop his course, he swims over the one and scales the other."

As ugly as homemade sin

Often without the 'As,' this is definitely an old Appalachian mountain slang saying which goes back generations It has been in use in the Blue Ridge Mountains since at least the 1950s. Some have suggested that it refers to incest which used to be prevalent but this is unlikely. For ugly, there seemed no worse thing to compare it to. An early printed example is from *The Atlantic Monthly, Volume 199*, 1957.

"He is as **ugly as homemade sin**. And his hair. His hair is falling out."

As useless as tits on a boar (hog or pig)

Obviously this saying originated on farms in the Southern U.S. According to a major phrase origin book, this simile, meaning totally useless, it has been in use since the 1940s. The earliest available citation in print says 'bull' rather than 'boar,' and is found in *The Marlet Magazine*, University of Victoria, November 18, 1965:

"The last six lines of the poem: They're about **as useless as tits on a bull**..."

As you may have guessed by now

Charles Dickens was an early citer of a form of this phrase in his *All the year round*: a weekly journal, in 1869:

"My business is bird-stuffing, **as you may have heard or guessed...**"

As you go through life two rules will never bend, never whittle toward yourself or pee against the wind.

Over the past sixty years or so this saying has been on signs or 'mottos,' as they were once called, all across America. It has become a very well-known and oft-quoted saying meaning 'Don't do something which is going to make matters worse for you.'

Atta boy!

A shortening of 'that's a boy. This expression is American and from the early 20th century. It is an enthusiastic expression of approval for a job well done by any male. It is commonly used at games when the male has scored points.

Two silent era movies contained the phrase: *Atta Boy's Last Race*, 1916, in which 'Atta Boy' was the name of a horse, starring Dorothy Gish and Keith Armour, and *Atta Boy*, in 1926 starring Monte Banks and Virginia Bradford.

At the drop of a hat

This means, of course, without notice. An example would be when someone is apt to take action on something when others expect it the least.

It is most accepted that this phrase originated in the old American West in the late-1800s, when the signal for the start of an event was often marked by the drop of someone's hat.

However, this 'drop of a hat' reference is years earlier. In quoting a Colonel which was addressing U.S. President Andrew Johnson, in a section called 'Editor's Drawer,' *Harper's New Monthly Magazine, Volume 32, Issue 191*, April 1866:

> He commented, "Mr. President, when I consider the momentous importance of this awful responsibility that now rests on me, and the fate of the millions of the rising generations to come that rests on the decision—yes as it were of **the drop of a hat**—I say, Sir, it almost overcomes my senses to think of it."

Some claim that it was also used in Ireland when it was stated that someone was ready to fight 'at the drop of a hat.'

In 1898, *Harper's Magazine, Volume 97*, in an article titled 'A Man and His Knife' used the phrase in its current sense in regard to fighting:

> The man who would not fight "**at the drop of a hat**, and drop it himself," was soon made to feel that he had very much better not have been born.

It means to act readily upon any signal, and is used to stereotype a person who is on edge and jumps at the slightest impulse.

At the eleventh hour

The basis for this idiom comes from the parable of the Vineyard given by Jesus in *Matthew 20:11-16*, in which the workers hired at the eleventh hour, received the same wages as those who were hired at the beginning of the work day.

Since the signing of the armistice at the end of World War I, at the eleventh hour, of the eleventh day, of the eleventh month of 1918, the phrase 'eleventh hour' has come to prominence as meaning the last minute.

A modern example is that of newscaster Natalie Morales, who, on NBC TV's Today Show on the morning of Friday, December 16th, 2011, announced, "An eleventh hour deal has been reached to avoid a government shutdown ahead of tonight's midnight deadline." The deal, however, proved short-lived and it was 'back to the old drawing board' (see).

At the end of one's rope

Coming to mean, out of patience, or 'up in the air' (see) about what action to take next, it is the American version of the British phrase, 'at the end of my tether,' and comes from animals who were tethered, or staked out, which have reached the maximum distance available and are straining to go farther. It has been in our jargon since the early 20th century.

In *The Saturday Evening Post*, April 5, 1915, Volume 187, Issue 7, in an article titled 'Hit the Line Hard,' on page 93, an early example of the expression is printed:

> "I think you've **reached the end of your rope**. I think you're about ready for a smash-up."

Typically, when one has reached 'the end of their rope,' they have exceeded their defined boundaries.

At the end of the day

This modern idiom means the same as the 'tried and true' (see) saying 'after all is said and done,' it did not come into popular usage with its present meaning until the dawn of the twenty-first century, although it could have been around in limited speech a bit earlier. Several earlier books have this as there title, but usage was usually in the literal sense. A 2002 nonfiction release, *At the End of the Day: How Will You Be Remembered?* by James W. Moore reflects the move to the figurative term.

Avoid it like the plague

The origin of this much-used expression is a bit vague. Apparently it was in use at least by 1699. William Penn used it in *Some Fruits of Solitude,* Edition 5:

"An able bad Man, is an ill Instrument, and to be **shunn'd as the Plague**."

Shortly later, in 1703, Mary, Lady Chudleigh, included this in *Poems Several Occasions, Together with the Song of the Three Children:*

"Those Ills we court, which we **as Plagues shou'd shun**."

Aw Pshaw!

The dictionaries, including *Merriam Webster*, list pshaw as an expression of irritation, contempt, disgust or disapproval. Though antiquated, and replaced by other terms of utter disgust, it is usually prefixed by 'aw.' *Merriam Webster* says it has been around since 1656. Since that's a specific year, it could possibly be Thomas Blount's *Glossographia.* Since Blount was, among other professions, a lexicographer, and this tome was a dictionary of over 11,000 words published that year; this seems likely, though the text seems illusive.

Many references occur in works of the 18th, 19th, and even 20th century. In 1720, William Congreve used pshaw in *Love for Love: a Comedy*, on page 108:

"**Pshaw**, O but I dream't that it was so tho."

In 1777, here is a quote using the saying from Richard B. Sheridan, in *School for Scandal*:

"**Pshaw!** He is too moral by half!"

axe to grind, An

According to *The Guardian: A Monthly Magazine, Volume X, No. 2*, February, 1859, published by the Reformed Church in America, in Pennsylvania, here is an abridged version of the origin claimed to be from Benjamin Franklin:

"When I was a little boy," says Dr. Franklin, "I remember one cold winter morning I was accosted by a smiling man with an axe on his shoulder. 'My pretty boy,' said he, 'has your father a grindstone?' 'Yes sir.' Said I. 'You

41

are a fine little fellow,' said he; 'will you let me grind my axe on it?' Pleased with the compliment... 'Oh, yes!' I answered, 'It is down in the shop.' 'And will you, my little fellow,' said he... 'get me a little water?' Could I refuse? I ran and soon brought a kettle full....Tickled at the flattery, like a fool I went to work, and bitterly did I rue the day... I toiled...till I was almost tired to death... I could not get away; my hands were blistered, the axe was sharpened...the man turned to me with, 'Now you little rascal, you've played truant; send for school or you'll rue it.' Alas! thought I, it is hard enough to turn the grindstone this cold day, but to be called a little rascal was too much. It sunk deep in my mind...When I see a merchant over-polite to his customers, begging them to take a little brandy, and throwing his goods on the counter, thinks I **that man has an axe to grind**. When I see a man flattering the people, making great profession of attachment to liberty, who is in private life a tyrant, methinks, look out, good people, that fellow would set you turning a grindstone..."

However, famed Pennsylvania newspaper editor, Charles Miner, actually wrote this provocative story. It is called, *Who'll Turn the Grindstone*. The reason it is so often attributed to Franklin, according to a 1916 book, *Charles Miner, a Pennsylvania Pioneer* by Charles Francis Richardson and Elizabeth Miner Thomas Richardson, is that he was a great admirer of Ben Franklin, and developed a publication very similar to his *Poor Richard's Almanac*, titled *Essays from the desk of Poor Robert the Scribe*. The saying means that someone has 'a method behind their madness' (see) or a hidden reason for their actions. Often they are seeking revenge against someone.

B

Back in the day

This is the latest rendition of a tradition which started long ago. This phrase, per se, evolved in the latter part of the 20th century by young to middle-aged urban Americans referring to the era in which they were growing up, likely 'in the hood' (see). An early example, which may have propelled the phrase onward to fame, is from a book from Messalonskee High School in Oakland, Maine published in 2001. The fitting title is *Back in the Day: Oral History, Folklore, and Outhouse Tales (or, Tales from the Three-holer) from Kennebec County, Maine, Volume 4*. The volume is packed with interviews and essays compiled by journalism students to describe the way of life in Maine during the 20th century.

Immediately before the introduction of this phrase, 'back in my day' was popular, and prior to *that*, 'in the old days' or in the 'good old days.' In time relation, it is like thinking that the 'grass is greener on the other side of the fence.' People naturally relate to the days of their youth as their prime time—as an era when life was better and they could 'write their own ticket.'

Backseat driver

Back in the early-to-mid-20th century, men almost always drove and women were expected to be only bystanders to the process. The saying is originally American.

The first known reference to someone being called a 'backseat driver' (in a literal sense) is from the *Daily Kennebec Journal* (Augusta, Maine), in May, 1914:

> "When New York pitcher Vernon Gomez retires as a smokeballer he wants to become a smoke eater. Here he gets a tryout as **a back-seat driver** on a hook and ladder truck at St. Petersburg..."

Later the phrase began to be used in a very figurative and derogatory nature. *The Bismarck Tribune* (North Dakota) a few years later printed the following in December 1921:

> "**A back-seat driver** is the pest who sits on the rear cushions of a motor car and tells the driver what to do. He issues a lot of instructions, gives a lot of advice, offers no end of criticism. And doesn't do a bit of work."

It appeared in the U.K. as well by 1930, when P. G. Wodehouse used it, without any explanation of its meaning, in his book of short stories, *Very Good, Jeeves!*

> "Quite suddenly and unexpectedly, no one more surprised than myself, the car let out a faint gurgle like a sick moose and stopped in its tracks ... the **back-seat drivers** gave tongue. 'What's the matter? What has happened?' I explained. 'I'm not stopping. It's the car.'"

Back to square one

This phrase began with some game. There are three distinct possibilities here.

The oldest seems to be hopscotch, which is played on a grid of numbered squares. This game has been around for centuries, and was referred to in the 1677 edition of Robert Winstanley's satirical almanac, *Poor Robin*, as Scotch-hoppers. The game involves players hopping from square to square, leaving out the square containing their thrown stone. They usually go from one to eight, and 'back to square one.'

The B.B.C. referred to listeners following the progress of football games in radio commentaries, dividing the pitch into eight squares. Commentators would describe the play by telling what square the ball was in. The practice was referred to in an issue from January, 1927. However, nowhere has the phrase back to square one been denoted. Despite this, the B.B.C. in the January, 2007 edition of the *Radio Times* claims that these grids gave us this phrase.

Another possible origin is board games, and particularly Snakes and Ladders, as the earliest printed citation of the phrase is from 1952 in the *Economic Journal*, published on behalf of the Royal Economic Society in London.

> "He has the problem of maintaining the interest of the reader who is always being sent **back to square one** in a sort of intellectual game of snakes and ladders."

Despite that comment, it isn't a feature of Snakes and Ladders that players are sent back to square one. Some say, however, that it has a close option. Regardless, going back to square one is a common way of saying 'start over.'

Back to the drawing board

On 1 March 1941 a cartoon, drawn by famed American cartoonist Peter Arno (Curtis Arnoux Peters, Jr.), was published by *New Yorker Magazine*. It depicted a World War II airplane crashing in plain view of spectators. Little did they know that the caption, 'Well, it's **back to the old drawing board**,' would create a cliché which would be used by their generation, and likely all generations to come.

Back to the salt mines***

This old expression is used to mean that after taking a break from work, particularly a difficult job, it is now time to return, though begrudgingly so. It was inspired by the tradition of Russian penal servitude for political prisoners in Usolye, at the Siberian salt mine owned by the Russian ruling class in the late 19th century, and up to the Bolshevik Revolution in October, 1917. Conditions there were very brutal, and the prisoners were housed in shanties which did nothing to protect them from the harsh weather. *Harper's Magazine*, in an article in 1888, cited Iletsk as a place where these Russian convicts also worked in salt mines. As an idiom, "the salt mines" has been used metaphorically for work since that time period. The earliest verifiable reference to "back to the mines" as a specific metaphor is from *Murder Day By Day* by Irvin S. Cobb, 1933:

"Well Gilly, it's **back to the mines** for me…"

Bad blood

Originally called 'ill blood' in the late 18th century by both Jonathan Swift in England, and Thomas Jefferson in America, it referred to stirring up ill will.

This idiom, per se, has been in use as such since the early 19th century Charles Lamb used it in *Essays of Elia* in 1823 and means that two parties, often family members, have reached a point in their relationship where communication is useless due to extreme conflict or differences of opinion on key issues. Several citations followed in the 1800s including James Finemore Cooper in *Wyandotte*, 1843:

"The government at home, and the people of the colonies, are getting to have **bad blood** between them."

Then even Mark Twain in *Tom Sawyer, Detective* in 1896:

"…here was **bad blood** between us from a couple of weeks back, and we was only friends in the way of business."

Several movies have been produced in various countries using the phrase as their title including an Australian 1982 flick starring Jack Thompson, a 1986 French film starring Juliette Bionche, and a 2011 American thriller with Slaine and Michael Yebba directed by Ben Affleck. A number of television shows also bear the name as all or part of their titles. At least eight songs and two albums also are named 'Bad Blood.'

Bait and switch

This cliché came into popular use in the U.S. in the latter half of the 20th century as a legal term for the illegal practice, usually of a retailer, offering a popular product for sale to entice buyers, then substituting another product, usually of considerably less value or less desirability, when the customers wanted to purchase the item. The term also may apply to the practice of the seller attempting to get the customer to switch to a more expensive product when the advertised item was not available.

An early reference is from *Consumer Health: Products and Services*, by Jessie Helen Haag, 1976, speaking of infractions from the previous decade:

"In one study, faulty electrical equipment in hospital operating rooms caused 1200 patients to be electrocuted during 1964 and 1965. Four current types of advertising used to fleece the consumer are (1) **bait and switch**…"

Baker's dozen

This old saying is said to come from the days when bakers were severely punished for baking underweight loaves. Some added an extra loaf to a batch of a dozen to be above suspicion. A baker's dozen thus means thirteen.

ball's in your court, The

Meaning, 'It's your turn to make a move' (I've done all I can do), this slogan is a metaphor for the tennis ball being on the opponent's side of the net. This sports idiom crept into general usage in the latter part of the 20th century. A very early example is from *Cincinnati Magazine*, July 1977:

"And now, as they say, **the ball's in your court**."

Other magazine references followed that year in both *Jet* and *Ebony*; then in the 1980s, it gained more frequent usage in a variety of genres.

Bang for the buck

This saying, which means 'value for the money spent,' is of political origin. With 'bang' referring to 'firepower' or 'weaponry,' it literally meant 'bombs for one's money.' The alliteration of 'bang' and 'buck' helps to make the phrase memorable.

The earliest confirmed reference to 'bang for the buck' is found in 1968 in the first edition of William Safire's *New Language of Politics*. Safire claims that the phrase was coined in 1954 by Charles E. Wilson, U.S. Secretary of Defense, in reference to his 'massive retaliation' policy of then Secretary of State, John Foster Dulles.

The phrase has certainly been used in all cases relating to getting more out of an investment of money or time.

Baptism by fire

This phrase's origin is from the biblical book of *Matthew*, in chapter *3*, verse *11*. The words are attributed to John the Baptist.

"I indeed baptize you with water unto repentance, but he that cometh after me is mightier than I, whose shoes I am not worthy to bear: he shall **baptize you** with the Holy Ghost and **with fire**." *(KJV)*

There are differing beliefs as to the baptism by fire mentioned here (some say power from God, some say persecution and martyrdom).

As an idiom in our modern world, a 'baptism by fire' means our worst nightmare has come true. It applies to the tests that life may bring our way to make us better people.

Barefaced liar

Shakespeare was the first one to use the term 'barefaced' in *A Midsummer Night's Dream.* It was said to be 'beardless, with no hair upon the face.'

In 1852, Harriet Beecher Stowe first used the term 'barefaced lie' in her classic novel, *Uncle Tom's Cabin.*

Barefaced lies are those told with no shame, audacious and impudent in intent.

Barking up the wrong tree

The earliest known printed citation is found in James Kirke Paulding's *Westward Ho!* published in 1832.

> "Here he made a note in his book, and I begun to smoke him for one of those fellows that drive a sort of a trade of making books about old Kentuck and the western country: so I thought I'd set him **barking up the wrong tree** a little, and I told him some stories that were enough to set the Mississippi a-fire; but he put them all down in his book."

The English is a bit less than perfect in this reference, but the phrase must have caught on in the United States quickly after Hall's book. It appeared in several American newspapers throughout the 1830s. One notable example is in this piece from the Gettysburg newspaper *The Adams Sentinel* in March of 1834:

> "Gineral you are **barkin' up the wrong tree** this time, for I jest see that rackoon jump to the next tree, and afore this he is a mile off in the woods."

basket case, A

This old expression refers to a person or thing which is unable to function properly. It originated in the American Military service during World War I, and that was not in the normal sense that it is now used. In March 1919, a bulletin was issued for Major General M.W. Ireland by the U.S. Command on Public Information, which was reported by the newspapers across the country.

> "The Surgeon General of the Army ... denies ... that there is any foundation for the stories that have been circulated ... of the existence of '**basket cases**' in our hospitals."

One paper, the *Syracuse* (NY) *Herald,* that month, explained:

> "By '**basket case**' is meant a soldier who has lost both arms and legs and therefore must be carried in a basket."

The term was again picked up in World War II, and came into popular culture to mean what it does today.

Bated breath

Some want to spell the first word in this expression 'baited,' even to J.K. Rowling in the Harry Potter novel, *The Prisoner of Azkaban.* However, it really should be 'bated,' as this is merely a shortened form of abated, meaning brought down, lowered or depressed. Bated breath is breathing that is subdued because of an emotional difficulty. Most often someone is likely to say, "I'll be waiting with bated breath," meaning that they will be anxiously anticipating an answer or response.

Here is another example of Shakespeare's ability to pass down a cliché. The first reference is in *The Merchant of Venice,* 1586:

> "...Shall I bend low and in a bondman's key,
> With **bated breath** and whispering humbleness..."

Bats in the belfry

Though it sounds like an old British movie, or from a Gothic novel of the 19th century, it isn't. Bats are busy little near-blind winged mammals which fly about in dark places. Belfries are in towers like church steeples, and were places in which bats dwelt. The earliest record of this is from American writers just after the dawn of the 20th century. For example, this is from an article in *The Newark Daily Advocate*, in Ohio, not New Jersey, in October, 1900:

> "To his hundreds of friends and acquaintances in Newark, these purile [sic] and senseless attacks on Hon. John W. Cassingham are akin to the vaporings of the fellow with a large flock of **bats in his belfry**."

The usage here has continued to this day. Someone who is confused and a bit dazzled may be said to have 'bats in the belfry,' or 'gone bats.'

Batten down the hatches

This is of nautical origin and had to do with preparing ships for inclement weather. The earliest known reference to this practice is in William Falconer's *An universal dictionary of the marine*, published in 1769:

> "**The battens** serve to confine the edges of the tarpaulings close down to the sides of **the hatches**."

Batten strips are narrow boards made to cover a gap. On ships, hatches were often either open or covered with grating, allowing the lower decks to ventilate. These were covered by tarps battened down to prevent them from blowing off.

The first exact citation of the phrase 'batten down the hatches' is from the *Chambers Journal* in 1883:

> "**Batten down the hatches** - quick, men."

Batting one thousand

This Americanism (also used as 'batting a thousand') means that one has done something better than thought possible. Literally, it is getting everything in a series of items correct. It was derived from the game of baseball, a true American sport. Someone who has 'a thousand batting average' has made a hit every time at bat in a specific time period, for instance, a game. Some sources claim usage before the game of baseball even started. Ironically, as a cliché it can also refer to the reverse, when someone has done everything wrong

Battle of the bulge

This humorous idiom meaning 'the struggle to control ones weight' is taken for the American name given to a major offensive by the Germans launched against the Allied forces toward the end of World War II (16 December 1944 – 25 January 1945) through the heavy forests in the Ardennes Mountains Wallonia in Belgium, simultaneously with France and Luxemburg on the Western front.

Despite the claim by a major book of American slang origins placing first figurative citation at 1956, this figurative citation is from *American Magazine*, Volume 54, January 1952:

"When he started dieting, Cecil weighed 195; the charts said he should weigh 150. That is what he is shooting for. ... One of the front fighters in **the battle of the bulge** in Louisville is Mrs. Cissy Gregg..."

A number of other references follow by 1958.

Some other early references showing the phrase associated with weight still use capital Bs. We find the same in April, 1961, in this citation from *Baseball Digest* in an article about San Francisco Giant's pudgy first baseman, Willie McCovey, regarding his time at the local YMCA.

"He was there primarily to work out, which he had been doing daily for weeks. He was there, upon request, to talk about 1960, a year in which he almost lost his 'life' in a lonely, losing **Battle of the Bulge**."

Beat around the bush

When hunting birds there was a common practice in olden days of taking a stick and beating around (or about) bushes to drive birds out into the open. Afterward, someone would attempt to catch the birds. 'I won't beat about the bush' came to mean 'I will get straight to the point without any delay.'

It first appeared in print in the medieval poem, *Generydes, A Romance in Seven Fine Stanzas,* in about 1440:

"Butt as it hath be sayde full long agoo,
Some **bete the bussh** and some the byrdes take."

The poet is unknown and the only copy is a single handwritten manuscript in the library of Trinity College in Cambridge in the U.K. Even in this poem, it is clear that beating the bush was a poor substitute for actually getting on with the hunt and taking the birds.

Then, in 1572, George Gascoigne adds 'about' to the phrase in *Works*.

"**He bet about the bush**, whyles other caught the birds."

Beaten within an inch of one's life

Though now meant to be symbolic when used as a warning, this was originally a fairly literal idiom meaning to attack someone so violently that they almost died as a result. It was initially to describe the results of a 'flogging' or whipping with a rod. 'Within an inch of one's life' has also been used to describe a close

50

brush with death from other means, or being frightened 'to within an inch of one's life.'

It has been found in print in this sense since the early 19th century as seen in the following lines from a story titled *Reverses* in *Blackwood's Edinburgh Magazine* in August 1827:

"'I overtook him within five miles of Canterbury, and **horsewhipped him within an inch of his life**.'"

Even prior to that, 'within an inch of their lives' was used to express other figurative scenarios, such as excessively tight garments, as in *Memoirs of the Life of Mrs. Elizabeth Carter*, 1807:

"After all there was a dispensation of going without hoops…They are laced **within an inch of their lives**, their stays excessively stiff, and their stomachers of an amazing length, nearly approaching their chins."

Beating a dead horse (See: **Keep beating** (or **flogging) a dead horse**)

Beat me to the punch

This old idiom originated in boxing and figuratively means that someone thought of an idea, accomplished a feat, or got to a destination before someone else. It is especially used when two or more persons are in competition or are trying to accomplish a goal before someone else.

This has been in our vernacular much longer, but it gained popularity by a song written by Smokey Robinson and Ronald White, which hit number nine on the pop chart on August 11, 1962 entitled *You Beat Me To the Punch*.

"You **beat me to the punch** that time; you beat me to the punch. Woah-oh-oh-oh, you beat me to the punch!"

Beat of a different drummer (See: **March to the beat of a different drummer**)

Beauty fades, dumb is forever

A 1999 book by TV's Judge Judy Sheindlin, ***Beauty Fades, Dumb is Forever: The Making of a Happy Woman,*** has made this a cliché on lots of people's lips. The book is based on true court cases and presents 'ten hard and true lessons for happiness.'

Beauty is in the eye of the beholder*

This means that while one person may not see the quality or loveliness of something or someone, another may feel quite differently. The root of this old proverb goes back much further than the current version. It is likely a trickle down from Shakespeare's 1588 line in *Love's Labours Lost:*

"Beauty is bought by judgement of the eye."

Then, in 1741, Benjamin Franklin, in an edition of *Poor Richard's Almanac,* included this rhyme:

"Beauty, like supreme dominion / Is but supported by opinion."

Other authors used similar phrases. The individual most often credited with this exact saying is Margaret Wolfe Hungerford, who wrote books under the pseudonym, 'The Duchess'. The initial publication of it is in her 1878 book, *Molly Bawn.*

Beauty is only skin deep

This one is attributed to Thomas Overbury. The text is in *Overbury's Wife,* written in 1613; published, 1614:

"All the carnall **beautie** of my wife, **Is but skinne-deep**."

Other references attributed to Overbury carry the same meaning.

A poem by John Daves, *A Select Second Husband,* in 1616, states:

"**Beauty's but skin-deepe**."

Many references have occurred since. The saying means that though outward beauty is alluring, it does not determine the true worth or character of the person. A related phrase is 'Beauty is as beauty does.'

Be careful what you wish for—you just might get it

Songs by Eminem and the Pussycat Dolls didn't start this saying. It's an old proverb which was popularized in the short story *The Monkey's Paw* by W.W. Jacobs first published in *The Lady of the Barge* in 1902 which was first performed in 1907 on Broadway as a one-act play.

It means, like 'be careful what you pray for' that sometimes what we think we want is not what is best for us.

Bee line

In past centuries most people believed that bees always flew in a straight line to their hives. Therefore, making a 'bee line' for something came to mean going straight for it. An early example is from Charles Dickens, in *All the Year Round, Volume 5*, page 271, 1871, and identifies the phrase as 'American.'

> "In America such a line is called **'a bee line,'** and sometimes an 'air line.' Bees, after having laden themselves with honey, have been observed always to fly back to the hive in a direct line, which is not always the case with crows…" (See: **As the crow flies**.)

Been there, done that

This phrase means that someone has experienced what is being discussed, it now bores them and they don't want to talk about it. The cliché began to take shape in the 1970s with the short form, 'been there.' An example in print is from New York Judge Edwin Torres' famed crime novel *Carlito's Way*, in 1975:

> "Money is only an object. I'll get it. Got it, **been there**."

Done that was added later. In February, 1982, *The Syracuse Herald American,* in New York, carried an article by Jerry Buck about actress Lauren Tewes. It called the saying 'Australian':

> "Miss Tewes, who has just got divorced, says she doesn't plan to get married at this time. Using an Australian expression, she says, **'Been there, done that.'**"

In spite of this, no notations are found in Australia until 1983. The phrase is used frequently in the U.S.

Before you could say Jack Robinson

This means 'to be done suddenly, with lightning speed.'

It is likely that this 'Jack Robinson' was just as mythical as Jack Frost (see) or Jack be nimble, or the Jacks of all trades. However, some have suggested that John Robinson, the Constable of the Tower of London in the late seventeenth century at a time when heads were quickly chopped off, was the inspiration for this famous or *infamous* Jack.

At any rate, in 1778, Fanny Burney used a form of it in her romantic novel, *Evelina, or the history of a young lady's entrance into the world.*

"'For the matter of that there,' said the Captain, 'you must make him a soldier, before you can tell which is lightest, head or heels. Howsomever, I'd lay ten pounds to a shilling, I could whisk him so dexterously over into the pool, that he should light plump upon his foretop and turn round like a tetotum.'

"'Done!' cried Lord Merton; 'I take your odds.'

"'Will you?' returned he; 'why, then, 'fore George, **I'd do it as soon as say Jack Robinson.**'"

Beggars can't be choosers

Like the other proverb in this book with a similar meaning, 'you can't look a gift horse in the mouth' (see) this was recorded and passed down to us by John Heywood, this one in his 1562 book of Proverbs. In Heywood's day, there was very little pity and provision for the poor, and if one were fortunate enough to be the recipient of a gift, he should appreciate it, even if it did not completely meet the need at hand. Here is the quote from Heywood.

"**Beggers should be no choosers**, but yet they will:
Who can bryng a begger from choyse to begge still?"

The actual meaning at the time was 'beggars ought not to be choosers, rather than 'can't be.'

Behind every great man is a great woman

This much-repeated cliché became a feminist movement slogan as early as the 1960s, but was in use considerably earlier. The earliest printed reference seems to be from the *The Port Arthur News*, a Texas newspaper, in February, 1946. The article had the heading: "Meryll Frost – 'Most courageous athlete of 1945'":

"As he received his trophy, the plucky quarterback unfolded the story of how he 'came back'. He said 'They say **behind every great man there's a woman**. While I'm not a great man, there's a great woman behind me.'"

The impression was left here that it was already well-known as a saying.

Behind the eight ball

This is a sports-related cliché, most commonly believed to have come from billiards. An eight ball is the pesky black ball which in certain games can't be touched without a penalty. If a ball which one is attempting to knock into a side pocket is behind the eight ball it can be a tricky shot. Figuratively, this means that someone is in a weak or losing position.

Another version of the origin of the cliché is that it derived from the game of Kelly Pool in which the players are allowed to use one of sixteen balls to pot, and the players with the lower numbered balls play first. Those who get balls with numbers larger than eight are likely to win. Hence, if you start after the eight ball you are in a weak position from the start.

The billiards origin makes more sense. In Kelly Pool it would likely have been 'after,' instead of behind and 'the *eighth* ball' in this case.

All early known citations of the phrase are from the U.S. and date from the early 20th century. This one is from the Wisconsin newspaper *The Sheboygan Press*, in December of 1929:

"Bill ['*Lucky' Bill McKechnie, manager of the Boston Braves*] figures he can finish **behind the eight ball** with any kind of a ball team, so there's no harm in trying out young talent as there's nothing to lose beyond last place."

Bend over backward

This phrase is used to metaphorically describe willingness to do anything necessary simply to make someone else happy. In the second half of 1968 Cuna Supply Cooperative applied to the U.S. Copyright Office in Washington DC for copyrights on several advertizing slogans. One was:

"When you need a loan we **bend over backwards** to help."

This is the earliest known citation of the phrase as an idiom.

Bend someone's ear

This applies to talking to someone about something which he or she may rather not hear, and may be boring. It would seem to indicate talking so much that the ear would move backward. Asking for permission to 'bend someone's ear' is a plea for indulgence. Originally it was telling someone to bend their *own* ear, and goes back to the 19th century. An early example is from *Klosterheim* by Thomas De Quincy, 1855:

"Prince, **bend your ear** a little this way."

Then from *Masonic Odes and Poems*, Robert Morris, 1880:

"Hark, Freemasons, I'm to tell you,— **Bend your ear** in earnest vow,— What we covenanted deeply…"

Bent out of shape

This expression for being extremely upset about something is very new compared to many. It never came into practical usage until the second half of the 20th century.

Bob Dylan used the phrase in his long satiric lyric *It's Alright Ma (I'm Only Bleeding)*, "**Bent out of shape** from society's pliers…" This is probably the genesis of its acceptance into pop culture jargon.

best is yet to come, The

This positive affirmation, often associated with the Christian hope of eternal life, has been in common use since at least the late 19th century, when William Garden Blaikie included the following lines in his biographical work of a Puritan minister, *David Brown, D.D., LL.D.: professor and principal of the Free Church College, Aberdeen: a memoir:*

"To be at home with the Lord at death is enough in the meantime. But **the best is yet to come.**"

A song composed by Cy Coleman with lyrics by Carolyn Lee in 1959 by this title helped to popularize the phrase among the masses and is best known for Frank Sinatra's rendition in 1964 (Reprise Records).

best laid plans of mice and men often go awry, The

Many likely thought that this was coined by John Steinbeck in his classic novel, later made into an epic motion picture, *Of Mice and Men*. However, as mentioned earlier in this book, it was Robert Burns who first penned these immortal words (or a close, rather Scottish, version) in his narrative poem, *To a Mouse*.

The section goes like this:

"But Mousie, thou are no thy-lane,
In proving foresight may be vain:
The best laid schemes o' Mice an' Men,
Gang aft agley,
An' Lea'e us nought but grief an' pain,
For promised joy."

The phrase relates to the fact that no matter how much planning someone does, 'a monkey wrench' can always be thrown into the equation foiling them. (See also: 'throw a monkey wrench into the works'.)

best of both worlds, The

The root of this phrase probably goes back to French philosopher, Voltaire, who in 1759 in his satire, *Candide,* quoted his mentor Pangloss:

*"...in **this best of all possible worlds**, all is for the best."*

The cliché is used when contrasting two lifestyles or situations yet advocating enjoying the advantages of each.

In 1853, Thomas Benny published a work encouraging Christian living entitled, *Is it Possible to Make **the Best of Both Worlds**? A Book for Young Men.* In 1895, he published a slightly different version, leaving off 'Is it possible to make...'

A 1925 three-act play by Monica Ewer had this catchy title.

Best thing since sliced bread

Sliced bread has been with us since 1928, when it was first packaged and sold in stores. According to the *Kansas City Star*, the original ad was "the greatest forward step in the baking industry **since bread was wrapped**." This led to the common cliché, 'The greatest (or best) thing since sliced bread.'

The phrase, as we know it, has been around in popular American jargon since the mid-20th century, and has come to be applied to anything thought to be revolutionary. It has been joined by other such phrases such as 'the best thing since the hula-hoop.'

Better a friend who is close than a brother far away

This is the most-used version of this old saying, but it is actually a paraphrase of a biblical proverb from King Solomon in *Proverbs 27:10*. It is very close to the *New American Standard Version* of last part of this verse:

> "Do not forsake your own friend or your father's friend, And do not go to your brother's house in the day of your calamity; **Better is a neighbor who is near than a brother far away.**"

The saying is pretty much an axiom. Sometimes having a friend or neighbor close in time of need is better than having to go a great distance for a family member who may not even be as willing to help as your friend.

Better late than never

This usually expresses one's disdain over the procrastination of another person. The first citation to this popular phrase seems to have been by Geoffrey Chaucer in *Canterbury Tales.* It's from the story titled *Yeoman's Prologue,* written about 1386. It is early Middle English.

> **"For bot than never is late.'"**

Better safe than sorry

Better safe than sorry is an axiom /proverb which first appeared in print in 1837 in Irish novelist Samuel Lover's *Rory O'More.*

> "Jist countin' them,-- is there any harm in that?" said the tinker: "**it's better to be safe than sorry.**"

Then on 14 April 1933, *Radio Times* included the following:

> "Cheap distempers very soon crack or fade. **Better be safe than sorry.**"

Better than a poke in the eye with a sharp stick

Said to be originally from Australia by one source, and possibly Celtic by another, it is often used in America. It has even been proposed that it came from Homer's *Odyssey*. There is no evidence of this, and the phrase was not even in use until the late 19th century. The earliest known citation is from *Uncle John,* a novel by George John Whyte Melville, Volume II, page 90, 1874:

> "Three sovereigns isn't much, but it's **better than a poke in the eye with a sharp stick**."

It has even been abbreviated with the acronym BTAPITEWASS.

Better to go to bed hungry than to wake up in debt

Though the above is often listed as a traditional proverb, Benjamin Franklin (1706-1790) is credited with a similar saying: "**Rather to go to bed without dinner than to rise in debt**." This is likely the true origin. The phrase stresses the importance of living within one's means.

Between a rock and a hard place

The basis of this expression has been said to arise from the Greek Classics. Odysseus, it is written, had to pass between the monster, Scylla, and the deadly whirlpool, Charydbis.

The phrase itself, however, is of American origin and was first recorded in *Dialect Notes V* in 1921.

> "To be **between a rock and a hard place**...to be bankrupt. Common in Arizona in recent panics; sporadic in California."

The 'recent panics' mentioned here no doubt refer to the events surrounding the Bisbee, Arizona mine worker deportations of 1917. Early in the 20th century a dispute developed between the copper mining companies and the mine workers. In 1917, the workers, some of which had organized labor unions, presented a list of demands, including more pay and better working conditions, to their bosses. Their demands were refused and many workers were deported to New Mexico. It is believed that the choice of these workers between poor working conditions at the rock-face, and unemployment inspired the original saying, 'between a rock and a hard place.'

Between the devil and the deep blue sea

This old saying is akin to 'The devil to pay' (see). In sailing vessels of old, the 'devil' was a seam between the planks which was quite inaccessible, and imperative to keep water-proofed. Often the devil referred to the board which was attached to the hull to support the heavy guns. Pitch was used in this process. Caring for the devil was hazardous, but better kept well-maintained than lost in the 'deep blue sea.'

Between the Devil and the Deep Blue Sea was the title of a popular song written by Ted Koehler and Harold Arlen, and recorded by Cab Calloway in 1931.

The idiom has come to mean any dilemma which seems unsolvable.

Beyond the pale

If someone is beyond the pale, they are incorrigible—beyond the acceptable standards of decency.

This may be better understood in Europe and the U.K. than the U.S. Originally a pale was an area under the authority of a specified ruler or government official.

In the fourteenth and fifteenth centuries the King of England ruled Dublin and the surrounding area known as the *Pale of Dublin*. The *Pale of Calais* was formed in France as early as 1360. Catherine the Great created a *Pale of Settlement* in Russia in 1791.

A pale has long been associated with a fence in which one is protected; a safe, enclosed area. Anyone 'beyond the pale' was seen as savage and dangerous.

Beyond the shadow of a doubt

A forerunner of this expression has been around since circa 1300. Other early references appear as 'shadow of a doubt,' sans the word beyond.

In 1850, Nathaniel Hawthorne included 'the shadow of a doubt' in *The Scarlet Letter.*

Then, the popular source for most researchers on the full phrase, 'beyond the shadow of a doubt' is Robert Frost in his brilliant poem, *The Trial by Existence* in 1915.

Harper Lee's highly acclaimed *To Kill a Mockingbird, 1960,* included Atticus Finch's well-known court statement:

> "The law says 'reasonable doubt,' but I think a defendant's entitled to **the shadow of a doubt**. There's always the possibility, no matter how improbable, that he's innocent."

This suggests that a 'shadow of a doubt' exceeds the requirement of law in court cases determining guilt.

Biblical proportions

Though a recent cliché, talk of events being 'of biblical proportions' meaning 'exceptionally large scale disasters,' has been documented back as far as the 1980s. One such example is from the movie, *Ghostbusters* (1989), when Dr. Peter Venkman, played by Bill Murray, said to the mayor, "Or can you accept the fact that this city is headed for a disaster of **biblical proportions**?"

Other examples are found in such publications as *Time Magazine*. Since then, the idiom has become utilized in pop culture to describe Armageddon-type cataclysms feared to happen, and actual disasters such as tsunamis and especially devastating hurricanes and tornadoes. The news media has 'eaten this phrase up' and uses it freely.

Big Apple, The

'The Big Apple' for the city of New York was coined by touring jazz musicians in the 1930s, who used the slang expression 'apple' for any town or city. To them, playing in New York City was to play the big time –The Big *Apple*.

Big fish in a small pond

A big fish in a small pond is someone with great abilities and much pull in a small company or geographical area. A reverse to this would be a small fish in a big pond.

The phrase is from the U.S. and the earliest reference seems to be in *The Galveston Daily News*, in Texas, in June 1881, and apply to local interests:

> "They are **big fish in a small pond**."

In 1919 both phrases were used in the *Engineering and Mining Journal*, Volume 107, published by the American Institute of Mining Engineers:

> "I would rather be a **big fish in a small pond** than a small fish in a big pond."

Since the 1980s the expression has gained much popularity and has been used by writers in books of almost every genre.

bigger they are, the harder they fall, The

This well-known proverb has been attributed to a quote from British boxer, and three-division world champion, 5' 11 ½" tall, 165 pound Robert "Bob" Fitzsimmons (1863-1917), in an interview in 1902. Though he had made headlines by beating larger men, including 305 pound Edward Dunkhorst, right after the statement, he lost to American James Jackson Jeffries, who stood 6' 1" and weighed 225 pounds. If Fitzsimmons didn't coin it, he certainly made the phrase popular.

It means that every person, no matter how important, is subject to failure. Those with the most clout are likely to have more to lose as a result of a possible downfall.

big picture, The

The big picture refers to the whole of a matter, not just one part of it. It requires us to take a step back and look at all options. In order to grasp 'the big picture' one needs to possess to a fair degree what is known as 'Gestalt.' This is a word we borrowed from the Germans and this ability can be helpful in many careers which require much deliberation and preparation. Gestalt literally means 'form or shape,' and Gestalt psychology teaches us wholeness, and developed from research in neurology and cybernetics in the 1940s and '50s. The idea of seeing the total picture, however, is even older. As early as August 1904, it was used in *The World's Work: A History of Our Time*, Volume 8, by Walter Hinds Page:

> "But you **see the big picture** and learn the big facts in the Palace of Agriculture itself. The total impression produced is not that this is the work of farmers who plow and sow and pluck and reap and produce everyone his little store."

As a cliché, 'the big picture' came into common use in the late 20th century.

Big shoes to fill

This was a quote from Andrew Jackson when he assumed the office of President of the United States in 1829, succeeding John Quincy Adams. The full quote was:

> "**I've got big shoes to fill.** This is my chance to do something. I have to seize the moment."

It is still in use and means that the the successor of a person who was a great individual and accomplished much will likely be judged accordingly.

Big Wig

Centuries ago, incredibly, men and women took baths only twice a year, traditionally in May and October. Women always kept their hair covered, while men shaved their heads to avoid lice and bugs and wore wigs. Wealthy men could afford high-quality wigs made from wool. They were not able to wash the wigs, so to clean them they would carve out a loaf of bread, put the wig in the shell, and bake it for thirty minutes. The heat would make the wig big and fluffy; hence the term 'big wig.' People often use the term 'Big Wig' to describe a person who appears to be powerful and wealthy.

An early figurative example is from *Littell's Living Age, Volume 1*, page 206, 1844:

> "Blest age, when lawyers ape the deeds Of Bayard and the Cid, And scorn the peaceful "Practices" Of Impey and of Tidd! When **big wigs** leave the courts and change (Of arms blood-thirsty takers,)"

bird in the hand is worth two in the bush, A

This common proverb, meaning a small advantage or known asset is more valuable to a chance at a larger profit goes back to medieval days when falcons were commonly used as birds of prey. It meant that the falcon was very valuable to its owner and certainly worth more than two birds not yet obtained (in the bush).

The first reference in print to the term as it is currently used was in John Ray's *A Hand-book of Proverbs*, published in 1670. How far back it was actually in use is debated. A similar proverb is found in Solomon's biblical book of *Ecclesiastes* chapter 9, verse 4. 'A living dog is better than a dead lion.' This was quoted by Henry David Thoreau in *Conclusion*, from *Walden*.

An even closer version is quoted in a book of proverbs by John Heywood in 1546 titled *A dialogue conteinying the number in effect of all the prouerbes in the Englishe tongue*. This version was printed as: '**Better one byrde in the hande than ten in the wood.**'

'The Bird in Hand' was used as a common name for English pubs in the Middle Ages, and several still exist with the name. In 1734, a hamlet in Pennsylvania was founded with that name.

Birds of a feather flock together

Meaning that persons of similar interests are likely to find each other and keep company, the phrase has been around at least since the mid-sixteenth century. William Turner used a form of it in his 'papist satire' (writing against the Roman Catholic religion) *The Rescuing of Romish Fox.*

"**Byrdes of an kynde** and coulor **flok** and flye always **together.**"

Bite the bullet

This old saying comes from the days before anesthetics. As far back as the American Revolution a soldier about to undergo an operation was given a bullet to bite. It now means to grin and bear a painful situation. It can also mean missing the worst case scenario.

The figurative meaning was pioneered by Rudyard Kipling in *The Light That Failed,* 1890.

"**Bite on the bullet**, old man, and don't let them think you're afraid."

Bite off more than one can chew*

This idiom originated in the U.S. in the mid to late 19th century and is thought to have been taken from children filling their mouths too full of food. It came to be used shortly thereafter for getting an excessively large plug of tobacco in one's mouth. The earliest known printed figurative reference, however, is in *Publisher's Weekly*, in an article titled 'Communications', January 6, 1877:

"I will admit that there is a show of reason in this statement, and to use a strong phrase of another friend of mine, in this successful effort I am afraid that "I have bit off more than I can chew."

As an idiom it means taking on too large a task or responsibility.

Bite the dust

This well-known phrase doesn't originate with American Western movies. Its earliest printed non-English reference comes from of the epic Ancient Greek poem, Homer's *Iliad* about the Trojan War with the Greeks, written circa 700 BC, as translated by William Cullen Bryant in 1870. To 'bite the dust' was a poetic way of describing the death of a warrior. Is seems uncertain whether to credit Homer or Bryant.

> "Grant that my sword may pierce the shirt of Hector about his heart, and that full many of his comrades may **bite the dust** as they fall dying round him."

The first citation of the phrase in English came from the Scottish author-translator, Tobias Smollatt, in 1750, in *Adventures of Gil Blas of Santillane*:

> "We made two of them **bite the dust**, and the others betake themselves to flight."

Bitter pill to swallow

This phrase, which now refers to any experience which is difficult to accept, originated in the days before coated tablets, when medicines often had horrid taste, and were unpleasant to get down. One such medicine was in the form of pellets made from the bark of the cinchona tree, and was successful in fighting malaria. The quinine in it, however, was extremely bitter.

An early figurative citation is from *The Leavenworth Medical Herald*, Volume 4 page 26, June, 1870 and refers to changes made as a result of the Civil War:

> "And this, say gentlemen from the South, is **a bitter pill to swallow**. It is a **bitter pill to swallow**, I admit; but is it any worse, any harder, any more humiliating, any more cruel for you than it is for us?"

Black as the ace of spades

The ace of spades has a special significance because in England, many years ago, playing cards were taxed. To be certain that the tax was paid by card companies, it was illegal for anyone but the government to print the ace of spades, then the card companies had to buy these from the government, thus paying the tax.

The card was, of course, black, but it was made especially ornate which made its black color stand out. Thus, the phrase came to be, as 'black as the ace of spades.'

Blackberry winter

An expression used in Southern and Midland America to describe a 'cold snap' which seems to arrive each spring about the time the blackberries bloom. Another such term is 'dogwood winter' which is when the dogwood trees are in bloom.

The term has been in use since at least the late 19th century, and the Illinois State Horticulture Society included this near reference in their Transactions in 1875:

> "We have had a very dry season, and yet the Kittatinny blackberry has ripened perfectly, while most other varieties have dried up. And this comes right in with my remarks last night. We have thought that our **blackberries winter**-kill."

Then, in *Highways and Byways of the South*, 1904, Clifton Johnson wrote:

> "Then, later, when the blackberries are in blossom, we have another cold spell what we call the **blackberry winter**."

A few years later, in 1915, the *American Botanist* included the following very clear reference:

> "In a similar way a cold spell in spring, after winter has apparently vanished, is variously named **blackberry winter**, dogwood winter, or redbud winter. Our little winter of this kind comes in May and according to the Monthly Weather..."

Black sheep

Black cats are traditionally a symbol of bad luck, and beware the chance that one may cross your path! Black was associated with mourning as early as the second century in Rome, something likely adapted from the ancient Egyptian culture. *Bête noire* is French for "black beast" and means something disliked or feared.

In the *Bible* (*Psalms 100:3, 23:1*), people were depicted as sheep, and the Lord as the shepherd. In pre-industrial times, black sheep were less valuable than white ones. Perhaps this was caused by the idea of black being associated with evil or the devil. As a result, a black sheep in a family became a term applied to a less-desirable member.

Bleeding like a stuck pig

"Bleeding like a stuck pig" is a cultural phrase to describe profuse bleeding caused by a hog slaughtering technique in which the swine is stabbed in a main artery, usually with an anticoagulant on the instrument used.

The metaphor was in use by 1857 when it appeared in a British short story book, *Bentley's Miscellany Volume XLI*, in a tale called *A Fisherman's Third Letter to His Chum in India*:

"You hit him, sir," said Tim, "for he is **bleeding like a stuck pig**."

After the turn of the century a version was listed in 1902 in *Slang and its analogues past and present:*

"**Bleeds like any stuck pig.**"

Novels soon included it, and then it was used in a 1921 issue of *Saturday Evening Post*.

Blessing in disguise

This line has been in usage in English at least since the 18th century, and the earliest known reference to it was in a song by British writer and clergyman, James Hervey, in *Reflections on a Flower Garden*, 1746, quoted in *The Puritan* magazine.

"Good when He gives, supremely good,
Nor less when He denies;
E'en crosses from His sovereign hand
Are **blessings in disguise**."

(*The Puritan, an illustrated magazine for free churchmen, Volume I and II*, page 36, February to December, 1899)

It clearly means that when a circumstance seems to be adverse, often the 'cloud has a silver lining' (see) and it will turn out to be a blessing.

Blind as a bat

Bats' eyes are very sensitive, and in daylight they are almost totally unable to see anything. That's why they are called 'blind.' But in the dark, which is when they are up and about, though they have erratic flight patterns, they definitely can see and sense where they are going. In fact, they have a sophisticated built-in sonar system, by which they detect objects around them by sending out ultrasonic sound waves. This simile started in the late sixteenth century, and has survived the tests of time.

Blind leading the blind

This one, like many common sayings, is from the *Bible*. In *Matthew 15:14*, Jesus criticized the Pharisees, who were the religious authorities of his day, saying they were 'blind leaders of the blind.'

Blood in the water*

As an idiom, this refers to the exhibition of apparent weakness on the part of one competitor in a match, causing a feeling of vulnerability and pressure on that person and an over-confident attitude on the part of the other. It is derived from shark and piranha attacks which leave the persons involved helpless. The sight and smell of blood in the water stimulates the predators into a nervous frenzy so they will attack anything in range. It came into usage after Stephen Spielberg's 1975 mega-hit movie, *Jaws*.

The earliest verifiable citation of the metaphorical usage of this phrase is found in *Over the Wire and on TV: CBS and UPI Campaign '80*, compiled by Michael J. Robinson and Margaret A. Sheehan, published in 1983, page 133:

> "After three years in close proximity, the press inevitably had more information about Carter on which to base their news coverage. The first reason Powell gave to explain Carter's press miseries was the idea of **'blood in the water'** –that more bad press goes to those who have just had bad press."

Blood is thicker than water

This saying means quite simply, relatives will stick together and hold up for one another when mere friends will not. Sometimes this proves true; sometimes not.

68

This was originally an old German proverb, *Blut ist dicker als Wasser.* It first appeared a medieval beast epic, *Reinhart Ficks* (Reynald the Fox), by Heinrich der Glîchezære in about 1180. The proper English translation of the term there was 'Kin-blood is not spoilt by water.' Then in 1412, English priest John Lydgate wrote in *Troy Book:*

"For naturally blood will be of kind / Drawn-to blood, where he may it find."

One rendering of this is 'Relationships within the family are stronger than any other kind.'

We get our modern saying from John Ray, in his 1670 *A Hand-book of Proverbs.* In 1815, Sir Walter Scott used it in his novel, *Guy Mannering* as:

"Weel – **Blud's thicker than water** – she's welcome to the cheeses."

According to *The Boston Globe*, experts tell us that the adult human body is 50-60% water and that blood itself is 83% water. But it is obvious that real blood *is* thicker than water.

Blood, sweat and tears

This expression, meaning excessive effort exerted under trying circumstances, is often attributed to famous favorite sons, such as Winston Churchill, Oscar Wilde and Mark Twain. Though these fine gentlemen certainly utilized it, none of them were its author. The root of it comes from the *Bible* in *Luke 22:44*:

"And being in an agony he prayed more earnestly: and his **sweat** was as it were great drops of **blood** falling down to the ground." *(KJV)*

Though this verse does not use the word 'tears,' it is implied, and was used in the first known printed reference to the phrase in the English translation of *Sermons on Various Subjects* by Christmas Evans (1766-1838), translated from the Welsh by J. Davis, 1837:

"Christ the High Priest of our profession, when he laid down his life for us on Calvary, was bathed in his own **blood, sweat and tears**."

Evans, sometimes dubbed 'the John Bunyan of Wales,' came about his Christian name due to his birth on 25 December 1766.

Blowing smoke

The literal term, 'blowing smoke' goes back to the 1614 introduction of Virginia tobacco to Western Europe.

Later, magicians used smoke as a means of obscuring the truth and making people believe that they had done something amazing.

Blowing smoke became a way of saying that a compliment was insincere and meaningless, and usually meant to gain favor from the other person. Another such phrase is 'jerking me around.'

Blow one's mind

This now somewhat outdated cliché came into American popular culture in the 1960s and was derived from the effects of mind-altering drugs like LSD. Though 'blows my mind' is a bit stronger expression, its modern replacement is 'surreal.' This term, most often used loosely, meant that something was so shocking or overwhelming that it was difficult for the mind to grasp. It faded from everyday use in the 1980s. A similar expression is 'blown away.'

Blow something to smithereens

The word smithereens is Irish, and is a variant of the modern Irish word, 'smiderin,' meaning small pieces.

One theory of the origin is that smithereens may refer to the shards of metal formed when iron is hammered in a smithy. The word smiodar means fragments in Irish. -een is a common ending for Irish words.

The idea of things being 'broken, smashed, or blown to smithereens' dates from at least the turn of the 19th century. Francis Plowden, in *The History of Ireland*, 1801, mentions a threat being made against a Mr. Pounden by a group of Orangemen:

> "If you don't be off directly, by the ghost of William, our deliverer, and by the orange we wear, we will break your carriage in **smithereens**, and hough your cattle and burn your house."

Blow the whistle on something or someone *

This idiom means to reveal to the proper authority facts concerning corrupt or dishonest activities going on so that they may be stopped. It is believed that this derived from the days when law officers blew their whistles to signify an illegal activity. Another thought is that it referred to referees blowing their whistles in the event of a foul or improper play in sports.

It was in use this way since at least 1933, when Franklin W. Dixon applied it in the Hardy Boys mystery, *Footprints Under the Window*, in Chapter 8:

> "My guess is he cut out from the gang and wants to **blow the whistle on** his pals."

Blue-bloods

This term means aristocratic. For centuries Arabs occupied Spain, but they were gradually forced out during the Middle Ages. The upper class of Spain had lighter skin than most of the population, as their ancestors had not inter-married with the occupying Arabs. As a result, the blue-looking blood running through their veins was more visible. Of course we know that all blood is red, but it sometimes appears to be blue when veins are visible near the skin's surface. As a result, blue-blooded came to mean 'upper class.'

Bob's your uncle

Commonly used in the U.K., it usually follows a set of instructions to mean, 'and there you have it,' or 'now you're all set.' The origin, however, seems to be anybody's guess, and there are multiple theories. According to some it has been around since the late 19th century.

One popular theory is that "Bob" refers to Lord Frederick Roberts, who was an Anglo-Irish soldier, born in India, who fought and commanded in his birth country, as well as Abyssinia, Afghanistan, and South Africa. He was one of the most successful military officers of the Victorian era and was cited for numerous acts of bravery. His most gallant effort was likely the lifting of the siege of Kandahar in 1878 when he marched 10,000 troops over three hundred miles from Kabul to a glorious victory. Well respected among his troops, Roberts was affectionately called 'Uncle Bobs.'

It is claimed that the phrase "Bob's your uncle" was originally used by Roberts' men to boost confidence among the ranks and imply that all would be well under his command.

Another explanation is that the phrase dates to 1887, when British Prime Minister Robert Cecil, Lord Salisbury made the appointment of Arthur Balfour to the high post of Chief Secretary for Ireland—a definite act of nepotism, in the truest form. You see, Lord Salisbury was Arthur Balfour's "Uncle Bob." The difficulty with either of these explanations, however, is that—despite extensive searching by a number of researchers—the earliest known *published* uses of the phrase are from 1932, two from 1937, and two from 1938.

But some say that the *root* of it is even older. Another theory is that it derives from the slang phrase "All is bob," meaning that everything is safe, pleasant or satisfactory. This dates back to the 18th century or so (it's in Captain Francis Grose's *Dictionary of the Vulgar Tongue* edition of 1785). Several other slang expressions contain the word 'bob,' some associated with thievery or gambling, and from the 18th century on it was also a generic name used for someone a person didn't know. Any or all of these might have contributed to its beginning.

Born leader

In a literal sense, this is a misnomer, there is really no such thing. Leaders are developed. But potential and characteristics of leadership may exist within one's personality. Without such potential and characteristics, a person will not become an effective leader.

On 4 September 1936, David Lloyd George met Adolph Hitler, and commented, "He is **a born leader** of men. A magnetic, dynamic personality with a single-minded purpose, a resolute will and a dauntless heart..." (*I Talked to Hitler* by the Right Honourable David Lloyd George, *Daily Express,* London, November 17, 1936)

This saying became popular with persons thought to have natural ability for leadership. Certainly Hitler was a leader—just tragically misguided—and one who changed the course of history.

Born with a silver spoon in one's mouth

This term is often applied to aristocrats born to inherited wealth, and seen as rather spoiled by their high-class heritage. In Australia, the common expression for one born to privilege is 'silvertail.'

Another alternate of this phrase was 'gold spoon,' used in the 1840 'Gold Spoon Oration' which criticized President Martin Van Buren for his perceived luxurious lifestyle.

A similar expression in Portuguese is translated 'born in a gold cradle.'

"Born with a silver spoon in their mouths" is often applied to the British Royal family, and has been for generations because of the perception of the average citizen of the U.K. to them as out of touch with the common people.

Botched up

This saying has evolved into a menagerie of variants. The origin of this idiom, however, is quite clear.

In 1879, British railroad engineer, Sir Thomas Bouch (1822-1888), designed a bridge that was built over the Firth of Tay at Dundee, Scotland. It was claimed to be the greatest structure ever built in Victorian England. In fact, the construction of the Tay rail bridge resulted in his being knighted. The bridge was nearly two miles long, consisting of eighty-five spans and at the time was the longest bridge in the world.

On the stormy night of 28 December 1879, only nineteen months after the bridge was declared safe by the Board of Trade and opened to traffic, the wind caused the collapse of some of its spans. A train and six carriages and seventy-five human lives were lost that night, making it the worst accident caused by structural failure in the history of England. Sir Thomas Bouch died only 10 months after the failure.

As a result of this disaster, seemingly only trumped by the sinking of the 'unsinkable' Titanic, anything which is put together in slipshod manner or substandard is said to be 'boutched up,' usually spelled 'botched up,' because of current pronunciation.

Bottom line

This idiom means the final figure on a profit and loss statement, also called 'net income.' Alternatively someone's bottom line is the lowest amount of money which someone is willing to accept for doing a job or accept for the price of an item. It is a relatively new expression.

The term has been used extensively since the mid-20th century and has become a title in numerous fields including a fabulously famous music venue in Greenwich Village in Manhattan started in the 1970s, which thrived until the economic decline of the early 21st century, a Southern California magazine highlighting Hollywood stars, a Kansas City Communications Marketing Firm and various other news and personal improvement tools.

Boy Howdy!

This phrase, (sometimes 'boy hidy' or 'boy, oh howdy') a variation of the simple exclamation, Boy! going back to the late 19th century, was in use as early as 1902 (which may be its coining) when it appeared in the May 13th edition of `the *News-Democrat* in Uhrichsville, Ohio in a poem called *Howdy.*

> "Man that sez it's good enuff—
> 'Ol' **boy, howdy!'**"

The saying became popular as early as World War I when it was in the October 18th 1918 issue of *Stars and Stripes*, in an ad on page 7:

> "**Boy howdy!**"—what a razor!

Around that time it showed up in a number of other publications.

Boys will be boys

This expression apparently was in print as early as 1589. Around the beginning of the seventeenth century, Thomas Deloney, in *The Gentle Craft*, made the statement a bit more generalized by stating, '**Youth will be youth.**' (This version appears in a later printing, dated 1903.)

In 1935, a British comedy film was made named *Boys Will be Boys*, and several rock groups have recorded songs by that name. There was even a short-run American TV sitcom, which began as *Second Chan*ce and revamped as ***Boys will be Boys*** in 1988.

The term implies that there are certain intrinsic characteristics which apply to all young male humans which remain constant, and we may as well accept them for who they are and let nature take its course. It has been over-used by parents and well-meaning friends of young boys for generation after generation; but for those enduring their antics, it gets no easier to bear.

Brand spanking new

Branding something shows immediately that it then belongs to a particular person or company. This expression as a verb has been around since the Middle

Ages. It is derived from the hot branding stake, later, iron—a term applicable since 900 A.D. 'Brand name' is a derivative of this.

The earliest printed reference to 'brand new' is from John Foxe's *Sermons*, in 1570:

"New bodies, new minds and all thinges new, **brande-newe**."

Some later citations were spelled differently, such as this line from the London paper, *The Times,* in 1788:

"The liquor spoiled a **bran new** pair of sattin breaches."

In 1830, bran-span new was used in Henry Angelo's *Reminiscences*:

"His feet were thrust into a **bran-span new** pair of fashionable pumps."

This seems to be a version of a later citation in *The Whitby Glossary*, 1855:

"**Brandnew, Brandspandernew**, fresh from the maker's hands, or '**spic and span new**'."

It would appear that the modern phrase 'brand spanking new' only evolved in the late 19th century as found in this earliest known printing in *Harper's New Monthly Magazine*, in April 1860, in the story entitled *Captain Tom: A Resurrection:*

"He had a new vessel, he had a new crew, he had **brand spanking new** fish-gear; but he had his old luck."

Break a leg

This idiom seems related to an oxymoron, for it states the exact opposite of what is being intended. It is utilized in the theater, reportedly out of the superstition that it was bad luck to wish an actor good luck before a show. It is most often used before the opening night of a play.

This oldest of uses supposedly has origins in ancient Greece and Rome. It is said that in ancient Greece spectators in the arenas would stomp rather than clap, and they would sometimes break a leg. In ancient Rome, gladiators would fight to the death in the Coliseum. One source says that spectators would shout, "quasso cruris," the Latin equivalent of 'break a leg.' This was said to be suggesting that the gladiators stay alive by only breaking the leg of their opponents.

Other ethnic origins are also reported, such as Elizabethan theater, Yiddish (Hatsloche un Broche) and German/Polish beginnings (połamania nóg). At any rate, it seems a universal saying which dates far back into the history of our world.

'Break a leg' also can mean, 'make a strenuous effort.' There are many references in which it is used this way as well. One is from the *Evening State Journal* in Nebraska in 1937.

"With all the **break-a-leg** dancing there are many who still warm to graceful soft shoe stepping."

Break the case wide open

This popular American saying was popularized in the late 20th century in reference to police cases which would incite great interest from the public. An early example is from *Cops and Constables, American and British Fictional Policemen* by Earl F. Bargainnier and George N. Dove, 1986.

"When cases do not break, Fellows is apt to chastise himself for the lack of results. Even when (as in The Late Mrs. D.) ... of his flashes of inspired reasoning and **breaks the case wide open**, he regrets not having thought of it sooner."

Break the ice

Anciently, all cities that grew from trade because they were built on rivers suffered when the cold winters froze over their gateway to the world. Small ships were developed to break the ice to 'forge a path for others to follow' so the large ships could get in and bring their precious cargoes.

The first recorded figurative use of this phrase, meaning 'to prepare the way' for anything, or to create a good relationship with a stranger, was by Thomas North in his 1579 translation of *Plutarch's Lives of the noble Grecians and Romanes.*

"The Oratour - At last **broke** silence, and **the ice**

Breath of fresh air

This means a sense of welcome relief caused by someone just met or something which has just happened, usually preceded by bad circumstances or events. Though used literally much earlier, it began to be used in a figurative sense in the mid-19th century. In May 1845, this citation appeared in *The Electric Magazine of Foreign Literature, Science and Art,* in an article previously published in the London Quarterly Review titled *The Improvisatore, or, Life in Italy* by Hans Christian Anderson as translated by Mary Howitt (first published 1835):

"At the sun's rise and setting alone was there **a breath of fresh air**..."

Bridle one's tongue

This jewel is from the *Bible*, thus the thought is 2000 years old! The verse is *James 1:26*:

"If any man among you seem to be religious, and does not **bridle his own tongue**, he deceives his own heart. This man's religion is vain." *(KJV)*

James, who was a leader in the church at Jerusalem, was a strict proponent of legality in the old school, and often clashed with the Apostle Paul on points of matters of faith versus the law according to church tradition.

Today this is quoted when telling someone to 'watch their mouth.'

Bright-eyed and bushy-tailed

Regardless of the inference by a major phrase origin encyclopedia that this refers to a cat (some say squirrels), this metaphoric idiom is originally a term used in fox hunting from the late sixteenth century. A fox which had dull eyes or has a shaggy coat will not provide the type of sport expected by classy experienced hunters who are out for the thrill of the hunt.

It means eager, alert and full of energy, and has reportedly been in oral use in this sense since the 1930s, possibly due to the popularity of the Shirley Temple movie, *Bright Eyes*, released on December 28, 1934. But the first known printing is from *Torpedo Junction* by Robert Joseph Casey, 1942:

"I muttered okay and Commander Chappell said: 'Tell Mr. Ford that Mr. Casey's been asleep but that he's now **bright-eyed and bushy-tailed** and will be with him forthwith.'"

77

Bring down the house***

This old figure of speech goes back to the 19th century and is used to mean that a performance or oration has been so outstanding as to excite the audience enough to garner great applause. The word 'house' in this sense refers to an auditorium or performance hall. It was also used to refer to laughter in the earliest available citation in *Annie Orme* by Rachel Sinclair, first published in *Sharpe's London Magazine* then in *Littell's Living Age*, Volume 45, 20 November 1852:

> "But, before I had done speaking, Annie was standing on the floor, laughing like to **bring down the house**."

Then in January 1870, *The XIX Century*, Volume 2, in the article, Early Literary Progress in South Carolina, has the following citation which uses it in a more usual sense:

> "He did not know, perhaps, that there was a famous buffo of that day, named Spiller, who could always **bring down the house** with a 'hurrah' from the groundlings that tore its way to the rafters."

Bring home the bacon

The roots of this common phrase may go as far back in the annals of history as early-12th century Essex, to the story of the 'Dunmow Flitch,' when a tradition was begun in 1104 which continues to this day. It is based on a local couple who impressed the Prior of Little Dunmow with their devotion to each other in marriage to the point that he awarded them a flitch (a side) of bacon. The ritual of presenting devoted couples a flitch each year is well documented and mentioned in Geoffrey Chaucer's *The Wife of Bath's Tale and Prolouge* in circa 1387. They are a part of *The Canterbury Tales*.

> "But never for us the flitch of bacon though, That some may win in Essex at Dunmow."

In early American county fairs, greased pig contests were held, and the winner kept the little porker, and 'took home the bacon.'

When Joe Gans and Oliver Nelson fought for the World Heavyweight Championship in 1906, the New York newspaper, *The Post Standard* reported on September 4th:

"Before the fight Gans received a telegram from his mother: 'Joe, the eyes of the world are on you. Everybody says you ought to win. Peter Jackson will tell me the news and you **bring home the bacon**.'"

Bringing home the bacon has long meant not only bringing home a desired prize, but doing well and earning a good living.

Bring out the 'A' game

This American cliché started showing up in the early 1990s, possibly in Chicago in reference to the Bulls, where it has been frequently used, and means 'come on, do your best this time, show us what you've got.' It certainly started in sports and quickly spread across the country and became a favorite of coaches and reporters in regard to a variety of games.

Now it is applied to persons in all professions who give a job their very best: in attitude and abilities—a job that would receive an 'A' grade. A related expression is 'Get in the zone' (see).

Brownie points [See: **Scoring** (or **racking up**) **brownie points**]

Bucket list

One of the newest clichés we are including, this is based on a 2007 movie with this title, starring Morgan Freeman as a man who is facing death with a list of things he wants to do before he 'kicks the bucket' (see). The phrase rapidly became a metaphor for those adventures a person must pursue in his or her lifetime.

buck stops here, The

President Harry Truman famously had a sign with this slogan on his desk, apparently to describe the finality of the responsibilities of the U.S. government ending in his office. The reverse side said 'I'm from Missouri,' and it was a gift from a friend. The slogan had been in use for a number of years before. Some card games use a marker called a buck. Different players act as dealer. When the buck is passed to the next player, the responsibility of dealing is passed. Stopping the buck is to accept the responsibility for dealing.

Bugger off!

This is a form of the originally very profane British term, 'bugger' which has now lost the original punch and is more accepted as common slang. (See: '**Bug off!**')

Bug off!

Bug off is a popular American term which says the same thing as a lot of other definitive sayings. Get lost, make yourself short, make like a tree and leave! It is probably short for the similar British term, 'bugger off!' Its first known American usage was in *The New York Magazine*, February 15, 1971.

> "This time the rapist left with the police. A method I have found personally helpful in discouraging the street molester is to embarrass the hell out of him — that is, turn around and in a loud voice say '**Bug off!**'"

Build a better mousetrap and the world will beat a path to your door

The root of this proverb is found in the writings of Ralph Waldo Emerson, before the invention of the mousetrap.

> "If a man has good corn or wood, or boards, or pigs, to sell, or can make better chairs or knives, crucibles or church organs, than anybody else, you will find a broad **hard-beaten road to his house**, though it be in the woods."

The invention of the mousetrap actually came in 1889, seven years after Emerson's death. His quote was then erroneously changed to include the mousetrap:

> "If a man can write a better book, preach a better sermon, or **make a better mousetrap** than his neighbor..."

The phrase has come to mean anything that can be made better and more efficiently will draw the customer to it. It likely spawned the saying in the 1989 Kevin Costner movie, *Field of Dreams*, "Build it and they will come."

Bumfuzzled

This curious word may not be used in all parts of the English-speaking world but where I was brought up, in the Southern U.S., it was often found in

80

conversations. It has been around in what is sometimes known as the 'South Midland' since the dawn of the 20th century, and means confused or flustered. Will Nathaniel Harben, in his Northern Georgia Sketches, 1900, used it this way:

> "'Well, I'll be liter'ly **bumfuzzled**!' he exclaimed. 'Ef it ain't John Ericson! I knowed yore company was in the fight last night, an' I thought o' you when I ...'"

The gist of the jargon sounds authentic to the region among locals with little education of the era.

Bummer

In the late 19th century, a bummer was what we now call a bum.

'That's a bummer,' though a bit older, didn't come into popular usage until the latter part of the 20th century. A bummer is a situation for which you had highest hopes, yet it flopped. When someone fails an important test or is not able to go on a much-anticipated trip, or worse, someone's sweetheart left him or her for a person of questionable character. Those circumstances could be described as bummers. An early printed example is from *Twisting the Rope*, a novel by Rebecca A. MacAvoy, page 14, 1986:

> "That's a **bummer**. But, you know, it gets better."

Burning one's bridges behind (him or her)

The root of this metaphor goes back to ancient military tactics when soldiers crossing rivers to invade hostile territories were instructed to burn the bridges in order to provide no way for any of their troops to turn back. As an idiom, it means cutting off all contact with one's past in order to embrace a more positive future. It first appeared in print in the late 1800s.

A very early example is from *Gleanings in Bee Culture*, an Ohio Christian publication promoting beekeeping, 1889, by 'A.I. Root' in a story entitled 'Our Homes':

> "He replied, 'Don't you think a person can be a Christian without Joining the church? .... He should rather **burn the bridges behind him**, and thus render It Impossible to retreat.'"

After this, similar references sprang up in a number of books and magazines throughout the 1890s and early 20th century.

Burning the candle at both ends

Today this metaphor refers to staying up late at night and rising early in the morning, thus loosing sleep, thus having an unsustainable lifestyle which dulls the senses and causes poor productivity. But this was not the original meaning. The earliest known mention in print is from Randle Cotgrave's *A Dictionary of the French and English Tongues*, published in 1611, and appeared in French:

> "Brusler la chandelle par les deux bouts" (To burn the candle by the two ends)

Thirty-one years later, the English version appeared in *Dictionarium Bratannicum* by Nathan Baily, 1730:

> "**The Candle burns at both Ends.** Said when husband and wife are both spendthrifts."

This begins to shape a figurative meaning, still somewhat variant from its present intent. *The Gentlemen's Magazine* in March 1771, used a near-modern citation in 'Debates of a Political Club':

> "Exhausting our strength therefore to crush her, if the vulgarism may be allowed, is **burning the candle at both ends**. It is suicide in politics..."

Burning the midnight oil

This is a metaphor which means working well into the night. It relates to the days when oil lamps and candles were the only means of lighting homes.

It is very old, for English author Francis Quarles wrote it in *Emblemes* in 1635.

> "Wee spend our mid-day sweat, or **mid-night oyle**;
> Wee tyre the night in thought; the day in toyle."

Burst one's bubble

This is 'knocking the wind' out of someone's hopes and dreams. This is a recent cliché comparatively, taking root in the late 20th century and 'gaining steam' on into the twenty-first. An early example is from the tabloid *Weekly World News*, March 7, 1989 in the Horoscope section on page 42:

> "Not to **burst your bubble,** Taurus, but you would be wise to check on this dreamboat's marital status before becoming involved."

82

Burying the hatchet

Unlike such Hollywood fanaticized Native American phrases as, "ugh, white man speak with forked tongue," burying the hatchet is actually of Native American traditional origin.

Hatchets were buried by the chiefs of tribes when they came to a peace agreement with another tribe or with white settlers. The phrase is recorded as early as the mid-17th century in English, but what it refers to is from much earlier, possibly even pre-dating the white settlement of the Western Hemisphere.

A translation of Thwaites' great work, *Jesuit Relations,* in 1644 suggests this practice:

> "Proclaim that they wish to unite all the nations of the earth and to **hurl the hatchet so far into the depths of the earth** that it shall never again be seen in the future."

The *New England Historical & Genealogical Register* for 1870 has a record that Samuel Sewall made in 1680, in which he recounts the burying of hatchets, or 'axes,' by Native American tribal leaders:

> "Meeting wth ye Sachem [the tribal leaders] the[y] came to an agreemt and **buried two Axes in ye Ground**; which ceremony to them is more significant & binding than all Articles of Peace the **Hatchet** being a principal weapon wth ym."

Actual references to this as a cliché come somewhat later, such as the one in *The History of the Five Indian Nations of Canada* by Cadwallader Golden, Esq., 1747.

> "The great Matter under Consideration with the Brethren is, how to strengthen themselves, and weaken their Enemy. My Opinion is, that the Brethren should send Messengers to the Utawawas, Twibtwies, and the farther Indians, and to send back likewise some of the Prisoners of these Nations, if you have any left to **bury the Hatchet**, and to make a Covenant-chain, that they may put away all the French that are among them."

The cliché has come to symbolize permanent reconciling of differences between opposing persons or groups.

Busier than a one-armed paper hanger

This humorous analogy has been in common use in the U.S. since at least the early 20th century. Sometimes it is expanded to say, 'with hives' or 'on a windy day.' The meaning is clear, too busy for one's own good. Despite the fact that someone who writes useless checks is also known as a 'paper hanger,' this applies to the obvious—hanging wallpaper—a task which requires both hands to perform properly.

An early example is found in *St. Nicholas,* an illustrated magazine for boys and girls, *Volume 45, Part 2* by Mary Maples Dodge, in a section called *Daddy Pat's Letters from the Front*, 1919:

> "Daddy has been **busier than a one-armed paper-hanger**, and it has been awful hard to find time to write."

Butterflies in one's stomach

Someone with butterflies in his or her stomach feels nervous, queasy and jittery. The person may be scared or excited by circumstances. Anxiety can cause a disruption of the body's enzymes. It is claimed that once a clever writer used the metaphor and it caught on. Some have used it to relate to the special emotion of new love. Many folks believe that they are only psychological, but an article in *Science News* by Joanne Silberner back on February 22, 1986 entitled '*Stomach Butterflies Scramble EGGs*' (erratic electrogastrograms) states, "**Butterflies in your stomach** aren't all in your head."

Buyer beware / Let the buyer beware

This saying is intended as a consumer protection warning on goods or services which may be unwise purchases. It has been in use since the early 20th century, and became more popular in the latter half of the century due to heightened concerns over con-persons and ponzi schemes. An early printing is from 1922 in *The Public Conscience: Social Judgments in Statue and Common Law* by George Clark Cox, page 235:

> "Caveat Emptor — Let the **Buyer Beware** WARREN v. BUCK Vermont Reports, October Term, 1898…"

84

Buying a pig in a poke

This saying is brought up again in the later expression 'letting the cat out of the bag' (see), and refers to the time when piglets were sold at market in bags. Since a cat was about the size of a young pig, unscrupulous merchants would sometimes defraud the buyer by placing a cat in the bag. Eventually it was no longer prudent to buy a 'pig in a poke.'

Today it is used to refer to buying anything 'sight-unseen.'

By and by

This now means 'after a while' or in the unknown distant future, and has been in use in its present form since the early 16th century and a version of it for a hundred years before. Originally in the 1400s it meant 'one by one.'

The phrase was actually used more than once in the *King James Version* of the *New Testament* (1611). The Greek word which it is translated in this way is *euthieos*, literally meaning 'immediately.' One such example is *Luke 21:9* when Jesus is speaking with his disciples concerning the end of the age:

> "But when ye shall hear of wars and commotions, be not terrified: for these things must first come to pass; but the end is not **by and by**."

The NIV reads:

> "When you hear of wars and uprisings, do not be frightened. These things must happen first, but the end will not come right away."

By and by has more recently been used in Christian lore to express hope in eternal life.

By and large

How this term came to mean 'on the whole,' or 'generally speaking,' is mysterious. It was originally a nautical command given to the captain of a sailing vessel, meaning 'sail slightly away from the wind.' There was a danger of being 'taken aback' when sailing too near the wind current.

It is said that it evolved from not wanting to 'sail directly into a statement.' Saying 'by and large' is a way of hedging a direct answer, and speaking in generalities. It is used both in America and Britain.

It was used in 1889 by Mark Twain in *A Connecticut Yankee in King Arthur's Court:*

> "Take it **by and large**, that spread laid everything far and away in the shade that ever that crowd had seen before."

By hook or by crook

Though other origins have been suggested, this old saying is almost certainly to come from a medieval English law stating that peasants could use branches of trees for fire wood if they could reach them and pull them down with their shepherds' crook or their billhook. It had nothing to do with someone being a 'crook.'

The first reference to this is in John Gower's *Confessio Amantis* in 1390.

> "**What with hepe** [hook] **and what with croke** [crook] they [by false Witness and Perjury] make her maister ofte winne."

Today it is used to mean that something will be obtained by whatever means is necessary, regardless if it is proper or legal.

By leaps and bounds

The two words here are near synonyms, so this serves as a double imperative for rapid progress. It has been used in English since 1796 when Alexander Pope used it in his translation of Homer's *The Iliad*.

> "High o'er the surging tide, **by leaps and bounds**, He wades, and mounts; the parted wave resounds. Not a whole river stops the hero's course, While Pallas sills him with immortal force."

By the skin of one's teeth

This popular metaphorical saying, meaning narrowly escaping disaster, comes from the biblical book of *Job*, chapter *19* verse *20*. The first English translation is from the *Geneva Bible*, 1560, and is a literal rendering of the Hebrew text:

"I haue escaped **with the skinne of my teethe**."

C

Can dish it out but can't take it

This means that someone is eager to say insulting and hurtful things to others, but when the slurs are hurled back the person is resentful. The earliest available verifiable citation is from *Boys' Life,* February 1938 in a sports article, *Winning Streak,* by B.J. Chute on page 8:

> "They have proved they **can dish it out. But can they take it**? That's what everyone is wondering."

can of worms, A

This metaphor is based on cans of worms which were sold for fish bait in the U.S. in the 1950s. Once they were opened, it was very hard to get the can shut so that the worms could not escape. Opening or getting into a can of worms became a figurative expression for bringing to light a matter which caused more problems than it did good and was not easily resolved. In spite of claims by other sources that the earliest citation is from 1955, *The Bulletin for Atomic Scientists,* January 1951, page 6, contains the following figurative connotation in "An address (by Robert J. Oppenheimer) delivered to the Awards Banquet of the Science Talent Institute in Washington, D.C., March 6, 1950":

> "Perhaps nowhere has the impact of science more clearly altered the specific terms of a great political issue in the effects of political development on warfare. This is **a can of worms** with which I have myself unhappily been engaged for some years. It would not be honest to say— though it would not be foolish to hope— that the very terror of modem weapons would in itself put an end to war…"

Can't carry a tune in a bucket

This phrase has several alternatives, like in a basket, a bushel basket (especially popular in the 1950s) or a bag or paper sack. It means that a person is tone deaf and unable to sing the simplest melodies properly.

It has been in use since at least the early 20th century. In 1922, Jim Tully wrote in his first book, *Emmett Lawler*:

"Emmett burst forth in song, but his comrade punched him in the side and said, 'Lord Sakes, shut up, you **can't carry a tune in a bucket**.'"

References to 'couldn't carry a tune' go back a bit farther. *The Winds of Chance* by Rex Beach, 1918 has this on page 35:

"He **couldn't carry a tune**

Can't hit the broad side of a barn

This has been used in both the literal and figurative ways. This hyperbolic expression dates from the late 19th to early 20th century in the military, and means that one has poor aim, or is greatly off in determining direction. The term broad side may have originally referred to battleships rather than barns according to some researchers. About 1900 it began being used in baseball for a pitcher with poor aim. The earliest known citation is found in *Ranier of the Last Frontier*, by John Marvin Dean, 1911:

"Those ladrones with Fagan yonder **can't hit the broad side of a barn** when they aim at it. If they was any good, they wouldn't let us follow 'em up like this."

Can't hold a candle to

The basis of this cliché goes back to the 16th century before street lighting existed. In those days, someone going home from a theatre or tavern at night was accompanied by a 'link boy' who carried a candle or a torch. These link boys were considered by those whom they served as very inferior individuals. Therefore, if someone 'couldn't hold a candle' to someone else, it meant that they were very inferior to them.

Can't see past the end of one's own nose

This humorous analogy has been in English speech and writing since the early-20th century. In 1907, the first printed example of a version of the phrase found is from *Druggists' Circular, Volume LI:*

"Proprietors are not blind, but they **won't see, any farther than the end of their own noses**."

In January 1912, in *The Dog Fancier*, Volume 21, Number 1, carried the following line on page 18 in a letter to the editor on 'That High Cost of Living':

"The editor of the Omaha Trade Exhibit, by the way, must be a bright sort of an individual who **can't see far past the end of his own nose**, else he would not have added his personal O.K. to such a statement as he apparently did do."

Can't see the forest for the trees

This applies to the problem of having so many small problems that take up one's time and efforts that the big picture of what is truly important is only a blur and undetectable.

On November 27, 1915, *School and Society*, Science Press, New York, edited by J. McKeen Cattell carried an early citation. Speaking of the modern young teachers he wrote:

"They **can't see the forest for the trees**; they can't see the facts for the facts."

Then in March, 1920, *St. Nicholas, a Magazine for Boys and Girls*, printed this citation in an article titled, '*An Airplane View of Russia*' in *The Watch Tower, a Review of Current Events* by Edward N. Teall:

"The history of ancient Rome is interesting; the history of modern Russia is more interesting—but harder to understand because we are so close to it. '**Can't see the forest for the trees.**'"

Can't walk and chew gum at the same time***

This old slang expression is used to mean that a person, usually a male, is unable to multitask. Strangely enough, the earliest citation for not being able to chew gum while doing something else refers to a woman. This could have been the original source for making this cliché. In an article in *The Dental Register,* Cincinnati, Ohio, June, 1892, we find the following:

"It is maddening to watch a talkative woman when she is chewing gum. Then, no woman has ever been able to look pretty **and chew gum at the same time.**"

The earliest citation of "can't walk and chew gum at the same time" is found in *The Record Chronicle*, Denton, Texas on 24 December 1956, in section 2, page 2, column 4:

"A classic comment by a local baseball player referring to a teammate's co-ordination: 'He **can't walk and chew gum at the same time.**'"

But a misquote actually popularized the expression, and some have heralded this as its origin. A statement made by President Lyndon Johnson in a private conversation about then House Majority Leader Gerald Ford, originally a bit differently, first printed in the *New York Times* in October, 1973, appeared in California's *Santa Cruz Sentinel* on Friday 17 May 1974 on page 32 as:

"He's so stupid he **can't walk and chew gum at the same time**."

Johnson was, of course, from Texas the state in which the article appeared. In his actual conversation, however, Johnson used the name "Jerry Ford," he said "dumb," not stupid, and didn't say "walk."

Can't win for losing

This Americanism, likely started by sports writers, meaning on a seemingly endless losing streak, has been around since the 1960s. An early example is from *Baseball Digest*, July 1967, page 81 in an article about Manager James Joseph Dykes:

"There had to be deletions and content reduction to stay in compact volume, because the man who was Mr. White Sox for 12 years when they **couldn't win for loosing** and who managed five other big league teams (A's, Indians, Tigers, Orioles and Reds) as well, is of strong and voluminous language."

Cardinal sin*

This term is usually used in a humorous context as an unforgivable error, usually deriding someone for committing such a deed. It is derived from the 'seven deadly sins' dating back to the 6th century originally grouped together by St. Gregory the Great. These sins were said to give rise to other sins.

The earliest known English reference in print is in William Crookes' *The Chemical News and Journal of Physical Science*, page 285, June 26, 1794, in Proceedings of Society:

"This fear of trouble is the ***cardinal sin*** of the English cuisine, and it plays admirably into the heads of 'pushing' tradesmen, by whom we are 'taken in and done for.'"

Carry a torch for

Carrying a torch for someone is a romantic term for keeping a 'flame of love' glowing in one's heart though no actual interaction is occurring. The first figurative reference to burning a torch is from the *Epilogue* to Irish playright Richard Brinsley Sheridan's comedy *The Rivals*, 1776:

> "In female breasts did sense and merit rule,
> The lover's mind would ask no other school;
> Shamed into sense, the scholars of our eyes,
> Our beaux from gallantry would soon be wise;
> Would gladly light, their homage to improve,
> The lamp of knowledge at **the torch of love!**"

Carrying a torch was a political practice in campaigns during the 19th century, exhibiting a burning care for the candidate. In November 1927 *Vanity Fair* carried the following:

> "When a fellow '**carries the torch**' it doesn't imply that he is 'lit up' or drunk, but girl-less. His steady has quit him for another or he is lonesome for her."

The first 'torch song,' a romantic ballad of unrequited love, written in 1912, was also first performed by Tommy Lyman in 1927; *My Melancholy Baby*. In nightclubs, female singers who made them their specialty became known as 'torch singers' during the 1930s.

Carte blanche

This literally means 'blank paper' and is adapted from the French. It means to give 'a blank check' or full discretionary freedom to do anything desired in the authority of the person giving the power.

It was first recorded by Raby in 1707 and was reprinted in the *Hearne Collection* in 1886:

> "Who sent **Chart Blanch** to make a Peace."

The term was later adapted to Gothic novels in the respect of a woman becoming a mistress with carte blanche of the man's wealth.

Cash cow

The term 'cash cow' was brought back to Britain from India by soldiers who noticed the natives in India offering money to temple idols in the form of sacred cows. It was coined in its present meaning in the 1960s by management guru, Peter F. Drucker.

Normally, a cash cow product has high market share in a slow-growing market, and is responsible for a large amount of the company's profit.

In 1977 *BPC Banker's Magazine, Ltd,* Volume 221 included the following on page 27:

> "Two recent mergers indicate the problems in growth markets with a high rate of inflation and without a **cash cow** to support them."

The term is also used in sarcasm by sales and business persons to describe customers who have no control over their spending habits.

Cash on the barrelhead

In medieval times, 'cash on the nail' was a common expression to mean what we in the U.S. now know as cash on the barrelhead, or immediate payment for goods or services at the time of receipt. A nail was not what we would think, but a shallow vessel mounted on a post at a place of business, into which the money must be deposited in order to receive goods.

Later, at seaports, a barrel of salt, tar, etc. was turned on end, and used as a countertop. The buyer and seller would face each other with the barrel between them. The buyer would place the money on the barrelhead to pay for the goods in the barrel.

Catawampus or catywampus

This Southern-midland slang expression now means positioned diagonally or 'kiddy-cornered' (originally 'cater-cornered'). Etymologists have had a time detecting its actual derivation, and especially how it came to have this meaning.

Cata or cater is a prefix meaning askew. In the early 20th century a 'wampus cat' was any wild cat. A mountain lion is sometimes called a catamount.

The original meaning of this word, in fact, according *Slang and Analogies Past and Present* by William Ernest Henley published in 1891 was, 'vermin, especially those that sting and bite.' An earlier spelling is listed as 'catawampous,' meaning fiercely, eagerly or violently destructive, and was a verb and by adding '-ly' it could be used as an adverb. Catawampus, it says, was apparently formed from the earlier word.

The first recorded usage known is from Charles Dickens in *Martin Chuzzleivit,* chapter, 21, page 216:

"There air some **catawampous** chawers in the small way too, as graze upon a human pretty strong."

Then in 1880 in Mortimer Collins' *Thoughts in my Garden:*

"Look at their [spiders] value in destroying wasps and blue-bottles, gnats, midges and all manner of **catawampuses**."

It was also used this way in *Littell's Living Age, Fifth Series Volume LX* in 1887:

"...as a fight between a crocodile and a **catawampus**..."

In fact, catawampus was used in this manner in recent times as seen in *The Old China Hands,* 1961, by Charles Grandison Finney:

"'Some sort of **catawampus** coming down the track, sir,' said the Sheriff. 'Nonsense,' said the lieutenant..."

In 1988, in *Morris Dictionary of Word and Phrase Origins*, the word is listed with cater-cornered, and in 1997, it receives the definition, 'In a diagonal position, crooked, not square' in *Hoi Toide on the Outer Banks: The Story of the Ocracoke Brogue* by Walt Wolfram and Natalie Schilling-Estes (page 40).

Catch 22

A catch 22 is a phrase which has come to mean a situation in which one seems to have no choice; either likely resulting in a negative or undesirable conclusion. It comes from the title of a 1961 book titled Catch-22 by Joseph Heller of which the first chapter was originally published in a magazine in 1955 under the title Catch-18, which presented a paradox.

Cat got your tongue?

This means, 'What's wrong, can't you say something about this?'

It is believed that this saying has its origin in the Middle East where thousands of years ago the practice of an eye for an eye was common. It was also customary to punish thieves by cutting off their right hand, and liars by ripping out their tongue. These body parts were fed to the king's pet cats.

cat's meow, The

This cute expression meaning 'the ultimate' was first coined by American cartoonist Thomas A. "Tad" Dorgan (1877-1929). He also coined the popular expression, "for crying out loud!" (See cat's pajamas)

Cats have nine lives

This common old saying is based on ancient fables. Nine is a mystical number in folklore and many religions. Cats were revered in Egypt. The ancient Egyptian priesthood in On, mentioned in Greek literature as Heliopolis, worshiped Atum-Ra, the sun god who was said to be the giver of life. Atum-Ra took the form of a cat when visiting the underworld, was claimed to embody nine lives in one creator. The following is from an Egyptian song from the 4th century BC:

> "O sacred cat! Your mouth is the mouth of the god Atum, the lord of life who has saved you from all taint."

Remnants from cat-worship lingered in Europe until the middle ages. Though the cat was no longer thought of as a divinity, they were seen as magical and otherworldly. The resilience of cats and their remarkable ability to survive falls still is an inspiration to humanity, so the myth of nine lives lives on.

cat's pajamas, The

In the U.K., it's 'the cat's pyjamas.' At any rate, it means a really good thing, and sometimes a really good *new* thing.

One unlikely theory is that this saying came from E.B. Katz, an English tailor of the late 18th and early 19th centuries, who made the finest silk pajamas for the nobility and wealthy. But there just aren't any printed references available before the early 1920s of the phrase.

The expression has definitely been around since at least that decade. Some people think that cartoonist Tad Dorgan, the originator of 'the cat's meow,' first came up with it, as well as several others that didn't stick around including "the flea's eyebrows" and "canary's tusks."

94

Popular Science, January 1926 edition, contained the following line in an endorsement for Daven radios by an editor:

> "Man! — of all the beautiful, round and full tones, this is **the cat's pajamas**."

Some other people say that this phrase was coined slightly earlier than the 1920s, and used by schoolgirls. Tad Dorgan didn't invent it; he just picked it up and made it popular. The 1926 movie, *The Cat's Pajamas* starring Betty Bronson, Sally Winton, Ricardo Cartez and Arlette Marchal didn't hurt either.

There's not really any logical explanation for how or why it started, unfortunately. It was part of a popular series of phrases coined in the 1920s about animals and their body parts, including the bee's knees, the snake's hips, the clam's garter, the eel's ankle, the elephant's instep, the tiger's stripes, the leopard's spots, the sardine's whiskers, and the pig's wings. 'When pigs fly' (see) was recorded back in 1616. All of these are a bit silly. Whoever first came up with the cat's *pajamas* (obviously not a body part) might have chosen the word 'pajamas' because they were new and viewed as cool in the 1920s; but basically, they were just sticking with the fads.

Caught on like wildfire

When something is 'trending,' like a video 'going viral' on YouTube, or a new dance or clothing fashion which is 'flying off the shelves,' it is said to have 'caught on like wildfire.'

This idiom originated from the literal wildfires which burn out of control, destroying thousands of acres of timberland annually. But it has been used metaphorically since at least the mid-19th century. *The Teacher's Visitor,* Volume 5, July-December 1846, edited by William Carus Wilson, had the following citation:

> "The words **caught like wildfire**, and a shout went round the hall, that as Lord Clarendon said, 'you would have thought the hall had cracked.' Such was the outburst of triumph."

An article in the *Washington Post* on December 1st, 1995 uses the analogy of Smokey the Bear, the U.S. Forest Service mascot and symbol of forest fire prevention, as '**catching on like wildfire**.' Smokey was originally drawn by artist Rudolph Wendelin in 1944, who, at the time of the article's publication, was 85 years old, and was featured in the article. Wendelin passed away in 2000.

Caught red handed

Various origins have been given to the expression 'Red handed,' (also used as red-handed) including an allusion to the culturist symbol of Ulster in Northern Ireland. The term originates very near there, indeed—from Scotland, and refers to having blood on one's hands after committing a murder.

The first use of 'to be taken with red-hand' dates back to a usage in the Scottish Acts of Parliament of King James I in 1432. Sir Walter Scott first used the term 'taken red-handed' in his classic novel, *Ivanhoe*. It was long after that before the term became more common as 'caught red handed.'

Some even claim earlier uses of similar phrases (in their native tongues) by the people of the Indus Valley between 800 and 900 BC, who determined a thief's guilt or innocence by putting the accused person's hands on an axe blade which had been heated until it was glowing red; or the Japanese, who were said to brush the sap from poison ivy on their money, and believed that thieves would break out in a rash and be caught 'red handed.'

Caught with one's pants down

This idiom is similar to 'caught red handed,' but does not necessarily indicate being caught committing a crime.

There is actually a consensus among researchers as to the meaning of this phrase. It means 'to be taken by surprise or caught unprepared.' There are three references as to the possible origin.

The first one, however, seems most likely. It relates to the Roman Emperor Caracalla, later known as Marcus Antoninus. He was viewed as one of the toughest Emperors around 200 BC. Historic legend tells us that while he was on an important journey his armed escort gave him privacy to relieve himself beside the road. A certain Julius Martailis, who had a grudge against the Emperor, took advantage of the opportunity to run forward and kill him with a single stab of the sword. He tried to give chase to the assassin but was killed by an arrow from one of the bodyguards of the now deceased Caracalla.

Hence, 'with your pants down' would conjure up visions of an embarrassed man who was caught at a most inopportune moment.

A related phrase is 'caught with your hand in the cookie jar.

C'est la vie

This expression, borrowed from the French, is often used by writers of English song lyrics (the list is exhaustive), articles, books and screenplays. It means, quite simply, 'that's life' or 'such is life' and is used to shrug off unfortunate circumstances in much the same way as 'get over it.'

Dante used the following in *The Divine Comedy* circa 1308-1321:

> "**c'est** le chemin de **la vie** contemplative..." (it is the way of the `contemplative life)

chain is only as strong as its weakest link, A

A proverb which can be used both literally and figuratively, this is often applied to a person who is a member of a group which functions as a whole. In business and family, if one fails to hold up their 'part of the bargain' the purpose is compromised and the entire organism falls apart. It's similar to 'one bad apple spoils the whole batch' (see).

The phrase dates back to at least the mid-to-late 18th century, as it was well established in usage when it was included in Thomas Reid's *Essays on the Intellectual Powers of Man* in 1786.

> "In every chain of reasoning, the evidence of **the last conclusion can be no greater than that of the weakest link of the chain**, whatever may be the strength of the rest."

Chairman of the Board

In the late 1700s, many houses consisted of a large room with only one chair. Commonly, a long wide board folded down from the wall, and was used for dining. The 'head of the household' always sat in the chair, while everyone else ate sitting on the floor. Occasionally a guest, who was usually a man, would be invited to sit in this chair during a meal. To sit in the chair meant you were important and in charge. They called the one sitting in the chair the 'chair man.'

Today in business, the head of a corporation is often called the Chairman or 'Chairman of the Board.'

Change one's tune

This idiom refers to reversing one's views or pattern of behavior. The first version of this expression, 'sing another song' dates back to circa 1300 when it is said that itenerant minstrels in England altered the words to songs in order to please their current audiences. By the early 1800s it was in frequent usage in English literature. One example is from *The Political History of England* Volume 1, 1808, by Thomas Hodgkin:

> "...Aldehelm, in his younger days...after which he **changed his tune**, gradually interwove with his song the words of Scripture, began to speak to them of serious things, and, in short, won back to sanity and devotion the citizens..."

Charity begins at home*

This old proverb, expressing the imperative nature of caring for family before others, is not from the *Bible*, but the basis of it is biblical. The following is from *I Timothy 5:8*:

> "But if any provide not for his own, and especially for those of his own house, he has denied the faith and is worse than an infidel." *(KJV, 1611)*

Famed British theologian, John Wycliffe, expressed the idea as early as 1382 in *Of Prelates*:

> "Charite shuld begyne in him-self." (Reprinted in 1880)

In John Fletcher's 1625 Comedy, *Wit Without Money,* he wrote:

> "**Charity** and beating **begins at home**."

The exact saying is first found in Christian physician Sir Thomas Browne's *Religio Medici*, a few years later; written in 1642, published properly in 1643:

> "**Charity begins at home**, is the voice of the world; yet every man his greatest enemy."

Charley horse

This is a sudden knot to swell up on a leg or arm, and may be caused by a knuckle-pounding. Actually, the term came from a horse kick. *The Doctor's*

Book of Home Remedies II, 1995, says, "This out-of-the-blue leg cramp is as intense as a kick from a palomino."

The earliest printed reference located is from January 1904 in *The Outlook Magazine, Volume 76*:

> "A **Charley horse** guard interprets itself as a peculiar stiff, padded guard of the large frontal muscle of the thigh, which is very amenable to the deep **'charley horse'** bruise, so called — tricksy players in earlier football epochs..."

Chasing one's own tail

This metaphoric animal-inspired idiom has been present in our language since at least the dawn of the 20th century. An early printed example of the phrase, yet more literal, is found in British author George Mottram Andrews Hewitt's humorous 'animal autobiography' *The Rat*, 1904:

> "I am afraid that I am rather like a kitten or a puppy-dog, **chasing my own tail**..."

A more figurative usage is found in the May, 1927 issue of the *Rotarian Magazine:*

> "Competing on price alone is just like a dog **chasing its own tail**. It certainly is hard work, but what does it gain the dog?"

By 1951, it had reached its current present meaning, as demonstrated in this citation from *Science: Sense and Nonsense* by John Lighten Singe:

> "To change the metaphor, the sages chase their own tails through the ages. A little child says, 'Gentlemen, you are **chasing your own tails**.'"

Chew the fat

This idiom means making small talk or simply having a conversation for a period of time; may also be applied to gossiping.

Although some sources attribute its origin to either sailors in olden days who would chew on salt-hardened fat, or Native Americans or Inuit tribesmen who were said to chew animal hides to soften them in their spare time, there seems to be no real evidence that either of these had a bearing on the original usage of the phrase.

A form of the expression first appeared in *Life in the Ranks of the British Army in India and on Board a Troopship*, a book by J. Brunlees Patterson, in 1885.

> "This select and volatile body of men is commonly designated by their more sensible and forbearing comrades as the 'grousers' from the fact that the chief elements of their composition seems to be made up of grumbling or **chewing the** rag or **fat**, as it is termed, at anyone and everyone, anything and everything generally, and dusky humanity particularly."

Chicken scratches

This idiomatic expression, another ignored by other phrase dictionaries, has been in use since at least the mid-20th century, when it began to be used by school teachers to describe incredibly poor handwriting of some students. It is derived from the fact that when fowls scratch in the dirt they produce odd markings. Usually only the writer can interpret what is meant by these scribbles. It may also be the derivation of the term 'scratch paper' used for doodling.

Children should be seen, not heard

Contrary to popular belief, this did not come from *The Bible*. The earliest version of this proverb applied to young women, or 'maids' and was recorded in Augustinian prior John Mirk's *Festial* like this in about 1389:

> "Hyt ys an old Englysch sawe (saying): '**A mayde schuld be seen, but not herd**.'"

Note the saying was 'old' at that time.

In Thomas Becon's *Works*, in 1560, we read:

> "This also must honest maids provide, that they be not full of tongue. **A maid should be seen, and not heard**."

This trend continued until the 19th century, when we find the following in John Quincy Adams' *Memoirs*, first published in 1876:

> "My dear mother's constant lesson in childhood, **that children** in company **should be seen and not heard**."

Chinaman's chance

This expression is believed to have originated from the fact that in the 19th century when Chinese migrant workers went to California to work in gold mines and construction sites and were assigned to the most hazardous job of igniting dynamite. Also, those which came to stake claims for gold in the goldrush of 1849 came late because of the length of time it took to arrive from China after hearing the news. By the time they arrived, they were destined to work in areas already rejected by the early miners. In both instances, the Chinese had little or no chance of striking it rich on California gold. It wasn't until the early 20th century, however, that the saying began to show up in magazines and books. The earliest available citation appears in July, 1914, in *Everybody's Magazine* in a story titled 'The Game of Light' by Richard Washburn Child on page 49.

> "'See here!' exclaimed poor J. B., snatching at the other's sleeve. 'There isn't **a Chinaman's chance** for that.'"

chink in one's armor, A

This expression has been used in a literal sense for over six hundred years to mean a crack or gap which may be penetrated by the enemy in a joust. It has been used figuratively since the mid-1600s, to mean that someone has a weakness or a problem which may prevent success. Sometimes it is used to refer to a minor flaw that is likely to cause problems for him or her. Some have confused chink and the incorrect form, kink, in this phrase.

chip off the old block, A

This, today, is clearly recognized as a reference to children inheriting the traits of their parents, most usually a son and his father.

The earliest variant of this cliché is 'chip of the same block.' The block may have been referring to stone or wood. It dates back to at least 1621, when it appeared in that form in London Bishop Robert Sanderson's *Sermons*:

> "Am not I a child of the same Adam ... **a chip of the same block**, with him?"

Actually, in the case of Adam, in *Genesis 2:7*, it could have referred to the earth, since Adam was said to have been fashioned by the Creator from the dust of the earth.

Another slightly different form, 'chip of the old block' comes not much later, in John Milton's work, *An apology against—A modest confutation of the animadversions upon the remonstrant against Smectymnuus* in 1642.

"How well dost thou now appeare to be **a Chip of the old block**."

Finally, in the 19th century, 'chip off the old block' is cited, and it is the parent, especially the father, that is being dubbed 'the old block.' The earliest reference known of to this is in the Ohio newspaper *The Athens Messenger*, in June, 1870:

"The children see their parents' double-dealings, see their want of integrity, and learn them to cheat ... The child is too often **a chip off the old block**."

Chip on one's shoulder

This one is interesting, because one would not automatically suspect the origin. In fact, there is a bit of a conflict as to exactly when it started. But the U.S. practice could have been a carryover from the English story.

The History of British Work and Labour Relations in the Royal Dockyards, 1999, tells of their 18th century practices. The book relates that the standing orders for the Royal Navy Board for August 1739 included the following ruling:

"Shipwrights to be allowed to bring [**chips**] **on their shoulders** near to the dock gates, there to be inspected by officers."

This mentions chips on shoulders, but not why the saying would be as it is. The American version explains the current usage much better.

In the 19th century, there was reportedly a practice in the U.S. of sparring for a fight with a chip on one's shoulder, daring others to knock it off.

Today, 'having a chip on one's shoulder' means that one is carrying a grievance against someone or something.

Chip shot

In golf (where the term is most often used) a chip shot is made when the ball lands close enough to the green to use a wedge or larger number iron, removing a divot, getting sufficiently under the ball to lift it on. It is considered (though not always) an easy play. In the 21st century, metaphorically, a chip shot can pertain to a simple maneuver which someone may make in order to better position themselves. In 2004, a book titled *Best 143 Business Schools* contained the following:

"Alternatively, professors ask for a volunteer to open a case, particularly someone who has had real industry experience with the issues. After the opening, the discussion is broadened to include the whole class. Everyone tries to get in a good comment, particularly if class participation counts heavily toward the grade. '**Chip shots**'— unenlightened, just-say-anything-so-you-can-get-credit comments—are common..."

Then on NBCs *Today* show, May 8, 2012, this comment was made metaphorically regarding a political candidate:

"This should be a **chip shot** for him."

Chomping / Champing at the bit

Champing or chomping at the bit figuratively indicates that someone is anxious to get started with a project which hasn't gotten 'off the ground' yet. Horses and mules which are ready to go often chew the metal bit in their mouths on the bridle which the rider or trainer controls. It's like a nervous sign of their impatience. This is typical of horses set to race. It is said that 'champ' is an indication of the sound made when the bit is ground in the horse's teeth. Chomp may derive from the munching down that the animal does. The word champ, however, dates from the 16th century, predating the word chomp. Regardless, the expression has been with us for at least a hundred years.

Clean as a whistle

There is no doubt that this simile has been around for hundreds of years, and likely was originated in the British Isles. There have been several suggestions ventured by etymologists as to the exact origin and connotation of the phrase.

A version of it was utilized by Robert Burns, the famous bard of Scotland in his poem, *The Author's Ernest Cry and Prayer*. He used the word 'toom' meaning empty, instead of clean.

"Paint Scotland greetan owre her thrissle; Her mutchkin stoup as **toom's a whissle**."

Other writers spoke of a pure, clear or dry whistle during this age. The intent, however, seemed to be that to achieve a pure sound from a whistle, it should be clear or dry. This certainly seems to be the origin. Later usage turned to 'clean as a whistle.' Some see it as merely the clear, clean tone of a whistle made from a reed.

103

This became a simile of anything to which this attribute applied

Cleanliness is next to godliness

This is not from the *Bible* as some have claimed, or from other ancient Hebrew writings. The first mention seems to have been from the English writer, Francis Bacon, with whom some equate Shakespeare. Though a slight variant, as is often the case with original citations, it is obvious that the meaning is here. In *The Advancement of Learning*, 1605, Bacon wrote:

> "**Cleanness** of body was ever deemed to **proceed from** a due **reverence to God**."

Around two hundred years later, John Wesley inferred in one of his sermons that the proverb, as we quote it today, was well known when he stated:

> "Slovenliness is no part of religion. '**Cleanliness is** indeed **next to Godliness**.'"

Clear as a bell

A bell is used as a model for clarity because of its unquestionable clear tone.

Its likely origin is from the ads of the Sanora Chime Company, which started manufacturing phonographs in the 1910s. They adopted 'clear as a bell' as their slogan, praising the clear quality of their record players.

Clear as mud

This old saying is often used to mean that someone's question or explanation is very obscure and needs a great deal of clarification. The first known citation is found in *The British Theater, or A Collection of Plays which are acted at the Theaters Royale, Volume 21*, 1808, in the play '*John Bull*,' Act II, Scene ii:

> "Dennis. Don't be bothering my brains, then, or you'll get it as **clear as mud**."

The New Monthly Magazine, September, 1829 in 'The Metropolis in Danger' has:

"It belongs to the subject to observe that this is "as **clear as mud**" to all who have any head for figures."

Clip someone's wings

Chickens used to have their wings clipped to prevent their flying out of an open coop or lot. As a metaphor, it applies to taking away someone's freedom, or even controlling their circumstances in life. It dates back to 1590-93, when it was used by Christopher Marlowe in his Elizabethan play, *The Massacre at Paris*.

"Away to prison with him, I'll **clip his wings**."

Cloak and dagger

This term has come to be associated with intrigue and suspense in novels. The oldest references to the use of cloaks and daggers were in the 16th century, and had to do with grasping a dagger in one hand and a cloak in the other, with which to hide the weapon. The cloak could also provide a degree of protection from an opponent's wounds. Because of hiding the dagger, this was considered a dishonest method of combat. Giacomo di Grassi, in *His True Arte of Defense*, first published in 1570, included a section called "The Rapier and Cloake."

Cloak and dagger began to be utilized by poets and authors in the 19th century, such as Longfellow and Dickens, and gradually evolved to mean something secretive and intriguing.

Close but no cigar

This is another saying coming into use in the early-to-mid-20th century. Back then fairs used cigars as prizes in some places, and this most likely spawned the term.

It is first found in print in Sayre and Twist's publication of the script of the 1935 film version of *Annie Oakley*:

"**Close**, Colonel, **but no cigar!**"

Then, from around 1949, citations appear in a number of U.S. newspapers. One such example is in a story from *The Lima News* in Ohio in November of 1949 which tells how The Lima House Cigar and Sporting Goods Store barely avoiding being burned down. The article was titled "Close But No Cigar."

Close enough for government work

This phrase originated during World War II, and initially had a positive connotation. Government work was required to be of the highest possible standards. The passage of the years eroded the meaning due to slacking of standards and government waste. Today the saying has taken a 180 degree turn to refer to shoddy workmanship sans the care and pride once implied. The term is also used to mean something done on company time for personal use.

Writers of various genres have put the term to use, and its meaning is clearly borne out by Stephen King in *Nightmares and Dreamscapes*, 1994:

> "The most inflexible measurement is also the most important: the distance between the pitcher's rubber and the center plate. Forty-six feet—no more, no less. When it comes to this one, nobody ever says, 'Aw, **close enough for government work** — let it go.'"

Close only counts in horseshoes (and grenades)

In most things in life, exact accuracy and skill are required to keep going. Questions on an exam or a quiz show unless answered properly are still incorrect.

This too-oft-spoken cliché has obvious origins. The game of horseshoes is played by tossing at a metal stake in hopes of ringing it with the metal shoe and scoring maximum points. When the shoe lands within a horseshoe's width of the stake, points are also added to the player's score. The phrase was used untold times before someone came up with another item which also could have noticeable results when landing close to its intended target. Hand grenades have a disastrous effect, possibly even death, even when merely close.

This version of the original phrase appeared as early as 15 August 1914, the *Lincoln Daily News*, Lincoln Nebraska, carried this citation:

> **"Close does not count only in horseshoes."**

Then on 8 July 1932 in the *Washington Post*:

> **"Close doesn't count except in horseshoe pitching."**

By 26 January 1970, grenades came into the picture in this quote from *The Guthrian* a paper in Iowa:

> **"Close only counts in horseshoes and grenades."**

Because baseball great Frank Robinson used the full phrase in an article appearing in print in *Time Magazine* on 31 July 1973, it is sometimes wrongly credited to him:

> "Close don't count in baseball. **Close only counts in horseshoes and grenades**."

Close shave*

This phrase came into usage in the early 19th century and means narrowly escaping an undesirable event. It was coined in an era when barbers provided much of the medical treatment in America, and often shaved the patient in anticipation of something such as surgery. The object was to get as close a shave as possible without irritating the skin. Sometimes the actual procedure was not possible after the shave and the results were very painful.

The earliest verifiable figurative reference in print is found in the November, 1820 issue of *The Philosophical Magazine and Journal* in an article titled 'Return of the Discovery Ships':

> "It was a **close shave** as to time. The sea, or the lanes of water amongst the ice, which we had hitherto navigated, were now entirely frozen over. The ships were housed over, and all things prepared for the winter, which, thank God, we passed..."

Clothes make the man

This phrase has been brandished by the fashion industry for many years to promote stylish dress for both men and women. It is originally a quote from American author and humorist Mark Twain who said:

> "**Clothes make the man**. Naked people have little or no influence on society."

coast is clear, The*

This is, as it sounds, an old nautical expression, later used metaphorically. It now is utilized to indicate that there is no reason not to proceed with a plan, particularly a dubious one; that there appears to be no opposition or obstruction, and no one will get in the way, either literally or figuratively. It originally meant that there was no fog or obstruction from a port or harbor, and a ship could be given the okay to depart, then later in war time regarding the absence of enemy ships. It was said to have been first in print in 1531 in describing a vessel safely clearing the coast, but this has not been verified. A form of it was certainly used by Shakespeare circa 1591, in *Henry VI*, near the end of Scene III, regarding visibility.

"MAY. See **the coast clear'd**, and then we will depart."

The first printed reference to absence of enemy ships is in 1797 in *The Poetical Works of William Summerville, Volume II*, 'The Night-Walker Reclaimed', line 264:

"And then reveal'd how all had past: Next thought is proper to explain His plot, and how he laid his train: '**The coast is clear**. Sir, go in peace, No dragon guards the Golden Fleece.'"

The earliest verifiable totally figurative use in print is from a letter dated in New York, December 4, 1875, found in *Louisa May Alcott's Life, Letters and Journals*, published in 1924:

"I wanted to see him; but he is a newsboy, and sells late papers, because, 'though harder work, it pays better, and **the coast is clear** for those who do it."

Cock a snoot (See: **Thumb one's nose**)

Cold cash / cold hard cash

This American idiom, sometimes used as was first 'coined' in about 1915 and means money which is liquid, or readily available to pay bills or make purchases. It comes from the fact that the first form of accepted money was coins, made from gold and silver which got cold when not in ones pocket. A lot of folks in the early 20th century didn't trust paper money. When coin handlers started receiving coins that had other content they were also harder, hence, 'cold *hard* cash' became popular later.

Two early citations are available. On 20 March 1915 the *Saturday Evening Post* printed this in an article by Albert J. Beveridge titled 'The Lincoln Highway':

"Take one illustration, and one that deals with to-day and with **cold cash**, 'with the present hour, and with actual dollars and cents.

The other is a quote from Ernest Baron Gordon in *Russian Prohibition*, 1916:

> "'Heads of large concerns employing labor,' said the Minister of Finance, 'have said they would pay in **cold cash** the sums necessary to cover the deficit in revenue, and could afford it easily from the larger incomes derived from the increased capacity of employees.'"

Cold feet*

This old idiom refers to someone having a lack of courage about taking some impending action. It is most commonly attributed to Stephen Crane in his 1893 novella, *Maggie, a Girl of the Streets*:

> "I knew this was the way it would be. They got **cold feet.**"

By the early 20th century it was being included in English college slang. It was used by some during the First World War to refer to those afraid to go into battle.

There was however, earlier usage of the term in a popular German novel by Fritz Rueter, *Ut Mine Stromtid,* or *An Old Story of My Farming Days,* written about 1862. When translated into English in 1878, in banter over a player backing out of a card game, another player says:

> "'If you suffer from **cold feet,'** said Brasig, 'I will tell you an excellent cure...'"

In another book written about the same time, *Seed-Time and Harvest*, Rueter refers to a shoemaker getting "cold feet," obviously as a pun.

But this *still* isn't the actual coining of the roots of this figurative expression. Italian playwright, Ben Jonson, used a form of it in his satirical work, *Volpore*, in 1605.

> "Let me tell you: I am not, as your Lombard proverb saith, **cold on my feet;** or content to part with my commodities at a cheaper rate than I am accustomed: look not for it."

Even as early as 1605, this was called a 'Lombard proverb' in Italy. In Italy, it meant figuratively, 'to be without money.' It is believed that it moved to English as 'unwillingness to continue.'

Cold hands, warm heart***

Contrary to publication by a major proverb dictionary that this expression was first cited in 1903 by V.S. Lean, *Collectanea, III 380* (which read as "a cold hand and a warm heart,") This saying was in use over half a century earlier. *Introduction to the Young Ladies Elocutionary Reader* by William and Ana U. Russell, James Munroe and Company, Boston, 1845, contains the following in Exercise LXII on page 136:

> "Oh! but it is cold. 'Seasonable weather,' says the stranger, 'warms the heart,—**cold hands, warm heart**.'"

A number of other citations were made in books before the turn of the century, yet numerous online sources still place its origin as early in the 20th century.

This proverb is based on an old myth that a person who has cold hands must be "warm-hearted" or a generous, good person. The actual fact is that your physical warmth has nothing to do with your interior personality. According to Dr. Mark Kestner, a chiropractor in Murfreesboro, Tennessee, in an article in the *Murfreesboro Post* published on January 20, 2015, however, scientific research on staying warm indicates that the opposite may be true in a physical sense. According to Kestner, "Cold hands are likely a sign that your heart and other organs are not as warm as they should be."

Cold turkey

Before cold turkey meant quitting drugs without help, it referred to 'talking cold turkey.' 'Going cold turkey' came later. The first known reference to this meaning is from a newspaper in Canada, *The Daily Colonist*, in October 1921.

> "Perhaps the most pitiful figures who have appeared before Dr. Carleton Simon are those who voluntarily surrender themselves. When they go before him, they [drug addicts] are given what is called the '**cold turkey**' treatment."

This analogy was made because during quick drug withdrawal the person's blood is forced to the inside organs making the skin appear white and giving the skin a goosebump-like appearance.

Come back to bite you (in the butt)

This is an alternate to 'what goes around comes around.' (See) and 'come back to haunt you.' (See) Another is 'be sure your sins will find you out.' When people make unwise choices, they have a way of boomeranging. This metaphoric idiom has been around since the mid-to-late 20th century and comes from the fact that a dog that is mistreated is likely to show its displeasure by tearing into its abuser when his or her back is turned. The moral of the phrase is 'deal with situations wisely before they deal with you.'

Come back to haunt you

This cliché / idiom generally means that a poorly-thought-out decision has lasting consequences. When a person is tempted to take some drastic action on the spur of the moment, or tell a lie, he or she should take time to think about the long-term result. Guilt is a poor bedfellow.

The idea of spirits of deceased coming back to earth has been prevalent for thousands of years. The word 'haunt' comes from the old French, 'hanter,' and was of Germanic derivation.

As a cliché, a form of it began to be used in print in the early 20th century in the vein of a person coming back after death to haunt someone when Lucy Maud Montgomery placed it in *Anne on the Island* in 1915:

> "If you won't let me cast in my lot with you I'll die of the disappointment and then I'll **come back and haunt you**."

On April 16, 1921 in a story called *The Golden Idol* by Christine Jope Slade in the *Saturday Evening Post* it was used in the same way:

> "And you'll make her a good stepson or I'll **come back and haunt you**, my lad. I've had a deal of experience haunting. I played the Ghost in Hamlet with Booth. Are all those children still playing that foolish game?"

In recent years, it is more often used in the more figurative sense, as in *Father's Rights: Hard Hitting and Fair advice for Every Father*, by Jeffrey Leving and Kenneth Dachman, 1998:

> "Tell the truth, or your attempts at deception will **come back to haunt you** at trial."

Come hell or high water

There have been earlier variations of this phrase. The original was 'hell *and* high water,' and later, 'through hell and high water.' The first printed examples appeared around the turn of the 19th century and tend to be linked to cattle ranching and herding cattle through tough trails and flooded rivers on the way to market.

The earliest known figurative example is from a story called 'A Red Haired Cupid' by Henry Wallace Phillips which appeared in *McClure's Magazine* in August, 1901:

> "'Do you, Kyle, take this woman, Loys, to have and keep track of, **come hell or high water**, her heirs and assigns for ever?' — or such a matter— says he, all in one breath"

Though in a wedding vow, this citation is from a ranching tale.

Come out of one's shell

This old saying is an allusion to either a snail or a turtle, which seem shy because they often withdraw when people are around them, especially when they feel threatened. People who have an introverted personality are compared to crustaceans and shelled reptiles, and when they are able to become more extroverted, they are said to be 'coming out of their shells.'

An early citation of this metaphoric expression, though not fully as it is used today, is from *Spirit of the English Magazines,* January 1, 1820 in an article titled 'Maurice and Berghetta.'

> "'From pure caution, Father,' says he, 'and forethought: you may unsay a lie if you find it distressing, but you cannot unsay the truth, if it is ever so inconvenient: lies are like snails horns, you throw out one or two just to feel your way, and if all's safe, then **come out of your shell**, and welcome.'"

In his celebrated Russian novel, *The Idiot*, published in London in English in 1887, Fedor Dostoieffsky used a form of the metaphor in speaking of the complexity of the human brain:

> "There is always a something, a remnant, which can never **come out from under your shell**, but will remain there with you, and you alone, for ever and ever, and you will die, perhaps, without having imparted what may be the very essence of your idea to a single living soul."

Come out of the closet

This figure of speech is used for 'gay' or homosexual persons of either gender admitting to their 'sexual orientation.' The term 'coming out' was coined in the early 20th century from the analogy of comparing gays announcing their homosexuality to the 'coming out parties' of débutantes, or young upper-class women presenting themselves to society, and announcing their eligibility to suitable bachelors. The addition of 'closet' was done later because so many had previously stayed incognito due to social stigmatism long associated with their suppressed lifestyle. An early application of this term was used by pop king Michael Jackson in his 1991 song, *In the Closet*. This was likely derived from skeletons in the closet (see), a term in use since the early 19th century.

Come out swinging

This common idiom came into usage in the mid-20th century and means to enter into a confrontation with the intent of clashing on ideas or objectives. Is is based on boxing in which the two opponents leave their respective corners making jabs into the air, ready for action. In the *Summary of Proceedings of the National Convention of the American Legion*, August 26 to September 1, 1949, page 35, we find an early citation:

"'**Come out swinging!**' he declared. The commission carefully considered the entire situation. It felt that The American Legion could square no other course with its basic principles but to '**Come out swinging!**'"

Come to Jesus meeting

Said to have originated in the religious camps on the New Jersey shore in the 19th century, this saying today has nothing to do with Jesus, and everything to do with a meeting of the minds. It is a much-used term in Southern America. It means something big is going down of which all parties concerned need to be informed and 'on the same page' (see)—a cold hard fact is likely to be revealed and it's probably 'put up or shut up' time.

The November 11, 2002 *Business Week Magazine* carried a classic example of the phrase in an article headed 'Is the Pen Finally Mightier than the Keyboard?'

"Leob feared he might pull back on the 2002 launch. She called a '**come-to-Jesus**' **meeting** in August in [Bill] Gates's conference room, with two dozen execs from the Tablet PC, Office, and Windows groups to answer any questions Gates might have."

113

Coming out of the woodwork

This phrase refers to vermin (bugs, mice, etc.) coming out of the walls of houses. It is used to mean unwanted people who show up in expectation of receiving something for themselves—often without cost.

The origin was from *"The Gnoors Come from the Voodvork Out,"* the first of a series of fantasy short stories by Reginald Bretnor from the 1950s originally published in *The Magazine of Fantasy and Science Fiction* (winter-spring 1950) which featured a crafty Swiss-American clock maker, Papa Schimmelhorn.

Connect the dots

Connect the dots as a metaphoric expression refers to using the known data to figure out the whole picture, usually obvious. The idiom originated as a type of puzzle often called 'dot-to-dot.' Each dot is numbered. By drawing a line from one dot to the next until all of the dots are connected, one can solve the puzzle.

In 1871, *The New York Teacher, and the American Educational Monthly, Volume 8* published a method of teaching children how to form letters, numbers, and basic shapes—triangles and squares, by making dots on a paper then connecting them, a technique proposed by Professor Louis Bail, a chart expert at Sheffield Scientific School at Yale who was already utilizing this process to develop graphs. The idea was picked up by others over the following decades as indicated in a number of educational publications.

Long before 1944 the idea of forming pictures by connecting dots had been devised. That year, in *The Spectator, Volume 152*, this appears:

"Do you remember…when you were a youngster? How, by **connecting the dots** numbered 1, 2, 3, 4, etc., in rotation, you were enabled to draw some intriguing animal such as an elephant, giraffe or monkey?"

Then, on 21 May 1953, Saalfield Publishing Company began submitting copyright requests for books with dot-to-dot formats to the Copyright Office, Library of Congress, Washington, DC, as shown on page 547 of the *Catalogue of Copyright Entries, Third Series, Volume 8*, January to June 1954.

By the mid 1970s the phrase had begun to be used figuratively. In 1974, a book entitled *American Writers*: *A Collection of Literary Biographies, Volume One* by Mary Weigel, edited by A. Walton Litz and Leonard Unger the following appeared:

"**Connecting the dots** is no simple task, and reading DeLillo is often like looking at one of MC Escher's visual…"

114

Continental breakfast

Countries in continental Europe, often known simply as the 'continent,' typically serve a cold breakfast consisting of cereal, cheese, and croissants as a self-service buffet. This is contrasted with a 'cooked breakfast' or 'full English (or American on this side of the pond) breakfast,' which typically includes fried or scrambled eggs, sausage, bacon or ham, and sometimes even tomatoes.

Cooler than the other side of the pillow***

This metaphor was coined by the late popular ESPN Sports Anchor Stuart Scott (7-14-1965 to 1-4-2015) while working at ABC TV station WPDE in Florence, SC in about 1987. It means that a person has such a great demeanor that if someone doesn't like the person there is something wrong with his or her thinking. When waking in the night, flipping a pillow often helps a person feel good and go back to sleep more easily.

Cop or copper

The old English word 'cop' meant grab or capture, so in the 19th century policemen became known as coppers, due to the fact that they were responsible for grabbing or catching criminals. The word 'cop' is actually an acronym for Constable on Patrol.

Copycat

This was likely started as a reference to how kittens copy the actions of their mothers. It is an Americanism and first known to appear in print in 1896 in poet S. O. Jewett's highly acclaimed book, *Country of the Pointed Firs*.

> "I ain't heard of a **copy-cat** this great many years... 'twas a favorite term of my grand-mother's."

Corner the market

Cornering the market is controlling a particular stock, product or commodity in order to control and manipulate the price. Examples are Jay Gould and Jim Fisk's attempt at cornering the gold market in 1869, and John Rockefeller cornering the oil market in 1872 by making deals with the railroads.

Concerning the stock market, in 1903, Frank Norris wrote in *The Pit, Volume 2*:

115

"'Sam,' he shouted, 'do you know—great God!—do you know what this means? Sam, we can **corner the market!**'"

On December 30, 1914, Mack Cretcher, writing from the Philippines on their agricultural policy with the U.S., published in 1918 in *A Tenderfoot in All the Topics* said:

"The Governor-General and Vice Governor Martin at once got busy and gave out the information that if any attempt was made to **corner the market** on rice, flour, milk, and other necessities, the whole resources of the government would be brought into play in order to check it."

Cotton-pickin'

This saying came about from picking cotton in the past era in Mississippi and Alabama. In fact, it was referred to in print in a literal sense as early as the 18th century. This citation appeared as a figurative term in a newspaper in a small town in Pennsylvania called *The Daily Currier,* in November 1942:

"It's just about time some of our Northern meddlers started keeping their **cotton-picking** fingers out of the South's business."

But it had been used in speech in a figurative connotation long before this. Cotton-pickin' or the proper spelling, cotton-picking has always been a contemptuous slang remark. Cotton pickers were originally slaves, and even later, usually of African descent, and it is likely that it was comparing the person to someone which was, unfortunately, not looked upon favorably in that day. In fact, in 1855, the following appeared in *Twelve Years a Slave: Narrative of Simon Winthrop: A Citizen of New York,* page 179 (rude word omitted):

"Practice and whipping were alike unavailing, and Epps, satisfied of it at last, swore I was a disgrace — that I was not fit to associate with a **cotton-picking** "n****r" — that I could not pick enough in a day to pay the trouble of weighing it, and that I should go into the cotton field no more.**"**

Today it is still primarily an Americanism, but not perceived as contemptuous.

Country mile

The meaning behind this is derived from the directions people used give in the country. When they told someone it wasn't but a mile or so, it might turn out to be closer to two miles. So 'better by a country mile' is a lot better.

In the U.K. a 'Welsh mile' is the term used, as Wales is largely rural, and it is nearest to the American 'country mile.'

Courage is fear that has said its prayers

This oft-quoted saying is often attributed to a number of famous persons who were not its author. The truth is, it is from a short verse titled *Courage* by Karle Wilson Baker, printed in a small publication titled *Poetry: A Magazine of Verse Volume XIX*, October – March, 1921-1922, on page 16. It is meant to encourage people to dispel fear through faith.

> *"Courage*
>
> "Courage is armor
> A Blind man wears,
> The calloused scar
> Of outlived despairs:
> **Courage is fear**
> **That has said its prayers"**

Most often credited are silent movie star, Dorothy Bernard (1890—1955) and iconic Swiss Theologian Karl Barth (1886—1968)—likely because of the similarity of his name to the author of the verse. Among others sometimes credited for coining it are famed American poet Maya Angelou, Christian author Max Lucado, evangelist Joyce Myer, inspirational writer Ruth Fishel and novelist and political activist Anne Lamott.

Devotional writer Norman Eugene Nygaard in *Strength for Service to God and Country*, 1942, Abingdon-Cokesbury Press, gave credit to Baker for the quote, as did Charles Langworthy Wallace in *A Treasury of Sermon Illustrations*, 1950.

Scores of other authors have inserted the proverb in their writings, and musician Stephen Tyler even voiced it on American Idol on May 8, 2012. It was also quoted in the United States Senate on Monday, September 28, 1998 in a prayer by Chaplin Dr. Lloyd John Ogilvie.

Crack a smile

In past centuries, women would apply bee's wax to their faces to smooth out their complexions. When they were talking to one another, if a woman began to stare at another woman's face she was told, 'mind your own bee's wax' (see).

Should a woman smile, the bee's wax on her face would crack, hence the term 'crack a smile.' This now means, begin a simper.

In February, 1914, the New York publication, *Yachting* (Vol. XV, No. 2) carried this citation to the figurative use:

"We should **crack a smile**!"

Cracked up to be (See: **Not all it's cracked up to be**)

Crazy as a betsy bug

A phrase which was once common in the American South, this refers to being uncontrollable, erratic, and irrational. The expression has been around since the late 19th century.

A betsy bug, aka bessie bug, is a member of the Passalidae family of beetles. It is big (about an inch and a half long), black and shiny, and has nasty-looking pincers. It can and will bite people and flies where it wants to.

In 1925, Bernie Babcock used the simile in *Booth and the Spirit of Lincoln: A Story of a Living Dead Man:*

> "A second time this angel came and spoke to Manoah's old woman and a second time he thought her **crazy as a betsy bug**. Then she went down to the water hole to wash — kind of a shady place like under trees."

Crazy as a loon

A loon is the North American name for a duck-like fowl which in Europe is called the Great Northern Diver. Their cry sounds eerie, and apparently not unlike the howling of someone who is insane. One unusual trait is the fact that loons emit their sounds at night, rather than in the daylight hours, likely another reason for the metaphor. The name is thought to have been given because they seem to be howling at the moon, and taken from lunar, from the same Latin source as the word lunatic. In Shakespearian times, 'loon' was a term of abuse.

When it comes to being 'crazy' the list seems exhaustive. Similar creatures referred to in this light are a bat, a bedbug, a betsy bug (see), a beetle, a barn owl, squirrelly and a peach orchard boar. Related phrases are nutty as a fruitcake, not playing with a full deck, doesn't have both oars in the water, lights are on but nobody's home, elevator doesn't go to the top floor, one card short of a full deck, one brick short of a load, one sandwich short of a picnic, one beer short of a six pack, half a bubble off plumb and bats in the belfry (see). All such terms are considered very 'politically incorrect' (see).

Crazy like a fox

As a phrase, this is an antonym of crazy as a loon, because someone who is crazy like a fox is not crazy at all, but very shrewd. The saying took root from the title of a book by American humorist, Sidney J. Perelman, first published in 1944.

Cream of the crop

This has been used for centuries as meaning the very best of anything. When butter was churned, the cream rose to the top of the churn, or jar. A traditional churn had a wooden dasher which was forced up and down to produce the butter.

Cream of the market was an early form of this expression. The earliest known printed reference to a form of this phrase, 'cream of the jest' was in John Ray's *Hand-book of Proverbs* in 1670.

Cream of the crop, per se, was probably borrowed from the old French phrase 'crème de la crème,' cream of the cream, meaning the best of the best. It was well-known in English by 1800.

Crocodile tears

'Crocodile tears' are a hypocritical show of grief or sadness. The saying derives from the old wives' tale which said that a crocodile wept insincerely if it killed and ate a person.

Crooked as a barrel of snakes

This decidedly Southern American expression first started showing up in print around 1914, when the August issue of *The Practical Druggist*, in an article by W.H. Cousins of Wichita Falls, Texas, titled 'Substitution' contained the following lines:

> "If a builder's plans drawn by an architect specified timbers of a given size, and because he could use timbers of much smaller size and have them covered from the sight of the superintendent the builder substituted the smaller timbers and got away with a hundred dollars of another man's money we would all agree that he was **as crooked as a barrel of snakes**."

119

The comical simile was quickly picked up and was used by a number of other writers in the early 20th century.

Cry all the way to the bank

This cliché means that in spite of negative circumstances, a person did well financially, which made it much more bearable.

The phrase is often accredited to Liberace, who used it in 1953, after a concert at Madison Square Garden for which he took a beating from critics, but made a tidy sum of money. It was quoted in 1954 by Hy Gardner in *Champagne Before Breakfast*.

> "Yet Liberace takes it all with a grain of sugar, commenting, in his sort of slushy style of speaking, 'Those jokes and bad notices affect me very deeply— they make me **cry all the way to the bank!**'"

Even earlier, however, it appeared in *Waterloo Daily Courier* of Iowa on September 3rd, 1946:

> "Eddie Walker perhaps is the wealthiest fight manager in the game ... The other night when his man Belloise lost, Eddie had the miseries ... He felt so terrible, **he cried all the way to the bank!**"

Though it didn't become popular until much later, the reverse phrase, laugh all the way to the bank was in print in *Peter, A novel of which he is not the hero* by F. Hopkinson Smith in 1908.

> "Some of them heard Mason **laugh all the way to the bank**."

Cry baby

The term 'cry baby,' also spelled crybaby or cry-baby, is an Americanism and is claimed by etymologists to go back to 1850-1855. Figuratively, it refers to a person who acts 'wimpy' and cries or complains over small insignificant issues.

Its use in America likely originated from more literal usage in urban legend tales which began around that time in Anderson, South Carolina, and have spread across the length and breadth of the United States.

A large number of states have stories of babies dying on bridges, producing rumors that these bridges were haunted and the cry of the babies could still be heard. In Anderson, South Carolina (1850s—a mother reportedly threw her baby off the bridge after her husband died in the war); on White Lick Creek in Anderson, Indiana (a baby died in a car crash); near Smyrna, Delaware (a mother reportedly threw her baby off the bridge). These bridges, and many others, are all nicknamed 'Crybaby Bridge.' Other states with such legends include Ohio, where there are no fewer than 24 'crybaby bridges,' New Jersey, Illinois, Oklahoma, Georgia, Alabama, and Texas.

Mark Twain first used the actual term figuratively in *The Adventures of Tom Sawyer* in 1876 when Tom was trying to shame Joe for wanting to go home:

> "Well, we'll let the **cry-baby** go home to his mother, *won't* we Huck? Poor thing—does it want to see its mother? And so it shall. You like it here, *don't* you Huck? We'll stay, won't we?"

Cry foul

This metaphoric expression means that something done is either unfair or illegal. It originated with 'foul play,' from which the sports term later evolved, meaning that someone had gone outside the boundries of acceptable behavior. The following was used in an article printed in *Blackwood's Edinburgh Magazine,* April, 1832, in a story titled 'Miss Fannie Kemble's Tragedy':

> "There shall be voices **cry foul** shame on thee!"

Though there is some doubt as to the exact implication of the above citation, Sir Walter Scott wrote this a few years earlier in *The Betrothed,* 1825:

> "We thank the Welsh assassin who hath rid us of him; but his adherents would **cry foul** play were the murderer spared."

The term remained dormant for many years, then was revived in the 1970s, possibly due to the baseball term, and has enjoyed much popularity since.

Cry wolf*

This idiom, meaning to give a false alarm, is derived from one of Aesop's fables (210, Perry Index, 6th century BC) "The Boy Who Cried Wolf." In the story, a shepherd boy repeatedly tricks residents of a nearby village into believing that a wolf is attacking his flock by hollering, "Wolf! Wolf!" Eventually they are wise to his deception, and when a wolf actually does attack, they do not respond and the flock is killed.

Curiosity killed the cat

This long-popular proverb means that being too inquisitive can get a person into deep trouble. Precursors of the phrase first appeared in plays in the latter 16th century. In 1598 British playwright, Ben Johnson, used the following in the comedy, *Every Man in His Humour*:

> "Helter skelter, hang sorrow, **care'll kill a cat**, up-tails and all, and Louse for the Hangman."

About the same time, Shakespeare wrote *Much Ado about Nothing*, containing this line:

> "What! Courage man! what through **care killed a cat**, thou hast mettle enough in thee to kill care."

The precise saying appeared in James Allan Meir's *A Handbook of Proverbs, English, Scottish, Irish, American, Shakespearean and Scriptural*, 1871, in alphabetical order on page 34.

Cut from the same bolt of cloth

This figurative term has been around in Europe and America for centuries. Cut from the same bolt of cloth is an idiom borrowed from the clothing industry. Hundreds of years ago families would buy a bolt of cloth and fashion their clothes from it. Every bolt of cloth was, and still is, given a number so that when a tailor or seamstress runs out and goes back to the supplier to obtain another piece to match whatever he or she is making, they will not get one even a tad different from the exact pattern and shading of the original.

When someone states that two persons are 'cut from the same bolt of cloth' it means that they have many similarities. They may have the same upbringing and culture, be close the same age and have had similar experiences along the path of life.

The Minnesota Dairymen's Association's *Proceedings of Annual Convention*, Volume 18, 1896, page 118 contains the following excellent example of the phrase:

> "There was quite a family of Butlers, and they were all **cut from the same bolt of cloth**

Cut off one's nose to spite one's face

This phrase, which we would think would never have been so, came from literal examples of pious women as far back as the 9th century actually cutting off their noses. The most famous of these was Æbbe the Younger, Mother Superior or Abbess of the Priory of Coldingham. In 867 AD, Viking pirates from Zealand and Uppsala landed in southeast Scotland. When news of this raid reached St. Æbbe she summoned all of her nuns, urging them to disfigure themselves, so that they might be unappealing to the invading Vikings. In doing this, she hoped to protect them from sexual assault. She demonstrated this by cutting off her own nose and upper lip. The nuns then followed suit. The Viking raiders were so disgusted that they burned the entire monastery to the ground.

Later other examples were recorded of this practice including St. Oda of Hainault and St. Margaret of Hungary.

The expression, 'cut off your nose to spite your face' became a term to describe any action of self-destruction motivated by anger or revenge. Often it has been used in jest to express someone's disgust over the unwise actions of another.

The 1796 edition of Grose's *Classical Dictionary of the Vulgar Tongue* included:

"He **cut off his nose to be revenged of his face**."

It is defined as "one who, to be revenged on his neighbour, has materially injured himself."

Cut (or give) someone some slack*

This idiom means to stop being so controlling; relax the rules—to figuratively back off a bit and allow the other person a little room or freedom to move around. It denotes the idea of one being tied to someone else by a rope and having complete control of his or her actions and movements.

The basis is hundreds of years old and nautical in origin. It derived from tying a ship to a pier. As one line was pulled to bring the ship closer, the other was released, or 'given slack'.

The earliest known verifiable figurative usage, however, of a form of this is from 1948 in *Mr. Roberts*, a play by Thomas Heggen and Joshua Logan, act 3, scene 3:

123

"That's too much! *Give him some slack* this time!"

Cut the mustard

The origin of this phrase is the subject of a long-standing debate among those who research common English euphemisms.

Perhaps the most likely origin is that 'mustard' is a corruption of muster. "Muster" in military vernacular, means to summon troops for inspection. Those who are up to standard are said to have 'passed muster.' Cut normally refers to being able to do something. Therefore to cut the muster would mean to come up to standard.

Cut to the chase

This familiar cliché comes from the American film industry, and actually goes back to silent films which often concluded with chase scenes proceeded by romantic storylines. The first preserved reference, though not its original coining, is from the script direction of an early 'talkie,' *Show Girl in Hollywood*, based on Patrick McEvoy's novel *Hollywood Girl*, re-leased in 1930.

"Jannings escapes... Cut to chase."

D

Damned if you do and damned if you don't

This is from 19th century American evangelist Lorenzo Dow. Dow decided as a young boy to devote his life to 'teaching the word of God' and began preaching when he was only nineteen years old. Although his views were similar to those of the Methodists, he was never formally affiliated with that denomination. He rode on horseback throughout both the North and South of the United States. Dow's dramatic sermons, eccentric manners, and odd-looking clothing made him a frequent topic of controversial conversation. He died in 1834, and in 1836 his written works were edited and published. They included *Reflections on the Love of God*, a strong criticism of preachers who supported the doctrine of Particular Election and confused their congregations by pointing out conflicting statements in the Bible. In his writings in a somewhat humorous rhyme, Dow chastened "those who preach it up, to make the Bible clash and contradict itself, by preaching somewhat like this: 'You can and you can't - You shall and you shan't -You will and you won't - **And you will be damned if you do - And you will be damned if you don't.'"**

The memorable quote stuck in pop culture with few people today realizing its true origin.

Damn the torpedoes, full speed ahead

On August 5, 1864, during the American Civil War, Navy Rear Admiral David G. Farragut was in charge of the Federal Fleet in the Battle of Mobile Bay on the coast of Alabama. When the ships were slowing, Farragut asked why their ship was not moving forward. He was informed that torpedoes were in their path. His reply reportedly was, "Damn the torpedoes!" The story took several years to appear in print, and by that time, it was printed, "Damn the torpedoes, go ahead!" What was actually said is questioned by historians. The quotation was altered in time to **"Damn the torpedoes, full speed ahead!"**

It is now used as a command to proceed regardless of obstacles present.

Damsel in distress

This term has come to typify a particular theme of stories, in which a female character is in dire need of rescue by a macho-type male hero. It is based on a French word, demoiselle, which suggests a delicate young woman. The roots of the idea of the 'damsel in distress' go all the way back to Greek tragedies and their harrowing encounters with gods and demigods. Naiveté usually characterizes such a fragile feminine character.

A 1919 novel by P.G. Wodehouse bore the title *Damsel in Distress*, and was made into a movie in 1937.

In cartoons, Minnie Mouse was characterized often in this role in the mid- 20th century.

Dance around the truth

When one dances around something they don't hit it. This is what happens in dancing around the truth. It means that truth is avoided by lying and or deceiving another party. As an idiom it came into popular use in the late 20th century.

Another related phrase is 'dancing around an issue,' also called 'skirting' it, therefore avoiding the true issue. Politicians are well known as masters of this art.

Beating about the bush (see) is a similar expression which is not always as negative in connotation, and can be used merely as evading something which one does not wish to discuss.

Dance around the Truth is the title of a 2009 country-rock song made popular by Jamie Lee Thurston. *Dancing Around the Truth* and *Dancin' Around the Truth* are also song titles.

A *New York Times* article on February 15, 2012 was titled, *Dance Around the Truth*, and featured a story of Tanaquil Le Clercq (1929-2000), a French ballet dancer of the 1950s.

Dance with the devil

This saying implies playing around with evil, and was born of reported activities of 'witches' in the 1600s. Charles Dickens, in *All the Year Round: A Weekly Journal* printed on April 17, 1887, Volume XV, wrote this in *A Seventeenth Century Assize*:

> "A certain Ann Armstrong, a witch-finder, deposed that she had seen one of the witches **dance with the devil**, at a meeting which, we may suppose, was of particular jollity."

Dangle a carrot in front of someone

This term, which began appearing in the mid-20th century, is used to mean offering a tempting proposal to lure someone to an agreement, contract or way of thinking. A great early example, which explains the origin, is from the novel *Island in the Sun* by Alec Waugh, 1955:

> "'Treat them like mules, **dangle a carrot in front of** their noses and keep a stout whip in a strong right hand.' She had heard hatred in the voices of her father's friends. But in Grainger's voice the mockery was friendly."

darkest hour is just before dawn, The

This old proverb means that at one's lowest state of being, there is always hope for a brighter tomorrow. The earliest printed reference is from *A Pisgah-Sight of Palistine and the Confines Thereof* by British theologian and historian, Thomas Fuller, 1650:

"It is always **darkest** just **before** the Day **dawn**eth."

Dark horse

This came from the logical circle—the racetrack. A dark horse was one of obscure origins which few people felt had a chance of winning a race. The term is usually applied after a 'miracle' alters fate. Later it caught on, like other animal phrases, and was applied to people.

The earliest known reference was from Benjamin Disraeli in *The Young Duke*, 1831.

"A **dark horse**, which had never been thought of ... rushed past the grand stand in sweeping triumph."

The figurative usage of the exact phrase seems to have first been applied to academia in 1865 in Sir Leslie Stephen's *Sketches from Cambridge by a Don.*

"Every now and then a **dark horse** is heard of, who is supposed to have done wonders at some obscure small college."

Dawn on (someone)

This figurative idiom means that some truth that one should have realized suddenly became clear, usually after much contemplation. It is taken from the dawning of day after a long period of darkness. It became popular in English writing in the 1830s. One example is from *The British Magazine* November 1st, 1832 in the story of Thomas à Becket:

"Let us hear his own account of the circumstances under which the idea first **dawned on him** that his friend and companion had ever worn a hair shirt in his life, — not that he was in the habit of wearing one — still less that this one was overrun with vermin, — but that he had ever, in any solitary instance, had any such garment on his person."

Day in and day out

Also 'day in, day out,' this means without ceasing a continual practice—every day without exception. Webster added this phrase to the dictionary in 1913, but it was already in print in 1895. *Proceedings of the American Medico-*

Psychological Association, Philadelphia, PA, May 15-18 1894, contained the following:

"She was restless and tossed about **day in and day out**..."

day late and a dollar short, A

This Americanism came into our pop culture in the mid-to-late 20th century, though it may have been in use somewhat earlier. It was already well-recognized when it appeared in the *New York Magazine* on November 15, 1971 in an article on the Associated Press by Fred Powledge:

"It's a difficult undertaking and as the reforms proceed at The AP, some staffers are saying that the changes are **a day late and a dollar short**. Criticizing The Associated Press is very easy."

It is a sarcasm regarding perpetual ill-preparedness. A similar phrase is 'too little too late.'

Days of wine and roses

This nostalgic expression, referring to past self-indulgent youthful years with no responsibility, was originally taken from an 1896 poem, *Vitae Summa Brevis* by Ernest Dowson:

They are not long, the weeping and the laughter,
Love and desire and hate:
I think they have no portion in us after
We pass the gate.
*They are not long, **the days of wine and roses**:*
Out of a misty dream
Our path emerges for a while, then closes
Within a dream

A 1958 television drama by that name was written by J.P. Miller, as well as a 1962 film adaptation. The title song from the movie was composed by Henry Mancini and Johnny Mercer.

Dead as a doornail

It is most likely that the 'door nail' in this idiom refers all the way back to 1350, and was a small metal plate which was nailed onto a door which served as a plate for the knocker. After so many visitors pounded on the 'door nail,' the life would just be pounded out of it, and it would no longer be effective.

128

Charles Dickens used the phrase in his immortal classic, *A Christmas Carol* to describe the ghost of his old partner.

"Old Marley was as **dead as a door-nail**."

Dead in the water

Something which is 'dead in the water' is stalled and not likely to be resurrected. It may be applied to anything out of commission.

This phrase is naval and was originally a literal term for a sailing ship which could not move due to calm winds. The cliché in a figurative sense appears to be of late 20th century American origin. An article in *The Boston Globe* in 1980 included this:

"For Arthur Lane, perennial president of the Boston Shipping Association, the Port of Boston is 'lying **dead in the water**.'"

Then, in 1982 the current Treasury Secretary, Donald Regan, described the national economy as being '**dead in the water**.'

Dead ringer

This has come to mean someone who looks 'exactly like' another person. (See: **Saved by the bell** for the origin.)

Dead set against

This common idiomatic expression means totally and irrevocable opposed to something. Noah Webster included the precursor of this, 'set against' in his 1845 *An American Dictionary of the English Language*, defining it as 'to oppose.'

In a *Harper's Magazine* article, *The Father of Railways*, in the fall of 1857 we find:

"George Stephenson was brought before the committee, and the lawyers made a **dead set against him**."

As time progressed, it evolved from a noun to a verb. In 1943, in *The Oxbow Incident*, Walter Van Tilburg Clark used it in the current sense:

"Though mostly by jokes, she'd been **dead set against** Osgood from the first day he came."

129

Dead to rights

This is certainly a curious expression, and dates back at least to the mid- 19th century, when many such clichés were coined. It first appeared in a collection of underworld slang jargon called *Vocabulum, or The Rogue's Lexicon* by George Matsell. The word 'dead' in this phrase was slang to mean 'absolutely, without any doubt.' The use of dead in this respect is more common in England where it dates back to the 16th entury. It is, of course, accepted in many cases to mean that in the U.S., like 'for dead sure,' 'dead broke,' etc.

The origin of the usage of 'to rights' here is not so easily pinpointed. Since the 16th century it has meant in a proper manner or order. To set to rights, for instance, means to make a situation right. Here it is to mean that every requirement of law has been met. The phrase therefore connotes that the arrest was properly executed and justifiable.

Dead to the world

Originally used as a synonym for 'forgiven of sin,' as in a book titled *Dead to the World, or, Sin and Atonement* by Klara Bauer, 1874, this now-comical idiom simply means sound asleep or totally exhausted. The initial principle was in a number of Christian books beginning as early as 1732 as seen in the Catholic theology tome, *The Cases of Polygamy, Concubinage, Adultery and Divorce.*

"They, likewise, who are baptized, are **dead to the World**, yea, and buried with Christ, and yet their Marriage is not dissolved..."

Though still retaining the original meaning in some religious circles, a modern example of the exhausted meaning is found in Scientology founder L. Ron Hubbard's long sci-fi novel, *Battlefield Earth,* 1982:

"He's **dead to the world** in the plane."

Deer-in-the-headlights look

The proverbial 'deer-in-the-headlights look' is a stunned, blank, lack-of-words facial expression when a person is asked a question that is foreign to his or her understanding or knowledge. The *Chicago Sun-Times*, in late 1999, printed the following:

"When I ask the tellers about Y2K, I get... **deer-in-the-headlights** stares..."

When a deer is stoically standing on a highway at night and a car approaches, its eyes gaze into the headlights and it seems immobile.

The cliché is American and late 20th century in origin. It came to public recognition during the 1988 presidential campaign of George H.W. Bush. His running mate, Dan Quayle, who of course became the Vice President, after comments made during a debate with Senator Lloyd Bentsen, displayed a blank look which was described by commentators the following day as "like a **deer in the headlights**, frozen in fear."As a result, the statement became a national catch phrase

Déjà vu

This French phrase, meaning literally 'already seen' is used by English speakers and writers frequently and is a mysterious feeling that something which has just transpired has happened before, though no memory of the prior event exists. The term was first found in *L'Avenir des sciences psychiques* (The Future of Psychic Sciences), a book by French psychic researcher, Émile Boirac (1851-1917). The experience of déjà vu is normally accompanied by an eerie feeling unlike anything else known to science.

Déjà vu all over again*

Unlike the original saying, this variant is purely figurative. It means that the "same old thing" is repeating itself. It is attributed to legendary New York Yankees MVP turned manager, Yogi Berra (1925—2015), and became known as one of his amusing anecdotes called "Yogi-isms." The actual quote is "It's like déjà vu all over again." It later was used by John Fogerty as an album title.

It came into more popular use by the media in 2013.

Den of thieves

This one is of biblical origin, and taken from *Luke 19:46*, when Jesus was driving the 'money changers' out of the Temple in Jerusalem:

> "Saying unto them, It is written, My house is the house of prayer: but ye have made it a **den of thieves**." (*KJV*)

The phrase is used as a metaphor to refer to places where individuals or groups who are questionable in their intent hang out. 'Living in a den of thieves' (taken from the dark 2006 anti-folk song '*Us*' by Regina Spektor) is used figuratively to draw attention to unintentionally associating with the baser element of society.

131

Desperate times call for desperate measures

The meaning of the phrase is clear, and it's certaain that many folks in America and Europe have used it during the recent economic upheavals.

Shakespeare passed on to us an enormous number of our clichés and proverbs. Below are some quotes which may be precursors of this phrase:

> "Diseases **desperate** grown,
> By **desperate** alliances are relieved,
> Or not at all."
> — *Hamlet, IIII.ii.*

> "I do spy a kind of hope,
> Which craves as **desperate** an execution
> As that which we would prevent."
> — *Romeo and Juliet, IV.i.*

Guy Fawkes, however, is alleged to have said to King James I on 6 November 1605: "**Desperate diseases require desperate measures**." This is definitely the original phrase.

The Oxford Dictionary of Proverbs, however, takes this back even farther to Erasmus:

> "1539 R. Taverner tr. Erasmus' Adages 4 '**A strong disease requyreth a strong medicine**.'"

Destiny is not a matter of chance; it's a matter of choice. It is not a thing to be waited for; it's a thing to be achieved.

This is a quote from famed American politician, William Jennings Bryan (3-19-1860—7-26-1925), who ran for President of the United States in 1896, 1900 and 1904, served in Congress and was Secretary of State under Woodrow Wilson. He rose to greater heights of fame when, as attorney for the State of Tennessee, he prosecuted John T. Scopes, the schoolteacher who went on trial for teaching evolution in Dayton, in 1925.

Devil-may-care

Meaning a flippant sense of responsibility and lack of concern for others, the earliest documented use of a form of this phrase is from 1793 in Thomas Hastings' *Regal Rambler*:

"**Deel care**, said Dr. Leveller, loud enough to be heard."

Then, in 1837, Charles Dickens wrote in chapter 49 of *The Pickwick Papers:*

"He was a mighty free and easy, roving, **devil-may-care** sort of person..."

devil to pay, The

Originally this old saying was 'the devil to pay and no hot pitch.' In a sailing ship, a devil was the seam between the planks, and it was imperative that it be made waterproof. Fibers from old ropes were hammered into the seam and then a tar-like substance known as pitch was poured (or paid) onto it. If a boatsman had the devil to pay and no hot pitch he was in big trouble.

Diamond in the rough

When diamonds are mined they are dark and unshapely. Only with precision cutting and polishing by highly skilled artisans do they become the desirable gemstones that have hypnotized humanity. Even then, there are some stones which do not have good enough color and clarity to capture a top price.

This metaphoric expression refers to a person who has great innate abilities but lacks the social graces and skills to fulfill his or her potential. A variation of the metaphor was first expressed as 'rough diamond' in 1624 by John Fletcher in *A Wife for a Month.*

"She is very honest, and will be as hard to cut as a **rough diamond**."

Though 'diamond in the rough,' per se, has been used down through the centuries in a literal sense, it only began to be used figuratively in the late- 19th century when it was meant to define human nature in *The Chautauquan, Volume 5*, number 1, published by the Chautauqua Institution Literary and Scientific Circle, Meadville, Pennsylvania, October 1884, in 'Editor's Outlook' on page 51:

"Human nature is a **diamond in the rough,** and it is worth polishing and setting for its own sake."

Then this citation was printed in *The Saturday Evening Post*, on January 2nd, 1915 in a story by Harry Leon Wilson entitled 'Ruggles of Red Gap.'

"It was really quite amazing, and I perceived for the first time that Cousin Egbert must be a **diamond in the rough,** as the well-known saying has it."

Diamonds are a girl's best friend

This much-quoted phrase was taken from the title of a song written by Julie Styne and first introduced by Carol Channing in the original Broadway production of *Gentlemen Prefer Blondes* in 1949 and most notably performed by Marilyn Monroe in the 1953 film version.

Since that time it has been used widely as a cultural cliché by diamond retailers to promote sales, and by women who want them.

Diamonds are forever

Based on the fact that diamonds are the hardest mineral known to man, and that jewelry made with them are often passed down as keepsakes, this saying is as popular today as ever. It was made famous by the 1971 James Bond movie starring Sean Connery.

But the Bond film was not the origin of the cliché. In her 1925 novel, *Gentlemen Prefer Blondes* by Anita Loos, which was made into the play and later the movie, a form of the phrase appears:

"So I really think that American gentlemen are the best after all, because kissing your hand may make you feel very, very good, but **a diamond** and sapphire bracelet **lasts forever**."

Then in 1948, the well-known diamond company, De Beers, adapted the phrase as their slogan and has continued to use it. The first was in the *New York Times* in August of that year read:

"De Beers Consolidated Mines Ltd., owner of diamond workings in South Africa, plans a fall campaign in leading national magazines which will stress the engagement-ring tradition. Four-color ads will reproduce paintings by well-known artists and carry the slogan '**a diamond is forever**.' N.W. Ayer & Sons, Inc., Philadelphia, is the agency."

Diddly-squat

This means a very small, insignificant amount. Nothing or next to nothing. It is often used with something meaning or someone having done or knowing 'diddly squat.'

The Rotarian, February 1975, on page 48 carries the earliest printed reference found, in a cartoon caption:

> *"Teasdale, I think I owe you an apology. This excellent report on the status of the company bowling league shows that you so know **diddly-squat** about something."*

An earlier phrase, 'doodly-squat,' however, is almost certainly the origin of this negative connotation. Squat was actually derived from a French slang word meaning 'to void excrement,' or release hard waste. *Jonah's Gourd Vine*, a first novel by Zora Neale Hurston, 1934, carried this jumbled line:

> "She ain't never had nothin' {em}not eben **doodly-squat**, and when she gits uh chance tuh git holt uh sumpin de ole buzzard is gone on uh rampage."

The *OED* gives this definition: 'Doodlely-squat, nothing, no more than the product of a child who squats to do his duty.'

Die laughing

This phrase is thought by most to be a humorous stating of an impossible situation, but in reality, it is anything but funny. In the 3rd century BC, Chrysippus, a Greek stoic philosopher, died of laughter after giving his donkey figs then watching it try to eat them.

In 1410, King Martin of Aragon died from a combination of indigestion and uncontrollable laughter.

It is recorded that in 1556 Pietro Aretino died of suffocation from excessive laughter.

Then in 1660 Scottish aristocrat Thomas Urquhart, the first translator of the works of François Rabelais into English, was reported to have died laughing upon hearing that Charles II had taken the throne of England, Scotland and Ireland.

But there is proof. Alex Mitchell, a fifty-year-old bricklayer from Kings Lynn, England, in 1975, died laughing from watching a *Kung Fu Kapers* episode of *The Goodies* featuring a Scotsman in a kilt with bagpipes doing battle with a master of Lancastrian martial art armed with a black pudding. After twenty minutes of unstoppable laughter Mitchell slumped on the couch, his heart failing him.

Then there was Danish audiologist Ole Bentsen who died laughing watching *A Fish Called Wanda* in 1989. Again, the uncontrolled laughter caused cardiac arrest.

In 2003, a fifty-two-year-old Thai ice cream salesman named Damnoen Saenum was reported to have died while laughing in his sleep. His wife tried unsuccessfully to wake him, and death came after only two minutes. Either heart failure or asphyxiation is blamed for his demise.

As an idiom, the first reference to the phrase known is from 1897 in a fiction article published in the *Hawke's Bay Herald* in New Zealand by American author, Jeanette Scott Benton about the Old West called *A Pair of Old Maids:*

"I was so full of **laugh** I thought I would **die**."

Versions of the cliché have been used in American literature since at least the early 19ᵗʰ century. One example is in *A Girl Named Mary* by Juliette Wilbor Tompkins published in Indianapolis in 1918.

"**Laugh**? I thought I'd **die**!"

Different strokes for different folks

This American proverb means different people enjoy different things and live dissimilar lifestyles. In short, everyone is unique. It likely originated in the African-American community in the 1960s. It has been heralded as America's quintessential postmodern proverb.

The earliest printed citation available is from a 1969 thesis by Michael William Jacobs, published by Jane Addams Graduate School of Social Work, University of Illinois at Chicago, titled, ***Different Strokes for Different Folks***: *An Analysis of the Urban Lower Class Negro's Personality and Culture as Revealed in His Music, Rhythm and Blues.*

In 1974 a Volkswagen ad parodied this saying with the words, 'Different Volks for different folks.' Then from November 3, 1978 to May 4, 1985, NBC ran a sit-com titled *Different Strokes* featuring a middle-aged affluent Caucasian man who had two adopted African-American sons. The show was then picked up by ABC who ran it one more season. The show's theme song included the entire phrase.

Dig one's own grave

This metaphoric idiom means to do something which will ultimately lead to one's own downfall. It was coined in the first half of the 19th century, and the earliest available figurative reference is from *Blackwood's Edinburgh Magazine*, August 1829, in 'Review of the Last Session of Parliament':

> "He has, as it were, **dug his own grave**: And even if we desired emancipation as much as we have ever deprecated it, we should consider it dearly purchased by the loss of his public reputation."

Ding-dong, Avon calling!

This is a famous slogan adapted by Avon Products Manufacturing, Inc. in 1954 which made door-to-door selling seem chic and catapulted the company to success. Though the slogan has been displaced by the soft modern approach 'Let's talk,' it has long been a cliché used in jest when ringing someone's doorbell.

Rebecca Johns' 2007 novel, *Icebergs*, contains a good example:

> "'**Ding-dong. Avon calling**,' his brother shouted. He was laughing, but Sam didn't see what was so funny about it. Three-fifteen in the morning."

Dire straits

A good clue to the origin of this term, believed to have originated in the 15th entury, is the spelling of 'straits,' which are passageways through which ships navigate. In early years of global exploration and trade growing via ships, navigation through the straits could be very treacherous, and the circumstance would be seen as dire when problems arose. Eventually, waterways were improved, and during normal weather, they are passable.

Now, any time a person is in an especially difficult situation, especially in a financial matter, they are said to be 'in dire straits.'

A 1980s rock band took this for their name.

Discretion is the better part of valor

The meaning is literal. It came from Shakespeare, in *Henry IV, Part One*, 1596:

"Falstaff: '**The better part of valour is discretion**; in the which better part I have saved my life.'"

Do as I say, not as I do

This phrase first appeared in John Selden's *Table-Talk, written shortly before his death in* 1654: "Preachers say, '**Do as I say, not as I do**.'" Not a good slogan, particularly when applied to 'men of the cloth.'

Dodge the bullet

This is an idiom which means to successfully avoid a potentially dangerous problem. The word 'dodge' itself is from the late 16th century, and is thought to derive from the Scottish word '*dodd,*' meaning to jog. The idea of dodging bullets in a literal sense came from the engrained image of the pioneer days. It was used this way in print as early as the late 19th century. One example is from 11 February 1892 in *Forest and Stream* magazine:

"A contends that a man standing 1000 yds. away with a Remington rifle could hit a man before he had time to **dodge the bullet**." (A represented one of two persons, the other being B)

It began to be used slightly figuratively toward the mid-20th century as in this citation from *Bullets for the Bridegroom*, 1944, by David Dodge:

"He had acted as Whit's bodyguard in an official capacity some years before when Whit was **dodging bullets** because of a little matter of half a million dollars in income tax refunds."

By the late 20th century it was in full usage as a metaphor, as in an article in *Computerworld*, May 12, 1986 on page 58:

"Comdlsco's Raymond Hipp until the board of directors brings enough focus to the question of "What if?" and the risks are acutely defined. Once that takes place, you can't **dodge the bullet** any longer."

Does a cat have a tail?

This is a classic rhetorical question. Though not a major cliché, in the U.S. South, it is another way of saying that one is stating the obvious. It seems to have started in the mid-20th century.

In Fanny Flagg's 2007 novel, *Can't Wait to Get to Heaven*, this cute quip appeared:

"When the waiter came up and asked if they would be wanting to order desert, the new bridegroom said, '**Does a cat have a tail?**' Bobby Jo thought it was about the wittiest thing she had ever heard."

A similar saying is 'Is the Pope Catholic' (see).

Doesn't hold water

Not holding water means that something has no solid basis in truth or reason. It indicates that a theory or story is 'full of holes.'

The origin is from British actor, playwright and poet laureate Colley Cibber in a 1702 comedy play named *She Would and She Would Not*, Scene IV:

"This will **never hold water**."

Dog Days of summer

Sirius, known as the Dog Star, which, to the naked eye appears to be the largest star other than the sun, is invisible between 24 July and 24 August because it rises and sets at the same time as the sun. The ancient Greeks believed that this is what caused the exceptionally hot muggy days of summer during this period and dubbed them 'Dog Days.'

Dog-eat-dog

The *Gentleman's Magazine and Historical Chronical*, Volume XIX, 1749, on page 448 references a poet who said, 'nor will dog eat dog. The Second Edition *Oxford English Dictionary* refers to a quote from 1858 of an old proverb, 'Dog does not eat dog.' Then in 1776, the following appears in *The Fall of the British Tyranny, or, American Liberty Triumphant* by John Leacock, on page 48:

"Kidnapper. Aye, so I've heard, but I look upon this to be a grand manœuvre in politics; this is making **dog eat dog**— thief catch thief— the servant against his master— rebel against rebel— what think you of that, parson?"

From this idea the current meaning likely evolved which was already understood by Saturday 25 December 1813, when this appeared in *The Examiner* published in New York:

"All the trade and commerce we are to have is among one another: if any body makes money, he must make it, not by his enterprise in foreign commerce, but out of his own countrymen. '**Dog eat dog**,' is now our commercial motto and practice..."

The phrase definitely refers to fierce competition, and this is often obvious among dogs fighting over bones or food.

dog is a man's best friend, A

This seems to derive from the well-accepted fact that dogs are intrinsically faithful to their owners, and we now know that those with pets are likely to live longer, according to those who do such studies.

The first known publication of this saying is from a poem published in *The New York Literary Journal,* Volume 4, 1821.

> "The faithful **dog**—why should I strive
> To speak his merits, while they live
> In every breast, and **man's best friend**
> Does often at his heels attend."

To paraphrase a quote from former British Prime Minister, Harold Macmillan, "Fido, 'you've never had it so good.'"

Dogwood winter (See: **Blackberry winter**)

Dollars to donuts

This phrase was meant as 'a sure bet' and was coined in America when a dollar was worth much more than a donut. The apparent first citation is in *The Daily Nevada State Journal,* in February 1876, which seems rather appropriate now, since Nevada is the state associated most with betting and gaming.

> "Whenever you hear any resident of a community attempting to decry the local paper... it's **dollars to doughnuts** that such a person is either mad at the editor or is owing the office for subscription or advertising."

At that date, donut was still spelled the old way, with 'dough' in its full form. It also seems ironic that 'dough' is a slang way of saying money now. Other similar phrases later sprang up in print like 'dollars to buttons' and 'dollars to cobwebs.'

dollar waiting on a dime, A

This figurative expression means that someone or something important is being held up by someone or something less important. The earliest known citation is from the *Engineering and Mining Journal*, Volume 129, 1930:

> "If so, here again is '**a dollar waiting on a dime**.' Safety First!"

Don't believe anything you hear and only half of what you see

This wisdom is from Ben Franklin. The actual quote is "Believe none of what you hear and half of what you see."

Don't bite my head off!

References to 'biting someone's head off,' meaning snapping at someone in an overly-aggressive manner, have been around since Charles Dickens used it in a literal manner in the August 15, 1868 edition of *All the Year Round* in a story titled *A Hard Road to Travel*, comparing a dentist pulling a tooth to a monster, or a bear, after his head:

> "...the sympathizing looks of my nurse; the deadly dew of terror that started from my pores as the monster seized me; and finally one circular wrench, as though some huge bear with red-hot jaws were **biting my head off**..."

After the turn of the 20th century it began to show up in a figurative sense as in *Atlantic Monthly*, in the biographical tale, *J.E.B. Stewart*, by Gamaliel Bradford, Jr. in 1913:

> "'Don't you understand? When those ladies arrived they were mad enough with me to **bite my head off**, and I determined to put them in good-humor before they left me.'"

Don't bite the hand that feeds you

This is another old one from at least the 18th century in England, for political writer, Edmond Burke, used a version of it.

> "...having looked to government for bread, on the very first scarcity they will turn and **bite the hand that fed them**."

This saying is likely much older, and means exactly what it sounds like. If someone is being kind to you, return the kindness, don't fight them.

Don't borrow trouble

The roots of this proverb go directly to the words of Jesus in *Matthew 6:34*:

> "Take therefore no thought for the morrow: for the morrow shall take thought for the things of itself. Sufficient unto the day is the evil thereof."(*KJV*)

This saying means that it is useless trying to worry about something that may happen when we have enough to be concerned about today. Other versions include, 'never meet trouble half way' and 'never trouble trouble until it troubles you.'

As early as 1803, an article titled *'Borrowing Trouble'* was in *The Liberal and the New Dispensation, Volume 12*.

In December 1854, *Harper's New Monthly Magazine* had this in *Loss and Gain; a Tale of Lynn*:

> "Don't be anxious; **don't borrow trouble**."

In the last half of the 19th century popular novelists such as Oliver Optic (in *Our Boys and Our Girls*, 1871) and Louisa May Alcott (in *Eight Cousins*, 1875 and *An Old Fashioned Girl*, 1902) picked up the phrase and it flourished in usage through the early 20th century. In fact, it is still used today.

Don't bury your head in the sand

This metaphor means not to try to avoid the inevitable, especially danger, by pretending it doesn't exist. The root of this comes from a story written by philosopher Pliny the Elder (23-70AD) in Ancient Rome suggesting that ostriches hide their heads in bushes. Later it was claimed that they hide their heads in the sand and that they think if they can't see people, then the people are not able to see them. On Friday evening, 11 June 1858, Charles Spurgeon, one of the most influential ministers of his day, used this illustration in his rousing sermon, 'A Free Salvation' on the Grandstand at Epsom Race-Course in London:

> "Did you ever hear of the ostrich? When the hunter pursues it, the poor silly bird flies away as fast as it can, and when it sees that there is no way of escape, what do you suppose it does? It **buries its head in the sand**, and then thinks it is safe, because it shuts its eyes and cannot see. Is that not just what you are doing? Conscience will not let you rest, and what you are trying

to do is bury it. You **bury your head in the sand**; you do not like to think..."

The next year this sermon was printed in *The Penny Pulpit: A Collection of Accurately Reported Sermons by the Most Eminent Ministers of Various Denominations*.

The truth is ostriches actually don't bury their heads at all. But this grand proclamation by such a famed minister likely spread the saying around the globe though others have reported its origin as later.

Don't cast your pearls before swine

This is from the *Bible*, and these are the words of Jesus to Peter in *Matthew 7:6*. He is making the point to not waste wisdom or truth on people who are not prepared to receive it.

Don't change horses in the middle of the stream

This means to not make a major change in the midst of a campaign or project. Throughout the years variations of this proverb have often been used to promote incumbents in American political campaigns.

Most often, Abraham Lincoln receives credit for coining this phrase. This is not true, though he did popularize it in the English language. On June 9th, 1864, he was making a speech in reply to a delegation from the National Union League who was informing him of his nomination for reelection to the presidency, and offering congratulations, when he spoke these words:

> "I have not permitted myself, gentlemen, to conclude that either the Convention or the league have concluded to decide that I am the best man in the country; but I am reminded in this conclusion, of a story of an old Dutch farmer, who remarked to a companion once, **it was not best to swap horses while crossing streams**."

A slightly different version of the speech was reported the following day in a number of newspapers, including the *New York Tribune*, leaving out his reference to the 'old Dutch farmer,' and leaving the readers to assume that he had coined the phrase. And there have been many variations since as to the actual quote.

Irrefutably proving that Lincoln did not originate this proverb, the *Hamilton Intelligencer* in Butler County Ohio, contained the following on September 10, 1846, as part of a story also in a political context:

> "No Time to Swap Horses. There is a story of an Irishman who was **crossing a stream** with mare and colt when finding it deeper than expected, and falling off the old mare. He seized the colt's tail in reaching the shore. Some persons on the bank called to him, advising him to take hold of the mare's tail, as she was ablest to bring him out. His reply was that it was a very unseasonable time for **swapping horses**."

The American Masonic Register and Literary Companion, however, had previously carried this tale on April 4th, 1840.

For an exhaustive study of the origins and evolution of this proverb and its use in other countries see *The Folklore Historian, Volume 24*, 2007, published by Indiana State University.

Don't cotton to

References to 'cotton' as a verb go back as far as 1648 (then spelled 'cotten'), when a pamphlet entitled *Mercurius Elencticus* which mocked the British Parliament, quoted poet George Wharton, himself a Royalist soldier, as saying "Unless Harry Marten and he cotten again, and make a powerful intercession for him…" It means to agree with, or be friendly with. Hence the common phrase, 'Don't cotton to,' popular in the 20th century, refers to being opposed to someone or something. Later references also used 'cotton up' in a sense of patronizing someone.

Don't count your chickens before they are hatched

This tidbit of wisdom is one of the oldest of this type of sayings. It was first recorded in Aesop's fable from 570 BC entitled *The Milkmaid and Her Pail*.

> "'Ah, my child,' said the mother, '**do not count your chickens before they are hatched**.'"

It was much later used by Thomas Howell in *New Sonnets and Pretty Pamphlets* in 1570. Obvious is the intent—don't be so quick to count on something that may not materialize, particularly financial gain.

> "**Counte not thy Chickens that vnhatched be,**
> Waye wordes as winde, till thou finde certaintee."

A little later there is a reference used by Samuel Butler in his narrative poem, *Hudibras* in 1664.

> "To swallow gudgeons ere they're catch'd,
> And **count their chickens ere they're hatched**."

Don't criticize your neighbor until you've walked a mile in his shoes / moccasins

The premise of this proverb is that no one should judge or criticize another person until they have experienced what that person has been through. Modern American comedian Jack Handley said, "Before you criticize someone, you should **walk a mile in their shoes**. That way when you criticize them, you are a mile away from them and you have their shoes." One of the top American proverbs quoted, the credit need not go to Handley, though.

Harper Lee also used a similar phrase in *To Kill a Mockingbird*, 1960, when the main character, Atticus Finch, said to his daughter, "Don't judge a man until you've got inside his skin and walked around in it."

The saying is actually from an old Native American prayer:

> "Great Spirit—Grant that I may **not criticize my neighbor until I have walked a mile in his moccasins**."

Hearsay among Western Native Americans attributes the prayer to Chief Joseph of the Nez Perce Indians who was born Hinmatóowyalahtq'it in Wallowa Valley, Oregon, and died at Colville Indian Reservation in Washington (1840-1904).

Don't cry over spilt milk

This saying means not to worry over unfortunate events which have already happened, and which you are unable to change.

This proverb has roots so deep that it's impossible to dig them all up. Researchers believe that it likely originated with folk lore about fairies. In the ancient world it was thought that laying out a 'shrine' with food for fairies would bring good fortune to a house. Needlessly wasting food added difficulty to feeding the family. However, when milk was spilled, if someone pined over it, it was considered that they were unwilling to give the gift to the fairies, so crying over the loss was scolded.

The earliest reference found is from England, in 1659, in *Paramoigraphy* by James Howell, brother of the Lord Bishop of Bristol:

145

"No weeping for shed milk."

Don't feel like the Lone Ranger

This cliché developed in the U.S. in the mid-to-late 20th century and was derived from the fictional masked ex-Texas Ranger who, with his 'Faithful Indian companion,' Tonto, went around doing good and righting wrongs in the Old West. He was first introduced on a radio program in 1933 premiering on WXYZ in Detroit, Michigan, written by Fran Striker. The show 'spread like wildfire' and spawned a popular TV show which was a Saturday morning favorite for youth growing up in the 1950s.

The Lone Ranger was the last surviving Texas Ranger of six who were ambushed by a band of outlaws, and while all odds were against him, almost singlehandedly defeated evil on the shows. When someone feels like everything is going against him or her, and no one cares about his or her plight, another person with a similar problem may state, "Don't feel like the Lone Ranger, I'm right there with you!"

Don't get your panties in a wad (or knickers in a knot, etc.)

Originally the phrase was "Don't get your knockers in a twist" and was coined on British TV on *The Basil Bush Show* which began airing in the late 1960s. Then in Australia the twist changed to 'knot.' Americans started saying panties later.

Don't give up the ship

James Lawrence, an American naval officer in the War of 1812 was in command of the *USS Chesapeake*. In a single ship conflict with *HMS Shannon* on 4 June 1813, after being mortally wounded by small arms fire, while dying in battle, he cried out, "Don't give up the ship!" This became, and remains to this day, a popular naval battle cry. It was invoked by Commodore Oliver H. Perry's personal battle flag, adapted to commemorate Lawrence.

This slogan became a set of rules for Napoleonic era war games, published by Guidon Games in 1972.

Don't have a leg to stand on

Someone who is crippled is not able to stand on their legs. This idiom refers to being figuratively crippled by not being able to support a theory or belief. The earliest known citation is from *Reason and Religion, or the Certain Rule of Faith* by Edward Worsley, 1672 on page 332:

> "Fail to do this and your Assertion hath not so much as one **leg to stand on**, besides fancy, or something worse."

Don't have a pot to pee in or a window to throw it out of

In medieval London, at the time this was coined, there was no indoor plumbing, and chamber pots were the common toilets. At that time, many people dumped them out their windows into the gutters beside the streets below. Even the very poor had these pots, so saying this was taking a person to the lowest rung of poverty.

Some areas of the world and some Amish communities still use chamber pots today.

Don't have the sense God gave a billy goat

This Southern Americanism evolved in the late 20th century from similar sarcastic insulting metaphors. An early example of this type phrase is in the writing of famed *Atlanta Constitution* humor columnist, Louis Grizzard, and is found in *Won't You Come Home, Billy Bob Bailey?* 1980.

> "This is a free country, and if somebody **ain't got the good sense God gave a** sweet potato, it ain't up to me to move ... Otherwise, you'll have lumps, and you don't want lumps. Salt and pepper and stir in enough butter to choke a **goat**."

Note the slightly later reference to a goat. Eight years later, Chapel Hill, North Carolina writer, Nancy Tilly included the following in her juvenile novel, *Golden Girl:*

> "But Penny felt as left out sitting next to Jack's sister as she had with Henry. There Tracey was, with the girls who dated football players. If I had **the sense God gave a billy goat**, I'da joined the Pep Club and be sitting with Tracey..."

Don't hide your light under a bushel basket

This proverb is a paraphrase of the words of Jesus in *Matthew 5:15:*

> "Neither do men light a candle, and **put it under a bushel**, but on a candlestick; and it giveth light unto all that are in the house." *(KJV)*

The quote is found worded slightly differently in both the Gospels of Mark and Luke. It means that we are given talents and abilities in order to help others. Selfishness only leads to sadness.

Don't judge a book by its cover

This wise metaphorical phrase, usually meaning someone should not prejudge a person by the way he or she looks or dresses, goes back at least to the mid-19th century. It can also be applied to things or situations being wrongly judged.

An early reference, in a quite literal sense, is in George Eliot's *The Mill on the Floss*, published in England in 1860. The character named 'Mr. Tulliver' used the phrase in discussing Daniel Defoe's *The Political History of the Devil*, noting the beauty of the book's binding. This is the opposite of what is usually the case in the figurative meaning, when persons of high character or intelligence are looked down upon by prejudiced individuals because of their race, creed or color.

It was first noted figuratively in the *Journal of American Speech* in 1929.

Don't kick a pullin' mule

This Southern Americanism is used by Jack Daniel Distillery in Lynchburg, Tennessee, to illustrate the importance of keeping something that aids the area where it is. Another old saying explains the reasoning behind this, 'When a mule is kicking, he is not pulling, and when he's pulling, he is not kicking.'

Don't kill the goose that lays the golden eggs (See: 'Your goose is cooked')

Don't kill (or shoot) the messenger

In Bible days as well as in the Middle Ages the messenger who brought bad news to a king or queen would be killed. Though it has been claimed to be used by Sophocles as early as 442 BC in the play *Antigone,* there seems no truth to this, though a messenger brought bad news twice. The closest was the statement, "No one loves the messenger who brings bad news."

In 1598 the principle *was* expressed by Shakespeare in *Henry IV, Part 2*. Later in *Anthony and Cleopatra* (1623), when Anthony married another woman, Cleopatra threatened the messenger and he retaliated.

148

It means that the bearer of bad news is not responsible for its content and does not deserve to be treated with contempt. Current application includes blaming news media for reporting negative stories.

Don't let a fox guard the henhouse

This proverb means that a job should never be assigned to someone who will then be in a position to use it for personal gain or to repay a vendetta. It first appeared in the French *'La contre ligue,'* translated into English by John Wolfe (1589), and is similar to the Latin saying: *'Ovem lupo commitere'* meaning 'to set a wolf to guard sheep.' The proverb was first printed in America by Arthur Guiterman in *A Poet's Proverbs* in 1924. It has been used in several similar forms.

Don't let the sun go down on your wrath

This is from the *Bible, Ephesians 4:6 (KJV)*:

"Be ye angry, and sin not: **let not the sun go down upon your wrath**."

It is meant to remind people not to harbor anger and let it fester. Before the end of any day a person should face the frustrations of that day and make amends for any angry tirades toward others.

Don't look a gift horse in the mouth

This proverb comes from the fact that by examining a horse's mouth, a person who is trained to do so can determine their age. Their teeth project a bit more forward each year. This phrase means 'don't examine too carefully the motives of a person who is making a gift to you without asking for something in return, or try to examine its worth before accepting it gratefully.'

This is an ancient saying of obscure origin which goes back to at least the 16th century. The first known printing of a similar proverb was 'Don't look a given horse in the mouth' in John Heywood's 1546 work, *a dialogue conteinyng a nomber in effect of all the prouerbes in the Englishe tongue.*

"No man ought to **looke a geuen hors in the mouth**."

Heywood's work is the source of early printings of many sayings. He was employed in the court of King Henry VIII and Mary I as a musician and playwright. His proverbs rank only second to those of the *Bible* in historic significance, it seems. (See others in this book.)

Don't open Pandora's Box

Pandora was the first mortal female created by Zeus in Ancient Greek mythology. She was given to **Epimetheus** as his wife, and presented with a mysterious box which she was forbidden to open. However, like Eve in the Garden of Eden, she disobeyed, releasing evil into the world. Hope remained inside the box.

The fear of someone opening Pandora's Box means that the person has the potential of inadvertently causing bad things to happen.

The phrase was used in *The Medical Times* on Saturday May 2nd, 1846 in the article, 'To Correspondents.'

> "If we give Hesiod credit for telling the truth, then are we to believe that all the ills that infest us poor mortals are due to that infatuated fellow Prometheus, who was silly enough to **open Pandora's box** to see what treasure was. The only treasure it had lay, like treasures in general, deep enough no to be got at, except at a sacrifice hardly worth the making."

Don't sweat the small stuff

This means not to worry about things that are not important. The cliché was coined by author Dr. Richard Carson in a best-selling book he wrote while flying across the Atlantic and published in 1997 titled *Don't Sweat the Small Stuff...and it's all Small Stuff.*

Don't take any wooden nickels

Collectable wooden nickels were minted in the U.S. beginning about 1888. A 'wooden nickel,' in more recent times, referred to a promotional coin issued by a merchant or financial institution. These were commonly used in the U.S. in the 1930s after the Great Depression. Sometimes chambers of commerce issued wooden nickels which had expiration dates after which they were worthless.

This Americanism is a jesting reminder for others to be cautious in their business dealings. Coins today, however, are of very little actual value, other than their backing by the government.

Don't throw the baby out with the bath water

This old idiomatic expression means that in attempting to get rid of something bad we should not also eliminate the good along with it. It came from the German proverb, 'das Kind mit dem Bade ausschütten.' The first printed record of this phrase is in *Narrenbeschwörung* (*Appeal to Fools*) by Thomas Murner in 1512. This proverb was common in past centuries in German, and was used in the writings of such notables Martin Luther, Johann Wolfgang von Goethe, Otto von Bismarck, Thomas Mann and Gunter Grass according to David Wilton in *Word Myths, Debunking Urban Legends*.

Thomas Carlyle utilized this idea in his essay on slavery titled *Occasional Discourse on the Negro Question* in 1849, admonishing slave owners to end slavery while retaining the dignity of the slaves:

> "And if true, it is important for us, in reference to this Negro Question and `some others. The Germans say, '**you must empty-out the bathing-tub, but not the baby along with it.**' Fling-out your dirty water with all zeal, and set it careering down the kennels; but try if you can keep the little child."

Don't try to teach your grandma to suck eggs

This old proverb means that people shouldn't try to give advice to someone with more experience than themselves, though this thought seems an absurd ensample. The earliest citation of a form of it is included in John Stevens' translation of *Quevedo's Comical Works*, published in 1707:

> "You would have me **teach my Grandame to suck Eggs**."

Tom Jones used it a bit later in *Henry Fielding* in 1749:

> "I remember my old schoolmaster, who was a prodigious great scholar, used often to say, Polly matete cry town is my daskalon. The English of which, he told us, was, That a child may sometimes **teach his grandmother to suck eggs**."

Dot all your i's and cross all your t's

This cliché means to pay close attention to all the details of your task. It also means make sure you have your facts straight before you proclaim your theory as fact so that others won't ridicule you. It originated with writing, where it is necessary to make certain that these letters are properly completed so as not to be confused with any other letter.

The earliest known printed reference, which seemed to indicate that in a literal sense the practice of checking 'crossing t's and dotting i's' was originally not important when submitting articles for publication, was in the January 1835 issue of Edgar Alan Poe's *Southern Literary Messenger*, in 'Extracts from the Letters of Correspondents':

> "But I shall do better in the future. While you continue to publish what I send you, I shall continue to cater to you. In doing this I shall henceforth **cross the t's and dot the i's** in my copies, although this should have been omitted in the original. 'I am wae to think' indeed, as Burns says, what critics would do for want of such mistakes."

[The word wae (pronounced 'whyh' meaning 'who') illustrates Robert Burns' use of Gaelic Scottish.]

Then in 1858 in the United States Congress *Abridgment of the Debates of Congress, from 1789 to 1856,* by Thomas Hart Benton, D. Appleton, page 387, the following figurative example is taken from a January 1820 debate:

> "Pray, sir, what is the object of referring a bill to a committee — merely to **dot the i's and cross the t's**?"

Do unto others as you would have them do unto you

Upon this proverb many religions have built their philosophy. It is one of the oldest sayings known to man. This particular version comes from the words of Jesus in *Matthew 7:12.*

It first appeared in English in 1535 in the *Miles Coverdale Bible.*

> "Therfore **what soeuer ye wolde that men shulde do to you, eue so do ye to them**."

In various forms, the principle expressed in this proverb is conveyed in the classic literature of ancient Greece, Rome and the holy writings of Islam, Taoism, Sikh and other religious texts.

It is universally known as the 'Golden Rule' and various businesses have adapted the name. Some use it as a slogan. A popular colloquial form is 'do as you would be done by.'

Down and out

It has been suggested that this term originated in American boxing in the late 19th century and applied at that time to a boxer who was knocked out in a match, the meaning coming from being knocked down and staying out or unconscious. There seems to be no printed evidence that the term was ever used in boxing circles in this manner during that era.

On February 10th, 1911, what appears to be a reprint of an early citation of this metaphor as it appeared in an Oklahoma newspaper was in *The American Economist* - (American Tariff League, NY):

> "There is no one to oppose it except Virginia. This eliminating process is continued — fighting each other — until Protection is all gone, everybody is idle and hungry, and all the people are **down and out**— Capitol Hill (Okla.) News."

In July 1915, however, the phrase appeared in the *American Bar Association Journal, Volume 1; Number 3* in a committee report referring to the current condition of a judicial movement.

> "It would be misleading to characterize the judicial recall movement as dead. It is **down and out** in the sense that a contestant is down and taking the count."

This would seem to indicate that perhaps this mention was in essence taken figuratively from a boxer being down in the ring.

In the early 1920s it began appearing in print frequently referring to someone who was destitute, without any means of financial support. In 1922 in *Writers of Today: Models of Journalistic Prose* selected and discussed by John William Cunliffe (Director of the School of Journalism, Columbia University) we find the following reference in an article reprinted by permission from the *New York Times*, January 21, 1922:

> "Not because she has more pride than the man has. She hasn't. But because cops haul in girls who would sleep on benches, and well-meaning organizations rescue girls who look **down-and-out**."

Down and Out: Studies in the Problem of Vagrancy by Mary Kingsland Higgs was published in 1924 by the Student Christian Movement examining the problem in America.

Down in the dumps

This is one of the most ancient phrases in the English language to express sadness and depression. In medieval days, 'the dumps' meant dejection. The earliest known reference is from *A dialoge of comforte against tribulation*, by Henry More, published in 1529.

> "What heapes of heauynesse, hathe of late fallen amonge vs alreadye, with whiche some of our poore familye bee **fallen into suche dumpes**."

Even Shakespeare made use of 'the dumps' in *The Taming of the Shrew* in 1596.

> "Why, how now, daughter Katharina! **in your dumps**?"

Sir Francis Grose was the first to define 'down in the dumps' in his *The Dictionary of the Vulgar Tongue*, 1785:

> "DUMPS. **Down in the dumps**; low-spirited, melancholy: jocularly said to be derived from Dumpos, a king of Egypt, who died of melancholy."

Down in the mouth

This, of course, is a variation of the same idea as down in the dumps. The idiom is taken from the sides of one's mouth being down when in a saddened state. The first known printed citation is from Bishop Joseph Hall in *Cases of Conscience* in 1649:

> "The Roman Orator was **down in the mouth** finding himself thus cheated by the moneychanger."

Down south in Dixie

Dixie is a shortening of the name of Jeremiah Dixon, surveyor of the Mason-Dixon Line which separated the North (non-slave) from the South (slave states) in terms of the pre Civil War days in America, and specifically the line between Maryland and Pennsylvania. Also, in 1860 a bank in New Orleans' French Quarter named Citizen's State Bank began issuing ten-dollar notes with the word 'Dix' (French for 'ten') printed on them, calling the bills Dixies. The practice spread to other Louisiana banks. The Confederate States which seceeded from the Union—North Carolina, South Carolina, Mississippi, Florida, Alabama, Georgia, Louisiana, Texas, Virginia, Arkansas, and Tennessee became known as Dixie, or Dixieland. Both of these uses of the word 'Dixie' are claimed to explain the term. A lot of Southern businesses still contain the word 'Dixie,' and the old theme song of the South is named '*Dixie.*'

Down the hatch

A hatch was initially an opening in a ship's deck through which the sailors went into the lower deck or compartments. In a literal sense it was in use as soon as the early 18th century. Down the hatch is a figurative idiom for drinking, often used in making a toast. It means to gulp something down one's throat. It was used in this manner as early as 1938 in *The University Review,* University of Missouri at Kansas City:

> "**Down the hatch**. Another drink up here for Mike from Steeltown."

Numerous bars have taken this name.

Down the tubes

Something which has gone 'down the tubes' is regarded as unrecoverable. Other variants worldwide are 'down the drain,' and the British equivalent, 'down the pan.'

It is from the U.S. and the earliest known citation referred to sports. *The Charleston Daily Mail* in May 1954, contained an interview with Parry O'Brien, in which he commented on his reaction to his earlier shot put record being broken by Don Vick.

> "Yes, that gave me another incentive. I was proud of that record. Then I had visions of all my records going **down the tubes**."

Down to a T

This means to the smallest detail. The root of this came from the *Bible* in *Matthew 5:18*. Here Jesus said:

> "Till heaven and earth pass, one jot or one tittle shall in no wise pass from the law, till all be fulfilled." (*KJV*, 1611)

Even in the Wycliffe translation of the Latin Bible in the 14th century, the word tittle was used. The term 'jot' as used here, is for the Greek 'iota' – the name of the small Greek letter "I," though Jesus was most likely speaking of the tiny equivalent Hebrew letter "yod."

This started the use of the term 'to a tittle' in reference to the most minute detail, which came into use in the early 17th century. Later this was shortened to a 't.'

Down to earth

Meaning practical and easy to understand for the everyday person, this cliché is from about the 1930s as no printed citation appears earlier than 1932. It most likely came into being as a result of the screenplay and motion picture that year, *Down to Earth*, by Homer Croy with screenplay by Edward Burke.

Down to the wire

This means coming down to the last minute or deadline at which something conceivably can be done. It is taken from horseracing where a wire or metal thread marks the finish line. It is used in all situations in which time is of the essence to complete the task. The first apparent mention of the phrase in a literal sense comes from *The Harvard Advocate*, Harvard University, March 7, 1901, in an article titled 'Kentucky Bell' (the name of a horse) on page 89:

> "As the horses surged **down to the wire** for the third time, for a clear start, the buzz of conversation stopped, and all eyes were fixed on the track."

Figurative use didn't develop until after the middle of the 20th century.

Draw a line in the sand

Basically, this metaphor refers to determining a physical point at which one may proceed no further. It can also mean that at this given point, the consequences for continuing will be irreversible and disasterous to the other party. It was first used in a more unembellished sense as early as 1527, when, during his second expedition for the conquest of Peru, the Governor of Panama sent two ships to Isla de Gallo to rescue the entourtage of Francisco Pizarro. Pizarro drew a literal line in the sand and said:

> "There lies Peru with its riches; Here, Panama and its poverty. Choose, each man, what best becomes a brave Castilian."

Only thirteen men continued with Pizarro, the others left at once for Panama.

In modern times, we find this citation in an article in the *Washington Post* on December 19, 1950:

*He **drew a line in the sand** with the toe of his boot, and said, "It's as though I told you 'I can punch you in the nose, but you can't reach across that line to hit me back.'"*

A very figurative example appears in *The Washington Post*, October 29, 1978:

"Notwithstanding the supposed public revulsion toward more federal spending, waste and bureaucracy-building, Congress seems to have gone out of its way to **draw a wide line in the sand** in front of Carter."

In more recent years it has been used often referring to ultimatums between America and nations in the Middle East in attempts to avert war.

Dressed to the nines

Someone who is 'dressed to the nines' is very flashily and smartly attired. They are certain to be noticed, even by the most casual observer.

In etymology, nine is the most difficult number with which to reckon. Quite a few catch phrases contain the number nine. Others include 'cloud nine,' 'the whole nine yards' and 'nine day's wonder.'

Some folks say that this cliché and 'the whole nine yards' both started because tailors of old needed nine yards of cloth to make a fashionable suit. The more cloth they used, the more elaborate, hence, 'to the nines.'

The earliest attempt to note a derivation of 'to the nines,' known, however, is *The Progressive Dictionary of the English Language* by Samuel Fallows, in 1835. He states that it 'may perhaps' be derived from 'to thine eynes'—*to the eyes.*

'To the nine' or 'to the nines,' was previously used to indicate near-perfection, the highest standards. That phrase was in print in the 18th century, well before 'dressed to the nines' was first used, as in this example from William Hamilton's narrative poem, *Epistle to Ramsay*, 1719:

"The bonny Lines therein thou sent me,
How **to the nines** they did content me."

This had nothing to do with either eyes, or clothing, but resultant satisfaction. Nine had been utilized in other contexts through history as a superlative—much like we would say a nine out of ten today.

The Poetick Miscellenies of Mr. John Rawlett, 1687, provides what is likely the earliest reference to 'to the Nine':

157

"The learned tribe whose works the World do bless,
Finish those works in some recess;
Both the Philosopher and Divine,
And Poets most who still make their address
In private **to the Nine**."

Drive a hard bargain

This means demanding that the other party in a transaction settle for less than asked or expected in exchange for a product or service. Contrary to other respected published sources stating this was first recorded in 1836 (there are two that year), the earliest year which it appeared was 1824 in *Reports of Cases Argued and Determined in the Circuit Court of the United States for the First Circuit*, compiled by attorney William P. Mason, in a case in Massachusetts in October 1819:

> "But there is a wide distinction between such a case and the case where a father, with a view to favour his son, and not to **drive a hard bargain** with him, makes a small deduction from his ordinary prices**...**"

Drive someone up the wall

This idiom means that someone is extremely annoying. It derived from the idea of two people being together in a locked room with no way to escape and one annoying the other to the point to wish for a means of escape. Since there is no way out the person is 'climbing the walls' figuratively. A similar phrase was used in *Tales and Novels* by Maria Edgeworth, 1833 in 'Drama' on page 239:

> "...since you **drive me** to **the wall** I must say no, and I do say no."

Here the meaning is somewhat ambiguous. The actual phrase started showing up in writing about 1970. A very early example is found in *Desperate Characters* by Paula Fox, published that year:

> "They **drive me up the wall**. Don't make wife jokes to me."

drop in the bucket, A

Like a number of familiar sayings, this one comes from the *Bible—Isaiah 40:15, King James Version*, 1611:

"Behold, the nations are as **a drop of a bucket**, and are counted as the small dust of the balance: behold, he taketh up the isles as a very little thing."

It means an insignificant amount when compared to the whole.

Drop the ball

This applies to failing to follow through on a project or endeavor. It also may refer to making any blunder which causes a problem for others. It originated from football when the ball is fumbled and costs the team a valuable play.

Figurative use dates from the mid-20th century. An early citation is from *Railway Age*, Volume 155 in 1963:

"A person can read the minutes of a board meeting from the spring of 1950; then pick up a copy of the minutes of the 1963... solicit and division freight agents to hand your rate problems, somewhere along the line they **drop the ball**."

Drunk as a skunk

We obviously know that this phrase has nothing to do with the lovable, yet oft avoided furry mammal. It is simply derived from the habit of rhyming our sayings. Though similar expressions in the English language date to the 15th century, 'drunk as a skunk' dates only to the late 1930s. Writers came close in 1938 with citations like this one from *Colliers Illustrated Weekly*, Volume 101:

"**Drunk** and disorderly. Can't you smell it? He was havin' a knock-down-that he was working on an important case, then settled down ... 'You finally sunk to booze and brawlin', eh, you **skunk**?"

A very early example of a version of the simile is from *American Nabob,* a novel by Holmes Moses Alexander, 1939:

"Half of 'em are **drunk as skunks**."

The next year *Stars on the Sea*, Frances van Wyck Mason, 1940 carried this dead-on line:

"Must have been **drunk as a skunk** not to have recognized him."

Dyed in the wool

Anciently, this was originated by wool that was 'fiber-dyed' before it was woven, because it kept the dyed color better than woolen cloth which was dyed after the weaving.

The 1909 *Journal of Geography, Volume 8*, page 64, explains the process:

> "If the material is to be **'dyed in the wool,'** it is sent directly from the dryers to the dye room, where it is dyed in large vats."

The very next year this example of figurative use, unchanging in purpose and belief, appeared in *The Friend, a Religious and Literary Journal*, March 10, 1910:

> "But the Mojaves have ever been **dyed-in-the-wool** pagans, and are not very promising material to work with."

E

eagle flies on Friday, The

Payday for most working class people is traditionally Friday. As a result, the phrase has come to be used as a cliché and songs have included it since 1947 when T Bone Walker's *Call it Stormy Monday* was released containing the following bluesy lyric:

> "Yes **the eagle flies on Friday**, and Saturday I go out to play
> **Eagle flies on Friday**, and Saturday I go out to play
> Sunday I go to church, then I kneel down and pray"

Eagles dare to win

This catch phrase has been used since the MGM 1968 World War II film, *Where Eagles Dare,* starring Clint Eastwood and Richard Burton brought the 'eagles dare' theme to front and center.

Eagles are a symbol of bravery, and the National bird of America. *Inc. Volume 2* in 1980 contained the following:

> "**Eagles Dare to Win** ... One of these 'psychological triggers' is the Eagle."

early bird catches the worm, The

This proverb means that when someone puts in the proper effort and prepares well, he or she will reap rich rewards.

Though it may be older, it was first recorded by, and came down to us from, John Ray in *A Compleat Collection of English Proverbs, 1678*:

"The early bird catcheth the worm."

Early to bed and early to rise makes a man healthy, wealthy and wise

This is one of the most recognizable proverbs of Benjamin Franklin in *Poor Richard's Almanac*. In those days it was important to rise early because the work day for most people began at dawn.

Earmark

The use of the term 'earmark' for designating something for a specific purpose came from the days when cattle and other livestock had their ears marked so that their owner could be identified. The *OED* states that it appeared as a noun in 1523. Edmund Spenser wrote of earmarking in *Prosopopoia, or, Mother Hubberd's Tale* in 1591.

"Least we like rogues should be reputed
for **eare marked** beasts abroad be bruted."

The first figurative use known was April 1860. In the Making of America Project in *Atlantic Monthly Magazine* published by Tichner and Fields, Boston:

"…we appeal to the common sense of everybody, whether those we have quoted above are not enough to make a man ashamed of his birthplace. They are the **ear-mark** of a roving, careless, selfish population, which thinks only of mill-privileges and never of pleasant meadows…"

Even in modern times some ranchers use tags on the ears of cattle to identify them in the stock sales. Most often this is now used in political matters

Earn one's keep

In the late 1800s when this phrase originated, room and board was often the only pay some persons might receive for their labors. Large families even had their children work to 'earn their keep,' especially on farms. Lucy Maud Montgomery used it in her best-seller, *Anne of Green Gables* in 1908:

"I'll expect you to **earn your keep**, and no mistake about that."

Easier said than done

This old bit of wisdom was in the English language by 1483 in the book, *Vulgaria quedam abs Torencio in Angelica linguam traducta* by Terrence:

"It is easyer to saye than to do."

It has been used in numerous forms through the years, depending on where and when. It means that someone merely saying something is going to be done doesn't mean that the task will be accomplished.

Easy come, easy go

This old axiom is often applied to money and the things it can buy, indicating no concern over them. It was used in the *Atlantic Monthly* in January 1868, Volume 21, on page 27 in an article labeled, 'Pittsburg':

"Exemplifications these of the old adage, '**Easy come, easy go**.'"

It was already called an old adage.

Originally the title of a 1928 film starring Richard Dix, it was also the name of a 1967 movie starring Elvis Presley and the title song from it, plus a number of other tunes through the years, including ones by Bobby Sherman and country superstar, George Strait.

Easy street

This Americanism was coined in the late 19th century, and is used to portray a life of wealth and want for nothing, similar to the 'life of Riley' (see). The earliest known citation is from Amy Nealy's *Favorite Poems from the Best Authors*, 1894, in a poem by E.N. Stevens by this title. The second verse reads:

"Now men start out with ready feet,
To reach that highway broad and gay—
A simple task, for **Easy Street**
Is only just a block away!"

Eat humble pie

The original expression was to 'eat *umble* pie.' In medieval times (5th to 15th centuries) in the Western Roman Empire, umbles were the internal organs and less desirable parts of an animal. Some sources suggest that if a deer was killed on a hunt the rich ate the tasty venison, while their lower class people and servants ate umble pie. No real historical record has been found proving this, however. In time the phrase became corrupted to 'eat humble pie,' and came to signify debasing oneself or acting with great humility. Though the English word humble seems related, this was accidental. 'Umbel' was originally a derivative of the French word, *numble*, meaning deer's innards. The phrase was being used figuratively by 1850 when Charles Dickens used it in *David Copperfield.*

> "When I was a young boy, Uriah said, I got to know what umbleness did, and I took to it. I **ate umbel pie** with an appetite...I am very humble to this very moment, Master Copperfield, but I've got a little power!"

In 1910 a one act comedy play, *Humble Pie*, was written by William D. Emerson and published in Chicago.

Eating crow

This is an idiom originating in the U.S. in the mid-19th century. It symbolizes the humility of someone who was overly sure about something, and found out that he or she was wrong.

The exact origin is obscure, but it may have begun with an American story published by that exact name in San Francisco's *Daily Evening Picayune* on 3 December 1851 about a simple farmer in Lake Mahopack, New York. Other tales with similar titles, however, were printed around that time, even a bit sooner.

Other such phrases include, 'eating your hat' and having to eat your words. The crow is one of the birds listed in the *Bible* in *Leviticus 11* which was considered unfit to eat, or 'unclean' under Hebrew law. The crow is in the scavenger class with the likes of the raven, the vulture and the buzzard. A Currier and Ives painting by Thomas Worth in 1883 is called "**Eating Crow** on a Wager."

Eat out of house and home

This is another phrase of Shakespearean origin. If comes from *Henry IV, Part II*, 1597.

> "Mistress quickly:

163

'It is more than for some, my lord, it is for all, all I have. He hath **eaten me out of house and home**; he hath put all of my substance in that fat belly of his, but I will have some of it out again, or I will ride thee o' nights like the mare.'"

Eat your heart out*

This expression is a taunt which means that the person speaking has accomplished a goal which the person being berated can never hope to obtain. As a result the other person's innermost being is doomed to be consumed by jealousy, bitterness or desire. In the 16th century the phrase 'to eat one's heart' meant to suffer in silence or anguish.

The earliest reference, however, actually connoted grief, and is from circa 700-800 BC in Homer's Greek classic, *The Iliad.* In the Greek myth, Bellerophon is described as 'eating his heart out' in grief when the gods Ares and Artemis kill his children.

Eight ways to Sunday (See: Ways to Sunday)

Either fish or cut bait

This is one of several either/or sarcastic ultimatums, such as 'put up or shut up.' It most commonly means to do something worthwhile or get out of the way so someone else can do the job.

The phrase originated in the U.S. in the mid-19th century. Cut bait is when a small fish is cut up to use for bait to catch larger ones. The Utica, New York publication, *The Opal: A Monthly Periodical of the State Lunatic Asylum,* printed this in 1852:

> "But delicacy is attacked with Epilepsy in depicting so faithfully the results of sane life; the truth needs no commentary; farther, the moral turpitude of such customs, among those who profess so loud, and long, their fortunate position among folks; and hence, their infallibility bids him who indulges his time to pass in their narration, to **fish or cut bait**."

Not exactly the best reference to judge the phrase. However, the very next year the expression made a larger splash when it appeared in a publicized land dispute between Caleb Cushing, then Attorney General for the U.S., and William Hungerford. The judge on the case was Levi Hubble, and Hungerford was so unhappy with his decision that he tried to have Hubble impeached. His response hit the national news. This is from the official record of impeachment proceedings in Wisconsin in June 1853:

> "Judge Cushing has commenced a suit in the United States Court. Judge Cushing must **either fish or cut bait**."

But the expression was so foreign to the attorneys that they didn't know what to say. One of many evidences of this was in the *Milwaukee Daily Sentinel* in August:

> "There was some discussion amongst counsel, without any conclusion, as to the meaning of this phrase."

But by 1856, the figurative usage seemed to have caught on and was appearing in various other American publications. A similar phrase is 'Lead, follow or get out of the way.'

Egg on one's face*

This idiomatic expression implies that something that one has done has left him or her embarrassed and appearing foolish.

There is a bit of disagreement as to the actual origin of the phrase. The late Italian-American poet, translater and etymologist, John Ciardi, suggested that it could have come from rowdy, lower class theatrical performances in which an actor was sometimes the target of eggs being thrown in his face. Another idea is that it applied to individuals with sloppy eating habits leaving egg around their mouths. Some others feel that it may have first been used as a crass comment when soft-boiled egg yolk showed up in a beard or mustache. A final theory is that it may have been derived from egg-sucking dogs which unwittingly revealed their guilt by traces of dried egg around their muzzles.

It seems, however, that whatever the inspiration, it most likely began as youthful slang. It has been in English jargon since the early-to-mid-20th century. A newspaper story in Danville, Virginia's *The Bee*, August 27, 1941 may have been the initial printed citation:

> "A peek at the script turned up these gems, which Jane says are in the vocabulary of most any 15-year-old these days: 'Hold your lava, Vesuvius!'

(To a talkative friend). 'There I was — with **egg on my face**!' (describing embarrassment)."

Elbow grease

This expression relates humorously to the fact that some tasks require manual labor to accomplish, and that use of special products does not always make the task easier. According to *B.E.'s New Dictionary of the Terms Ancient and Modern of the Canting Crew*, published about 1698, 'Elbow grease has been a term of hard manual labor since 1639.'

Elbow room

This refers to having enough room to enjoy what one is doing without bumping into something or being annoyed by someone else while doing it. It originally literally meant being able to move one's elbows freely without hitting something, and has been in English at least since 1598 when it appeared figuratively in Shakespeare's *The Life and Death of King John*, and was spoken by the king himself in Scene vii:

"Ay, marry, now my soul hath **elbow-room**."

Sometimes wrongly attributed to him because it is one of the most-noted quotes from Daniel Boone (1734-1820), even in *World Book Encyclopedia*, 1987 is:

"Too many people! Too crowded, too crowded! I want more **elbow room**."

Elementary, my dear Watson

Normally this is attributed to Sherlock Holmes, the character in Sir Arthur Conan Doyle's classic crime series. But he never actually said it in any of them.

Holmes did refer to logical conclusions as 'elementary,' and on occasion he called his sidekick, 'my dear Watson.' But the two were never spoken together in any of Doyle's novels, and was not of his making.

The first coining of the phrase was in the 1910 serial in *The Captain Magazine*, released in 1915 as a comic novel by P.G. Wodehouse, *Psmith Journalist*. Then at the very end of the first Holmes 'talkie' film, *The Return of Sherlock Holmes*, 1929, the phrase appeared. The actor playing Sherlock on stage and in radio broadcasts, had used a similar phrase previously, "Oh, this is elementary, my dear fellow."

But where the phrase was actually used, and gained popularity, was in Edith Meiser's scripts for *The New Adventures of Sherlock Holmes* radio series broadcast between 1939 and 1947.

Now this serves as a popular cliché for a conclusion which seems foregone.

Elevator doesn't go all the way to the top floor

This is one of many politically incorrect clichés usually mouthed in jest in conversation or cited by writers in novels to suggest that someone is mentally handicapped. It originated in the late 20th century, and has been followed by such phrases as 'two fries short of a happy meal,' which is claimed by Yvonne Lehman of Tennessee. An early sad example is in *Anatomy of a Nursing Home* by Mary Elizabeth O'Brien, 1989, but it gets the meaning across well:

> "But just because you can't get around doesn't mean your brain has gone soft! Sometimes they treat you like the **'elevator doesn't go all the way to the top floor**...'"

Elvis has left the building

At the close of Elvis Presley concerts, this phrase was routinely employed to convince lingering fans to leave. Now it is quoted metaphorically simply to announce that a show or performance is over.

The first time this phrase was used at an Elvis concert in December, 1956, however, at the Louisiana Hayride show, by Horace Logan, the announcer, it was quite the opposite. Elvis had performed early, and the younger members of the audience who weren't big fans of country music began to leave, possibly hoping to get a glimpse of Presley. Logan said:

> "Please, young people ... **Elvis has left the building**. He has gotten in his car and driven away ... Please take your seats."

The regular announcer picked up on the phrase, and during the 1970s, this version can still be heard on several of Elvis' live recordings:

> "Ladies and gentlemen, **Elvis has left the building**. Thank you and goodnight."

Emotional rollercoaster

Though R&B singer, Vivian Green, made this phrase popular when she released the song by this title in 2002 in her album, '*A Love Story,*' she was not the one to coin it.

An emotional rollercoaster is when one's emotions go up and down to an extreme. Persons for whom this becomes a way of life usually end up on medications for depression and/or anxiety. Usually the term is applied to individuals in relationships which are less than desirable. Addicts to alcohol, drugs, etc. are also subject to such problems. The phrase came into usage in the late 20th century. An early citation is from a heading on page 89 of *Marriage: How to Keep a Thing Growing* by John W. Drakeford, 1979:

"Action Strategy #7 GET OFF THE **EMOTIONAL ROLLER COASTER**"

empty barrel makes the most noise, An (See: **It's the empty can that makes the most noise/rattles the most**)

end justifies the means, The

This is a philosophy going back to the ancients. It means that whatever is necessary to achieve the desired positive result is not wrong.

The original basis of this belief and this saying, later popularized and put in its current form by Prince Niccolo Machiavelli, came from the Greek playwright Sophocles, who wrote in *Electra*, circa 409 BC, 'The end excuses any evil.' Later this was rendered by the Roman poet Ovid as *Exitus acta probat*, 'The result justifies the deed' in *Heroides,* circa 10 BC.

Even a blind squirrel finds a nut once in a while

Sometimes this is used with hog or pig, the animal usually favored in older texts, and sometimes it is a truffle, a chestnut or an acorn. This saying infers that no matter how inept at what someone is doing he or she will get lucky every once in a while and do something right. Its origin, however, is obscure, though Jon R. Stone in *The Rutledge Book of World Proverbs* (2006) calls it Russian. It is used a lot on websites, in business, and most particularly concerning sales people who don't adapt well to the business, and by those inclined to think gambling or playing the lottery just might pay off some day.

Versions of it have been around in English since before it appeared in print as a saying in *Golden Hours*, a magazine for boys and girls, in January 1877:

"If 'a **blind pig finds an acorn now and then**,' as the saying goes, do you think we may safely say a blind hen finds a corn occasionally?"

A similar cliché is 'Even a stopped (or broken) clock is right twice a day.'

Even a stopped clock is right twice a day

This facetious saying is usually quoted to mean that just because someone is correct on one point doesn't mean they are always right.

This well-known aphorism is credited to Austrian writer Baroness Marie von Ebner-Eschenbach (1830 –1916). Noted for her excellent psychological novels, she is considered to be one of the most influential German language writers of the 19th century.

Even Steven

The most plausible origin of this is that it was first coined in Jonathan Swift's *Journal to Stella* (1710-1713). It was composed of letters written from London to Esther Johnson, who was 'Stella' in the journal. The character, named Steven, gave his wife six blows to one; then, said Steven, "Now we are even." (Swift also wrote the classic *Gulliver's Travels*.)

Some believe that it was merely started because of the rhyming of even and Steven.

'Even Stevens' became the title for a popular Disney Channel TV show airing from 2000 to 2003.

In Australia, an unstoppable and very famous horse named Even Stevens won the Melbourne Cup in 1962. But the horse was obviously not the origin of the phrase, though some Australians seem to believe that, but it was the other way around, because the expression has been in use in America since long before 1962.

Every advantage has its disadvantage

This is the converse viewpoint to 'every cloud has a silver lining.' Though a proverb claimed by some to be of ancient Ukrainian origin that is widely used in the Netherlands, it was Holland's most famous football (soccer) player, Johan Cruijf, who brought it to the forefront in 2007. (Dutch, *Ieder voordeel heb z'n nadeel)*

Every cloud has a silver lining

The thought behind this positive proverb was given graciously to us by the classic poet, John Milton in *Comus: A Mask Presented at Ludlow Castle* in 1634.

> "...Was I deceived, or did a sable **cloud**
> Turn forth her **silver lining** on the night?
> I did not err; there does a sable **cloud**
> Turn forth her **silver lining** on the night,
> And casts a gleam over this tufted grove."

Clouds with silver linings appear frequently in literature after Milton's day, usually calling them 'Milton's clouds.' But not until Victorian days did it begin to be quoted as a proverb.

In 1840, the first such reference appeared in *The Dublin Magazine, Volume 1*, in review of the novel, *Marian; or, A Young Maid's Fortunes*, published that year by Mrs. S. Hall.

> "As Katty Macane has it, **"there's a silver lining to every cloud** that sails about the heavens if we could only see it."

Obvious is the fact that the proverb's meaning is that every situation, no matter how hopeless it may seem at the time, shall eventually pass, and that some good result will ultimately prevail.

Every day of the week and twice on Sunday

This phrase has been used in the American South for decades, but did not originate there.

It goes back to Vaudeville days, from the 1880s to the 1930s. Show companies would advertise that they did the show '**every day of the week and twice on Sundays**.' Even in the '30s, the shows would only cost a nickel, and it had to be split between the producers, performers, stage hands and everybody, so the more shows they could put on, the more everyone got paid.

Every dog has its day

Desiderius Erasmus (a medieval Dutch scholar) stated that this saying came about as a result of the death of Greek playwright, Euripides, who in 405 BC was killed by a pack of dogs loosed upon him by an enemy. It means that even a person whom others view as incapable of such action will at some time get revenge upon his oppressor, no matter how powerful the person may be.

Greek biographer Plutarch recorded a version of this proverb for what appears to be the first time in *Moralia* in circa 95 A.D., as 'Even a dog gets his revenge.' Richard Taverner, however, included the first English rendering, '**A dogge hath a day**,' in 1569 in his *Proverbes or Adages by Desiderius Erasmus Gathered out of the Chiliades and Englished*. The modern form of the saying appeared in John Ray's *A Hand-book of English Proverbs* in 1670 as '**Every dog hath his day**.'

Every man has his price

This saying means that it is possible to bribe anyone—it's just a question of how much it will take to accomplish it.

The exact phrase is credited to British statesman, Sir Robert Walpole, the 1st Earl of Orford, and regarded as being the First Prime Minister of England (1676 –1745). A three-act comedy play by Baron Edward Bulwer Lytton first performed in London in 1869, in his memory, was titled *Walpole, or, Every Man Has His Price*.

President George Washington (1732-1799), who no doubt was familiar with Walpole's statement, came close with this comment in a letter to Major-General Robert Howe on 17 August 1779:

"Few men have virtue to withstand the highest bidder. "

Everyone has a cross to bear

This common English proverb was inspired by the story of Jesus related in *John 19:17*, who carried his own cross when being crucified, though the phrase itself is not found in the *Bible*.

Some may confuse this saying with *Luke 9:23* when Jesus is quoted as saying, "Whoever wants to be my disciple must deny themselves and take up their cross daily and follow me..."(*NIV*)

It is utilized in various forms, but usually when someone is complaining about the adversity which life has thrown his or her way. The meaning is that we all have our burdens in life, and we shouldn't 'feel like the Lone Ranger' (see) when we have problems.

Everyone is a genius, but if you judge a fish by its ability to climb a tree, it will spend its whole life thinking it is stupid

This quote from Albert Einstein (1879 –1955) is a thought-provoking reminder to not judge anyone by your personal abilities or agenda. All of us have different talents and those are the criteria by which others view us.

Everything but the kitchen sink

It is not certain as to exactly when this phrase evolved, but it was early in the 20th century. During World War II it became a popular cliché, likely because of families moving having to pack every possible belonging. It must have seemed that they were taking 'everything but the kitchen sink.' The problem with moving a kitchen sink was that it was connected by pipes and difficult to remove. The first verifiable citation was in *Billboard* in the January 8, 1944 issue as a heading over a section of an article on page 15 titled *"March of Time" Pays Visit to Music Row—Sees Everything, Tells Almost Nothing.*Thereafter it began to appear in a number of publications.

An early quotable figurative usage was on the radio/TV show, *Queen for a Day*, in 1945. A contestant had racked up an enormous collection of prizes. The host stated that she had 'won **everything but the kitchen sink**.'

Everything's coming up roses

This saying originated in the U.S. and became a cliché in the 1950s. It was the title for a popular song in the Broadway musical 'Gypsy' in 1959 and the movie in 1962. It means everything is great, and could have been inspired by the 1932 campaign slogan of F.D.R. "Everything will be rosy with Roosevelt."

Every Tom, Dick and Harry

This is a catch-all phrase meant to include everyone, and like the term 'guys' is often used to include females. The root of it came from Shakespeare in *Henry IV, Part 1*, 1597.

> "I am sworn brother to a leash of Drawers, and can call them by their names, as **Tom, Dicke, and Francis**."

The first printed citation of the actual current version is from 17th century English theologian John Owen who, in 1657, told a governing body at Oxford University, "Our critical situation and our common interests were discussed out of journals and newspapers by every Tom, Dick and Harry."(Peter Toon, *God's Statesman, The Life and Work of John Owen*, p. 52, 1972)

Every tub must stand on its own bottom

Largely a British proverb, this means that every person should be self-sufficient and not depend so much on others. The first printed reference appeared in 1564 in William Bullein's *A Dialogue Against the Fever Pestilence:*

"Let **euery** Fatte [vat] **stande vpon his owne bottome**."

Then in 1639, John Clarke included a near-modern version in *Paroemiologia Anglo-Latina* (66):

"**Every tub must stand on his owne bottome**."

Excuse my French

Everyone around is aware that a person just used a swear word, but 'French' is a more polite term. The point being, that term was foreign to the normal speech of someone present.

This meaning of the phrase is of 20th century origin, and from England. A slight variation was used by Michael Harrison in *All Trees were Green*, in 1936:

"A bloody sight better (**pardon the French!**) than most."

The precise cliché comes only four years later in *The Pronunciation of English Words derived from the Latin* (S.P.E. Tract No. IV) by John Sargeaunt, 1940:

"**Excuse my French!** (Forgive me for my strong language)."

The initial source of the phrase is considerably earlier, deriving from a literal usage of the exclamation. In the 19th century, when English people used French expressions in conversation they often apologized for it—likely because many of their listeners wouldn't have been familiar with the language. An example of this was in *The Lady's Magazine*, in 1830:

"Bless me, how fat you are grown!—absolutely as round as a ball: — you will soon be as enbon-point (**excuse my French**) as your poor dear father, the major."

'*En bon point*' is French for 'plump; well nourished.' It seems a bit strange that the speaker, having been rather rude about her acquaintance's appearance, felt obliged to apologize for doing so in French, but not for the act of rudeness itself.

Extend an olive branch

An olive branch is a universal symbol of peace. This means to offer a truce or propose a treaty of peace. The earliest mention of greenery from an olive tree is in the *Bible*, in *Genesis 8:11*, when the dove brought back an 'olive leaf,' possibly a twig containing leaves, to Noah after the waters of the great deluge subsided, which, like the rainbow, served as an emblem that the disaster was over and men could once again live at peace on earth.

> "Then the dove came to him in the evening, and behold, a freshly plucked **olive leaf** was in her mouth; and Noah knew that the waters had receded from the earth." (*NKJV*)

Then, in Ancient Greece and Rome, olive branches became symbols of peace. Defeated armies traditionally would carry with them literal olive branches to signal their surrender. The Ancient Roman poet, Virgil (70 BC to 10 BC), in *Aenid*, used the olive branch as a sign of peace:

> "High on the stern Aeneas his stand,
> And held a **branch of olive** in his hand…"

eyes are the window to the soul, The

The basis of this proverb is so ancient that it is impossible to surmise its exact time and place of origin.

The eyes give clues to what someone is thinking. The underlying theme of this old adage is expressed in the *Bible*, in *Matthew 6:22-23*:

> "The **lamp of the body is the eye**. If therefore your eye is good, your whole body will be full of light. But if your **eye** is bad, your whole body will be full of darkness. If therefore **the light** that is in you is darkness, how great is that darkness!" (*ASV*)

Cicero (106-43 BC), over 100 years before the New Testament was even written, has been quoted as saying, "*Ut imago est animi voltus sic indices oculi*" (The face is a picture of the **mind** as **the eyes** are its interpreter).

The Regiment of Life, 1544, was a translation by Thomas Phaer from a French text of *Regimen sanitatis Salernitanum*, written sometime between 1050 and the early 12th century. Quoting from this translation:

"A person's thoughts can be ascertained by looking in his or her eyes."

Then in circa 1591, Shakespeare used this in *King Richard III, Act V, Scene iii, Line 117*:

"To thee I do commend my watchful soul,
Ere I let fall the **windows of** mine **eyes**."

eye for an eye and a tooth for a tooth, An

This is an ancient Babylonian philosophy and legal code called the Code of Hammurabi (1780 BC). 'An eye for an eye' is found in several passages in the *Hebrew Bible*, and refers to just punishment based on the crime. This principle has been a basic factor considered in the formation of laws of countries for thousands of years, including Judaism, ancient Roman law, British Common Law, and a consideration in the American Justice System.

Jesus, however, is quoted as saying in the 'Sermon on the Mount,' "You have heard that it was said, 'An eye for an eye and a tooth for a tooth.' But I say to you, Do not resist an evildoer. But if anyone strikes you on the right cheek, turn the other also." (*Mathew 5:38-39, RSV*)

The sentiments of Jesus have been carried forward by modern non conformists.

Mahatma Gandhi said, "**An-eye-for-an-eye-for-an-eye-for-an-eye** ... ends in making everybody blind." – Louis Fischer, *The Yale book of quotations*, Fred R. Shapiro, 2006

Martin Luther King concurred with Gandhi when he later used this phrase in the context of racial violence: "The old law of **an eye for an eye** leaves everyone blind." – *The Words of Martin Luther King, Jr.* by Coretta Scott King

F

Face the music

Like 'pay the piper' (see), this phrase is referring to owning up to an unpleasant situation; accepting the truth.

It is believed to come from the practice by the old British military of playing the drums when someone was court martialed. It was said that they were 'drummed out' of their regiment in disgrace.

The first actual reference in writing to the saying, however, was in the *New Hampshire Statesman and State Journal,* in August 1834.

"Will the editor of the *Courier* explain this black affair? We want no equivocation—'**face the music**' this time."

Face value

In a literal interpretation, this is the amount printed on the face of a stock, bond or legal financial instrument or document. In this sense, it has been around since at least the mid 1800s.

Hunt's Merchants' Magazine and Commercial Review, June 1855 had the following citation in an article titled *Railroad Enterprises and Their Detractors*:

"In judging the real loss on these bonds, therefore, we are able to pay no attention to their **face value**."

Figuratively, it has been in use since the early 19th century, and means the apparent value of something based on what it is thought to be worth, whether in regard to financial investments, statements or beliefs.

On 7 March 1908, this citation was printed in *The Black Diamond*, a magazine published by Lehigh Coal and Navigation Company in Pittsburg:

"The gentlemen at the United Mine Workers of America wish to say that we take them at their words. The coal operators accept their statements at their **face value**."

Failure is not an option

This modern statement of resolve came fully into our vocabulary in the 1990s, especially after Ed Harris used it playing Gene Kranz in *Apollo 13* in 1995 (The phrase was not actually used by Kranz during the mission, though he did write a book by that title that strengthened the use of the saying). But at least one printed example predated that decade. The following citation is from an ad in *Field and Stream* in October 1988.

"When one shotgun has to do the job of three, **Failure is not an option**."

Fair and square

In the late 16th century, when this analogy originated, square meant 'honest in one's dealings.' The earliest known reference in print is from 1589, when George Puttenham used a form of it in *The arte of English poesie*:

> "[Aristotle] termeth a constant minded man—a square man."

A few years later, Francis Bacon made use of the actual phrase 'fair and square' in his essay, *Of Prophecies*:

> "**Faire, and square**. The gamester calls fooles holy-day."

Fake it till you make it

This adage means believe in what you expect, act successful and exude confidence even when things are down so that success will ultimately come. The idea is sometimes called 'positive affirmation' and the root of this is found in the *Bible* in *Proverbs 23:7a* (*KJV*): "As a man thinketh in his heart, so is he."

It is often associated with Alcoholics Anonymous but doesn't appear in their material. Though heralded as an 'old saying' by some, it really isn't that old. Printed references only go back to the early 1980s.

A book by Phil Kerns, ***Fake It Till You Make It****: Inside Amway* (Victory Press), published in 1982, helped to popularize the phrase, and may have been the first printed citation.

Fall from grace

Today this is used in a figurative manner to mean withdrawl from a position which is viewed as prestigious or looked up to with respect. The origin of this term is in the *Bible*, the writings of St. Paul in *Galatians 5:4*:

> "Christ is become of no effect unto you, whosoever of you are justified by the law; ye are **fallen from grace**." *(KJV)*

Michelangelo's classic painting, circa 1508-1512, ***Fall from Grace***, depicts Adam and Eve eating from the forbidden fruit in the Garden of Eden.

Fall into place

This idiomatic expression is used to describe a situation in which a number of factors come together in a satisfactory, and usually unexpected, way to make something better or more understandable.

Though references to 'fall into' appear in print in the early 19th century, there are no available printed citations to 'fall into place' in this meaning until near the end of the century, when Newell Dunbar uses it in the biographical work, *Phillip Brooks, the Man, the Preacher and the Author,* in 1893.

> "Whatever he writes is written to be spoken. He has the extemporaneous instinct. The main thought or feeling he wishes to express is jumped at at once, and struck out first, leaving the details to **fall into place** afterwards."

Fall on one's sword

Figuratively, this idiom means to take responsibility, even though it causes personal harm, for the greater good. In a literal sense, it is derived from soldiers committing suicide by falling on a sword when death was inevitable as far back as ancient Israel. The first mention of this practice printed in English was in the *Cloverdale Bible*, 1535, in the account recorded in *II Samuel 31:4-5* of the death of King Saul.

> "...Then tooke Saul ye **swerde and fell** therin.

> "Now whan his wapenbearer saw that Saul was deed, he **fell also vpon his swerde** and dyed with him."

This practice has been followed throughout history, in ancient Rome and in Japan, for example.

After Peter, Lord Carrington resigned as Margaret Thacher's Foreign Secretary on 5 April 1982 this phrase began to be used metaphorically about him, because by so doing he was taking his share of personal responsibility for Argentina's invasion of the Falklands, as other high ranking British polititons had already done.

Familiarity breeds contempt

This saying, like others in this volume, has its origins in *Aesop's Fables*, from the 6th century. After the English translation of the fable called *The Fox and the Lion*, it reads:

*"Moral of Aesop's Fable: **Familiarity breeds contempt"***

This means that being too close to others often causes us to become acutely aware of their faults and resent them rather than be tolerant.

Famous last words

Before this phrase was used with sarcastic overtones, it was a way of remembering the dying words of well-known individuals. Perhaps the quote which forever altered the destiny of the way the cliché would be viewed was the timely final sentence spoken by U.S. Civil War Union Major General, John Sedgwick, immediately before he was killed by a sniper's shot at the Battle of Spotsylvania Court House in Virginia:

"They couldn't hit an elephant from this distance."

Now, it is easy to see why this would fit our common conception of 'famous last words.' The phrase roughly means that what was said was out of touch with truth or reality.

The earliest figurative uses of the cliché suggested in jest that what had just been spoken might cause offense and result in the one speaking being placed in a precarious position. The first printed references to it being used as we know it are found in a series of cartoons in a newspaper from the 1920s and '30s. Here is an early example from *The Milwaukee Sentinel* published in July, 1928.

"**Famous last words**: I don't want much to eat—just a little cold guinea hen and some imported caviar under glass."

The meaning was later expanded to refer to more general, potentially deadly, situations for anyone, as in this quote from *Shell Aviation News* in 1948:

"Leopoldville is easy to find because you cannot miss the Congo River. (**Famous last words!**)"

It is now used in an even broader sense to refer to situations which are not necessarily deadly at all.

Fan the flames***

This popular idiom means to make an already difficult situation even worse, usually intentionally. Other similar expressions are "add fuel to the fire" and "feed the fire." It is derived from the fact that a small fire left alone may dwindle and go out, but fanning the flame will cause it to flare up.

This idiomatic expression was in use by the early to middle 19th century, as it was used twice in *The Works and Remains of the Reverend Robert Hall* (an English Baptist Minister 1734-1831) compiled by Olinthus Gregory, printed by Henry G, Bohn, London, 1846. This comes from page 41 and was taken from "Politics and the Pulpit" from the *Journal of Commerce*, 1 June 1830:

> "And yet, because we cannot unite in this habitual breach of the Ninth Commandment; because we will not **fan the flames** of sectional excitement, already blazing around the pillars of our glorious Union; we are called Pro-Slavery men ..."

Add(s) fuel to the fire appeared even earlier in books being printed in London. The earliest citation was in the autobiography of a British actress, *An Apology for the Life of George Anne Bellamy*, published in 1785. In speaking of a person's reputation being harmed unfairly she stated the following:

> "It only **adds fuel to the fire**."

fate worse than death, A

Originally a euphemism for rape, it means that some things linger in the mind and make life seem unbearable. When it was first coined, in the 18th century, it was believed that a woman who was the victim of a sexual crime would be better off dead. A version of it was used in this vein in Edward Gibbon's *Decline and Fall of the Roman Empire* in 1781:

> "The matrons and virgins of Rome were exposed to injuries **more dreadful**, in the apprehension of chastity, **than death itself**."

More recent references have been less literal, and show a hint of irony, such as in Edgar Rice Burroughs' initial Tarzan novel, *Tarzan of the Apes*, 1914:

> "[The ape] threw her roughly across his broad, hairy shoulders, and leaped back into the trees, bearing Jane Porter away toward **a fate a thousand times worse than death**."

feather in one's cap, A

Putting a feather in one's cap is an idiom which indicates finding favor with a person who may be able to help in the future.

It is believed to have been derived from the ancient custom in some cultures of a warrior adding a feather to his headgear for each enemy slain. The custom was found in Native American tribes in Alberta, Canada, and North and South Dakota. Similar practices go back as far as the Mongols, the ancient Hungarians and the Incas in South America.

Feathers in caps related to hunting were also used by highlanders in Scotland and Wales. It is still customary in Wales for the hunter who kills the first woodcock to pull out a tail feather and stick it in his hat.

Fed up

This expression dates to the early 19th century when the plump gentry in England were compared to farm animals which had been fattened up for market. While the lower class was suffering for want of food, they loathed those who appeared 'fed up.'

The following, from an article in *The Middlesex Currier* in February 1832 speaks of a court case in which it was argued that the Duke of Bourbon couldn't have hanged himself, since he was unable to either stand on a chair or tie a knot. The attorney involved referred to the awkwardness of princes.

> "Every thing being done for them, they never learn to do anything. They are **fed up**, as it were, in a stall to exist and not act. It is rare to find a Prince who can walk decently across a room."

This phrase caught on, and later in the 19th century, other groups of 'idlers' were said to be 'fed up,' and the phrase crept into general parlance. Later usage included 'fed up to the eyeballs,' and 'fed up to the teeth.'

It has since come to be used when anyone has 'had enough.'

Feeling one's oats

This means feeling robust, but the saying did not originate with humans. It had to do with the common feed of horses which were well cared for. When one feels their oats, they are 'full of vim and vinegar' (see) so to speak, peppy and energetic. Horses were fed with beans and fodder back as far as ancient Rome, and when they were peppy they were 'full of beans.' The expression 'feeling your oats' only came into use about two hundred years ago.

General Mills used 'He's feeling his Cheerios' (an oat cereal) in their ads from 1950 to 1953.

Feeling the heat

Figuratively, this means encountering uncomfortable situations which cause undue pressure, and originated from the idea that getting too close to a fire has unpleasant results. It was used in this respect as far back as 1845 by Arthur Louis Keyser in *Our Cruise of New Guinea*:

> "One would have thought that the climax of astonishment had been reached, but a new wonder was in store for them, for one of us **feeling the heat** oppressive, innocently removed his hat and disclosed to view a head of very white hair..."

In modern times it has been frequently used in the U.S. in regard to Presidents 'feeling the heat' from Congress.

Fight fire with fire

The roots of this phrase were passed down to us by Shakespeare in *King John*, 1595.

> "Be stirring as the time; **be fire with fire**;
> Threaten the threatener and outface the brow
> Of bragging horror."

The origin of the saying as we know it came from actually fighting fire, when it was done by settlers in the U.S. in the early 19th century. In order to put out or prevent additional grass fires, they set small controllable fires called 'back fires.'

In the novel, *A New Home, Who'll Follow, Or Glimpses of Western Life,* by Caroline Kirkland, using the pseudonym, Mrs. Mary Cleavers, based on frontier experiences in Michigan in the late 1840s, we find the following citation:

> "The more experienced of the neighbours declared there was nothing now but to make a "back-fire!" So homeward all ran, and set about kindling an opposing serpent which should "swallow up the rest;" but it proved too late. The flames only reached our stable and haystacks the sooner..."

The earliest known usage of the actual term, 'fight fire with fire,' is American also, and is in Henry Tappan's *A Step from the New World to the Old and Back Again,* 1852.

> "Smoking was universal among the men; generally cigars, not fine Havanas, but made of Dutch tobacco, and to me not very agreeable. I had some Havanas with me, and so I lighted one to make an atmosphere for myself: as the trappers on the prairies **fight fire with fire**, so I fought tobacco with tobacco."

It came to mean to respond to an attack by combating it with the same or a similar method.

Fighting chance

Defined as a possibility of success with much effort, the phrase has been in use since the late 19th century. Early examples, though figurative, are mostly set around military conflicts, such as this citation from the American Civil War History of the 14th New Hampshire Regiment, *A Memorial of the Great Rebellion,* 1882, by Francis Henry Buffum:

> "To be drowned between decks in the night, like rats in a trap, with no **fighting chance**, was a fate from which the stoutest quailed."

Fight tooth and nail

A Latin phrase was the seed of this thought. It was '*dentibus et vnguibus,*' literally meaning 'tooth and nail.' In the sense that we know it (as fighting), it appeared in English in 1562 in Ninian Winget's *Certain Tractates*:

> "Contending with **tuith and nail** (as is the prouverb)."

In the sense of 'holding fast,' it is of equal age, and is listed in Erasmus' *Enchiridion Militis Christiani* (another of our frequent sources) in 1533.

> "Take and holde this **toth and nayle**, that to be honour onely which springeth of true virtue."

Finders keepers, losers weepers

This old saying means that when something is found, even if the person who lost it wants it back, the finder may claim full rights to ownership. A related saying is 'possession is nine-tenths of the law' (see). It is a colloquial variation of a proverb originating at least in the early 19th century. The earliest known mention is in John T. Brockett's *Glossary of North Country Words* in 1825.

"No halfers—**findee keepee, lossee seekee.**"

Then in 1856, Charles Reade, in his novel, *It is Never Too Late to Mend* said:

"We have a proverb—'**Losers seekers finders keepers.**'"

Finders, keepers was again brought out in 1874 by Edward Eggleston in *A Circuit Rider: A Tale of the Heroic Age*:

"If I could find the right owner of this money, I'd give it to him; but I take it he's buried. '**Finders, keepers,**' you know."

A modern example of the exact phrase comes from the *Daily Express*, in London, March 17, 1969:

"Where I come from it's **finders keepers, losers weepers.**"

Find one's niche

This is applied to discovering one's particular segment in life or the business market. The word niche has been in use in English since the early 17th century. The earliest usage available for the phrase in this respect is from a prayer in the *Proceedings of the Annual Meeting of the State Association of Young Men's Christian Associations* (YMCA), New York, February 17-20, 1887:

"Let me **find my niche**. Let me make a joint with the life of things. Let me help in some way, small or great, to make the world I live in better, the circle I move in cheerier, heartier; to bring a better hope amongst my nearest life-comrades..."

Fine and dandy

In this saying, 'dandy' does not derive from the noun meaning a male who is overly concerned with physical appearance, which did not evolve as a shortened form of jack-a-dandy until the late 18th century. Dandy in this phrase comes from the dandelion, which in Middle-Age England represented prosperity. Fine and dandy came to mean that all was doing well. Now the term is sometimes used sarcastically to mean just the opposite.

Fingers were made before forks

This comical proverb is sometimes used jestingly to mean that it is alright to eat some foods holding them in the hands because before utensils were invented, this was common practice.

In ancient Egypt, large bronze forks were used in sacrificial offerings to their gods. The first report of dinner forks existing was in Constantinople circa 400 AD, and one of these is in the Dumbarton Oaks collection in Washington, D.C. In the 7th century, they were reported in Middle Eastern courts. In 1075, the daughter of Byzantine Emperor Constantine X Ducas, Theodora Anna Doukaina, received a small, gold one as a part of her dowry when she married Domenico Selvo, Doge of Venice, in Constantinople, which then went with her to Venice. The church harshly condemned the princess's use of this fork, stating that it was contrary to God's intentions for use of fingers for eating. However, they slowly caught on in Italy, being utilized only by the upper class during the late Middle Ages.

Forks were not known in England until 1608, when writer Thomas Coryate returned from a walking tour bringing back one of these 'Italian eating implements.' Even then, the British were not anxious to adapt to their use. The saying, if not coined, was made famous, and first printed by Jonathan Swift in *A Compleat Collection of Genteel and Ingenious Conversation*, 1738, "They say **fingers were made before forks**, and hands before knives." He didn't say who 'they' were, but, Swift, being an Anglo-Irish satirist and Dean of St. Patrick's Cathedral in Dublin, could have meant it as a facetious throwback to the censures of the princess by the church six centuries earlier.

Fish and company stink after three days

This well-used proverb may have been gleaned from 'the wisdom of the ages,' but was passed down to us by Ben Franklin as '**fish and visitors stink after three days**' and was included in *Poor Richard's Almanac*.

Fit as a fiddle

In the early 17th century, when this expression was first coined, 'fit' didn't mean healthy, but rather, 'suitable.' A fiddle, of course, is another name for a violin— one which is still commonly used in bluegrass, Cajun and country music circles. What folks were saying is that something or someone, in most cases, was suitable for the purpose.

Written in 1598, but not published until 1601, William Haughton's comedy play, *Englishmen for my Money*, uses it in the current form:

"This is excellent ynfayth (in faith), as **fit as a fiddle**."

Then shortly afterward, in 1603, Thomas Dekker, in *The Bachelor's Banquet*, utilized a slight variation of this phrase.

"Then comes downe mistresse Nurse as **fine as a farthing fiddle** in her pettycoate and kertle."

Some say that Haughton's play inaugurated a sub-genre of drama that was exploited and developed by Thomas Dekker and Thomas Middleton over the following years.

Today someone 'fit as a fiddle' is a person in top notch health who is capable of competing with 'the best of them.'

Fits like a glove

Scottish physician Tobias G. Smollett's use of this in *The Exposition of Humphry Clinker* in 1771 is the first known citation of a form of this simile:

"'I would willingly give him a pair of new shoes,' said he, 'and half a guinea into the bargain, for the boots, which **fitted me like a glove**, and I sha'n't be able to get the fellows of them till the good weather for riding is over.'"

It refers to anything which seems to be a natural match, whether actually a physical fit or a figurative one.

Fit to be tied

This expression is used of anyone who is very angry or frustrated. It originated in the mid-19th century and derives from the use of strait jackets to restrain mental patients who appear to be out of control.

The earliest known printed citation to this figurative phrase is from *The Gentleman's Magazine,* London, in September 1869 in 'Will He Escape?'

"The fox-bearded men contemptuously put aside, sometimes by him, were, in their own slang, '**fit to be tied**.'"

Five will get you ten

This idiomatic expression began in the early 20th century, and is a betting parlance for even odds. It is a way of saying 'Do you want to bet on it?' The first known printed reference is 1927 in *Forum: Volume 77:*

"'**Five will get you ten**!' Those ten dollars were the hardest money I ever earned."

This example in 1929 in *The Saturday Evening Post, Volume 201* is more clearly figurative:

"Thornton Pymm, if he has any gift at all, **and five will get you ten** that he hasn't, is a director of rough, slapstick motion-picture comedies with actors throwing whipped cream on one another. That is what Nature made him."

By the late 1940s and early 1950s the saying was widely used.

Flash in the pan

This refers to something which offers a lot and delivers nothing. The term has been around since the late 17th century, despite attempts to attach its origin to the California gold rush, to which it was applied, and certainly was true. In *Reflections on several of Mr. Dryden's plays,* printed in London, dated 1687, Elkanah Settle wrote these words:

"If Cannons were so well bred in his Metaphor as only a **flash in the Pan**, I dare lay an even wager that Mr. Dryden durst venture to Sea."

Flew the coop

This is American slang for 'ran away.' Often now it is merely used when someone leaves home. It is derived from chickens flying out of a coop to avoid impending danger. Foxes and hawks are a very real threat to poultry. Now caged fowls usually are totally enclosed to prevent this disaster, though other threats often take their tolls. It has been in use as an idiom since the late 19th century. Used here as a dialect expression, an early example is from Frank Leslie's popular New York *American Magazine* in a story by Victor Speer titled *Vision in Baxter Bay*, December 1893:

"She didn say dat we wuz dead skins, an dat she wuz tipped off for heaven, but she jes come right out in de middle of de room an sez: 'Men, wo all kicks over de traces an **flies de coop** sometimes, but de Boss is alius ready ter take us back.'"

Then in 1900, it was listed in the American Dialect Society's *Dialect Notes*:

"**fly the coop**, v. phr. To leave suddenly; to run away. 'He got in debt to everybody and then flew the coop.'"

Flogging a dead horse (See: **Keep beating** (or **flogging**) **a dead horse**)

Flying by the seat of one's pants

Until the development of the skip/skid indicator near the end of World War I, pilots had no instruments to help them to turn easily and sufficiently. If the aircraft skipped, their bottoms would be sliding 'down hill' in their seats. If they skidded, they would be pushed 'uphill.' Thus the expression came about, 'Flying by the seat of your pants.' This required heightened awareness. Today this term applies to developing a sense of being able to perform well under less than desirable conditions.

Fly in the face of

Primarily used to mean to go diametrically against an accepted belief or practice, this metaphoric expression alludes to a mother hen flying in the face of a dog or other animal which threatens her chicks. A similar phrase, 'fly in the teeth of,' is often used in regard to harsh winds.

It has been around since the 18th century, and was used in the religious publication, *The Monthly Review, or Literary Journal,* September 1785:

"They worship private authority, while they **fly in the face of** universal."

fly in the ointment, A or One*

In ancient days, ointments were used for anointing, rather than medicine. This figurative expression, meaning a tiny irritating flaw which causes harm to the whole actually is based on a quote from the *Bible,* in a time when anointing was common. It is found in the 1611 *King James Version* of *Ecclesiastes 10:1*:

"Dead **flies** cause **the ointment** of the apothecary to send forth a stinking savour: so doeth a little folly him that is in reputation for wisdom and honour."

Less than 100 years later, in 1707, John Norris used this scripture to form the exact phrase in *A Practical Treatise Concerning Humility*:

"'Tis that dead **fly in the ointment** of the Apothecary."

Fly off the handle

This is but one of what seems like a never-ending supply of idioms meaning 'to get angry.' Others include, 'flip your wig,' 'blow a fuse,' 'boil over,' 'blow your top,' 'have a conniption,' have a hissy,' 'blow a gasket,' 'crack up,' 'throw a fit,' 'go haywire,' (see) 'go batty,' 'go ballistic,' (see) 'go bananas,' 'go into a rage, a rampage or a rant,' etcetera, ad infinitum. This is not a flattering scenario in which to find oneself, on either side of an issue.

This one, however, has old roots. Axes and hammers have been around for thousands of years, and when the head of one flies off the handle, it may cause injury. The phrase has been used metaphorically in English since the early 1800s. *Slang and its Analogies, Past and Present*, by John Stephen Farmer, 1893, page 259, lists the earliest reference as 1825; however, this citation is not for 'fly off the handle,' per se, but for a line from *Brother Jonathan* by John Neal, 'Most **off the handle**, some o' the tribe, I guess.'

But, eight years later, in a *"letter to the Editor* of the *Portland Currier"* (Maine), dated September 14, 1833, written by American humorist Seba Smith (1792–1868) as coming from fictional Major, Jack Downing, one of dozens of such satirical letters sent to newspapers in the 1830s, '40s and '50s, the following is included:

> "Let a feller be all worn out and as wilted down as a rag so that the doctors would think he was jest ready to **fly off the handle**, and let him go down to the Rip Raps, and stay there a fortnight, and he'd come back up again as smart as a steel-trap."

It was listed in *A Glossary of Words and Phrases Usually Regarded as Particular to the United States, Second Edition* by John Russell Bartlett published in 1859:

> "To **Fly off the Handle**. To break out, become excited; also, to break a promise."

fly on the wall, A

Being 'a fly on the wall' means someone having the ability to observe a situation without anyone knowing he or she is around. This idiom was started in the early 20th century in the U.S., and the first known printed reference is from the *Oakland Tribune* (California) in February 1921.

> "I'd just love to be **a fly on the wall** when the Right Man comes along."

Nowadays this is used for 'Fly on the wall documentaries' which are filmed of real-life situations supposedly without affecting the day-to-day normal lives of the participants—a type of 'reality show.'

Fly under the radar

This term was coined in a literal sense as a military phrase in the 1950s. It was derived from planes escaping detection of radar equipment before electronic counter measures were developed. In the late 20th century it came to be used figuratively to mean to be invisible or stealthy, or to keep from standing out.

Follow suit

It seems that the obvious origin for this is the correct one as the *Oxford English Dictionary (O.E.D.)* has no earlier meaning for 'follow suit' than the one from card games, 'to play a card of the same suit as the leading card; hence often, fig., to do the same thing as somebody or something else.'

The phrase originally used was 'follow in suit,' which has long since gone the way of the dinosaur. Earliest literal usage goes back to the 16th century rules for piquet. By 1779 *Hoyle's Games Improved* has the phrase, in a literal connotation, used as it is today:

> "If a Person happens not to **follow Suit**, or trump a Suit, the Partner is indulged to make Enquiry of him, whether he is sure he has none of that Suit in his Hand..."

The origin of 'siute,' 'suite' and 'sute,' precursors of the word suit, derived from Anglo-French, and go back to the Middle English of the late 13th century.

'Follow suit' has been used figuratively since the early 19th century. In *Niles' National Register*, a publication of documents, essays and facts, 12 May 1838, in *Mr. Barney's Letter*, this citation is found:

> "...other banks will **follow suit** within a limited time, say sixty days after the 10th May, and why not **follow suit**?"

Food for thought

This classic metaphor means a provocative idea. As food is imperative for us in a physical sense, new thoughts are the mother of philosophies and inventions and keep us ever growing mentally. The premise of the phrase is that we mull a new idea over and give some time for it to digest, thus determining its worth for ourselves.

In 1825, English Poet Laureate, Robert Southey, Esq., LLD, wrote, in his lengthy narrative poem, *A Tale of Paraguay*: 'A lively tale, and fraught with **food for thought.**'

fool and his money are soon parted, A

A proverb from the 'wisdom of the ancients,' its thought was well known by the late 16th century when it was brought to light in poetry by Thomas Tusser in *Five Hundreth Pointes of Good Husbandrie* in 1573.

> "**A foole and his money,**
> **be soone at debate**:
> which after with sorrow
> repents him to late."

This exact wording of the saying is dated at 1587 in Dr. John Bridges' *Defence of the Government of the Church of England*.

> "If they pay a penie of two pence more for the reddinesse of them... let them look to that, **a foole and his money are soone parted**."

This speaks of the folly of putting one's entire hope and effort into obtaining money and the things it will buy, while leaving out love of family and faith in God, as outlined in the Bible stories of rich men who demanded more and more and died, taking nothing with them.

Fool me once, shame on you; fool me twice, shame on me

This axiom means that once someone has been duped, it's usually pretty tough to pull the same trick on him or her again.

When President George W. Bush was in Nashville, Tennessee making a speech on 17 September 2002 he said this:

> "There's an old saying in Tennessee—I know it's in Texas, probably in Tennessee—that says, **fool me once, shame on—shame you. Fool me—you can't get fooled again.**"

He was obviously aiming at this saying. *Random House Dictionary of Popular Proverbs* states that it was originally a child's saying. It has also been attributed to an ancient Chinese proverb. It goes back to at least the 17th century. There are several early citations, but the first form known is from 1611 as quoted in *Tarlton's Jests and News and Out of Purgatory,* by James O. Halliwell in 1844:

> "For Who **deceives me once**, God forgive him; if **twice**, God forgive him; but if thrice, God forgive him, but not me, because **I could not beware**."

Then Sir Anthony Weldon said it was from Italy in *The Court and Character of King James I* published first in 1650:

> "The Italians having a Proverb, **He that deceives me Once, it's his Fault; but Twice it is my fault**."

A similar expression is 'Once beaten, twice shy.'

Fools rush in where angels fear to tread

It was Alexander Pope who coined this in Part III of his epic poem, written in 1709 and published two years later, *An Essay on Criticism*. Then in 1905, E. M. Forster had a change of heart, and renamed his novel, *Montenano, Fools Rush in Where Angels Fear to Tread*. Pope was a master of word and phrase coining.

As a cliché, it means that those who are least prepared for the consequences will likely take a greater risk, especially on love.

The Elvis Presley hit song by this name was written by Rube Bloom and Johnny Mercer, and was first recorded in 1940 by Bob Crosby and his Orchestra; first released that same year by Tony Martin. It was followed by Frank Sinatra, Steve Allen, Tony Bennett, Brook Benton, Dion, Doris Day, Ricky Nelson, Dean Martin and a host of others during the 1950s and '60s. Elvis' version wasn't until 1972.

Footloose and fancy free

This term per se came into usage in the early 20th century referring to persons who are unattached romantically and free to do whatever they want without fear of retribution. The first known reference is in *The Saturday Evening Post,* in an article titled *Who's Who and Why*, November 6, 1909:

> "The idea of not allowing a Kansas patriot to run **foot-loose and fancy-free** through the halls of Congress does not appeal to Murdock? What, he inquires, is a Kansan for, if not to be **foot-loose and fancy-free**?"

Individually the parts have been in use much longer. The word 'footloose' has been around since at least 1863, as it was listed in the *Oxford Dictionary* at that publication. It is noted as having its origin in the U.S.

'Fancy-free' is from Shakespeare in *A Midsummer Night's Dream*, 1598 in dialogue by Oberon:

"...In maiden meditation, **fancy-free**."

Foot the bill

This phrase came from signing a bill or account for merchandise or services at the bottom, or foot, to accept responsibility for paying it. It has been in use in English since the 19th century. Mark Twain gave us an early example in *The Adventures of Huckleberry Finn* in 1884:

"Looky here, you break for that light over yonder-way, and turn out west when you git there, and about a quarter of a mile out you'll come to the tavern; tell 'em to dart you out to Jim Hornback's, and he'll **foot the bill**."

For all intents and purposes

This means 'for all practical purposes,' and originated in Britain in an act of Parliament under the infamous King Henry VIII in 1546 in a broader and slightly different form:

"*to* **all intents, constructions, and purposes**..."

The law was actually made retroactive to 1539 when this particular Henry took the throne. It meant that whatever Henry said was the final and indisputable law of the land. And he used this power freely and without reservation or respect to the rights of others, including execution of his wives. Later it was reduced and recorded in British law as 'to all intents and purposes' as in *Commentaries on the Laws of England Volume 2* by William Blackstone in 1768. One example:

"The enjoyment of it must indeed be deferred till hereafter; but it is **to all intents and purposes** an estate commencing in *praesenti*, thought to be occupied and enjoyed in *futuro*."

The use of the phrase continued to be recorded this way in legal matters both in the U.K. and the U.S. until well into the 20th century. One example post dating this was in A General Collection of the *Most Interesting Voyages and Travels in All Parts of the World Volume 8*, by John Pinkerton, 1811:

"I heard a missionary assert, that far from Limpoa, in the province of Chequiam, he saw some trees that bore a fruit pretty hard on the outside...which being put awhile in the air, becomes good white tallow; and it serves **for all intents and purposes**, for the same uses that tallow is put to, only with this advantage, that it does not defile the hand..."

The literal meaning of this modern term, 'for all intents and purposes,' per se, which came into popular use in the late 20th century, is that the statement in question may not be in and of itself true, but for the purpose in play, it will be deemed as such, because it falls to the intent rather than the exact wording.

Forbidden fruit

Meaning 'anything which is considered taboo,' this metaphoric expression derived from the story in the *Bible* which starts in *Genesis 2:17*. There it is recorded that after God placed the first man (Adam) and woman (Eve) in the Garden of Eden, all fruit was good to eat except for that growing on the tree of knowledge of good and evil. Later, the text states that the couple partook of the fruit in disobedience to the Creator. Though it is often pictured as an apple (hence, the Adam's apple), most scholars believe it to have been symbolic.

force to be reckoned with, A*

This idiomatic term is applied to ideas, people or things which are considered so important or strong that they cannot be ignored and must be confronted at some point. The word, 'reckon' is from the Middle English *recenen,* before 1000 AD, a derivative of the German *rechnen.* When used as reckoned with, means 'dealt with.' The idiom itself became popular in the late 19th century, but its usage began much earlier. The first printed reference known is from the *Journal of the Senate of the United States of America*, 1804, in an article titled *William Duane & Son* on page v:

"William Duane worked chiefly as a printer in London, and in 1787 moved to India where he established the *Indian World*. Controversial and hot-tempered by nature, Duane became **a force to be reckoned with** in British India. He acquired both wealth and prestige — and the enmity of the East India Company, whose operations he castigated in his paper."

Forever and a day

In 1596, when Shakespeare wrote *The Taming of the Shrew*, in which he used this enchanting phrase for the first time, 'for ever' was two words. Forever is for eternity, so to speak, and there is no time frame any greater, but saying it this way serves to magnify the immensity of the thought that something will never end. Here are the words of the master playwright, spoken in the play by Biondello:

"If this be not that you look for, have no more to say, But bid Bianca farewell **for ever and a day**."

Later, he used it again in *As You Like It* (1599):

"ROSALIND: Now tell me how long you would have her after you have possessed her.

"ORLANDO: **For ever and a day**."

Forewarned is forearmed

This is an old proverb dating back to at least the 16th century. In this case, the meaning is literal, and was originally written as simply 'forewarned, forearmed.' It is found this way in Robert Greene's *A Notable Discovery of Coosnage* in 1592:

"**forewarned, forearmed**: burnt children dread the fire."

A man named John Farmer in 1831 published *The History of New Hampshire* in which were reprinted some letters originally written in the 1680s. One of these was from Captain Francis Hooke in which he warned of danger from the Indians. In that letter he wrote the following which includes two proverbs:

"A word to the wise is enough. The old proverb is, **forewarned, forearmed**."

Then, Abraham Tucker used the present form in *The Light of Nature Pursued* in 1768:

"Knowing that **forewarned is forearmed**."

Forgive and forget

The roots of this saying come from the *Bible*. Forgiving is a command of Jesus, as in *Matthew 6:14*, but forgetting wrongs is attributed to God in *Hebrews 8:12*.

The saying itself, however, in reverse, was first coined in English by Shakespeare in *King Lear* written between 1603 and 1606, and published in 1608:

"Pray you now, **forget and forgive**."

Then used by Miguel de Cervantes in *El Ingenioso hidalgo don Quixote de la Mancha,* first published in Spanish also in the early 17th century, (1605, 1615) and translated into English shortly thereafter (1612, 1620).

"Let us **forget and forgive** injuries."

Forgone conclusion

This is an idiom for something which is bound to happen. It was coined in 1604 by Shakespeare in *Othello*, III, 3, 434:

"But this denoted a **foregone conclusion**."

This is a response to Iago who was saying that what he was telling him was just a dream of Cassio's. Iago, of course, was the villain.

For Pete's sake! / For the love of Pete!

These have been easy for researchers to follow. Both phrases are euphemisms for 'for God's (or Christ's) sake' and 'for the love of God (or Christ)' and were coined in an era when those phases were considered blasphemous. Nowadays the original phrases are commonly used, but the replacements are also still around. 'Pete' most likely is a reference to St. Peter.

But here may be another explanation. The exclamation 'for the love of Pete' is recorded in print from 1918. In turn that reminds us of 'for the love of Mike,' which is older, recorded from the 1880s. This last expression seems to have been a euphemistic cry to replace 'for the love of God,' which is known from the early 18th century as an irritated exclamation. The expression 'for pity's sake' may have been an influence on the choice of Pete. As a result, somewhere around 1918, Pete joined Mike as the name to invoke when you were annoyed, frustrated or disappointed; both men being stand-ins for the deity that it would be blasphemous to mention.

Free for all

This is another term for a brawl, melee or fracas. It is used most often when a group of people get wildly out of hand and end up in an uncontrolled fight. The expression may also be used in a bit more figurative sense, and has been in use since the 1880s. A very early example is found in *The United States Medical Investigator*, 1883, Volume XVII, on page 225:

> "It would seem that physical protection, or more regard to security from gross treachery upon the public health should find some position in 'the science of government.' Instead we find a *free for all*."

Freelance

Now used primarily of writers or reporters who work on their own under contract, this saying had its genesis in the Middle Ages. 'Freelances' were Italian and French knights who fought for whomever would hire them: for good or bad. They were literally free lances. But the term didn't originate then, but with Sir Walter Scott as 'free lance' in his classic novel, *Ivanhoe* in 1820.

Freudian slip

This phrase, named for noted neurologist and psychologist, Sigmund Freud (1856-1939), is an inadvertent remark or mispronunciation of a word which is believed to reveal the true thoughts or feelings of the speaker, usually distinctly different from the way the individual wants to be perceived.

Though not scientifically proven, it reflects the teachings of Freud.

friend in need is a friend in deed, A

This is another of the oldest proverbs known to man. The principle was stated in writing as early as the 3rd century BC. Famed Roman Era writer, Quintus Ennius wrote, *"Amicu certus in re incerta cernitur."* The literal translation from the Latin is "A sure friend is known when in difficulty."

The Oxford Dictionary of Quotations lists it as existing in the English language from the 11th century, but the earliest verifiable reference is from William Caxton's translation of *Four Sonnes of Aymon*, 1489.

"It is sayd, that **at the need the friende is knowen**.

Then, in the 16th century, like so many others, it was recorded by John Heywood, this one in *A Dialogue Conteynyng Prouerbes and Epigrammes,* 1562.

"Prove thy **friend ere thou have need; but, in deed.
A friend is never known till a man have need**."

Friendly fire

This idiom seems contradictory—like an oxymoron. But it actually is from a military origin, and means fire from one's own forces rather than enemy fire. Though certainly not the first time in history when it occurred, this phrase began to be used during the Viet Nam conflict in the 1960s and '70s, when this sad scenario became known, and was even more widely used during the Gulf War of 1991.

Friends don't let friends drive drunk

Although the phrase may have been coined earlier, this began as an ad slogan created by the Outdoor Advertising Association of America. It was first used in this capacity shortly before New Year's Eve in 1982. It developed into a variety of sayings regarding things that friends don't let friends do.

Friends with benefits

This 21st century idiom is based on an increasing number of friends becoming involved sexually with no long-term commitment. The term and practice spawned a short-lived 2011 television sitcom produced by Imagine and 20th Century Fox and a 2011 movie starring Justin Timberlake and Mila Kunis showing the complications which arise from such a relationship, which also suffered at the box office.

From pillar to post

When a child is orphaned, abandoned or neglected, he or she has too often been placed into numerous foster homes or children's homes. This practice is known by the idiomatic expression, (pitched) 'from pillar to post.'

The root of the phrase is from an early game of tennis, which has been played in one form or another since the 13th century. Originally it was actually a type of volley which was then called 'from post to pillar,' which referred to the post that supported the net, or rope, as it was then. The name evolved as a saying as 'from post to pillar' until the 16th century, when it was changed to its present form, 'from pillar to post.'

In 1864 the phrase became the title of an anonymous novel published in London which skyrocketed it to fame as a figurative term. In the 1902 edition of *Slang and its analogies past and present; Volume 5,* by John Stephen Farmer and William Ernest Henley, it was defined as 'hither and thither, with aimless effort or action.'

From the cradle to the grave

This saying, used to mean 'one's entire life experience,' is from the title of Hungarian Romantic Period virtuoso Franz Liszt's last symphonic poem composed in 1881-1882.

From the get-go

Meaning from the very inception of an idea or concept, according to *Merriam Webster* it was coined in 1966; however, it was used in an article in 1962 by Langston Hughes in the *Chicago Defender*. Also the following appeared in *Revista Hispanica Moderna: Boletin del Instituto de las Hispanas*, English Version, (Hispanic Institute in the United States, Columbia University), 1962 Volume 58-59:

> "Our lives are affective **from the get-go**: from infancy to death, from getting out of bed in the morning to getting back in it at night."

From the sublime to the ridiculous

This cliché is adapted from a statement in Thomas Paine's *The Age of Reason*, in 1773.

> "**The sublime and the ridiculous** are often so nearly related that it is difficult to class them separately..."

Then Napoleon Bonaparte likely aided its popularity as a phrase in 1812 when he retreated from Moscow. He is quoted as saying, "**From the sublime to the ridiculous** there is only one step."

Front and center

This was used as early as 1743 by British Brigadier General Humphrey Bland in *A Treatise of Military Discipline*, as "Front and Center Ranks," also known as bearings, which is the source of its figurative meaning.

"**Front and Center** Ranks, move forward to Close Order, March. XIII. **Front and Center** Ranks, move forward to Order…"

The common usage of this term to mean 'in the forefront' has been a part of the English culture since September 22, 1951 when "*Front and Center On the Town*" appeared in Billboard Magazine. However, the military command 'front and center' has been around considerably longer. In September, 1922, in an article titled *The Curious Tribe of McFee* by Peter B. Kyne in *Cosmopolitan Magazine* we have these lines in three places on the same page (misspelling copied):

"'Private Kelleher, **front and center!**' Kelleher hopped down from the lorry, marched down the front of the batthery and come up, … Then says I, 'Private McFee, **front and center!**' Out shteps me poor misguided Kevin **front and center**."

Full steam ahead

Derived from operating the controls of a steam engine on a ship or train, it means full power, with the throttle wide open straight ahead. Figuratively it indicates going into a project with great enthusiasm, refusing to be discouraged. It has been in figurative use since the early 19th century. One example is from an article in *Dry Goods Reporter* published in Chicago on January 2nd, 1915: *Full Steam Ahead for 1915*. The article suggests that businessmen adapt this as their slogan for the year.

Funny as a crutch

This obviously sarcastic oxymoron was used on a voice-over commercial for the 1970s sitcom, *Happy Days*, in which Potsie was put down by Richie Cunningham, to which he responds with "**Funny as a crutch**, Rich."

It was stated that this was the origin, but it had been around much longer. Burton Braley used it in *Sonnets of a Suffragette* on page 188 in 1913:

"Cut out the comedy. You ain't so much. You're just about as **funny as a crutch**."

200

G

Gag a maggot

This refers to something totally disgusting or revolting. It came into use in the mid-1960s. The earliest citation available is found in *Design with Type* by Carl Dair, 1967:

> "'But come on, let's go take a run around the set. Brace yourself, though. I warn you, man, it's terrible — it's ghastly.'

> "'Yes, exactly. Ward Four would **gag a maggot**.'"

Gag at a gnat and swallow a camel

This metaphoric expression, meaning being overly concerned about insignificant matters, while allowing more important ones to escape attention, comes from the *Bible*: Jesus' words to the scribes and Pharisees in *Matthew 23:24*:

> "You blind guides, who **strain out a gnat and swallow a camel**!" (*KJV*)

Game of cat and mouse

This common idiom is defined as a contrived action which entails constant chases, near catches and escapes. The basis is taken from an Indian Sanskrit tale of a lion, a cat and a mouse attributed to Hitopadesha about 1675, not to be confused with a much earlier fable by Aesop, *The Lion and the Mouse.*

Its use, as we know it, dates to the mid-to-late 19th century. It was first a literal game played in schools based on cats chasing and playing with mice as described in 1868 in *Chronicles of St. Mary's* by 'S.D.N.'

> "Presently a girl left the players, who had just started a **game of 'Cat and Mouse**,' and seating herself by Lydia, showed she wished to make her acquaintance."

By World War I it had begun to be used figuratively as seen in this snippet from the *Typographical Journal* in September 1917:

> "In those days it was a **game of cat and mouse**. We were the mouse and the Germans were the cat. They played with us. We never had any doubt as to the final outcome of the war, but we knew that for the time we were outnumbered, outgunned and outmunitioned**.**"

201

Get above one's raising*

This bit of American Southern colloquialism means that a person is acting in a way that indicates that he or she feels he or she is better than other family members or that is incongruous with the person's family of origin. It has often been used contemptuously and is understandably resented by the other party who feels that he or she is merely attempting to rise above poverty and or ignorance. The earliest known printed citation of a form of this idiom is found in Richard Malcolm Johnston's 1889 novel, *Ogeechee Cross-firings*, page 9:

> "There's no good in a fellow trying to rise too far **above his raising**. It's well for Tom Doster that he could not go to the bar. He's proud enough, hard as he has to work, and he cannot, if he ever tries, conceal his aspiring nature."

In 1905, the following example, with 'gotten' rather than 'rise' was printed in The University of Virginia's publication, *Corks and Curls, Volume 18*:

> "One of them actually called me 'a fat voting idiot who had gotten **above his raising**.'"

Get a life*

This now-common Americanism is usually spoken in a taunting manner to indicate that the person being addressed is using an uncommonly inordinatet amount of time on trivialities. The earliest known citation is found in January 1983 in a *Washington Post* article:

> "Gross me out, I mean, Valley Girl was, like, ohmigod, it was last year, fer sure! I mean, **get a life**! Say what?"

Get a room!

This derisive comment is used when a couple is displaying overt sensual affection toward one another in public. It is meant to discourage them from continuing this practice which is likely embarrassing to the speaker. The term came into usage in the U.S. in the late 20th century.

Get down to brass tacks

This debated phrase, meaning getting to the heart of a matter, is from the 19th century. One possible origin is that it refers to the brass tacks on fine upholstery; another, that it is a Cockney rhyming slang for 'hard facts,' which seems unlikely since it seems to originate in the U.S. Still another argument, likely correct, is that it alludes to tacks hammered into a sales counter to indicate exact points of measuring, particularly of cloth. The first known printing comes from the *Tri Weekly Newspaper* in Galveston, Texas in January 1863:

> "When you come **down to 'brass tacks'** - if we may be allowed the expression - everybody is governed by selfishness."

In November 1911, an ad for Cooper Hewitt Lamps in *The Illuminating Engineer* showed that even then the origin of the expression was uncertain:

> "'**Getting down to brass tacks**' is a characteristic American slang phrase, full of suggestion but of obscure origin..."

Get down to business

This means to seriously apply oneself to the job at hand. It has been around since the late 19th century, as we see from this example which clearly shows that it was understood and in use in *The West Virginia Bar* in February 1896:

> "Let us **get down to business**. We want those who are willing to subscribe to such a position to stand up and be counted."

Get in the zone

This is a term which arose from a psychology known as 'flow,' proposed by Hungarian professor Mihaly Csikszentmihalyi in a 1990 book, *Flow: The Psychology of Optimal Experience*. Flow is defined as a mental state in which a person is energized to focus on a given task. Getting in the zone or tapping into the zone indicates being mentally prepared or positively charged and has been applied largely to athletes preparing for tough competition.

Get off your high horse

For hundreds of years, one definition of 'high' has been 'powerful,' and 'out of touch with the common people.' The 'High Kings' of old often held commoners in contempt. Ancient rulers and lords rode large expensive steeds when surveying their kingdoms. Great military men throughout history rode such animals as well. They were viewed as above the law, haughty and untouchable.

To say 'get down off your high horse' implies that the speaker feels that the person being addressed is acting in a haughty or self-righteous manner.

The earliest references to high horses, like many idioms, were literal. The original ones were huge, and in medieval England they were known as 'great horses.' In Old English, John Wycliffe wrote thusly of them in *English Works*, circa 1380:

"Ye emperour... made hym & his cardenals ride in reed on **hye ors**."

'Hye ors,' of course, translates to '**high horse**.'

By the 18th century, the term, 'mounting one's high horse,' was used in a figurative sense. In 1782, Admiral Sir Thomas Pasley penned his *Private Sea Journals,* which contained the phrase in this light. They remained unpublished for about a century and a half. In 1931, they were finally published by his great-great-great-grandson.

"Whether Sir George will mount **his high Horse** or be over-civil to Admiral Pigot seems even to be a doubt with himself."

Get one's ducks in a row

This is making certain that all of the details of a project are taken care of before beginning the job. There is controversy among etymologists as to the origin of this metaphoric phrase, some relating it to carnival games involving moving images of ducks to be shot down to win prizes, others stating that it came from resetting early short bowling pins, nicknamed 'ducks,' by hand. What seems the most likely origin, however, is that it is taken from nature. Mother ducks are followed by a straight line of ducklings when marching from one place to another.

Contrary to sources dating its coining to the middle or latter 20th century, it came into use early in 20th century and the first known example is from 1919 in chapter 20 of Kate Langley Bosher's novel, *His Friend Miss McFarlane* from Harper & Brothers, New York:

"He's been away for some days **getting his ducks in a row**, and you can bet your last bit he's got 'em there, all right."

Then three years later in *The Lumber Trade Journal*, New York, on 15 January 1922 we find:

"...there is no question but that many buyers are **getting their ducks in a row** and will soon be on the market for more stock."

Get one's fill of something

This idiom means to be so overwhelmed with something that one wants no more part of it. It has been around since at least the early 18th century. The first known citation is from *Mystery of godliness considered in LXI sermons wherein the diety of Christ is prov'd upon no evidence than the Word of God and no other View than for the Salvation of Men* by Thomas Bradbury, 1726:

"Good old Simeon deliver'd himself on that occasion like one who had **got his Fill of** Lise, and had no more to stay sot in this World..."

Get one's giggle box turned upside down

This phrase means to get started laughing and not be able to stop. Also, to laugh so hard that one cries. It originated in America in the latter 20th century. The term 'giggle box' has been used since the mid-20th century for a person who laughs a lot, as well as for a forum of humorous children's stories, as in the *Publisher's Weekly* printed in Philadelphia, and other publications beginning in the 1950s, as well as a game.

Get someone's goat

Getting someone's goat (usually used in the past tense) is getting up their 'ire.'

To discover what a goat has to do with getting upset about something, a little American book, written under the pseudonym, "Number 1500" published in 1904 called *Life in Sing Sing* has the answer. Therein the word 'goat' is given as slang for anger.

The first mention of the phrase, per se, seems to be from a Wisconsin newspaper called *The Stevens Point Daily Journal* in May of 1909.

"Wouldn't that **get your goat**? We'd been transferring the same water all night from the tub to the bowl and back again."

It made its way 'across the pond' (see) to England by at least 1924, when it was used in a story by Nobel Prize winner John Galsworthy called *White Monkey*, clearly seen as a recently coined expression.

"That had **got** the chairman's **goat**! – **Got his goat**? What expressions they used nowadays!"

Get the hell out of Dodge

Dodge, of course, refers to Dodge City, Kansas, which was the site of so many Western shows and movies in the 1950s and '60s. The most prominent of these was the long-running television series, Gunsmoke, originally airing from 1955 to 1975. The phrase was commonly used when outlaws were commanded to leave town.

In the mid-1960s this became popular slang among street gangs for getting out of any location.

Get the kinks out

This means to rid something of difficulties or quirks, thus enabling success in a venture.

Kink is a Dutch word meaning twist, as the twists in a knotted-up rope. Kinks are considered anything that causes confusion or obstruction. This saying originated in the 17th century, and fits all connotations, whether mental, emotional or physical.

Get the lead out

This idiom originated in the U.S. about 1930. During the Second World War, this phrase caught on in the military, as used by sergeants and other commanders, and had reference to soldiers getting going faster. It meant get the lead out of their feet, not their posterior, as it has apparently come to be viewed today.

Getting sidetracked

Understanding the origin of why we call getting distracted 'getting sidetracked' goes to the etymology of the word 'sidetrack.' It is, of course, a compound of the words 'side' and 'track,' and comes from railroad siding. It is from the literal verb coined in 1880, which means to move a train car onto a 'sidetrack.' It has been used figuratively since 1889, and means 'to divert from the main purpose.'

The first known reference is from *Debates: Official Report, Volume 2,* Canadian Parliament House of Commons, 1889:

"Clearly we must get to the root cause of this problem and not **get sidetracked** by surface issues."

Getting the short end of the stick

This saying goes all the way back to medieval Europe, and a technique known as the 'split tally' used to record money exchange (at the time, coins) and debts. The fund was regularly short, and a squared stick was used which was marked with notches and split lengthwise. Each party was given one of the equal halves to record the debt and had proof of the amount according to the number of notches. Later, this method was altered in order to prevent tampering.

One refinement was to make the two parts of the stick of different lengths. The longer part was called 'stock' and was given to the party which had advanced money to the receiver. This is actually the origin of the word 'stockholder.' The debtor, on the other hand, 'got the short end of the stick.'

Today 'getting the short end of the stick' indicates getting the bad end of a deal in any type of transaction.

Getting up on the wrong side of the bed

This is a superstition which can be traced back to the Roman Empire, when it was claimed the wrong side of the bed was the left side. People have been saying that other folks got up on the wrong side of the bed for well over three centuries now to indicate that they got up in a bad mood, most likely unaware of the origin. There is another saying, 'got up with their left foot forward,' that might give a hint of this. A lot of English superstitions resulted from the inferiority of the left from the right, which is even older than Rome. One says that it is bad luck to put your left shoe on first. It is said that Augustus Caesar was very particular to arise each and every morning on the right side of the bed.

As long as three thousand years or more ago, left handed persons were looked down upon as being inferior—something that southpaws are often 'up-in-arms' about. Alexander the Great, Julius Caesar, Napoleon, Michelangelo, Leonardo da Vinci, Beethoven, Benjamin Franklin, Mark Twain, Albert Einstein, Paul McCartney, Bruce Jenner, John McEnroe, and Bill Clinton were all born left-handed.

Get to the bottom of something

This means finding out what really happened in a situation which is mysterious or sketchy as to details; to determine the underlying cause. The term came into use in the late 18th century. The earliest known printed reference to the figurative

207

use is from *The Life and Opinions of Tristam Shandy, Gentleman*, by Lawrence Sterne, 1787:

> "Bridget had pawned all the little stock of honour a poor chamber-maid was worth in the world, that she would **get to the bottom of** the affair in ten days; and it was built upon one of the most conceivable *postulatum* in nature; namely that whilst my Uncle Toby was making love to her mistress, the corporal could find better things to do, than to make love to her... "

Get under someone's skin*

This common idiom means to persistently annoy someone to an immense degree or affect someone deeply, even in a good way, making forgetting the person, place or thing responsible nearly impossible. The first known reference to the term is found in the British novel, *Griffith Gaunt*, by Charles Reade, first published in *The Argosy*, as a serial, Chapter XVI, in the November 1866 issue:

> "So with me hearing 'Mercy, Mercy' called out to me after so many years, I do think the quality hath somehow **got under my skin**; for I cannot abide to see folk smart, let alone to strike the blow."

The saying picked up steam in the early 20th century.

Get up on a soap box

In the 19th century wooden boxes which were designed to hold soap and other merchandise for wholesale shipment, because of their availability, were often used to make platforms on which speakers stood during impromptu political speeches.

The term came to metaphorically mean someone making an unofficial, often flamboyant, public speech. It also can relate to a person's stance on a subject as expressed by someone of a varying opinion.

Since 1872, for example, each Sunday, speakers have assembled in Hyde Park in London to make such addresses in regard to topics like religion and politics.

Get wind of

Meaning to learn about or hear a rumor regarding, this expression has been common since the early-to-mid-19th century, and was famously popularized by William Makepeace Thackeray in *Paris Sketch Book,* 1840:

"If my old aunt **gets wind of** it, she'll cut me off with a shilling."

Four years later a form of it was used by his principle competitor and contemporary, Charles Dickens, in *The Life and Adventures of Martin Chuzzlewit*, 1844:

"If this story should **get wind**, their country relation had, by his imprudence, for ever disgraced…"

Gift of gab

Here we must explore a bit of etymology. The word gab is a shortened form of gabble, meaning loquacious jabbering. The gift of gab means the ability to talk readily and in a persuasive manner. This is a prime feature of a salesman, a public speaker or a man or woman of the cloth. Random House places the origin of 'gab' at 1675-1685. The first recorded use of the phrase was in 1839 in Charles Dickens' *Oliver Twist* (Chapter 43).

"'Ay, that he shall,' replied Fagin, 'and we'll have a big-wig, Charley: one that's got the greatest **gift of the gab**: to carry on his defence; and he shall make a speech for himself too, if he likes.'"

Give a leg up

This figurative expression is from helping someone cross a hurdle or mount a horse by boosting his or her leg over its back. This came to mean any boost or support to aid one's progress in any venture. The earliest known metaphorical reference to the phrase in print is from William Clobett's *A Complete Collection of State Trials and Proceedings for High Treason*, Volume 32, 1824:

"In answer to a question put by me, he says, 'I did not know Thomas Turner;' it seems by the testimony of Thomas Turner, that he was the other man who **gave him a leg up.**"

Give me a break!

This is a request to grant someone special consideration when the person feels pressured, hemmed in, or bothered. The expression came into popular use in the mid-to-late 20th century. In a very early example in 1949, in *The Prison World*, Volume 11, page 18, the word break is in quotation marks in a poetical prayer:

"Oh, please Lord!
Give me a chance in court
Give me a jury's rapport,

Give me a 'break' that is real
Or, give me some grounds for appeal!"

Twenty years later it is evident that the phrase was in common use in *Negro Digest*, June 1969:

"Look, Jenkins, I ain't done nothing to you, why don't you **give me a break**?"

Give someone an inch and he, she or they will take a mile

Originally this proverb was used with reference to the Scottish ell, not a mile. There is a big difference. An ell was about two cubits. A cubit was measured by the length from the tip of a person's fingers to their elbow, which could vary greatly. For this reason, standardized measurements became necessary. Scottish measures were not made obsolete and replaced by English ones until 1824.

The first printing was from John Heywood's *A dialogue conteining the number in effect of all the proverbs in the English tongue* in 1546.

"For when **I gave you an inch, you tooke an ell**."

The Middle English term became "Gie 'im an inch, an he'll tak an ell." As time went on and the ell was no longer understood as a measurement, it was quite simple to exaggerate the term to a dimension with a similar sounding name, a mile.

This cliché means, quite naturally, that it is easy for someone who has been granted special privileges to take advantage of their benefactor and step out of the boundaries intended.

Give someone the cold shoulder

In days of yore, when an unwanted visitor came, the host would give him or her a cold shoulder of mutton instead of hot meat as a hint not to call again.

The first printed reference to the phrase is in Sir Walter Scott's *The Antiquary,* 1816.

"The Countess's dislike didna gang farther at first than just **showing o' the cauld shouther**."

Note that the 'cauld shouther' (Scottish dialect for 'cold shoulder') is shown, not eaten. In a just slightly later work, *St. Ronan's Well*, 1834, Scott, who coined several of the clichés we know today, also uses the phrase in its current form.

"I must **tip him the cold shoulder**, or he will be pestering me eternally."

Give someone the third degree

This phrase is derived from the ritual in the Freemasons, having been conducted since the 18th century, of granting degrees upon members of the fraternity who have earned them. The third degree is an especially grueling one, in which the Lodge Brother is blindfolded, led through the lodge in a prescribed manner, questioned at length, and warned not to divulge the secrets to which they have been made a party by virtue of their degree. The ceremony can last up to forty-five minutes, and is so intense that 'giving someone the third degree' has come to be synonymous with telling a person very sternly what they should or should not do. The term has also come to apply to a harsh interrogation given by law-enforcement agencies

Give up the ghost

This expression, still applied to death, is from *Mark 15:37, King James Bible*, 1611. Referring to the death of Jesus on the cross, it reads:

"And Jesus cried with a loud voice, and **gave up the ghost**."

glutton for punishment, A

A glutton is someone who constantly overeats without thinking of the abuse to his or her body. 'A glutton for punishment' is an idiom of obscure origin which means that one continues to take on tasks that most people would avoid. The phrase has been in use since the early 20th century in the U.S.

The 1918 *Cap and Gown*, the yearbook of the University of the South in Sewanee, Tennessee, has the following citation on page 72 under the heading 'Football Players':

"SATTERLEE, 'Cypers.' –Saterlee suffered from malaria throughout the season, and never did reach the form he might have attained otherwise. He tried hard, was exceedingly willing, **a glutten for puninhment**, and faithful to the nth degree."

Go ballistic

This is an idiom meaning to become excessively enraged, irrational and possibly violent. The etymology of the word 'ballistics,' from which the term is taken, going back to circa 1775, pertains to the science of the motion of projectiles, such as bullets and bomb detonations. The idiom itself, however, wasn't coined until the mid-1980s, and was largely linked to the controversy over ballistic missiles.

An abbreviated early example is from the *New York Times*, March 22, 1985:

> "The Second Circuit upheld Griesa's ruling that the United States Army Corps of Engineers... He can **go ballistic**."

God helps those who help themselves

There are many phrases that people *think* come from the *Bible*, but don't. This is probably at the top of the list—right up there with 'cleanliness is next to godliness' (see). Many of these actually came from Shakespeare, Ben Franklin, or some other historic writer. This one is from Franklin, and was included in the 1757 edition of *Poor Richard's Almanac*. In fact, this is thought by many to be the most common of Franklin's proverbs.

Go Dutch

This means that each person in a group or couple pays for his or her own meals rather than one individual footing the entire bill. This is one of many terms which originated as far back as the 17th century based on English negative stereotypes of customs in Holland during the Anglo-Dutch Wars.

God (or Good Lord) willing and the Creeks don't rise

The old adage "God willing and the Creeks don't rise" originally referred to the Creek Indians and not streams of water. This phrase was coined by a politician and Congressional Indian diplomat named Benjamin Hawkins in the late 18th century. While in the South attempting to negotiate a treaty, Hawkins was requested by President George Washington to return home. In his response, he was said to write, 'God willing and the Creeks don't rise.' Because he capitalized the word "Creeks' it is deduced that he was referring to the Creek Indians, a tribe with which he was negotiating.

God works in mysterious ways

This literal proverb is from a poem by William Cowper (1731-1800) *God's Mysterious Way*, the first verse of which reads:

"**God works in a mysterious way**,
His wonders to perform;
He plants His footsteps on the sea,
And rides upon the storm."

Goes to show

Goes to show, just goes to show, goes to show you, goes to show you never can tell, and other related idioms indicate that what has just happened is proof or an indication that something is an evident or obvious truth, or that it has an important message. It has been used in this way since the early 19th century, and was printed often in legal records. An early example from 1819 is in *Reports and Cases Argued and Determined in the Supreme Court of Judicator* (New York) in the case of Skilding and Haight v Warren, May 1818:

"The proof offered must be such as **goes to show** the note void of its original inception, or original creation, and to destroy it totally."

An example from *Report of the Forest Divorce Case* by Catherine Norton Sinclair Forest, 1852, this one from the New York State *Superior* Court, uses 'goes to show you.'

"If such is the case, gentlemen— if you have these prejudices against the defendant, let me call your attention for a moment to a portion of the testimony in this case, which **goes to show** you— not what I say of the defendant or what anybody else says of him—but which **goes to show** you his heart itself."

Go figure!

This vogue idiom is derived from the Yiddish (Hebrew) expression, *Gey vays,* which literally means, 'go know.' The intention is 'who would have thought of it in that way?' Or 'how do you justify that?' It came into usage in the late 1970s to early '80s as seen in this statement from *Perspectives of American English*, 1980, by Joey Lee Dillard, citing the *Jewish Digest* and the *New York Times*:

"'**Go figure** it out!' (I'll be darned, can you match that?) This is a frequent heading for oddities presented in the *Jewish Digest*. It has appeared in other places, sometimes cut to '**Go figure**', as in the conclusion of a recent *New York Times* article on culture in Indianapolis..."

Go fly a kite

The idea of telling someone to go fly a kite came from colonial America, and the idea that Ben Franklin allegedly discovered electricity while flying a kite. Telling someone to go fly a kite was originally intended to be a way of telling someone to go find a better idea—make a new discovery. It has come to mean, 'get lost' or 'make yourself scarce.'

Go for broke

This means to take a great risk and wager everything in order to have a desired item or service, or to spare no expense in obtaining a desired goal. Originally a Hawaiian Pidgin slang reference to betting everything on one roll of the dice in the game of craps, this idiom was made famous because it was the motto of a World War II Japanese American military unit, the 442nd Infantry Regiment, and the title of a 1951 film about that unit.

Go for the jugular

Obviously referring to the jugular vein in the neck, which when cut can cause near-immediate death; this idiom means to attack someone at their weakest point, swiftly and deliberately inducing great harm.

Early printed references often used 'vein' as this was originally a quote from West Virginia politician, diplomat and attorney, John W. Davis, in this first known citation from *The Florida Law Journal* in 1950 referring to preparing for a case in court and writing legal briefs:

> "Again, **go for 'the jugular** vein,'** as John W. Davis puts it, or for 'the hub of the case,' as Rufus Choate expressed it. 5 Hit the key point or the two key points. Put the others in your brief; but avoid them in oral argument."

Mario Pittoni quoted it, not knowing it came from Davis, in his book on composing legal briefs, *Suggestions on Brief Writing and Argumentation,* 1951:

> "Always '**go for the jugular** vein.' I do not know from what source I quote that phrase but it is of course familiar."

Go haywire

Meaning to go wrong, this idiom is derived from a light wire used in baling machines to bind hay bales. It originated in America in the early 20th century from the earlier term, hay wire outfit, used to describe companies which cheaply patched up botched machinery using wire similar to that used in baling. In 1905 *The U.S. Forestry Bureau Bulletin* defined a hay wire outfit as:

"A contemptuous term for loggers with poor logging equipment."

In 1920, the 'hay wire' was listed in The American Dialect Society's *Dialect Notes, Volume V, Part III* in 'A Word List from the Northwest':

"Hay wire. Gone wrong or no good. Slang."

Then, 'to go haywire' was recorded in an article about a basketball game in *The Helena Independent*, in Montana in January 1928:

"...their anxiety to score let their passing game **go haywire** with many wild heaves finding marks in the bleachers."

Going over or through something with a fine-toothed comb

The fine-tooth(ed) comb was devised as early as 1830-1840 and used to check for head lice. By the late 1800s the term began being used in a figurative sense to mean investigating anything very carefully. The following reference appeared in *The American Homoeopathist*, June 1, 1893:

"He went for a case, not 'With brains, sir,' but **with a fine tooth comb**."

Going to hell in a handbasket

This saying started in America—but not in the 21st century, or even the latter 20th century. It was coined back in the *early 20th century*. A hand-basket is just a basket with a handle. Whatever is being carried in one goes wherever it is being taken with no resistance.

James Rader, an editor with *Merriam Webster* writes in *The Dictionary of American Regional English* that the saying 'to go to heaven in a handbasket' was recorded much earlier than 'to go to hell in a handbasket' which he indicates appears to have come about in the 1950s. Because of a reference to 'head in a handbasket' from Samuel's diary in 1714, Mr. Rader presumed that the saying could have been around 'much longer than our records indicate.'

An earlier example, however, is from *The American Magazine*, Volume 105, 1928:

"'They can all **go to Hell in a hand basket!**' Lem burst out."

Going to the dogs

This has been used figuratively for anything going to ruin; for example, something which shows moral decay, since at least the late 18th century. A play entitled *Germanicus, A Tragedy* by 'A Gentleman of the University of Oxford' was published in *The London Review of Literture* in 1775, and included this citation of the phrase:

"Sirrah, they are prostitutes, and are civil to delude and destroy you; they are painted Jezabels, and they who hearken to 'em, like Jezebel of old will **go to the dogs**; if you dare to look at 'em, you will be tainted, and if you speak to 'em you are undone."

Going to town

This means doing something with wholehearted gusto, or excessive fervor. It was coined in the 19th century in reference to going from a rural area to the nearest center of activity for an outing, and meant engaging in a very jubilant event. It has changed somewhat in meaning. It became very popular in America in its present figurative form by the 1950s. As early as January 1938, the term was being re-invented as seen in this authoritative citation from the Reader's Forum of *The Rotarian*:

"Goin' to Town

"I fear that some of your readers will acuse Dr. Vizetelly and me of 'not knowing our onions' on current American slang in the inadequacy of the expression '**going to town**,' as used in your November issue [q.v. footnote to *"Goin' to Town, Vocally* by James L. Waller]. Slang terms just won't 'stay put.' A new expression comes into being today, receives immediate approbation, and tomorrow has aquired a dozen shades of meaning.

"Hence, my interpretation of '**going to town**,' though basically correct as a synonym with 'making good,' is not quite that intended by Mr. Waller in his article. He uses it, as the article indicates, to mean 'getting across; being there with the goods; bringing home the bacon' or in common prose, creating a highly favorable impression."

Down a bit further, the letter states:

"Hence, **going to town** not only indicates 'making good,' but usually 'making good in a big way'; highly favorable, highly satisfactory or agreeable— 'something to write home about.'"

Charles E. Funk, *Associate Editor*, *Funk and Wagnalls New Standard Dictionary, New York, New York*

Go in one ear and out the other

This common phrase means to be heard but not heeded, to be ignored or forgotten or to make no impact or impression. The implication here is that whatever is being said does not stay inside the listener's head because he is empty-headed; information just passes straight through to the other side. It is brought down to us in 1396 by Geoffrey Chaucer's *The Canterbury Tales Book IV, l. 435*:

"**One eare** it heard, **at the other out** it went."

Go jump in the lake

Like 'go fly a kite,' this cliché was used freely in the mid-20th century to ask someone to 'bug off.' It originated in the U.S. Unlike the other saying, this one gave no hint of finding a 'better mousetrap.' As the years passed, it became outdated by less flattering ways to say the same thing, though some authors still pull it out and brush it up.

A very early example was from the Kiplinger Magazine, *Changing Times*, August 1950, in an apparent quote from Pennsylvania department store mogul, E.T. Hager:

"If they will tell the boss to **go jump in the lake**, they are apt to start telling the customers to **go jump in the lake**."

Gone to Texas (See: **Things went south**)

217

good beginning makes a good ending, A

This proverb refers to the fact that in order to achieve effective results we must have a worthy start. It goes all the way back to a 1350 English Book of Proverbs, *Douce MS (52* number 122), and has changed very little in almost eight centuries.

> "Of a **gode begynnyng comyth a gode endyng**."

Its beginnings revert to similar sayings as early as 1300.

Goodbye

This most popular of parting words was originally a contraction of 'God be with ye.' Shakespeare used 'God be wy you' in *Love's Labour's Lost*, 1598. Over sixty years later, in 1659, a letter penned by Gabriel Harvey contains the first actual known usage of a close form of the word 'goodbye.'

> "To requite your gallonde [gallon] of **godbwyes**, I regive you a pottle of howdyes…"

Good fences make good neighbors

This cliché can refer to the fact that even when someone is a trusted friend or associate, caution needs to be observed with regard to being too close and free with information, personal belongings or even relationships. It definitely advocates well-defined borders. *Oxford's Dictionary of Quotations* lists it as a 17th century proverb.

It was popularized in Robert Frost's 1914 poem, *Mending Wall*, though it is used as coming from another person in the verse:

> "He will not go behind his father's saying,
> And he likes having thought of it so well
> He says again, '**Good fences make good neighbors**.'"

A similar French proverb is 'a hedge between keeps friendships green.'

Good judgment comes from experience, and a lot of that comes from bad judgment

This is a quote by American Vaudeville performer, humorist, actor and social commentator Will Rogers (1879—1935) which has been adapted as an American proverbial saying.

Good luck with that!

While it can be used with a sense of sincerity, this cliché began to be a regular part of American pop culture in the early 21st century to factiously indicate the speaker's feeling that a specified goal was useless.

A classic example is in *One Trick Pony*, 2008, by Daniella Brodsky.

"'All right,' he said, '**good luck with that**.'

"*Good luck with that*? What was *that* supposed to mean? Was there something wrong with a girl who was confident about herself, who just happened to have an instinct about things?"

Good night, sleep tight

The earliest known reference to the phrase, 'sleep tight' was in an entry written on 2 May 1866 in Susan Bradford Epps diary (published later), *Through Some Eventful Years:*

"All is ready and we leave as soon as breakfast is over. Goodbye little Diary. '**Sleep tight** and wake bright,' for I will need you when I return."

Though not a literal reference, it seems that it inferred sleeping soundly. The original nursery rhyme from at least the late 19th century was:

"**Good night, sleep tight**,
Wake up bright,
In the morning light
To do what's right
With all your might."

Note the congruent wording with the diary citation on waking bright. An addition was sometimes inserted for the second line: 'Don't let the bedbugs bite.'

In 1881, *Boscobel,* a novel by American writer Emma Mersereau Newton contained this clip:

> "'**Good-night, sleep tight**; And don't let the buggers bite,' said Fred with a comical twinkle in his brown eyes.'

The rhyme was present in the U.K. as well, as evidenced by this 1901 extraction from *The Games and Diversions of Argyleshire* by Robert Craig Maclagan:

> "On Going to Bed
>
> "**Good night, sleep tight;** Don't let the bugs bite..."

Good ole boy

This American slang expression may be taken in either a positive or negative connotation depending on the circumstances of its use. Usually it applies to rural Southern men who are easy-going, humble and well thought of. In the negative sense, it can apply to someone who is deviant and determined to fight the organized social system.

The earliest known printed citation is in the Oklahoma Folk-Lore Society's publication, *Folk-say, Volume IV* in 1932:

> "Some of the people cried unrestrainedly, 'Yessir, Booger was a **good ol' boy.**'"

Use of the term didn't become widespread until the early 1970s.

Good Samaritan

The term 'Good Samaritan,' now used for any doer of good deeds, is from a parable in the *Bible* (*Luke 10:25-37*), when Jesus was using the example that often the person who does the right thing is not the one whom we would expect to do so. The story goes that a certain Jewish man was beaten and robbed (modern usage, 'mugged') and left by the road for dead. A priest and a Temple worker came by, and went across the street to avoid helping. Technically, 'they didn't want to get involved.'

Then a mixed-race man from a group against whom the Jews had great prejudice saw the injured man and had mercy on him, treated his wounds, took him to the inn and put him up, and then offered to pay any cost of caring for him until he was well. Jesus said this man, not the 'holier than thou' (see) Jews, was the one who was doing right.

Good wine needs no bush

In spite of earlier researchers dating the coining this proverb to the late 17th century, it comes directly from *Act V, Scene IV* of Shakespeare's *As You Like It*, in the epilogue, spoken by Rosalind, written in late 1599, published, first folio, 1623:

> "If it be true that **good wine needs no bush**, 'tis true that a good play needs no epilogue; yet to good wine they do use good bushes, and good plays prove the better by the help of good epilogues."

In those days in England, ale houses hung out greenery to let travelers know that they could come in for enjoyment. The meaning reflects the idea that if the wine is good enough, it would need no advertising with hanging boughs—word of mouth would do the trick. Today we would more likely say, 'quality speaks for itself.'

Goody-two-shoes

This idom is used in sarcasm by someone who felt the other individual was trying to pretend to be saintly when in fact he or she was far from it.

It comes from the title of a long-forgotten anonymous 'Cinderella-type' tale published in 1765, *The History of Little Goody Two-Shoes*, sometimes accredited to Oliver Goldsmith due to style and period. The book was intended to illustrate the Christian teaching that diligence reaps its reward in the next life.

'Goody Two-Shoes' is the handle ascribed to a poor orphan girl named Margery Meanwell. She is so terribly impoverished that she only owns one shoe. When a rich gentleman bestows her with a pair of shoes, she keeps repeating that she has two shoes.

> "She ran out to Mrs. Smith as soon as they were put on, and stroking down her ragged Apron thus, cried out, 'Two Shoes, Mame, see two Shoes.' And so she behaved to all the People she met, and by that Means obtained the Name of **'Goody Two-Shoes**.'"

This gift placed within her the desire to press forward, so she worked very hard and eventually married a wealthy widower.

From the turn of the 20th century, people considered self-righteous have been dubbed 'Goody-goody,' which eventually gave way to 'Goody Two-Shoes.'

Go off half-cocked

In the U.K. where this was originally coined, it is 'go off at half-cock,' and originated in the 18th century with flintlock guns which have a cocking mechanism which may be set at half-cock for security. If a firearm with this feature went off at 'half-cock' it would be entirely by accident.

The earliest known printing of the British phrase 'going off at half-cock' is from *London and Its Environs Described*, a set of books published by R. and J. (Robert and James) Dodsley in 1761:

> "Some arms taken at Bath in the year 1715, distinguished from all others in the Tower, by having what is called dog locks; that is, a kind of lock with a catch to prevent their **going off at half-cock**."

Gradually, the phrase changed in printings in America to 'half cocked' and came to mean acting without proper preparation. The earliest known citation of this version is from *The Register of Debates in Congress*, in 1833, in this statement made by Rhode Island Representative Dutee Pearce:

> "I regret that the gentleman from Maryland has **gone off half cocked**."

It was used two years later in *An Account of Colonel Crocket's Tour to the North and Down East* by David "Davy" Crocket, 1835.

> "I writ the letter and sent it there to be printed, to show that I didn't **go off half cocked**, and keep people from thinking that I had refused before I was ready."

Go off the deep end

Figuratively this means to become irrational in ones thoughts and act on those feelings without regard to responsibility. It is taken from jumping into the deepest part of a swimming pool, especially where the water is over ones head and the person is unable to swim. The earliest known citation, in spite of other published origins in the early 1920s, is in an article titled *The Desert Air* by Dornford Yates in *The Windsor Magazine,* August 1919:

> "'They're all right, as a rule,' Berry was saying, 'but every now and then they **go off the deep end**.'"

Go out on a limb

This indicates someone putting himself or herself at a disadvantage in order to help someone else or a cause.

This metaphor is derived from climbing a tree and edging farther and farther out on a bough in order to get a fruit, nut, bird nest, cat, etc. The indication is that by going too far out, the limb may break. The earliest known printed figurative reference is from *The Stubenville* (Ohio) *Daily Herald*, in October 1885:

> "We can carry the legislature like hanging out a washing. The heft [main part] of the fight will be in Hamilton country. If we get the 14 votes of Hamilton we've got 'em **out on a limb**. All we've got to do then is shake it or saw it off."

Gospel truth

This, of course, is derived from the term applied to the first four books of the *New Testament*, known as the Gospels. 'Gospel' doesn't actually mean 'truth,' though. It is from the Old English *god spel* which means 'good news.' It became associated with 'truth' because of the Christian belief that the teachings and mission of Christ, told in the Gospels, comprise the truth that should be spread to all mankind, and supersedes all previous religious teachings. Because of this the message has been called 'the gospel' since the 14th century. The idiom 'gospel truth' originated in the 17th century, as applied to biblical truths, and since the 19th century for any unquestionable truth.

Gossip

Early politicians needed feedback from the public to determine which issues people deemed important. Since there were no media devices, such as telephones, televisions or radios, the politicians sent their assistants to local taverns, pubs, and bars, telling them to 'go sip' some ale and listen to people's conversations and political concerns. The two words 'go sip' were eventually combined when referring to local opinion and, thus the term 'gossip.'

Go to pot

We think of this term as going bad, downhill, or to ruin. In past centuries, any farm animal that had outlived its usefulness, such as a cow which could not bear calves and give milk, or a hen that no longer laid eggs, would literally go to the owner's pot. It was cooked and eaten.

Go viral

This modern expression has to do with Internet videos placed on sharing websites which receive inordinate numbers of plays, bringing them to the attention of television and marketing executives. It was coined in the 1990s.

Go west, young man

Legendary Newspaper editor, Horace Greely, who founded the *New York Tribune,* is most often credited with this quote which was actually first stated by John Babsone Lane Soule. The quote was originally the title to the *Terre Haute Express* editorial written in 1851 by Mr. Soule. Along with being *wrongly credited* to Mr. Greeley, it has also often been *misquoted.* It was actually written not as 'Go west, young man, go west!' but as:

"**Go west, young man**, and grow up with the country."

It was credited to Greely because he later used it in his own editorial in 1865. It has been often quoted and has become an American cliché.

Go with God (Vaya con Dios)

This familiar benediction, or statement made upon parting, is often used in many languages. It originally came from the Hebrew thousands of years ago as the name 'Danyael' or Daniel, which literally means "Go with God."

The Spanish word, '*adios*,' meaning 'goodbye,' is an abbreviation for "a" (to) and "*Dios*" (God), from the old Spanish phrase "*A Dios vais*" ("You're going to God"), '*Vaya con Dios*,' the Spanish phrase for "Go with God" is a familiar parting statement as well.

Go with the flow

This metaphoric idiom derives from moving along with the tide or current of the ocean and figurative use dates from the 1960s. It means to not fight prevailing thoughts or behavior patterns and agree to comply with the normally accepted attitudes. Another version is 'go with the tide.'

In a literal sense it had long been used, as in this example from the *Quarterly Journal of the Geographical Society of London*, in 1877, Volume 33, regarding experiments made with corked bottles loosed in the ocean.

"These will **go with the flow** of tide (though not with its ebb) across a whole gale of wind."

The first known figurative example is found in *The Electric Kool-Aid Acid Test* by Tom Wolf, 1967:

"But one could see the larger pattern and move with it — **Go with the flow**!—and accept it and rise above one's immediate environment and even alter it by accepting the larger pattern and grooving with it."

The principle, however, is actually from ancient Chinese Taoism which was practiced as early as the 4th century BC.

grand jury will indict a ham sandwich, A*

Variations of this adage are often used to indicate that a competent district attorney can obtain an indictment from a grand jury in virtually any case, and guilt should not be presumed merely because of an indictment.

Though it was made famous by Tom Wolfe in his 1987 best-selling novel, later turned blockbuster film, *Bonfire of the Vanities*, it appears to have originated with Solomon "Sol" Wachtler, then chief judge of the New York Court of Appeals. In an interview on January 31, 1985, appearing in the *New York Daily News* on page 3, Wachtler suggested that district attorneys, at least in New York, had so much influence over grand juries that "by and large," they could get a grand jury to "indict a ham sandwich."

Grandma was slow but she was old

This phrase is used when belittling someone for being slow in his or her actions or reactions. It is American and began to be used in the late 20th century.

Grasp at straws

Grabbing or grasping at straws is a term which has been around since the mid-18th century to mean a desperate and almost certainly futile attempt to save oneself in a time of great adversity. The term lives on.

The first known reference in print to this adage is in Samuel Richardson's lengthy novel, *Clarissa*, in 1748.

"A drowning man will **catch a straw**."

The meaning was derived from the fact that reeds which grew by the sides of rivers were hollow, and if a man who was being pulled down by the current could grasp one, he may be able to breathe through it as he went under, helping him to survive until he could paddle ashore.

grass is always greener on the other side of the fence, The

This is certainly a metaphoric proverb, and one of the most widely used sayings in the English language. It speaks of the urge of humanity to be dissatisfied and always look for something they don't have. It's what makes us want to 'keep up with the Joneses'(see).

This idea was expressed in the Latin proverb, "*Fertilior seges est alieno semper in arvo,*" used by Erasmus of Rotterdam and translated by Richard Taverner in 1545 as "The corne in an other mans ground semeth euer more fertyll and plentifull then doth oure owne." Having gained a bit of notoriety in the 16th and 17th centuries, this earlier version never quite caught on in the main stream of British culture, but certainly seems to be the source of the current proverb. In 1959 a play debuted by Hugh and Margaret Williams titled *The Grass is Always Greener,* with the variant, 'on the other side of the hedge.' Other mid-19th century variants are 'Distant pastures always look greener,' and 'Cows prefer the grass on the other side of the fence.'

Grass roots

Sometimes used with 'movement,' this expression means the people at a local level rather than at the center of a major arena, political or otherwise. Because of this, it is often associated with the basic fundamental elements of, or believers in, a social movement, cause, genre or belief system. It has been in use since at least the early 20th century. The earliest known figurative citation is in the title of a 1905 book by Jay Elmer House titled, *At the Grass Roots,* and contained the memoirs of his life from childhood in rural Kansas.

Graveyard shift

The origin of this expression actually had nothing to do with graveyards or burying people. Back in the old days, when sailors and ocean-faring folks went to sea, those who worked the late night hours got blurry-eyed, and their eyes watered trying to stay awake. Since any thick liquid was called 'gravy' the saying 'gravy-eyed' came to be among sailors. The late-night shift was then called 'the gravy-eyed shift.' When the sailors were in at port and went into pubs, they told others that they were pulling 'the gravy-eyed shift.' 'Land lubbers' somehow didn't get the phrase, and among themselves, thinking in the superstitious notions of the era, began calling it the 'graveyard shift,' believing it to be a late-night watch for the dead spirits, or something of that sort. Evidently, the imagined phrase caught on, for this is what it is still called today.

Great minds discuss ideas; Average minds discuss events; Small minds discuss people

This astute statement is one of many noteworthy quotes from American First Lady, diplomat and social activist, Eleanor Roosevelt (1884-1962). It is a self-explanatory axiom.

Great minds think alike

This is a well-known proverb, but has not been around as long as many of them; but still, for hundreds of years. The root dates to at least 1618. Dabridgcourt Belchier wrote the following in his comedy, *Hans Beer-Pot*, that year:

"Though he made that verse, Those words were made before. Good wits doe jumpe."

Here 'jump' meant 'agree with,' something we would never use today. British novelist, Laurence Sterne, also used it that way in *Tristram Shandy* in 1761:

"Great wits jump: for the moment Dr. Slop cast his eyes upon his bag the very same thought occurred."

The 'think alike' wording wasn't found in print until quite a while later. The earliest example known is in Carl Theodor von Unlanski's short biography, *The woful history of the unfortunate Eudoxia*, published in 1816:

"It may occur that an editor has already printed something on the identical subject - **great minds think alike**, you know."

U.S. founding father, the English-born Thomas Paine, like many today, had a different way of looking at the idea that 'great minds think alike', i.e. "No, they don't," he implied in the 1792 political pamphlet, *The Rights of Man, edition 2*:

"I do not believe that any two men, on what are called doctrinal points, think alike who think at all. It is only those who have not thought that appear to agree."

Green around the gills

This is a statement sometimes made jestingly and good-naturedly to someone who appears sick, usually because of a reaction to something eaten or done, and that he or she may regurgitate. Gills are the respiratory organs of aquatic animals and fish, which enable them to breathe underwater. This metaphor has been around since at least 1906 when it appeared in *The Motorboat,* a bi-monthly New York magazine, in the July 10 edition:

"The effect was so very marine that, when Mrs. Willie Reefer Jibb and Mrs. Shiver R. Timbers, of Gowanus, saw the costume they were both seized with a violent attack of nausea and turned **green around the gills**."

Green with envy

The plays of Shakespeare had a tremendous influence on our modern conceptions of the English language. Before Shakespeare, the color 'green' brought to mind other emotions than envy and jealousy, such as fear, ill-humor and illness. But he changed it all with the flick of a quill.

In a famous passage Iago warns Othello to 'beware, my lord, of jealousy; /It is the green-eyed monster which doth mock/The meat it feeds on' (*Othello*, III, iii, lines 169-171). This was obviously derived from a green-eyed cat playing with a mouse victim.

Grin and bear it

This means to accept an unpleasant situation when there is nothing we can do to change it. Though this saying was brought to light in the 20th century in a daily syndicated cartoon which was started in 1932 by George Lichty, the saying goes back to at least the late the 18th century. The earliest known citation is in William Hickey's *Memoirs* 1749-1830, in which it is credited to sailors:

"I recommend you **grin and bear it** (an expression used by sailors after a long continuous of bad weather)."

Ground zero

'Ground zero' has become synonymous with the World Trade Center terrorist attacks of 9-11-2001. But it is much older, and has been dated to 1946. It was likely coined to describe the devastation of the atomic bombs dropped on Hiroshima and Nagasaki which effectively ended World War II.

Ground zero is the spot in Manhattan where the blast occurred, and the term is used to specify the area which surrounds the point of an explosion. In both cases huge pits of devastation resulted. Both of these incidents were acts of war, changed the course of history, snuffed out countless human lives and will always be remembered by the families of those involved.

It has since been utilized as a metaphor for all kinds of things, many of them non-destructive. For example "Milan is **ground-zero** for raised hemlines."

guilty dog barks first, The

Also, 'the guilty dog barks loudest,' this old saying means that people try to cover up their wrongs by feigning innocence. Often when a group of people are confronted about which one did something, the one who immediately tries to point a finger and blame someone else is often the one who is guilty.

Guilty pleasures

This expression refers to something a person enjoys in spite of feeling guilty about it. These could range anything from sex to smoking to a fattening dessert or even something as seemingly harmless as music, a video game or dance style. Though it is experiencing a surge of popularity in the 21st century, it has been in use in English since the early 18th century. The first known citation is from *Examen poeticum* by John Dryden, 1706:

> "Next Night their **guilty Pleasures** they repeat;
> Another follow'd, and another yet:
> When he, desirous to behold, at last
> Thy soft kind Nymph whom he so oft embrae'd."

Guinea pig

Metaphorically, a guinea pig is someone who is used, often to their own chagrin, as a test model for an experiment, the outcome of which may be iffy at best. It is unclear how the furry little cavy obtained this name back in the 17th century, for it is not a pig, nor did it originate in Guinea.

229

The earliest usage of this term to describe a person had nothing to do with the subject of an experiment, but was a novice worker on a ship in *The Adventures of a Kidnapped Orphan*, published in London in 1747:

"He sent his nephew, at the age of fourteen, on a voyage as a **Guinea-pig**."

In the form which we now know it, it was first utilized by George Bernard Shaw in *Quintessence of Ibsenism*, in 1913:

"...to the schoolmasterly vanity and folly which sees in the child nothing more than the vivisector sees in a **guinea pig**: something to experiment on with a view to rearranging the world."

Gung ho

This expression is now accepted as meaning "zealous and eager". It is the anglicized pronunciation of the Chinese "gōng hé" (工合), sometimes spelled "kung ho." "Gōng hé" is a shortened version and slogan of the "gōngyè hézuòshè" (工業合作社) or Chinese Industrial Cooperatives, abbreviated as INDUSCO as an English acronym.

Individually these words mean "work together." Gung ho became widely used in World War II as a slogan for the U.S. Marines under General Evans Carlson. In on October 25, 1943 *Life* carried this quip around a photo on page 6:

"The title of the picture will be **Gung Ho**! (Work Together), the Chinese motto which Colonel Carlson adopted as his own. The picture above shows Colonel Carlson as he met Randolph Scott..."

Gung ho had been in print for the first time two years earlier, though, in October 1941, in California's *Oakland Tribune*, in a story about some captured short war films:

"Other shorts are 'Information Please' and '**Gung Ho**' with Regan McCrary."

Gun shy*

This idiom means wary or mistrusting. It is originally derived from hunting dogs which had been frightened by a gun fired near them and would run at any loud noise. The first verifiable citation in print, however, refers to a breed of birds, and is in *Ornithological Rambles in Sussex* by Arthur Edward Knox, page 227, 1849:

> "Godwits then appear in their plain grey garb, and are all equally wary and *gun-shy* from repeated persecution..."

The earliest known totally figurative reference in print is found in *Peck's Red-headed Boy* by George Wilber Peck, page 42, 1901:

> "He has always been back with the women, taking up a collection. He has cared for nothing but money, and you will find if they catch him, that his baggage consists of specie that he has stolen. *He is gun shy*, that is what ails Aguinaldo."

H

Hale and hearty

This time-tested descriptive phrase most commonly refers to someone who is healthy and strong, usually in spite of advancing age or physical drawbacks. It has been in use in English popular culture since the late 18th century as illustrated in this earliest known citation from A. Thompson's 1799 English translation of the German play, *The East Indian: A Comedy*, by Baron August von Kotzebue:

> **"Hale, and hearty! hale, and hearty!** father! father!**"**

And even more clearly in this line regarding Richard Cromwell, from *The European Magazine and London Review*, November 1801:

> "He was so **hale and hearty**, that at fourscore he would gallop his horse for several miles together..."

It is of interest that in Charles Dickens' poetical offering, *The Posthumous Papers of the Pickwick Club,* 1838, it refers to plants as well:

> "Whole ages have fled and their works decayed,
> And nations have scattered been;
> But the stout old Ivy shall never fade,
> From its **hale and hearty** green."

Handle with kid gloves

This means to treat a particular situation with care and tact. Watch what you say and do regarding it, because it could have disastrous results to do otherwise. The first printed reference to this metaphorically was in the 1830s according to the *O.E.D.* That was around the time that boxing gloves were invented by Jack Braughton, called the 'father of modern boxing.' Kid gloves were made of the hide of young goats, and were very soft. Later, in the mid-19th century, saying that someone 'wore kid gloves' was a way of insinuating that the person was soft and dainty.

Hand over fist

As the phrase implies, this refers to something which is occurring rapidly and in continuous succession. It has been in use since the 18th century, and the earliest known citation to a related expression comes from England's Royal Society's *Philosophical Transactions* for 1736:

> "A lusty young Man attempted to go down (**hand over hand**, as the Workmen call it) by means of a single Rope."

Other such references continued, but the first appearance of the actual phrase occurred in 1825 in *The Naval Sketchbook* by William Glascock:

> "...but it oftner favoured the French—for at daylight, you see, they weathered our wake, coming up with us, '**hand over fist**', in three divisions." Henry Colburn, London

It was only eight years later when money was introduced into the equation by Seba Smith in *The life and writings of Major Jack Downing*, 1833:

> "They run into Mr. Harris' room and clawed the money off of his table, **hand over fist**."

Handsome is as handsome does (See: **Pretty is as pretty does**)

Hand to mouth (See: **Living hand to mouth**)

handwriting is on the wall, The

It is recorded in the *Bible,* in *Daniel chapter 5,* that when Belshazzar had replaced his father, Nebuchadnezzar, as King of ancient Babylon, he prepared a great feast for a thousand of his lords. At the feast, he became intoxicated and he and his wives and concubines and lords drank from the sacred vessels of the Temple in Jerusalem, and praised their gods.

Suddenly, the finger of a man's hand appeared and wrote four foreign words on the wall of the palace, *'mene, mene, tekel, upharsin.'*

When this happened, the king went into panic, and he ordered his servants to bring the fortune tellers and anyone who might be able to interpret these words, promising that anyone able to do so would be given great gifts and prominence in his kingdom. No one who came had a clue to the meaning of the writing. Then the queen told him that a prophet in his kingdom had 'the spirit of the holy gods' in him, and had interpreted dreams for his father, so he sent for him. His Hebrew name was Daniel, but Nebuchadnezzar had named him Belteshazzar. So the king called for Daniel.

Daniel told the king that he did not want his gifts, but he would interpret the writing for him. He told Belshazzar that there was but one God, and He had given the kingdom to his father, Nebuchadnezzar, who had miserably failed and had become insane like a wild animal. Now, Belshazzar had also failed as king, and gone after heathen gods. As a result, 'the writing was on the wall.' Paraphrased, the words meant, 'God has measured your days as king and you have been weighed in the balance (or scale) and found wanting,' or 'come up on the short end of the stick' (see) so to speak.

If it is said that 'the handwriting is on the wall' today, it means that there are clear signs that something or someone is surely doomed to fail.

Hanging by a thread

This metaphoric idiom refers to something which is ready to fall apart, much as a button which is coming loose and dangling by a single attachment to a garment. The thought behind this saying originated in classic Greek legend. Damocles, a courtier of ancient Syracuse, Italy, it is told, annoyed King Dionysius with constant flattery. The king invited him to a banquet, where Damocles was seated under a sword suspended at the pommel by a single hair from a horse's tail, symbolizing his tenuous position in the court. Fear kept him

233

from enjoying the banquet. Finally, after much begging, he was allowed to leave.

Early literal use of the actual phrase can be found in the 1771 *Encyclopedia Britannica, Volume II*, Society of Gentlemen in Scotland, in an article on hydrostatics:

> "There are some things which cannot be weighed in this manner, such as quicksilver, fragments of diamonds, etc. because they cannot be suspended in threads; and must therefore be put into a glass bucket, **hanging by a thread** from the hook...**"**

An excellent early example of the figurative use is found in the novel, *Chums,* by Harleigh Severne, 1878:

> "It would be cruel kindness for me to try to hide it from you, Mrs. Royce,— her life is **hanging by a thread**."

Hanging in the balance

This metaphoric phrase alludes to someone being in a precarious state, figuratively speaking, in which the outcome is unclear, and may go one of two ways depending upon circumstances. The derivation is from a set of scales which may be tipped either way. It is actually found in the *New Living Translation of the Bible,* in *Deuteronomy 28:66*:

> "Your life will constantly **hang in the balance**. You will live night and day in fear, unsure if you will survive."

The 1611 *KJV* uses 'hang in doubt,' but the meaning is still there.

The exact phrase was in use by the early 19th century as seen in the excerpt from Jane Porter's 1832 novel, *The Pastor's Fire-side*:

> "Hostilities were at this time **hanging in the balance** between Great Britain and Spain, on account of Gibraltar..."

Hang in there***

Some claim that this originated with baseball. That it came about in this sense from the fact that pitchers prefer batters to stand a good distance from home plate because it makes it easier to strike them out. Therefore pitchers will often throw a ball or two close to the body of the batter in the hope of instilling the fear of being hit. As a result, the batter's teammates may holler. "Hang in there!" to encourage the batter to not be intimidated by the pitcher.

Though it is certainly common in baseball, there is evidence that this phrase was likely used earlier in both French and Russian. In 1826, according to HubPages writer, D. Mitchell, it was uttered first by French inventor and early photographer, Nicéphore Niépce, in regard to a cat hanging from a tree limb. This type of image was later used on numerous "Hang in there" posters which became popular in the early 1970s, sometimes as "Hang in there, baby."

In the 1971 English translation of *One Day in the Life of Ivan Denisovich* by Aleksandr Isaevich Solzhenitsyn, Farrar Straus Giroux, NY, original copyright by Soviet Literary Magazine *Novy Mir*, 1962 we read:

> **"Hang in there**, shipmates! It's a good thirty below!"

Some sources indicate that it was originally a nautical expression meaning that help was on the way. The modern meaning is definitely an encouragement to be firm and brave, believing that in a bad situation, things will improve.

Hang one's hat on something

This expression means to depend on something; to put one's trust in or hopes on it. The earliest known citation is from the *Saturday Evening Post*, April 22, 1905:

> "I groaned and conceded **he could hang his hat on** a dozen such points, but without profit, and so, following him, I called court to order."

Hang out to dry

This means to abandon, or leave someone 'suspended,' who is in serious need of help. It is derived from clothes hanging on a clothes line, which was still common in some areas when the figurative phrase was coined in the mid-to-late 20th century.

Hang ten*

This expression originated in the early 1960s in the world of surfing, referring to a specific impressive maneuver on the surf board, and is still used around the world in that context by surfing enthusiasts. In this move, the surfer positions his or her surf board so that the back of it is covered by the wave and he or she is free to walk on the front of the board and hang all ten toes off the board. Hang Ten, a company with a distinctive logo label was soon formed in California for surf garments which began an ad campaign in 1962. The surfware was worn by cast members on the TV comedy, *The Brady Bunch,* followed by those of *Melrose Place* and *Beverly Hills 90210.* The brand swept the surfing world marketplace by the 1980s.

The phrase soon began to be used in a figurative context. In a *Popular Mechanics* Yamaha ad, April 1968, page 227, the following metaphoric usage appeared:

> "For these are the exciting new cycles from Yamaha. If you want to 'trip with the light fantastic,' **hang 10** on this new 180 Street Scrambler."

In the 1980s Mutual of Omaha Insurance Company introduced their 'Hang Ten Campaign' in which their field reps would go into desirable neighborhoods hanging bags on doorknobs labeled 'Hang Ten' with promotional material for their major products, largely targeted at Homeowners and Auto coverage.

Hanky-panky

Originally this nonsensical term did not apply in a connotation of mischievous sexual shenanigans, but had to do with trickery. The earliest known printing comes from the first edition of *Punch, or the London Charivar*, published in September 1841:

> "Only a little **hanky-panky**, my lud. The people likes it; they loves to be cheated before their faces. One, two, three—presto—begone. I'll show your ludship as pretty a trick of putting a piece of money in your eye and taking it out of your elbow, as you ever beheld."

Then in 1938 George Bernard Shaw gave it a whole new flavor in political satirical play, *Geneva:*

> "She: No **hanky panky**. I am respectable; and I mean to keep respectable. He: I pledge you my word that my intentions are completely honorable."

Happily ever after

The origins of this phrase actually came from ancient Greco-Roman mythology, and evolved through the fairy tales of English literature. The phrase became the epitome of the 'happy ending' and has been the title of numerous books, songs and albums, television shows and Hollywood films, both animated and using real people in their casts.

Happy camper

This modern metaphoric expression is applied to someone who is content with their present situation, and is likely used sarcastically in the negative more than the positive. In spite of numerous claims that it originated on a 1982 episode of *Silver Spoons* when Ricky (Schroder) and his grandfather went on a camping trip, there are two flaws in this. First, it was already in use at least a year earlier; second, the *Silver Spoons* use is a literal reference to camping.

Though it is likely that in a literal sense it started in summer camps earlier, the first citation of the phrase 'happy campers' in a non-camping context is from an article by David Bird in *The New York Times* regarding homeless men in 1981:

"It is not a group of **happy campers** that gets off the bus."

harder you work, the luckier you get, The

Although this is certainly a quote from golfer Gary Player, the first person who said it was much earlier, just in a slightly different way.

"I am a great believer in luck. **I find that the harder I work the more of it I seem to have.**"

It's from the third President of the U.S., Thomas Jefferson.

Hard to come by

This phrase means difficult to find or obtain. It has been in use in this respect since the early 19th century, as seen in this reference from this reference from Matthew Henry's *Exposition of the Old and New Testament, Volume 2*, written circa 1708-1710:

"But what must they do for bread? Truly that was as **hard to come by** as any thing…"

Then this from *The Gentlemen's Magazine*, by Sylvanus Urban, Gent, January 1839:

> "Let not the great-bellied Sistern now long for strawberries or cherries, for I assure ye they are very **hard to come by**; money also will be **hard to come by**…"

Hard work never hurt anybody

A symbolical proverb, this is meant to convey the thought that work performed for the greater good is always in some way beneficial to the worker. Though Ronald Reagan used a form of it in a sarcastic manner, he is certainly not the originator of the phrase. What Reagan actually said was:

> "They say **hard work never hurt anybody**, but I figure why take the chance."

Other versions include 'Hard work never killed anyone,' 'A little work never killed anyone' and 'A little hard work never hurt anyone.'

The killed version was used as early as May 1918 when it was used in *The Photographic Journal of North America:*

> "Real Hard Work versus Useless Slavery
>
> **REAL hard work never killed anyone.**"

Then in June 1920 when it appeared in Kansas City (MO) Public Service Company's *The Railwayan* Magazine:

> "It is a mistaken idea that hard work kills men. **Hard work never killed anyone**. It is the improper care of oneself when he is not working that does the damage."

Haste makes waste

This ancient rhyming proverb has been in its present form since circa 1575. Many versions, however, preceded it. The first was in 1386 in Chaucer's *Tale of Melibee, I:*

> "The proverbe seith in wikked **haste is no profit**."

Then in 1546, John Heywood included it in *A dialogue containing the number in effect of all the proverbs in the English tongue,* I. ii. A3:

"Som things show after weddyng, that **haste maketh waste**."

It was also in John Ray's *A Compleat Collection of English Proverbs* in 1678 as it is today.

"**Haste makes waste**, and waste makes want, and want makes strife between the goodman and his wife."

It is to say that rushing is useless and causes more trouble than it is worth.

Have a bone to pick with someone

This metaphor dates to the 16th century, and was first recorded in 1565 by James Colfhille:

"I will add this, which may be **a bone for you to pick on**."

It was inspired by a dog chewing unceasingly, picking a bone clean of every possible morsel of meat. 'Having a bone to pick with someone' smacks of a weighty topic of discussion which will take, like the dog with the bone, a considerable amount of chewing and digesting. A similar phrase, 'a bone of contention,' is of like age. This is a subject over which two persons argue, like a pair of canines over a choice bone.

Have front row seats to

This modern metaphoric expression is derived from the advantage of obtaining seats at an event which are close to the action where it is easy to determine what is happening. It means that someone is in an excellent position to have knowledge of important information.

An early example is from *Russia on our Minds: Reflections on another World*, 1970, by Delilah and Ferdinand Kuhn:

"And we, as reporters on foreign assignments, happened to **have front-row seats** to watch the Russians in a brand-new role."

Have one's heart set on something

This means to want something so much that obtaining it becomes a person's focus. Setting one's heart is an ancient expression, in English going back to the late 14th century. Chaucer used a form of it in *Troilus and Criseyde*, 1385:

"Why not love another sweet lady, who may **set your heart** at ease?"

Several *Bible* verses use the essence of it. *Hosea 4:8*, which was written in Hebrew between 755 and 725 BC, translated into the King James Version, 1611, is one:

> "They eat up the sin of my people, and they **set their heart on** their iniquity…"

Have one's work cut out for him or her

This common saying has been linked to the tailoring business as far back as the early 17th century. A good tailor would lay out his work and then carefully cut out the parts of a suit before beginning the sewing process. Through the years it came to mean any job that was tedious and implies that someone may have difficulty getting the job accomplished. It also is likely the origin of being 'cut out' for a job.

It was included in *A Christmas Carol* by Charles Dickens, which was published in 1843.

Have someone coming and going

This figure of speech is applied to catching someone any way they turn and giving him or her no way out of doing something the other party wants them to do. It has been in use since the mid-20th century. A good early example is from *Amendments to the Natural Gas Act* from the U.S. Senate Committee on Interstate and Foreign Commerce, 1955:

> "In other words, they would **have you coming and going**."

Have someone in one's pocket

This means to have control over someone. It was in use by 1931 when it appeared in Francis Henry Gribble's *Emperor and Mystic: The Life of Alexander I of Russia*:

> "Some of his colleagues — notably those Prussians who called him 'their Alexander' and believed that they **had him in their pocket** — were playing an undisguised game of grab, and wanted to annex territory without the least regard for any…"

Have something sewed up

To have something, for example an election, sewed or sewn up means to have gained control over the situation or the future results. The earliest known citation is from *The Life and Opinions of Tristram Shadny, Gentleman* by Laurence Sterne, chapter 43, 1787:

> "The nymphs joined in unison, and their swains an octave below them. I would have given a crown to have **had it sewed up**. — Nannette would not have given a sous, — Viva la joia was in her lips…"

Having a heyday

A heyday is the time of greatest vigor or success that someone has. Though a bit archaic now, this cliché was often used as a metaphor for someone who was being perceived as exploiting someone else or exhalting themselves to success at someone else's expense.

'Heyday,' as such, goes back to at least the late 16th century and is a variant of high-day. A high-day, even in Bible days, was a feast day—a day of celebration. In Middle English in the late 12th century it was spelled 'haye da.' This is the term which gave way to our understanding of a holiday, which derived from 'holy day.' The term has also been related to the use of 'hey' as an expression of great enthusiasm; but the mere fact of the Middle English spelling seems to explain why the figurative word became changed from high-day to heyday.

Head on a platter

This analogy is used to express a desire to punish someone out of anger.

This phrase came from the Biblical story of the beheading of John the Baptist, a version of which is found in *Matthew 14*. Herod, the puppet Roman-sponsored king in Israel, was condemned by John for his adulterous relationship with his brother Phillip's wife, Herodias. Herod had John thrown into prison, and wanted to kill him, but because of John's popularity, was afraid of the backlash. On his birthday, the daughter of Herodias, Salome, pleased the king so much in her seductive dance that he vowed to give her anything she asked. *Verse 8* says:

> "Prompted by her mother, she said, "Give me here **on a platter the head** of John the Baptist."(*NIV*)

Even more afraid of his mistress, Herod reluctantly agreed to grant Salome her hideous wish.

Head on the chopping block

Someone's head on a chopping block means that they are in danger of exposure, being made a scapegoat, severe criticism or firing. The essence of it was derived, as 'Heads are gonna roll,'(see) from the practice in Ancient France of beheading people with the guillotine.

The actual expression was used in a literal sense in the fairytale, *Buttercup*, from *Popular Tales from the Norse* by Christian Asbjornsen, George Webbe Dasent, with translations from the Norske Folkceventyr into English in London in 1859:

> "'Stop a bit,' said Buttercup; 'I'll soon show you how to do it; just lay your **head on the chopping-block**, and you'll soon see.'

> "So the poor silly thing laid her head down, and Buttercup took an axe and chopped her head off just as if she had been a chicken."

An early figurative example comes from *The Proceedings of the National Convention* of the Industrial Union of Marine and Shipbuilders of America, Baltimore, 1943. But it is apparent that the expression was already in use.

> "It put its **head on the chopping block**, and now we are going to affirm that we do put our **heads on the chopping block**, just because we will make this commitment here today, that we approve of an amendment like that."

Head over heels

When the phrase was originally coined it meant something was upside down, or 'topsy-turvy.' It came from flipping 'head-over-heels' when turning cartwheels, which seems like the opposite. The first known reference to this phrase is in Herbert Lawrence's *Contemplative Man* in 1771.

> "He gave [him] such a violent involuntary kick in the Face, as drove him **Head over Heels**."

Love wasn't brought into the equation until 1834, when the legendary American frontiersman and Congressman, David Crockett, used it in his personal memoirs, *Narrative of the life of David Crockett*, 1834.

> "I soon found myself **head over heels** in love with this girl."

Head over heels after this came to mean 'all shook up' over something. Overwhelmed, so to speak, by something exciting—particularly love.

Heads are gonna roll

Even more than 'head on the chopping block,' this means that employees are going to be fired over some specific infraction, misjudgment or incident. It came into usage in the mid-to-late 20th century. An early reference is from *The Kenyon Review*, Kenyon College, Volume 31, 1969:

> "...one slat of fence in this district without Mason's picture on it by tomorrow morning, well, some **heads are gonna roll** around here."

It later inspired the titles to musical offerings by Los Angeles punk rock group, The Hippos (*Heads are Gonna Roll*, Interscope Records, 1999) and British heavy metal band, Judas Priest (*Some Heads are Gonna Roll*, Columbia Records, 1984).

Heads I win, tails you lose

Derived from tossing a coin to determine the winner in a competition, this expression means that the speaker will win regardless of any attempt by the opposition to prevent it. The coin toss originated in the late 17th century, and this idiom was coined in the mid-19th century. The earliest known citation comes from *The Exhibition Speaker*, by P.A. Fitzgerald, 1856, in a one-act romantic comedy play, *Hob and Nob* by Madison Morton:

> "*Nob.* Now then, sir, heads win?
>
> *Hob.* Or tails lose—whichever you prefer.
>
> *Nob.* It's the same to me, sir.
>
> *Hob.* Very well, sir. **Heads I win—tails you lose.**"

He ain't heavy, he's my brother

Used as a reminder of the common roots, heritage and bonds of all mankind, this was made famous in modern times by a wildly popular ballad written by Bobby Scott and Bob Russell, and originally recorded in 1969 by Kelly Gordon at the legendary Abby Road Studios in London, later recorded by the Hollies, Neil Diamond and Elton John.

But this phrase goes back much further. It was first used in print in 1884 by Rev. James Wells in his children's book, *Parables of Jesus* (from *Luke 15:1-6*). He makes a comparison of the shepherd carrying his lost sheep back to the fold to a

243

little girl carrying a big boy who was asked if she were not weary from her load, to which she surprisingly replied:

"No: he's not heavy; he's my brother."

The story was retold in 1909 by Frank Tappan Bayley, D.D., in *Little Ten Minutes, or A Pastor's Talks with Children* in the talk *Love's Scales, Why the Baby Wasn't Heavy;* published in London, Edinburgh, New Chicago and Toronto. Here it was related that the incident occurred in a Scottish city.

In 1918 Ralph Waldo Trine published *The Higher Powers of Mind and Spirit,* therein making obvious reference to the same tale, using a young Scottish lass straining to carry a younger lad. When someone commented to her about how heavy a load she had, in this version she replied:

"He's na heavy. He's mi brither."

Apparently the tale was older than all of the references.

Roe Fulkerson, the first editor of *Kiwanis* Magazine, used the saying as the title of an article in 1924. The December 1941 edition of the *Louis Allis Messenger* had a black-and-white sketch of a boy carrying his brother with the caption 'He ain't heavy, he's my brother.' It was the work of Van B. Hooper. Father Edward Flanagan, the founder of Boys Town, Nebraska, saw the drawing and felt that it was representative of the Boys Town effort. He got permission to have it reprinted in color and altered the caption to read, '**He ain't heavy, Father...he's my brother.**' This consequently became the motto for Boys Town.

Heard it through the grapevine

After the invention of the telegraph in 1844, it became clear that the rural communities already had a pretty effective system of communications through the mouth-to-mouth method. A saying developed that it was a 'grapevine telegraph'—a humorous allusion to the fact that grapevines were the nearest thing to wires in those areas.

In 1876, *The Reno Daily Gazette* ran an article about the bumper corn and grape crops that year. They commented on the fact that the people then known as 'Indians and Negroes' seemed to already be aware of it. It seemed that they did not realize that they were likely the ones who had done the labor of harvesting the crops.

"It would seem that the Indians have some mysterious means of conveying the news, like the famous **grapevine telegraph** of the negroes in the [American Civil] war. The Pioneer Press and Tribune says that, while the first telegraphic news of Custer's death reached them at midnight, the Indians loafing about town were inquiring about it at noon."

Hearing news 'through the grapevine' came to mean from an informal contact or spread mouth-to-mouth by those who are free to repeat gossip. Like so many clichés, it became the title of a hit song—first released by Smokey Robinson in 1967 and soon after by Gladys Knight and the Pips. It became a signature song in 1968 for Marvin Gaye, who actually recorded it before Gladys Knight. In 1970 it was also released by CCR (Creedence Clearwater Revival).

Heart is in the right place

This metaphor is used to mean that someone's intention is proper and that he or she is a good individual regardless of appearances. The earliest known printed references are in missionary publications in 1833, the first being Proceedings for the *Church Missionary Record*, detailing the proceedings of the Church Missionary Society, London, in the *February* issue:

"A well-educated Hindu Christian is worth a great deal to our work, if his **heart is in the right place**; but such are rare."

On 9 November 1833 it also appeared in *The Religious Intelligencer*, a weekly missionary paper by Nathan Whiting, New-Haven:

"The man whose **heart is in the right place** will fall down in the dust to praise and pray…"

Heavens to Betsy!

This was originally an exclamation of surprise, like 'my goodness!' or 'gracious sakes,' and all are rather archaic now. It originated in America in the mid-to-latter 19th century, and was mostly restricted to the US. It faded to near oblivion during the 20th century. Though its origin was seen as unsolvable in a 1955 book on the origin of curious phrases, the first known example is from *Ballou's dollar monthly magazine Volume 5*, January 1857.

"'**Heavens to Betsy**,' he exclaims…"

Heavens to Murgatroyd!

This is a variant of the previous exclamation, 'heavens to Betsy!" In the 1960s it was made popular by a cartoon character called 'Snagglepuss.'

But the lovable cat with a lisp didn't start it. It was first uttered by Bert Lahr, later famous for his role as the cowardly lion in *The Wizard of Oz*, in the later 1944 film, *Meet the People*. The voice of Snagglepuss was actually patterned after Bert Lahr's voice as the unforgettable big cat in *Oz*, and the saying, 'heavens to Murgatroyd' borrowed from *Meet the People*.

Though there is no definitive origin for this particular 'Murgatroyd,' it has a long-standing place as a surname in British aristocracy. Likely these nobles are the source for a number of Baronets in Gilbert and Sullivan plays with this name in the late 19th century and the likely reason for the use of 'Murgatroyd' in this exclamatory saying.

He has enough money to burn a wet mule

This old Southern American saying is from the 1880s. Through the years it has often been used in negative political confrontations, particularly when referring to someone with a large sum of disposable funds, especially when the money may have been obtained dishonestly. It was used in 1935 by Carleton Beals in a quote from *The Story of Huey P. Long*:

> "Huey described the battle graphically. 'They have filled up the city with **enough money to burn a wet mule**... They are laying their plans to try to ruin me...'"

Long was a controversial Louisiana Governor.

A similar popular expression is simply 'money to burn.'

Hell hath no fury like a woman scorned

This axiom is not, as some have claimed, a quote from Shakespeare, but rather from a play by William Congreve, *The Mourning Bride* (1697). The complete quote is:

> "Heaven has no rage like love to hatred turned
> **Nor hell a fury like a woman scorned**."

246

Help! Murder! Police!

This common comical expression is the first line of an old children's game rhyme from the early-to-mid-19th century:

> **"Help! Murder! Police!**
> My wife fell in the grease!
> I laughed so hard
> I knocked over the lard,
> **Help! Murder! Police!"**

The saying itself, however, without the rhyme, has been used in books since at least 1848 when Richard Brinsley Sheridan used it in a two-act tragedy play titled *The Critic*.

> "I say, — stop the fight ! — **help** ! — **murder** ! — **police** !"

In 1850, it appeared in a paper called *The Minor Drama*, in another play titled *A Good Fellow*:

> "Here, **help** — **murder** — **police!** [Runs up to gale inr., opens it, and Captain Hazard enters hastily, followed by two Policemen. Dust. Help — murder — poison — fire!"

Hem and haw

This is stalling to keep from giving a direct response to someone's query. In etymology, to hem, making such an utterance dates to the 15th century, and haw is from the 17th century and summarizes the meaning of the phrase, and is defined as 'an expression of hesitation.' Hem and haw used together dates to a letter penned by Fanny Burney on 16 October 1786 published in 1842 by Charlotte Barrett in the *Diary and Letters of Madam d'Arblay*.

> "I **hemmed and hawed**—but the Queen stopped reading."

Here's the scoop

Again the etymology is needed. The informal term, 'scoop,' primarily used in journalism, is first referenced in 1874, when a paper in Danbury, IA, *The Maple Valley Scoop*,' was first listed in *Edwin Alden & Brothers American Newspaper Catalogue*. It refers to publication of 'the real story,' often in conflict with what was reported by someone else. The paper's name was later changed to the "Danbury News," but reverted to *The Maple Valley Scoop* again before becoming the "Criterian" in 1888.

In the same year that *The Maple Valley Scoop* was listed under that name, patents were applied for a long-handled scoop in both the U.S. and Canada. A scoop is a useful instrument for acquiring ice cream. Scooping is reaching out and getting something that others naturally want. The term came to be applied in journalism on a permanent basis, even though the newspaper no longer went by that name.

Here today and gone tomorrow

A reminder of our mortality, this phrase refers to anything which is only temporary. It was first printed in John Calvin's *Life and Conversion of a Christian Man,* 1549: `

"This proverb that man is **here today and gone tomorrow**."

He said, she said

This modern cliché is from the title to an NBC TV game show hosted by Joe Garagiola from September 15, 1969—August 21, 1970.

The saying is frequently used to highlight the differences between opinions and differences between males and females, largely in relationships. But what he said and she said have long been a matter of contrast, as in William Faulkner's *Light in August*, 1932:

"'I'll buy you another one,' **he said. She said** nothing."

And Flannery Conner used this in *Everything that Rises Must Converge* in 1956:

"'Mr. Parker,' **he said she said**, 'I hired you for your brains.'"

He who fights and runs away may live to fight another day

It may seem cowardly to some to run, but there are cases when it is the only alternative; especially when survival is the main objective. This proverb is ancient and was first printed in similar form in Nicholas Udall's 1542 translation of Erasmus' *Apophthegms II;*

"That same manne, that renneth awaye, Maye again fight, an other daye."

Similar printed references occurred over the next 400 years, and then on June 2, 1981, it appeared in its current form in *The Daily Telegraph* in London as a caption to a picture.

He who has the gold makes the rules

In a 1967 *The Wizard of Id* cartoon strip the king remarks: "Remember the Golden Rule!" to which a peasant replies: "What's that?" A different peasant barks back, "**He who has the gold makes the rules**!" The strip's creators, Brant Parker and Johnny Hart, featured this edition in their 1971 book, *Remember the Golden Rule*. A new cliché was born. It is used to remind people that 'money talks' (see) and unless they have the funds to compete, they may be 'left out in the cold' (see).

He who laughs last, laughs best

Though also from Tudor era England, this phrase was not coined by Shakespeare, as some believed. It is initially found in print in the play *Christmas Prince,* whose author is uncertain, but may have been Oxford founder, Sir Thomas White, which was first performed at Cambridge about 1608:

> "Laugh on laugh on my freind
> **Hee laugheth best that laugheth to the end**."

Often stated as "He who laughs best laughs longest," this proverb expresses the feeling of surprise and disappointment felt by someone who feels that he or she has won an argument or battle only to find that their opposition is the true victor.

He who lives by the sword will die by the sword

This is a slight variation of the admonition of Jesus in *Matthew 26:52*, to Peter (according to the parallel verses in *John 18*), after he cut off the right ear of the priest's servant, Malchus, following the arrest of Jesus:

> "Then said Jesus unto him, Put up again thy sword into his place: for **all they that take the sword shall perish with the sword**." *(KJV)*

It is used to remind people that violence begets violence.

He who loses money, loses much;
He who loses a friend, loses more;
He who loses faith, loses all

These are the final lines of a longer quote by former first lady, Eleanor Roosevelt. Though self-explanatory, it emphasizes the importance of friends and faith above the temporary value of money.

249

He who plants a garden, plants happiness

This is an ancient proverb of controversial origin, some saying German, most saying Chinese. It expresses the fact that tilling the earth reaps rewards, not only in the literal harvest, but also in the personal satisfaction one gains through the experience.

He who seeks revenge should remember to dig two graves

This is another anonymous proverb claimed without proof to be of ancient Chinese origin, emphasizing the futility of believing that 'two wrongs make a right.' The same principle is in the scriptural proverb, 'He who lives by the sword will die by the sword' (see).

He, who travels alone, travels fastest

A form of this was first printed in *Walden* by Henry David Thoreau in 1854:

> "**The man who goes alone can start today**; but he who travels with another must wait till that other is ready."

But it was Rudyard Kipling who actually coined the phrase closer to the way we know it in *The Story of Gadsby*, published in 1889:

> "Down to Gehenna, or up to the Throne, **He travels fastest who travels alone.**"

Hide nor hair***

This very old figurative expression, usually "neither hide nor hair," refers to something or someone who has seemingly dropped out of sight. The earliest verifiable English usage of the phrase, in a somewhat variant manner, is from page 27 of *The Fables of LaFontaine*, translated by Elizur Wright in 1842:

> "But with so little thought or care,
> That neither horns, nor **hide, nor hair**
> Reveal'd to them the stag was there."

Then, two years later, in the *American Agriculturist*, July 1844, Volume 3, Number 7, we have a precise example of common usage of the phrase:

"We presume others came to the same conclusion,
as we have seen neither **hide nor hair** of said convention,
nor any reports of its doings since it,
adjourned in this city last October."

High as a kite

High as a kite is seldom preceded by 'as,' hence it goes here in the alphabetical order of things.

'High' has been used in the sense of intoxication since the 1600s, and this simile has been around since 1859 when Charles Dickens used it in a bit different sense (with 'as') in the ghostly tale *The Haunted House*:

"This dough will rise as **high as a kite** in a south wind."

This is now used for any form of 'being high,' whether regarding exorbitant prices or emotionally as by alcohol or drugs.

Highway robbery

In the mid-20th century, this indicated being charged a shamefully ridiculous amount for some badly needed item or service. It meant that the persons being taken unfair advantage of had no choice but to pay the exorbitant rates.

As long ago as the 14th century, when people with money traveled the roads in England, or when the church was transporting gold, etc., the poor would resort to 'holding up' the coaches, horses, wagons etc. Famous thieves, including Robin Hood, from whom the American term 'hood' or 'hoodlum' derived, were made legends through this practice. The phrase 'your money or your life' was coined by highwaymen. 'Highway robbery' was what the practice was dubbed in England.

It is likely that this happened by at least the 15th century in continental Europe. Later the tradition continued in the U.S., and Mexico, where the thieves were known as banditos.

Hindsight is always 20-20

Also stated as 'hindsight is better than foresight,' this factious cliché means that it is easier to see mistakes after-the-fact. The earliest citation of a form of it is from Robert J. Burdette in *Hawk Eyes*, 1879:

"If a man had half as much foresight as he had **hindsight**, he'd be a lot better off,"

The Century Magazine, April 1884, carried the following in the article, 'Topics of the Time':

"There is a homely maxim that '**hindsight is better than foresight**.'"

"Always" followed in *Readings in Guidance* by physiology textbook authors Lester D. and Alice Crow, 1962:

"The influence of personality theory on the work of the vocational counselor is well known. Indeed, **hindsight, always 20-20**..."

Hip, hip, hurray!

Also spelled 'hooray,' this is a cheering approbation for someone or something being praised, and is often accompanied by 'three cheers for...' It was first recorded in England in correlation with making a toast while lifting a drink.

In memory of the Treasonous Gunpowder Plot of 5 November 1605 and the failed assassination of King James I of England, formally James IV of Scotland, aka Guy Fawkes Night, the first poem was composed in 1742 and has evolved through the years. It incorporated the cheer, '**hip, hip, hoorray!**' added in the 19th century.

"REMEMBER, REMEMBER THE FIFTH OF NOVEMBER

"Remember, remember the fifth of November
Gunpowder, treason and plot
I see no reason why gunpowder treason
Should ever be forgot

"Guy Fawkes, Guy Fawkes, 'twas his intent
To blow up the King and the Parliament
Three score barrels of powder below
Poor old England to overthrow
By God's providence he was catched
With a dark lantern and burning match
Holloa boys, holloa boys
God save the King!
Hip hip hooray!
Hip hip hooray!
A penny loaf to feed ol' Pope
A farthing cheese to choke him

A pint of beer to rinse it down
A faggot of sticks to burn him
Burn him in a tub of tar
Burn him like a blazing star
Burn his body from his head
Then we'll say ol' Pope is dead.
Hip hip hooray!
Hip hip hooray!"

His words were smoother than butter

This 'proverb,' used as a warning against 'cons,' is actually *Psalm 55:21.*

"**The words of his mouth were smoother than butter**, but war was in his heart: his words were softer than oil, yet were they drawn swords."

His (or **her**) bark is worse than his (or **her**) bite

This means that the person being spoken of has a reputation of 'spouting off at the mouth' but doesn't follow through with his or her empty threats.

This old proverb has been around since at least the mid-17th century and was first printed by a Welch-born English poet and Anglican priest named George Herbert, in his *Jacula Prudentum, or Outlandish Proverbs and Sentences &c (no. 49)* in 1651.

History repeats itself

Philosophical quotes regarding history and its significance in regard to the present are sprinkled throughout history itself, and were originated by many colorful characters, including Henry Ford.

It was the German author of the Communist Manifesto, Karl Marx (1818-1883), however, who first coined the phrase as we know it. The translation of his statement is, "**History repeats itself**, first as tragedy, second as farce."

Another well-used, related statement was made by Spanish philosopher, poet and novelist, George Santayana, birth name, Jorge Agustín Nicolás Ruiz de Santayana y Borrás, who was born in Madrid in 1863. Santayana was reared in the U.S. and educated at Boston Latin School and Harvard University, and wrote mostly in English, thus he identified himself as an American.

Santayana's statement in *The Life of Reason, Volume 1*, 1905, "Those who cannot remember the past are condemned to repeat it," has gone down as one of the most quotable quotes of the 20th century.

From the study of history itself, the fact that the mistakes of history are often repeated has been all too evident.

Hit me like a ton of bricks

This cliché has been utilized by folks from as varying worlds as Catherine Lloyd Burns, as a title for her witty, vindictive memoir, *It Hit Me Like a Ton of Bricks*, to J. Cole as rap lyrics, "It took me all day to find some inspiration, it just **hit me like a ton of bricks**, no renovation."

This common American idiom has been around since at least the mid-20th century, and means that an idea or fact which was previously not thought of suddenly 'dawned on'(see: Dawn on someone) the speaker or hit him or her 'out of the blue,' (see) in a shocking way.

Hit the ground running

This phrase was coined in a literal sense in the latter 19th century, in America. An article titled 'The King of All Liars' in *The Evening News,* in North Tonawanda, New York on 23 April 1895 contained the following paragraph:

> "I turned to run and figured to a dot when he shot. As he cracked loose I jumped way up in the air and did a split, just like what these show gals does, only mine wasn't on the ground by six foot. The bullet went under me. I knew he had five more cartridges, so I **hit the ground running** and squatted low down when his gun barked a second time."

Thereafter, in the early 20th century, many references sprang up in other publications. The cliché had hit the ground running, and there was no stopping it. It evolved to include any project or business that had just experienced an exceptional startup and was operating as it was intended. A related phrase is 'up and running.'

Hit the nail on the head**

Meaning that what a person did or said was precisely correct, the first printed citation is from the earliest surviving autobiography known written in English, *The Book of Margery Kempe*, about 1438.

> "Yf I here any mor thes materys rehersyd, I xal so **smytyn ye nayl on ye hed** that it schal schamyn alle hyr mayntenowrys."

In intelligible modern English, this would read:

"If I hear any more these matters repeated, I shall so **smite** (hit) **the nail on the head** that it shall shame all her supporters."

This reference remains cloudy as to intent; however, this line from *The Cosmographical Glass* by William Cunningham in 1559 is as we portray it today:

"**You hit the naile on the head** (as the saying is)."

Hobnob / Hob-knob

Hobnobbing with someone is keeping company. It is mostly used by folks in talking about others who are perceived as being of 'lower social status' associating with those of higher society. But this meaning evolved from a much simpler origin.

Originally the term was hab-nab, from the Old English habbe (meaning hit) and nabbe (meaning miss). This seems strange, but it was from giving and taking of drinks with others.

Around the beginning of the 19th century, the phrase came into play in England as 'Will you hob or nob with me?' An answer of nob indicated that they had agreed to a drink of wine together.

Hobson's choice

The saying comes from a famous British postman and livery stable operator named Thomas Hobson (1544-1631), sometimes called 'the Cambridge Carrier.' When Hobson's horses were not needed for mail delivery, they were rented to staff and students of nearby St. Catherine's College. The fastest horses were in high demand, and became overworked. Because of this, he developed a strict next-in-line horse policy. He would never veer from this decision, so it was 'this horse or none.' The word got around the university that one had no choice in a rental horse; it was always 'Hobson's choice.'

From the mid-17th century, when there is no choice at all in some matter, it may be called a 'Hobson's choice.'

255

Hocus pocus

This phrase resulted as a magician's ridiculous imitation and corruption of Latin words '*hoc est corpus*' used by Catholic priests to declare transubstantiation and was concocted in the 17th century. In the world of magic it has since been used to introduce an illusion aimed at convincing the audience that the magician has special powers.

Shortened forms of this resulted in the words hoax and hokum.

Hold something over someone's head

This idiomatic expression means to use one's knowledge about someone else to control him or her. The earliest available citation appeared in *An African Millionaire* by Grant Allen in *The Strand Magazine* in a syndicated series published in 1896-1897:

"...Charles said, 'to **hold** this one last coup **over my head** in terrorem.'"

Hold the gun to someone's head

This hyperbolic idiom is from the mid-20th century, and means exerting extreme pressure on someone. An early printed reference is found in *Critical Teaching and Everyday Life* by Ira Shor, originally published in Canada in 1945.

"After all, no one forced you to go to college; no one **held a gun to your head**."

Hold your horses

This means 'hold on' or 'wait,' and was taken from pulling back on the reigns of a horse to bring it to a halt. Of 19th century American origin, the earliest citation of a form of it is from the New Orleans newspaper, *Picayune* in September 1844:

"Oh, **hold your hosses**, Squire. There's no use gettin' riled, no how."

Holier than thou

This is just what it sounds like: an expression from the *Bible*. In *Isaiah 65:5*, the Old Testament prophet condemns people who say 'stand by thyself, come not near me for I am **holier than thou**' *(KJV)*. It now has a negative connotation.

Holy Grail of, The

This 21st century expression for the quintessential example of anything desired or sought after is derived from the name in Arthurian legend most often applied to the utensil from which Jesus drank and shared wine with his disciples at the Last Supper before his crucifixion, also said to be the chalice used by Joseph of Arimathea to catch 'the blood of Christ' while taking him down from the cross. Due to a revival of the legends of the Quest for the Grail, and renewed speculation as to the actual meaning of 'Holy Grail' in modern times, the term became synonymous with the ultimate in any genre.

Home-court advantage

This term in a literal sense has been used since early in the second half of the 20th century in sports for basketball teams and tennis players (and some others) improved chances of winning on their home court. As late as 1965, it was sometimes seen in quotation marks. It has, since the late 20th century, as early as the 1980s, often been used figuratively to refer to anyone having the 'upper hand' (see) when competing in any field from dating to politics when they are in familiar territory.

Home is where the heart is

This proverb derives from the fact that where one longs to be is the true home of that person. It is attributed to Gaius Plinious Secundus, aka Pliny the Elder, (23 AD –79 AD), Como, Italy, who died during the eruption of Mount Vesuvius.

Home, sweet home

This phrase, used to express the importance, primarily of the place to which one is devoted because of heritage and birth, is from the title to a famous song written in Paris by American-born John Howard Payne and melody by British composer, Sir Henry Bishop, first performed in London in 1823. The tune may have been based on a Sicilian folk song.

Honesty is the best policy

This proverb is not from the *Bible*, as some may think. It is first found in Aesop's Fable, *Mercury and the Woodcutter*, in the 6th century BC, about two woodcutters, one honest, one not. Mercury, the Greek god of commerce, was also seen in ancient mythology as the messenger of the gods, and pictured with wings on his feet, swiftly bringing his positive vibes to earth. The story was a children's favorite in both ancient Greece and Rome.

A form of it was later found in the writings of Sir Edwin Sandys, an English politician and colonial entrepreneur, prominent in the Virginia Company which founded Jamestown, Virginia, the first English settlement in America. In *Europae Speculum*, in 1599, he wrote:

"Our grosse conceipts, who think **honestie the best policie**."

The phrase was later used by many dignitaries in America, including Benjamin Franklin, Alexander Hamilton, Thomas Paine, and Presidents George Washington, Thomas Jefferson, John Quincy Adams, James Monroe, and Andrew Jackson.

This most well-used of sayings also appeared in classic works such as Dickens' *David Copperfield*, and Alcott's *Little Women*.

Honeymoon

Traditionally the word moon has been used for 'month' by native tribes in various lands, because of the complete changes of the moon each 30 days. It is no different here. The word honeymoon originally meant 'honey month' in ancient Britain, where the newly-married couple was to drink mead, made with honey, for a full month after the wedding in celebration.

Honor among thieves

The Oxford Dictionary of Proverbs tells us the concept is found in circa 1622–1623 and cites *Soddered Citizen,* which was a comedy play by Maramion Redux, performed by the King's Men at Blackfriar's Theater, likely about 1630.

"**Theeues haue betweene themselues, a truth**, And faith, which they keepe firme, by which They doe subsis."

The phrase was close to its modern form by 1802 according *The Works of Jeremy Bentham Volume IV*, page 225, 1843.

> "A sort of **honour** may be found (according to a proverbial saying) **even among thieves**."

It is in the familiar form, with an addendum, in 1823, according to "J. Bee" in *A Dictionary of the Turf,* page 98.

> "'There is **honour among thieves**, but none among gamblers,' is very well antithetically spoken, but not true in fact.

Hook, line and sinker

This common idiom, sometimes 'swallowed (something) hook, line and sinker,' and other times 'fell for (something) hook, line and sinker' means to believe something at once without considering its source or testing its authenticity. It is often used to describe how someone thought to be gullible reacts to stories told them by others.

Originating in the United States in the mid-19th century, it is an extension of an earlier English saying, 'to swallow a gudgeon.' A gudgeon is a tiny fish used for bait. The idea implies that the gullible person is like a starved fish which swallows not only the bait, but the entire hook, line and sinker.

Hope for the best and prepare for the worst

This `16[th-]century English proverb initially appeared in a slightly different form in the British play, *Gorboduc,* by Thomas Norton and Thomas Sackville, first performed before Queen Elizabeth I on 18 January 1562:

> "Good is I graunt of all to **hope the best**, But not to liue still **dreadles of the worst**."

A few years later, in 1581, it had become closer to what it is today in W. William Averell's *Charles and Julia*:

> "To **hope the best, and feare the worst**, (loe, such is Loouers gaines)."

Horse Feathers!

Originally a single word, this term was coined in the U.S. in the late-1920s as a euphemism for horses**t by cartoonists. It was used by T. A. Dugan, who often went by TAD, as evidenced in a 1927 annotated dictionary of his clever work, *A TAD Lexicon*, published by etymologist Leonard Zwilling. Then Billy de Beck, creator of *Barney Google* cartoons, assumed credit in the December 1928 issue of the journal, *American Speech*.

The changing of the term to two words was accomplished in 1932 in the Marx Brothers film by that name.

This is also used to express disbelief.

Horse of a different color

Popular enough to use in the classic movie, *Wizard of Oz* in 1939, the origin of this thought goes all the way back to 1601; Shakespeare in *Twelfth Night, II, iii.*

"My purpose is, indeed, **a horse of that color**."

Although this referred to something being of the same matter, rather than a different one, the 'stage was set' and by the end of the 18th century, the 'tables were turned,' and it began being used to denote the opposite. For example, in 1798, an article in *The Philadelphia Aurora* used the phrase of President John Adams, sarcastically dubbing him King John I in comparison to the monarch of England, King James I.

"Whether any of them may be induced… to enter into the pay of King John I is **a horse of another color**."

Horsing around (See: **Quit horsing around**)

Hot on the heels of

This originally came from a hunter's closeness to his prey. It means getting very near to whatever one is seeking, whether facts or a literal goal. The earliest citation of this metaphoric idiom known is from Edmund Bailey O'Callaghan's *History of New Netherland or, New York Under the Dutch*, 1848, page 168:

"In Holland, Van de Donck was still **hot on the heels of** Van Tienhoven."

260

Hotter than a two dollar pistol

This metaphor is now applied to something believed to be stolen. In the early 20th century, when this was coined, cheaply made and priced pistols were constructed of inexpensive metal which would retain heat after firing. An early citation is from *Esquire* Magazine, Volume 19, 1943, and seemed to indicate being great:

> "Because of its tremendous power and short wing spread, this cigar-shaped Martin bomber is known to be **hotter than a two-dollar pistol**."

Hot to trot

This slang expression has two meanings intrinsically related. The rude definition, most often thought to be primary, is 'ready and willing,' which may be applied to sexually promiscuous males or females.

The gentler rendering is 'poised and ready for action' of any kind. Its derivation is from horseracing, envisioning an eager racehorse 'chomping at the bit' (see), anxious for a contest to begin.

The term dates from the mid-20th century. Despite a publication of the first citation of this phrase from 1961 in a major cliché origin dictionary, the 1955 U.S. *Library of Congress Catalogue of Copyright Entries* contains a copyright for *Hot to Trot* as a musical composition. Alabama-born artist, Forrest Fields, aka Terry Fell, recorded a hillbilly song written by Gene Tabor that same year titled '*I'm Hot to Trot*.' From the lyrics it did not seem to reflect the rude connotation at that time.

house divided against itself cannot stand, A

This is another biblical paraphrase that has come into popular contemporary use. It means that any nation, organization, family, club, church, etc., which has a great rift is destined to fall.

> "And Jesus knew their thoughts, and said unto them, Every kingdom divided against itself is brought to desolation, and every city or **house divided against itself shall not stand**."(*Matthew 12:25, KJV*)

How do you like them apples?

This rhetorical question expresses vexation over some situation. In spite of another dictionary's claim that this has been around since the 1920s, it appears that the earliest citation is later. Back in the glory days of radio a popular similar phrase was 'How about that?' used by Mel Allen between 1939 and 1964. There is a feeling among researchers that the 'apple' referred to in this 'poor English' saying was a mortar bomb fired by a Stokes gun used in World War I, called 'the toffee apple.'

This line has been popular in movies and on TV. In the Howard Hawks Western film, *Big Sky,* in 1952, starring Kirk Douglas, this is used. In another Howard Hawks Western, *Rio Bravo,* in 1959, Walter Brennan's character, Stubby, throws a hand grenade and says. "How do ya like them apples?" Then, Jack Nicholson's character in *Chinatown,* 1974, says this line. And more recently, Homer Simpson used it in a 1991 *Simpsons* episode, as well as Matt Damon's character in *Good Will Hunting* in 1997.

How's your copperosity segaciating?

The earliest printed reference to any version of this now-antiquated humorous phrase was in *The History of the Republic of Texas from the Discovery of the Country to the Present Time; and the cause of her separation from the Republic of Mexico* by N. Doran Maillard, Esq., Smith, Elder & Co., Cornhill, London, 1842. Maillard was a British-born attorney who had lived in Texas. Here is a snippet from the book:

> "The usual salutation of the Texas gentleman is, '**How does your copperosity segacerate** this morning?'—'How are you?' (this is all after an absence of some years.) A pretty considerable of a jug full of sun this morning,—A tarnation upstreet sort of a day this I calculate."

Because the words "copperosity" and "segashuate" (spelled this way) were picked up by Joel Chandler Harris in *The Tar Baby and other Tales of Uncle Remus,* published in 1881, he is often wrongly credited for coining them. Another author to use a version of this phrase James Joyce in *Ulysses:* "**Your corporosity sagaciating OK?**"

The word 'copperosity,' also spelled and pronounced corperosity is a play on the word corporality, which had been in the English usage since the 14th century, meaning 'the quality or state of being or having a body.' Segaciate,' segacerate and Harris's version, segashuate, are corruptive derivatives of the word

262

sagacious, meaning 'having or showing acute mental discernment and keen practical sense.' The phrase expressed beliefs of Caucasians of the perceived slave pronunciations of these words. To the Southern gentleman of the 19th century, this was a way of asking, 'How well does your body seem to harmonize with your mind and spirit?'

hurrier I go the behinder I get, The

This is a quote from Lewis Carroll in *Alice in Wonderland*. It has been used ever since to illustrate the fact that 'haste makes waste.' (See)

Hurry up and wait

This saying originated in the United States Military during World War II and means rushing around to get somewhere or to an appointment with a sense of urgency then ending up having to wait in line or on someone.

News and Views, the publication of GMAC in New York, in June 1944 included the following:

> "We adopted the slogan "**Hurry up and wait**" which, believe you me, was most appropriate."

On 9 April 1945 Randall Jefferson Culver of Evansville, Indiana applied for, and was granted, a copyright on a song titled *Hurry up and Wait*, published in the catalogue that year on page 581.

I

Icing on the cake

When this cliché first came into usage, in the 1940s, it was to show frustration or disgust, such as, 'that's the last straw,' or the 'straw that broke the camel's back' (see).

The story is told that the wife of a wealthy movie producer was throwing her daughter a party for her sixteenth birthday in 1942. It was a grandiose, catered event with an exhaustive guest list. However, for various reasons, the girl's mother was disgusted with the party and spent much of the day criticizing the caterer, and yelling at the other participants in the activities.

Then came the anticipated time when the girl was to be given her expensive cake. Everyone gathered around, but when the caterer wheeled in the cake, the mother went berserk. Rather than a multi-layered cake with beautifully colored frosting, the caterer simply drizzled icing over the cake. The mother screamed out, "You put ICING on the cake? Nobody puts icing on cake!" after she stormed out, everyone was silent and the poor birthday girl left the room crying.

The story, it is claimed, became a joke among the attendees of the wrecked party. Whenever something went wrong, they would say, 'that's the icing on the cake.' From there, it spread as a cliché.

Eventually, the meaning evolved to what it is today—the finishing touches to something good.

I could (couldn't) care less

The original form of this idiom was, of course, 'I couldn't care less,' meaning 'There is no way that I could have the least bit of interest about this subject.'

The original saying is British, and the first verified reference to 'I couldn't care less' is in 1946 as the title for a book by Anthony Phelps. The topic is Phelps' experiences in Air Transport Auxiliary during World War II. It was obvious that the expression was already well-known by that date. It had reached the U.S. during the 1950s, and was common.

The earliest known publication of "I could care less" was in 1956 in the *Alaska 1955 U.S. Congress House Committee hearings before the Subcommittee on Territorial and Insular Affairs*:

> "…I have had no dealings with them. I don't even know who they are, and **I could care less** because they have been a source, frankly, to me personally of embarrassment."

Attempts to apply logic to 'I could care less' have failed and it is obvious to researchers that the original intent of the change was 'sarcastic.'

I could tell you, but then I'd have to kill you

The suggestion has been made that the root of this came from the story in *Genesis* when God told Adam and Eve in the Garden of Eden that if they ate from the tree of the Knowledge of Good and Evil they would surely die (*Genesis 2:17*).

This comical expression actually originated in movies in which a person was killed because 'he knew too much'. The first use of 'He knows too much' was in *The Man Who Knew Too Much* released in 1934. The actual quote of this phrase comes from *Top Gun* in 1986.

> *"Maverick: Uh, sorry Goose. WE happened to see a MiG 28 do a 4g negative dive.*
> *Charlie: Where did you see this?*
> *Maverick: Uh, that's classified.*
> *Charlie: It's what?*
> *Maverick: It's classified.* **I could tell you, but then I'd have to kill you.**"

It has been utilized in themes of espionage, and comedy in movies and on television since the 1980s. It has become a joke as a metaphor when someone is avoiding relating a personal matter to an inquisitive party.

I cried because I had no shoes, until I saw a man with no feet

This saying, as we know it, first started appearing in publications in the early 1950s, such as *The New Catholic World, Volume 180*, 1954.

It was the credo of Helen Keller's life, and was condensed from the following excerpt from the ancient book by the Persian poet, Sa'di, *The Gulistan, or Rose Garden*, written in 1259:

> "I never complained of the vicissitudes of fortune, nor suffered my face to be overcast at the revolution of the heavens, except once, when my feet were bare, and I had not the means of obtaining shoes. I came to the chief of Kufah in a state of much dejection, and saw there a man who had no feet. I returned thanks to God and acknowledged his mercies, and endured my want of shoes with patience."

The Gulistan has been translated into English many times, the first complete translation being by James Dumoulin (Calcutta, 1807).

The condensed version was attributed to Tolstoy in *Effective Living, an Interdisciplinary Approach* by Lois Smith Murray, 1960.

I cut my teeth on...

The literal expression, used for babies when their first teeth break through their gums, goes back to 1677 according to the *Oxford English Dictionary*. Babies chew on things during this process, which may have been the inspiration for the way it came to be used. It actually evolved, with similar figurative expressions coming into usage earlier, like 'cutting one's eye teeth' and 'cutting one's wisdom teeth' meaning to acquire wisdom. But in a figurative sense, this phrase means to learn something as a beginner. It has been in usage in the U.S. since at least the mid-19th century. This version was used by Ralph Waldo Emerson in *Society and Solitude*, a collection of essays, published in 1870:

> *"..... boy 'when he cuts his eye-teeth,' as we say, childish illusions passing daily away, and he seeing things really and comprehensively, is made by tribes..."*

Emerson alluded to the fact that the saying was in common figurative use.

idle mind is the devil's workshop, An

This is not in the *Bible*, as some have thought. The nearest verse, which carries the thought in the Christian canon, is in *II Thessalonians 3:10*:

> "For even when we were with you, this we commanded you, that if any would not work, neither should he eat."

This proverb rather evolved. Chaucer, in the 12th century, called the hands the devil's tools. In 1715, Isaac Watts made reference to Satan using idle hands. The first close printed version of this proverb comes from 1721, in James Kelly's *A Complete Collection of Scottish Proverbs:*

> "If **the Devil** finds a Man **idle**, he'll set him at **work**."

Then the brain is used in *Gnomologia* by Thomas Fuller, 1732:

> "**Idle brains are the devil's workhouses**."

The 'idle brain' and '*workshop*,' per se, came from H.G. Bohn in his 1855 *Hand-Book of Proverbs*:

> "**An idle brain is the devil's workshop**."

I don't give a tinker's dam

This saying, contrary to common thought, originally had nothing to do with the curse word. In Britain during the reigns of the Yorks, Tudors and Stuarts, many tinkers were knavish drunken men. They would travel about earning their living mending pots and pans and sharpening knives. They 'dammed up' the leak inside the pots with clay, using a more permanent material, like a solder, on the

266

outside. When it was finished, the clay would be taken out and thrown away. The clay was called 'the tinker's dam.' The dam was also known as a 'cuss,' as it was worthless. Thus, the saying developed.

I'd rather die on my feet than continue living on my knees

This saying is a quote from Mexican Revolution leader, Elimiano Zapata, born Elimaino Zapata Salazar (1879 –1919), according to *Libertarian Theologies in North America* (1979) by Gerald H. Anderson and Thomas F. Stransky, p. 281. The actual quote, of course, is in Spanish: *"Prefiero morir de pie que vivir de rodillas."*

It was so popular that other rebels have used it. It is meant to convey the passion for change in present conditions, as Patrick Henry's famous statement, "Give me liberty or give me death."

If (or when) all else fails read the instructions

The earliest available reference in print to this saying is from the U.S. Library of Congress' *Catalogue of Copyright Entries*, Third Series, 1976: January—June:

"(**When all else fails, read the instructions,** 33rd installment)"

This was the title of a book by James W. Moore, Abingdon Press, 1993.

If a rooster crows after sundown, he will get up with a wet head

This is an old superstition from folklore. A book by Fletcher Bascom Dresslar, 1907, *Superstition and Education* from the University of California at Berkley includes it this way:

"**If a rooster crows when he goes to bed,
He's sure to get up with a very wet head.**"

If at first you don't succeed, try, try again

This proverb first appeared in *Teacher's Manual* in 1840 by American educator Thomas H. Palmer who wrote:

"'Tis a lesson you should heed, try, try again. **If at first you don't succeed, try, try again.**"

Some sources believe that the phrase dates to well before this, to the time of Robert I of Scotland, best known as Robert the Bruce, the 14th-century king popularized in the movie *Brave Heart*, who suffered a major defeat at the hands of the English. Legend says that he then hid in a cave near Gretna, close to the border of Scotland and England. While there, according to legend, he watched a spider attempting to spin a web. Each time the spider failed, it simply began again. So inspired was the Bruce by the little arachnid that he left the cave and returned to lead his troops in a series of victories against the English. Whether Bruce actually used the phrase is questionable, but the tale may have inspired Palmer.

The saying was brought into popular culture by British hymnist, educational writer and *Westminster Review* editor, William 'Edward' Hickson in 1857 when the entire quote from Palmer was used in his *Moral Song*. It is now applicable to much more than lessons in school.

I feel it in my bones

Also used with 'can,' this old saying originated from the changes in the weather affecting someone's joints, especially with arthritis, but is figurative and refers to getting a hunch about something.

The earliest known citation is from the weekly publication *The Automobile* December 30, 1909, in an article titled *How to Make My Car Pay for Itself*:

> **"I feel it in my bones**, and until a man does feel his health resident within himself, until he knows as a man that he is healthy without waiting for the physicians certificate to enable him to draw his accumulated lodge benefits he has not gained that surplus of vigor which the machine is designed to assure."

Forms of the saying have been used in many films; the first in 1919, *La Giana Blanca*. Others include *Pride and Prejudice*, 1940, and *Chitty Chitty Bang Bang*, 1968. A song by Earth Wind and Fire, *I Can Feel it in My Bones*, was released by Warner Brothers Records in 1971 on their album, *The Need of Love*.

If God had wanted us to fly he'd have given us wings

This popular cliché is a common quote from the era before the Wright Brothers invented the airplane. One early example of the principle is from *The Practical Works of Richard Baxter*, Volume III, 1838:

"If a man desire to fly with wings, or to be as God, these desires God is not to fulfil."

If ifs and buts were candy and nuts, we'd all have a Merry Christmas

Also quoted as "If 'ifs' and 'buts' were candy and nuts, wouldn't it be a Merry Christmas?" and "...what a wonderful Christmas it would be," this quote from the late Don Meredith, former Dallas Cowboys quarterback turned commentator, has become a catchphrase in the vein of 'If I had a nickel for every time I heard that I'd be rich.' It has the effect of 'If we could all get around to everything we would like to do we could all celebrate.' Meredith used the phrase several times in the early 1970s. It must have been used before this, either by Meredith or someone known to both him and Howard Cosell, however, based on this early conversation from the *Ada Evening News*, in Oklahoma, December 17th, 1970, page seven, column one:

> "Howard: 'If Los Angeles wins, it's a big one, but San Francisco is still very much in it.' Dan: **'If ifs and buts were candy and nuts, we'd all have a merry Christmas**.' Howard: 'I didn't think you'd remember that old canard. 'Dan: 'Is that what it was?'"

If I had a (unit of currency) for every time I heard that...

Often with varying units of currency, and sometimes ending with a phrase like, 'I'd be rich,' this catchphrase is from at least the early 20th century. It is used to illustrate how often something is said or done.

In the 1932 crime film, *Under-Cover Man,* the following dialogue took place:

> "Lora Madigan: 'I wouldn't think of doing such a thing.'
> Kenneth Mason: **'If I had a dollar for every time I heard that**.'

If is a big word

This cliché reminds us that speculation sometimes is in vain. It appeared in *Moody's Monthly Magazine*, May 1907, in an article titled *Mortgage Indebtedness Increasing:*

> "'Everything is booming and if the good times continue we will all get rich.'

> **"'If is a big word.'"**

If it ain't broke, don't fix it

Bert Lance, the Director of the Office of Management and Budget under President Jimmy Carter, was quoted in the newsletter of the U.S. Chamber of Commerce, *Nation's Business,* in May 1977, as believing he could save the government billions of dollars by adopting a simple motto.

"'**If it ain't broke, don't fix it**.' He explains: 'That's the trouble with government: Fixing things that aren't broken and not fixing things that are broken.'"

He wasn't the one who first said it, though, but he did popularize it. Here, however, is a citation from the Texas newspaper *The Big Spring Herald* from December 1976:

"We would agree with the old Georgia farmer who said his basic principle was '**If it ain't broke, don't fix it**.'"

If it had been a snake it would have bitten you

This old saying, though now somewhat archaic, is often used when a person walks right by an obvious item and does not see it. It can also apply to not seeing something in print, etc. It goes back to at least the late 19th century. It was used by Opie Percival Read in *Emmett Bonlore*, 1891:

"…I didn't see any shirt."

"**If it had been a snake it would have bitten you**."

"Glad it wasn't a snake."

If it sounds too good to be true, it probably is

The earliest citation of a form of this comes from 1578 in George Whetstone's early English comedy, *Promos & Cassandra,* B3,

"I thought thy talke was **too sweete to be true**."

Only two years later, in 1580, Thomas Lupton made it a bit more like we have heard this used in *Siugila, Too Good to Be True.*

The phrase 'too good to be true' was used by a number of authors over the next few centuries. It wasn't until December 5th, 1954 that Victor H. Hyborg, president of the Association of Better Business Bureaus in the U.S. and Canada, in an article in the *Oakland Tribune*, made the statement:

"Remember if a bargain **seems too good to be true, it usually is**."

If it walks like a duck, swims like a duck and quacks like a duck, then it probably is a duck

Though this seems like merely a statement of common sense, the phrase is used to let people know that they need to exercise a bit of good judgment when dealing with persons who exhibit characteristics which are typical of charlatans or other undesirable characters.

American poet, James Whitcomb Riley (1849–1916), coined this comical phrase when he wrote, "When I see a bird that **walks like a duck and swims like a duck and quacks like a duck, I call that bird a duck**."

Later Riley's quote was popularized by Richard Cunningham Patterson, Jr., the U.S. Ambassador to Guatemala, in 1950, during what was commonly called 'the cold war.' He accused Guzman's government of being Communistic, stating:

"Suppose you see a bird walking around in a farm yard. This bird has no label that says 'duck'. But the bird certainly **looks like a duck**. Also, he goes to the pond and you notice that he **swims like a duck**. Then he opens his beak and **quacks like a duck**. Well, by this time you have probably reached the conclusion **that the bird is a duck**, whether he's wearing a label or not."

This became known as the 'duck test' and was used in 1964 by Cardinal Richard Cushing in regard to Fidel Castro.

If I've told you once, I've told you a thousand times

This saying goes back to 1730, and a version is in *A Complete Collection of State Trials and Proceedings for High Treason*, London; Volume 2, page 68, in the Trial of John Lilburne:

"...for that I must tell you again and **once is as good as if I told you a thousand times over**..."

Then in 1866, in *Inside: A Chronicle of Secession* by Presbyterian Minister, William Mumford Baker, (published under the alias G. F. Harrington) page 194, came a lot closer to the actual saying as we use it today:

"Of course you won't remember it; you never do anything I say, but **if I said it to you once**, don't touch confiscated property, **I told you ten thousand times**."

If looks could kill

The first known printed reference is from Bram Stoker's *Dracula* in 1897.

"If ever a face meant death—**if looks could kill**—we saw it at that moment."

Obviously, this expression is used to indicate an especially vicious stare intended to convey an unmistakable message of disdain.

If the shoe fits, wear it

The roots of this saying go back to England even further than when this first appeared in *The New York Gazette and weekly Mercury* on May 17, 1773 before the U.S. declared its independence.

"Why should Mr. Vanderbeck apply a general comparison to himself? Let 'those whom **the shoe fits wear it**."

The phrase was first 'if the cap fits wear it.' 'If the shoe fits, put it on' is also sometimes used. Recent spins on this proverb include 'If the shoe fits, you're lucky,' a quote from Malcolm Forbes, and 'If the shoe fits, it isn't on sale.'

If you can't beat 'em, join 'em

Seen in several variants, this proverbial saying is from at least the late 19th century, and means if all attempts have been made to be victorious against an adversary, it is better to lay aside your differences and make a truce.

A book titled ***Beat 'em or Join 'em*** by Clemett Garibaldi Lanni was published by the Rochester (NY) Alliance Press in 1931. It was the first of three books he was to write about George W. Aldridge, notorious city boss of the late 1800s to early 1900s, who may have coined the phrase. The *Rochester Sketchbook*, by Arch Merrill, published in the 1946, has a section about Aldridge which states:

"'**If you can't beat 'em, join 'em**,' was one of his maxims."

The saying must have taken root in the political system, because the *Atlantic Monthly*, February 1932, notes as one of Indiana Senator James E. Watson's 'favorite sayings':

"If you can't lick 'em, jine 'em,"

If you can't stand the heat, get out of the kitchen

Flamboyant U.S. President Harry S. Truman was famous for saying what he meant whether anyone liked it or not. What the implication is, and always has been, is that if you can't cope with a situation, step aside and let someone else handle it.

Before serving as President, in July 1942, in fact, this quip appeared in *The Soda Springs Sun,* an Idaho newspaper:

"Favorite rejoinder of Senator Harry S. Truman, when a member of his war contracts investigating committee objects to his strenuous pace: '**If you don't like the heat, get out of the kitchen**'."

In 1949, after becoming President, he told his staff, when warning them not to be too concerned over criticism regarding their appointments:

"I'll stand by [you] but **if you can't take the heat, get out of the kitchen**."

However, it was Truman's close friend and advisor, General Harry Vaughn who actually originated the phrase, according to an article in *Time*, April 28, 1952.

If you can't take Mohammed to the mountain, bring the mountain to Mohammed (also Muhammed in some cultures)

This is often quoted for doing whatever is necessary to get the job done. The original statement, however, was a little more practical: "If the mountain won't come to Muhammad, Muhammad must go to the mountain." This saying was based on a late 16th century story that Mohammad once sought proof of his teachings by ordering a mountain to come to him. After all, Jesus had said that if anyone had enough faith he could move mountains. When the mountain didn't move, he reasoned that God had been merciful, for if it had indeed moved they all would have been crushed by it in the process.

If you catch my drift*

When this expression is used it means that something is inferred which may not be completely understood at first. 'My drift' to indicate proper meaning, or purpose, was used as early 1599 in *The First Book of the Preservation of Henry VII* by John Payne Collier, page 25:

"For my delight (O Queene) **my drift** and only my purpose, Is to record Chronicles; metricall verse fitly to compose, And to refyne our speach, to procure our natural English Far to be more elegant; that verse may skilfuly florish."

A bit later it was cited by Shakespeare in *Hamlet,* in *The Second Quarto*, 1604:

"*Pol*. Marry sir, heer's **my drift**, And I belieue it is a fetch of wit…"

It was likely derived by the 'drift' of a river, meaning its flow or direction of movement. This saying refers to a current of thought, often difficult to follow.

This indeed seems to be the case in the earliest known figurative use of 'catch my drift' in *Blackwood's Edinburgh Magazine* in December 1849, in *The Green Hand, a "Short" Yarn, Part VI*:

"Finch was too much of a fair seaman not to **catch my drift** at once, but in too great a passion to own it at the time. "D'ye think, sir," said he, with a face like fire, "so much sense as there is in this long rigmarole of yours, that I'm such a— that's to say, that I didn't know it before, sir?"

If you find yourself in a hole, the first thing to do is stop diggin'

This funny quip is a quote from American humorist and social commentator, Will Rogers (1879 –1935). It is typical of his home-spun humor. It is to remind us that we can't borrow ourselves out of debt, and we can't lie ourselves out of another untruth.

If you play with fire you'll get burned

This proverb means that doing something known to be dangerous will inevitably bring undesirable consequences. Similar sayings are if you lie down with dogs you'll get up with fleas (see), and 'if you play with a snake you'll get bit(ten)!'

The saying has been popular since the mid-20th century. An early printed reference is from 1964 in *Intermarriage, Interfaith, Interracial, Interethnic* by Albert Isaac Gordon:

> "I can still remember them saying, 'It's all well and good that you go out with that girl, but **if you play with fire, you'll get burned**.'"

If you snooze, you lose

This phrase is an ever-popular ad campaign slogan extolling the virtues of acting immediately in order to get the best values and selection. The earliest on record is from a classified ad placed by Holmes Motor Company on June 6th, 1950 in the *Daily Courier*, Waterloo, Iowa:

> "**If you snooze you lose**. So BUY NOW from us."

If you step on a crack; it will break your mother's back *

Stepping on a crack in the sidewalk has carried with it a stigma of bad luck since the late 19th century, especially among children. The first known printing is from April 1890 in *The Teacher*, Volume II, Number 24, New York City, under the heading 'Children's Lies,' which was reprinted in later educational pamphlets:

> "If they **step on a crack** when walking on the sidewalk, they are 'going to have bad luck' or are 'poisoned.'

A subsequent rhyme sprang from the now-shocking racist view point prevalent in the American South after the Civil War, according to tradition. The earliest chant was "Step on a crack and your children will be black," which soon gave way to, "your mother will turn black." Other superstitions also sprang up a bit later and lasted through the mid-20th century. 'Step in a hole, you'll break your mother's sugar bowl,' 'Step on a nail, you'll put your father in jail,' and other such rhymes also were used by the mid-1920s.

An early example of the current chant dates to 1907 in *Superstition and Education* by Fletcher Bascom Dresslar.

> "**Step on a crack—**
> **Break your mother's back!**"

If you've got it, flaunt it

This cliché meaning 'show off your assets and abilities to the highest advantage' was originally a famous line by Zero Mostel in Mel Brooks' popular 1968 comedy film, *The Producers*:

"That's it baby, **when you got it, flaunt it! Flaunt It!**"

It inspired an ad slogan of Braniff Airways, beginning by the end of that year.

"We're Braniff. **If You've Got It, Flaunt It.**"

If you want something done right, do it yourself

The first printing of a variation of this proverb is in *The Chirsten State of Matrymonye* by Myles Coverdale in 1541:

"That whych thou cannest do conueniently thyselfe commytte it not to another."

An updated version was used by famous minister, Charles Spurgeon, in *John Ploughman's Pictures*, page 33, published in 1880:

"**If you want a thing well done, do it yourself.**"

If we do not learn from our mistakes, we are bound to repeat them

This is a rephrasing of a famous quote by Spanish-born philosopher, George Santayana, "Those who cannot remember the past are condemned to repeat it." (See: **History repeats itself**)

If wishes were fishes, we'd all have a fry

The following is found in *Harper's Magazine* in September 1874, in a story titled *In the Abess's Parlor* by Frank Lee Benedict:

"Jem once more quavered out, '**If fishes were wishes**—"

This is derived from an age-old rhyme appearing in *The Children's Pew* by J. Reid Howatt, 1893, where it was referred to as an 'old rhyme':

276

"**If wishes were fishes,
We'd all have some fried**;
If wishes were horses,
Beggars would ride."

Another version is found in the London literary publication *Pick-Me-Up*, *27 August 1892*, in a poem titled, "*If Wishes Were Aught*," of which this is one verse:

"If wishes were horses, Beggars would ride;
If wishes were fishes,
We'd swim with the tide;
If wishes were aught but a fanciful thought,
Love only would abide."

This is a variation of an earlier Scottish proverb from James Kelly's *A Complete Collection of Scottish Proverbs*, *1721* which says "If wishes were horses, beggars would ride."

All rhymes and proverbs regarding wishes remind us that they are illusive.

If wishes were horses, beggars would ride (See: '**If wishes were fishes…**')

If you lie down with dogs, you'll get up with fleas

This proverb goes back to Latin, *Chi va dormir con i cani, si leua con i pulici, and* the earliest English version is in the 16th century translated by James Sanford in *Garden of Pleasure* in 1573:

"He that **goeth to bedde wyth Dogges, aryseth with fleas**.

Then, in George Herbert's *Outlandish Proverbs* (no. 343), 1640:

"Hee that **lies with the dogs, riseth with fleas**."

It means that if you associate with someone questionable, that person's problems will affect you in the long run.

If you think you can do a thing, or if you think you can't do a thing, you're right

This is a thought-provoking quote from Henry Ford. It is another way of saying, *Proverbs 23:7a (KJV)*: "**As a man thinketh in his heart, so is he**." Believing he or she can't do something will keep a person from succeeding.

I gave at the office

This is a catchphrase originating in the mid-20th century as an excuse not to donate to some cause for which one is being solicited. Usually it is a way of saying 'I don't want to contribute.' Season 4, Episode 13 of the *Mary Tyler Moore Show*, first aired 8 December1973, was named *I Gave at the Office*.

Ignorance is bliss

This sarcastic cliché has been in general usage in the English language for close to 300 years.

The phrase 'Ignorance is bliss' was lifted from the little-known poem (today) *Ode on a Distant Prospect of Eton College* by the English poet Thomas Gray, published in London in 1742. The context of the quote reads as follows:

"Thought would destroy their paradise. No more. Where **ignorance is bliss**, 'tis folly to be wise."

I'll be a monkey's uncle!

This saying is derived from a slam against Darwin's theory of evolution. It has a similar meaning to 'I can't believe that!' Obviously it didn't come into being until after Charles Darwin's theory was published in *On the Origin of the Species* in 1859. The famous 'Scopes Monkey Trial' (The State of Tennessee VS John Thomas Scopes) was held in 1925 in Dayton, Tennessee, when the high school biology teacher went on trial for teaching evolution in violation of Tennessee's Butler Act. Scopes was found not guilty. This trial inspired the movie, *Inherit the Wind*, starring Spencer Tracy, Frederick March and Gene Kelly, 1960.

I'll be dadgum! / doggone

These are American euphemisms for GD, and, like 'Well, I'll swanny' (see) 'for Pete's sake' (see) darn, and so many others, were used by 'decent folk' in the nineteenth and especially early-to-mid-20th century to avoid swearing.

I'll cross that bridge when I come to it

This is a way of telling someone that you will deal with a problem when it happens, and not before. It has been around since the mid-19th century. A form

278

of it was used as the title and initial line of an article in *The Sailor's Magazine and Naval Journal* in October 1849, American Seaman's Friend Society:

"'**Never cross a bridge until you come to it**' was the counsel usually given by a patriarch in the ministry to troubled and over-careful Christians."

I'll eat my hat

For hundreds of years, in fact, since the late 18th century, 'I'll eat my hat' has been an expression of someone's confidence and certainty of an event happening.

The promise to eat one's hat is, of course, not something anyone would hold the speaker to. The earliest citation of the phrase known in print is from Thomas Brydges' *Homer Travestie (A Burlesque Translation of Homer)*, in 1797:

"For though we tumble down the wall,
And fire their rotten boats and all,
I'll eat my hat, if Jove don't drop us,
Or play some queer rogue's trick to stop us."

Charles Dickens used a longer version of this phrase in *The Pickwick Papers*, published forty years later, in 1837:

"If I knew as little of life as that, **I'd eat my hat** and swallow the buckle whole."

I'll give you three guesses and the first two don't count

This humorous expression is intended to make someone realize that the question at hand has a simple obvious answer. It has been used since the mid-20th century. An early citation is from *American Flint*, The American Flint Glass Workers' Union publication, 1950, Volume 39, page 58:

"Naturally when the party was over, who do you think got stuck with all the work of cleaning up the hall? **I'll give you three guesses and the first two don't count**."

I'll knock you into the middle of next week

Also followed more recently by 'and meet you coming back on Sunday.' This sarcastic figurative expression has been in use since the mid-19th century. An early example is found in *The Australian Journal* for the week ending June 30, 1866 in *Thoughts on Threats*:

> "Absurd: 'If you say that again, **I'll knock you into the middle of next week.**'

I'm all ears

The earliest known citation for this saying is from John Gideon Milligan's British play, *The Bee-hive: A Musical Farce*, 1811:

> "Speak — **I'm all ears.**"

In 1939 a copyright was applied for at the U.S. Copyright Office by Maude S. Moulton, Los Angeles. '18159 **I'm all ears**; song'.

When someone says that they are all ears, they are likely responding to someone who has indicated that he or she has something important to say. The speaker is stating that the individual has his or her undivided attention—that he or she won't be using his or her hands to send a text, or using his or her eyes to scan the room—the individual is 'all ears' to hear what the other person has to say. When someone says this, the speaker can usually feel confident that the other person believes that the message is important. At times, however, it is used sarcastically.

I may be dumb, but I'm not stupid

This comical phrase is often used as a quote from former Steelers quarterback, analyst and actor, Terry Bradshaw. Actually it had been around quite some time before it was picked up by Bradshaw while working as a commentator. As early as 1976 it appeared in *Executive Decisions* by Rossall James Johnson;

> "You haven't discussed that with anyone have you?

> "Ron: Not at all. **I may be dumb, but I'm not stupid!** I've got enough problems."

I'm from Missouri—you'll have to show me

Harry Truman was a Missourian, and was quoted as using this phrase on occasion, also. The famous saying was not from Truman originally, however, but was a quote from U.S. Congressman, Willard Duncan Vandiver, in 1899. But the root of it didn't start with the Congressman. Westerners liked to tease folks from Missouri back then, painting them as slow witted. The Missourians, however, being above their taunts, turned the tables on the expression, saying that 'Show me' meant that they were exceptionally alert and would not be outsmarted.

Congressman Vandiver made his famous statement before a meeting of the 'Five O'clock Club' in Philadelphia. Being a member of the Congressional Committee on Naval Affairs, Vandiver was in town to inspect the city's naval yards. The dinner at which he spoke was after the inspection. Vandiver and Governor Hull were the only two guests not in proper evening attire—the governor reemerging at the last minute. Somehow Hull had managed to acquire an evening suit, but one which was not a proper fit. Hull and Vandiver were both scheduled to speak. During the governor's speech he made a joke about why his suit didn't fit properly then introduced the congressman. Vandiver was embarrassed by the fact that he was now the only person in attendance without evening wear, and, after his speech concluded, made this playful remark aimed at Hull:

> "He tells you that the tailors, finding he was here without a dress suit, made one for him in fifteen minutes. I have a different explanation. You heard him say he came over here without one, and you see him now with one that doesn't fit him. The explanation is that he stole mine, and that's the reason why you see him with one and me without any. This story from Iowa doesn't go at all with me; **I'm from Missouri, you've got to show me**."

The statement was spread across the nation by the news media, and since then, Missouri has been known as the 'Show Me State.' It has also become an oft-repeated catchphrase for others, in admiration of the way a negative was turned into a positive.

I'm going to jerk a knot in your tail

This old Southern American figurative expression was used as early as 1946 in Harry Allen Smith's *Rhubarb*. It means that there will be serious consequences to disobeying a command.

I'm going to see a man about a horse (or dog)

This euphemistic saying was derived from the days when someone was going to settle a bet on a horse or dog race. Though now archaic, through the years it came to be used as a way to conceal what a person was actually leaving to do, such as going to the restroom or to purchase an alcoholic beverage.

The earliest known citation is the 1866 Dion Boucicault's play, *Flying Scud*, in which a character dances around a situation by saying:

281

"Excuse me Mr. Quail, I can't stop; **I've got to see a man about a dog**."

Imitation is the sincerest form of flattery

The meaning of this was captured in one of noted Austrian writer, Baroness Marie von Ebner-Eschenbach's quotes (1830-1916): "**Authors from whom others steal should not complain, but rejoice. Where there is no game there are no poachers.**"

I'm just sayin'...

Sometimes followed by 'is all,' this modern cliché means that the speaker or blogger wants the audience or readers to mull over what has just been brought out, as they may not have thought about the subject in a certain way, and the conclusion is worthy of consideration. The exact origin is unclear, but it seems to have evolved from humorous Yiddish speech, as it was used as far back as Vaudeville (1880s to 1930s) by Jewish entertainers at the end of their jokes. Then in the 1980s, two comedians, Paul Reiser and Eddie Murphy, popularized it, though it was not in the exact context as it is used today on television and Internet blogs. It conveys the meaning of "I'm just saying what I think."

In a coon's age

The expression, 'I haven't seen you in a coon's age' dates to the 19th century, and came about from the belief that raccoons lived a long time. Actually, the life expectancy of a healthy raccoon is only from five to seven years. They may have surmised this because their skin is durable and was good for 'coon-skin hats' and the like back then. The raccoon was the figurehead for the Whig party. They were a bit akin to the modern Republicans who chose the elephant, also having a tough hide.

In a New York minute

The time and person who first coined this phrase have evidently been lost somewhere on the streets of the city that never sleeps. It likely originated there, but not by a native New Yorker. The saying is derived from the perception that folks in other parts of the country have of New Yorkers—that they have no time for anyone or anything but themselves. Thus a New York minute passes in a flash.

Fortunately, New Yorkers are much like people in other cities—varied in their views, their use of time, and their way of showing their feelings toward others, though they do for the most part live a rushed lifestyle.

The following is the earliest known citation of 'New York minute', but does not relate to time. It's from *Galveston News* (Texas), 15 August 1954, page 22:

> "Betty Jean Bird of the Pirate Club has what she claims the smallest French poodle in the nation…It's no bigger than a **New York minute** and that's only thirty seconds."

The earliest known printing in which it refers to time is found in *New York Magazine, Volume 4,* 1971, in an ad for Laura Pells Theatre:

> "Health and Wellness Showcase Life happens **in a New York minute**."

In a nutshell

This figurative expression means 'to sum it up briefly.' In *Curiosities of Litterature,* by Isaac Disraeli, Volume 1, page 370, 1833 we find the following:

> "The Iliad of Homer **in a nutshell**, which Pliny says that Cicero once saw, it is pretended might have been a fact, however to some it may appear impossible."

This is mentioned in a number of 19th century publications, and would have occured in the first century B.C.

Shakespeare used it in 1602 in *Hamlet,* when he spoke the words:

> "O God, I could be bounded **in a nutshell**, and count my selfe a King of infinite space."

In the sense that it is used today, the earliest available citation appears in the April 13, 1839 issue of *The Atheneaum* in Murray's 'Journal of the English Agricultural Society,' Volume 1, Part 1:

> "The whole question, and its effects, may be comprised **in a nutshell**; and the following sentence, with which the work before us opens, is quite enough for the purpose of our argument…"

In a pinch

This term originated in Britain in the late 1400s as 'at a pinch' and means in difficulty, an emergency, or when nothing else is available. It was included in John Heywood's 1562 book of Proverbs:

"May I be holp forth an inch **at a pinch.**"

In a tizzy

This colloquial term means in a frenzy, or nervously frustrated about circumstances. The word 'tizzy' may have been a corruption of the word 'tester,' a slang name for a sixpence coin used in the early 20th century.

The use of the term in this vein has been around since the mid-1930s, and a very early citation is from *Time, Volume 27,* 1936:

"So for days at a time I couldn't bear putting pencils to paper — one scratch got me **in a tizzy.**"

Indian giver

The figurative definition is a person who gives something then takes it back. The term evolved from 'Indian gift' which was first coined by Massachusetts Loyalist politician, Thomas Hutchinson, in 1765 during American colonization when Natives gave gifts to the white Europeans in anticipation of receiving a gift in return.

In 1848 historian and linguist John Russell Bartlett published his *Dictionary of Americanisms* which first cited the phrase 'Indian giver':

"**INDIAN GIVER.** When an Indian gives anything, he expects an equivalent in return, or that the same thing may be given back to him. This term is applied by children in New York and the vicinity to a child who, after having given away a thing, wishes to have it back again."

Note the figurative application already existed by 1848. It is likely that some Europeans accepted gifts from Natives who expected something in trade, and when nothing was received, demanded the return of the gift.

In front of God and everybody

This is another cliché that others avoid. This saying arose to popularity in the mid-20th century, and the earliest known printed reference is found in *The Saturday Evening Post*, 1947, Volume 219, page 137:

> "I straighten up. I wink. I do not make him answer right there **in front of God and everybody**..."

It was used in the Warner Brothers romantic drama, *A Summer Place* in 1959 starring Richard Eagan and Dorothy McGuire, with young Troy Donahue and Sandra Dee.

> "**In front of God and everybody** this time?"

It became even more widely popularized by jokes and sarcastic remarks, and the 1986 book, *Confessions of April Grace, In Front of God and Everybody*, by K.D. McCrite, brought it to the forefront of popular culture.

The idea behind this is based on the biblical teaching that God is omniscient—He sees everything we do. One such reference is from *Jeremiah 23:23-24*.

> *"Am I a God who is only in one place?" asks the Lord. "Do they think I cannot see what they are doing? Can anyone hide from me? Am I not everywhere in all the heavens and the earth?" asks the Lord.* (NLT)

In high cotton

Those who owned the expansive cotton plantations in the Deep South, particularly in antebellum days, were 'filthy rich,' and those who worked the fields were originally slaves, and later, seasonal or migrant workers. The highest, healthiest plants produced the most cotton. Therefore being 'in high cotton' became a catchphrase for the envied landowners of the day. The earliest known citation is from *Railroad Magazine*, Volume 46, July, 1948, in an article titled 'In the Days of the Old Eighty-Five' by J.W. Hinds:

> "I WAS really living **in high cotton** along about 1911, when I was firing the 85 for L. G. (Louie) Rodefeld on a Galveston, Houston & Henderson local and through freight during the week and on passenger every Sunday."

In hot water

Notes and Queries: A Medium of Enter-communication for Literary Men, General Readers, etc., Fourth Series, Volume Nine, published in London in 1872 dates 'hot water' meaning trouble to 1537. In the book there is a letter written by John Hussey dated June 22, 1537 to his mistress, Lady Lislie, in which he noted that he 'could get into no **hot water**...' Indications are that the phrase was already in use in England at that date.

The derivation is plain. Someone in overly hot water is bound to get burned if the person doesn't realize the predicament and get out quickly.

There are quite a few 'hot' idioms, including, 'hot under the collar,' 'hot and bothered,' 'hot and heavy,' and 'to make it hot for someone.'

In like Flynn

This expression originated in the first half of the 20th century in America. The popular Hollywood leading man, Erol Flynn, was a real 'ladies' man.' He was suave and debonair. Young men who wanted to be popular with the girls developed the saying 'In like Flynn' to denote that they were able to gain access to a girl's heart. A very early example is in *Glory for Me* by MacKinlay Kantor, 1945:

"By God," said Derry. "That's the place I live! I'm **in like Flynn!**"

In (or at) one fell swoop

Fell, used in this sense, comes from a Latin word meaning cruel or savage. Shakespeare coined the expression 'one fell swoop' in *MacBeth, Act 4, Scene 3*, in 1605:

"Macduff:
He has no children.—All my pretty ones?
Did you say all?—O hell-kite!—All?
What, all my pretty chickens, and their dam,
At one fell swoop?"

Today the phrase suggests suddenness of action.

In one's heart of hearts

This symbolic phrase means in one's deepest thoughts or feelings. The heart has long been used to relate to the center of one's spiritual, emotional, intellectual and moral being. The use of the word in this manner is found in *Exodus* chapters *5* through *12* when Moses is pleading with the Egyptian Pharaoh to release the 'Children of Israel' the text repeatedly states that Pharaoh's heart was hardened. In Egyptian mythology the heart was a portion of the soul weighed in a balance against the 'feather of Ma'at' which symbolized truth.

Shakespeare, however, coined the phrase 'heart of hearts' in *Hamlet, Act 3, Scene 2,* 1602:

"**Hamlet**:
Give me that man
That is not passion's slave, and I will wear him
In my heart's core, ay, **in my heart of heart**,
As I do thee."

In the bag

This common phrase, meaning 'as good as in one's possession,' came into usage early in the 20th century—by 1900 in Australia, and in a citation there in 1945 in a reference book by Sidney John Baker, called *The Australian Language*.

"A horse set to lose a race is said to be **in the bag**."

The current version, however, was coined because of a New York Giants tradition. In *The Mansfield News*, a paper in Ohio, in May 1920, the following appeared:

"An old superstition was revived at the Polo grounds, New York, recently when Eddie Sicking was dispatched to the clubhouse with the ball bag at the start of the ninth possession of one run lead. This superstition originated during the run of twenty-six consecutive victories made by the Giants in 1916, the significance of it resting in a belief that if the bag is carried off the field at that stage of the game with the Giants in the lead the game is **in the bag** and cannot be lost."

In the black*

This phrase refers to doing business in a solvent manner. It was first used in a *Wall Street Journal* news story in 1923. (See: **In the red**)

In the cards

This metaphoric expression means 'destined to happen' and is taken from the practice of using Tarot cards introduced between 1420 and 1440 in northern Italy to 'tell fortunes' or claim to look into someone's future. The practice is often associated with the occult. Originally this was 'on the cards' and dates from the early 19th century.

A prime example is from *Letters of Harriett, Countess Granville, 1810-1845*, Volume II published in London, 1894, edited by her son, Edward Frederick Leveson-Gower;

> "I am morally quite unequal to a journey of six days without Granville, when if anything was to go amiss I should go into a nervous madness. St. Germain? Very easy, still **on the cards**, but hardly enough, as I want bathing, des eaux and sea air."

In the doghouse

In chapter 16 of Sir J.M. Barrie's *Peter Pan*, 1911, Mr. Darling, the father of Wendy, ended up chained in the dog's kennel as an act of personal penance for allowing the children to be 'kidnapped.' This is the first incident in literature of someone being 'in the doghouse' as a punishment.

The actual phrase, however, first appears in *Criminalese*, James J. Finerty's glossary of criminal jargon, in 1926:

> "**In dog house**, in disfavor."

The idiom is often used as the place a man ends up when he has sorely offended his wife or significant other.

In the driver's seat

This metaphoric phrase was derived from the obvious literal meaning, and is used to refer to being in charge of a situation. Figurative use began in the mid-

20th century. A very early example which is semi-figurative is from *The Rotarian Magazine*, August 1945:

> "We can design better motorcars, engineer safer highways, and pass wiser laws until we are blue in the face, but unless we can put Intelligence **in the driver's seat**, we shall in postwar years see such records as that of 1941..."

A purely metaphoric citation is from *Readings in Marketing* by Phillip R. Cateora, 1967:

> "...the overall activities of a business are working hard to bring computer programming and utilization under their control. A handful of others, perhaps a bit more perceptive and far-sighted are already firmly established **in the driver's seat**."

In the grand scheme of things

This idiom means that something is relatively unimportant compared to the entire scope of everything or the 'plan of the universe.' The phrase has been used in English since the early 20th century. An example is from an article titled 'An American System of Economics' by C.A. Bowsher in *Moody's Magazine*, May 1912:

> "Land, gold and collective man are derivative relations **in the grand scheme of things** when contrasted with value."

In the hood

This saying became popular in the 1980s referring to the urban neighborhood. Originally it was used as a slang term for a primarily black residential area in the city. Eventually it came to mean the ghetto, or rough parts of town, where gangs form and which many people avoid who don't live there. The term has been used frequently on TV shows and in movies. An early example in print is from *Ebony Magazine*, May 1977 in a Navy ad on page 43:

> "And with 30 days paid vacation each year, He can afford to spend a few of them here With Sonny and Skip, back home **in the hood**. Thanks to the Navy, Woody's future looks good."

In the pink*

Today the meaning of this expression is 'in perfect health or condition.' Use of 'the pinke' to indicate top form can be traced as far back as 1597 when William Shakespeare used this in *Romeo and Juliet*:

"Murcurio: I am **the very pinke** of curtesie."

Then, the following is taken from *Kensington Gardens,* a comedy by John Leigh, 1720:

"'Tis **the Pink** of the Mode, to marry at first Sight—And some, indeed, marry without any Sight at all."

The usage here of 'the pink of the mode' indicated the top form of fashion or excellence, giving much the same meaning as 'in the pink' today. This was used by numerous writers of the 18th and 19th centuries. In 1770, the following was on page 405 of *The Works of the Rev. Phillip Skelton*:

"It would be acting like coxcombs, a character, of all others, the most absurd in the professors of religion, either to set ourselves out **in the pink of the mode** for so short an appearance…"

Then in 1905 we find the following in the British *Kynoch Journal:*

"Makers may dispatch explosives from the factory **in the pink** of condition."

In the red*

This is an accounting term which means 'in debt' as opposed to being 'in the black' or financially solvent. It comes from the practice of using red ink in financial balance sheets to indicate negative balances. Black ink was used at least three years earlier to refer to positive figures. The earliest citation of this expression is found in 1926 in *Wise-Crack Dictionary* by George H. Maines and Bruce Grant:

"*In the red*, losing money in show parlance."

In the right place at the right time (See: **In the wrong place at the right time**, below.)

290

In the toilet

The derivation is obvious. It means totally doomed, wasted, worthless and useless. Metaphorically it came into use in the mid-to-late 20th century. An early example is from the Hoke Communications publication, *Direct Marketing: Volume 37,* 1974:

> "But our principal business is **in the toilet...**"

In the wake of

This means 'following' or 'in the aftermath of.' It is derived from the use of 'in the wake of a ship' as early as the 18th century. *The New Universal Dictionary of the Marine,* 1830, under 'wake' on page 616 explains:

> "A ship is said to be **in the wake of** another, when she follows her upon the same track, or on a line supposed to be formed in the continuation of her keel..."

The earliest known references in a figurative respect are in *Orbital System of the Universe* by Anthony Welsch, 1875, in several places, including this on page 122:

> "Perceptive organs **in the wake of** the very remote past, will perceive the dark past, as light in the future..."

In the wrong place at the right time

This phrase is one of a number having to do with logistics. The earliest was 'the right place at the right time,' which was used as early as 1960 in the American Marketing Association's *Marketing Keys to Profits in the 1960s*:

> "The U. S. answer is the application of the proper amount of power **in the right place at the right time.**"

This one came several years later and means to be where one is unable to take advantage of some opportunity due to unfortunate timing, bad choices or luck. It appeared in 1981 in *Labor Markets: Theories and Practices in the United States during the 1970s* from the John F. Kennedy School of Government in a discussion paper by Gordon L. Clark and Meric S. Gertler in relation to workers of the previous decade. The article was reprinted later in more than one publication.

Into the drink

This slang term meaning into the sea originated in the early 19th century. The earliest known citation is from James Kirk Paulding in *The Banks of the Ohio*, 1833:

"Shut pan, and sing dumb, or I'll throw you **into the drink**."

I only drink when I'm alone or with someone

Though the phrase is often used as a comical saying to excuse someone's alcoholic habit, it is actually a bit twisted quote from football superstar, Joe Namath:

"I only drink on two occasions, when I'm with people and when I'm alone."

Iron out the kinks

This expression means getting the problems fixed. When *The Calendar Act* passed in 1751 in Great Britain and in North America, eleven days were removed from the year. It was stated that this Act, presented to the British Parliament by Lord Chesterfield, Philip Dormer Stanhope, was passed by the British Parliament in order to "**iron out the kinks**" in the Gregorian calendar. This was the earliest known citation of the figurative phrase.

I smell a rat

To 'smell a rat' means something is suspicious; like the Shakespearean quote, "Something is rotten in the state of Denmark" (see).

This goes back centuries, to the time when rats were common pests and carried diseases. Wealthy people would obtain dogs, which had a keen sense of smell, to sniff out the rats and get rid of them. When one of these dogs would perk up his ears and begin sniffing around, it was believed that he 'smelled a rat.'

This came, as many sayings regarding animals have, to be personified.

Is the Pope Catholic?

When something is questioned as being true, this phrase expresses the utmost confidence in its validity. It was coined in the 1960s.

The earliest known citation of this phrase is in *The United States Congress record of The Quality Stabilization Hearings*, April and May 1962:

> "My little boy has a saying, '**Is the Pope Catholic?**'"

It was also printed in *The Oshkosh Daily Northwestern* in Wisconsin in November 1969:

> "An avid sports fan Tom Pech of Oshkosh was asked before the library board meeting if he planned to attend the Packer-Lion game at Green Bay come Sunday. His reply? '**Is the Pope Catholic?**'"

I think this is the beginning of a beautiful friendship

Often used as a cliché, this is a quote from the end of the 1942 Humphrey Bogart / Ingrid Bergman big screen blockbuster, *Casablanca*. It is the final line when Rick is speaking to Louie, and is prefaced by 'Louie.'

It is better to be thought of as foolish than to open your mouth and remove all doubts

Several persons have been quoted as saying this; however, the root is from the *Bible* in *Proverbs 17:28*:

> "Even a fool, when he holdeth his peace, is counted wise: and he that shutteth his lips is esteemed a man of understanding." (*KJV*)

Logically, this means that one should think before speaking.

It is more blessed to give than to receive

This is from the *Bible: Acts 20:35*. The most usually quoted version of the entire verse is from the *Authorized King James Version* of 1611.

> "I have showed you all things, how that so laboring you ought to support the weak, and to remember the words of the Lord Jesus, how he said, **It is more blessed to give than to receive**."

293

It is what it is

Versions of this thought have been around from time in memorium. One of the first such phrases is found in the biblical book of *Exodus*, where it is recorded that God told Moses to tell the Israelites that I AM THAT I AM sent you. The name of 'G-d' is so sacred to Orthodox Jewish people that they will not say it aloud. In Hebrew, since there are no vowels, it is spelled YHVH or YHWH.

A clown in Shakespeare's *Twelfth Night* said, "That that is, is."

The phrase also typifies a belief in phenomenology, part of a metaphysical science known as ontology, which teaches that anything of itself cannot be what it is not. It is also known in French, and is **c'est ce que c'est.** This phrase has become associated with football and other sports.

It'll all come out in the wash

Many clichés and proverbs which are similar either came from an earlier saying or their meanings overlap. This one is no exception. An earlier version was from *Don Quixote,* by Cervantes, 'all will away in the bucking' (soaking cloth in lye).

Henry Festing Jones, a friend and collaborator with novelist Samuel Butler, quoted him as saying in 1876, "**It will all come** right **in the wash.**"

It means in the end everything will work out satisfactorily.

It matters not if you win or lose; it's how you play the game

Now heralded as an 'old saying,' a form of it appeared in print around the early 20th century. In 1912, in Alfred E. Chirm's *Burton Dane* he wrote:

> "Father used to tell me that whether **you win or lose** counts but little compared to the kind of fight you put up."

It rains on the just and on the unjust

This old adage is from the *Bible* in *Matthew 5:45, KJV*. It is used to mean that good and bad come to all people.

"That ye may be the children of your Father which is in heaven: for he maketh his sun to rise on the evil and on the good, and **sendeth rain on the just and on the unjust**."

It's a jungle out there!

Having been used as the titles of various musical compositions, and books, this phrase figuratively means that life is trying, at best, and both physical and mental preparedness are needed for a chance at success.

The first known book by this title was by Susan Dodson published by Harper Collins on 28 December 1924.

It became very popular as a metaphoric term in the 1970s as seen in this citation from Kiplinger's *Changing Times* April 1976 in an article on job hunting:

"Then we say, 'Now look, **it's a jungle out there**. And somewhere out there is a job you can get. But everybody else is after that job, too, so what you've got to do is beat out the competition for the job you want.'"

It's all Greek to me

Like many other idioms, this came from Shakespeare. It was first spoken by Casca, one of the conspirators against *Julius Caesar* in the first act of the play. He used it in regard to statements made by Cicero after Caesar refused the emperor's crown three times. Cicero had actually spoken in Greek to make sure that the average-Roman-passer-by didn't understand.

The phrase is used to mean that the person speaking has no understanding of what has just been said by a third person.

It's all relative

Originally this was a quote from Einstein who came up with the 'theory of relativity.' It has come to be an idiom meaning that everything, even truth, is different for different people with different concepts and abilities. For one, something may seem absurd and impractical; to another, it makes perfect sense. For a person who makes $10,000,000 a year, for example, something may seem relatively inexpensive, when to someone making $25,000 a year the same item would likely seem outlandish in price.

It's always darkest just before dawn

This is not from the *Bible*, as some have assumed, but is from English theologian and historian, Thomas Fuller (1608-1661). The actual quote is:

"It is always darkest just before the day dawneth."

It has long been used as a proverb meaning no matter how bleak a situation may become, there is still hope. Usually when one is ready to give up, the solution is at hand.

It's a man's world

This phrase was originated as early as May 1912 in the New York Magazine, *The Smart Set:*

"You must like your world, to take such a risk," she said wistfully. "A man's world! Ah, **it's a man's world!**" he cried.

She nodded. "I have heard," she said, and eyed him indulgently. "And when do the ships go?"

Then a 1915 play in four acts accentuating the male-dominated society which had existed through the previous millennia was titled *A Man's World* written by Rachel Crothers.

It gained great popularity after the release of the number one hit song by James Brown in 1966, entitled *It's a Man's, Man's, Man's World*, co-written years earlier by Betty Jean Newsome, as merely *It's a Man's World*.

Modern advances in women's rights in Western society have made this phrase rather antiquated in the big picture in the English language.

It's a nice place to visit, but I wouldn't want to live there

This 'old saying' is also a truism. Its meaning is literal and it is used of any place which has conditions not conducive to year-round living for most people. The earliest version was most likely coined by Captain Jack Abernathy regarding the city of New York, as published on 9 June 1910, in *The Times*, on page 7:

"New York **is a nice place to visit, but you couldn't hold me there** with a two-inch rope. There isn't enough breathing room."

It's an ill wind that blows no good

The original version of this proverb, meaning 'having a definite negative effect on everyone', obviously older, was first recorded by John Heywood in his 1546 book, *A dialogue conteining the nomber in effect of all the prouerbs in the Englishe tongue:*

> "**An yll wynde that blowth no man to good**, men say."

It's a small world

This old saying is used when two persons discover an unknown connection. The Spanish equivalent, 'El mundo es un panuelo' has also been in use for many years.

The earliest known printed reference to the phrase is from George Ade's *In Pastures New*, 1906.

Built for the 1964 New York World's Fair, "**It's a small world**" takes you to countries inhabited by appropriately costumed audio-animatronic dolls singing "*It's a small world after all*," written by the Sherman brothers, Richard M. and Robert B. It's a small world is now a popular musical boat ride at Disneyland in California, which opened on May 22, 1968.

It's better to light a candle than curse the darkness

This saying is listed in numerous places as an 'ancient Chinese proverb', but its exact origin is illusive. The *Bible*, however, has numerous references referring to light and darkness, and *Romans 13:12* bears resemblance to the principle herein:

> "The night is far spent, the day is at hand: let us therefore cast off the works of darkness, and let us put on the armour of light." *(KJV)*

It means that complaining about a bad situation does no good; only taking positive action can help.

It's easier to get forgiveness than permission

This famous statement is attributed to U.S. Naval Rear Admiral Grace Hooper (1906—1992) and was quoted in an interview published in *Chips Ahoy* Magazine in July 1986. It means that there are times when action is necessary for which one has no time to receive permission. In such cases, it is better to take action and face the consequences later.

It's like talking to a brick wall

This old saying means that a person has no interest in what is being said. The thought was around as early as 1893, when Oscar Wilde included the following in his play, *Linda Windermere's Fan*:

> "CECIL GRAHAM But I like **talking to a brick wall** — it's the only thing in the world that never contradicts me!"

It's not how you start, it's how you finish

This proverbial saying, though sounding older, is actually a quote from the NHL's St. Louis Blues General Manager, Doug Armstrong, when he was General Manager of the Dallas Stars. This philosophy, in contrast with 'It matters not if you win or lose, it's how you play the game' (see) is the attitude that rocketed the stars to their Stanley Cup victory when he was Assistant General Manager in 1999, and his father, NHL linesman Neil Armstrong, to Hall of Fame status.

It's not over till the fat lady sings

The precursor of this proverb was 'the carnival isn't over till the fat lady sings.' Its use in sports journalism is attributed to broadcaster Don Cook. His original saying was 'the opera isn't over till the fat lady sings,' shifting the focus of where 'the fat lady' performed to a more common stage of song. It was first used by Cook in April 1978, after the first basketball game between the San Antonio Spurs and the Washington Bullets, now called the Washington Wizards, during the National Basketball Association playoffs, to illustrate that even though the Spurs had won one game, the series was far from over.

It is said to be derived from the operatic performances which generally feature overweight sopranos at the climax. The meaning is that we should never assume the outcome of any activity until it is fully played out.

It's not rocket science

This Americanism is often used when explaining the simplicity of a task to a concerned individual. Because of the highly technical nature of the rocket program, developed by such geniuses as Warner Von Braun following WWII, it became regarded as the most complex of scientific achievements by most Americans, in particular. In the 1980s, when the term first appeared, it was largely related to football. A very early example is from Philadelphia suburb paper, *The Daily Intelligencer*, in Doylestown, Pennsylvania, December 1985:

"Coaching football is **not rocket science** and it's not brain surgery. It's a game, nothing more."

It's not the cough that carries you off, but the coffin they carry you off in

This proverb is an old Scottish rhyme of unknown origin. Though meant to be humorous, it is a reminder that if one takes proper precautions, one can live a longer life. It means, when we have a controllable ailment we should treat it soon enough that it will not become a serious problem. It has been around since before April 8, 1911 when it appeared as a quip in American Meat Packers Association's New York and Chicago weekly trade publication, *The National Provisioner,* in the Chicago Section:

"It's not the cough that carries you off, but the coffin they carry you off in. — Perpetrated by Lew Hawkins."

Note the use of 'perpetrated by,' meaning in this sense, submitted by or responsible for, not indicating origination.

It's not the fall that hurts, it's the landing

This old saying has been applied to all types of falls, from falling from horses to out of trees and even boats, as is the case in this early citation from *Popular Boating Magazine*, February 1965.

"But as they say, **it's not the fall that hurts, it's the landing**."

It's not the size of the dog in the fight, but the size of the fight in the dog

This Mark Twain quote means that it is a person's courage and determination that determine his or her victories in life, not size, money, or any obvious advantage.

It's not what you know; it's who you know

This phrase has been in popular use in the U.S. since at least the early 20th century. It is self-explanatory, and often relates to job-placement, as it did in the earliest known printed reference, which was in *The Electrical Worker*, a

299

magazine published by The International Brotherhood of Electrical Workers, in May 1914:

"Many devious forces apparently also control the conditions of advancement and preference, and a phrase that is often heard is to the effect that **it's not what you know that counts so much, as who you know!**"

Four years later, on 22 September 1918, *The New York Tribune* printed the following:

"PHILADELPHIA, Sept. 21.—The shipyard workers along the Delaware River have adopted a war slogan all of their own. It is: '**It's not what you know; it's who you know.**'"

It is clear from the first citation in the trade paper that the saying was already being used to some degree. By the late 1930s it was in common use across America.

It's the empty can that makes the most noise / rattles the most

Originally 'An empty barrel makes the most noise,' it is a quote attributed to Benjamin Franklin. It is derived from the fact that an empty metal pot makes more noise when hit than a full one. It means that just because someone is sounding off about a subject that they don't necessarily have the right ideas about how to handle the situation. It has been rephrased as both vessel, and can.

It's the only way to fly!

This famed ad slogan was used by Western Airlines, starting in 1956, and became a familiar saying used figuratively for the most popular method of doing anything.

It's the thought that counts

Originally 'It's not the gift, but the thought that counts,' which came from American author, poet and theologian, Henry Van Dyke (1852 – 1933), who was a professor of literature at Princeton University, and received numerous honors. The meaning is literal, and it has been used by multitudes of people to enforce the fact that thoughtfulness is a most worthy attribute.

Like so many other such clichés, this can also be used sarcastically.

It's time to pay the piper

This comes from the 16th-century tale of the *Pied Piper of Hamelin* (Germany) which inspired the immortal Robert Browning poem in 1842. In 1284, according to the story, the town was infested with pesky rats, and the village people hired the piper to play his pipe and lure the pests away. But when time came to pay the piper, they refused to keep their end of the bargain. He then retaliated, and lured the children away in the same manner.

The moral is, when we agree to a product or service and receive what we request, we must be willing 'to pay the piper.' If we refuse to pay, we must be prepared for the consequences. Also used when one has done something unwise.

It takes one to know one

This idiom is usually used in a derogatory manner meaning that only a person of similar traits would recognize another. A similar phrase is the 'pot calling the kettle black' (see). It was in use by at least 1927 when the English Version of the French political publication, *Les Réalités*, issue 50, printed this:

> "His cartoons hit home and drew blood from politics, business, religion, justice, the theater. Apparently, **it takes one to know one**."

It stems from a much older adage, "no one is better at finding a wrongdoer than another wrongdoer."

It takes two to tango

This phrase was originated and made popular by a 1952 song composed by Al Hoffman and Dick Manning with this title. Two versions of the song were released that year, one by Pearl Bailey (a *Billboard* magazine best-seller for 17 weeks), the other by Louis Armstrong.

This expression has come to mean that in order to succeed at relationships both sides must be working together in unison, and that when a joint venture fails, it was because they weren't in agreement.

I was born ready

This phrase was made famous by Hollywood movies. And it was in a number of films. But contrary to popular belief that it was first spoken by Jack Burton in

Big Trouble in Little China in 1986, Hal Needham in *Smokey in the Bandit*, 1977 or even Gator McKlusky in *White Lightening* in 1973, it was first uttered in *Hondo* (John Wayne) in 1953:

> "Like I told you, **I was born ready!**"

I won't hold my breath

Sometimes 'wouldn't,' this means a person doesn't expect a particular thing to happen. It is used in sarcastic humor. The earliest known reference in print is in a letter to the editor from page 2 of *The Rotarian*, April 1944:

> "P.S. **I won't hold my breath** waiting for the reissue of the February Rotarian."

I wouldn't be caught dead

This idiom means that a person would be too embarrassed to ever do a particular thing, wear some type of clothing or go to some particular place. The earliest known citation is from the humorous magazine, *Judge's Library*, December 1900, in a caption under a cartoon of mice:

> "Humph! **I wouldn't be caught dead** in your old trap."

I wouldn't touch that with a ten foot pole

The earlier version of this figurative phrase, meaning 'I don't want anything to do with it, at all' was first printed in John Clarke's *Paroemiologia Anglo-Latino* in 1639:

> "Not to be handled with a paire of tongues."

Then in 1846 the 'ten foot pole' version was used by Caroline Matilda Kirkland in *Western Clearings:*

> "I know you did, and I expected you'd come back so big that a man **couldn't touch you with a ten foot pole**."

J

Jack Frost

This term, used to denote the horrid freezes in the dead of winter, derived from a character in ancient Viking lore originally known as 'Jokul Frosti' (icicle frost), a variant of which is 'Old Man Winter' (see). This personification of winter's deep chill is said to leave frosty patterns on windows which sometimes resemble ferns. In English literature, he was around at least by the early 19th century and appeared in the *Balance and Columbian Repository*, Hudson, New York, on 22 October 1805:

> "On Tuesday night last the vegetable world was attacked with great severity, and great havoc made in the fields and gardens in this quarter by that destructive old veteran, **Jack Frost**."

Wizard of Oz creator, L. Frank Baum, in *The Life and Adventures of Santa Clause*, 1902, where he is mentioned several times, portrayed Jack Frost as the son of 'the Frost King.' Here is one citation:

> "At night **Jack Frost** rapped at the door. 'Come in!' cried Claus.
>
> "'Come out!' answered Jack, 'for you have a fire inside.'"

Jack of all trades and master of none

Jack, here, is generic for a common man. The expression, 'Jack of all trades,' which has a negative connotation, goes back to the 14th century. An example is in John Gower's poem *Confessio Amantus* (The Lover's Confession), 1390.

> "Therwhile he hath his fulle packe,
> They seie, 'A good felawe is Jacke.'"

The Oxford English Dictionary defines the medieval name 'Jack' at pretty much the bottom of the social ladder:

> "Jack - A man of the common people; a lad, fellow, chap; especially a low-bred or ill-mannered fellow, a 'knave.'"

Various trades were called 'jacks.' Lumberjacks, steeplejacks, and sailors were called Jack-tars. In the Middle Ages, about all trades used the word jack. 'Jack of all trades' was coined in 1612. It was then that Geffray Marshall wrote of his prison experiences in *Essayes and characters of a prison and prisoners.*

"Some broken Cittizen, who hath plaid **Jack of all trades.**"

'Master of none' was not added until the late 18th century. Martin Clifford, head-master of Charterhouse School, in notes on the poems of Dryden, 1677, wrote:

"Your writings are like a **Jack of all Trades** Shop, they have Variety, but nothing of value."

Then in 1770, *The Gentlemen's Magazine* included the line:

"**Jack of all trades** is seldom good at any."

The earliest known mention of the phrase as we know it today is in Charles Lucas's *Pharmacomastix*, in 1785.

"The very Druggist, who in all other nations in Europe is but Pharmacopola, a mere drug-merchant, is with us, not only a physician and chirurgeon, but also a Galenic and Chemic apothecary; a seller of druggs, medicines, vertices, oils, paints or colours poysons, &c. a **Jack of all trades, and** in truth, **master of none.**"

Jinx, you owe me a coke*

Jinx is a children's game thought to have originated in America during the 'Vaudeville days' of the early 20th century. Jinxing someone (causing the person bad luck) was an expression used as early as the 1930s. Jinx was played when two youngsters (or even adults) unintentionally spoke the same words at the same time. It has a number of variants or penalties, all proceeded by 'jinx': 'you owe me a malt, because it wasn't your fault,' 'you owe me a soda,' 'buy me a coke,' 'pinch or poke, you owe me a coke.' Some even said 'ten cents or a coke.' It was rarely taken literally, as hardly anyone actually bought the soda, though pinches and pokes were common. It became quite popular in the 1960s, particularly in the North and Midwest.

Johnny come lately

In old 17th-century English Johnnie or Johnny meant just a fellow, chap or 'bloke.' In the British army a new recruit was known as 'Johnny Raw.' Like 'Jack,' it was a common term for an average sort of male. By the 1880s it could refer to a man about town. Johnny come lately began being used in America by the 1830s to mean a new person in the area.

By October 1920 it was already considered a phrase used by 'old-timers,' as per this citation from an article titled 'The Little Big Horn or Why Custer Lost' in *Fur News and Outdoor World:*

> "Many a young officer from West Point ('**Johnny come Lately**' as the old-timers used to call them) asked for transfer to Ft. Lincoln for the good morals that reigned there.

Johnny on the spot

This means 'front and center,' or ready to do whatever, when it is needed. The first known printed reference is in *The New York Sun*, in April of 1896.

> "**JOHNNY ON THE SPOT**. A new phrase has become popular in New York."

Other citations began appearing around the same time in newspapers and authors' works.

Join the club!

Also 'welcome to the club!' This idiom is used to express a common unfortunate experience. Figuratively, it originated in the U.K. and has been in use since the late-1940s.

journey of a thousand miles begins with a single step, A

This saying, dating in the original Chinese to the 6th century BC, has never lost its validity. It is from *The Way of Lao-tzu*, a much quoted Chinese philosopher (604 BC - 531 BC). It reminds us that in order to accomplish any goal we must take the initiative to begin the effort.

Jumpin' Jehoshaphat!

Jehoshaphat is a king in the *Bible* who was the son of King Asa, and the fourth king of the nation of Judah in the divided kingdom of Israel (873-849 BC)—but this is not the true origin of the phrase. Jumping Jehoshaphat was used by the middle of the 19th century as a mild oath, and a euphemism for Jehovah, 'Jeho' being the initial sound of both names.

The phrase was first printed in the novel, *The Headless Horseman, or a Strange Tale of Texas,* by Thomas Mayne Reid, published in 1866, but is likely older. Today it is seldom used.

Jumping over the broomstick

This now-archaic comical expression for marriage was started in the ancient traditions of various nations known as simply 'jumping the broom.' These include African, Scottish, Hungarian and Gypsy cultures—which all included brooms at wedding rituals. This was most notably associated with the Rmoani Gypsy people of the United Kingdom, particularly those centered in Wales. In this culture, couples often eloped and would jump over a branch of flowering broom shrub to show that they had made their vows.

In Alex Haley's *Roots* TV mini-series in 1977 the slaves were depicted jumping the broom at the culmination of their nuptial ceremonies. This practice declined after the end of slavery in America due to the stigma.

Jump on the bandwagon

The word 'bandwagon' was coined in the U.S. in the mid-19th century for the wagon that carried a circus band. Circus great, Phineas T. Barnum used the term in his autobiography in 1855, *The Life of P.T. Barnum.*

> "At Vicksburg we sold all our land conveyances excepting four horses and the '**band wagon**.'"

The figurative term, 'getting aboard' or 'jumping on' the bandwagon came later, in the 1890s. Theodore Roosevelt made reference to this in one of his letters in 1899, which were published in 1951.

> "When I once became sure of one majority they tumbled over each other **to get aboard the band wagon**."

Jump ship

This phrase in a figurative sense means to abandon a job or a project before it is complete. It is derived from crew members in the past centuries that would jump overboard without authorization to avoid completing an undesirable voyage and attempt to swim to shore. An early figurative citation is from the *Bulletin of the Atomic Scientists*, December 1951, in an article titled *Scientists Have a Duty to Society* by Murray S. Levine:

"The human impulse to **jump ship** can be understood and be even be forgivable…"

Jump start

In a literal sense this is boosting off an automobile, or other mechanical device, by hooking booster cables to a battery which is low on power. Figuratively, it has come to mean reviving or giving new life to anything which has lost its ability to function on its own. It has been in literal use since the late 1970s, and figurative use since the 1980s. An early metaphoric example is from *The Museum Studies Journal* at John F. Kennedy University, Volume 1, Issue 4, 1984:

"The first year of the Seminar was the result of a strong '**jump start**' from academia, with Williamsburg representing one terminal and prestigious academic institutions the other.

Note that jump start is in quotes, usually indicating a fairly new, but known, expression.

Jump the gun

This idiomatic expression means to begin a project before the necessary preparations have been completed. The Americanism which preceded it, 'beat the gun,' derived from track and field events which were cued by the firing of a pistol, which began in the early 20th century. A very early example of a form of the phrase is from Crowther and Ruhl's *Rowing and Track Athletics*, 1905:

"False starts were rarely penalized, the pistol generally followed immediately on the signal 'Get set!' and so shiftless were the starters and officials that '**beating the pistol**' was one of the tricks which less sportsmanlike runners constantly practised."

The earliest known citation of the figurative phrase as known today is from *The Iowa Homestead*, November 1921:

> "Give the pigs a good start; **jump the gun**, so to speak, and get them on a grain ration before weaning time."

A clearer example comes from *Muncey's Magazine, Volume 83*, January 1925:

> "He might have hit the leading man, instead, and then I'd have felt responsible to his widows — all of 'em; so I decided to **jump the gun**."

Jump through hoops

This idiom, figuratively relating to overcoming obstacles to accomplish a goal, though used literally from the early 19th century, began being cited in this respect in the early 20th century from circus animals jumping through hoops at the command of their trainers. An early example is from *The Man Next Door*, 1918, by Emerson Hough:

> "The servants didn't look up to her pa and me very much, but they'd **jump through hoops** all the time for her."

Jump to conclusions

This means to make an assumption, usually incorrect, before obtaining all of the relevant facts. It has been around since the early 19th century. In *The Farmer's Magazine*, Boston, Friday, 31 August 1821:

> "They deal in broad assertains and flat denials—state premises to suit themselves and then **jump to conclusions**, at which they could never arrive any other way."

Ambrose Bierce wrote the following in what could have been a tale from an earlier day in *Fantastic Fables*, 1899:

> "Two Frogs in the belly of a snake were considering their altered circumstances.

> "'This is pretty hard luck,' said one.

> "'Don't **jump to conclusions**,' the other said; 'we are out of the wet and provided with board and lodging.'

"'With lodging, certainly,' said the First Frog; 'but I don't see the board.'

"'You are a croaker,' the other explained. 'We are ourselves the board.'"

jury is still out on that, The

This figuratively means that there is still not sufficient information to make an intelligent decision about a questionable subject.

This phrase was first used by *The New York Daily Times* in May 1850 in a literal sense.

> "The [Gardiner Trial] **Jury are still out**, with no prospect of immediate agreement."

Note the incorrect usage of a plural verb with a singular subject. It has continued to be used by newspapers in cases of trials to this day. The figurative usage, however, began in the U.S. in the 1940s, and has since become quite trite. One such example is from *The Terre Haute Star* in Indiana in a published report of a baseball game in July 1949.

> "**The jury is still out** on his [Orestes (Minnie) Minoso's] batting ability."

In the forties and fifties there are a number of such examples, but the infamous Finch-Tregoff murder trials from 1959-1961 in Los Angeles brought the phrase to full usage in the U.S., as it was then that it became a cliché that no one would forget. The juries in each of the three trials 'took their sweet time' in coming to a verdict.

Just chicken feed

Used to mean a paltry sum, especially in regard to money, and often in contrast with a larger amount. The earliest known citation is from *Life Magazine*, October 27, 1941, on page 39 in an article titled *A. F. of L. Ditches a Racketeer but Cannot Ditch its Critics*:

> "The misdeeds of Mr. Browne and his kind may cost the U. S. public millions of dollars, but this is **just chicken feed** to Thurman Arnold (right), head of the Department of Justice's anti-trust division."

Just desserts

This means 'what is deserved,' and originated in the 13th century when the word 'deserts,' spelled then with only one s, but pronounced like desserts, meant 'things deserved.' Hundreds of years later, in 1599, we find a printed citation in *A Warning for Faire Women*:

"Upon a pillory - that al the world may see, A **just desert** for such impiety."

Just give me the Reader's Digest (abridged) version***

Beginning in the spring of 1950, *Reader's Digest* began producing a series of what would become four books each season, in condensed form. These were initially called Reader's Digest Condensed Books. Over time it became popular in America to use the phrase, "Just give me the Reader's Digest Abridged (or Condensed) Version" when someone was dragging a story out too long. Many shortened this to merely "Just give me the Reader's Digest Version."

The saying was likely spawned from a comment made in *Reader's Digest* itself in 1975, Volume 106, page 2:

"Tell your story as succinctly as you can, then cut it by a third. If you think it cannot be done, take a novel you enjoyed and compare it page by page with the **Reader's Digest Condensed** Books **version.**"

An early example of this is on page 15 in Act 1 of the Australian play *Down an Alley Filled with Cats* by Warwick Moss, 1987:

"Timothy. It's a long story.
Simon. Could you **just give me the Reader's Digest version?**"

Just in the nick of time

A nick on something is a very small notch. This phrase has to do with a tiny notch of time in which something is accomplished before it would be too late to make a difference.

Around the 1560s 'in the nick' began to be applied regarding a critical moment. Arthur Golding used possibly the first example of 'nick' in this context in his translation of Ovid's *Metamorphosis*, (originally Latin and French) in 1565:

"Another thing cleane overthwart there commeth **in the nicke**:
The Ladie Semell great with childe by Jove as then was quicke."

It was a bit later that 'of time' was added to make the meaning clearer as demonstrated in Arthur Day's *Festivals*, (a book of sermons) in 1615:

"Even **in this nicke of time**, this very, very instant."

And it has been utilized that way ever since.

Just skin and bones (See: **Nothing but skin and bones**)

Just (or only) the tip of the iceberg (See: **Tip of the iceberg****)

Just what the doctor ordered

This means 'exactly what is needed at the time,' and has been an English idiom since at least the 1930s. An early printed example is found in *From a Colonial Governor's Note-book* a history of the Caribbean and West Indies by Sir Reginald St. Johnson, 1936:

"And the captain, who was thirsty, said: 'That's **just what the doctor ordered**,' and heroically tossed his down at a gulp, while the rest of us took a preliminary sip in order to get the full benefit of the new flavour."

From the contents, it could have been in use much earlier.

K

Katy bar the door

This phrase was in a poem by James Whitcolm Riley published in 1894, but was already in use prior to this time.

" *When Lide Married Him*

"When Lide married him – w'y, she had to jes dee-fy
The whole poppilation! - But she never bat an eye!
Her parents begged, and threatened - she must give him up - that he

Wuz jes 'a common drunkard!' - And he wuz, appearantly.
Swore they'd chase him off the place
Ef he ever showed his face
Long after she'd eloped with him and married him fer shore!
When Lide married him, it wuz **"Katy, bar the door!"**

It may have come from the traditional Scottish folk song. *Get up and Bar the Door*, published in 1776, in which a stubborn couple was arguing about who should 'bar the door.' However, this poem never uses the name 'Katy.'

Another suggestion is that it originates with Catherine Douglas and her attempt to save the Scottish king, James I. When he was attacked in Perth in 1437, the room in which he was kept had a missing lock bar. The story goes that 'Katy' Douglas tried to save him by barring the door with her arm. The discontented attackers broke her arm and murdered King James. Her story was told by Sir Walter Scott, and afterward the 'lass that barred the door' became known as Kate Barlass, and her descendants still use that name to this day.

Keep a stiff upper lip

From the height of the British Empire came the feeling that to do one's duty required that no emotion be shown. A stiff upper lip indicates such an attitude.

In 1935, P.G. Wodehouse published a novel titled *Stiff Upper Lip, Jeeves. The* first printed reference to this phrase, however, is actually American. It was in *The Massachusetts Spy* in Worchester on June 14, 1815.

"I **kept a stiff upper lip**, and bought license to sell my goods."

Later printed references are clearer as to the intended meaning of the phrase, though, such as one from the *Huron Reflector* in 1830.

"I acknowledge that I felt queer about the bows; but I **kept a stiff upper lip**, and when my turn came, and the Commodore of the P'lice axed [sic] me how I came to be in such company…I felt a little better."

Keep beating (or flogging) a dead horse

Originally 'flogging,' this phrase has been an English idiom since the mid-19th century. It means to keep 'harping' on an issue which has already been resolved.

The origin may most aptly be revealed in *The Fireside, Annual* published in London in 1877 by Rev. Charles Bullock:

"The man that was on his way, with a friend, to "Islington, N.," had heard many a time and again the allegory about **flogging a dead horse**, but here was the very sign and symbol, fact and parable, experience and moral."

And down a bit in the text the allegory is stated:

"Here was this nearly **dead horse**, and there was this stupid and cruel flagellator trying to whip it up into standing posture, **to flog it** back into life and power."

It had appeared in *Watchman and Wesleyan Advertiser* newspaper in London in 1859.

"It was notorious that Mr. Bright was dissatisfied with his winter reform campaign and rumor said that he had given up his effort with the exclamation that it was like **flogging a dead horse**."

Keeping up with the Joneses

This was inspired by a comic strip by Arthur 'Pop' Momand named 'Keeping up with the Joneses' in the *New York Globe,* first published in 1913. He had originally chosen 'Keeping up with the Smiths,' but changed the title before it was published. By September 1915, a short silent film had been produced by the same name, highlighting women's styles.

Jones, like Smith, was picked as a generic family because the name was so common, and the term merely means trying to keep pace in social standing with those in society that many may admire and/or idolize.

The idea spawned the E! Reality TV Series which began airing in 2007, *Keeping up with the Kardashians.*

Keep it under your hat

This odd-sounding but well-known saying originated at a time when it may have not sounded quite as strange as it does in the 21st century. It is recorded in a collection of stories published in London as *The Adventurer* in 1793, on page 309.

"By a sudden stroke of conjuration, a great quantity of gold might be conveyed **under his hat**."

It has commonly been told that the conception of hiding items under someone's hat came from the belief that British archers in medieval times used to store spare bowstrings under their hats to keep them dry. But the question would remain, what did this have to do with keeping secrets?

It seems more likely that this referred to keeping the secret in one's head. The earliest known printed reference to this is in *Nuttie's Father*, a novel by Charlotte Mary Yonge, published in 1885.

"Alice Egremont's loving and unsuspecting heart was so entirely closed against evil thoughts of her husband... while Nuttie, being essentially of a far more shrewd and less confiding nature, was taking in all these revelations... It was all **under her hat**, however, and the elder ladies never thought of her, Alice bringing back the conversation to Mrs. Houghton herself."

Afterward it was utilized by other writers in similar context. Another such expression is 'Keep it on the down low.'

Keep one's fingers crossed

The admonition to keep one's fingers crossed came from a custom which existed before the advent of Christianity, when in early European cultures the cross was a sign of unity and it was thought that peaceful spirits dwelt at the point of an intersection. It began by two persons crossing their index fingers to anchor a wish until it was fulfilled. Over the centuries the custom became simplified so that a person could make a wish on his or her own by simply crossing the index finger with the middle finger. In some circles the practice of two persons linking index fingers as a greeting still exists. Eventually it was sufficient to simply say, 'keep your fingers crossed' as a symbol of believing something will happen without actually doing it.

Keep the ball rolling

The original version of this phrase was British: 'Keep the ball up.' It alluded to keeping a ball in the air, or simply put, 'keeping an activity going.' An early figurative use of this phrase is found in a letter from social philosopher Jeremy Bentham to George Wilson in 1781 in regard to keeping a conversation going:

"I put a word in now and then to **keep the ball up**."

The Americanized version was made popular, as was the campaign slogan, 'Tippecanoe and Tyler too,' during the Presidential election of July 1840. Martin Van Buren had become unpopular, and was up against Whig candidate William Henry Harrison, who had become famous for his war against the Shawnee Indians at the Battle of Tippecanoe, and his running mate, John Tyler. Harrison was pictured with a log cabin, which could not have been further from his actual upbringing on a Virginia plantation. The theme song of his campaign, *Tippecanoe and Tyler Too,* went like this:

> *"Don't you hear from every quarter, quarter, quarter,*
> *Good news and true,*
> *That swift **the ball is rolling** on*
> *For Tippecanoe and Tyler Too."*

His caravan rolled from town to town with shiny ten-foot-diameter globes which were kept 'up in the air,' and his enthusiastic team chanted, 'keep the ball rolling.' Harrison was in, and 'Tyler too.' But when the newly elected sixty-eight-year-old leader gave a rousing two hour inauguration speech in the rain, he caught pneumonia and died, spending just over a month in office—the shortest presidency in U.S. history.

Keep the faith

This term in modern speech means continue to have hope regardless of what happens. It inspired songs by Michael Jackson and Bon Jovi. It is, however, of biblical origin. It is derived from *II Timothy 4:7* in which St. Paul writes to Timothy:

> "I have fought the good fight, I have finished the race, I have **kept the faith**." *(NIV)*

Keep those cards and letters coming in, folks

In early 1964 the song ***Keep those Cards and Letters Coming In*** was first released by Johnny and Jonie Mosby on Columbia, and first appeared in *Billboard* at number 48 in country hits for the week ending April 18. It was up to 16 by June 13.

On January 1, 1965, Ernest Tubb and Loretta Lynn released an album titled *Mr. and Mrs. Used to Be*, which included the song ***Keep those Cards and Letters Coming In***.

In 1968, Dean Martin brought together a group of young ladies who sang, danced and acted on his TV show, *The Dean Martin Comedy Hour*. They were

315

named the Golddiggers. They became so popular that they received much fan mail. Martin coined this phrase as we know it, in relation to their great popularity. The exact quote is:

"**Keep those cards and letters coming in, folks**, to these kids. They're great!"

As a result, it became a catchphrase meaning 'keep showing your appreciation for a job well done,' or 'continue sending in your contributions.'

Keep your chin up

This is another proverb with American origins. The first known printed reference to this was found in a Pennsylvania newspaper called *The Evening Democrat*, printed in October 1900 in a section on '…the health giving qualities of mirth.'

"**Keep your chin up**. Don't take your troubles to bed with you—hang them on a chair with your trousers or drop them in a glass of water with your teeth."

Apparently this section of the paper appealed to those of a certain age who had nothing better to do than to be amused with such stuff…especially considering the reference to 'teeth in a glass.'

Keep your eyes peeled***

This old idiom means that one should keep a vigilant watch out, and has been in use since the mid-19th century. The suggestion has been made that the idiom was coined during Robert Peel's organization of the first British Police force in the 1820s. The British police are called "Bobbies" in honor of Mr. Peel, and it has been said that were also called "Peelers" in the beginning, and that watching for them was keeping one's eyes "peeled." This derivation is problematic, as it ignores the obvious etymology of not allowing anything to come over the eyes, thus being clear-eyed and observant.

The premier version was actually "keep your eyes skinned," thus exhibiting this origin. The first citation of this form is from the *Congressional Record of the United States*, the First Session of the 22nd Congress, 7 December 1831, in the *Diary of Alphonso Wetmore* from 1828, used by the Secretary of War, Hon. Lewis Cass:

"'**Keep your eyes skinned** now,' said the old trapper, 'We are now entering upon the most dangerous section of the trace, the war ground of the Fanis, Osages, and Kansas.'"

The earliest printed reference known of "keep your eyes peeled" is from the Amherst College publication, *The Indicator*, Volume III, Number 7, February 1851, by Aaron Burr;

"My young friends," he would say, "women is dangerous. In the lump, they are to be kept clear of. However, **keep your eyes peeled**, and if you come across a virtuous woman to your taste, why, just blaze her."

Keep your friends close but your enemies closer

This means that one should keep close tabs on anyone whom he or she suspects may turn against or betray him or her, whether a supposed friend or an admitted enemy. In keeping such folks close a person may even have them feeling that they are considered friends and thus lull them into a false sense of security.

Claims of the origin of this cliché go back to Machiavelli in *The Prince*, published in 1515 and most commonly to Chinese military strategist, Sun Tzu in the sixth century BC. He did say something similar in *The Art of War*:

"It is said that if you know your enemies and know yourself, you will not be imperiled in a hundred battles; if you do not know your enemies but do know yourself, you will win one and lose one; if you do not know your enemies nor yourself, you will be imperiled in every single battle."

But, it is actually a quote from Michael Corleone in *Godfather II* in 1974.

"My father taught me many things here — he taught me in this room. He taught me — **keep your friends close but your enemies closer**."

Keep your nose clean

This American idiom, preceded by the British term, 'keep your hands clean,' relates to keeping away from undesirable influences which would bring down one's reputation and influence, and is applied most particularly to crime. The earliest known citation is from *The Globe* in Kansas City, Kansas, in May 1881:

"Mr. Lowell commenced railroading about sixteen years ago, as superintendent's private secretary, and by **keeping his nose clean**, brushing his clothes, and attending Sunday school regularly, he has succeeded..."

Keep (or hold) your nose to the grindstone

This term means to stay so very busy with work that there is little time for other activities. In spite of a theory that this was derived from millers checking millstones used in grinding grain to smell when it was burning by placing their noses to the stones, the most likely true origin is from the practice of knife sharpeners bending over the stones with their faces nearly touching the grindstones. The earliest known citation in print is from *A mirrour or glasse to know thyselfe*, by John Frith in 1532:

> "This Text **holdeth their noses so hard to the grindstone**, that it clean disfigureth their faces."

In *The Present State of Europe*, Volume 12, January 1701, we find the following statement:

> "Alas! poor Popes! they would fain preserve the Remainder of that usurp'd Authority which formerly they had over Sovereign Princes, so that when they meet with a Bigotted Zealot, they will be sure to **hold his Nose to the Grindstone**."

The phrase was common in Europe in the 18th century and in rural America by the early 20th century.

Keep your powder dry

This idiom means to save your resources until they are needed in order to be prepared for the genuine shortage.

It goes back to the 19th century and Oliver Cromwell's campaign in Ireland, when the soldiers had to keep their scarce gun-powder dry and be prepared for battle.

In *Ballads of Ireland*, in 1856, Edward Hayes wrote:

> "There is a well-authenticated anecdote of Cromwell. On a certain occasion, when his troops were about crossing a river to attack the enemy, he concluded an address, couched in the usual fanatic terms in use among them, with these words – 'put your trust in God; but mind to **keep your powder dry**.'"

Wet or wasted gunpowder could have spelled defeat.

19th century references to this phrase always gave the full context of the original—'Put your faith in God and **keep your powder dry**.' It seems that the primary admonishment was that they place faith in God first and foremost, as evidenced in this 1908 article from *The Times Literary Supplement* (London):

> "In thus **keeping his powder dry** the bishop acted most wisely, though he himself ascribes the happy result entirely to observance of the other half of Cromwell's maxim."

Kicking the can down the road

This is a 21st century universally understood metaphor for putting off something that needs badly to be done and which will have to be brought up again very soon, and possibly under more stringent circumstances. It began to be utilized by the news media in late 2010 in regard to the U.S. Congress and Senate moving financial reforms forward on their agenda. Then it blossomed in regard to the Bush Tax cut controversy and increasing the National Debt Limit forward into 2011 and in reference to the 'fiscal cliff' at the end of 2012.

It is derived from children playing a game with a tin can which is kicked a little at a time down a road or city street.

Kick someone to the curb

This metaphoric slang term indicates abandoning or getting rid of someone physically and emotionally as if the person were garbage placed out with the trash for removal. Though in use earlier, it started appearing in printed sources in the early 1990s.

Kick the bucket

One theory is that an ancient method of slaughtering a hog was hanging it upside down from a beam in a barn designed for this purpose, called a 'bucket.' In its death throes, the porker would naturally 'kick the bucket.'

Another belief is that a method of hanging oneself was to stand on a bucket after placing the noose around the neck, and kick the bucket away. The first theory has more merit.

The earliest mention available in print is from the *Gentleman's Monthly Intelligencer*, May 1780:

"Wentworth, *poor man*! he died very rich; his disease stuck so close to him that it has obliged him to **kick the bucket**, upon which there is a strange dust raised, and reflections are bandied about by his relations touching the will, who suspect there has been a good deal of shuffleing..."

Eight years later it was listed by Francis Grose in his *Dictionary of the Vulgar Tongue*, defined as 'to die.'

Kill two birds with one stone

Even killing one bird by throwing a stone would likely be rare. The intent, of course, is taking care of two needs with a single effort.

Though there were similar phrases used in English and French literature in the 16th century, the earliest known printed reference to this idiom, as we use it today, was by Thomas Hobbes in *A Work on Liberty* in 1656.

"T. H. thinks to **kill two birds with one stone**, and satisfy two arguments with one answer."

Kissing cousins

This is a Southern Americanism which goes back to before the Civil War. It means a distant cousin known well enough not only to be kissed when greeted, but also which could legally be allowed for consideration of marriage. (However, before the Civil War even first cousins could wed.) In the South, this still doesn't generally have to go very far back, and in the not-so-distant past, relationship was not viewed in the proper way. In reality, the children of first cousins are second cousins, and they have been deemed by past generations as third cousins, and even persuaded by other family members to marry. In many Northern states only eighth cousins are accepted as being distant enough to be legally joined. But the matter of cousin marriage is decided by individual states.

This practice, however, is much older in its beginnings. Cousins marrying each other was openly encouraged in the royal lines of Europe and even ancient Israel and Egypt. Some couples were even closer in relationship, such as the parents of King Tut, which were shown by DNA testing to have been siblings. Close relatives marrying has been known to cause a wide range of genetic disorders.

Worldwide, 10% of all marriages are still between first and second cousins.

Kit and caboodle / Whole kit and caboodle

These two words actually have similar meanings. A kit is almost like it sounds—contents in a pouch or container with necessities inside, such as a first-aid kit. It actually started with a soldier's kit-bag. The word caboodle, also called just 'boodle,' is now archaic. However, in the 1968 Oscar-winning movie, *Rachel, Rachel,* starring Joanne Woodward in the title role, when she had placed an order at a store she told the clerk, "I'll write you a check for the whole caboodle." It meant a group or collection, and usually referred to people. It had its origin in America, which is the only country where caboodle was ever used, except with kit, and similar terms are from as early as 1884. In *Grose's Dictionary of the Vulgar Tongue,* 1785, 'The whole kit' is recorded as 'the whole of a soldier's necessities, the contents of his knapsack.'

As early as the 1830s, citations are found in books and papers using just 'boodle.'

In the *Syracuse Sunday Standard*, in New York, in November 1884 we find this:

"More audiences have been disappointed by him and by the **whole kit-and-caboodle** of his rivals."

Then, in September 1888, *The Dunkirk Observer-Journal,* also in New York, contained an article titled '*The Origin of Boodle.*'

"It is probably derived from the Old-English word bottel, a bunch or a bundle, as a bottel of straw. '**The whole kit and boodle** of them' is a New England expression in common use, and the word in this sense means the whole lot. Latterly, boodle has come to be somewhat synonymous with the word pile, the term in use at the gaming table, and signifying a quantity of money. In the gaming sense, when a man has 'lost his boodle,' he has lost his pile or whole lot of money, whatever amount he happened to have with him."

Note that 'kit and boodle' was in 'common use' in New York by that date.

Kith and kin

Kith is derived from an Old English noun, cȳth, meaning familiar country, acquaintances and friends. It came from an old Germanic root noun. Kith is now obsolete as a word except in the idiom 'kith and kin', which as a phrase originally meant 'native land and people.' It first appeared in print circa 1377 in William Langland's *Piers Plowman,* an early source of Robin Hood legends.

321

Knee-high to a grasshopper

This means short, young, or both. The saying was one of many metaphoric analogies originating in the 19th century. One, 'knee-high to a toad,' may have been used as early as 1814. But the first known record in print of this phrase was from the U.S. Magazine, *The Democratic Review,* in 1851.

> "You pretend to be my daddies; some of you who are not **knee-high to a grass-hopper**."

Knock it out of the park

This figure of speech derived from hitting a homerun in baseball at a stadium when the ball goes outside the walls, thus bringing home all current runners. Metiphorically it means 'doing a great job.' When related to business it implies excelling beyond expectations. The phrase originated in America, as did the game of baseball. It has been used literally since the 1930s.

The figuratiuve usage took hold in the late 1990s, and an early example is from an ad for the 1998 Corvette published in magazines such as the July 1998 issue of *Yachting* on page 1:

> "We set out to design the ultimate Vette for enthusiasts and I think we **knocked it out of the park**."

Knock on wood

This expression, related to superstition, is used, usually with the speaker actually knocking on a wooden object such as a table or desk, to ward off bad luck. "I hope that never happens again, knock on wood."

This saying is of ancient origin, and likely related to the worship of trees by various civilizations. Some tribes believed that spirits either dwelt in, or guarded, trees, and these spirits protected the living.

Greeks felt that the oak tree was sacred to Zeus. Celtic peoples believed in tree spirits, and both taught that touching sacred trees would bring good fortune. The Irish folk lore states that touching wood is a way to thank the leprechauns for their luck. Pagan religions had similar beliefs. Both Chinese and Koreans taught that the spirits of mothers who died in childbirth returned to nearby trees.

The wooden cross as a symbol of good luck is actually an adaptation of the older Pagan belief, much like the Christmas tree being brought into the home around the winter solstice.

Perhaps a more direct cause for the current practice is that of the Jewish version. During the Spanish Inquisition, Jews took refuge in synagogues built of wood. To gain admission, they had to know and use a coded knock. Since this practice saved so many lives, it became common practice to 'knock on wood' for good luck.

Knock the wind out of someone's sails

This obvious nautical expression was derived from positioning one ship in front of another to slow it down by blocking the flow of wind to its sails. In a near-literal sense it means to hit someone so hard that their breath is cut off momentarily, thus bringing their movement to an abrupt halt. Another form is 'take the wind out of someone's sails.' Metaphorically, it means to destroy a person's advantage in an endeavor. It appeared in *Boy's Life* Magazine as early as October 1920 in an article titled *Courage* by Earl Reed Silvers:

"His announcement **took all the wind out of Tod's sails**."

Knock yourself out!***

The phrase "Knock yourself out" is now used in speaking to someone who is desperately seeking a way to accomplish something. It means, "Go ahead and try all you want, but you may not get it done, and it's probably not worth the effort." It is said to have originated in Harlem in the 1930s. The OED, however lists it as from 1942, meaning "to have a good time." Like many colloquialisms, the meaning has evolved over the years.

Know beans

There was an old riddle which would be told in country stores which went like this: How many blue beans does it take to make seven white beans? The answer was seven. When the seven blue beans are pealed, you have seven white beans. When the person said 'I don't know,' they were told, 'You don't know beans.'

The saying has come to mean that the person doesn't know anything about the subject at hand.

Knowing which side one's bread is buttered on

This was passed down by John Heywood in *A dialogue conteinying the number in effect of all the prouerbes in the Englishe tongue,* 1546:

"**I knowe on whiche syde my breade is buttred**."

It means 'I know where my loyalty lies. I realize who is responsible for my good fortune, and I will show that person or persons the greatest of respect.'

Knowledge is power

This quote from British author and philosopher, Sir Francis Bacon (1561 - 1626) appeared in *Religious Meditations, Of Heresies*, 1597. It has become a catch phrase for the fact that education gives much greater leverage in life and helps one to gain higher goals.

Know something like the back of one's hand

This means to know something so intimately that it feels like it is a part of you. The earliest known reference is from Robert Louis Stevenson's *Catriona* or *David Balfour*, 1893:

> "Thanks to Johnnie Cope and other red-coat gomerals, I should ken this country **like the back of my hand**; and if ye're ready for another bit run with Alan Breck, we'll can cast back inshore, and come to the seaside again by Dirleton."

Kudos*

This expression is singular, not plural as some have mistakenly supposed. It came from the Greek *kydos,* meaning honor, glory or praise, and entered into British university slang in the late 18th to early 19th century. The earliest known English citation in this vein is in the January 1794 edition of *Anthologia Hibernica*, Dublin:

> "Bassett expects **kudos** from the dean this term; but I think he will be badger'd for not attending Hornlby."

It first appeared in America in the early 20th century. It was in British author, Florence Luisa Barclay's *The Mistress of Shenstone*, published both by G. P Putnam in England and by Grosset and Dunlap in New York in 1910, where it was found on page 181:

> "...then the powers-that-be have a way of taking all the **kudos**..."

In the 1920s and '30s, *Time Magazine* cited it frequently, thus popularizing it in the U.S.

L

Lame duck

This metaphoric expression refers to any person or thing which is now unable to perform properly, especially one which was previously able to do so. It is most often applied to politicians who are in their final term in office, and even more likely to be used when the current office-holder has just lost an election. The original meaning, however, had to do with the Stock Market in London and refered to investors who were unable to pay their debts. The earliest known citation is from Horace Walpole's *Letters to Sir Horace Mann*, 1761:

> "Do you know what a Bull and a Bear and a **Lame Duck** are?"

A Selection of Leading Cases on Various Branches of the Law, 1855, makes the meaning clear:

> "'He is a **lame duck**,' meaning that he was incapable of fulfilling his contracts…"

Then in a few years later, though still used in the previous manner we see the present meaning come into play in *The Congressional Globe* entry for 14 January 1863:

> "In no event could it be justly obnoxious to the charge of being a receptacle of '**lame ducks**' or broken down politicians."

Land of milk and honey

This phrase is of biblical origin. In the Book of *Exodus*, Moses referred to the 'Promised land' of Canaan as a land flowing with milk and honey. The first reference is in *3:8:*

> "So I have come down to rescue them from the hand of the Egyptians and to bring them up out of that land into a good and spacious land, a **land flowing with milk and honey**—the home of the Canaanites, Hittites, Amorites, Perizzites, Hivites and Jebusites."

Other verses continue this theme, such as *Exodus 3:17, and 33:3.*

It is intended to represent a land of plenty, in which the descendants of Israel would want for nothing.

Through the centuries the term has been used to describe a place of great abundance. The phrase has spawned a number of songs, a motion picture, a novel and even a bar. Most notably, '*Milk and Honey*' was the title of a Broadway Musical in 1961 by Jerry Herman and Don Appell, and an album by John Lennon and Yoko Ono, released after Lennon's death, in 1984.

Land o' Goshen! (See My land o' Goshen!)

Last but not least

This phrase is used when the final performer or speaker is coming out to assure the audience that the reason for his or her being last was not because of inferiority. A similar phrase is 'we saved the best for last' (see). The idea in principle is biblical. In *Matthew 19:30* (John Wycliffe's version), published in 1382, we read:

"But manye schulen be, **the firste the laste, and the laste the firste**."

The earliest printed citation of a form of this phrase, however, comes from John Lyly's *Euphues and His England*, 1580.

"I have heard oftentimes that in love there are three things for to be used: if time serve, violence, if wealth be great, gold, if necessity compel, sorcery. But of these three but one can stand me in stead - **the last, but not the least**; which is able to work the minds of all women like wax."

Shakespeare also used a similar version of it in *King Lear* published in 1608, in a line spoken by Lear, himself:

"Now, our joy,
Although the last, not least; to whose young love
The vines of France and milk of Burgundy
Strive to be interess'd; what can you say to draw
A third more opulent than your sisters? Speak."

Laugh all the way to the bank (See: Cry all the way to the bank)

Laughter is the best medicine

Although the saying is not a direct quote from the *Bible*, the origin is there.

"A merry heart does good, **like medicine**, but a broken spirit dries the bones." – *Proverbs 17:22 (New KJV)*

In 1937, the BBC printed the following in Volume 18 of *The Listener*:

"Revival of Totem-worship —
Laughter is the best medicine for tyranny; but the world of 1937 rarely dared to laugh."

The thought was picked up by *Reader's Digest* (which began publication 2-5-1922) as the title for one of their regular features, which began appearing in the mid-1940s.

Lay an egg

In the early days of playing cricket, it was determined that 'a duck's egg' meant you had no runs. No score was a zero, which looked a lot like an egg. Now we use the term 'goose egg' to mean zero.

Today the term 'lay an egg' signifies failure.

Lead someone down the primrose path

This now somewhat archaic metaphoric saying stems from Shakespeare's *Hamlet*, Act III, Scene ii, 1602, in which Ophelia is speaking harshly to her brother, Laertes, regarding his near demands for her to resist the advances of Hamlet:

"Do not, as some ungracious pastors do,
Show me the steep and thorny way to heaven,
Whiles, like a puff'd and reckless libertine,
Himself the **primrose path** of dalliance treads
And recks not his own rede."

The term 'primrose path' refers to a life of luxury. The admonition against leading others into this lifestyle has to do with giving deception of false security by placing them into a situation in which a life of ease will be harmful by drifting them into irresponsible hedonism. It wasn't until the late 19th century when the phrase gained popularity, and 'leading someone down the primrose path' caught on. The earliest known example of this is in *A Tangled Chain* by Jane Ellen Panton, 1887:

"Yet when she became acquainted with Mrs. Verney, and recognised how much livelier and pleasanter her life would be now she had someone near her who 'knew all the ropes,' and could **lead her** triumphantly **down the primrose path** of pleasure, she forgot all her ideas on the subject of Mrs. Buckworth's virtues, and could only be thankful that she was not leaving home hampered by a girl..."

leap of faith, A

According to the Encyclopedia Britannica, 'Leap of faith' is "a metaphor used by the nineteenth-century Danish philosopher Søren Kierkegaard in his *Afsluttende uvidenskabelig Efterskrift* (1846; Concluding Unscientific Postscript) to describe commitment to an objective uncertainty, specifically to the Christian God. For Kierkegaard, God is totally other than man; between God and man there exists a gulf that faith alone can bridge..."

Kierkegaard, who lived from 1813 to 1855, formed a philosophy based on the importance of the individual and individual choice.

This premise is, however, a basic tenant of the Christian faith, and in order to totally embrace Christianity, this leap is necessary. Faith is the acceptance of a principle or belief without hard scientific proof.

The cliché spawned songs by Michele Branch and Kenny Loggins and a comedy film starring Steve Martin in 1992.

Learn the ropes

On sailing vessels in past centuries it was imperative to learn which ropes were for which purposes and know how to control them. This could prove a life-or-death situation in the event of a storm at sea.

Today it is used to refer to learning the ins and outs of any new venture.

Leave well enough alone

This cliché is a lot like 'If it ain't broke, don't fix it' (see). When a situation is going well, don't try to change it. When a product or service has reached a level of success that is difficult to top, there is no need to 'reinvent the wheel.'

It has been in use since at least 1917, when Canadian novelist, Lucy Maud Montgomery made use of it in a volume of her Anne of Green Gables series, *Anne's House of Dreams*:

328

"Don't you meddle with the matter. **Leave well enough alone**."

Left hand doesn't know what the right hand is doing, The

The thought of this originates in the *Bible*, in *Matthew 6:3;* in Jesus' much vaunted Sermon on the Mount:

"But when thou doest alms, let not thy **left hand know what** thy **right hand doeth**." (KJV)

Here, the purpose was the idea that gifts of charity should not be done so that others would see and give glory to the giver.

That view of selfless giving was reiterated by Henry David Thoreau in *Walden; or life in the woods,* published in 1854:

"If you should ever be betrayed into any of these philanthropies, do not let **your left hand know what your right hand does**, for it is not worth knowing."

Through the passage of time, the current cliché was developed, meaning that one member of an organization or a family wasn't aware of the actions of another.

Left holding the bag

To leave someone 'holding the bag' is a metaphor for someone who should be responsible walking away from another person, leaving him or her defenseless, taking the blame for something that had gone wrong. It dates to mid-18th century England, and was originally 'giving someone the bag to hold.' It referred to a gang of robbers who had stolen money, and as they were on the verge of being apprehended the one who had the bag of loot would hand it to another one, leaving him to take the blame while making a run for safety.

Left out in the cold

Figuratively, this means excluded or not informed about what is happening. In spite of printed origins in another major dictionary that this is from 1920, it has been used figuratively since February 26, 1875 when it appeared in Sir William Crookes' *Chemical News Journal of Physical Science* in an article on the Society of Public Analysts about the Sale of Food and Drug Act that year in Britain:

"At present, Scotland and Ireland are **left out in the cold**, although they have derived great benefit from the old measures; but I am sure that a provision will be made in the Bill to remedy any such inconvenience."

Even Harry S. Truman used it in his *Rear Platform Remarks in Montana* on September 30, 1952, later published in *Public Papers of the Presidents*:

"They want to get back in power so they can make this country the happy hunting ground that it was for the millionaires, so that the farmer and the workingman can be **left out in the cold** again, like they were back in the twenties and the early thirties**."**

Lemon (auto)

A lemon is an automobile which is found to be defective after it is purchased, and may apply to either new or pre-titled autos. The word 'lemon' in this fashion goes back farther than its usage as relating to cars. It was coined early in the 20th century in describing any defective item. Then, Julian Koenig, a highly acclaimed ad executive, used it in his 1950s Volkswagen 'Think Small' advertising campaign.

In the 1970s economist George Akerloff, a later Nobel Prize winner for this work, used the term in his 1970 paper, *"The Market for Lemons: Quality Uncertainty and the Market Mechanism."*

The attention Akerloff gave to the problem was instrumental in first 'lemon law' being proposed in California in 1980.

Lend me your ear(s)

This line, spoken by Mark Antony from Act III Scene II of Shakespeare's *Julius Caesar,* 1599, has become a cliché for asking someone to pay attention to what one has to say. The actual quote is:

"Friends, Romans, countrymen, **lend me your ears**."

The Beatles picked the line up in their popular 1967 song, *With a Little Help from my Friends*.

"…**lend me your ears** and I'll sing you a song."

leopard cannot change its spots, A

The meaning of this proverb is easy to decipher. Someone is what they are by their intrinsic nature. They don't usually change. Although some people really *do* change, the point is generally well-taken. You shouldn't fall 'hook line and sinker' (see) for someone's claim that they have changed until you examine their motives, and until they prove themselves.

This is another biblical paraphrase, and is from *Jeremiah 13:23a*.

"Can the Ethiopian change his skin, or **the leopard his spots**?"

Lesser of two evils

The saying 'the lesser of two evils' is an idea in politics and political science that of two poor choices, one is not usually as bad as the other.

Originally called 'the lesser evil,' the principle began as a Cold-War-era (between 1946 after the close of WWII, and 1991) pragmatic foreign policy belief utilized by the United States. To a somewhat less significant extent, it was also used by other countries during this time. It dealt with the way third-world dictators should be handled.

In our modern era, the idiom is often applied to political elections, but may be used of any derisive choice.

Let sleeping dogs lie

This metaphoric expression means once a scenario has played out it is usually better to 'let well enough alone' than to try to change it and possibly instigate trouble and make matters worse for all concerned. It is a quote and favorite saying from first British Prime Minister, Sir Robert Walpole (1676 –1745).

But Sir Robert is not the originator of the saying. A form of it was used earlier by Geoffrey Chaucer in *Troilus and Criseyde*, published in 1374.

"It is nought good a **sleepyng hound** to wake."

Then, John Heywood, in his second book of phrases, *A Dialogue Conteynyng Prouerbes and Epigrammes*, in 1592, recorded it much the same as:

"It is ill wakyng of a **sleapyng dogge**."

The thought actually has its roots in the biblical book of *Proverbs, 26:17* (KJV):

"He that passes by, and meddles with strife belonging not to him, is like one that takes a dog by the ears."

Let's run it up the flagpole and see if anyone salutes

This catchphrase, now a cliché, became popular in the U.S. in the mid-20th century (late 1950s and early '60s) and means 'let us present an idea and see whether it receives enough favorable reaction to proceed.'

Sometimes it is still used humorously with the knowledge that it will be seen as outdated, even by old-timers. It was associated with ad agencies on Madison Avenue in New York, and utilized by comedians poking fun at corporate America, along with such expressions as 'the whole ball of wax' (see).

It was used in the movie *Twelve Angry Men*, starring Henry Fonda, and Stan Freberg's 1961 comedy album, *Stan Freberg Presents the United States of America: The Early Years*.

Allan Sherman used this cliché in his 1963 parody of Gilbert and Sullivan's *When I was a Lad*.

"I worked real hard for the dear old firm, I learned most every advertising term. I said to the men in the dark gray suits, '**Let's run it up the flagpole and see who salutes**.'"

Let the cat out of the bag

There are two commonly accepted origins for this idiom. The first and most likely is that it came from the days when piglets were sold at markets in bags, and some would put cats in the bags instead. To let the cat out of the bag would expose the fraud. This is also where the saying 'buying a pig in a poke' (see) came from, and is referenced as early as 1530.

Another theory is that the cat referred to a cat o' nine tails which was used to flog unruly sailors in olden days. Though doubtful, this is remotely possible, as there are references to the cat o' nine tails for centuries before any use of letting the cat out of the bag. The nine tails are from the three ends of rope which were each tied off in three more knotted ends. The 'cat' refers to the scratches made by the horrible lashes it cut in the flesh of the victim's back.

Let the chips fall where they may

This metaphoric phrase originated in the late 1800s. What is certain is that it alluded to woodcutting and the falling of the chips made by the axe, but may have been coined in the medical profession. The idiom is usually prefaced by stating a current situation of which the outcome is uncertain. The speaker is indicating that regardless of the consequences, whatever happens will be left as is. There is likely nothing that can change fate. A related phrase borrowed from Spanish is 'que sera, sera' (what will be, will be).

The earliest known citation is from *Albany Medical Annals* (NY), Volume 17, 1896, and the quote is from the obituary of Doctor Henry M. Burtch, who had used it as his motto. Another very early reference is from *Transactions to the State Medical Society of Wisconsin*, 1899, Volume 33:

> "'Hew to the mark, **let the chips fall where they may**,' but let all discussion be prompted not merely by a desire to criticise, to find fault, or to differ with others, but by a firm determination on the part of every member to do his full share towards the advancement and diffusion of scientific knowledge, the promotion of public good, the elevation of our profession, and the furtherance of good fellowship."

This line may have indeed been the coining of the phrase, for it is repeated in a number of publications in the years immediately following, in several professions, and in *Medical Advance*, Volume 45, 1907, we find:

> "There was a time when Dr. Frank Kraft was animated by a noble enthusiasm for Homeopathy and the journal of which he is editor with its motto 'Hew to the line, **let the chips fall where they may**,' was a staunch defender of its truth."

Let the dead bury the dead

Figuratively, this means that we should not grieve about the past and should live in the present. It is another phrase of biblical origin. There are two records in the gospels which may or may not have referred to the same incident. In each case, a disciple asks Jesus for permission to leave and bury his father. Both scriptures state that Jesus answered by saying basically the same thing.

> "Follow Me, **let the dead bury their own dead.**" *Matthew 8:22, NIV*.

"**Let the dead bury their own dead**, but you go and proclaim the kingdom of God." *Luke 9:60, NIV.*

Many have called this a 'hard saying' of Jesus. It seems likely that Jesus sensed that the disciple was looking for an excuse to shirk duty in his service. Taking care of family in times of emergency was never forbidden in biblical days.

Let the punishment fit the crime

Different ideas have been passed around about the origin of this precise phrase. It is a very old principle in regulating judicial systems. The earliest form of this was in the Code of Hammurabi, which predated the Mosaic law of ancient Israel. The basis of the Code, as recorded earlier in this volume, was 'an eye for an eye and a tooth for a tooth.'

There is another story which relates to an old Chinese tale about a restaurant owner who sued the tenant of the apartment above his establishment who ate his rice while enjoying the smells wafting upward from his restaurant. The suit charged the man with stealing the smells of his food. The judge ordered the accused man to take a handful of gold coins and pass them from one of his hand to the other. The verdict seems to make the point that smells cannot be stolen. It may have been a prime example of the punishment fitting the crime in a frivolous case.

Let your hair down

Even the most sophisticated folks likely still enjoy 'letting their hair down' on occasion. In fact, members of the highest society are the ones who coined this phrase way back as early as the 17th century when women's hair was pinned up in elaborate hairdos. This meant spending hours fixing their hair, and multitudes of hairpins.

It was said that in 19th century France during the reign of Napoleon, the women of French nobility would have been fiercely condemned if they had appeared in public without their hair properly pinned. When they returned home, it was quite a relief to take out the pins and 'let their hair down.'

The earliest known reference to the look of women not properly groomed is John Cotgrave's *English treasury of wit and language*, 1655.

"Descheveler, to discheuell; to pull the haire about the eares."

Today, letting one's hair down means relaxing and having a good time.

Levelheaded

Originally 'level-headed,' it dates back at least to October, 1873 when it was used in regard to British professor, John Tyndall in *Popular Science Magazine*:

> "We regard him as one of the ablest physicists of the time, and one of the most **level-headed** philosophers that England has ever produced — a man whose intellect is as symmetrical as the circle, with its every point equidistant from the centre."

It means 'intelligent, calm and likely to make common-sense decisions.'

Level the playing field

This is derived from an earlier Americanism, 'on the level,' which first appeared in 1872 in George Burnham's *Memoirs of the United States Secret Service:*

> "On the level, meeting a man with honorable intentions."

To level the playing field means to give all involved in an endeavor equal chances of success. In a metaphoric sense, the earliest known reference is found in the *Tyrone Daily Herald* in Tyrone, Pennsylvania in January 1977:

> "Our philosophy is that we have no problem competing with the mutual savings banks if they **start from the level playing field**," Bolger said.

John Bolger was a lobbyist for the U.S. Bankers Association.

Liar, liar, pants on fire!

This is the most commonly quoted part of a derisive rhyme used by children. The entire chant is:

> "**Liar, liar, pants on fire**, hang them up on a telephone wire."

In theory, the idea was likely contrived from the idea of a liar burning in hell, as described in the *Bible* in *Revelation 21:9* (KJV):

> "...and **all liars**, shall have their part in the lake which burneth with **fire...**"

In reality, it is a short paraphrased version of the 1810 poem *The Liar* by William Blake. Here is the first verse:

"Deceiver, dissembler
Your trousers are alight
From what pole or gallows
Shall they dangle in the night?"

lick and a promise, A

This figurative phrase means that the person would do as little as possible now and come back and finish the task when they had more time. It was first recorded in print in 1860, by Walter White in *All round the Wrekin*.

"We only gives the cheap ones **a lick and a promise**."

Lick one's lips / chops / chomps

All versions of this old idiom refer to showing great pleasure over the anticipation of a future event, particularly when personal gain is expected. It is derived from animals, particularly dogs, licking their lips when awaiting a tasty meal or treat. It was used in a literal sense regarding people as early as the late 1700s.

The first known figurative citation is in *The Abridgement of the Debates of Congress from 1789 to 1856*, published in 1857:

"…but even then the trans-Alleghanian wilderness was rustling with the preparation of the savage, **licking his chops** in ambush, and hankering for the promised repast."

Lick one's wounds

This figurative term means to recover from hurt feelings after a defeat, rebuke or criticism. It is based in the ancient Greek and Roman belief that saliva has healing powers, and the fact that animals do indeed lick their wounds to heal them. In *The Works of Samuel Johnson, L.L.D.*, 1787 we find:

"Politics, the most vulgar of all topics, were alone excluded, The British lion was then **licking his wounds**, and we drank to the peace of old England."

336

Life begins at forty

This cliché has been around since at least 1932 when a book with that title was published, authored by W.B. Patkin, professor of journalism at Columbia University in New York. In 1937, a song sung by Sophie Tucker, written by Jack Yellen and Ted Shapiro also had this title, and the cliché was 'up and running' (see). 40 is an age often accepted as the beginning of midlife—a point which some dread worse than the proverbial 'seven year itch' (see). The fortieth birthday ushers in a time when some women refuse to divulge their age and men want to prove that they still retain abilities they had when they were younger.

Life is just a bowl of cherries

Life Is Just a Bowl of Cherries was the title of a popular song with music written by Ray Henderson and lyrics by Buddy G. DeSylva and Lew Brown. It was first published in 1931, performed by George Gershwin and revived in 1953 by Jaye P. Morgan.

The original song gave rise to the review of composer Henderson's music labeled *'It's the Cherries'* which launched the American Composer's Series in 2002.

The phrase came to be used as an expression meaning that all is going well and life is carefree.

Life is what you make it

"**Life is what you make it**, always has been, always will be" is a quote attributed to two strong American women from the same era: folk artist, Grandma Moses (September 7, 1860 – December 13, 1961), and U. S. First Lady Eleanor Roosevelt (October 11, 1884 - November 7, 1962).

The July 1930 issue of *Boys' Life* included the following in an ad on page 55:

"Vacation, like **life, is what you make it.**"

Actress Marilyn Monroe later said, "This **life is what you make it**. No matter what, you're going to mess up sometimes, it's a universal truth."

337

Life's a journey, not a destination

This reminds us that we are on a constantly changing voyage through life, and our goals and needs may change from time to time. Also, it means that we should enjoy it because we never know when it will end. It is a quote from American essayist, lecturer and poet, Ralph Waldo Emerson (May 25, 1803 – April 27, 1882).

Light as a feather

This simile is of ancient origin and means extremely light in either physical weight or texture. It was included in *Dictionary of Phrase and Fable* by E. Cobham Brewer in 1894.

Light at the end of the tunnel

This figurative expression has reference to going through dark tunnels along the road of life, and finally being able to discern a glimmer of hope. It was first coined in the early 1920s, and the earliest known citation in print is from *The Christian Register*, 1 September 1921:

> "Mr. Lloyd George is confident that the Washington Conference will not end in mere resolutions, but in a real pact of peace. He sees the **light at the end of the tunnel**."

It was popularized by American President John Fitzgerald Kennedy in the early 1960s in referring to U.S. involvement in the Viet Nam conflict.

Lightning never strikes twice in the same place

This proverbial saying can be either literal, or figurative. Literally, it has been proven untrue, though not very likely to actually occur. Figuratively, it means that an unusual event never happens twice to the same person. It was first recorded in *Thrilling Adventures of the Prisoner of the Border* by P. Hamilton Myers, 1857.

Then in *Orchard and Garden* magazine published by J.T. Lovett in Little Silver, New Jersey in July 1888 we find:

> "They say **lightning never strikes twice in the same place**."

338

It also appeared in *The Man in Lower Ten* by Mary Roberts Rinehart, 1909.

Lights are on and nobody's home

This is one of a number of hateful clichés used to indicate the belief that someone is failing to comprehend or react in the expected manner, often because they are preoccupied. It became popular in the late 20th century.

Like a bat out of hell

This has nothing to do with bats' supposed connection to blood-sucking vampires getting away from their victims to escape capture. The bat is essentially a harmless creature.

This earliest known citation of 'a bat out of hell' appeared in 1915 regarding the speed of a car. It is in *The Southwestern Reporter,* Volume 177, concerning decisions by the Supreme and Appellate Courts:

> "They went down onto Main Street and drove out south to Twenty-Third going at so rapid a rate that when they passed Henry McCain and J. H. Martin in another car McCain's attention was attracted to the speed, and he exclaimed: 'It's going **like a bat out of hell!'**"

The article later states that the speed of the car was estimated at 40 to 50 miles an hour—breakneck for 1915. This caused a fatal accident which resulted in a suit (Madding vs. State) which ended up in the Supreme Court of Arkansas on 17 May 1915.

The phrase refers to the uncanny speed of a bat in flight, and the 'out of hell' part is likely to have been added for effect, and probably referred to their abode in dark caves. The Greeks envisioned 'Hades' as underground. Others say it may have come from the German word höhle meaning cave.

Like a bull in a china shop

This means that the actions of a person are overly clumsy and/or careless, insinuating that he or she would break fragile items easily. This simile has been in use since the early 19th century. Some claim that the earliest known citation is from Frederick Marryat's novel, *Jacob Faithful* in 1834, however, it had appeared in many publications years before. As early as 1811, in *Heads of the People: or, Portraits of the English*, in an essay titled *Tavern Heads*, by Charles Whitehead, the following appeared:

"Wang Fong wouldn't much like John Bull to invite himself to tea in his territories; that would be **a bull in a china shop**, with a vengeance! we should pretty soon crack their canisters..."

Like a chicken with its head cut off

This, of course, is merely figurative, since chickens are not able to even walk after their heads are removed. Their nerves do jerk a bit though.

This phrase was known in the United States as early as the late 19th century, and appeared in print as a simile by the 1880s. It was used in an article about an escaped prisoner in *The Atlanta Constitution* in July of 1882.

"Finding himself free from the heavy shackles, he bounced to his feet and commenced darting about **like a chicken with its head cut off**..."

Like a fish out of water

This simile refers to someone in a position for which he or she is totally unsuited. It is very old, and a form of it was used by Chaucer in *The Canterbury Tales*: *Prologue,* 1386:

"...a monk, when he is cloisterless;
Is **like to a fish that is waterless**."

The earliest known reference to the current idiom is in *Pilgrimage*, by Samuel Purchas, 1613:

"The Arabians out of the desarts are as **Fishes out of the Water**."

Like a lamb to the slaughter

This means a person has been 'sacrificed' for a cause. It is taken from the *Bible* and referred to the sacrificial death of Christ. It is found both in the Old and New Testaments. In *Isaiah 53:7*:

"He was oppressed and he was afflicted, yet he did not open his mouth; **like a lamb that is led to slaughter**, and like a sheep that is silent, so he opened not his mouth." *(ESV)*

Then in *Acts 8:32*, when 'the eunuch' was reading the verses from Isaiah.

340

Like death warmed over

This means little better than if a person were dead. The earliest version of this expression, either following 'look' or 'feel' was 'like death warmed up,' which first appeared in *The Soldier's War Slang Dictionary* in 1939, which suggests that it may have a military origin. During the late 1940s, however, both 'warmed up' and 'warmed over' began to coexist in English slang. In 1947, Mary Collins published a book titled **Death Warmed Over**.

Like shooting fish in a barrel (See: **Shooting fish in a barrel**)

Like two peas in a pod

Also 'as alike as two peas in a pod,' this simile derives from the fact that peas in the same pod are virtually indistinguishable. A lot of times this has not only been said of twins, but of two friends or a couple who are inseparable due to their common interests.

Versions of this phrase date to the 16th century. John Lyly used a form of it in *Euphues and his England* in 1580.

> "Wherin I am not unlike unto the unskilfull Painter, who having drawen the Twinnes of Hippocrates, (who wer as **lyke as one pease is to an other**)."

'Pease' in the Tudor English of Lyly's day was the singular form, not plural. This brings to my mind the children's rhyme still being circulated as late as in the 1980s:

> "Pease porridge hot, pease porridge cold,
> pease porridge in the pot, nine days old.
> Some like it hot, some like it cold,
> some like it in the pot, nine days old."

The earliest version of this rhyme was in John Newberry's *Mother Goose Melody*, circa 1760.

Like water off a duck's back

This metaphoric saying has been in popular culture since at least the late 19th century and derived from the fact that ducks have oily feathers. When rain falls, or they are doused all over with water; even when they have been in a pond, lake

341

or river for hours and waddle ashore, the water not only runs off, but they appear totally dry.

The first printed reference known is from 23 May 1874 in *The Grey River Angus* reporting on a serious situation existing in Nelson, New Zealand regarding the Provincial Council and the government-owned Brunner Mine. Here is a clip containing the idiom:

> "This is one of the advantages of a non-responsible Government — that it can afford to allow hostile motions to glide **like *water off a duck's back*,** or rather like a pellet from the scales of an alligator."

In 1893 another article appeared in a New Zealand newspaper using the phrase. Then on 25 September 1894, the first reference known in an American publication was printed in the *Lawrence Daily Journal* in Kansas, in an ad for Pearline Soap placed by James Pyle.

> **"Like *water off a duck's back*** – so dirt leaves, when Pearline gets after it. No matter where it is, the easiest, safest, quickest and cheapest way to get rid of it is with Pearline. Washing clothes is Pearline's most important work."

'Like water off a duck's back' can refer to anything intended to cause adverse effects, but which the supposed victim ignored and allowed to have no effect whatsoever.

Like white on rice

All rice is originally brown, then by abrasive action the bran is removed and the rice appears white. To expose the white on the rice it requires decisive action. Usually this term is used to emphasize that a person is onto something or someone in a very quick and decisive manner.

This metaphoric expression began in the Deep South of the U.S. sometime in the mid-20th century. It was likely coined in Louisiana Cajun country and carried across the South. Then it was picked up by Kentucky-born Muhammad Ali, in the 1960s just after he changed his name from Cassius Clay. It was not intended to have racial implications, although some used it to apply to romances between Caucasians and Asians. It means being on top of the situation. It was picked up by Ike and Tina Turner in *Baby Get It On* in their album, *Acid Queen* in 1975.

> *Ike: "Now you're the finest girl I ever saw in my life. I want to stick to you **like white on rice**, so come on."*

> *Tina: "Ah-huh."*

It was also used in Whodini's dance hit; *The Freaks Come Out at Night* in 1984:

"Now the party's jumpin,' the place is packed
And when the crowd's like this, I'm ready to rap
But before I could bust a rhyme on the mic
Freaks are all over me **like white on rice**."

Lion's share

The idiom 'the lion's share' means the greater portion of anything. It has its origin in a number of *Aesop's Fables*, in which the lion claimed the greatest portion on the spoils when hunting with other animals. Aesop lived from 620 to 564 B.C., and is credited with several of our common idioms.

little bird told me, A

The basis of this saying is from the *Bible*. Solomon wrote in *Ecclesiastes 10:20* that we should not curse the king, or the rich, even in private, or 'a bird of the air' may report what we say. Being one of the most powerful kings of the day he had the authority to squelch such gossip aimed his way.

little knowledge is a dangerous thing, A

The two synonymous proverbs, 'a little knowledge is a dangerous thing,' and 'a little learning is a dangerous thing,' have been around since the 18th century.

The latter, the original, is attributed to Alexander Pope (1688-1744). It was first printed in *Essay on Criticism*, 1709:

"**A little learning is a dangerous thing**; drink deep, or taste not the Pierian spring there shallow droughts intoxicate the brain and drinking largely sobers us again."

In an article in *The monthly miscellany; or Gentleman and Lady's Complete Magazine, Vol. II*, 1774, the writer misquoted Pope, using the word 'knowledge' instead of 'learning':

"Mr. Pope says, very truly, '**A little knowledge is a dangerous thing.**'"

Still, it was claimed that Francis Bacon originated the saying earlier.

Little pitchers have big ears

This is a word play on the fact that the handle of a pitcher looks a bit like an ear, and children are likely to be about when adult conversations take place that are not intended to enter their 'pitchers.' This is another one recorded by John Heywood in *A dialogue conteinyng the nomber in effect of all the prouerbes in the Englishe tongue*, his first such book, in *1546*.

"Auoyd your children, **smal pitchers haue wide eares**."

Live and let live

This saying is first referenced as a 'Dutch proverb' in 1622 by Gerald De Malynes in *Ancient Law-Merchant* (The Merchants' Almanac):

"According to the Dutche prouerbe…Leuen ende laeten leuen, To **liue and to let others liue**." (To live, let others live)

A few years later, in 1641, it was listed by David Fergusson in *Scottish Proverbs*. Then, in 1678 by John Ray in *A Compleat Collection of English Proverbs*.

Live the life of Riley

Though archaic now, in the 1950s this was still very common in the U.S. to mean a life of ease and prosperity. This phrase, according to some, was popular as far back as the 1880s in England, when the poems of James Whitcomb Riley depicted comforts of prosperous home life. Indeed, he may have been the original 'Riley.' It was spread with the Irish /American soldiers in the U.S. Army during WWI.

The first known published citation is in a letter from a Pvt. Walter J. Kennedy who was stationed at Camp Dix, New Jersey, which was published in *The Syracuse Herald* on June 29th, 1918 under the heading, 'Great Life, Writes Soldier at Camp.'

"This is surely one great life, We call it ***the life of Riley***. We are having fine eats, are in a great detachment and the experience one gets is fine."

Later that year *The Bridgeport Telegram* published a letter from Pvt. Samuel S. Polley, who was stationed in France.

"They [German officers] must have led **the life of Reilly** as we caught them all asleep in beds…"

The phrase reached the wider public via the 1919 song by Howard Pease:

> *"My name is Kelly*:
> "Faith and my name is Kelly, Michael Kelly, but I'm **living the life of Reiley** just the same."

Living hand to mouth

This means not knowing where one's next meal will come from and originated during great famine in the 16th century in Britain. It was called this because people were so desperate that when someone was able to obtain any small amount of food it literally was taken by the hand and placed directly in the mouth. It was referenced in print as early as 1658 in *Two Books of Mr. Sydrich Simpson*, Minister of Cambridge, in the second book: *Faith or, believing, is Receiving Christ* on page 154:

> "It is a mean thing in its self for a man to live dependantly, & to have nothing but **from hand to mouth**."

Now this may be used much like 'living paycheck to paycheck.'

Living high on the hog

'High living' has been in English vocabulary for many centuries as the lifestyle of the wealthy. 'High on the hog,' however has only been used since the early 20th century and is thought to have been derived from the fact that the better cuts of pork come from higher on the hog, as mentioned in this excerpt from the *New York Times* in March 1920:

> "Southern laborers who are 'eating too **high up on the hog'** (pork chops and ham) and American housewives who 'eat too far back on the beef' (porterhouse and round steak) are to blame for the continued high cost of living, the American Institute of Meat Packers announced today."

Eight years earlier, in 1912 in *History of Roanoke County,* page 29, by George S. Jack and Edward Boyle Jacobs this variant appeared:

> "With all the tenderloin, spareribs and backbones, we **lived 'high off the hog.'**"

Living on borrowed time

This phrase is used to indicate that one has lived beyond the normal life expectancy. The earliest known printed reference is from *The Indiana Progress*, in Indiana, Pennsylvania, in September 1886:

> "We may be care-worn and aged, forsaken of the world, **living on borrowed time**, useless so far as any activity is concerned, dependent on children, or friends; yet Jesus has loving acquaintance with us."

Even more figurative use includes anything which has lasted past its expected duration.

Living on the edge

Usually applied to 'living dangerously' without concern to the results, though at times it may mean that one is figuratively in a precarious position involuntarily. The earliest known citation in print is from *Sylla, a tragedy*, 1829, a play in five acts translated from the French of Etienne de Jouy by Victor Joseph, scene VIII, page 111:

> "From crime to crime — Ah! I indeed am tired
> Of **living on the edge** of such a precipice!"

Loaded for bear

Loaded for bear is a cliché meaning to be ready for whatever comes, even when anticipating a fight, or the worst case scenario in the challenge at hand. It is derived from the old frontier days when barrel-loaded muskets were used for all sorts of game, but when hunting bear, the woodsman knew to pack in a powerful amount of gunpowder before adding the metal shot. The earliest known printed reference to the figurative phrase is from the Masonic publication, *Transactions of the Annual Convocation of the Grand Chapter of R.A. Masons* (Michigan), 1881, page 107, and is rife with of figures of speech:

> "The report on Foreign Correspondence is the work of a veteran, but can not say now whether a neophyte could have wielded those sissors as ably as did the veteran chairman—fact is, Companion Innes is always **'loaded for bear'** when his game is nothing but chipmunck or prairie hen..."

The quotations represent the fact that the idiom was already known to some degree.

Lo and behold!

This somewhat archaic expression has a meaning like 'Look! That is astonishing!' It first appeared in English between the 8th and 11th centuries in the anonymous epic poem, *Beowulf*, at the beginning of Chapter XXIV:

"BEOWULF, SON OF Ecgtheow, then spoke: '**Lo and behold!**'"

A similar context is found in the 1611 *King James Version* of the *Old Testament* scripture text of *Genesis 15:3*, attributed to Moses about 3000 BC in words quoted as being spoken by the patriarch Abraham even earlier.

"And Abram said, **Behold**, to me thou hast given no seed: **and, lo**, one born in my house is mine heir."

Locking the stable door after the horse has bolted (or **the mule has gotten out**)

In the American South the form used is 'after the mule has gotten out,' but in other locales 'after the horse has bolted,' is more common. This humorous metaphoric proverb applies to taking action on an important matter after it is too late to make any difference. It has been around in English since Medieval times. It all started by the idea of a stolen horse. The first version of this proverb is from William of Wykeham in the Franciscan manuscript known as *Douce MS 52* (no. 29), in 1350:

"When the hors is stole, steke the stabull-dore."

Other versions followed including John Lyly in *Euphues* I. 188, in 1578:

"It is to late to **shutte the stable doore** when he **steede** is stolen: The Trojans repented to late when their towne was spoiled."

Other citations using 'stolen' remained to be printed even through the 19th century. The term 'bolted' only appeared in the 20th century as in the two following references.

From the crime drama, *Death of a Peer* by 'Dame Edith' Ngaio Marsh, in 1940:

"**The horse** having apparently **bolted**, I shall be glad to assist at the ceremony of **closing the stable-door**."

Then we get to our modern version in the language quarterly publication, *Verbatim* Winter, 1979-'80:

"It is too late to **shut the stable door after the horse has bolted**."

Lock, stock and barrel

The first known recorded mention of this expression, meaning 'the whole thing' was British from *Major Jones' Courtship* by W.T. Thompson, published in 1842.

"All moved, **lock stock and barrel**."

The saying is derived from the three parts of a musket, the common gun of that era, a simple devise consisting of a lock, or latch and pin to release for firing, the stock, or stick, a wooden handle used to place against the shoulder when firing, and the cylindrical metal barrel (a name derived from a beer barrel) through which the ball fired.

This book is also the source of the coining of the word 'goatee,' which was adapted from the appearance of a goat's beard.

Long row to hoe (See: **Tough row to hoe vs. Long row to hoe**)

Look before you leap

In spite of the belief that this originally applied to being cautious when jumping on a horse's back, the original meaning seems to have nothing to do with horses. This proverb was first recorded in the 1350 Franciscan manuscript, *Douce MS 52* (no. 150):

"**First loke and aftirward lepe**."

This 1528 entry in William Tyndale's *Obedience of Christian Man,* it is evident that it was used both literally and figuratively:

"We say '**Loke yer thou lepe**,' whose literall sence is, doo nothinge sodenly or without avisement."

In John Heywood's *A dialogue conteinyng the nomber in effect of all the prouerbes in the Englishe tongue,* 1546, it plainly has to do with entering too quickly into a marriage; exactly how it is often used today:

"And though they seeme wives for you never so fit,
Yet let not harmfull haste so far out run your wit:
But that ye harke to heare all the whole summe

348

That may please or displease you in time to cumme.
Thus by these lessons ye may learne good cheape
In wedding and all things to **looke ere ye leaped**."

Look down one's nose at

This means to consider another person inferior to one's self. It has been used figuratively in English since the 1920s, and an early example is from *Ladies' Home Journal*, Volume 43, Part 1, April 1926:

"You at least do not **look down your nose at** the journalist."

Looking at the world through rose-colored glasses

A major dictionary states that this was first recorded in 1861, in Thomas Hughes' sequel to *School Days at Rugby, Tom Brown at Oxford,* posted here:

"Oxford was a sort of Utopia to the Captain. He continued to behold towers, and quadrangles, and chapels, **through rose-colored glasses**."

However, it appeared at least twenty-six years earlier in Mary Baddington's *Slight Reminiscences of the Rhine, Switzerland and a Corner of Italy*, Volume 2, page 125 (1835).

"What a delicious thing it is to be young, and to **see every thing through rose-colored glasses!**"

Looking for a needle in a haystack

This 'old saying' means that finding something is virtually impossible. It has been around since before November 1840 when it was printed in *Southern Literary Messenger* in a story titled "The German's Daughter": Thomas White, Richmond, VA:

"To seek for us abroad, would be '**looking for a needle in a haystack**.' We are therefore separated forever!"

The quotation marks indicated that the saying was known earlier.

Looks like the cat that ate the canary

This means a person who appears smug, especially while hiding something mischievous or private. The earliest known reference in print to a version of it is from 1910 in as article titled 'Cotton Bulls Stand Shock of Deliveries' in the *New York Times*, April 30th, on page 2:

"He talked freely and carried the smile of the **cat that swallowed the canary.**"

Look what the cat dragged in

Until the last few decades, it was common for house cats to go out in search of prey, whether mice, chipmunks, birds, or other small, helpless creatures. They had a tendency to proudly drag their find into the house all covered with their saliva, and a bit tattered, and knock it around playfully.

When someone not around for a while would visit, possibly appearing weatherworn, a humorous greeting became, "Look what the cat dragged in."

Though the exact origin is unclear, this common saying has been around since the early 20th century and is freely used in both the U.K. and the U.S. An early example is from *The Railroad Telegrapher*, Volume 30, Part 1, 1913:

"Minnesota Division Notes:
"**Look what the cat dragged in**. Brother D. J. Mahoney has resigned and the duties of division correspondent has fallen on my head."

Loose cannon

Beginning in the 17th century, the British ships of war had cannons as their primary offensive weapons. They were mounted on rollers and secured to the ship with ropes. The phrase 'loose cannon' derived from actual cannons on the ships which came loose from the ropes and were rolling about the deck causing danger to the crew. In a different sense, speaking of the balls, 'loose cannon' was used in 1838 in *Damascus and Palmyra* by George Greenstreet Addison (pages 165-166):

"Piles of marble cannon-balls and some '**loose cannon**' were laying about them..."

The English translation of Victor Hugo's 1874 French novel, *Ninety-three* described such a scene in regard to the weapon itself, without using the actual phrase. Then in 1875, the first literal English use of 'loose cannon' came in Henry Kingsley's novel, *Number Seventeen,* giving credit for the thought to Hugo:

"At once, of course, the ship was in the trough of the sea, a more fearfully dangerous engine of destruction than Mr. Victor Hugo's celebrated **loose cannon.**"

The earliest known figurative use is found in *The Galveston Daily News* in Texas, December 1889:

"The negro vote in the south is a unit now mainly because it is opposed by the combined white vote. It would in no event become, as Mr. Grady once said, "a **loose cannon** in a storm-tossed ship."

Loose lips sink ships

This idiom, which means 'Be careful what you say, for it may fall upon the wrong ears and be used against you,' was coined during WWII as an American slogan to encourage people to be cautious not to give information to someone who could be an enemy of the country. Originally, it was 'Loose lips *might* sink ships.'

Below is an example found in a Maryland newspaper called simply, '*The News*' and was printed in May 1942:

"As countians [attendees at the local county school] registered in the high school lobby before the opening of the meeting, they were surrounded on all sides by placards bearing such admonitions as '**Loose Lips Might Sink Ships,**' 'Defense On The Sea Begins On The Shore,' 'Defense In The Field Begins In The Factory' and patriotic creeds and slogans."

Lose one's marbles

This idiom for indicating that one's mental capacity is waning evolved from the idea that for a lad in the 1800s, marbles were extremely important. It would be like saying today that a child lost his DS or his iPod. Marbles were often a child's most prized possession. An early citation of this figurative usage is from an August 1886 edition of the *St. Louis Globe-Democrat*:

"He has roamed the block all morning like a boy who had **lost his marbles.**"

Around this time, 'losing one's marbles' began to be used for getting upset or angry. In Lawrence, New Zealand, *The Tuapeka Times*, carried the following statement in August 1889:

"For I tell you that no boy ever **lost his marbles** more irrevocably than you and I will lose our self-respect if we remain to take part in a wordy discussion that ends in a broil. *[a quarrel]*"

The change in meaning to 'losing one's mind' began in the U.S. around the same time and the Ohio newspaper, *The Portsmouth Times*, did a story in April 1898, referring to marbles in the context of 'mental capacity':

"Prof. J. M. Davis, of Rio Grande college, was selected to present J. W. Jones as Gallia's candidate, but **got his marbles mixed** and did as much for the institution of which he is the noted head as he did for his candidate."

Both meanings were used simultaneously for a number of years, and by 1927, the loss of sanity definition had taken precedence, and one edition of Duke University's journal, *American Speech* defined the phrase without any doubt in this manner:

"Marbles, doesn't have all his (verb phrase), mentally deficient. 'There goes a man who **doesn't have all his marbles**.'"

Losing face

In the 18th century, women wore bees wax on their faces to smooth out their complexions. When they sat too close to the fire, the wax would melt. Therefore, the expression 'losing face' came to be in a literal sense in Europe and Colonial America. Figuratively it came to indicate declining in popularity or honor in the eyes of others, and was first commonly used in this manner in China. This early example is from William Jennings Bryan's *The Old World and Its Ways*, 1907:

"The most grievous misfortune that can befall a Chinaman is to '**lose his face**.' Its meaning is mortification at failure.

In the Presbyterian publication, *The Chinese Recorder and Missionary Journal,* Volume 39, Shanghai, 1908, we find:

"There is a Chinese expression about '**losing face**.'"

Loud enough to wake the dead

Though this may have its origins in the cry of Jesus when commanding Lazarus to 'come forth' from the grave (*John 11:44*), as an English idiom it goes back to the late 18th century. The earliest known printed reference is from *Saratoga: an Indian Tale of Frontier Life* by Daniel Shepherd, 1787, page 64:

"But there was no other way; so, jumpin' on a big stone in the middle of the path, I gives a screech **loud enough to wake the dead**."

Love conquers all*

This is from the old Latin platitude, *amor vincit omnia*. In circa 1599 the Italian artist, Agostino Carracci, painted a striking work named *'Onmia vicit amor.'* But the saying goes back much further, to Virgil's *Tenth Eclouge*, line 69, 70 BC. The thought of love conquering all is paramount to religion and philosophy throughout history, and blends with the writing of St. Paul in *chapter 13* of the *First Epistle to the Corinthian Church* written circa 96 AD. Particularly see *verse 8*: "Love never fails." Also his Epistle to *Titus, 1:15*: "To the pure, all things are pure…" (*Omnia munda mundis*) (*Both, NIV*)

Love is blind

This one is from Shakespeare. It must have been a favorite line, because he put in several of his plays. Here are a few lines from *Merchant of Venice*, 1586.

"JESSICA: Here, catch this casket; it is worth the pains.
I am glad 'tis night, you do not look on me,
For I am much ashamed of my exchange:
But **love is blind** and lovers cannot see
The pretty follies that themselves commit…"

Love makes the world go 'round

This proverbial saying is based on the fact that love, in its truest form, is the primary source of contentment for mankind. The phrase has been the title of a number of songs, beginning with one in 1896 with lyrics by Clyde Fitch and melody by William Furst (which was the coining of the phrase).

Love me, love my dog (or cat)

More often than not, it seems, females are cat people and males are dog people, if they are both prone to pets.

The original, however, was 'dog.' It was first coined in a time when males dominated relationship, and cats could stay in the barn and catch mice. Though it was passed down by John Heywood in his 1546 book of proverbs, it is quite a bit older, and was used in a sermon by St. Bernard of Clairvoux in Latin in the 12th century:

> "...*qui me amat, amat et canem meum*," which means, 'who **loves me, also loves my dog**.'

Heywood's version read thusly:

> "He that **lovyeth me lovyeth my hound**."

A word play on this was used by MGM as the title of a Tom and Jerry Cartoon in 1966, "*Love Me, Love My Mouse*."

The phrase with 'cat' came into usage in modern days when women cat owners began to take greater dominance in the conditions of relationships. This new twist spawned everything from T-shirts to patchwork quilts.

Lower than a snake's belly (in a wagon rut)

The fact that a snake slithers on the ground made this the perfect simile for low. Then adding 'in a wagon rut' gets below ground level. It means 'you can't get lower than this' and usually refers to a person's corrupt character, but can also mean that someone feels really poorly.

The metaphor is an Americanism which qualifies as an 'old saying' and the wagon rut indicates about how far back it goes. The earliest known citation in print, however, is from *Everybody's Magazine*, December 1924:

> "I could handle six like you, if they didn't have guns! Men? The only thing about you that's a man's is your pants! You're **lower than a snake's belly**, and that's pretty low!"

The idiom was also used to refer to military planes flying extremely near the ground.

Lower the boom*

This idiom is used to indicate a harsh scolding or punishing for an infraction. It is originally, like many terms, nautical, from booms or long beams used on ships. In the theater this refers to a large pole used backstage to move furniture. But the most dangerous boom is the one used on a crane or hoist. Lowering a hoist boom on someone's head would be disastrous, even ending in death.

The earliest known printed figurative reference is from *A Merchant Seaman Talks: My Name is Frank*, by Frank Laskier, 1941, page 41:

> "They pulled their boat alongside, and McCarthy climbed up the blistered side of this tramp, up the Jacob's ladder, on to the deck and up on to the bridge, and there, to use our own expression, he **lowered the boom** on the ship's company..."

Low man on the totem pole

The last person to be hired by an employer usually gets 'no respect' like comedian Rodney Dangerfield always harped about—but he's not the one who thought up this one. It was likely an earlier funnyman named Fred Allen who first coined it in his act, and it 'went viral,' as we would say today. But it has nothing to do with a totem pole. In fact, the opposite is true—the bottom carving on a totem pole is actually considered the most important figure. Lowest is highest in honor.

Luck is when opportunity meets preparation

This is a quote from modern American composer Eric Beheim. It is based upon the fact that 'luck' is normally a misnomer, and a similar phrase is 'we make our own luck.'

Lying through one's teeth

This figurative expression has been in use since at least 1950. An early example is from *American Magazine*, Volume 150, that year, on page 140:

> "...there," Keane said, his tone a trifle grim, "before we swallowed a classic red herring, hook, line, and sinker. The boy was **lying through his teeth**. We all know it."

The meaning seems clear. Lying through one's teeth indicates that the untruth is very intentional. The person speaking is putting on a façade of friendliness and smiling while hiding the wicked truth. It seems that this expression is the same in a number of societies.

M

Madder than a wet hen

Again, similes and metaphors are difficult to pin down for origin, but it is likely that this originated in the Southern Appalachians. It is common mountain belief that chickens get angry when they are dumped into a tub of water. When Southerners use this phrase they mean that someone is as irate as one can imagine.

Maintain the status quo

This is one of several using Latin expressions commonly referred to by English-speaking people, likely as often as many all-English idioms. This means keeping things just the way they are, often refusing new ideas, even if for the better. It has been in use since at least the early 19th century when an article in the *Edinburgh Review* (Scotland) stated:

"**The status quo was to be maintained** in Luxembourg during negotiations regarding that duchy."

Make a clean breast of it

Meaning to be truthful and confess everything, this goes back to 1753, when *The Scots Magazine* printed the following:

"He pressed him to **make a clean breast**, and tell him all."

Make a long story short

Often, when telling an anecdote, this old English idiom is used to get to the point. Originally it was 'to cut a long story short,' a version still used in England and Australia. The idea of making long stories short dates as far back as the 14th century when Chaucer wrote the Canterbury Tales. The current version was used by Henry James in his comic short story, *A Bundle of Letters* published in the *Parisian Magazine* in 1878; Robert Louis Stevenson in *Treasure Island* (1883), and by Edgar Rice Burroughs in *Tarzan of the Apes* (1914).

Make a mountain out of a molehill

This oft-used saying refers to making a 'big deal' out of something insignificant. The first recorded English usage was in 1548. Before that, a mole was known as a 'wand,' later changed to 'want.' A molehill was called a 'want thump.' Still later the name for mole was changed to 'moldewamp,' meaning 'earth thrower.' This was shortened to 'molle.'

The idiom is first found in Nicholas Udall's English translation of *The first tome or volume of the Paraphrase of Erasmus vpon the newe testament*, 1548, recorded below:

> "The Sophistes of Grece coulde through their copiousness **make** an Elephant of a flye, and **a mountaine of a mollehill**."

It was later recorded in *Foxes Book of Martyrs*, 1570.

Make ends meet

This applies to surviving financially in difficult economic times. It goes back to at least the 17th century. Though from the context it seems that the phrase was already in use, the earliest known citation is from Thomas Fuller's *The History of the Worthies of England,* circa 1661:

> "Worldly wealth he cared not for, desiring only to **make both ends meet**; and as for that little that lapped over he gave it to pious uses."

Make hay while the sun shines

This may be used either literally or figuratively. It comes from John Heywood's *A dialogue conteinyng the nomber in effect of all the prouerbes in the Englishe tongue*, 1546.

> "**Whan the sunne shinth make hay**. Whiche is to say.
> Take time whan time cometh, lest time steale away."

Quickly becoming a cliché, like many other such proverbs, in 1673 it was cited in a figurative, non-farming context by Richard Head in his glossary containing phrases formerly used by thieves and vagabonds, *The Canting Academy*:

> "She ... was resolv'd ... to **make Hay whilest the Sun shin'd**."

Make heads or tails of...

This saying is derived from the coin toss to decide a matter. It either lands on heads or tails. If one 'can't make heads or tails' of something it means that it is impossible to understand the situation.

This has been used figuratively since the early 19th century. The earliest available citation is from October 1832, in *Blackwood's Edinburgh Magazine*, in chapter 14 of a serial titled *Tom Cringle's Log* by Michael Scott which was later published in 1834 as a novel:

"Confound me if I can **make heads or tails of** it either..."

In 1861, George Eliot used it in *Silas Marner*, chapter eleven, in dialogue from Mr. Lammeter to Solomon Macey:

"There's a many tunes I don't **make head or tail of**, but that speaks to me like the black-bird's whistle."

Make new friends, but keep the old;
One is silver, the other is gold

The original proverb was derived from a hymn by Welch-American musician and composer, Dr. Joseph Parry (5-21-1841—2-17-1903) named *Make New Friends, but Keep the Old* or *New Friends and Old Friends:*

"**Make new friends, but keep the old;**
Those are silver, these are gold.
New-made friendships, like new wine..."

Parts of the song were published in a number of books in 1906, including *A Conspectus of American Biography* on page 739.

"Cherish friendship in your breast.
New is good, but old is best;
Make new friends, but keep the old. —
Those are silver, these are gold."

Make new friends, but keep the old; One is silver, the other is gold became the first verse of the Girl Scout song, *Make New Friends,* and has been a well-used proverbial reminder of the importance of friendship.

Make no bones about it

This cliché connotes an emphatic statement. The roots of it go back to 15th-century England, and possibly earlier. The original thought was 'finding bones in it,' as in stew in which small bones could have been included which might cause bodily harm if swallowed. Discovering no bones in food was an indication that it had been well-prepared.

The first figurative printed reference to 'finding no bones about a matter' was in *The Paston Letters* in 1459, a collection of correspondence between members of the gentry in England, acquired and published by the executors for William Paston, 2nd Earl of Yarmouth. Paston included this phrase:

> "And fond that tyme **no bonys in the matere**." [*and found that time no bones in the matter*]

The phrase is somewhat archaic now, but in the 1980s it made a brief comeback and enjoyed rather frequent usage.

Make one's mouth water

This common idiom relates to something which one wishes with all of their being that they could have. In 1555, the earliest known reference is from Richard Eden, speaking of cannibals, who wrote in *New Worlde*:

> "These crafty foxes beganne to swallow theyr spettle as thyre **mouthes watered** for greediness of theyr prey."

Make someone's blood boil

This means to cause someone to become extremely angry. The earliest reference known is from *Alcibiades* by Thomas Otway, published in England in 1675.

> "I am impatient and my **blood boils high**."

Male chauvinist pig*

This somewhat archaic derogatory term was coined in the early 1960s and used extensively in the 1970s by feminist groups to describe a man who exhibits an attitude of male superiority and disdain for women, especially in an aggressive manner. The word chauvinist is derived from the French *chauvinism*, after Nicholas Chauvin, proclaimed to be a legendary French soldier in Napoleon's

'*Grand Armée*' (1805-1815). The word was popularized in Cogniard's vaudeville in the early-to-mid 19th century.

The earliest verifiable citation of this expression is in Mel Brooks' musical play, *All American*, 1962:

> "TRISH. Maybe he isn't a **male chauvinist pig**."

Man among men

Meaning a very special person with unusual abilities or qualities, the root comes from Shakespeare in *Anthony and Cleopatra*, 1609.

> "By Isis, I wilt give thee bloody teeth, if thou with Caesar paragon again my **man of men**."

Man cave

This is a modern day expression which became cliché in the early 21st century. It means a special room, or place which is set aside for the use of a man which is not readily available to his spouse or 'significant other,' or to children, in which he can involve himself in work, play or hobbies without interruption from others.

The expression was started from the idea in John Gray's runaway best seller regarding improving relationships, *Men are from Mars, Women are from Venus*, 1992, where a man's special place is dubbed 'a **man's cave.**' The phrase carried through into later books by Gray.

Man does not live by bread alone

This cliché actually came from the words of Moses to the grumbling Israelites in the *Bible*, in *Deuteronomy 8:3*:

> "And he humbled thee, and suffered thee to hunger, and fed thee with manna, which thou knewest not, neither did thy fathers know; that he might make thee know that **man does not live by bread alone**, but by every word that proceedeth out of the mouth of the Lord doth he live."

'Manna' literally meant 'what is it?' The saying implies, in a literal sense, that we have spiritual needs as well as physical ones. It has come to be used as meaning figuratively that we need a well-rounded diet. A mid-20th century joke was to add 'he must have peanut butter.'

Man may work from sun to sun,
but woman's work is never done

This is an ancient folk rhyme of unknown origin which has been used throughout the ages to illustrate the exhaustive nature of the duties of a housewife and mother. A woman who chooses this important alternative need never be thought about in a poor light.

A well-known lady named Martha Ballard wrote the following in her journal on 26 November 1795:

"**A womans work is Never Done** as ye Song Says, and happy Shee whos Strength holds out to the End..."

It seems that the rhyme may have been put to music at one time from this remark.

An episode of *The Honeymooners*, starring Jackie Gleeson and Audrey Meadows, in 1955 was entitled "A Woman's Work is Never Done."

man's got to do what a man's got to do, A

This much-used phrase means that a person has to follow what he or she feels is right regardless of the outcome. It is often credited to John Wayne in John Ford Copula's *Stagecoach*, 1939, but what he actually said was, "Well, there's some things a man just can't run away from."

The actual verbatim reference is from a film, though. Fred MacMurray said it in *The Rains of Ranchipur* in 1955.

In the book version of *Grapes of Wrath*, in 1939, John Steinbeck came very close, so he should actually have credit for the thought. In chapter eighteen, it has the line: "I know this man. **A man got to do what he got to do**.

man's home is his castle, A

This phrase was originally British, and was oft-quoted as "An Englishman's home is his castle." In the U.K. it is still used by right-wing reporters who are upset by the supposed vanishing rights of a homeowner to do what he pleases with his own home. They perceive this as an inalienable right.

In England the right of a homeowner to protect his property was established in Common Law by Sir Edward Coke, an attorney and politician, in *The Institutes of the Laws of England*, 1628:

"For **a man's house is his castle**, *et domus sua cuique est tutissimum refugium* [and each man's home is his safest refuge]."

Several British authors after that took up the saying and made it commonplace. Then in 1890, American author, Joel Chandler Harris' *Life of Henry W. Grady*, a biography of the Managing Editor of the *Atlanta Constitution* for which Harris was the Associate Editor, included the phrase as well, bringing it to prominence in the States.

"Exalt the citizen. As the State is the unit of government he is the unit of the State. Teach him that **his home is his castle**, and his sovereignty rests beneath his hat."

man who is his own lawyer has a fool for a client, A

The reasoning behind this modern proverb is that one cannot be objective when representing his or her own interests. It has been in use since the 19th century. It first appeared in print in *The flowers of wit, or a chance collection of bon mots,* by Henry Kett, in 1814.

"…observed the eminent lawyer, I hesitate to pronounce, that **every man who is his own lawyer, has a fool for a client**."

In *The Canada Law Journal*, Vol. 5, Toronto, ON, March, 1869, we find that this phrase was already common in that country:

"It is a saying among lawyers, that '**a man who is his own lawyer has a fool for a client**;' but there are very few fools of this description in the world."

Many hands make light work

The root of this proverb comes from *Ecclesiastes 4:6*:

"Two are better than one,
because they have a good return for their labor." *(NIV)*

But the actual quote is from John Heywood's *A dialogue conteinyng the nomber in effect of all the prouerbes in the Englishe tongue*, 1546.

"**Many hands make light warke**."

It means that the synergy of more than one person working in harmony can accomplish more than one trying to do a job alone.

March to the beat of a different drummer

This is from American author, poet and philosopher Henry David Thoreau (July 12, 1817 – May 6, 1862). The entire quote is:

> "If a man does not keep pace with his companions, perhaps it is because he hears **the beat of a different drummer**."

Marching to the beat of a different drummer has become synonomous with being a non conformist and blazing trail for others to follow.

Mark my words

The word 'mark' since the twelfth century has been used by writers and in conversation to mean 'head.' The earliest example of "mark my words" known is in *Coverdale's 1535 translation of the Bible, Isaiah 28:23:*

> "Take hede, and heare my voyce, pondre and **merck my wordes** wel."

This is also used as 'mark my word,' but in every case the speaker intended for the hearer to pay close attention, because what he or she was saying was most definitely true, in the speaker's opinion, and usually a prediction of something certain to happen because of the chain of events which had already transpired.

Marry in haste, repent in leisure

The originator of this proverb is playwright William Congreve in his comedy of manners, *The Old Batchelour*, produced in 1693:

> "Thus grief still treads upon the heels of pleasure: **Married in haste**, we may **repent at leisure**."

It is also a truism which needs no explanation.

Mayday! Mayday! Mayday!

Mayday is the international radio distress signal for ships in serious trouble introduced in 1923 by Fredrick Stanley Mockford, a senior official at Croydon Airport in London, and made official in 1948. It is the anglicized form of the French m'aider, meaning 'help me,' and is a shortening of venez m'aider, 'come help me.' The call is given three times in a row, to prevent a misinterpretation or misunderstanding under less than perfect conditions. Other officially recognized calls of distress are SOS (see) and the Morse code signal CDQ (Come Quickly, Distress).

Measure twice, cut once

This is an old English proverb which dates to at least the late 16th century. Its meaning is clear: carefully consider all of the options before making a final decision, especially in important matters, because in some issues, once the choice is made, you won't have another chance to change the course of the matter.

The first reference known is in *Second Frutes* by linguist John Florio, tutor at the Court of King James I (compared to and supposed by some to be the real Shakespeare), in 1591:

"Always **measure marnie before you cut anie.**"

Men seldom make passes at girls who wear glasses*

This is a quote from American humorist, author and poet, Dorothy Parker (1893-1967), in the 1920s. Also used as 'Boys don't make passes at girls who wear glasses,' this is actually a prejudiced assumption. In fact, glasses are now often worn as a fashion statement, and true beauty still shows through. Wearing or not wearing eyewear is not a major factor in most men's attraction to a lady. Personality, intelligence and attitude are of prime importance.

Me Tarzan, you Jane

Contrary to popular belief, this famous catchphrase, often used in jest when a man is laying claim, so to speak, on a woman, was never in a Tarzan movie or in any of Edgar Rice Burrough's popular Tarzan books. In the original offering which spawned the series, *Tarzan of the Apes*, 1914, in chapter 18, the ape man's words are, "I am Tarzan of the Apes. I want you. I am yours. You are mine."

In the Johnny Weissmeuller 1932 film version, Jane was teaching Tarzan to speak English. She pointed at herself and said "Jane" then at him saying, "Tarzan." His on-screen response was to 'ape' her by doing the same. In an interview in the June, 1932 issue of *Photoplay Magazine*, Weissmeuller actually did say it, though. He told the reporter:

"I didn't have to act in *Tarzan, the Ape Man* — just said, **'Me Tarzan, you Jane.'"**

After that, his quip became a comic cliché that many people mistakenly assumed came from one of Weissmuller's Tarzan movies.

Mexican Wave

This curious term, outside of North America, refers to the wave effect experienced when crowds in stadia rise up and sit down in successive groups. Though the phenomenon had been experienced as early as October 31, 1981, during a section by section cheer during a major league championship baseball game in Oakland, California, it was previously only 'the Wave,' worldwide, and still is in the U.S. The term 'Mexican Wave' was coined during the FIFA football World Cup held in Monterrey, Mexico in 1986.

Mind your own bee's wax

As noted in the 'big wig' explanation, personal hygiene in the olden days was often poor. As a result, many persons, both women and men, had developed acne scars before they reached maturity. The women would apply bee's wax to their faces to smooth out their complexions. When they were talking to one another, if a woman began to stare at another woman's face she was told, 'mind your own bee's wax.'

Now it is humorously used for 'mind your own business.'

Mind your p's and q's

Various explanations have been given through the years about this expression; including being cautious when drinking alcoholic beverages to distinguish pints from quarts, but the most logical one is that of the printer's apprentice when learning to set type. The lower case p and q were so similar, that the printer would warn the novice in the trade to watch to not confuse them. Hence, 'mind your p's and q's' became synonymous with behaving, not becoming confused and getting one's facts straight.

Misery loves company

This cliché alludes to the belief that if someone is in anguish, having another to share it with lessens the pain. The first reference in print to a form of it seems to be from Chaucer in *Troyless*, written in 1374:

"Men seyn, to wrecche is consolacioun, to have another felawe in his peyne."

In *The Friend of Peace* by Philo Pacifious, 1816, the exact saying is mentioned in the following manner:

"It is a common maxim, that '**misery loves company**,' and perhaps it is not less so with error and vice."

Misery makes strange bedfellows

This is from Shakespeare. It means that unfortunate circumstances tend to cause us make unlikely alliances. It comes from *The Tempest*, 1611.

TRINCULO:

"Alas! The storm is come again! My best way is to creep under his garberdine; there is no other shelter hereabout; **misery** acquaints a man with **strange bedfellows**."

miss is good as a mile, A

The first printed example of the proverb as we know it is in a journal called *The American Museum*, Volume 3, 1788.

"A smart repartee…will carry you through with éclat such as '**a miss is as good as a mile**.'"

But the thought behind it did not originate in the U.S. Similar proverbs were in usage in the British Isles more than a century earlier. The following, from William Camden's *Remaines of a Greater Worke Concerning Britaine* was published in 1614.

"An ynche in **a misse is as good as** an ell."

It was also present in Scotland in the early 18th century as a proverb. James Kelley included it in his publication of *A Complete Collection of Scottish Proverbs* in 1721.

"An inch of **a miss is as good as a** spaw (span)."

Miss the boat

This idiom means to lose out on an opportunity because of ignorance of it. The idea behind it can be traced back to the biblical story in *Genesis* 6:9—8:22, which was echoed in other ancient civilizations, in which a large boat, or ark, was built to save people from a great impending flood. Only a few people heeded the warning, the rest 'missed the boat' and were washed away in the deluge. The earliest available verifiable citation for the figurative form is in *What We Found behind the Scenes in European Research*, from *The First Annual Reunion Dinner of the National Research Council, European Labratory Tour*, The Waldorf-Astoria, Friday, October 29, 1937:

> "Where France has '**missed the boat**' in making itself an industrial success is in bringing industry into line."

Moment of truth

This is the precise second that a decision must be made or that a crucial fact is uncovered. Ernest Hemmingway made the first English reference in *Death in the Afternoon* in 1932. Here it is credited to Spanish origin.

> "The whole end of the bullfight was the final sword thrust, the actual encounter between the man and the animal, what the Spanish call the **moment of truth**."

Monday morning quarterback

This Americanism applies to a sports fan who seems to always know after a football game what the quarterback *should have done* to win the game or improve his performance. It was first used in print in 1932 when it appeared in at least two publications, one being *What Price Football: A Player's Defense of the Game* by William Barry Wood:

> "Fortunately, this genus of sports-writer is comparatively rare. Yet one '**Monday morning quarterback**' in the ranks of the press can cause..."

Money begets money

Sounding for the world like *Poor Richard* who said, 'a penny saved is a penny earned,' (see) Ben Franklin also gave us this one in 1748 in *Letter to my Friend A.B.*

"Remember that money is of prolific generating nature. **Money can beget money**, and its offspring can beget more."

A similar common saying is 'It takes money to make money.'

Money burning a hole in someone's pocket

This saying goes all the way back to Thomas More in *Works*, 1530:

"A little wanton **money, which burned out the bottom of his purse**."

It is used when someone has a problem saving and can't resist the slightest whim.

Money can't buy happiness

No truer proverb has ever been coined. Genuine contentment and peace of mind must come from spiritual means. The root came from Rousseau's *Discours in Spain* in 1750.

"Money buys everything, except morality and citizens."

Money doesn't grow on trees

This saying was coined early in the 19th century and refers to the fact that trees were plentiful, but money had to be worked for and earned. There have been several theories as to its origin, including the creation of paper money, and *Pinocchio* (Carlo Collodi, 1883), but the earliest known reference in print is actually from the *Daily Advertiser*, in Boston, Massachusetts, 17 July 1819, in 'From the Connecticut Courant,' on page one:

"**Money does not grow on trees**; and I verily believe, if the philosopher's stone which turns every thing into gold, could be found in every field, it would serve rather to increase the vices, follies and miseries of mankind."

After that, the phrase became popular with authors over the next hundred years.

Money greases the axle

Axle grease is Australian slang for money. In *Western Folklore*, from the California Folklore Society, 1947, this is listed with other old sayings. It has also been attributed to Colorado lore. Popular English author and playwright, William Somerset Maugham (25 January 1874 – 16 December 1965), who also coined "Money is like a sixth sense without which you cannot make a complete use of the other five" (*Of Human Bondage*, 1915), was quoted as telling American politician, author and playwright, Clare Boothe Luce (March 10, 1903 – October 9, 1987**)**, "Love may make the world go round, but **money greases the axle**."

Money is the root of all evil

This is a *misquote* from Bible, *I Timothy 6:10*, where St. Paul is writing to his protégé, teaching him the pitfalls of which he must be aware, that could derail his ministry. *The King James Version* says, "The love of money is the root of all evil." The more proper rendering of the original Greek of this verse is that found in the *New International Version, The American Standard Version*, and *The New Living Translation*, "For the love of money is a root of all kinds of evil."

In any translation, it involves 'love of money,' not money per se, which has no ability in itself, of course. The intention of the verse is to warn Timothy and future readers of the text against one of the 'seven deadly sins,' greed. In fact, the Catholic *Douay-Rheims Bible* uses the word 'desire' rather than 'love'—a bit closer to lust, which would be a quite proper rendering. A splendid way to interpret this is the fact that the lust for personal gain causes great corruption in human character.

Money talks

The first printed reference to this saying is in Giovanni Torriano's *Piazza universale di proverbi Italiani (A common place of Italian Proverbs and Proverbial Phrases)*, 179, 1666. The first American reference is in *Saturday Evening Post*, 3 September 1903.

It means that talk, per se, does not accomplish many goals, but when someone invests enough money, things happen. A related saying is 'Put your money where your mouth is!' (See)

Monkey see, monkey do

This figurative phrase means whatever one does, someone else will mimic. The earliest printed reference to it is from February 1922. *Transactions of the Commonwealth Club of California,* San Francisco, printed the following explanation in Minutes of the Year 1921:

"Harry B. Reynolds argued on both sides to establish the celebrated psychologic law discovered by Pythagoras, '**Monkey see, monkey do**.'"

The person mentioned here is ancient Ionian Greek philosopher, mathematician and religious movement founder Pythagoras of Samos (c. 570-495 B.C.). It seems that this had reference to child psychology in which parents teach children to imitate their actions.

Month of Sundays

The earliest printed usage of this phrase is from *The Real Life and Adventures of Hamilton Murray*, 1759:

> "…he exhibited the various contorsions and wreathings of a rattle snake with surprizing velocity, to the no small edification of the commander, who swore he should dance to the second part of the same tune, for **a month of Sundays…**"

From the context, this idiom was not likely coined by Mr. Murray, but something he was already familiar with. The meaning is 'a very long while.'

Moral compass

This metaphor relates to anything which serves as a guide for decisions relating to morality or virtue. Though not its coining, the earliest known reference to a moral compass appeared in *Essay on Liberalism*, by Andre Vieusseux, 1823, page 130:

> "…the people have lost their **moral compass**, and are now like mariners on a wreck, wandering in unknown latitudes and at the mercy of the buffeting waves."

More dollars than sense (cents)

This is a double entendre, and a well-known play on words. The exact origin of this cliché is unknown; however, it is obviously American, and according to one source, showed up in newspapers in the late 19th century. The earliest available citation of the exact phrase is from the weekly publication, *The Judge,* 29 June 1912:

> "Many a woman's figure represents **more dollars than sense**. A frivolous woman draws the line nowhere but at her waist."

The point: people who use their fortunes to finance follies lack common sense.

An alternate which may be used in other cultures where dollars aren't the accepted currency is 'more money than brains.'

More fun than a barrel of monkeys

This figurative saying, which seems to have undergone a transformation in more recent years to a felicitous application, meaning 'not fun at all' similar to the old phrase 'like fun!' is a later version of earlier phrases, which literally meant 'extremely cleaver and loads of fun.' The earliest known citation of a version of it is from George Darley's dramatic play, *Thomas à Becket*, 1840:

> "De Traci chatters **More than a cage of monkeys**: we must wait."

Then, forty-nine years later, we find a reference in print which gets us nearer to the current version in *Harper's Bazaar* on 21 December 1889:

> "My brother... says the American girls are perfectly fascinating... He says they are **more fun than a box of monkeys**."

Other variations followed including a bushel, bag and cartload of monkeys. Then in December of 1895, Willard C. Gore used 'barrel' in the University of Michigan student magazine, *The Inlander* in a collective definition of the term under 'Student Slang':

> "**Barrel of monkeys**, or bushel of monkeys, to **have more fun than**, to have an exceedingly jolly time."

More or less

This idiom is one of the oldest in the English language, predating Shakespeare, Thomas More and most other progenitors of these sayings. It was around in 1225 as used in the notable anonymous prose work, *Ancren Riwle*:

> "**More oder lesse**."

It connotes an approximation.

More (questions, excuses, etc.) than Carter has liver pills

In 1868 Dr. Samuel Carter of Erie, Pennsylvania developed a tiny, white-coated pill which he claimed was good for a number of afflictions ranging from a sick headache to constipation and even torpid liver, which was supposedly 'positively cured' and gave them the name, 'Carter's Little Liver Pills.' The ingredients were taken from nature. By 1880, millions of them were being sold worldwide. The saying thus came into usage because of the enormous number of them marketed. Though obviously not it's coining, the earliest known citation is from *Machinist's Monthly Journal*, January, 1920:

> "Not all of us have the same ambition, and it is just as well that we do not, because we would have more Presidential candidates **than Carter has liver pills**."

After the pill was studied in 1951 it was proven to be no more than an 'irritative laxative,' with no value to liver problems, so in 1959 the name was changed to simply Carter's Little Pills. They were removed from the market in the 1960s.

More than you can shake a stick at

Today meaning 'abundance,' its origin is uncertain, and what specifically was meant by shaking a stick. But it seems to have arisen from a term of hostilities. Shaking a stick at something would indicate scolding. The earliest known version of it appeared in print in 1818 in the *Lancaster Journal* (Pennsylvania):

> "We have in Lancaster as many taverns **as you can shake a stick at**."

In March 1830, in *The Casket, Flowers of Literature, Wit and Sentiment*, had the following:

> "His slang curses were ultra Kentuckian on a ground of yankee; and he had, says my informant, **more** of this **than you can shake a stick at**."

Both of these references have to do with subjects toward which some would have harbored resentment in the areas indicated during the 19th century. Lancaster was settled by the Amish, and many Kentuckians resented Northerners.

more things change the more they stay the same, The

This proverb is the English translation of an old French saying used by novelist Alphonse Kerr (1808 – 1890), "plus c'est la même chose." It means that things do not truly change on a basic level.

more we sweat in peace the less we bleed in war, The

This is an old Chinese proverb which is often credited to Sun Tzu author of *The Art of War*, aka *Military Strategy and Tactics*. It is also quoted with 'training' for 'peace' and 'battle' for war. It became popular after it was quoted by General George Patton.

Move into high gear

This figurative phrase is used to illustrate an immediate increase in activity of anything or any project which is designed to bring it to a higher level of operation. It is derived from 'straight transmissions,' the only type available in early automobiles, which need to be manually changed, and reach peak performance when in 'high gear.' It has been used to refer to both mental and physical efforts, and often to political campaigns. The earliest known citation is from *The Harvester World*, International Harvester Company, Volume 20, 1929:

> "Service is **moving into high gear** on the Indianapolis, Indiana, territory. Under the direction of Branch Manager J. A. Brookbank the organization is making gratifying progress in getting local service stations established."

Movers and shakers

This idiom means people who are known for getting tasks accomplished. Alfred O'Shaughnessy coined the expression in the first stanza of his 1873 poem, *Ode* published in *Appleton's Journal*.

> "We are the music-makers,
> And we are the dreamers of dreams,
> Wandering by lone sea-breakers,
> And sitting by desolate streams;
> World-losers and world-forsakers,
> On whom the pale moon gleams:
> Yet we are the **movers and shakers**
> Of the world for ever, it seems."

The phrase is now most often used of the rich and powerful elite, or those quickly moving 'up the ladder' of success.

Mum's the word

Meaning keep quiet about this, the phrase is from Shakespeare in *Henry VI,* 1590:

HUME:

"Seal your lips, and give **no words but mum**."

Music soothes the savage beast

Often wrongly attributed to Shakespeare, the quote is actually "Music has Charms to soothe a savage Breast" and was coined by the Playwright/Poet William Congreve, in *The mourning bride*, 1697:

"ACT I. SCENE I:

"A Room of State. -
The Curtain rising slowly to soft Music, discovers ALMERIA in Mourning, LEONORA waiting in Mourning. -
After the Music ALMERIA rises from her Chair, and comes forward. -
ALM. **Music has Charms to sooth a savage Breast**,
To soften Rocks, or bend a knotted Oak."

Must be something in the water*

This expression, used jokingly, is based on the fact that if something strange is happening to numerous people in a specific locale, especially where everyone gets their water from the same source, the problem could be caused by the water.

It has been used in a literal sense since at least the mid-19th century. The book, *The Midshipmen's Trip to Jerusalem and Cruise in Syria* by Augustus Adolphus Lynne, 1872, contains the following on page 162:

> "It has been asserted that there is **something in the water** which renders the people sturdy, hard and fearless; and it is curious enough that people of this kind have never been found in connection with Bethlehem."

The joke, which implies that the problem could affect everyone, seemed to take hold after the 1975 film, *Stepford Wives*, in which Johanna notices that all of the women are behaving strangely and arranges to have the water tested to determine if that is the source of the problem.

My bad

This modern cliché means that the person speaking made a mistake which affected others and is admitting fault. The best evidence is that it was coined in the NFL, possibly by Sudanese-American football star, Manute Bol in the early 1980s, after coming to the U.S., but before he joined the NFL, and that it spread through the league. This assessment is from reports of those hearing the phrase earlier than the first citations and possibly due to Bol's changing to the English language from the Dinka tongues.

The first reference in print is Chuck Wielgus and Alex Wolff's, *Back-in-your-face Guide to Pick-up Basketball*, 1986:

> "**My bad**, an expression of contrition uttered after making a bad pass or missing an opponent."

The above doesn't identify the first player to use the phrase. An article in *The St. Louis Post-Dispatch*, on January 10, 1989 contained the following:

> "When he [Manute Bol] throws a bad pass, he'll say, '**My bad**' instead of 'My fault,' and now all the other players say the same thing.

My land o' Goshen!

Largely in the Southern U.S. this is an archaic mild oath (like 'my goodness!') derived from the *Bible*. The Land of Goshen was an area in northeastern Egypt which was occupied by the Israelites before the Exodus. It is referred to in *Genesis 47:27* specifically in this way in the English Revised Version:

> "And Israel dwelt in the land of Egypt, in the **land of Goshen**; and they gat them possessions therein, and were fruitful, and multiplied exceedingly."

The earliest known citation, however, to this as an expression of surprise or disgust in print is from *Sketch of Connecticut, Forty Years Since,* 1824 by Lydia Huntley Sigourney and Jerusha Lanthrop (Oliver D. Cooke and Sons, Hartford) page 116:

> "**Land o' Goshen**! why Lady! You don't think that all the crutters, who call themselves Christians, are as right as we, do ye? There's the Episcopalians, I went to their church, once at the landin' a' Christmas I think they call'd it."

My lips are sealed

Used to mean that one will swear secrecy to some information entrusted to him or her, in spite of the claim of another phrase origin dictionary that this was first cited in 1909, it appeared in print many times in the 19th century. The earliest known reference to this application of the phrase is from page 5 of *The Evangelical Magazine and Missionary Chronicle*, January 1834:

"Her power of articulation soon became much impeded; but, as her relatives assembled round the dying bed, she said, 'I wished to have spoken to you each separately, but **my lips are sealed**; I can only commit you to God.'"

In chapter 25 of Charles Dickens' historical novel, *Barnaby Rudge: A Tale of the Riots of 'Eighty,* 1841, he wrote:

"Having said that, **my lips are sealed**, and I can say no more."

My two cents worth

There is a lack of agreement on the origin of this phrase, meaning a person's personal opinion, whether wanted or not.

The earliest reference to two small coins is in the *Bible* in both the Gospels of *Mark* and *Luke* in the story told by Jesus about the poor widow who had only two 'mites,' like our two cents today, to put in the Temple offering. Because this was all she had, Jesus stated that it was of more value than the great sums given by those with so much more money. This would indicate that one person's 'two cents worth' may be of more value than someone else's opinion. It is possible that this premise is the basis of the saying.

The American phrase, 'my two cents worth' is predated by the British one, 'two pence worth,' but is more widely used today.

Some believe that the idiom arose from a minimum ante into a poker game.

Others believe that it is derived from the much older 16th century English phrase, included in this volume, 'a penny for your thoughts,' 'two cents worth' possibly indicating more than asked for.

The first known printed reference to the American saying was in *The Olean Evening Times*, (New York) in March, 1926 and was written by Allene Sumner. The heading was: "**My two cents' worth**."

My way or the highway

Sir Thomas Eagleton (1540-1617), Lord Chancellor under Queen Elizabeth, wished to gain favor with the new monarch, King James I. To assure King James of his loyalty, he wrote:

"I have learned no **waye** but the King's **highway**."

From this evolved our current cliché, 'My way or the highway.' The meaning is that 'if you don't like the way I want it done, you can hit the road.' It joins a lot of similar sayings, like 'Don't let the door hit your butt on the way out.'

N

Nature of the beast

This cliché usually means that a specific trait is normal for a person of a given group, or in a certain position or circumstances. It is derived from the fact that animals have certain characteristics which hold true of their species. It had long before been a literal phrase, but it has been used figuratively of people since at least the early 19th century. The earliest known figurative citation is in the London political publication, *The Examiner*, Sunday, 7 March 1819, in a letter:

> "Mr. Hazlitt has got him fast by the ribs, forcing him with various ingenuity of grip, to display unwillingly all the deformities of his moral structure. They now see **'the nature of the beast.'**"

Note the use of placing the phrase in quotation marks, indicating that the phrase is relatively new, but known. It may also refer to professions or things with set characteristics.

Neat as a pin

In the very early 1800s many manufactured items were irregularly produced, but pins were always uniform, and had a reputation for their neat appearance. It became cliché to use it as an example of neatness. It was cited as early as June 1812 in *La Belle Assemblée*, or *Bell's Court and Fashionable Magazine,* London.

> "The child too has quite the family air, both in dress and address, for it is nearly swaddled in its accoutrements, but apparently justly dressed, and **neat as a pin** (*rangé*) as the old nurse, no doubt, would have said."

Necessity is the mother of invention

Few other proverbs have as much truth as this one. Though its author is unknown, Plato sometimes gets the credit, and the first version was in Latin. William Horman, the headmaster of Winchester and Eton, included the Latin form in *Vulgaria,* a book of aphorisms for the boys of the schools to learn by heart, which he published in 1519:

"Mater artium necessitas."

In 1545, Roger Ascham came close to our English version of the phrase in *Toxophilus*:

"Necessitie, the inuentour of all goodnesse."

The earliest actual citation of the phrase as we know it seems to be from Richard Franck's *Northern Memoirs, calculated for the meridian of Scotland.* According to the version which was republished in 1821, with a forward by Sir Walter Scott, the original was written in 1648.

"Art imitates Nature, and **Necessity is the Mother of Invention**..."

Then Frank Zappa gave this phrase an extra 'zap' by naming his American 1960s to 70s classical jazz-rock band *The Mothers of Invention.*

Ne'er do well

This is a contraction of never do well, and originated in Scotland in the 18th century or before. A reference to it is found in Scottish poet and playwright Allan Ramsay's *A collection of Scots proverbs,* 1785.

"Some ha'e a hontla faults, ye are only a **ne'er do well**."

The phrase refers to a worthless person; one in whom others have no hope for a fruitful future.

Nest egg

The practice of placing eggs into hens' nests to encourage their laying more was recorded in print as early as the 14th century. Figurative use of the term 'nest egg' to refer to savings has been around since at least 1686. In 1927, Locke & Clarke published a collection of letters bearing that date including the following:

"The rest, I perceive, he is not troubled should remain as a **nest egg** till a farther occasion."

Never a borrower or lender be

This oft-quoted cautionary advice is from Shakespeare's Hamlet, 1602.

"LORD POLONIUS:
Neither a borrower nor a lender be;
For loan oft loses both itself and friend,
And borrowing dulls the edge of husbandry."

Never cross a bridge until you come to it (See: **I'll cross that bridge when I get to it**)

Never put off until tomorrow what you can do today

This is a warning against procrastination. Good intentions rarely reach fruition. It is a quote from third U.S. President, Thomas Jefferson (April 17, 1743—July 4, 1826), the principal author of the Declaration of Independence, who died on the fiftieth anniversary of U.S. Independence Day.

Never say never

This phrase means that anything, no matter how unlikely it may seem at the time, may happen. It has been at use since at least 1769 when a version of it it appeared on page 60 of *The Lovers; or, The Memoirs of Lady Sarah B___ and the Countess P___* by Pierre Henri Treyssac de Vergy: J. Roson, London, U.K., 1769:

"Although a woman of rank she is delicate and generous. F- is still the man she loves. **Never say, never** write 'I love thee not.'"

Never try to teach a pig to sing; it irritates the pig and wastes your time

This is a quote from *The Notebooks of Lazarus Long*, by Robert Heinlein (1907-1988), which has become proverbial. It is used to refer to someone with an annoying habit which they are unable or unwilling to change.

new broom sweeps clean, A

This is another proverb passed down by John Heywood. It seems to have been an old Irish proverb before this as "A new broom sweeps clean, but the old brush knows all the corners."

Heywood included it in his 1546 book of Proverbs, *A dialogue conteinyng the nomber in effect of all the prouerbes in the Englishe tongue*. It means that when new leadership takes over in either government or business, they are likely to get rid of those who were in strategic positions with the previous administration or management.

An alternate usage is when a new person takes over a position he or she will try to please everyone possible for a period of time, or do a good job for a while, then slack off, lagging back to mediocrity. Either way, there is likely to be a marked difference in the performance of someone after 'the new wears off.'

new wrinkle, A

Meaning a clever novelty, something hitherto unthought of, it has been used since before May 1835, when the earliest known citation appeared in *The New York Farmer and American Gardner Magazine*:

"This improving the character of hired men by means of agricultural publications is, to me, 'quite **a new wrinkle**.'"

It spawned a product name by 1918. This is from *Electrical Review* on Saturday, January 19:

"The Bryant Electric Company, Bridgeport, Conn., has added to its '**New Wrinkle**' line of wiring devices a novel canopy tap of wide application which ... The new tap receives any '**New Wrinkle**' body and many useful combinations can be made."

Nine ways to Sunday (See: Ways to Sunday)

Nip in the bud

In order to be more productive, trees and flowers have to be pruned. One item in proper pruning is nipping a number of less significant buds and allowing the healthy ones to receive a greater amount of the flower or tree's life-giving sap for nourishment.

The original phrase was 'nip in the bloom' and the earliest known reference to it was in a symbolic sense is in Henry Chettle's romance *Piers Plainnes Seaven Yeres Prentiship,* in 1595.

"Extinguish these fond loues with minds labour, and **nip** thy affections **in the bloome**, that they may neuer bee of power to budde."

Therefore, the idea of nipping undesirable notions 'in the bud' before they took the place of something more productive became a phrase to be commonly utilized.

No brainer

This expression means requiring very little or no actual reasoning to reach a conclusion or make a decision. Other sources site later origins; however, the first known reference in print is from *The Congressional Quarterly*, Volume 55, Washington, DC, 1956:

> "Of course, the vote will be a philosophical '**no brainer**' for members who have long supported — or opposed — a compromise along the lines proposed."

No good deed goes unpunished

Accomplished journalist and playwright, Claire Booth Luce (1903-1987), often gets credited as this phrase's originator. The earliest citation available is actually from playwright and novelist, Oscar Wilde, who lived before Luce (1854-1900) in *Lady Windemere's Fan*, a play first produced on 22 February 1892 at the St. James's Theatre in London.

Wealthy banker and noted philanthropist, Andrew W. Melon (1857-1933), is also sometimes attributed as coining the popular cynical phrase, but no proof seems to exist of this claim.

The sardonic meaning is that the practice of doing good deeds often backfires.

No harm, no foul***

The original proverb, coined in the 1950s, was **no blood, no foul**, and originated in basketball. It is still commonly used in Streetball, a street version of the game, where pushing and shoving is allowed as long as it doesn't lead to greater acts of aggression. Since about 1972, **no harm, no foul** has used been in medical malpractice considerations. In this case it insinuates that as long as violence does not leave marks, it is not able to be prosecuted. The term has since bled over into many other circumstances, particularly legal matters, when mistakes made are not held accountable.

The earliest use of the original words together, though not in this sense, are from William Shakespeare's *Troilus and Cressida* near the end of Scene II in words spoken by Cressida, circa 1602:

"No kin, no love, **no blood, no foul** so near me,"

This could have been the inspiration for the phrase. In its current form, it first appeared in print soon after the original was being used in basketball, on 2 December 1956 in the *Hartford Courant,* Hartford, Connecticut:

"The conference coaches also agreed that Big Ten officials this winter should emphasize a principle of '**no harm, no fou**l.'".

No hill for a stepper

The actual origin is unclear, but may be from high-stepping show horses, such as Tennessee Walkers. This snippet from the 1948 *Publication of the American Dialect Society* gives good insight into the intention of this phrase:

"That's **no hill for a stepper**. (That's not too hard a task for a good worker.)"

A similar phrase is 'no hill for a climber.'

No holds barred

This expression, which was derived from wrestling holds, has been in literal English since the early 19th century and means having no restrictions or rules. But it had obviously been in use longer. A verifiable printed citation is from *Current Opinion*, June 1892, in Travel, Adventure and Sport:

"Unquestionably, with unprincipled men as opponents, a weak-minded referee, and **no holds barred**, a catch-as-catch-can bout may become a brutal and very serious affair."

The first known figurative use was in *Observations by Mr. Dooley* by Finley Peter Dunn, 1906, page 149-150:

"Bailey is more iv a nachral debater. **No holds barred** with him."

No man can serve two masters

This proverb has a biblical origin. The meaning is literal, but also applies in the text to serving self and money while pretending to serve God. It is a quote from Jesus in *Matthew 6:24(KJV).*

"**No man can serve two masters**: for either he will hate the one, and love the other; or else he will hold to the one, and despise the other."

No man is an island unto himself

This is from *The Meditation XVII,* a classic Renaissance poem by John Donne (1572-1631). It points to the fact of the brotherhood of all mankind and the need of one for another.

No matter how you slice it (it's still baloney)***

This basic idiom, "No matter how you slice it," refers to no matter how one views something, and indicates that the conclusion is the same. A reference to slicing a loaf any way, metaphorically, was made as early as 1915 in *What is the Fletcher Music Method* by Mrs. Evelyn Ashton Fletcher Copp, Brookline, Massachusetts, page 52:

> "Better give us the loaf and let us **slice it up any way we like,** Herr Von Schollen-Bosshen will deal it out. He is both deaf and blind, so that he will not hear the whailing of the disappointed children..."

Another, slightly later version, attributed to Carl Sandberg, is "no matter how thin you slice it, it's still boloney." This refers to something which is obviously nonsensical. The term baloney, referring to something obviously untrue, was popularized by Variety slang writer, Jack Conway, in the early 1920s, then by New York Governor, Al Smith (1873-1994), who was a 1928 candidate for U.S. President.

The Baltimore Sun, on 9 May 1926, had an article, "No Matter How Thin You Slice It: Gab Of Collegiate Papas And Self-Starting Flappers Is Always Bolognie Anyhow And In Sort Of Code" by Katherine Scarborough, on page MS1. The article contained another reference to the expression.

On 29 November 1933, the *New York Times* had an article titled "Topic of the Times" on page 33 which had the following reference speaking of the 1920s:

> "Some of our leading scholars trace it back to a favorite American saying of that time, '**No matter how thin you slice it, it is still boloney.**'"

No news is good news

The earliest version of this old saying was attributed to King James I of England, in 1616:

> "**No newis is** bettir than evill **newis.**"

The modern variation, only a slight bit different, appeared some years later in about 1645 in *Familiar Letters* by James Howell.

"I am of the Italians mind that said **no news, good news.**"

It carries the meaning that when nothing new has been revealed regarding a tense situation, there should be no need to worry about a woeful conclusion.

No one will know the difference a hundred years from now

This old saying means that most of the things people are so concerned about are temporal and do not make a lasting difference. It was perhaps put best by Boy Scout administrator, scholar and teacher, Forest E. Witcraft (1894-1967), from his profound statement about life, *Within my Power*.

"**A hundred years from now it will not matter** what my bank account was, the sort of house I lived in, or the kind of car I drove...but the world may be different because I was important in the life of a child."

No pat answers

This means that there are not quick easy answers to the hard questions in life which are always the same regardless of circumstances. The earliest known citation is from *Kiplinger's Personal Finance*, January 1954, page 31:

"Because families and houses differ, there are **no pat answers.**"

It became the title of a 1983 book by Eugenia Price from Zondervan Publishing Company.

No man is worth your tears, but once you find one that is, he won't make you cry

This oft-quoted proverb is attributed to President Dwight D. Eisenhower (1890 – 1969). It is literal and pensive in nature.

No problemo

This is used by English speakers as Spanish for 'no problem;' however, that is actually 'no hay problema.' Problemo is neither Spanish nor English. But this Americanism took the place of the ever popular 'no problem,' meaning 'don't worry, I have everything under control' in the late 20th century when other true

Spanish phrases were becoming commonplace in our culture due to the large influx of Hispanic immigrants into American society.

No rest for the wicked*

This old saying has its roots in the biblical book of *Isaiah*. Two identical verses (*48:22* and *57:21*) read:

"'There is **no peace**,' says the Lord, '**for the wicked**.'" *(KJV)*

Another, similar verse which uses the word 'rest' in the 1611 *King James Version,* immediately precedes one of these, *57:20*:

"But **the wicked** are like the troubled sea, when it **cannot rest**, whose waters cast up mire and dirt."

The first time this appeared in English, only slightly differently, was in the *Miles Cloverdale Bible* in 1535.

The saying became quite popular in the U.K. in the late 18th and early 19th century, mostly with literal references to wrongdoing. One early example is from a letter printed in *The British Magazine and Review*, August 1783:

"Osnabrigs and ashes, at the electorate court in Hanover. They that fed the swine fled. There, is **no rest for the wicked**. The sceptre, of their government is not the Shebet of Righteousness."

In 1933 the figurative phrase was popularized by Harold Gray in a *Little Orphan Annie* comic strip under that heading.

No spring chicken

No spring chicken, as an idiom, was first recorded in 1906 in *The Encyclopedia of Word and Phrase Origins.*

One story is that in the early days of settling New England, chicken farmers discovered quickly that chickens born in the spring brought a better price that fall than older chickens which had gone through even one winter. Occasionally a farmer would try to pass off an older chicken for one born that spring. Upon examination, the buyers would remark, "That's no spring chicken!"

The phrase caught on and has long been used to apply metaphorically to people.

Not a dry eye in the house

The etymology of this idiom is based on a special meaning of the word 'house' as everyone attending a performance in a theater or other meeting place. It was coined in the U.S. and means that the general mood of an audience is one of strong emotion to the point of tears.

The saying came into popular usage late in the 20th century and inspired a song by that title, written by Duane Warren, and recorded by Meat Loaf, released in 1995.

Not all it's cracked up to be

This idiom means something does not live up to its reputation. Originally 'crack up,' now archaic, meant 'to praise.' This term originated in the early-to-mid-19th century and appeared in *Speeches, Poems and Miscellaneous Writings* by Charles Jewett, M.D., 1849, page 146 in relation to a jovial game in a bar:

"CRACK UP! CRACK UP!!"

It seems to be used here in the sense of laughter and happiness, like one would say, "That cracks me up!" But in *Slang and its Analogies, Past and Present;* Volume 2, page 201, 1891, by John Stephen Farmer and Ernest Henley, it was defined as to praise, dating to 1843:

"To **CRACK UP**, verbal phr. (colloquial). — To praise; eulogize. A superlative is TO **CRACK UP** TO THE NINES. Fr., faire Farticle, (commercial travellers') and faire son boniment or son petit boniment (cheap jacks' and showmen's). 1843."

By at least 1875, however, 'not what it's cracked up to be' was already in use with its current meaning, as seen in *The Gypsy Queen's Vow* by May Agnes Fleming, page 308:

"'This being taken captive and carried off to a romantic dungeon by a lot of bearded outlaws is **not what its cracked up to be** after all,' said Pet, gaping fit to strain her jaws."

Not by a long shot

This expression is from at least the early 19th century, and was born out of bets with great odds. A long shot indicates virtually out of reason. The earliest verifiable citation is from *Knickerboker, or New York Monthly Magazine*, Editor's Table, October 1851:

"So shall you see what the riversteamers are; what themes of just what pride they are to every New-Yorker—to every American! *Is* there anything like them for speed, comfort, luxury?—any thing in the wide world? '**Not by a long shot**!'"

Not by the hair of my chinny-chin-chin!

This cliché is from the children's story of *The Three Little Pigs*. It means 'under no circumstances!'

Nothing but skin and bones

Meaning extremely thin or emaciated, this expression has been in use since the mid-17th entury. The earliest known reference is from Edward Browne's *Sacred Poems or Brief Meditions Of the day in generall and all the days in the weeke*, 1641 in a poem titled 'Of the Night,' page 14:

"**Nothing but skin and bones** upon him are. See how that lazie slave doth turne the wheele…"

Nothing to write home about*

This idiom means that something is ordinary and unremarkable, possibly not living up to hype. It has been in our vocabulary since the late 19th century. It is believed to have originated in the military, as it became widely popular during World War I. The earliest known citation is from an early edition *The Windsor Magazine*, June 1896, which was not a military usage:

"On arrival at Lanua, Bowman, who believed in surprise visits, proceeded to make his manager's life rather less attractive than it was under ordinary circumstances, and those were **nothing to write home about**."

Nothing ventured, nothing gained

This old proverb means if a person does not make an effort at a venture, there is no chance of success. It goes back to Geoffrey Chaucer in about 1374-1384, in *Troylus and Chriseyde,* book V, st. 112:

"'But for to assaye,' he seyde, 'it nought ne greveth;
For he that nought nassayeth, nought nacheveth.'
['But to attempt it,' he said, 'should not grieve:

387

for he that attempts nothing will nothing achieve.'
i.e., **Nothing ventured, nothing gained**]"

It was adapted as a late 14th-century French proverb: *Qui onques rien n'enprist riens n'achieva* (He who never undertook anything never achieved anything). It was later included in John Heywood's 1546 book of proverbs, *A dialogue conteinyng the nomber in effect of all the prouerbes in the Englishe tongue.* It was first printed in America in the *'Letters and Papers of Cadwallader Colden'* in 1748.

Not my cup of tea

This idiom, meaning 'not something which I can enjoy or to which I can relate readily,' goes back before 1939, when it was used figuratively in *The Amazing Theater* by James Agate:

"For assuredly immersion in medieval legend is **not my cup of tea**."

It was preceded by 'he's my cup of tea' in use in Britain in the late 1800s.

Not on my life!

Similar to 'not by the hair of my chinny-chin-chin!' (see) and 'over my dead body!' (see), this also has a meaning of 'under no circumstances.' The earliest known reference in print of the words in succession is from *The British Drama*, 1804, in *Tancred and Sigismunda* by Thomson; Act IV, Scene i, page 602:

"What are we? In a land of civil rule, Of liberty and laws? **Not, on my life**, pursue them? — Giddy prince! My life disdains thy nod."

The earliest known figurative example of this phrase is from *The Century illustrated monthly magazine*, Volume 48, October 1894:

"**Not on my life**! Out of curiosity these rustics would have ransacked it during the night, and their heavy paws would have ruined my studies, and destroyed my beautiful open-air color-notes."

Not on my watch

Meaning 'this will not happen while I am in charge,' this is a nautical term derived by day and night watches on ships. When an officer is on watch he or she is in charge and responsible for whatever transpires on board. An early citation in print is from *Shipwreck: the Strange Adventures of Renny Mitchum, messboy of the trading schooner "Samarang"* by Howard Pease, 1957:

"The mate gave a grunt of disgust. '**Not on my watch**,' sir. I won't have lubbers like this young wharf rat."

Note the quotes around the phrase, indicating a known but fairly new idiom.

Not playing with a full deck

In olden days, playing cards was popular entertainment. However, there was a tax levied on the purchase of cards, only applicable to the Ace of Spades. To avoid paying the tax, people would purchase only the other 51 cards. Yet, since most games require all 52 cards, these people were thought to be stupid because 'they weren't playing with a full deck.'

Not ready for prime time*

This modern idiom which has come to mean second-rate or crude was derived from the name applied to the original cast of the popular late-night NBC television comedy variety show, *Saturday Night Live* which premiered on October 11, 1975, the **"Not Ready for Prime Time** Players." These included Lorraine Newman, John Belushi, Dan Aykroyd, Chevy Chase and others.

Not so much*

This modern cynical expression was first coined on the ABC TV comedy show *Brady Bunch*, Episode 73, season 4, which aired September 22, 1972. It caught on within a couple of years, and after it used by ex-President Richard Nixon in a 1975 speech, it became a well known catchphrase. It faded away for some time then it was picked up in the 1990s by Jewish comedian Paul Reiser, who used it repeatedly in the NBC Sit Com, *Mad About You*. Later it was carried to greater heights of popularity by comedian Jon Stewart, also Jewish, on Comedy Central's *The Daily Show* (1996-   ). Because of their Yiddish slant on the enunciation it has been associated with Jewish culture. In the 21st century it has become cliché and made a huge impact on pop culture. It is now used after anything being unfavorably compared to something popular or previously favorable.

Not the sharpest knife in the drawer

One of the many 'dimwit' expressions, this was first introduced in the late 1980s. It was used in *Almanac of the Federal Judiciary* in 1988, page 149:

"She is **not the sharpest knife in the drawer**."

Then Gary Hofler used it in the feature 'Get Smart!' in the September 5, 1994 issue of *Sports Illustrated*:

"You can block or tackle, or you can do some exotic things with a football cradled under your arm, but you're **not the sharpest knife in the drawer** when it comes to book learning."

Not worth a flip

Meaning totally worthless, this idiom has been in use since at least the late 19th century. It seems to have derived from flipping one's fingers. The phrase was printed in *Great Hours, a magazine for boys and girls*, June 1879, in a poem called 'Making it Skip':

"Now somehow, that is our Charlie's way. He takes little troubles that vex one so, **Not worth a flip**, And makes them seem to frolic and play."

Not worth a hill of beans

This old adage is somewhat akin to 'don't know beans,' (See: **Know beans**) since beans have for centuries been classified as among the most worthless of the farm harvest. This is a poor premise, as beans are good for many things, and there are countless varieties of them. Soy beans, for example, have multiple uses and are among the most nutritious of crops.

The phrase 'a hill of beans' is of American origin, and refers to the yield from one dropping of beans in a row—usually two. It was used in a literal sense as early as 1858. The earliest known figurative citation is in the 1921 publication of *The Indiscretions of Archie,* a novel by P. G. Wodehouse, published first in the U.K., and immediately afterward in the U.S.:

"Here have I been kicking because you weren't a real burglar, when it **doesn't amount to a hill of beans** whether you are or not."

Not worth a plug(ged) nickel

Meaning similar to 'not worth a flip,' this saying derived from one cent and three cent coins made in the early 20th century with a small silver plug added to the center of the planchet before striking to increase the value of the coin to five cents. When the plug was removed, it devalued the coin, so it became standard practice to examime these coins to make sure they were complete. In *Collier's Magazine*, Volume 74, 1924 we find a near-citation:

> "'I understand it's worth two million dollars,' I said. 'Yeah, but with water in it that comes on faster than it can be pumped out, the mine is **not worth a nickel**,' said Sam. 'You can **plug a nickel**, but how…'"

Then in 1935, in *The American Kennel Gazette*: Volume 52, part 1, we find a perfect reference:

> "He was a dog for which any fastidious sportsman would give his bankroll, but here at a field trial he was **not worth a plugged nickel**."

Not worth one's salt

Millennia ago, all or part of people's salaries would be paid in salt. There is a mention of this in the biblical book of *Ezra, chapter 6, verse 9*, in reference to the pay for the Persian king's servants. Also, according to the writings of Pliny the Elder in *Plinius Naturalias Historia XXXI*, the Roman soldiers were paid in salt. In fact, the Latin word 'salarium' is the root of the English words salt, soldier, and salary.

No walk in the park

This idiom seems to have evolved in the mid-20th century. A walk in the park is something like 'a piece of cake,' just a plain, simple task. But more likely you will hear someone bemoaning a difficult task as 'no walk in the park.' Evidently it comes from the fact that a walk in the park is a leisurely and enjoyable event. The first available citation is from *Billboard*, November 4, 1950:

> "'Producing a television show's **no walk in the park**,' said Billy Rose, after putting three programs in front of the camera."

Now you're talking (or speaking) my language

This means 'on the same page' (see) or 'what you are saying makes sense to me.' It came into usage in the 1920s, and one of the earliest known citations is from *The Dividend* by Joseph Knox Stone, 1927:

> "**Now you're talking my language**. Let me ask you some things first."

Nutty as a fruitcake*

This simile was first coined in the early 20th century in the United States based on the term 'nutty,' already in use as slang for 'crazy,' and the fact that fruitcakes, first made in the mid-19th century, had a lot of nuts. The earliest known citation is from *The Saturday Evening Post*, July 10, 1912, page 12 in a story titled On Main Street:

> "…the defendant's Aunt Jane, in Wilkes-Barre, was as **nutty as a fruitcake**, and his grandfather, in Oskaloosa, had to wear cotton in his ears to keep his brains from blowing his side-whiskers off—"

O

Off the cuff

In olden days, dress shirt cuffs were made of celluloid. Writers on some occasions failed to have paper to take notes and writing them on the removable cuffs of their shirts became an accepted common practice. Later they would incorporate their notes into their journals or jot them down for use in their stories or novels. Hence, they were said to be 'off the cuff.' This has come to mean anything that is improvised.

The earliest known citation is from *Royal Commission on the Press* minutes of Great Britain's Parliament, 1812:

> "Mr. Ross: It is a question I cannot answer **off the cuff**."

Off the top of my head

This expression means impromptu or impetuously. It originated in the U.S. in the mid-20th century. It first appeared in Harold L. Ickes's *Secret Diary* in 1939:

> "He was impetuous and inclined to think **off the top of his head** at times."

It soon became a favorite way to explain how an idea suddenly occurred to someone.

Of milk and water drink you a-plenty, but not tea or coffee until you are twenty

Though its origin may be forever lost, this short rhyme was used in the Southern U.S. in the early-to-mid-20th century to teach children to abstain from caffeine.

Of that ilk

This one is rarely heard in America, except by those of Scottish or Scots Irish descent who keep up with sayings of the old country. The word ilk is still in use there and in other places only when this cliché comes up.

It means 'of the same kind or class.' It is actually a twisting of the original meaning, and comes from the Old English 'ilca,' for 'the same,' and is correctly used only in referring to a person whose last name is the same as that of his estate. For example, MacDonald of that ilk means MacDonald of Donald.

Oh! what a tangled web we weave When first we practice to deceive!

Often mistakenly attributed to Shakespeare, this well-known proverbial rhyme comes from Sir Walter Scott's *Marmion, Canto VI, Stanza 7*, 1808, which reads in full:

"Yet Clare's sharp questions must I shun
Must separate Constance from the nun
Oh! what a tangled web we weave
When first we practice to deceive!
A Palmer too! No wonder why
I felt rebuked beneath his eye."

O.K.

The first known printed example of this expression is from a 1790 court record in Sumner County, Tennessee. The record was discovered in 1859 by a Tennessee historian named Albigence Waldo Putnam. In the records, Andrew Jackson said that he:

"...proved a bill of sale from Hugh McGary to Gasper Mansker, for an uncalled good, which was **O.K.**"

An early notation of our modern usage appears in 1815 on the handwritten diary of William Richardson, who had traveled from Boston to New Orleans about a month after the famous battle fought there by Jackson. In the note he stated, "We arrived ok." Here it is used to mean 'all well.'

It is believed that the actual derivation of the term was from a frequent misspelling of 'all correct' as 'ole korrect.'

The Boston Morning Post on 23 March 1839 carried an article using the term with the insinuation that this was indeed the origin. It ended this way:

"…and his *train*-band, would have his 'contribution box,' et ceteras, *o.k.*— all correct—and cause the corks to fly, like *sparks*, upward."

One year later, when Martin Van Buren was running for his second term as President of the U.S., the initials O.K. became a part of his campaign slogan. He was born in Kinderbrook, N.Y., and his nickname was Old Kinderbrook. His friends formed a committee for his campaign, called "The Democratic O.K. (Old Kinderbrook) Club." The slogan took off and he won the election.

Then on 23 October 1862, when James Pyle, placed an ad in *The New York Times,* referring to 'James Pyle's O.K. Soap' the term received even greater precedence, plunging it into everyday accepted English. Pyle's soap recipe was later purchased by Proctor and Gamble, and the name was changed to 'Ivory Snow.' Pyle's obituary in January, 1900, said that he was the first to use O.K. in an advertisement.

As a result of these varied events, O.K. came to mean what it does today. It may also be spelled 'okay.'

Old battle ax

A battle ax was used by the ancient Vikings as a weapon in battle. As they wore down, they would loosen on the handle and begin to rattle. The phrase 'old battle ax' was coined from an American Women's Rights group in the 19th century to refer to a person who rattled on and on and didn't have much to say.

The phrase caught on in the early 20th century, and an early example in print is from Chapter 13 of *The Job* by Sinclair Lewis, 1917:

"Home's the place for a woman, except maybe some hatchet-faced **old battle-ax** like the cashier at our shop."

Old enough to know better

Of course, this means mature enough to utilize good judgment. Sometimes 'but young enough to learn,' is added. It dates from the 19th century.

Oscar Wilde alluded to it in *Lady Windermere's Fan* in 1892:

> "My experience is that as soon as people are **old enough to know better**, they don't know anything at all."

Older than (or As old as) the hills

The intent came from a verse in the *Bible, Job 15:7*, in a dialogue recorded as being between God and Job. God asks Job:

> "Are you the first man ever born, or were thou made before **the hills**?"

The first known example of the phrase in English, as we know it, is found in Francis Hutchinson's *A Defense of the Ancient Historians*, 1734.

> "As vales are **as old as the hills**, so loughs and rivers must be as old as they."

This seems likely to be a literal reference to hills. However, a figurative citation does come soon afterward in *The Edinburgh Magazine*, in Scotland, in 1787.

> "If an unlucky gamester brought on his papyrus a combination of letters already known, every body abused him saying 'That has been already said' – 'That is **as old as the hills**' – 'all the world knows that.'"

old grey mare ain't what she used to be, The

This metaphoric cliché, which has come to mean that some particular person is growing old and but a shadow of his or her former self, is from a traditional folk song which is believed to have been based upon the extraordinary performance of 'Lady Suffolk,' the first horse recorded as trotting a mile in less than two and a half minutes. This transpired on 4 July 1843 at the Beacon Course racetrack in Hoboken, New Jersey, when the mare was more than ten years old. The lyrics to the song begin:

> "Oh, **the old gray mare, she ain't what she used to be**,
> Ain't what she used to be, ain't what she used to be.
> The old gray mare, she ain't what she used to be,
> Many long years ago."

Speculation as to the author includes Stephen Foster, but is uncertain.

Old hat

This alegorical expression means outmoded, old-fashioned, and uninteresting. The term likely comes from the fact that hats go out of style long before they are actually worn out. It began to be used in a figurative sense during the late 19th century. George Bernard Shaw cited it in his diplomatic criticism, *Platform and Pulpit,* in 1932:

> "If I mention that sort of thing I am told that is **old hat**."

Old Man Winter

This personification of the season, referenced in a number of poems, has been around for hundreds of years in Russian folklore. He is identified with Ded Moroz, the Russian Santa Claus. The earliest available reference in English is from *Leisure Thoughts in Prose and Verse* by Thomas Palmer Moses, 1849:

> "THE SEASONS
>
> "The stern **old man Winter**, with finger of steel,
> And with rude frosty mantle has fled;
> And the air-winged minstrels, with stirring appeal,
> Come to tell us of Spring in its stead."

Old stomping grounds

This old pioneer day saying came from the observations of settlers on the prancing of prairie chickens during their mating dances. They stomped and carried on so much that they wore out the ground, and soon the settlers could tell when an area had been their old stomping grounds. It came into full usage early in the 20th century. An early example is from *Business Directory and History of Jackson County* (Kansas) by Elizabeth N. Barr, 1907:

> "Another claim to honor is the fact that the town is located near John Brown's and Jim Lane's **old stomping grounds**."

Old warhorse

This has come to mean a variety of things depending on who's talking. It can be an old standard well-loved play or piece of music which has lost its luster in the modern age; it may also apply to a retired person, often military, who was highly respected.

As far back as the 17th century, a warhorse was originally a vigilant charger employed by a gallant knight which dashed valiantly into battle. Later it was applied to a cavalryman. The following is from a journal published in June 1887 titled *The Nation, Volume 44, Number 1146:*

> "The theatre of the war which broke out in 1653 between England and Holland, then at the height of her ... was the first land; to a son of the Anglo Saxon race, it was the old home. ... He had bestridden the **war-horse** to good purpose ..."

During the American Civil War, in the 1860s, Confederate Commander, General Robert E. Lee greeted his close friend, General James Longstreet, calling him, 'my old war horse.' Afterward, 'War Horse' became Longstreet's nickname.

This likely catapulted the term into popular usage as we know it.

Old wives' tale

This refers to a teaching, thought to have been born from superstition and passed down by 'gossip' (see).

'Wife,' in this sense, meant any woman. This originated from the feeling that old people tend to live in the past, and what they say is to be 'taken with a grain of salt' (see). *The King James Bible,* translated in 1611, uses a version of this. 'Refuse profane and old wives' fables' (*I Timothy 4:7*). But this saying was in use in England even before 1611—and strangely enough, this is the literal translation of the Greek—indicating that the thought had been around since at least the 1st century AD.

On again, off again

This old cliché refers to something done intermittently. It can also be used to mean capricious or fickle. This is a 19th century Americanism which was originally a railroad term referring to minor accidents, in which a train went off track and then back on again.

A popular song of about 1910 gave it credence. *Finnigin to Flannigan,* by Strickland Gillilan, rang out, "Bilin' down his repoort, wuz Finnigin! An' he writed this here: 'Muster Flannigan—**Off agin, on agin**, Gone again.— FINNIGIN.'"

Today this expression is frequently applied to romantic relationships which are uncertain and sporadic.

On a roll

This is what every gambler dreams about. It means enjoying a series of successes or a run of good luck; 'a winning streak.' Claims that it was in use in the 19th century hold no water. Etymology Online states that it was coined in 1976. Several citations appeared in the 1980s which still have it in quotes. One great example is in the University of Alberta publication, *The Gateway*, January 5, 1988, in an article on page 7 about the movie Wall Street highlighting a young stockbroker namned Bud Fox:

"Soon Fox is **"on a roll"**

This phrase has become a part of the name of a number of groups, products and projects.

On a shoestring

A lot of folks around the world have had to return to this sort of budget during our recent financial upheavals. A shoestring indicates very tight or limited financial funds. Sometimes it is used when relating to beginning a new business enterprise.

According to the *OED* the idiom originated in America in the late 19th century. A 1904 issue of *Cosmopolitan* printed this:

"He speculated **on a shoestring**—an exceedingly small margin."

Once bitten, twice shy

This expression is similar to 'Fool me once, shame on you; fool me twice, shame on me' (see). The first English version of a form of this was in 1484 in William Claxton's translation of *Aesop's Fables*:

"He that hath ben ones begyled by somme other ought to kepe hym wel fro(m) the same."

The earliest exact citation, once bitten, twice shy, is from *Folk Phrases of Four Counties* by G.G. Northall published in 1894 before appearing in a few novels in the early 20th century.

Once in a blue moon

The moon only appears to be blue on certain occasions, like following a volcanic eruption, for example. Small dust particles in the atmosphere after an eruption of a volcano usually diffract blue light and make the moon appear red at sunset; larger ones diffract red light, giving the moon a blue glow—hence, a true blue moon.

It was once thought that blue moons never occurred. This belief dates back to mediaeval England. The Bishop of St. Asaph, St. David's, Bath, Wells and Chichester, William Barlow, in his *Treatyse of the Buryall of the Masse*, published in 1528, wrote the following sarcastic note:

"Yf they saye **the mone is belewe**,
We must beleve that it is true."

Then in 1529, John Frith's essay, titled, *A pistle to the christen reader*, 1529, included this:

"They wold make men beleue... that ye mone is made of grene chese."

But the idiom 'once in a blue moon' didn't come into play until centuries later. This near example appears in Pierce Egan's *Real Life in London*, in 1821:

"How's Harry and Ben? - haven't seen you this **blue moon**."

The fact that since 1819 *The Maine Farmer's Almanac* has listed dates for future blue moons seems rather comical. The writers of this almanac seem to have their own definition of what 'blue moons' are. This appears to be based only on rarity, since it is the thirteenth full moon in a year, when this occurs. Some, therefore, have dubbed the second full moon in a calendar month as a 'blue moon,' though this doesn't mean that it will appear blue.

On cloud nine

One popular belief of the origin of this phrase has to do with cloud types. In the 1950s, the U.S. Weather Bureau classified clouds using numbers for each type. Nine was the number of the fluffy cumulonimbus type which most people consider to be beautiful as they float through the heavens. Someone on cloud nine would be enjoying a leisurely trip through the atmosphere.

A much older explanation is from Buddhism. Cloud Nine is one of the stages to Enlightenment of a Bodhisattva (one destined to become a Buddha).

The actual expression origin is in doubt, and earliest references are to other numbers for clouds, such as seven, eight and even thirty-one, and come from the mid-20th century in the U.S. One such is first listed in Albin Pollock's directory of slang, *The Underworld Speaks*, published in 1935.

"Cloud eight, befuddled on account of drinking too much liquor."

Perhaps this was saying that the person fell a bit short of **cloud nine**.

Actual printed references to 'cloud nine' come a bit later. In August 1946, the following appeared in the *Oxnard Press Currier* in California:

"I think he thought of everything, unless the authorities put something new on him out of **cloud nine**."

The early favorite, however, was cloud seven. In *The Dictionary of American Slang*, originally published in 1960, we find:

"Cloud seven – completely happy, perfectly satisfied, in a euphoric state."

This may have been influenced by the popular saying, 'seventh heaven' (see).

One bad apple spoils the whole barrel

Also used as 'spoils the whole bunch,' or 'bushel' as well. But the origin of the thought was something a bit different entirely. It seems to have been a Chinese proverb. The oldest version was 'One mouse dropping ruins the whole pot of rice.' But the core idea remains the same: one person's bad or negative example can rub off on many more.

It is a little uncertain exactly when this was converted to the English version with apples. It likely is a variant from the quotation from a 14th century Latin proverb translated, 'The rotten apple injures its neighbors.'

It may be that it first appeared in English when Geoffrey Chaucer used the idea in his unfinished work, *The Cook's Tale:*

"Better take **a rotten apple** from the hoard
Than let it lie to **spoil the good ones** there."

These proverbs carry the meaning that the solution is ridding the 'barrel' of the bad 'apple:' banishing a person with a 'rotten' attitude.

One foot in the grave (and the other on a banana peel)

This humorous hyperbole about a serious subject means 'on the verge of death.' It was already in use (with an alternative to the banana peel part) during the 16th century, when William Painter, in *The Pallace of Pleasure*, wrote in 1566:

"Takyng paines to visite him, who hath **one of his feet** alreadie **within the graue, and the other stepping after** with conuenient speede."

One for the road

There has been a common teaching that this saying, meaning a final drink before a trip, had its origins with the supposed practice in the 16th century of offering condemned felons a final drink at a hotel pub in Marble Arch en route to execution in London at the Tyburn tree.

Historic record doesn't bear out this theory. In fact, this phrase didn't appear until the mid-20th century, and seems to have related to taking a final drink in the English pubs and immediately hitting the road with alcohol in one's system. The first known reference in print is from *The Times* (London) in March 1939:

"Propaganda should be employed to train and fortify public opinion in the condemnation of persons who drink before driving - above all to discourage the practice of '**one for the road**'."

Other similar citations followed. But when Johnny Mercer used it in the title and lyrics of *One for my Baby (and One More for the Road)* which was crooned by Fred Astaire in *The Sky's the Limit* in 1943, it took off.

"We're drinking, my friend,
To the end of a brief episode.
So make it one for my baby
And **one** more **for the road."**

In more recent years the phrase has been utilized heavily as a title for a play, a short story, an album and more.

One good turn deserves another

A very early precursor of 'pay it forward,' this truism means 'I owe someone for the favor done for me previously.' According to *John Ryland's Library* (1930) XIV. 92, it dates as far back as circa 1400, appearing in a French manuscript of that period as *lune bonté requiert lautre*, and in the 1546 it was included in *A dialogue conteinyng the nomber in effect of all the prouerbes in the Englishe tongue*, John Heywood's first book of proverbs.

One in a million

This hyperbolic phrase means something or someone very rare and special. The saying became the title of more than one song, several books, a 1967 Scottish Psychedelic rock band and a Maylasian TV series running from 2006 to 2009. As early as 1769, in *The Life of Alexander Pope Esq.*, by Owen Ruffhead, the ability of Pope was described in this light:

"We have already seen, that he complimented Mr. Pope as one endowed with a gift given to **one in a million**, and that only to the true poet."

One man's trash is another man's treasure; one man's meat is another man's poison

The original version of this was '**one man's meat is another man's poison**,' which flipped in the opposite direction from the current phrase. This was in use since the late 17th century, and the earliest known citation is from *Several Sermons on the Fifth of St. Matthew* by the Reverend Dr. Anthony Horneck (1641-1697). This is from Sermon XI, delivered much earlier than the print date, as Dr. Horneck was already deceased and this is the second edition printed in 1706:

"...it's no absurdity to say, That a thing which is a Sin to one is a Blessing to another, no more than we count it a Solicism to say that what is **one Man's Meat is another Man's Poison**."

The Washington Post, 17 May 1924, carried the following citation:

> "Mrs. Gouverneur Hoes will be chairman for the opportunity table at the House of Mercy garden party, Wednesday, and promises to have the usual tempting bargains under the caption, '**One man's trash is another man's treasure.**'"

One red cent

Some have supposed that this came from the original Native American, called at that time a 'red man,' on the front of the 'Indian head penny.' Not so.

This term is derived from the red color or the pure copper that 'pennies' or cent coins in America were originally made from. Now they are more of a brown color, because they are minted from an alloy of copper, tin and zinc. And of course, they are not nearly worth as much. The figurative usage began in the 1840s and was printed in *Josiah Craig's Commerce of the Prairies* published in more than one periodical including *Littlle's Living Age*, Volume 2, 1844:

> "After the ordeal is over, the creditors declare themselves perfectly satisfied: nor could they, as is said, ever be persuaded thereafter to receive **one red cent** of the amount due, even if it were offered to them."

One step forward and two steps back

This is a cynical rearrangement of the popular catchphrase 'Two steps forward and one step back' (see). In 1904, Russian communist revolutionary wrote and distributed a pamphlet by this name.

only stupid question is the one not asked, The

This anonymous saying is intended to keep people from holding back from asking questions which others might feel they should already be able to answer. It began appearing in print in the mid-to-late 20th century, and was used by Leonard D. Goodstein and J. William Pfeiffer in *The 1983 Annual for Facilitators, Trainers and Consultants*:

> "Certain guidelines are always in effect and are agreed to by all members, for example: (a) criticize ideas, not people: (b) **the only stupid question is the one not asked**; (c) everyone in the group is responsible for the group's progress and process..."

Another way this is often worded is, 'There is no such thing as a stupid question.'

only things that are certain are death and taxes, The

Daniel Defoe was the first to coin a form of this phrase in 1726 in *The Political History of the Devil*, a book mentioned earlier in this volume.

"**Things as certain as death and taxes**, can be more firmly believed."

Since that time, other famous writers have picked up the torch and carried it forward to our modern vernacular. One was Ben Franklin.

In a letter to Jean-Baptiste Leroy written in 1789, reprinted in *The Works of Benjamin Franklin*, 1817 he stated:

"In this world **nothing can be said to be certain, except death and taxes**."

Margaret Mitchell, in her immortal Civil War epic, *Gone with the Wind,* in 1936 wrote:

"**Death, taxes** and childbirth! There's never any convenient time for any of them.

On one's toes

To tell someone to keep 'on (his or her) toes' is a metaphoric cliché meaning that one should stay alert and aware of his or her situation and surroundings. It has been in use since at least the turn of the last century, and its exact origin is obscure, but likely came from baseball outfielders or other sportsmen who need to be on their toes in order to move immediately to meet the objectives of the game. An early example, which could be deemed semiliteral, is from *The Forum*, Volume 29, 1900:

"What with the squash courts, the game rooms and gym, the health baths, music and entertainments, added to year-round golf, riding and hundreds of other resort attractions, there's enough to **keep you on your toes**."

By January 1919, this example from 'Meet Don Strong in March' in *Boys' Life* is most figurative:

"We can let you in on the secret that it is a dandy story that will keep you **on your toes** from month to month."

On shaky ground

This metaphor derived from the fact that earthquakes cause much tension and damage. When something or someone is on shaky ground, it means 'insecure and apt to collapse or cause harm.' On firm ground would be the opposite, meaning secure. It began being used figuratively by the early 20th century. The following appeared in *Brick and Clay Record*, 1 February 1912:

"'Who's been giving you a crooked deal?' Dietrich blustered. He felt himself **on shaky ground**. I think we've been fair with you. You can't expect to hog things from the start.'"

On the fence

Being or setting 'on the fence' is an idiom used to figuratively describe someone who is undecided about what to do about something, or unwilling to take sides in a vital issue. The phrase was perceived in this way as early as 1830 when it was used in the first person novel, *Lawrie Todd* by John Galt, page 247:

"'...I won't be a **sitting on the fence** no longer.'

"By this I could perceive he had some intention of making me a proposal of business, inasmuch as **sitting on the fence** means looking on in neutrality from a rail at others fighting."

This reference seems to give insight into the origin of the idiom. (See also: Straddle the fence)

On the lam

Going to the etymology of the word 'lam,' often wrongly spelled as lamb, it is derived from an Old Norse word, 'lamja,' meaning 'to make lame.' When this word was first introduced in English, it meant 'to beat soundly.' Other English derivations include lame and lambaste; the latter syllable from the Scandinavian for 'flog.' 'On the lam' began as what we would now call 'street slang' by the late 19th century, but was in full usage by the 1930s.

A good early example in print is from *Boy's Life* May 1936 in a story titled 'Arm of Guilt' by William Hayliger on page 6:

"Looks to me like he's taken it **on the lam**. You got a line out for him, Cap?"

It means to run away from facing responsibility.

On the level (See: **Level the playing field**)

On the other hand*

This old metaphor means 'from a different point of view.' Sometimes it is preceded by "On one hand..." but this is not necessary. It was likely derived from counting fingers one hand for reasons to do or believe something, then contrasting them by the number of opposing reasons on the other hand. In sales, this line of reasoning in closing is known as the "Ben Franklin close," based on a letter which Franklin wrote to Joseph Priestley on 19 September 1772, concerning the process he used in decision making, balancing the pros and cons.

The saying, however, goes back much further than Franklin, to at least the early 17th century Protestant Reformation, for the German equivalent was used by Martin Luther more than once, as indicated in the English version of *An Open Letter to the Christian Nobility of the German Nation Concerning the Reform of the Christian Estate*, 1520, translated by Charles Michael Jacobs, one of which is found on page 65 of the text published in 1915:

On the other hand, if they had a different faith, I would rather have them outside the Church; yet I would teach them the truth.

By 1645 the phrase was being used in English language publications, as found in *Hidden workes of darkenes brought to publike light* by William Prynne, on page 47:

"Religion without the least impeachment on the one hand; and debarring his Highneflê and all others, so much as once to open their lips to speake against Popery, or to attempt the conversion of the Infanta to our Religion **on the other hand**."

On the same page

This began in the mid-20th century as an idiom, and is derived from multiple copies of a document being distributed to a group. Being on the same page, in a literal sense, is making certain that all members of the group are looking at the same sheet of the report or document. This came to mean figuratively, being in agreement with an idea or principle. An early literal example, speaking of a syllabus prepared for teachers, is from *The Texas Outlook*, Volume 44, 1960:

"It is an exaggeration to say we are **all on the same page**, the same day, the same way..."

On the tip of my tongue

This means that something which one intended to say was almost brought to memory, but escaped before it could be uttered. Although it is used in *The Living Bible* translation of *Job 33:21* (1984), this is not its origin.

"I am about to open my mouth; my words are **on the tip of my tongue**."

'Tip-of-the-tongue' actually was derived from the French expression, *presque vu* meaning 'almost seen.' The tip of the tongue experience was first described as a psychological phenomenon in the text *Principles of Psychology* by American psychologist and philosopher, William James, (January 11, 1842 – August 26, 1910) in 1890, although he didn't label it as such.

Before this the phrase was often used to describe a statement which one was about to say, but thought better, or did not have a chance, in the early 19th century. In August 1823, this example appeared in *The Scots Magazine,* in a story titled 'The History of John and His Household':

"...and the words, 'you impudent, beggarly scoundrel, how dare you—' were just **on the tip of my tongue**, when I bethought myself that I might as well pick a quarrel with a puff of smoke out of my chimney..."

The current application seems to be in play by 1910 in this citation from *The Flint Heart, a Fairy Story* by Edin Phillpotts:

"'**On the tip of my tongue** too!'

"'So were the answers to all your questions **on the tip of my tongue**, I do assure 'e. But I couldn't manage to get 'em off!' said the Galloper."

On the warpath

Taken from the literal 'war-path' of Native Americans when going to battle against invading white settlers in the 18th and 19th centuries, it has now come to mean figuratively that someone is angrily coming out against someone else's practices. The first verifiable citation of 'the war path' is from *Geographical, Historical, Political, Philosophical and Mechanical Essays* by Lewis Evans, B. Franklin and D. Hall, Philadelphia, 1855, page 29:

"Canoes may come up to the Crossing of **the War Path**, or something higher, without a Fall."

And in the next paragraph:

"Its Navigation is interrupted with some Shoals, but passable with Canoes to the Gap, where **the War Path** goes through the Ouasioto Mountain."

On Saturday, 22 November 1800, the term 'on the war path' appeared in the LDS publication *The Deseret Weekly,* in the article 'The Indian Scare':

"Buckley came in today and says that every Indian on the reservation will shortly go **on the war path**, and they have got possession of Ouster's rifles, which the United States Army never found."

In 1911 the term 'on the war path' was used in Alfred J. Morrison's English translation of Johann Davis Schöepf's 1788 German book, *Travels in the Confederation,* indicating that 'on the war path' may have been used in English in the late 18th century.

"It is never the custom of the Indians to take with them children and women when they are **on the war path**."

By the 1940s, it began to be used figuratively, as in this citation from *Billboard* in August 1946, on the page headed 'Dressing Room Gossip':

"As others did a quick fade-out, leaving the guy talking to himself, someone remarked, 'Let's have a rabbit stew,' putting Saluto **on the warpath**."

Ooo, la,la!

The origin of this expression, meaning 'Wow, how lovely!' is the French *ô là! Là!* and is often used in a humorous tone when referring to a sensuously attractive female.

The eclamation has inspired numerous songs. The earliest known citation by an English publication is under the heading 'Current Misconceptions' on page 12 of *Life Magazine* on 6 July 1929,

"The favorite French feminine expletive is "**Ooo-la-la!**"

Opportunity knocks but once

The true sentiment behind this old saying may be so ancient that finding it is impossible. Latin writer Pubilius, circa 43 BC, *may* have been the first to present the idea when he said, "Opportunity is seldom presented, easily lost." About 370 AD, Roman scholar Ausonius wrote an amusing quip about the 'goddess Opportunity' who was claimed to be covered with hair in front and bald behind. Portions of the quote from Opportunity was, "I am a goddess seldom found and known to few…that none may catch me…as I flee…"

British author and politician, Sir Geoffrey Fenton, gave us an early English version in his translation of the work of *Fenton Bandello* about 1567:

> "Fortune once in the course of our life dothe put into our handes the offer of a good torne…"

Several others came close, including Thomas Seldon's translation of *Don Quixote* and a quote from William Penn. But it wasn't until John Dos Passos' novel, *The 42nd Parallel* in 1930 that the saying was written verbatim to the way we know it today.

This proverb was frequently used during the 20th century, and is to urge us to be quick to take advantage of opportunities that present themselves. A related saying, from Francis Bacon's *Essays*, is also noteworthy: "A wise man will make more opportunities than he finds."

Opposites attract

This implies that people are more attracted to others who are different from themselves—a theory which is much debated. The origin of this phrase is uncertain, however, the earliest citation known is from *The Great Harmonia; Being A Philosophical Revelation of the Natural, Spiritual and Celestial Universe;* Volume 1; page 118, by Andrew Jackson Davis, 1850.

> "The male attracts the female, and vice versa; but what we must not fail to notice is, that likes repel, and **opposites attract**, each other. Hence, two of the same gender can not associate so harmoniously as two of directly opposite relations."

One principle of nature should be noted. Magnets have a north pole and a south pole. When the two opposite poles meet, they do attract.

ounce of prevention is worth a pound of cure, An

It is likely no surprise to most that this proverb was passed down to us by none other than Ben Franklin. It is actually an axiom, because in order to head off disaster we must prepare for the worst, but to have the most positive result we should expect the best. Though this is often used in issues of health, and rightfully so, Ben was originally using it in relation to fire safety. Franklin actually wrote this using an assumed name. The statement went like this:

"In the first Place, as **an Ounce of Prevention is worth a Pound of Cure**, I would advise 'em to take care how they suffer living Coals in a full Shovel, to be carried out of one Room into another, or up or down Stairs, unless in a Warmingpan shut; for Scraps of Fire may fall into Chinks and make no Appearance until Midnight; when your Stairs being in Flames, you may be forced, (as I once was) to leap out of your Windows, and hazard your Necks to avoid being oven-roasted."

Ours is not to reason why

This thought provoking saying is a rewording of Alfred Lord Tennyson's lines from the 1854 narritive poem, *The Charge of the Light Brigade:*

"'Forward the Light Brigade!'
Was there a man dismay'd?
Not tho' the soldier knew
Some one had blunder'd:
Theirs not to make reply,
Theirs **not to reason why**,
Theirs but to do & die,
Into the valley of Death
Rode the six hundred."

It means that each person must face duties with resolve, knowing that the end result may not be easy to accept.

Out of sight, out of mind

The reverse of 'absence makes the heart grow fonder,' this means that when something or someone is not around it is easier to dismiss the memory attached. Based on 'in and out of mind,' which had been in use for at least two centuries prior, the earliest printed reference to this proverbial phrase is found in John Heywood's second book of proverbs, *Woorkes. A dialogue conteynyng prouerbes and epigrammes*, 1562:

"Out of sight out of minde."

Out of the blue

When something comes 'out of the blue,' it means that there was no indication that the event was going to happen. Sometimes this is used with 'like a lightning bolt...' because of the fact that lightning strikes can't be predicted and no one knows when one will strike an object, building, animal or person.

The earliest reference in print of this phrase is in Thomas Carlyle's *The French Revolution* in 1837.

"Arrestment, sudden really as a bolt **out of the Blue**, has hit strange victims."

Out of the frying pan and into the fire

This idea goes back to many ancient civilizations. In second century Greece, it was 'Out of the smoke and into the flame.' In Italian, as well as Portuguese, it was roughly, 'Out of the frying pan and into the coals,' The Gaelic equivalent is 'Out of the cauldron and into the fire.' The French version is more like today's English one. It would be translated, 'To leap from the frying pan into the fire,' and may be the immediate forerunner of our phrase.

This cliché means that a situation is bad and about to get worse.

Out of the gate

This modern idiom means from the very beginning, and is derived from horses coming out of the starting gate in a race. An early example is from *The Grants Game* by Lawrence Lee, 1981:

"If you said yes to all four of these questions, you look like a winner right **out of the gate**."

Out of the mouths of babes

This old saying, used to mean that children often realize important truths and bring to our minds astute thoughts is from the *King James Version* of *Psalm 8:2*:

"**Out of the mouth of babes** and sucklings hast thou ordained strength because of thine enemies, that thou mightest still the enemy and the avenger."

411

Out of the woods

This commonly used expression, now referring to being out of imminent danger, particularly of death or financial ruin, had its origin in Roman times, when it had to do with an actual forest.

Its first known written usage in England was in the 11th century by Charles Kingsley in *Hereward the Wake*. The British version is 'out of the wood.'

As a proverb, however, it originated in the United States, and was referenced in the papers of Benjamin Franklin. It was used by Abigail Adams in a letter dated 13 November 1800.

Out the ying yang

Though etymologists find it difficult to pin down the origin of the phrases 'out the ying yang,' meaning having an abundance of something and 'up the ying yang,' the meaning of which seems a bit obscure, it likely derived from the Chinese symbol, yin yang.

This ancient philosophical symbol represents a balance in humans and in all of nature between light and dark, and good and evil. It is a Tao symbol which has been around since the Yellow Empire (2698B.C. to 2598B.C.). The possession of this balance represents an abundance of peace in one's life.

An Atlanta based American crunk rap duo debuting in 2000 took the name 'The Ying Yang Twins,' and has enjoyed popularity in the hip-hop community.

The term 'ying yang' is likely a corruption of yin yang, and could have been coined by young people who were bothered by comparisons of the 'great wisdom' of the ancient cultures, and meant it as a sign of being 'fed up.' (See) This is often used in the connotation of "I've had it up the ying yang with this," which may have been enlarged to mean anything in abundance.

Over a barrel

This saying, which has been around since at least 1938, is American in origin, and means under someone else's emotional or financial control and unable to do anything about it.

The first known reference to the phrase is in a cartoon in *The Clearfield Progress*, a newspaper published in Pennsylvania. From the caption of this cartoon, "You've got him **over a barrel**, Major" it appears that the phrase was in use prior to the publication.

There seems to be some confusion as to whether this meant a wooden barrel, which may be smothering someone, or a gun barrel, as seemed to be the case in a later reference.

Over my dead body!

This figurative phrase implies that the one being addressed would have to kill the speaker in order for something to happen. This was the title of a 1940 Nero Wolfe novel, but this was by no means its coining. It first appeared in a rather literal form in Peter Porcupine's *The Bloody Bouy*, page 47, 1797:

> "I drew my my sword, continues the witness, and told Pinard that he should pass **over my dead body** to come at the woman."

Then this was in Frederich Schiller's tragic German five act play, *The Death of Wallenstein,* translated into English in 1800 by Samuel Taylor Colerage:

> "SCENE V.
> "To these enter Macdonald, and Devereux, with the Halberdiers.
> "Gordon. *(throwing himself between him and them.)*
> "No, monster!
> "First **over my dead body** thou shalt tread.
> "I will not live to see the accursed deed!"

Over the hill

Obvious origins point to reaching the summit of a peak and beginning descent. It means the decline in physical condition and ability which begins in mid-life, and has often been applied to reaching the age of 40, and as age expectancy has increased, now may refer to 50. The figurative usage came into play in the early 1950s. A very early example in print is from an ad in *Esquire's Apparel Arts*, Volume 23, 1953:

> "Any man who can wear his old sports shoes when there are new Nunn-Bush SUBURBANS like these ... is **over the hill**, brother, **he's over the hill**."

O ye of little faith!

This is another common saying from the *Bible*, and more specifically, Jesus. After leaving the Pharisees and Sadducees which had been testing him, Jesus made a metaphoric statement to his disciples concerning the 'leaven of the Pharisees,' a biblical type of sin. They misunderstood him, believing it was because they had taken no bread with them. Jesus was not pleased with their lack of perception. He responded with, "**O ye of little faith**, why reason ye among yourselves, because ye have brought no bread?" *Matthew 16:8b, KJV.* Jesus also used the rebuking phrase with his disciples in *Matthew 8:25, 14:31,* and *Luke 12:27.*

The first time it appeared in English was in the *Miles Cloverdale Bible* in 1535.

Now, when someone doubts something which it seems they should readily accept, this is used as a cliché.

P

Packing heat

This urban slang expression for carrying a concealed firearm became popular in the 1980s, but appeared in *London Charivari,* Volume 265, as early as 1973:

"Liddy shoulda been **packing heat**. I always said it, carry a rod, I said."

Paddle your own canoe

This means to take charge of your own life, and is, for the most part, good advice. It has been in use since the early 19th century. At least two poems in the mid-1800s went by this title. The following lines are the first two verses from one of them, which is anonymous, and was published in 1852 in the *Crawford County Courier* in Wisconsin:

"*Paddle Your Own Canoe*

"My father die, God rest his soul,
When years I numbered two,
And left me 'midst this world alone,
To paddle my own canoe.

"A step-grand-daddy, now no more,
Taught me my P's and Q.
And ever in my ears he dinned,
You'll **paddle your own canoe**."

Paint the town red

Excitement and having a good time, regardless of the consequences, are associated with 'painting the town red.'

The most likely place of origin for this phrase is in Melton Mowbray, Leicestershire, in the U.K., based on a well-documented event which took place in 1837. That year, Henry de la Poer Beresford, the Marquis of Waterford, a 'notorious hooligan,' took a group of his friends and 'ran riot' throughout the town, painting the tollbar and several buildings red.

Par for the course

Par is the term in golf for the average number of strokes acceptable on a hole. This phrase became figurative and is often facetiously used for what is normal and can be expected under the given circumstances. It soared to popularity, beginning in the early 1940s, as seen from this example in *Billboard*, March 28, 1942, page 13:

> "If you would have that box office remain **par for the course** or even bettered, get down to cases with yourself and decide what you, as an editor, would use under the conditions..."

Party pooper

This expression means someone who spoils the social climate for others and exhausts or dampens their spirits. It began showing up in the mid-20th century. It is likely that it derived from the earlier phrase 'pooped out' meaning exhausted, which had been in use since the 1930s. In spite of claims by a major dictionary dating it to 1954, it was in use by teenagers at least by 1950, as validated by this quote from *The First Two Decades of Life* by Ralph Vickers Merry and Frieda Kiefer Merry, published that year:

> "Other popular expressions are **'party pooper'** for one who spoils the fun for others; 'gab-jazz' for teen talk; 'booped out' for dressed up; 'digging the scene' for doing the town; and 'prehistoric' or 'upper plate' for those over 21."

Passing the buck

Passing responsibility on to someone else rather than doing the job yourself is called 'passing the buck.' It is a phrase that comes from card games where bucks are used to indicate the dealer (see: **buck stops here, The**).

Patience is a virtue

The idea that patience is a virtue can be traced back to the *Bible*, as it is listed as a 'fruit of the Spirit' in *Galatians 5:22, 23*:

"[22] But the fruit of the Spirit is charity, joy, peace, **patience**, long abiding, benignity [benignity, *or good will*], goodness, mildness, faith,

"[23] temperance, continence, chastity; against such things is no law."

Wycliffe Bible (WYC)

But the first citation of the proverb comes from William Langland's poem, *Piers Plowman*, 1377 and was expressed even earlier in Latin... *Maxima enim...patientia virtus* (patience is the greatest virtue). This means that the ability to wait for the fulfillment of a desire without complaining is important in the development of character.

Paying through the nose

This is akin to 'highway robbery' (see) in meaning. The origin, though, is not quite so 'set in stone' (see). There are also a number of other possible explanations, but only one that seems correct. Since it first appeared in English in the 17th century, and since the British slang word rhino, used in that era, means money, and 'rhinos' is the Greek word for nose, like in rhinoceros, the nose-horned beast, this likely triggered the expression. A nosebleed is a metaphor for being bled dry of money. Also, in that time period, the expression 'led around by the nose' was established, meaning forcing control on someone. This was used by Shakespeare in *Othello I: iii*:

"The Moor is of a free and open nature,
That thinks men honest that but seem to be so,
And will as tenderly be led by the nose
As asses are."

The earliest known actual reference is from 1708, in the English translation of *The Life of Guzman d'Alfarache or the Spanish Rogue* by Mateo Aleman:

"**...**and that nothing permanent was to be expected from that God, who, when ever he did a Favour, made us **pay through the Nose** for't."

416

Peeping Tom

According to a well-known legend, a man named Leofric taxed the people of Coventry, England excessively. His wife, the famous Lady Godiva, begged him to let up on the taxation. Leofric said he would end the tax if she rode through the streets of the city naked; so she agreed, and did so.

Peeping Tom is a much later addition to this story. Everybody in Coventry was told to stay indoors with the shutters closed. However, it is told that one man, later dubbed 'Peeping Tom,' sneaked a look at Godiva and was struck blind.

The term came to mean any man who looked in on women who were indisposed without their knowledge or consent.

Peer pressure

Meaning literally 'pressure felt by an individual to give in to expectations of persons in their age group, social status, or occupational classification, in spite of personal misgivings,' this phrase became popular in the mid-20ᵗʰ century. An early example in print is from *Popular Aviation* magazine, July 1939, in an article titled 'Aftermath' on page 106:

> "The hazy ambiguities of proper conduct soon are resolved by **peer pressure** and tradition, not by the strict protocol and regulations of the pilot's handbook."

pen is mightier than the sword, The

This metonymic adage was coined by British author Edward Bulwer-Lytton in Act II, Scene ii of his 1839 play, *Richelieu* loosely based on a cardinal by that name:

> "True, This! —
> Beneath the rule of men entirely great,
> **The pen is mightier than the sword."**

Penny-ante***

This American idiom refers to a very insignificant, unimpressive or trifling amount, often used regarding an investment.

Originally meaning, and still referring to, the minimum amount required to be dealt into a poker game, the first known use, in spite of other sources stating 1865, was in 1857, from S.W. Cushing's novel, *Wild Oats Sowings; or the Autobiography of an Adventurer,* page 141:

> "Barker had often used his utmost endeavors to induce me to try my luck, commencing so moderately as to propose the game of poker at a **penny ante**; but finding me fixed in my determination, he gave me an expose of the whole art, very coolly..."

Just after the turn on the next century the term was used as the name of such a game, as defined in *The Dictionary and Cyclopedia, New Volumes,* page 964:

> **"penny-ante** (pen'i-an'te), n. The game of poker when the amount of the ante is limited to one penny (one cent)"

By the mid-20th century the expression was beginning to be used in a metaphoric way. An early example is found in *Billboard*, July 6, 1946 in an article titled 'For Peanuts' on page 109:

> "Nearly everyone I knew was getting rich over night playing the market, but I kept plugging away on what seemed to them a smalltime **penny ante** game..."

Then, two decades later, the term was even being applied to people, as in *Life*'s extensive article about the accused assassin of Dr. Martin Luther King, James Earl Ray, May 3, 1968, on page 27:

> "'He's innocuous,' said the warden. 'He's **penny ante**.' That is, James Earl Ray, slight and round-shouldered, who flinched, smiled a crooked, private grin and sometimes even seemed to walk on a slant, was once **penny ante**."

penny for your thoughts, A

This statement originated in a time when a penny was something more to be sought after—even earlier than the time of the next proverb.

It was mentioned in 1522 by Sir Thomas More in *Four Last Things.*

Playwright John Heywood included 'A penny for your thoughts' in his catalogue of proverbs in 1546, in which the reference to 'A byrde in the hande' was made.

The saying likely dates further back, as the penny has a long history in Britain. The silver penny was first made about 757 AD, and by the reign of King Edward III in the 14th century, it was the most important coin in circulation, worth 1/12 of a shilling.

In purchasing power, it was about two to four dollars in today's American currency. Still, in John Heywood's day, a penny for one's thoughts may have been something to consider.

penny saved is a penny earned, A

The credit for this bit of wisdom goes to Benjamin Franklin, and appeared in his publication *Poor Richard's Almanac* in the 18th century. Were it coined today it would likely be 'a dollar saved,' at the very least. The point of the proverb is to encourage guarding against waste, and spending that which may be laid back 'for a rainy day.'

Penny wise, pound foolish

This one to a citizen of the U.K. is a bit like 'more dollars than sense' (see) to an American. It implies saving a small sum of money and not being wise enough to keep it, loosing even more. Figuratively it means being overcautious about trivial matters and letting more important ones go unheeded. A similar saying is 'gag at a gnat and swallow a camel' (see).

The earliest symbolic citation is in *The Historie of Foure-footed Beastes* by Edward Topsell, 1607:

> "If by covetousnesse or negligence, one withdraw from them their ordinary foode, he shall be **penny wise, and pound foolish**."

People in hell want ice water, too

This saying dates back to the mid-20th century, and probably was coined in the American South. The most likely derivation is from the parable of 'Lazarus and the rich man' in *Luke 16:19-31* in the *Bible*. In the parable, Lazarus was a sore-infested beggar who lay by the gate of a rich man. He asked for only the scraps from the rich man's table. Both men died, and the beggar went to his reward, while the rich man was in torment in hell, gazing upward at the beggar with Abraham. He cried for 'Father Abraham' to dip his finger in water and cool his tongue. Abraham refused, telling the desperate man that he had much good in life while Lazarus had none. In other words, 'People in hell want ice water, but they aren't getting it.'

This seems a logical origin, since preachers in the American South have taught this parable for generations.

People who live in glass houses shouldn't throw stones

This proverb reminds us that we all have faults and we should not be overly critical of others. It goes back to Geoffrey Chaucer's *Troilus and Criseyde* in 1385.

Then, George Herbert wrote in 1651:

"Whose house is of glass, must not throw stones at another."

This saying is first cited in the U.S. in 1710 in *William & Mary College Quarterly*.

Twenty-six years later Benjamin Franklin wrote in *Poor Richard's Almanac*:

"Don't **throw stones** at your neighbors', if **your own windows are glass**."

Perfect storm

Figuratively, this means an event in which a set of rare circumstances will have profound adverse influence over a situation. Though literal references date as far back as the early 18th century, regarding an actual phenomenon which causes an astronomical event, in a metaphoric sense, the first known citation is from the March 20, 1936 issue of the Texas paper, *Port Arthur News:*

"The weather bureau describes the disturbance as '**the perfect storm**' of its type. Seven factors were involved in the chain of circumstances that led to the flood."

Pet peeve

Though the word 'peevish' has been around in English since the 1300s, the first verifiable reference in print to 'pet peeve,' meaning something which is particularly annoying to an individual which may not bother others to the same degree, however, is from *The Illinois Chemist*, November, 1915, in a footnote on page 57:

> "'Originality is a prime virtue.' (So is original investigation.) Our **pet peeve**: 'Yes, and he talked about the paraffin series, methane, ethane, and propane.'"

The phrase had obviously already been in use for a while at this time.

Philadelphia lawyer

This term is used metaphorically to describe an attorney who is exceptionally well-versed in all points of law and more competent in defending clients, even at the expense of truth. It is thought to have been inspired by Andrew Hamilton, a Colonial attorney based in Philidelphia best known for his victorious defense in the libel suit of Peter Zanger, a newspaper publisher, in 1735.

According to *Merriam Webster*, the earliest actual figurative reference of the phrase is from 1788. This figurative example is from *The Americans, in their Moral, Social and Political Relations*, Volume One, by Francis Joseph Grund, 1837:

> "The prerogitaive of the general government, and those of the governor and legistator of each independent state, present often the nicest points of distinction, and afford ample scope for the ingenuity and discrimination of American lawyers. The most fertile in argument and scientific distinctions are, I suppose, those of Philadelphia, their fame being established by the adage, 'This will puzzle a **Philadelphia lawyer**;' which is expressive of the same difficulty as the squaring of the circle in mathematics."

Phone ringing off the hook

This idiom means that a telephone is ringing incessantly and repeatedly. It began to appear in print in the mid-20th century. This early citation is from *Milk Plant Monthly*, Volume 46, 1957, page 126:

> "The phone begins **ringing off the hook...** 'Susie won't drink her milk... my husband is going on a diet... the Dodgers lost three games in a row.'"

Today's smart-phone-possessing youth have a new saying, 'blowing up my phone.'

Physician, heal thyself

This phrase, literally referring to doctors who are attending to others diseases while not being able to cure their own ills, figuratively means 'take care of your own problems rather than finding fault with others,' and is often used sarcastically. It is from the *Bible*; *Luke 4:23, KJV*, and was spoken by Jesus:

> "And he said unto them, Ye will surely say unto me this proverb, **Physician, heal thyself**: whatsoever we have heard done in Capernaum, do also here in thy country."

Note, it was already a proverb in Israel in the first century AD.

Pick of the litter

Now applying to getting first choice at a most-sought-after item, this idiom was derived from having the first pick of a litter of puppies, kittens or even piglets in the mid-19th century. The earliest known literal citation, speaking of Greyhound puppies, is from *Manual of British Rural Sports* Fourth Edition by 'Stonehenge,' page 161, 1859:

> "I should care little as to the **pick of the litter** at weaning time."

The earliest known figurative reference is found in *If I were King* by Justin Huntley McCarthy, 1901:

> "''Tis you who lie now,' grunted Tabarie. 'There's no gold issue in the world that would make you as cunning as François. You would never have done as he did if the king had made you **pick of the litter**.'"

picture is worth a thousand words, A

In spite of claims that this is an old Chinese proverb, or that it even came from Confucius, there seems to me to be no supporting evidence of this. The root likely came from Russian writer Ivan Turgenev in *Fathers and Sons*, published in 1862. His version was:

> "A picture shows me at a glance what it takes dozens of pages of a book to expound."

The near-perfect versions of our modern proverb, however, are from Fred R. Bernard's ad title in the December 3rd 1931 edition of the advertising trade journal, *Printer's Ink* which promoted use of images on the sides of streetcars:

"One Look **is Worth a Thousand Words**."

But on March 10, 1927, Barnard used the phrase again, as "One Picture is Worth Ten Thousand Words," labeling it 'a Chinese proverb.' By his own admission this was done so people would take it seriously. It seems that the perception caught on, and some folks still quote this as an old Chinese proverb.

Piece of cake

The idea for this phrase originated in the southern United States in the mid-19th century, when cakes were given out as prizes for winning competitions. Slave couples used to walk in a circle around a cake at a gathering. The most graceful pair would win the cake. This is also the origin of 'cake walk,' both meaning that something was easy to accomplish.

The first written usage of the cliché was in *Primrose Path*, in 1936, by the outstanding American poet, Ogden Nash.

"Her picture's in the papers now, and life's **a piece of cake**."

Pie in the sky

Pie in the sky has often been suffixed with 'by and by,' or the original, 'when you die.' This saying comes from the first verse of an early 20th century folk song titled *The Preacher and the Slave* written by labor activist Joe Hill, aka Joe Hillstrom, born Joel Emmanuel Hillgglund, a legendary member of the labor group, Industrial Workers of the World. The song, a parody of the hymn *In the Sweet By and By,* was written in 1911 and is a satire on the Salvation Army, the preachers of whom Hill decried for lulling workers into complacency.

"You will eat, bye and bye,
In that glorious land above the sky;
Work and pray, live on hay
You'll get **pie in the sky when you die**."

Hill was executed for a murder of which he was likely not guilty in 1915. While the song sank into oblivion, lost in the annals of forgotten history, the saying 'caught on like wildfire' (see) and came to mean any empty promises which would never be fulfilled. Flowery political speeches prior to elections were often placed into the category

Pigeon hole / pigeon-hole / pigeonhole

Through the ages this term has changed drastically in perceived meaning. In medieval times, pigeons were raised domestically for their meat. Pigeon holes were openings in walls or cotes in which they nested. By 1785, when the following reference appeared in *The Case of Christopher Atkinson, Esq.*, this term had come to be applied to compartments in desks and offices in which items were stored, because they resembled the pigeon cotes.

> "The sale-notes of purchases for the Board were put upon a file, and those of what was bought towards the execution of what I had sold the Board, were put into a **pigeon hole** in his desk."

Then by the mid-to-late 19th century pigeon hole was being used as a verb for classifying something, or setting a matter aside with intent to return to it later. An example is from *The Galaxy*, page 93, January 1874:

> "He belongs to a class who, if a certain combination of sounds or letters has been uttered by somebody, somewhere, at some time — no matter who, where, or when — pounce upon it, classify it, label it, and **pigeonhole** it for preservation…"

Pinching pennies

Penny pinching has the air of stinginess, or being excessively cautious and saving with money, even to the point of grudgingly spending for necessities. Though some have pointed to the 1920s as the date of coining this expression, it was actually somewhat earlier, as seen from this reference to Dickens' *Christmas Carol* in *The LatterDay Saints Millinnial Star*, Thursday, 10 August 1905:

> "Have you forgotten that word in the 'Christmas Carol'? When Scrooge, in his terror, wakens he pleads his business, the necessity of **pinching pennies**, the making of a name for himself, the rising up early and sitting up late, to hoard and hoard."

Pipe dream*

This idiom is used to refer to an unrealistic hope or fantasy, and in its current application derived from illusions received from smoking an opium pipe. This term has evolved somewhat, and in what appears to be the original intent, British author, Hon. Grantley F. Berkley in his *Tales of Life and Death*, 1870, on page 71, uses it this way:

"Mrs. Mantisser proceeded to render up her accounts, the housemaid, who had been ordained for the present to succeed her, having been ordered by Mr. Hastings, in a very feverish and peculiar manner, never to leave the room during the course of these proceedings, as if he had some reason or other for dreading a *tête-à-tête,* lively in his remembrance—perhaps the unwelcome conclusion to last night's **pipe-dream**."

In the above tale, which is the earliest known printed citation, Hastings had only been smoking a 'pipe of tobacco' the previous evening.

Then, this more current example appeared in the Cleveland, Ohio railroad magazine, *The Station Agent,* September 1890:

"'When a man begins to talk about aerial navigation,' said E. J. Rennington of Mount Carmel, 111, 'he might just as well own up that he is crazy and a fit subject for the straight-jacket. It has been regarded as a **pipe-dream** for a good many years...'"

Five years later, an article in the *Fort Wayne Gazette* in September of 1895 contained the following, which linked the phrase to opium smoking, perhaps for the first time:

"There are things taking place every day in Chicago which are devoid of rational explanation as the mysterious coinings of the novelist's brain. Newspaper men hear of them, but in the rush for cold, hard facts, the 'pipe stories', as queer and unexplainable stories are called, are at a discount. Were it not for this the following incident, which can be verified by the word of several reputable men, would have long ago received the space and attention it merits instead of being consigned to the wastebasket as the '**pipe dream**' of an opium devotee."

Pitch black

Pitch is a substance originally made from tree sap, now also derived from coal tar or petroleum. It appears like tar, and was anciently used as waterproofing. It is mentioned in the *Bible* as the agent applied to Noah's ark to make it shed the water of the great flood. Since it is undeniably dark, the original saying was 'black as pitch.' Over the years it became simply, 'pitch black.' Sometimes this is used to describe a night at its darkest hour, when the heavenly bodies are obscured by dense clouds. Also, this could be utilized as a metaphor of a person's worst life experiences. In Latin it was pic; in Old English it was pich.

The phrase has been around for hundreds of years, and its exact origin is rather obscure.

Pitching woo

This somewhat archaic slang expression is derived from use of the word pitch as making a sale, and woo as referring to courting or making love. Woo was originally from the Old English *wōgian* (1050) and refers to making attracting ventures toward a person or group of people—a drawing toward. In the University of Alabama's *American Speech, Volume 12*, 1937, we find the introduction of the phrase:

> "To goose the ghost, for 'to hitchhike' and To **pitch woo**, for 'to neck,' are reported by John Galvin, a student at Columbia University."

Then that year, a film was copyrighted titled *Let's Pitch Woo* to star Charles Boyer and Danielle Darrieux which was released as a French production the following year, beginning on screen in France on 3 March.

Pitter-patter of little feet

Coined to be a humorous referral to the arrival or presence of a baby in a home, this phrase is taken from the rapid tapping sound of a toddler's feet on a floor. It has been in use since the mid-19th century. An early example is from *Once a Week*, edited by Eneas Sweetland Dallas, 22 June 1867 in a story titled 'The Walking Posters':

> "But then my ear was caught by another sound—which as long as there is life left in this broken down old body will never fail, to rouse me from any day dream—**the pitter patter of little feet**..."

place for everything and everything in its place, A

This quote, indicating that being well organized is important, is attributed often to *The Book of Household Management* by Isabella Mary Beeton, 1861. But it was around before Ms. Beeton's book. It was most likely a quote from Benjamin Franklin (January 17, 1706 – April 17, 1790), but the earliest printed nod for his coining the proverb seems to be on page 2 of *Niles Weekly Register*, Baltimore, 5 February 1820. The first known reference to the actual saying is from a book published by the Religious Tract Society in 1799 titled *The Naughty Girl Won*:

> "Before, however, Lucy had been an hour in the house she has contrived **a place for everything and put everything in its place**."

A number of publications contained the proverb in the 19th century and then in 1857 a book titled *A Place for Every Thing; and Every Thing in Its Place* was published in New York by Alice Bradley Haven.

In *Chemical News and Journal of Industrial Science*, Volume 33, by Sir William Crookes, 1876, page 38, it has exact wording and calls this a 'good old motto':

> "The pervading idea of these tabular studies is the good old motto — '**A place for everything, and everything in its place**' but it is extremely difficult to construct any."

Play both ends against the middle

This metaphoric expression means to manipulate two opponents against each other in order to gain advantage and benefit oneself. The earliest known citation is found in *Recollections of a New York Police Chief* by George Washington Walling, 1887. The quotes indicate that the saying was known but relatively new.

> "'So that where a precinct commander wishes to gain occasional glory by the capture of a sneak thief he must, in gamblers' parlance, '**play both ends against the middle**' — that is, his conscience and reputation against 'optional intelligence' in regard to persons he knows to be in the league with the criminals."

Play fast and loose

This means to ignore proper social behavior when it suits one's purpose. The earliest known figurative use of a form of this phrase is from Richard Tottel's poetical anthology, *Songes and Sonettes,* aka *Tottel's Miscellany*, 1557:

> "Of a new maried studient that **plaied fast or loose**."

Then only a few decades later, Shakespeare used the exact term in *King Lear*, 1608 in a statement by King Philip:

> "So newly join'd in love, so strong in both,
> Unyoke this seizure and this kind regreet?
> **Play fast and loose** with faith? so jest with heaven…"

Play hooky

The word 'hooky,' originally 'hookey,' likely came from the Dutch word 'hoekje' which was a game of hide-and-seek in the 17th century. It came to be called 'hookey' in English. Later 'hook' meant to escape or run away. It wasn't until the 19th century that skipping school started being called 'playing hookey,' likely because it was running away and escaping from school. It first appeared in *Dictionary of Americanisms: A Glossary of Words and Phrases* by John Russell Barrett in 1848 on page 180:

"To **play hookey**, is to play truant. A term used among schoolboys."

Play it by ear

Anyone who has ever been around musicians would recognize the source of this as the ability to produce music on an instrument with no formal training. There are a number of talented performers who can both play instruments and 'sing like angels' who have never studied music in any form. Quite a few popular singers in recent generations would fall into this category.

The cliché, however, means that one can handle any situation without reference to prior instructions. A play-it-by-ear sort of person might be able to take a complicated task and make it appear like child's play.

The literal use of ear in reference to music goes back to the 16th century. 'Having a good ear,' is found then. Jan van Wynkyn assistant to William Caxton, said in William Bonde's, *The Pilgrimage of Perfection,* in 1526:

"In the psalmody... haue a good eare." [*The psalmody was the former name for what we call the choir.*]

The actual phrase came much later, in 1839 in *The Edinburgh Review:*

"Miss Austen is like one who **plays by ear**, while Miss Martineau understands the science."

The figurative usage, as we know it today, however, originated in the 20th century, in the America, in a sports context. It was in a story about the proposed sale of the Brooklyn Dodgers in *The Coshocton Tribune*, in February 1934:

"Before going further In this direction, perhaps I can believe that awful suspense by stating that I am reliably informed today that the Brooklyn

Dodgers, otherwise the daffyness boys, otherwise the young men who **play by ear**, are for sale."

Play 'possum

This Americanism is a metaphoric expression used for anything or any person which pretends to be asleep or dead. It is based upon the instinct of opossums which roll over and feign being dead to protect themselves against predators. The date of origin is unclear, but it was in use by 1866 when it was printed in *American Horticulturist*, Volume 25, Orange and Judd, New York in an article about Barn Weevles:

> "They are very active in their motions, and, when alarmed, quickly hide themselves, or if touched, '**play possum**' — feigning dead, The female lays her eggs upon the surface of the kernels of grain…"

plot thickens, The***

This metaphor has been used in recent history to not only refer to an actual storyline in a play, show or movie, but has become common in real-life situations to indicate an unexpected turn of events which makes one feel that a scenario is not what has been expected.

It goes back to 1671 in *The Rehearsal*, a satirical play by the second duke of Buckingham, George Villiers. In making a mockery of poet laureate John Dryden's "heroic plays," Villiers, is depicting the actions of Byers, a type of Dryden, the playwright of the "play within the play," who, in considering his play, commented, "Ay, **the plot thickens** very much upon us."

Villiers was successful in his attempt to defame poor Dryden, who found himself so embarrassed again soon after writing *The Hind and the Panther* in 1687 in which animals debated religion. Two of his other critics, Matthew Prior and Charles Montagu, composed a parody called *The Hind and the Panther Travers'd to the story of the Country-Mouse and the City-Mouse*. In this play the Dryden "Byers" playwright says, "But now, gentlemen, **the plot thickens**, here comes my t'other mouse, the City Mouse."

Plugging along

This means that someone is barely functioning, and/or that the person is being stubbornly persistant. The word 'plug' was originally a seaman's term going back as far as the early 17th century, and plugging along could have been derived from being persistant to plug up holes in a ship to keep water from leaking in. When a ship is leaking it is barely functioning in its intended capacity.

The earliest known citation of the idiom is from *Forty Liars and Other Lies*, by Bill Nye, page 119, 1883:

"**Plugging along** in comparative obscurity is good enough for me."

Poet and don't know it

This sordonic statement is invoked when someone has apparently made an unintentional rhyme. It has been around in varying forms since the late 19th century. The earliest known citation is from Niagara University's (New York) *Niagara Index*, page 27, 1 October 1895:

"The author of that German poem, placed under our door must come to our office and identify himself with no less than three witnesses before we will pass judgement on its merits for publication.

"'We have **a poet and don't know it**. If he had whiskers he'd be a goat.'"

The fact that the entire expression was in quotes leads to the opinion that it was already in use. Then in 1926 the following variation, which became more popular, appeared in Volume 20 of the Washington, DC, literary journal, *Gargoyle Magazine* as a part of a 'Pat and Mike' joke:

"Pat: 'You're **a poet and don't know it**, your feet show it; they're Long-fellows.'"

Poetic justice

The British literary critic and historian, Thomas Rymer, coined the phrase 'poetic justice' in his essay, *The Tragedies of the Last Age Considere'd* in 1678. It means the allocation of an ideal form of justice, where virtue is rewarded and infamy punished, as befitting a poetry of drama.

Poetic license

This term applies to the liberty taken by a writer or artist to deviate from the normally accepted facts, grammer or procedures in order to arrive at a desired result. Sometimes this is refered to as 'articstic license,' particularly with artists. The first known use of the expression is in Daniel Defoe's *The Political History of the Devil*, 1726:

"This is so contrary to the nature of the thing, and so great an absurdity, that no **Poetic License** can account for it; for tho' Poesie may form Stories…"

Point blank range

Delving into etymology we find the origin of the word 'blank.' It came from the French word for white, which is *blanc*. In Spanish, their word is *blanca*.

In the Middle Ages archery was a popular sport for young men in England, and proper families encouraged their sons to attend archery schools. The center of a target was not always known as a 'bull's eye;' then it was called the blank, or the white in the center of the target.

When the students were taught how to hit the blank, they were told to 'aim high' which has become a catchphrase for life, aiming high to reach our goals. Aiming high would take care of the drop caused by gravity when archers were a distance away from the target. When they would get closer to the target—so near that gravity had little effect—they were at the point that they could aim directly at the blank. This became known as 'point blank range.'

Politically incorrect

This stemmed from the term, 'politically correct,' coined by Leon Trotsky (1879-1940) in the early 20th century to refer in a favorable light to those in agreement with the shifting views of the Bolshevik cause, which faded away for some time. Then in the 1960s it was revised by New Left radicals which desired to be viewed as revolutionaries. This was first reversed to 'politically incorrect' in the 1980s by conservatives to champion their free speech against campus leftists after the publication of *Closing of the American Mind* by Allan Bloom. It was around this time that 'not politically correct' and its acronym, 'not PC' came into use.

Today 'politically incorrect' is used as a cliché for anything which does not suit itself to protocol under the commonly accepted modern worldview, and may be offensive to others.

Poor as a church mouse

This phrase, meaning 'impoverished,' originated, and was very popular, in the 17th century. It seems that there was a tale told of a mouse which took refuge in a church, and looked everywhere for food. Since churches of that era had no kitchens, the poor mouse was destined to go hungry.

The following quote is from *Political Ballads*, 1731:

"The owner, 'tis said, was once **poor as a churchmouse**."

Poor as Job's turkey

The word 'poor' has been around since 1200 AD, and Job is a biblical character. This expression is credited to a Canadian judge and humorist named Thomas Halliburton (1796-1865), using the pseudonym Sam Slick, and appeared in the mid-19th century. He described Job's turkey as so poor he had only one brother, and so weak he had to lean against a fence in order to gobble.

The book of *Job* in the *Bible* is believed to be the oldest of biblical writings, even before there was such a thing as an Israelite. It is the tale of a wealthy man who was taunted by the devil with the permission of God. After he had everything taken away and was lying in ashes with boils all over him, he still had faith in the Supreme Being. He was used as an example of patience. To be 'poor as Job's turkey' indicated the lowest estate imaginable. Job, of course, would not have had a turkey, as they are native to North America.

Poot or get off the pot

Used in various versions, this hateful challenge implies that the person being addressed should follow through on his or her stated intentions with explicit action. Thirtieth U.S. President Calvin Coolidge (July 4, 1872 – January 5, 1933) was quoted as saying of his successor Herbert Hoover:

"For six years that man has given me unsolicited advice—all of it bad. I was particularly offended by his comment to '**s**t or get off the pot**' in reference to my delay in calling for action in the Boston police strike."

No earlier citaions are available. A similar expression is 'Fish or cut bait' (see).

Possession is nine-tenths of the law

This statement goes back at least as far as Old English Common Law, which began to develop after 1066, when William of Normandy conquered England, and came into full effect during the reign of Henry II (1154-1189) when it became one of the precepts of the land. It means that when someone has possession of property it is much easier to retain that possession than when someone else has control of it. It does not imply that the person in possession of any property is the rightful owner. The earliest actual printed reference available, however, is from *Memoir of the Life of Leiutenant General Daniel Burr*, 1821:

> "A great number of persons are disposed of, and it would be extremely difficult, now, if Sir E. Stanhope gets the possession without any further evidence, it would be hard if Sir E. Stanhope were to say, **Possession is nine-tenths of the law**; it is not necessary for me to give further evidence and he might throw every difficulty in the way of Mr. Jackson's title."

Pot calling the kettle black

This idiom refers to a person pointing out a flaw in someone else that he or she personally has or is guilty of. This saying has been universal in meaning in languages and countries around the globe for thousands of years. The *fable of Aesop, The Snake and the Crab*, from the 6th century BC signified this principle.

In more than one biblical story the fallacy of this idea is brought out. One prominent example is from the words of Jesus from the Sermon on the Mount in *Matthew 7:3*:

> "Why do you look at the speck of sawdust in your brother's eye and pay no attention to the plank in your own eye?" (NIV)

The first person recorded as using the actual phrase in English was the founder of the state of Pennsylvania, William Penn, in his *Some fruits of solitude*, in 1693:

> "For a Covetous Man to inveigh against Prodigality... is for **the Pot to call the Kettle black**."

Potluck

This term actually had its origin in the Middle Ages in Europe. The *original* potluck was a celebration in which the host would give away his possessions.

The tradition of potluck comes from the frugal idea of never throwing anything away. In days of old, meal leftovers were thrown into a pot together to feed unexpected guests. If you were to share a meal with a family you often had to take 'the luck of the pot,' as you could never be quite sure what you would be served.

Pound of flesh

This phrase is from Shakespeare's *Merchant of Venice*.

"SHYLOCK:
The **pound of flesh** which I demand of him Is deerely bought, 'tis mine, and I will haue it."

The insistence of Shylock that Antonio pay with his very flesh is central to the plot of the play.

Though *Merchant of Venice* debuted in 1586, the idiom did not become a part of our culture until the late 18th century. It is used to refer to a lawful but unreasonable payment of anything thought to be owed, and likely long overdue.

Powder keg

Powder kegs were primarily used for storing and moving large qualtities of black gunpowder until 1870, when modern bullets were developed. They had to be handled with great care, because even a small spark or excess heat could cause the powder to deflagrate. Powder keg, used metaphorically, means a situation is explosive and the least upset could be disasterous. It is often used of political and socio-ecconomic circumstances.

Power tends to corrupt and absolute power corrupts absolutely

This quote, often misquoted, is from English historian, politician and writer, John Emerich Edward Dalberg-Acton, 1st Baron Acton (10 January 1834 – 19 June 1902), aka Lord Acton in a letter to Bishop Mandell Creighton in 1887. It was followed by, "Great men are almost always bad men."

This proverbial statement is a truism and is still brought up in conversation and writings to remind others of the tremendous harm inflicted by monarchies throughout the span of our existance upon this planet. But the idea had preceded his famous proclamation, as a number of previous authors had utilized the principle. What may have been the first was William Pitt the Elder, Earl of Chatham, the Prime Minister of Great Britain from 1776 to 1788. In a speech in the House of Lords in 1770, he said:

"Unlimited **power** is likely to **corrupt** the minds of those who posess it."

Practice makes perfect

This proverb is one of the very old and often carried forward sayings and goes back to at least 1340, when a form of it appeared in Dan Michel's *Ayenbite of Inwyt:*

"Uor wone maketh maister" (For use makes mastery)

This was then included in John Heywood's 1546 book of Proverbs as 'Vse makes maistry.' By 1560 it was near to its present form in *Arte of Rhetorique* by Thomas Wilson.

"Eloquence was vsed, and **through practise made perfect**."

When John Adams wrote the saying in his Diary, it was as we know it.

Practice what you preach

The obvious meaning is that one should do the things they tell others to do—the opposite of 'Do as I say, not as I do' (see). Jesus in the *Bible* is also the oiginator of the principle behind this common idiom, in *Matthew 23:3*:

"So you must obey them and do everything they tell you. But do not do what they do, for they do not **practice what they preach**." *(NIV)*

There is no clear-cut answer to who said it exactly the way we use it today, but the verse from *Matthew* clearly conveys the point.

Preaching to the choir

This metaphoric expression is American in origin, and means giving instructions to someone who is already well aware of the lesson you are attempting to promote. Persons singing in a choir have usually heard the preacher's messages many times, and have demonstrated their acceptance of faith. The first known reference to a literal meaning of this exact phrase is found in *The Theater of Bernard Shaw*, Volume 1, 1961:

"Crowded intercession service at Westminster Abby brought to a close by disappearance of the congregation at such a rate that the rest fled, leaving the Dean **preaching to the choir**."

Though the intent had been expressed much earlier, the earliest figurative use is in the Ohio paper, *The Lima News*, in January 1973:

"He said he felt like the minister who was **preaching to the choir**. That is, to the people who always come to church, but not the ones who need it most."

This is likely when and where it was coined, as many other citations showed up soon afterward.

Pretty is as pretty does (Am.) / Handsome is as handsome does (Br.)

This saying means that just because someone is good-looking doesn't mean that they are a good person. The first reference is from Geofrey Chaucer's *The Wife of Bath's Tale*, 1387.

pretty penny, A*

In this quite antiquated idiomatic expression, a 'penny' is representative of money, in general. But when this first came into usage in the 18th century, a British penny had a purchasing power greater than today's American dollar (see 'a penny for your thoughts'). Entomology online places it at 1768. However, it was in usage long before that. *The Spectator*, London, Wednesday, 30 July 1712, reprinted in a volume in 1729 by J. Tonson, has the following (obviously a known expression at that date):

"But *Charles Ingoltson*, next Door to the Harp in *Barbacan,* has made **a pretty Penny** by that Asservation."

Pride goeth before a fall

This is a misquote of *Proverbs 16:18* which in the *KJV* reads, "**Pride goeth before** destruction and a haughty spirit before **a fall**." It is used to mean that when people allow themselves to be controlled by selfish desires they are sure to reap unwanted results.

Procrastination is the thief of time

This proverbial statement means that by prolonging doing something that has to be accomplished one is only wasting valuable time. It is a quote from British poet Edward Young (1683-1765).

Proud as a peacock

Peacocks are the male peafowl, and the appearance of their strutting about to show off their bright iridescent fan-like tail plumage led to the feeling that they were 'proud.' The earliest reference to the saying is from *The Reeve's Tale* the third story in *The Canterbury Tales* by Geoffrey Chaucer, circa 1395:

"As any **peacock** he was **proud** and gay."

Pull a fast one

This expression was first coined in the early 19th century when paper currency was first coming into usage, after centuries of reliance on coining of precious metals.

To 'pull a fast one' refers to what was known in those days as palming, which was pulling a banknote during a short-changing maneuver. This comes from an analogy to card playing. But short-changing is more likely the origin due to the time frame.

Pulling a rabbit out of a hat

The source of this metaphor is easily understood. Pulling a rabbit out of a hat is one of the 'oldest tricks in the book' of the magician. This illusion was popularized by French magician, Herman the Great, in the 19th century, but because so many new illusions have been developed which are much more thrilling, it is no longer a delight to audiences. Actually, it was not nearly as simple a trick as one would think. As a cliché it has been around since at least the early to mid-20th century and means that someone has success at a task which is totally unexpected. It comes from the idea of getting magical results.

Pulling someone's leg

To pull a person's leg means that someone is making fun of him in a good-natured way—especially in America. But that wasn't the original thought behind the expression. When it first turned up in Scotland, in the 19th century, it didn't have the lighthearted touch it has today. In those days 'pull one's leg' meant to make of a fool of him or her, often by outright cheating. At the origin of the phrase it indicated that by tripping a person or pulling his leg a person could throw him or her into a state of confusion, making that person look very foolish.

The origin is found in an 1867 Scottish rhyme. In it, 'drew' is used in the sense of 'pulled' rather than that word itself.

"He preached, and at last drew the auld body's leg,
Sae the Kirk (church) got the gatherins o' our Aunty Meg."

When Meg in the poem was hanged for a crime, the preacher pulled her leg to make certain that she was dead.

The following reference, a few years later, is from *Blackbirding in the South Pacific, or, The first white man on the beach,* by W. B. Churchward, in 1888.

"Then I shall be able to **pull the leg** of that chap Mike. He is always trying to do me."

In the British application of the term there is still more of a sense of deception than there is in the American usage of it. In England 'stop pulling my leg' means to stop lying and start telling the truth.

Pull no punches

This figurative phrase comes from boxing. Pulling a punch is holding back rather than letting go full force on an opponent. To not pull any punches means to give your enemy the full force of your fury, whether by direct action or verbally. Figuratively, this became popular in the 1940s as illustrated by this early example on page 10 of *Billboard Magazine*, March 28, 1942 in an article by Alan Brock, 'The Stage Actor in Radio':

"However, you can always rely upon the verdict from the control room — they **pull no punches** there."

Pull oneself up by his (or **her**) own bootstraps

This metaphorical phrase, meaning to do better solely as the results of one's own efforts, is from at least the mid-19th century, though no exact origin is evident. The first verifiable citation is from *The Dial* (magazine), November 1860, in Critical Notices in the opening remark of a lecture by Sir William Hamilton, Bart, Professor of Logic and Metaphysics at the University of Edinburgh:

"We have for sometime shared Mr. Carlyle's prejudice against metaphysics, seeing in the attempt of the mind to analyze itself an effort analogous to one who would **lift himself up by his own bootstraps**…"

Pull strings

This idiom goes back to the 17th century, and was coined from the old days of stringed marionettes. The man behind the curtain pulled the puppet's strings or manipulated him or her to make the show happen. The *American Heritage Dictionary of Idioms,* page 517, gives the following as 'from the first half of the 1800s,' but offers no source:

"His father **pulled some strings** and got him out of jail."

The earliest verifiable figurative reference is from 1904 in the English translation from French shorthand of *The Extraordinary Confessions of Diana Please* by Bernard Edward Joseph Capes, page 198:

"I have **pulled some strings**, sitting in my boudoir, with results as far-reaching as St. Stephen's."

It means using one's influence to help someone else.

Pull the rug out from under someone

This metaphoric expression is of unknown origin. It has been around in the English language since at least the early 20th century. Pulling the rug out from under someone would leave him or her defenseless. This would indicate a willful attack on someone intended to cripple his or her ability to recoil.

In a literal sense, pulling a rug out from under someone's feet unexpectedly would surprise the person and cause him or her to stumble and likely fall flat on his or her face or posterior.

Pull the wool over someone's eyes

This, of course, means to deceive someone. This analogy is somewhat related to 'big wigs,' in that both likely derived from the wearing of woolen wigs by both men and women as far back as the 16th and 17th centuries. This phrase, however, is 19th century American in origin.

The earliest known printing is from the *Milwaukee Daily Sentinel and Gazette,* in October 1839.

439

"And we ask one question that they dare not firmly answer, whether they are not now making a tolerable attempt to **pull the wool over the eyes** of the people."

The only element of doubt as to whether this is the true origin of the phrase is the fact that in the U.S. even most 'big wigs' had stopped wearing wigs by the 19th century. Thomas Jefferson, however, did wear one in the early part of that century, but gave the following advice to members of the U.S. court system:

"For Heaven's sake discard the monstrous wig which makes the English judges look like rats peeping through bunches of oakum."

Perhaps that's why they faded out of existence after that.

Pull up stakes

This figurative phrase means to leave one's place of abode and move to another. It began as a literal event. In the first colonization of America in Jamestown, Virginia, in 1607, stakes were put down forming a wooden fort all about the settlement to protect it from native invaders. The same procedure was followed in Plymouth, Massachusetts a few years later. In a *letter* in 1640, Thomas Lechford, planning to leave New England wrote:

"I am loth to hear of a stay, but am **plucking up stakes** with as much speed as I may."

By the early 19th century it was being used often metaphorically as seen in the poem 'Advice' from *The Balance and Columbian Repository*, 29 May 1805:

"'Twas wise in you, I ween, to say
'I'll **pull up stakes**, and run away.'
But since you're fled, I much am griev'd
You find yourself no more reliev'd..."

Pushing the envelope

Now used to mean carrying anything beyond the reasonable point, this idiom had its beginnings in the 1940s United States Air Force test pilot program. It originally meant flying an aircraft beyond its known performance 'envelope' or recommended limits.

Pushing up daisies

Daisies and other flowers of the field have long figured in the botanical image of dying and being buried. Flowers are sometimes planted on graves. Daisies seem to be most common. In *The Babes in the Woods,* a narrative poem about the Norfolk tragedy, included in *The Ingoldsby Legends* (written in the early 19th century), Rev. Richard Barham tells us to:

"…be kind to those wee little folks
When our toes are turned **up** to the **daisies**."

In 1866 George Macdonald polished this cute phrase by saying:

"I shall very soon hide my name under some **daisies**."

Today, in America, we use 'pushing up daisies' to mean the time when a person is no longer among those running through the meadows, looking down upon them, and the mortal shell lies below the soil.

Pussyfooting around

This figure of speech is derived from the ability of cats to walk softly without alerting other animals and even humans of their presence. It means metaphorically walking around the true aim of one's intentions or opinions without coming to the point. It has been in use since at least the late 19th to early 20th century. *The Atlanta Constitution* used the term in an article on 20 March 1903:

"Vice President Charles Warren Fairbanks is **pussy-footing it around** Washington."

Put all the cards on the table

The origin of this phrase, unsurprisingly, is from card games in which placing all of one's cards open is an act of honesty and truthfulness. This is not something done before the end of the hand in poker or blackjack!

The saying has been around since at least the early 20th century. The first verifiable citation is from *The Electrical Review*, London, 23 June 1906 in 'The Work of Scudamore' by Rollo Appleyard:

441

"In his negotiations with the companies for the purchase of property, Mr. Scudamore was at the disadvantage of having to **put all his cards on the table**."

Putting all of one's cards on the table means to be completely honest about one's purpose and intentions

Put on airs

This means to be haughty or pretensive of being better than one actually is. The earliest known use in print is from 1782 in *The Modern Part of an Universal History from the Earliest Accounts to the Present Time* in *The History of Leon and Castile* which was written a bit earlier:

"In a short time, however, after the king's arrival, disputes arose: for the nobility could not bear, that Don Pedro de Lara should **put on airs** of state and dignity in the presence both of his and their master."

This brings to mind the phrase 'holier than thou' (see).

Put on one's thinking cap

This metaphor was originally a 'considering cap,' (now quite archaic) which pinpoints its intent. Putting on one's thinking cap means taking the facts into consideration before reaching a conclusion—the opposite of 'snap-judgement' (see).

The earliest known citation of 'consideration cap' is from *Foole upon Foole* by Shakespearian actor Robert Armin in 1605:

"The cobbler **puts off his considering cap**, why sir, says he, I sent them home but now."

The first record of the use of 'thinking cap,' per se, is from *The Kenosha Times*, Kenosha, Wisconsin, in July 1857:

"This tendency is a very good thing as the safeguard of our independence from the control of foreign power, and it obliges every man to keep **his thinking cap on**."

Put out to pasture

The word pasture is from the Middle English, and derived from the Latin *pastura*, meaning 'grazing.' Cows or horses which are thought to be past the age to bare young and, in the case of cattle, give milk, are put out to pasture, and sometimes sold for various purposes...food for carnivorous animals, dog food, etc.

This term, in a literal sense, was used as early as 1735 in *The Complete English Copyholder* (A guide to lords of manors, etc.) Volume 1, page 155:

"For this reason a horse, &c, **put out to pasture** by Way of agiftmant may be distrained."

In the 20th century, the term 'put out to pasture' gradually came to apply to humans who were past their productive years, and means 'forced to retire.' It is equally popular in both England and the U.S. An early reference leading up to this is from *Billboard Magazine*, November 3, 1945, in an article about the end of American Tobacco subsidiary, Kay Kyser's 'lend-lease' to Colgate Palmolive by G.W. Hill on page 5:

"Hill let Kyser **out to pasture** at a time when cig manufacturers generally were putting in their horses..."

Put that in your pipe and smoke it

The first known citation was made by R. B. Peake in his two-act comedy, *American Abroad*, in 1824. It was exactly as we know it.

Then, in *The Lay of St. Odille,* 1856 by the same author as *The Babes in the Woods*, mentioned before, Rev. Richard H. Barham:

"**Put that in your pipe**, my lord Otto, **and smoke it!**"

It means 'digest that!' 'Think about what I have said very carefully.'

Put the fear of God into someone

This means to cause someone to have a great deal of reverence or profound respect for someone or something, or to terrify someone to the point they are ready to take action about something. Fear of God is biblical and is first found in *Genesis 22:12* when God tests Abraham as to sacrificing his son, Isaac, then tells him to not follow through:

> "Do not stretch out your hand against the lad, and do nothing to him; for now I know that you **fear God**, since you have not withheld your son, your only son, from Me..." *(KJV)*

A number of other verses use forms of the term. It is cited in a somewhat literal term in English as early as 1699 in Simon Patrick's *The Heart's Ease*:

> **"Put the fear of God in their hearts**, and this will preserve them more than a Father. When the guard is set within, they will less need one without."

By the late 19th century it was being used figuratively as in this example from a story on George Fox, founder of the Quaker faith in the 17th century, found in various magazines including *McMillian's*, September 1893:

> "Sometimes, however, Fox obtained a victory which, it is to be feared, he was sufficiently human to enjoy. As when he **put the fear of God into** the lame wife of the jailer at Leicester who was wont to beat her husband with her crutch."

Put the pedal to the metal

This idiom became popular in the U.S. in the 1950s when V8 engines with super power were all the rage. When the gas pedal was pressed to the floor, the throttle was wide open and teenaged daredevils hit the lonely stretches of highway to drag race.

It came to mean go at any task with all gusto, as fast as possible.

Put two and two together

This means considering the evidence in an elementary situation and deducing an obvious conclusion or explanation. It is derived from the most simple of problems: adding two digits. The earliest available printed reference is from *Facts and Evidences on the Subject of Baptism* by Charles Taylor, 1816:

> "The Scripture is plain enough, to proper attention. Any who can **put two and two together** to make four, may, and indeed *must* understand it."

Put up your dukes

This is a challenge to fistfight someone. It goes back to Prince Frederick Augustus, the Duke of York and Albany at the time of King George III of England in the late 18th and early 19th centuries. Prince Frederick, it was said, loved to duel, so fighters nicknamed their fists 'Dukes of York.' This was eventually shortened to simply 'dukes.'

Put your best foot forward

The Random House Dictionary of Popular Proverbs and Sayings dates the origin of this back to 1495, but offers no documentation.

The first known printed reference to a similar phrase is from a poem titled *A Wife* by Thomas Overbury in 1613.

"Hee is still setting the **best foot forward**."

This, of course, applied to the *right* foot (see 'getting up on the wrong side of the bed'). Your best foot is actually an incorrect adage, and should have been coined as 'better foot,' since it implies a person has more than two feet. Shakespeare, who has given us a number of our popular idioms, used a form of this one in *King John* (1623).

"Nay, but make haste; **the better foot before**."

This means that a person should embark on a task with singleness of purpose and determination to succeed.

Put your money where your mouth is

This figurative phrase means 'support your claims by action.' It is believed that it is Irish in origin, and originated in backing up boasts by betting in pubs in Dublin. It also has been applied to playing cards and putting in an ante to enter the game. The earliest actual citation available, however, is in dialogue from an American author, Howard Washington Odum, in his 1928 novel, *Rainbow Round my Shoulder*:

"Bet your money, go to hell."

"**Put your money where your mouth is**."

"It is down, turn them dam' cards you have, fell."

As is clear, this reference does apply to betting, and on cards.

Q

Quality time

This phrase, coined in America, gained popularity around the time it first appeared in print in 1973, when people started wanting to 'have it all.' This example is from the Maryland newspaper, *The Capitol*, in January of that year. The headline read, 'How to Be Liberated.'

> "The major goal of each of these role changes is to give a woman time to herself, Ms. Burton explained. 'A woman's right and responsibility is to be self fulfilling,' she said. She gives **'quality time'** rather than 'quantity time' to each task, whether it be writing, cleaning the house or tending the children."

quick and the dead, The

This is a biblical reference to the living and the dead, and is found in the *Bible* in several places, all referring to the final judgment of man. The first time it appeared in English was in the *Wycliffe Bible* in 1385 (*II Timothy 4:1*). Later it appeared in the *King James Version* in 1611. The phrase *The Quick and the Dead* became the title of a movie released in 1995 staring Sharon Stone. Here it referred to being either literally quick or dead in a Western town containing gunfighters.

Quick as a wink

This saying was first recorded on 1 August 1825 in *The United States Literary Gazette,* in a poem titled 'To Fancy' by 'Lonnol':

> "The brains o' ladies makin' dizzzy
> Withouten drink,
> Begone, you fausse deceitfu' hizzie,
> **Quick as a wink**!"

A more modern variant is 'quick as a flash.' Another such phrase is 'in the twinkling of an eye,' taken from the *Bible (I Corinthians 15:52)*.

Quick as greased lightening (See: **As fast as greased lightening**)

Quid pro quo

Though not exactly a cliché, and not really English, either, it is certainly a phrase to know, not only the meaning, but the origin. Indicating doing a deed in return for something the other does for you, 'You scratch my back, I'll scratch yours' comes to mind (see). It is Latin, and dates to the day when Shakespeare used a version of it in *Henry VI* in 1591.

> "I cry you mercy, 'tis but **Quid for Quo**."

Quiet as a mouse

This idea dates back to the 1500s. A mouse was viewed as the quintessential example of a quiet creature. The thought was expressed in 1562 in *Proverbs, Essays and Miscellanies of John Heywood* in a poem:

> "A **Quiet** Neigheour. ... I never heard thy fire once spark; I never heard thy dog once bark; I never heard once in thy house So much as one peep of one **mouse**; I never heard thy cat once mew — These praises are not small nor few."

Then we find the exact simile in 1750 in Charles Leslie's translation of alchemist Philalethes' 17th-century Latin writings, which he deemed 'pernicious,' *A View of the Times, Their Principles and Practices: Volume I,* which he called *The Rehersal*, page 78:

> "And if we had been let alone, we should have been as **quiet as a mouse** in a cheese."

Quit horsing around

This metaphoric animal-based idiom was derived from the obvious. It is similar to the term 'horseplay,' meaning mischievous antics. When horses are together in a pasture or a corral, they wag their heads, buck around and playfully nip at one another. When children are together they do a lot of the same things on a more human level. They pretend to fight and cut up with one another, hence, 'horseplay' and 'horsing around' were coined to describe this activity. The term 'horseplay' is said to have originated in the late 16th century. The *O.E.D.* states

1589. However, actual printed evidence of usage of 'horsing around' per se does not appear until the early 20th century, as in this first available citation in the January 1904 issue of *The Threshereman's Review*, St. Joseph, MO, in an editorial review on page 24:

> "The method of working live steam in the low pressure cylinder is a good thing when you get in a tight place. But **horsing around** over these rough Illinois roads we have here with so much steam pressure as required is dangerous and shortens the life of a boiler."

Even this seems a bit semi-figurative. Then in the January 6[th,] 1909 issue of New York's *Puck* magazine, there is mention of 'hobby-**horsing around** the room on the broomstick,' which may have led to the more metaphoric usage of merely 'horsing around' as we know it. In 1925, Corey Ford's witty tale, *Three Rousing Cheers for the Rollo Boys*, had the apparent first actual example of 'quit horsing around':

> "'Come on, **quit horsing around** now, Ben,' warned Dick in a voice that boded ill. Whack! went Tom's bat against the third ball..."

Quit your bellyaching

This popular saying in America means 'stop whining and complaining.' It may have evolved from 'quit telling me about your belly ache.' The earliest known citation is from Maritta Wolff's award-winning 1941 novel, *Whistle Stop*:

> "And you can **quit your bellyaching** to me about Joe Sibley, too."

R

Rack and ruin

This cliché means 'complete distruction' and dates back to an earlier version 'go to wreck' from as early as 1548 in a sermon by Ephriam Udall:

> "The flock **goeth to wreck** and vtterly (utterly) perisheth."

But the alteration to 'wrack and ruin' was just around the corner in 1577 when Henry Bull used it in his translation of *Luther's Commentarie* (Martin Luther) *upon the fiftene psalmes:*

"Whiles all things seeme to fall to **wracke and ruine**."

The current spelling came in 1599 in *The History of Corpus Christi College* by Oxford Historian Thomas Fowler:

"In the mean session the College shall goe to **rack and ruin**."

History proved him wrong.

Raining cats and dogs

There are a number of theories as to the origin of this phrase, but it's been in use for centuries. One belief is that thunder and lightening represent a dog and cat fight.

Some say that in London in the time of the bubonic plague during hard rains bodies of infected cats and dogs would wash up in the gutters. Perhaps.

But this phrase was around back in the dark ages according to historians. Cats were believed by superstitious sailors to have a lot to do with producing storms. And the witches who were said to ride the storms were often pictured on black cats.

Dogs and wolves were symbols of winds, and the Norse storm god, Odin, was frequently shown with dogs and wolves hovered around him. In the saying, 'raining cats and dogs,' cats symbolize the rain and dogs, the wind.

Rain on someone's parade

This idiom refers to saying or doing something to ruin someone's happy attitude, or spoil an otherwise joyous event. Parades are used because they are normally pleasurable, and precipitation puts a damper on them. The exact origin is unknown, but it began showing up in print in the last quarter of the 20th century. One example is found in *Big Bucks* by Pat Cook, 1982.

"I don't mean to **rain on your parade**, Buck, but you still owe the government a bundle."

Raising eyebrows*

This idiom means to cause people to be shocked or arouse suspicion or disapproval. It is derived from the fact that people often literally raise their eyebrows when startled or surprised. The figurative usage came into common use in the mid-20th century, and an early example is from *Princeton Alumni Review,* May 11, 1951, in a letter to the editor on page 4:

"But when you come to the statement that football will be continued on 'as large a scale as possible' **I think there** would be a **raising of eyebrows."**

Raring to go

The word raring, in such a sense, has been around since 1909 according to *Merriam-Webster*. It is thought that raring to go derived from the fact that horses 'rear up' lifting their front feet off the ground when they are excited and determined to run off. Raring is probably a form of rearing, as that is what the term means—anxious to get on the move.

The earliest available citation to this phrase, per se, is from *The Texas Railway Journal*, November 1913, in which it is in quotes as a known but fairly new idiom:

"As the time for the opening of the Texas Cotton Palace, at Waco, approaches, interest in the wonderful exposition grows keener, and the young folks are **'raring to go...'"**

Rattle someone's cage

This relatively recent idiom refers to annoying someone purposely just to unsettle the person. The earliest verifiable citation is from *Black Belt Magazine*, February 1975, on page 40 in a story by Dan Ivan titled 'Honor among Thieves':

"The only answer was to go straight to the guy responsible for it all and **rattle his cage** a little bit."

Read between the lines

The story is told that this phrase came from the early days of sending secret messages. Communications would be written on regular paper but hidden to be revealed only when a substance called a 'reagent' was applied.

Since delivering a blank sheet of paper was a dead giveaway, letters would be sent by currier containing a memo of little or no importance, but to read the true message, the recipient would have to apply the reagent to the spaces between the lines, where the intended message would then appear, perhaps when held up to light.

Another way of achieving this in the early 19th century was to write something where the recipient could read in the true meaning based on knowledge which they had and others did not. This was a simple form of cryptography of the day.

An early example of this phrase in text was found printed in the *New York Times* in August 1862 in which the saying is in quotes.

> "Earl Russell's dispatch does not recite the terms of the note to which it is a reply, the letter assumes a somewhat enigmatical character, and the only resource we have is, as best we may, to **'read between the lines'** of this puzzling, but important, communication of the British Foreign Secretary."

Reading between the lines today means understanding from the context of what has been spoken or written a hidden meaning not intended for everyone to surmise.

Read 'em and weep

The origin of this term is from gambling. It is most often used in poker when someone lays down a winning hand. It has been in use in dice as well since the early 20th century as seen in this example from *The Atlantic Monthly*, in 'Flying Thoughts' by Charles Bernard Nordhoff, April 1918:

> **"Read 'em and weep!** Ten francs — let 'er ride. I'll fade you!' The crap-shooting circle is always either stuffed with banknotes or reduced to a few sous — which latter predicament is a bit serious here, where we have to pay eight to ten francs a day to get sufficient nurishing food."

Read the Riot Act

Today this is used in jest and means to be scolded or told off for something.

But the real Riot Act was no joke. Following this law, enacted by the government in Britian in July 1715 (The full title was *An act for preventing tumults and riotous assemblies, and for the more speedy and effectual punishing the rioters*), if a rowdy group of twelve or more people gathered, a magistrate would read an official statement ordering them to disperse at once. It was enacted in haste to prevent Catholic Jacobite rebels from protesting against George I. Anyone who did not comply, after one hour, could be arrested and punished. The Jacobites supported the Scottish House of Stuart, and were a real threat to the new Hanoverian king.

real McCoy, The

The real McCoy is the genuine article. No fakes or imitations will do. This cliché was coined from a nickname for the middleweight boxing champion of 1897, Charles 'Kid' McCoy (October 13, 1872 – April 18, 1940), who would sometimes feign sickness and then show up to fight in good health and spirits. His promoters would have to convince the audience that he was the 'Real McCoy.' When accused of murder, McCoy reportedly took short-term refuge at a Christian shelter in California.

An ABC TV comedy series produced by Danny Thomas in Desilu Studios named *The Real McCoys* brought the already popular cliché to national prominence in the U.S. It starred Walter Brennon, Richard Crenna and Kathlene Nolan, and ran from 1957 to 1962.

Recipe for success

This idiom means a workable plan which if all ingredients are properly put together, will produce a positive result. It is also applied in the reverse as 'recipe for disaster.'

The term was coined by Sir Walter Scott in one of the *Waverly Novels*, in the Introduction to *The Abbot* in 1831:

> "A taking title, or the announcement of a popular subject, is a **recipe for success** much in favour with booksellers, but which authors will not always find efficacious."

Red letter day

On some modern calendars, Sundays are in red numbers, and other days in black. The practice began in ancient times when monks made, and were the only ones who kept, calendars. They were made by hand in monasteries or convents. Scribes often emphasized Saints Days, or festival days by marking them with a reddish ink made with ocher, a mineral of ferric oxide.

Later, when calendars began to be printed for common use, those in Christian countries often made the numbers of Sunday in red. This pattern caused the adaption of the idiom 'red letter day' for an important day in someone's life, like their wedding day, birthday, or graduation from college.

The first specific reference to this term comes from America, from the diary of Sarah Knight in *The Journals of Madam Knight and the Reverend Mister Buckingham*, written in 1704 and 1710, and published in 1940 in *American Speech*.

Red sky at night is a sailor's delight, red sky in the morning is a sailor's warning

The British say 'shepherd' rather than sailor. But there is more than one source to the thought behind this proverb.

The earliest is from Jesus in *Matthew 16:2-3*:

"When in **evening**, ye say, it will be **fair weather**: For **the sky is red**. And in the **morning**, it will be **foul weather** today; for **the sky is red** and lowering." *(KJV)*

Then there is the other favorite source, Shakespeare. He said something very similar in *Venus and Adonis:*

"Like a **red morn** that ever yet betokened, **Wreck to the seaman**, tempest to the field, **Sorrow to the shepherds**, woe unto the birds, Gusts and foul flaws to herdmen and to herds."

The rhyme, it seems, started long ago in England, with the shepherd version, likely because it was adapted from the reference in Shakespeare's play (though he also mentioned the seaman). Later, when many sailors were going to sea for commerce, 'sailor' replaced 'shepherd' for them.

Red Tape

The origin of this popular cliché goes back to the 16th century. King Henry VIII sent eighty petitions to Pope Clement VII asking that his marriage to Catherine of Aragon be annulled. The petitions were bound with red tape.

The expression was popularized in America after the Civil War, when veterans' records were bound in red tape and were overly difficult to access.

Now, anything which is fraught with difficulty and tied up in problems is said to have too much red tape.

Rein it in

This is a metaphor used to portray bringing something or someone under control. It is derived from controlling a horse by pulling the reins. As such, the phrase came into usage in the late 17th century. The first reference known is from *An Exposition on the Lord's Prayer* by Ezekiel Hopkins, Lord Bishop of London-Derry, page 133, 1692:

"Grace doth not **rein it in** with a hard hand."

Reinvent the wheel*

Usually spoken in a negative connotation, such as "Don't try to reinvent the wheel," this idiom means that it is unnecessary to try to rethink technology or methods that are already well-established and working properly.

This expression has been in use since the late 19th century, and the earliest known printed reference, therein enclosed in quotes, often to indicate a recent coining, is from *The Mechanics of Surgery* by Charles Trux, 1899:

"Perusal of The Mechanics of surgery will also assure that proper credit is granted inventors, chiefly surgeons and instrument makers of the 19th century, and that no contemporary surgical instrument designer will henceforth be compelled to '**reinvent the wheel**' owing to a lack of available historical sources that document the present day armamentarium."

Resting on one's laurels

In the ancient world, winners in athletics and other heroes were distinguished by awarding them wreaths of laurel leaves. If they rested on their laurels it meant that they were relying on their past achievements, and not reaching out for new goals. The earliest known figurative example of a form of this in print is from T. W. White's *Southern Literary Messenger* in February 1836 in Chapter VIII of 'Lionel Granby':

> "'Certainly, sir,' said he, 'you may retire, and **rest in** the shade of **your** victorious **laurels**; but remember—'and here his hollow voice increased in volume and quivered with passion, 'that if you again approach my sister in any shape or form, I will put you to death, even in her hallowed presence.'"

Rich get richer and the poor get poorer

This proverbial catchphrase is frequently used when discussing economic inequality in a society, and social criticism of free market capitalism. The first known coiner of the phrase was British poet, Percy Bysshe Shelly, who made the following observations in *A Defence of Poetry* written in 1821, but not published until 1840:

> "They have exemplified the saying, 'To him that hath, more shall be given; and from him that hath not, the little that he hath shall be taken away.' **The rich have become richer, and the poor have become poorer...**"

The saying to which Shelly referred was a rephrasing of *Matthew 13:12*.

Although a similar comment was made by seventh U.S. President, Andrew Jackson, in his 1832 bank veto, a closer statement was voiced by the ninth President, William Henry Harrison, who died shortly after taking office, in a speech on 1 October 1840, before becoming President:

> "It is true democratic feeling, that all the measures of the government are directed to the purpose of making **the rich richer and the poor poorer.**"

Riding a hobby horse

As a cliché, a hobby horse is something that one dwells on, a fixation. Someone riding a hobby horse is harping on something that a lot of other folks would rather not hear about.

A literal hobby horse is a child's toy and consists of a long slender stick, much like a broomstick, with an imitation horse's head for a top. In the U.K., more detailed and lifelike hobby horses vary in style, one of which has been around since at least the early 17th century. They are particularly associated with May Day celebrations, and what are known as Mummers Plays (seasonal folk plays) and the Morris dance (a form of English folk dance accompanied by music).

Right around the corner

This idiom refers to an event which is very near. In a literal sense, when something is right around the (street) corner, it is close at hand. The earliest verifiable reference is from *The American Stone Trade* magazine, August 1921:

"Spring is **right around the corner**."

Right as rain

Similes with 'right as' have been used since medieval days of knights and castles. This one means that something is secure and comfortable to those who put their faith in it. In the epic poem, *The Romance of the Rose*, in 1400, the phrase 'right as an adamant' was used. Today most people wouldn't have a clue what was meant, but an adamant was a magnet. According to one popular source, 'right as a line' is from 1546, which smacks of John Heywood, which is the source quoted by Frank Jenners Wilstach in *A Dictionary of Similes*, 1917. It is true that 'right as a gun' appeared in John Fletcher's 1622 play, *Prophetess*. Many others followed.

Like so many other clichés, this one came to us by way of the printed word, though some were using it slightly earlier. In Max Beerbohm's *Yet Again*, published in 1909, the same sentence catapulted two famous phrases onward into our vocabulary:

"He looked, as himself would undoubtedly have said, 'fit as a fiddle,' or '**right as rain**.' His cheeks were rosy, his eyes sparkling".

Right off the bat

This means that something occurred immediately when initiated. It is derived from baseball. The earliest known verifiable citation of this actual idiom was in George Putnam Upton's *Letters of Perigrine Pickle*, 1869:

"The Devil is not only a hard hitter with the bat, but he is a quick fielder, and he will pick a soul **right off the bat** of one of these soft muscle men while S. M. is wasting his strength on the air."

From the context, it seems that the phrase was already in use prior to this date.

A similar term, 'hot from the bat,' was used in a near-literal sense as early as 25 June of the following year in Yale's weekly journal, *The College Courant*:

"Wright taking the ball **'hot' from the bat** and throwing it to Piatt."

Right on!

This cliché is an exclamation of enthusiasm meaning 'You have hit the nail on the head' or 'You couldn't be more right about that.' Its origin is debated but some feel that it derived through African American slang as it was recorded first in Howard Washington Odom and Guy Benton Johnson's *The Negro and His Songs,* in 1925. The other primary theory is that it is a shortening of right on target or 'right on cue.'

It went on to national multiracial usage in the U.S. when it became the title of a magazine founded in 1971 targeted at African American teens which continued in publication until 2011 and was designed to focus on pop culture and the lives and careers of teen idols. It faded to near archaic statis near the end of the 1980s.

Right up one's alley

This idiom is now used both as 'right up' and 'right down' one's alley. Of course it means one's special field of expertise. The word 'alley' has been applied in this way at least since the early 17th century. Francis Bacon used a form of it in his essay *Of Cunning* in 1612:

"Such men…are good but in their own Alley."

"Up one's alley," however, came into usage in the first half of the 20th century. Margaret Carpenter used it in her novel *Experiment Perilous* in 1943:

"It isn't **up my alley** at all."

Ring true

Contrary to popular belief, this saying came into being, not from the toll of a bell, but from the quality of a coin.

During the Middle Ages, due to the scarcity of precious metals and equipment, metalworkers were not able to produce coins that were uniform in size and appearance. Because of this, criminals took advantage of the situation, and counterfeit coins were common. When there was any doubt as to a coin's authenticity, a merchant would drop it on a stone slab to observe its sound. If the coin was phony, it would make a dull tone. A true coin would make a clear sound, or ring. Thus the saying 'ring true' was born. A hollow sound was called 'ringing false.'

Today if something seems true based on known facts, it is said to 'ring true.'

Ripple effect

This is derived from the reaction of a stone thrown into a pond which initiates a series of rings or ripples which continually widen until they extend far out around the penetration point. Metaphorically, it refers to the resultant diffusion of a series of consequences brought about by a single event or action.

Though this was used in a more literal sense decades earlier, the first verifiable references of figurative use came in the mid-1960s, like this in quotes citation from page 15 of the U.S. Department of Agriculture report *Rural Areas Development at Work*, 1964:

> "The $125 million in rural housing funds moved through the economy with a **'ripple effect**,' creating an estimated 10,000 man-years of construction work and a demand for lumber, plumbing, heating and electrical fixtures, concrete, paint and furniture."

Rise and shine

This is a call to awaken someone and provide motivation to face the duties of a new day. The earliest reference to rising and shining in English is from the *King James Version of the Bible, Isaiah 60:1*:

> "**Arise, shine**, for thy light is come and the glory of the LORD is risen upon thee."

From this verse, the earliest actual usage of 'rise and shine' developed, as seen in *The Testimony of William Erbery*, 1658. In speaking of Christians, the Welch clergyman and radical theologian wrote:

> "They shall so **rise and shine** that the glory shall rise upon them."

Risk one's neck / Stick one's neck out

These figurative idioms refer to taking great risk. The earliest of these is 'risk one's neck,' which goes back to the mid-19th century. The earliest known citation is from a poem from *Martialis Epigrammata selecta:* (Select Epigrams of Martial), Book XII, Ep. LXIV, translated into English by Gulielmus Hay, 1755.

"A thief for this will hardly **risk his neck**:
Nor easily will scalding water break.
The servant brings it in no pain at all,
Nor have you any, lest you let it fall."

The original epigrams were much older, dating to just after the time of Christ. Marcus Valerius Martialis (known in English as Martial) (March 1, 40 AD – between 102 and 104 AD), was a Latin poet from Hispania (the Iberian Peninsula) best known for these books, the last of which contained these lines.

Though it had been in use a while earlier, the earliest verifiable citation of sticking one's neck out as a figure of speech is from *The Rotarian*, October 1937, on page 38 in an article titled 'Illegal Lending is Bad Business' by William Trufant Foster:

"BOLD as the unlawful lender often becomes, he tries not to **stick his neck out** too far."

road to hell is paved with good intentions, The

Contrary to the belief of many, Samuel Johnson did not coin this proverb. Though he came close with, 'Hell is paved with good intentions,' he was quoting earlier folks. The first known form was from Saint Bernard of Clairvaux (1091-1153), who said, 'Hell is full of good intentions or desires."

Then in 1670, John Ray listed it in his book, *A Hand-book of English Proverbs* as, "Hell is paved with good intentions."

Just where it picked up, 'The road to...' is anyone's guess. But it likely came about after most roads started actually being paved.

road to the house of a friend is never long, The

This old Danish proverb reminds us that the journey to visit a friend is always worth it, regardless of the distance or separation.

Rob Peter to pay Paul

Most would understand that this sarcastic idiom refers to borrowing from someone to pay a debt to another. In reality, this has happened for centuries.

A printed reference to this cliché was in *Ecclesia Restaurata by Peter Heylyn,* first published in 1661.

> "Most of the lands invaded by the great men of the court, the rest laid out for reparation to the church of St Paul - pared almost to the very quick in those days of rapine. From hence first came that significant by-word (as is said by some) of **robbing Peter to pay Paul.**"

The phrase was being used in England, however, for centuries before this. The ecclesiastical work, *Jacob's well: an English treatise on the cleansing of man's conscience,* circa 1450, includes this phrase in its primal form:

> "To **robbe Petyr & geve it Poule**, it were non almesse but gret synne."

And it may have been a bit older, as it was used in John Wyclif's *Selected English Works,* which could arguably have been written as early as 1380.

> "Lord, hou schulde God approve that you **robbe Petur and gif is robbere to Poule** in ye name of Crist?"

For certain John Heywood gave it a place in *A dialogue conteinyng the nomber in effect of all the prouerbes in the Englishe tongue* in 1546:

> "**Rob Peter and pay Paul**: thou sayest I do;
> But thou robbest and poulst Peter and Paul too."

In an entry in a French text in 1611, Saint was used before Peter and Paul, so it was obvious which Peter and Paul were meant in this popular phrase. It is likely, however that these two were chosen from the fact that both names begin with the same letter.

Rob the cradle

This saying seems to have derived from the 1925 Broadway comedy play by Russell Medcraft and Norma Mitchell titled, *Cradle Snatchers.* After having caught her husband with an attractive 'flapper,' a woman convinces her two female friends that their husbands are chasing women on the weekends. As a result, the ladies throw a champagne party and invite three attractive college boys to entertain them.

The phrase applies to either a man or woman who is in a relationship separated by an unusually large span of years. Sometimes it is jokingly used by men whose wives are not so much younger, but when they wish to flatter them.

A 2009 study by the Max Planck Institute in Germany suggests that men who marry significantly younger women live longer. Conversely, the study found that women who marry younger men die sooner, reducing their lifespan by twenty percent on the average.

Rocky Mountain high*

The term, 'Rocky Mountain high' is taken from the title and lyrics to the 1972-1973 pop-culture hit song of the late legendary balladeer John Denver, inspired by his move to Aspin in 1972. The final chorus, sung five times, is:

> "It's Colorado **Rocky Mountain high**
> I've seen it rainin' fire in the sky
> Friends around the campfire and everybody's high
> **Rocky Mountain high**."

This refrain was inspired by an actual event when Denver, his ex-wife and some friends went up in the mountains in Colorado to view a meteor shower. The high was both natural and figurative, as the Rocky Mountain grandeur makes many feel a sense of euphoria.

Some subsequently twisted this to mean a high obtained by marijuana, and the song was banned by a number of radio stations. There is nothing in the lyrics to indicate this, though the phrase is often now used to refer to such, particularly since Colorado, on 1 January 2014, became the first U.S. state to legalize the sale of marijuana for recreational purposes.

Rode hard and put up (or away) wet

This saying means someone has been treated badly or abused. It is derived from horses being ridden past the logical limit, then being put in the stall without even being brushed and allowed to cool down, thus being treated very poorly.

The oldest verifiable printed reference to the American form is in *Texas Magazine*, March 1974 on page 44, in 'Rodeo Madness' by Gary Cartwright:

"In cowboy talk, he looked like he had been **rode hard and put up wet**."

The earliest available, however, of the version normally thought to be British, is also from an American publication, *Field and Stream*, May 1989, in an article titled 'Thoughtless Packing' by Steve Netherby on page 76:

"It's been '**rode hard and put away wet**' over many years and has always come through."

Note that both versions utilize the incorrect verb tense.

Roger Dodger

Roger, in both military and civilian radio terminology, means 'I have received all of the last transmissions.' It was derived from the word indicating the letter 'R' in radio and spelling alphabets in use by the military at the time of the invention of the radio near the end of the 19th century.

This phrase was coined in the U.S. military during World War II in conjunction with a humerous antidote about a soldier, often called a pilot, who added his own flair to radio jargon. The punchline of the joke was, "Roger Dodger, you old codger!" It was circulated through all branches of service culminating with the Coast Guard.

rolling stone gathers no moss, A

This 16th century proverb is based on a principle well-known in that era. Moss is a very slow growing organism. The easiest way to keep it from forming on rocks is to move them about on a regular basis. The first known printing of it is by our old friend and publisher of curious English phrases, John Heywood, in 1546, in *A dialogue conteinyng the nomber in effect of all the prouerbes in the Englishe tongue*. It means that unless one settles down, they will never really accomplish anything.

"The rollyng stone neuer gatherth mosse."

Heywood may have garnered the 'mosse' idea from the poem, *A Spending Hand*, written a few years earlier by Thomas Wyatt to Sir Francis Bryan, the first of which reads:

"A spendyng hand that alway powreth out,
Had nede to haue a bringer in as fast.
And on **the stone** that styll doth turne about,
There growth no mosse. These prouerbes yet do last:

Reason hath set them in so sure a place:
That length of yeres their force can neuer waste."

Even before this a form of it was included by Erasmus in the third volume of his Latin proverbs, *Adagia*, in 1508.

Roll up the sidewalks***

Though other versions have been used like 'fold up the sidewalks,' 'roll up the pavement,' or the version reportedly used in Australia and Ireland, 'roll up the footpath;' in America it has been 'roll up the sidewalks' for over a century. There is even a German rendering of this saying.

Many years ago the streets in America were unpaved and often muddy, and the 'sidewalks' in front of buildings were made of mats or planks, which could literally be taken up. The term in the U.S. has been used since the late 19th century, and has been cited many times since the early 1920s. It is often used of towns in which businesses close at night and nothing is happening in the way of nightlife, but not always.

The earliest known printed reference is from pp 96, 97 of *A Bundle of Burnt Cork Comedy* by Harry Lee Newton, 1905, published in Minnesota:

"We had to take the girls home early because they **roll up the sidewalks** there at nine o'clock. She said that all the curbstones were to be removed because everybody was kicking against them."

Rome wasn't built in a day

This well-worn proverb is another for which 16th-century British playwright and writer John Heywood must receive credit for passing it on to us. It was also in *A dialogue conteinying the number in effect of all the prouerbes in the Englishe tongue*, published in 1546.

It means that nothing good happens overnight. It takes time to build relationships, businesses, etc.

rose by any other name would smell as sweet, A

Also used as 'a rose by any other name is still a rose,' and 'a rose is a rose is a rose,' but the 'smell as sweet' version is the proper one...at least the original.

This is because it is a quote from Shakespeare's immortal bittersweet romantic tragedy, *Romeo and Juliet*. It means that what something is called doesn't matter, but rather what it really is. The following is from Juliet speaking to Romeo:

"What's in a name? that which we **call a rose**
By any other name would smell as sweet;
So Romeo would, were he not Romeo call'd,
Retain that dear perfection which he owes
Without that title…"

This spawned a number of other uses of the phrase, 'a rose by any other name.'

Roses are red, violets are blue,
sugar is sweet and so are you

This short lyric, often followed by various other rhyming lines was inspired by the following is from a poem in Edmund Spenser's 1590 book, *The Fearie Queene*.

"She bath'd with **roses red, and violets** blew,
And all the sweetest flowres, that in the forrest grew."

A Valentine's Day nursery rhyme using this theme, and adding what was likely the initial version of the 'sweet' lines was printed first in *Gammer Gurton's Garland* in 1783:

"**The rose is red, the violet's blue,**
The honey's **sweet, and so are you**.
Thou are my love and I am thine;
I drew thee to my Valentine…"

Rough as a cob

In the American pioneer days, and even later, cobs were used by some for personal hygiene including cleaning after bowel movements. Obviously, this was unpleasant, envoking this thought. This means that an individual is unpolished in basic communication skills, etiquette and mannerisms. It didn't come into use, however, until the early 1940s and the earliest known example is from *Texas: a World in Itself* by George Sessions Perry, 1942:

"A tough man or an abrasive object are either one 'as **rough as a cob**.'"

Note the quotes, here, in this case, indicating a known local saying.

Rough it

This idiom refers to doing without the normally accepted comforts and conveniences. It was first recorded by Francis Grose in *A Clasical Dictionary of the Vulgar Tongue*, 1785:

> "Rough, to lie rough, to lie all night in one's clothes; called also **roughing it**."

Rub salt in the wound

In the past centuries in England, punishment of sailors for disobedience would often be whipping with a cat-of-nine-tails—a whip with particles of bone tied on the ends of nine strands of leather. After one of these beatings, salt would be rubbed into the wounds to help combat infection. Of course, this would bring on a great deal of pain, but would be better than developing gangrene, which may have caused death. The cliché 'rubbing salt in the wound' means adding more pain to an already bad situation. Sometimes 'rub it in' is used to relate the same meaning.

Rub the wrong way

This term now means to cause someone to become angry by making statements which are offensive or taking adverse action against someone. But it was originally something else entirely. In colonial America, floors of the better homes were made of wide oak boards which were polished by the servants once a week so that when company came they would look their best. It was imperative that this be done by rubbing with the grain, because 'rubbing the wrong way' would cause unsightly streaking. It was in use as a cliché before January, 1823, when it appeared in *The London Magazine* in a long, letter-type article titled 'Janus Weatherbound':

> "Truly 'without affectation,' for nothing **rubbed him the wrong way** so much as pretence; — then the sparks Hew about!"

Also, rubbing the hair of a cat the wrong way will upset it.

Rude awakening

This is the result of discovering the shocking truth of a situation. Its origin is uncertain, but it was coming into use in the early 19th century as seen from this earliest available citation in *Alla Giornata, or To the Day* by Lady C.S.M. Bury, 1826:

> "It was a **rude awakening**. She blushed at his approach, and betrayed a confusion of manner, as though he could have read her inmost thoughts."

Ruffle someone's feathers

This metaphoric expression is similar to 'rub the wrong way' (see). It means to irritate, or annoy someone. It comes from fowls getting offensive when people intentionally rub their feathers in an unpleasing manner. An early literal reference is found in Henry Headley's, *Select Beauties of English Poetry*, Volume 2, 1787, in *Lesbia on her Sparrow* by W. Cartwright:

> "O how eager would he fight,
> And ne'r hurt though he did bite:
> No morn did pass
> But on my glass
> He would fit, and mark,
> and do What I did, now **ruffle** all
> **His feathers** o'r, now let 'em fall
> And then straightway sleek them too."

The earliest available figurative citation comes in 1842, in *Museum of Foreign Literature, Science and Art*, Volume 44, In Charles Lever's *Jack Hinton, the Guardsman,* on page 419:

> "'...he went down to the gate and took a sitting shot at the sub-sheriff who was there in a tax-cart.'
> "'Bless my soul! Did he kill him?'
> "'No, he only **ruffled his feathers** and broke his thigh; but that was bad enough, for he had to go to France till it blew over.'"

Rule of thumb

This means 'an estimation based on common sense and practicality rather than an exact science.' The popular belief is that this was based on a law that allowed a man to beat his wife so long as the stick was no thicker than his thumb. In 1782, Judge Sir Francis Buller reportedly made such a legal ruling. The next year, James Gillray published a satirical cartoon which denounced Buller and pictured him as 'Judge Thumb.' In the cartoon, a man is beating his wife and the Judge is carrying two bundles of sticks.

Edward Foss, a respected historian, later concluded that though Buller was harsh in his rulings, there is 'no substantial evidence' that he actually made such a ruling, or that anyone ever called this principle 'the rule of thumb.'

British Common Law, however, did once hold that a man could chastise his wife in moderation. Moreover, any actual law called 'the rule of thumb,' also never existed.

Though the exact origin remains unknown, the phrase, itself, has been in circulation since the 1600s. In 1692, it appeared in print in Sir William Hope's manual, *The Compleat Fencingmaster*:

"What he doth, he doth by **rule of Thumb**, and not by Art."

It seems logical, and that is the basis of the rule, logic, that the rule of thumb likely was derived from the width of the thumb being used by carpenters in measuring small spaces.

Rule the roost

This is another chicken metaphor. The word 'roost' is from the Middle English of the 11th century, and 'ruling the roost' has been said of 'roosters,' a common term for a male chicken, for hundreds of years. It is used metaphorically for a person who dominates a family or group of people. A similar metaphor would be 'cocky,' which is derived from the other word for a rooster. The phrase, however, is not restricted by gender, but can be a female family member who 'wears the pants.'

The expression originated in the 16th century in a bit different light. The first known version is from English poet John Skelton in *Why Come ye not to Courte* (published c. 1550), line 198:

"He **ruleth all the roste**."

Elizabethan playwright and author, Thomas Heywood, in *Gunaikeion* (a poetic history of women), page 286, in 1624, recorded it this way:

"Her that **ruled the rost** in the kitchen…"

Then John Heywood in his 1546 book of proverbs, part i chapter iv:

"**Rule the roast**."

Shakespeare also had this in *Henry VI Part 2* (1:1) 1596-1599:

"The new-made duke that **rules the roast**..."

It wasn't until the mid-17th century that 'roost,' per se, began to also be used, and by the 20th century, displaced roast altogether.

Run into a brick wall

This American idiom has been molded into many shapes over the last few decades. Come up against a brick or stone wall, run into or hit a brick or stone wall, etc., means that you have encountered insurmountable obstacles in achieving a desired goal. A brick or stone wall is an excellent example of an obstacle which would stop someone 'dead in their tracks.'

This phrase was used as a metaphor as early as 1922 in *On Nature's Trail: A wonder book in the wild* by F. St. Mars:

> "And the old bird stopped dead — literally dead — in full career, stooped with a rending sound, and a suddenness as if she had **run into a brick wall**."

By the early 1950s it was being used as a figure of speech as in this example from *Billboard*, March 17, 1951:

> "Jake's increasingly desperate attempts at a reconciliation **run into a brick wall**."

Run of the mill

This expression means only basic, average or commonplace, with no augmentation to distinguish it or set it apart. It is American in derivation from mills which made standard products in the 19th century. The earliest known citation is from an ad in the *Lowell Daily Sun*, in Massachusetts, placed by Cook, Taylor and Co. in December 1895:

> "Seconds and the **run of the mill**, but for all wearing purposes, the same as firsts at twice the price. Fleeced Jersey vests in white or Ecru. 2 for 25c."

Run someone out of town on a rail

In a literal sense, this practice, aka 'riding a rail' was a punishment in 19th century America in which a man was forced to straddle a split fence rail held on the shoulders of at least two other men and paraded around town, then usually taken out of the city limits and dumped by the roadside. Later it was also used as a hyperbolic term when someone had committed a seemingly atrocious act, as seen in this citation from 'Through the Fire,' *Boys' Life*, March 1917:

"'He **ought to be run out of town on a rail**,' he said in a low tone. 'He's as bad as his father, I'll warrant.'"

Run something into the ground

This has two definitions. First, it can mean that a topic has been discussed so much that it has been exhausted and is no longer worthy of bringing up. Secondly it can refer to treating something so badly or using something so much that it is completely destroyed. The earliest known figurative usage in print is from *The American Review: A Whig Jouranal, Volume 5*, 1847:

"Even if he begins with a good thought, well expressed, he is pretty sure to **run it — into the ground** — before he gets through. Here is an instance."

Run the gauntlet

Running the gauntlet is defined as going through a series of harsh criticisms at the hands of one's detractors.

In medieval days, gauntlets or 'gantelettes' formed part of the suits of armor and were usually covered with plates of steel and were for both attack and defense. When a member of the British nobility would be attacked he would throw down the gauntlet as a challenge.

The phrase 'throw down the gauntlet' is first recorded in *Hall's Chronicles of Richard III*, 1548:

"Makynge a proclamacion, that whosoeuer would saie that kynge Richard was not lawefully kynge, he woulde fighte with hym at the vtteraunce, and **threwe downe his gauntlet**."

In another form of ancient punishment, the victim would run, stripped to the waist. A row of men on either side of him as he ran would whip him as he passed. This is like the use of the cat-of-nine-tails a few pages back. Many actually died from these beatings. This is where the term, 'running the gauntlet' originally came from. It was utilized in both the British army and navy.

But gauntlets were not used in these beatings. It was originally called 'running the gantelope,' an Anglicized form of the Swedish word 'gatlop,' referring to the gate of soldiers that the victims had to pass through.

The First Earl of Shaftsbury recorded the phrase in his *Diary*, in 1646:

"Three were condemned to die, two to run the gantelope."

By 1661, gantelope was changed to gauntlet in British writing. Likely it was because of the similar sound, and the familiarity of the English with the word 'gauntlet.' That year, Joseph Glanvill used the phrase in *The vanity of dogmatizing, or confidence in opinions etc.*:

"To print, is to **run the gantlet**, and to expose ones self to the tongues strapado."

Gauntlet, in this phrase, was first spelled as we use it today by Increase Mather in *The history of King Philip's war*, 1676:

"They stripped them naked, and caused them to **run the Gauntlet**."

S

Sadder but wiser

This cliché came into its own as a result of the 1962 version of *Music Man*, starring Robert Preston. The title to a song in this popular Rogers and Hammerstein musical extravaganza was *The Sadder-But-Wiser Girl for Me*. The song ended like this:

"I hope, and I pray, for a Hester to win just one more 'A'
The **sadder-but-wiser** girl's the girl for me.
The **sadder-but-wiser** girl for me."

The term has come to mean that as a result of an unpleasant event or circumstance, a person has become more aware and acceptant.

Safe and sound

This phrase means unscathed. The earliest mention of it in English is from the *King James Version* of the *Bible, Luke 15:27*, in which the father is rejoicing because the 'prodigal son' has returned:

"And he said unto him, Thy brother is come; and thy father hath killed the fatted calf, because he hath received him **safe and sound**."

Saved by the bell

The most logical explanation for this saying is the boxer who is being 'beaten to a pulp' and the bell announces the end of the round. This came into use as a boxing term in the late 19th century, but its origins may go back to as early as the 17th century.

The term is said to have originally applied to being rescued by a ringing bell attached to a coffin to keep people from being buried alive due to a lack of medical understanding and unconsciousness. People were often pronounced dead when they were in comas, seizures, and other states of near death. There were several patients in England and early America who opted for 'safety coffins' with bells incorporated into the designs which would ring in the event of body movement. There is no record of anyone actually being saved by one though. But these special coffins were registered in the late 1800s and as late as 1955. This is where the saying 'dead ringer' (see) originated.

Save it for a rainy day

Surprisingly, this saying has been around in English since 1580, when it was used by Francis Kinwelmersh in his frightening tale, *The Bugbears*.

"'Wold he haue me kepe nothing against **a raynye day**?'"

This joins such favorites as 'A penny saved is a penny earned,' and is reminiscent of the Perry Como lyric, 'Catch a falling star and put it in your pocket, **save it for a rainy day**.'

Save the best for last

In centuries gone by archers used to shoot arrows at the enemy soldiers in times of war. The supply of arrows in their quivers varied in quality, the best ones being the very straight, well-balanced ones with the finest torque and feathers. Most, however, were mass produced, with low-to-average quality shafts. Some were even made from branches of trees to insure enough when supplies were low. The poorer quality arrows were used first, when the opposing forces were at a greater range, and an actual hit was less likely. As the battle became closer, they would begin using the better ones, and master archers would instruct the soldiers to "**save the best for last**."

Say uncle!

Many believe that this expression came from the old Irish word 'anacol,' meaning the act of deliverance, protection, or mercy, as it is used to beg for mercy when someone has carried a friendly induction of pain a bit too far.

Another theory is that it goes even further back to a Latin expression used by Roman youth who got into trouble, *patrue mi patruissime,* meaning uncle, my best of uncles. They are thought to have been required to call for their uncle in order to be freed.

A number of newspapers in the late nineteenth and early twentieth centuries carried jokes with reference to this practice, often in the children's section.

One such example is from the *Iowa Citizen*, October 9, 1891:

> *A gentleman was boasting that his parrot would repeat anything he told him. For example, he told him several times, before some friends, to **say "Uncle,"** but the parrot would not repeat it. In anger he seized the bird, and half-twisting his neck, said: "Say 'uncle,' you beggar!" and threw him into the fowl pen, in which he had ten prize fowls. Shortly afterward, thinking he had killed the parrot, he went to the pen. To his surprise he found nine of the fowls dead on the floor with their necks wrung, and the parrot standing on the tenth twisting his neck and screaming: "**Say 'uncle,'** you beggar! say 'uncle.'"*

Say what you mean and mean what you say

Although this is not from the *Bible*, it is based on a principle found there—the words of Jesus when he said, "Let what you say be simply 'Yes' or 'No'; anything more than this comes from evil." (*Matthew 5:37, ESV*). This cliché is actually a rewording of a quote from Lewis Carroll's *Alice in Wonderland,* 1865. It was said by Alice to the March Hare at the Mad Hatter's tea party.

"'Then you should **say what you mean**,' the March Hare went on.

"'I do,' Alice hasitily replied; 'at least—at least I **mean what I say**—that's the same thing, you know.'"

The March Hare then told her that her logic was wrong.

Scared the bejeebees out of me!*

This is a further corruption of "Big Jesus," originally spoken as "bejesus," started among African American Christians as far back as the American Civil War when speaking of spirits. Children were taught that Jesus lives in us. Frightening someone badly was "Scaring the Big Jesus out" of the person. This was picked up by the general public in the U. S. and was a popular euphemism by the mid-20th century.

An early example in print is found in the February 11, 1955 issue of *Princeton Alumni Weekly,* on page 21:

> "But treasurers are funny guys—they *scare the bejesus out* of us—real treasurers, we mean."

Because this was thought by some to be blasphemous, by the 1970s it was usually altered to bejeebers or bejeebees.

Another corruption of a similar sort is hebejeebees or heebie-jeebies, thought to be from "Baby Jesus," which is also said by some to go back to slavery days. The terms are extremely close in spelling and pronunciation. This expression means being very jittery and anxious, and was popularized by American cartoonist William Morgan "Billy" De Beck (1810-1942), the creator of Barney Google and Snuffy Smith, in a 1923 cartoon. Many attribute its coining to him as a part of the rash of rhyming expressions of the 1920s. It is possible, however, that it was derived from the thought of someone stealing the Baby Jesus from a crèche, which would make the thief very nervous if he were to be suspected.

Scoring (or **racking up**) **brownie points**

Meaning receiving praise and or favor for specific acts or statements, often used in school slang, this term is traceable to at least the mid-1950s. *Brownie* by itself is recorded in the journal, *American Speech* as early as 1944 as 'a person who is always asking and answering questions in class to impress the instructor.' Brown-nose dates from even earlier—pre war.

Civil-Military Relations: An Annotated Bibliography 1940-1952, first published in 1954, has the following citation:

> "...points of order, view, and no return; of **brownie points** and point spreads; of vowel points, those dots that reader-friendly users of Hebrew and

Arabic scripts put in under the appropriate consonantal letters to tell you which vowel comes next..."

Though the meaning here is ambiguous, that same year, on April 15, *The Daily News*, Newport, Rhode Island, printed the following, citing several recent slang expressions:

"'We want more new lingo' writes a Missouri column fan who wants to be the first to spring new vernacular on her group. So here goes: Miami young people keep their teachers agog with their lingo says Sanford Schnier, of the *Miami Daily News*. He offers these 'cool' expressions: 'Flake out' — Too much study is tiring. 'Browse me on the scene' — Request for information. 'Pull a boo boo' — Make an error. **'Racking up the Brownie points'** — Teacher's pet. 'Toe Dancers' — High school sissies. 'Calories' — Plump girls. 'Fluffs' — Fat boys."

There is one reference, however, which is even earlier. The first known is from the *Los Angeles Times* in March 1951; and this one is not about school:

"You don't know about **brownie points**? All my buddies keep score. In fact every married male should know about 'em. It's a way of figuring where you stand with the little woman — favor or disfavor. Started way back in the days of the leprechauns, I suppose, long before there were any doghouses."

Scot free

This is a not a slam against the Scottish people, having to do with penny pinching. It's actually form the Old English word *sceot*, which meant a tax or a penalty. People in England who avoided taxes in olden days were said to have gotten off 'scot free.'

Scrape the bottom of the barrel

This idiom means to settle for the worst or lowest quality available because there was no choice. It is derived from the sediment in the bottom of a wine barrel. When the supply of wine became low, it was necessary to either throw out the dregs or scrape the bottom of the barrel.

The term was first used figuratively by Roman philosopher, lawyer and statesman, Marcus Tullius Cicero (January 3, 106 B.C. – December 7, 43 B.C.). In 70 B.C., he attacked Gaius Verres, the currupt Governor of Sicily, for scraping the bottom of the barrel (using the lowest elements within the society) to form an advisory council for trials.

Seal the deal

This means to finalize an undeniable agreement which will not be cancelled by either party. The earliest known example in print is from the novel, *Pigs to Market* by George Agnew Chamberlain, 1920:

> "The contractor's eyes narrowed, he transferred his cud thrice, and then murmerred the single word, 'Ballast.' After a longer and still more deliberate pause than usual he turned and held out his horny hand to **seal the deal** for the laying of the 'Mlidini spur roadbed.''

Second fiddle

This has a similar meaning to 'taking a back seat' to someone or something else, or be subordinate to them. Some people equate it to a 'sidekick' of an important person, and it evolved in the same time frame (see that entry below).

In an orchestra, the second 'fiddle,' or violin, plays more of a harmony than that played by the more prominent lead violin. Therefore the second fiddle is somewhat overpowered by the lead, though it still plays an important part to the value of the music.

It has been used figuratively since at lest the mid-19th century as evidenced by this citation from *Graham's Magazine*, in a story titled 'Meena Dimity,' by N.P. Willis, September 1843:

> "Harriet liked him, for he was the only beau in Slimford whose manners were not belittled beside her nose. ... to Meena Dimity, (for he was too proud to play **second-fiddle** to a town dandy) was walking with her, on a dark night, past the Diapers..."

Security blanket

In a literal sense, security blankets are small, familiar blankets carried by toddlers and young children for reassurance. The term originated in the 1920s, and was popularized by Charles Shultz in his beloved *Peanuts* cartoon strip as first mentioned in June, 1954. The earliest known mention of the phrase was in the *Official Gazette of the United States Patent Office*, 1924 when stating that a patent had been applied for on January 5, 1920, for a 'security blanket fastener' by Security Blanket Fasteners Co., in New York.

The following as appeared in newspapers in 1925:

Crib Blankets for the Little Folks
Security
Blanket Fasteners
for your baby's comfort keeps
covers on children. No matter how restless.
59 cents the Pair

Then during World War II 'security blanket' began being used figuratively to refer to strict security measures taken by Allied forces to prevent secrets from leaking to the Germans. *The Dothan Eagle*, Dothan, Alabama, printed the following in September 1944:

> "Reports being issued at Gen. Dwight D. Eisenhower's headquarters sometimes were as much as 48 hours behind the armies because of a **security blanket** thrown over the operations."

In a broader sense this term refers to anything which makes a person feel less threatened.

seed hidden in the heart of an apple is an orchard invisible, A

This Welsh proverb means that we can provide the foundation that our children need to become role models for the next generation by planting within them truths and principles of inspiration and leadership.

Its time of origin is uncertain, but it was quoted by Kahil Gabrin in *Jesus, the Son of Man*, 1928:

> **"A seed hidden in the heart of an apple is an orchard invisible**. Yet should that seed fall upon a rock, it will come to naught."

Seeing is believing

The principle of this proverb is thousands of years old, but the earliest printing in English is from S. Harward's *MS*, 1609 (Trinity College, Cambridge), which also appeared in John Clarke's *Paroemiologia Anglo-Latina* in 1639:

> **"Seeing is beleeving."**

It was then included in Lewis Baboon's *Arbothnot* in 1712 with an explanation of a sort:

> "There's nothing like Matter of Fact; **Seeing is Believing**."

See no evil, hear no evil, speak no evil

This ancient proverb is based on the Japanese tale of the three wise monkeys or three mystic apes. In order, they are Mizaru, covering his eyes, Kikazaru, covering his ears, and Iwazaru, covering his mouth. An optional monkey named Shizaru, crossing his arms, symbolizes the all-encompassing principle, 'do no evil.'

A 17th century carving over a door of the famed Toshogo shrine of the Shinto religion in Nikko, Japan popularized the proverbial maxim.

In Japan, this proverb is regarded as the Japanese Golden Rule. In Buddhism, it refers to refraining from dwelling on evil thoughts. In other traditions it is to emphasize avoiding the spreading of evil. In the Western world, both the three monkeys and the proverb refer to a lack of moral responsibility on the part of those who look the other way when others are committing horrendous acts.

See you later, alligator, after while, crocodile

This rhyme started as simply, 'see you later, alligator,' and was popularized by Bill Haley's hit classic, *See You later, Alligator,* released December, 1955.

It then appeared in *New Campus Writings* by Judson Jerome and Nolan Miller, second edition, in Tillie Olsen's '*Hey Sailor, What Ship,*' 1957.

> "Didn't know you were sick, Whitey, thought you were like… some of the other times. From the top stair, **See you later, alligator**."

'After while, crocodile,' or 'In a while, crocodile,' developed as a response to this.

Self-fulfilling prophecy*

This expression refers to a prediction which causes itself to come true, either directly or indirectly because of positive feedback between belief and behavior patterns being exhibited. Such examples may be seen in history as far back as ancient times and in such varying civilizations as Greece and India. 20th century sociologist Robert K. Merton is credited with coining the phrase in his book *Social Theory and Social Structure,* first published in 1949, and revised in 1957 and 1968.

Merton's concept, however, stems from Thomas theorem; W.I. Thomas, in his 1928 book, *The Child in America, Behavior Problems and Programs*, p. 572:

"If men define situations as real, they are real in their consequences."

But thee roots are much deeper. A variation of this idea, a self-fulfilling dream, is in medieval Arabic literature. A classic example is *The Ruined Man Who Became Rich Again through a Dream*. A man dreams of leaving Bagdad for Cairo and finding hidden treasure. He goes in search of it, experiencing misfortune, and is jailed. After telling an officer of the dream, who convinces him that his quest is futile, he returns to Bagdad and the officer discovers buried treasure beneath his home.

Sell oneself short

Novices are often admonished by their leaders not to sell themselves short in a business deal, or not to lack confidence in their own abilities to perform a task when they have the capability to do so.

This expression came from selling stock. Selling a stock short actually means to sell stock that one doesn't own. These shares can be bought later before the transaction is completed. This is practiced when investors believe the price of stock is going down and they hope to profit in that drop. This is one reason that insider trading is forbidden.

Since selling stock short is in anticipation of decline in price, selling oneself short came to mean that a person feels that he or she is loosing some ability.

Set in stone

Alternatives of this are 'written in stone' and 'carved in stone.' Millenniums ago, long before papyrus, and the invention of paper, history was recorded by carving the characters in stone.

In 1780 BC, the Code of Hammurabi stated that the law as written cannot be changed by anyone that follows and it was also 'written in stone.'

Another prime example to which most people today can relate even better is the Ten Commandments which Moses brought down from the mountain a couple of hundred years later in circa 1450 BC. When something was recorded in stone it was, quite naturally, very permanent, a factor emphasized about these sacred tablets which the *Bible* states were carved by 'the finger of God.'

Today this is likely referred to in the negative more than the positive. When we say that something is 'not set in stone' it means that, fortunately, it can still be changed.

Set one's cap at (for or on) someone

This term is usually applied to a woman who is attempting to gain the affections of a man. It is supposed by some to have derived from a French nautical term '*mettre le cap sur*' meaning 'to set a course for.' 'Cap' here, of course does not mean what our English term implies, so this is unlikely.

It could actually have come from placing a cap on a woman's head, since in the 18th century when the phrase was coined women wore white caps made of either linen or muslin adorned with lace or frills. It made sense that a woman who was vying for a man's attention would don her best cap and set at such an angle as to appear most attractive. In Oliver Goldsmith's *She Stoops to Conquer* in 1773 the following would seem to bear this out:

> "Well, if he refuses, instead of breaking my heart at his indifference, I'll only break my glass for its flattery, **set my cap** to some newer fashion, and look out for some less difficult admirer."

By early in the 19th century, the figurative usage was in print. Popular novelist Jane Austen included this in the classic, *Sense and Sensibility* in 1811:

> *"Aye, aye, I see how it will be," said Sir John, "I see how it will be. You will be **setting your cap at him** [Willoughby] now, and never think of poor Brandon."*

> *"That is an expression, Sir John," said Marianne, warmly, "which I particularly dislike. I abhor every common-place phrase by which wit is intended; and '**setting one's cap at a man**,' or 'making a conquest,' are the most odious of all."*

Set the record straight

This idiom means to provide accurate information or make an honest and fair statement regarding some circumstances or situation, especially when previous inaccurate information has been given. Contrary to other sources dating the coining of this phrase in the early 20th century, it was in use as early as the mid-19th century as seen in this citation from *The Congressional Globe* for the Second Session, Thirty-third Congress, 1855, page 244:

"Mr. BENJAMIN: I think, Mr. President, I have a right to **set the record straight** upon that point."

Setting on a powder keg (See: **Powder keg**)

Setting on the fence (See: **On the fence**)

Seventh heaven

This expression is used to represent a state of ecstacy or great joy. It is derived from a tenant of Islam. It is the farthest of the concentric spheres containing the stars, constituting the dwelling place of Allah and the angels, and ruled by Abraham in the Muslim and kabbalist systems. It is believed to be the ultimate reward for those who have earned it on earth and beyond all description.

Seven year itch

If you thought that the origin of this phrase was Billy Wilder's runaway hit movie starring Marilyn Monroe and Tom Ewell about men having affairs after seven years of marriage, you're wrong. Though this iconic film which contained the infamous image of Marilyn on the street over the hot air with her white dress blown up brought the cliché to a higher level of usage worldwide, it had been around since the early 19th century. The literal contagious skin condition was well enough known in the U.S. to be used in print as a metaphor for anything annoying as early as 1845, when it was used prejudicially in the *Wisconsin Herald and Grant County Advertiser*:

"When Illinois caught Mormonism off Missouri, she caught something worse than the **seven year itch**. Job sitting in the ashes and scratching himself amongst the pot-sherds, was infinitely more comfortable than poor Illinois now is, burning and festering under the scab of Mormonism."

Obviously a biased article, but a good example of early usage of the cliché.

Shake a leg*

In modern times this expression means 'get a move on' or 'hurry up.' This has been the case at least since the early 20th century when it was so defined in 1904 in *The New York Magazine*:

480

"**Shake a leg**...meaning hurry up."

This is used often for getting out of bed. An earlier similar naval phrase, 'show a leg,' was used for a wake-up call for sailors. It was said that in the beginning, when women boarded a ship, showing a leg for a woman would prove her gender and she was permitted to sleep later. This one could have evolved from that saying, but not necessarily, since the term 'shake a leg' in the mid-19th century was used of dancing. The earliest known figurative example of 'show a leg,' here in a non-naval context, in print is found in Edward Bradley's *The Adventures of Mr. Verdant Green*, 1854, written under the pseudonym, Cuthbert Bede:

> "I would answer Robert when he hammered at the door; but, instead of getting up, I would knock my boots against the floor... But that wretch of a Robert was too old a bird to be caught with this dodge; so he used to sing out, 'You must **show a leg**, sir!' and he kept on hammering at the door till I did."

Another theory is that the phrase 'shake a leg' became used like this first in the American Civil War when medics would come out to retrieve the dead and wounded after a gruesome battle, sometimes they could only tell if the soldier was still living was to lift and shake a leg to see if they detected movement. After that the phrase took on a new meaning.

Shaking like a leaf

This is another of many metaphoric expressions likely originating in the latter half of the 20th century in America. It is used most commonly by someone who is terrified of a given situation into which they are thrust. It indicates that they are trembling with anxiety, like a leaf on a tree blowing in the wind. A form of it (quake like an aspen leaf) was first used as shaking in anger by Chaucer in The Prologe of *The Somonours Tale,* one of his famed *Canterbury Tales*:

> "That **lyk** an aspen **leef he quook** for ire."

Share and share alike

This means to give equal portions to all persons concerned. The first mention in print of a form of this (share and share *like*) was in Richard Edwards' comedy play, *Damon and Pithias*, 1566:

> "Let vs into the Courte to parte the spoyle, **share and share like**."

The earliest known citation of the current form is in *Cases in Parliament: resolved and adjudged, upon petitions and writs of error*, 1698:

> "Brother Benjamin; and being thus charged, upon his dying before Age or Marriage, his Share, with the Profits thereof thus charged, is given to his younger Brother and Sisters, the Survivor and Survivors of them, **Share and Share alike.**"

Twenty-one years later Daniel Defoe used it in *The life and strange adventures of Robinson Crusoe,* 1719:

> "He declar'd he had reserv'd nothing for the Men, and went **Share and Share alike** with them in every Bit they eat."

Sharp as a tack

This idiom is, of course, a play on words with a dual meaning. 'Sharp' in this phrase refers to having a keen, witty mind while alluding to the fine point of a tack. Several sources report this since 1912. The actual origin is from New Orleans native Dominic James 'Nick' LaRocca (1889-1961), leader of the Original Dixieland Jazz Band who was active from 1912 to 1959 in the industry with several labels including Victor and Columbia. The band gave him the nickname "Joe Blade" in 1917 and they published a song titled *Joe Blade, Sharp as a Tack*. This was the earliest citation.

Variants, such as 'sharp as a thorn' and 'sharp as a needle' are from the mid-19th century.

shoe is on the other foot now, The

The root of this metaphoric phrase meaning 'the circumstances have now reversed' first appeared on 30 May 1861 as '*The Boot on the Other Leg,*' an editorial in the *New York Times*. Later it was part of the title to a book by Matthew Carey, *The Boot on the Other Leg: or Loyalty above Party* (1863). This is said to have originated years earlier. The inference here is that when a shoe is on the wrong foot it is very uncomfortable. It usually applies to someone who felt that they were above another in status and when the shoe is on the other foot, the person originally in a sad state is now in an improved position; while the other one, who felt superior, is taken down a peg or two (see) by the winds of fate (see).

Shoo-in

Some misspell this as shoe-in. It has come to mean a sure winner, but was not originally defined this way. The verb shoo meant to take someone or something in a specific direction by making noises or gestures.

The shift of this expression to horse racing occurred some time in the early 20th century. It meant winning a rigged race. George E. Smith related how this came about in his highly acclaimed, *Racing Maxims and Methods of Pittsburgh Phil* in 1908.

"There were many times presumably that 'Tod' would win through such manipulations, being '**shooed in**,' as it were."

Shoot fire and save matches!

The origin of this saying or who coined it is obscure, but it likely started in the American South around the mid-20th century. It, or the profane alternative, was used as an expression of surprise, alarm or disgust when something didn't go the way it was anticipated. The earliest known printed reference is from Guy Owens' classic novel of rural North Carolina, *The Ballad of the Flim-flam Man*, 1965, page 66:

"**Shoot fire and save matches**! You talk about running. Shucks, you've not seen nothing like it in all your born days, the way them two moonshiners lit out of there."

Shoot for the moon; even if you miss, you'll land in the stars

This popular saying is attributed most often to American motivational speaker and author, Les Brown (1945-). It means set high goals and exert the effort to reach them and even if you fail you are still ahead of where you would be if you hadn't put in the effort.

The earliest known verifiable citation of 'shoot for the moon,' in a figurative sense, is from *Changing Times,* the Kiplinger Magazine, February 1952:

"It's okay to **shoot for the moon** if you have some means of hitting it. But if you lack the know-how and the skill, you are wasting your time. Most interviewers know what is required to fill every job on their list..."

Shoot from the hip

Someone who 'shoots from the hip' speaks or reacts impulsively without regard to the feelings of others. It is derived from gunfighters in American pioneer days shooting from the hip to get the first shot against an enemy, and was used freely in print of shooting without aiming through the early 20th century. Later it also included doing other things without taking aim, such as snapping photos, as seen in this citation from *Popular Photography*, March 1947 in a subheading under 'Make Some Grab Shots':

> "Make technique automatic, then **'shoot from the hip'**"

By the early 1960s it was being applied in the current fashion, as in this reference from *Life*, April 12, 1963, in the article 'You Can't Fool an Old Bag Like Me' about author Hedda Hooper:

> "For better or worse, I'm doomed to **shoot from the hip**. Some people say I should give more attention to the saints of Hollywood and less to the sinners. That would mean hear no evil, see no evil and speak no evil, all three of which I do."

Shooting fish in a barrel

This phrase, meaning that something is ridiculously easy, is derived from the fact that fish used to be packed in barrels. When someone shoots, particularly a shotgun, into a school of fish, many will die from the mere shock of the blast. This practice is, of course, illegal in many locales, but it has been done by unscrupulous persons many times, and is undoubtedly the best way to kill the most fish at once. The earliest known citation is from 1949 in *American Business, Volume 19*:

> "LIKE **SHOOTING FISH IN A BARREL** It's a cinch to get urgently needed facts and figures when all you have to do is call STATISTICAL.**"

Then the term took off in 1958 when UCLA folklore and music teacher Donald K. Wilgus published ***Shooting Fish in a Barrel**: the Child Ballad in America*.

Then, Sonny Liston talked of a fight with Joe Frazier, claiming "it'd be like **shooting fish in a barrel**." (November 18, 1958: Auditorium, Miami Beach, Florida)

In the October 20th issue of *Billboard* that same year, the following appeared on page 42:

484

"Bentley said that if the weather is good, that date PHONEMEN ADDING 4 MORE PHONES Like **shooting fish in a barrel**."

Shoot the breeze

This idiom refers to talking about anything or nothing merely to pass time. It was preceded by the expression 'throw the bull con' (a form of shoot the bull, meaning saying something in a joking manner) recorded in 1903 in *The Judges Library*, a monthly magazine of fun.

> "He let this go for about a week, all the while chuckling in his sleeve, and then he told them he had only been kidding them. What little boy can tell me the definition of 'kidding'?"

> "It means to **throw the bull con** into some one..."

Then in *Popular Aviation and Aeronautics* Magazine, February, 1929, we find the following:

> "We often congregated in unfrequented nooks of the bay to '**shoot the breeze**' and smoke, until we saw a plane in which we thought an instructor might be..."

The saying is in quotes indicating a fairly recently coined expression.

Shoot the bull (See: **Shoot the breeze**)

Shot one's wad

This term originated in the 19th century when muzzle loader guns had to be stuffed with a cloth 'wad' in order to retain the gunpowder charge. A person had to be careful not to shoot too soon or at an inappropriate target because when they 'shot their wad' it was a difficult task to reload.

In the early 20th century it began to be applied figuratively to represent money, in a sense of spending all one had or 'betting everything' on one chance at high stakes. The earliest known reference in print to this meaning, plainly showing it as a recent usage from slang, is from *Memory and the Executive Mind* by Arthur Raymond Robinson, 1912:

> "In the vernacular of the street, if it may be pardoned in this instance, he has '**shot his wad**' at thirty, and why? Just on this account: He started out with a fearfully small supply of persistence, and by the time he reached the age of thirty, he had lost all that he once possessed; then like an old farm horse,

whose usefullness is past, he settled down to await patiently his turn, to depart from the world and its activites. He failed miserably!"

In recent years it also began to be used in a vulgar, sexual sense.

Show a leg * (See: Shake a leg)

Show your true colors

Early warships often carried flags of many nations aboard, in order to deceive the enemy and possibly ward off an attack, or get the jump on the enemy before they realized who they were. However, the rules of warfare required the ship to hoist the country's true colors before firing on another ship. It has come to mean showing forth one's actual personality or intent, especially when it is not what the other expected.

Shuckin' and jivin'

This term originated to represent the jargon used by African-Americans intended to mislead racist European-Americans during the era of slavery and the post-slavery years to be able to communicate ideas which would be unexceptable to those in power. According to some sources, it was in full use in the 1920s. Actual documentation available in print, however, dates from the 1960s. This early example from *Jet* magazine, April 16, 1968, referring to incidents surrounding the asassination of Dr. Martin Luther King, Jr. shows the expression in quotes:

> "In short, and in soul phraseology, it was a '**shucking and jiving**' scene that only brought discredit to the preachments of the slain advocate of nonviolent protest."

Sidekick

This term, as we know it, originated at the turn of the early 20th century and sometimes indicated a close confidant in crime, but not always. This appeared in *The Bridgemen's Magazine* in September 1903, on page 33 in 'The Wanderings of Two Backerups':

> "'Clams' Brodrick and **sidekick** Torn McCormick are also there."

How it came to first be coined is in question. To a pickpocket, a kick is a pair of trousers, and most specifically denoted as being trouser pockets. 'Kick' (a word used to mean pockets) first appeared in the mid-19th century, and even today 'kick' is used for a roll of bills or a stash of money. The term sidekick could have developed as someone who was kept up by a thief who divided up the spoils and provided a home for those who would come up beside a victim and snatch the 'kick.' It came to mean a person who was kicked to the side.

Sight for sore eyes

This phrase means that someone is glad to see some other person or thing. The first printed reference to a close version of this saying was by Jonathan Swift, in *A complete collection of genteel and ingenious conversation*, in 1738:

"The **Sight** of you is good **for sore Eyes**."

This seems to make even more sense than the way it is said now. It was apparently in use in Britain prior to this date.

The version we know was first recorded by William Hazlitt, in *New Monthly Magazine*, in 1826:

"Garrick's name was proposed on condition he should act in tragedy and comedy... What **a sight for sore eyes** that would be!"

Signed, sealed and delivered

Under English law, it has traditionally been required to have important documemnts such as laws, rulings and deeds signed, impressed with the proper wax seal then delivered to the intended party in person. Today this usage is obsolete. The earliest known example is from *The History and Life and Death of His Most Serine Highness* by Samuel Carrington, 1659.

"...the Articles of Peace were **signed, sealed, and delivered** on the behalf of both parties, and were accordingly published and proclaimed, to the general satisfaction of all men."

In a figurative sense it has come to mean that something has gone through proper channels and has been properly executed.

This phrase spawned a 1968 country LP on AllMusic label by Lefty Frizzell, *Signed, Sealed and Delivered*, including a song by that name written by Cowboy Copas and Lois Mann, and a Stevie Wonder hit song, '*Signed, Sealed Delivered, I'm Yours*,' released by Motown's Tamla label in June 1970.

487

Silence is golden

The topic of silence as a good thing goes back two thousand years and perhaps longer. In the biblical book of *Revelation*, it speaks of silence in heaven:

> *"...when He had opened the Seventh Seal, there was silence in heaven about the space of half an hour"* (*Revelation 8:1*).

There are even reports that versions of this proverb date to Ancient Egypt. The first citation in English, however, is from poet Thomas Carlyle, who translated it from German in his major work, *Sartor Resartus* (The Taylor Re-tailored), in 1831. To understand completely what is being said, it seems necessary to quote this entire refrain:

> "Silence is the element in which great things fashion themselves together; that at length they may emerge, full-formed and majestic, into the daylight of Life, which they are thenceforth to rule. Not William the Silent only, but all the considerable men I have known, and the most undiplomatic and unstrategic of these, forbore to babble of what they were creating and projecting. Nay, in thy own mean perplexities, do thou thyself but hold thy tongue for one day: on the morrow, how much clearer are thy purposes and duties; what wreck and rubbish have those mute workmen within thee swept away, when intrusive noises were shut out! Speech is too often not, as the Frenchman defined it, the art of concealing Thought; but of quite stifling and suspending Thought, so that there is none to conceal. Speech too is great, but not the greatest. As the Swiss Inscription says: *Sprecfien ist silbern, Schweigen ist golden* (Speech is silvern, **Silence is golden**); or as I might rather express it: Speech is of Time, Silence is of Eternity."

Silver bullet

Through the past several centuries the term 'silver bullet' has evolved to mean 'a quick and sure solution' to a problem. This fantasy was derived from the 19th century folklore, and earlier, that silver bullets were the only means of killing werewolves. They were made popular in America in the adventures of that mysterious legendary masked man who won great fame on the radio show beginning in 1933, and later whisked across every TV screen in America in the 1950s, mentioned earlier in this volume. The Lone Ranger's two defining marks were his black mask and the fact that he only used silver bullets, an allusion to the solutions which he brought to the troubled citizens of the Old West.

Much more ancient and likely a precursor of the idea that silver contained the magic cure for the ills of mankind is the use of silver spears in war. In 359 BC, when Philip of Macedonia consulted the Oracle of Delphi, he was told, "With silver spears you may conquer the world."

Use of silver bullets themselves actually dates from the late 17th century. Among numerous 19th century references to the belief that silver bullets would kill supernatural beings is from Sir Walter Scott's *Tales of My Landlord*, 1816:

> "The superstitious fanatics looked upon him as a man gifted by the Evil Spirit with supernatural means of defence. Many a whig that day loaded his musket with a dollar cut into slugs, in order that a **silver bullet** (such was their belief) might bring down the persecutor of the holy kirk, on whom lead had no power."

This continues to prevail in citations sprinkled throughout the 20th century, concerning silver and 'magic' bullets. The figurative usage, however, didn't actually catch on until the days of the legendary masked man.

The Bedford Gazette, in Pennsylvania, included the following in a September 1951 issue:

> "There are those who warn against viewing the atom as a magic weapon... I agree. This is not a **silver bullet** which can deliver itself or otherwise work military miracles."

After that, the phrase went 'shooting' into history.

silver lining, A (See: **Every cloud has a silver lining**)

Sink one's teeth into something

This idiomatic expression means to enter into a venture with great enthusiasm; to become deeply involved. The earliest available figurative reference is found in *The Washington Merry-go-round*, 1931:

> "Stimson actually began to **sink his teeth into** naval negotiations."

Sink or swim

This idiom means 'succeed or fail' because of one's own abilities to do so under less-than-perfect circumstances. It was preceded by 'float or sink' which was coined by Geofrey Chaucer in 1368 in *The Compleynte until Pite* as 'flete or sinke.'

The earliest citation of sink or swim was in *England in the Reign of King Henry the Eighth, the Life and Letters of Thomas Starkey*, circa 1538:

> "'They care not'(as hyt ys commynly sayd) 'whether they **synke or swyme**.'"

In about 1597, Shakespeare used it again in *Henry IV* (I:iii):

> "Or **sink or swim**."

Sitting duck

When ducks light on a pond or lake they are usually away from any protection and thus are easy targets for hunters. A sitting duck, figuratively, is someone who has left himself or herself open to criticism or adverse action from his or her enemies. It started being used in this way in World War II, as in this early example from an article on page 4 of *Boys' Life*, October 1944, titled 'Danger in the Air' by Richards Bennett:

> "Randolph knew that the general had been right when he had said he would be a '**sitting-duck**' for any Jap plane."

Sitting on one's hands

This idiom originally, in the 1920s, meant to withhold applause; later it expanded to failing to take appropriate action—doing nothing when something needed to be done. Here is an example from *Are You Decent?* by Willaim Smith, 1927:

> "Other performances when they **sat on their hands** and dared the performer to make 'em like it."

Then here is the earliest known example of the change in meaning from *Public Papers of the Presidents of the United States; Harry S. Truman*, 1940:

> "The Republicans **sat on their hands** in 1930, 1931, and 1932, and they did nothing to get us out of that depression."

Sitting pretty

This Americanism means to be in an advantageous position, especially financially. It came into use in the early 20th century. The earliest available reference is from *Typographical Journal*, February 1915, in which the phrase appears in quotes as with a recently coined expression:

> "'Los Angeles, America's Dreamland, 1915,' sounds pretty good....

> "Roy Heisler, who spent the Christmas holidays in one of those dry parts of southern Illinois, says if Kansas City ever goes dry like that town did, he will be '**setting pretty**.'"

Six of one, half a dozen of the other

The earliest citation of this phrase was likely in a book titled *The Comic Latin Grammar*, Second Edition, in 1840.

Then it was used as the title of a story in *Popular Science,* April 1883, in an article titled 'The Legal Status of Servant-Girls' the following appeared:

> "In other words, the legal and illegal ways of settling for the damaged or lost articles end in similar results. 'It is **six of one** and **half a dozen** of the other.' As a matter of practice and advisability, the illegal method of deduction, although it overrides the servant's rights, is better for her, as it saves her the expense of a lawsuit merely for a principle."

The phrase gained great popularity thereafter as meaning that two choices made little or no difference.

Sixteen-penny nails

There have been various theories presented for why nails are sized in 'pennies' rather than length. Here is the correct one.

The word 'penny,' in this case, was an old English term used to describe the number of *English pennies* required to purchase one hundred nails. Today the term is used only as a measurement of the length of the nail. A common sixteen-penny nail used in general construction today has a standard length of 3.5 inches, a number eight gauge diameter shaft (0.162 inches), a head diameter of $11/32$nds of an inch and forty-four such nails will weigh one pound. Other sizes were determined in like manner.

$64,000 question

This term had its roots in the CBS radio quiz show, *Take It or Leave It*, which ran from April 21, 1940, to July 27, 1947. The show was first hosted by Bob Hawk, who passed it to Phil Baker in '41. In 1947, the series switched to NBC, with various hosts including Baker, Garry Moore, Eddie Cantor and Jack Paar. On September 10, 1950, *Take It or Leave It* changed its title to *The $64 Question*. Paar continued as host, and then was followed by Baker from March to December of 1951, when Paar returned. The series continued on NBC Radio until June 1, 1952.

On both shows, contestants were asked questions written by researcher Edith Oliver. After answering correctly, the contestant was asked to either take or leave the prize money offered, or move on to a more difficult question which offered double the money. The first was worth $1 USD, and the final was the '$64.00 question.'

During the 1940s, 'That's the $64.00 question' became a common catchphrase meaning the answer to a difficult situation.

From 1955 to 1958, a version of the show aired on television under the title, *The $64,000 Question.* A spin-off show called *The $64,000 Challenge* was on between 1956 and 1958.

Nowadays the inflationary phrase is 'That's the $64,000,000 question.'

Six ways to Sunday (See: **Ways to Sunday**)

Skating on thin ice

This metaphoric saying was derived from the literal implication that when one skates on ice which is too thin to hold up his or her weight that person is sure to fall through and be in terrible trouble. Skates have been around since the mid-17th century, and originated in Holland, being taken to England after the Restoration by followers of Charles II.

This saying means that by broaching a touchy topic or edging into a situation which is a 'powder keg' waiting to explode, a person is unnecessarily placing himself or herself in a dangerous position. In a figurative sense, the phrase has been around in the U.S. for over fifty years, and was the title of a children's book in the U.K. by Nicholas Walker in 1988.

Skeleton in the closet

This was originally coined in England, but since the British use the word 'closet' to mean a water closet, or commode, there it is now stated as 'skeleton in the cupboard.'

The meaning of the phrase is 'a deep secret, that is being hidden, which, if exposed might cause irrefutable harm.' The first reference to this idiom is in the early 19th century. It is in an article by William Hendry Stowell in the U.K. monthly periodical *The Electric Review* in 1816. It is figurative in nature and the 'skeleton' was the supposed need to keep a hereditary disease secret.

> "Two great sources of distress are the danger of contagion and the apprehension of hereditary diseases. The dread of being the cause of misery to posterity has prevailed over men to conceal **the skeleton in the closet**..."

The dramatic use of hidden bodies was found quite frequently in the Gothic novels and short stories of the Victorian age. Edgar Allan Poe was a master of such tales. Here is an example from *The Black Cat*, first published in the *Saturday Evening Post* on 19 August 1843:

> "'Gentlemen, I delight to have allayed your suspicions,' and here, through the mere frenzy of bravado, I rapped heavily upon that very portion of the brick-work behind which stood the corpse of the wife of my bosom. The wall fell bodily. The corpse, already greatly decayed, stood erect before the eyes of the spectators."

Some feel that this phrase is derived from the era of the body snatchers, prior to 1832, when England allowed more extensive medical research of corpses due to the Anatomy Act.

Popular Victorian author William Makepeace Thackeray referred explicitly to 'skeletons in closets' in *The Newcomes; memoirs of a most respectable family*, 1857:

> "Some particulars regarding the Newcome family, which will show us that they have a **skeleton or two in their closets**, as well as their neighbours."

Skinny as a rail

This simile was first used as 'thin as a rail,' and appeared in Mark Twain's *Roughing It* in 1872.

"You'll marry a combination of calico and consumption that's as **thin as a rail**."

The rail spoken of was a fence rail, and many in the 19th century were cut pretty thin. Later, some changed it to 'skinny.' Though some have applied this to the Virginia Rail, a thin bird, indeed, this is an incorrect assumption.

Slam Dunk

This figurative expression comes from a player jumping with a basketball in his or her hand above the basket and literally dunking the ball in. Figuratively, it means someone has made an impressive move which has resulted in a great advantage. The phrase was coined in the 1970s in a literal sense, as evidenced by this early citation in quotes from page 48 of *Jet Magazine*, June 3, 1976 in *'Dr. J' Leads New York Jets to ABA Championship*:

"Erving, who has turned the '**slam dunk**' into an art form, captured Most Valuable Player honors for his record-setting 226-point performance during the six-game series, 31 in the last contest."

The earliest figurative example available is on page 24 of *New York Magazine*, February 2, 1987, in 'A Wolf in the Kitchen,' which relates the success of a café to a slam dunk:

"…broke through a wall in Arizona 206 to create a grazing café that went, as he says, '**slam-dunk** hit city."

Slap someone into next week or next year

This is a figure of speech, also sometimes 'next Tuesday,' used sarcastically by someone who is excessively angry and wants to make a clear point. It figuratively indicates that the slap would be so hard as to propel the individual forward in time. It came into usage at the late 20th century.

Slapstick comedy

Slapstick is a type of comedy which was popular in the 1930s, involving wide, boisterous moves, farce, and feigned violence outside the boundries of common sense. To understand why it was so called, we must look at the etomology of the word 'slapstick' which derived from the Italian *batacchio* or *bataccio* — called the 'slap stick' in English — a clublike object made of two wooden slats used in *commedia dell'arte* which produces a loud smacking noise. The batacchio dates back to the Renassiance, and historians argue that slapstick has been somewhat present in all genres of comedy since the rejuvenation of theater in church lithargical dramas in the Middle Ages.

Sleeping with the enemy

Sleeping with the enemy is an idiom used to describe a person who is fraternizing or dealing treacherously and unadvisedly with someone in a competing enterprise or with an opposite belief system. It is used in business, politics and religion—dangerous avenues in which to be cutting shady deals.

The phrase has been in common usage in America over the past several decades, and in 1991 a movie by this title starred Julia Roberts and Patrick Bergin.

Slick as an eel

This simile for 'so slippery it is difficult to hold' has been in usage since at least the 1830s. The earliest known example in print is from *Philadelphia Scrapbook and Gallery of Comicalities*, Saturday, 17 May 1834:

> "Well, as I could git no satisfaction from the Captain, I took a good pull of switchel and laid down on a hen coop to look out for squalls, when I didn't soon see one, leaning towards us, that in an hour made the *beauty* hoe it off through the water jist as **slick as an eel** — though the poor thing lost the bonnet from her gib in the confusion."

Slim Pickings

This cliché originated in the early 17th century, and alluded to the remainder of a carcass which had been picked clean by wild animals.

It has come to symbolize the meager amount of food, clothing, etc. after the bulk has been plundered through. It is applied to the poorest of persons and their desperate attempts to survive in a 'dog-eat-dog' (see) world.

The expression inspired American rodeo performer turned comedy character actor, Louis Burton Lindley, Jr. (1919-1983), to take the stage name 'Slim Pickens.' Pickens 'epitomized the tough, profane, sardonic cowboy' in such films as *Dr. Strangelove* and *Blazing Saddles*.

Slip through the cracks*

This old expression means to fail to be noticed because of neglect or lack of sufficient evidence. It is derived from coins or small articles falling between boards in old wooden floors in homes, barns or wagons in centuries past. The earliest known figurative usage was in *The Poetical Works of Alexander Pope* published in 1788, from *The Dunciad, Book 1,* on page 109:

> "Nonsense precipitate, like running lead,
> That **slip'd through.cracks** and zigzags of the head"

Small fish in a big pond (See: Big fish in a small pond)

Smart as a whip

'Smart' in this play on words refers to 'bright and clever.' When someone or some animal is hit by the crack of a whip, one way to describe the feeling is that it 'smarts.' In the 19th century when this phrase was coined, carriages were drawn by horses whose drivers urged them on with a whip. When cracking it near the horses didn't obtain the desired results, they were touched as lightly as possible to get them moving.

'Smart as a steel trap' was used in the early 1800s. It would be easy to see how much that could 'smart.' In 1860, however, the current phrase was printed in the *Mountaineer* in Salt Lake City:

> "Mr. A___ was a prompt and successful businessman, '**smart as a whip**,' as the Yankees say."

Smarter than the average bear

This is from the popular Hanna-Barbera cartoon character, Yogi Bear, and his little sidekick, Boo-boo. Yogi, whose name was a takeoff on baseball great, Yogi Berra, first appeared in 1958, when Berra was a top Yankee Hall of Famer, and World Series champ. Yogi Bear had a number of catchphrases in his vocabulary, the best known of which is this one. He proclaimed himself 'smarter than the average bear,' and sure enough, he was. Yogi was a talking bear who had no problem with the English language. Now, the phrase is used to describe someone who seems a notch above the crowd in intelligence and /or ingenuity.

A similar phrase is 'a mind like a steel trap.'

Smells like cyarn*

This old Southern American expression is used of something that emits a very strong, offensive odor. Its origin is debated. Some say that it comes from a corruption of the word carrion, which meant something dead or decaying. It has been proclaimed by others to have been originally of Scottish origin, as *kyran*, meaning manure. McFarlane's Gaelic English dictionary defines the word *cairbh* as carcass or a dead body.

Cairns (also from the Gaelic), or piles of stones, heaped on top of flat stone coffins, filled with human bones, are to be found all over Scotland.

Any way you define it, it comes from something that smells rank and is likely of Scottish Gaelic origin, many of whom settled in the Southern U.S.

Smile and the world smiles with you; cry and you cry alone

This proverb may not be true, but it is certainly good advice. Smiling beats crying 'hands down.' There is another saying, 'Misery loves company' which flies in the face of this one, but it's like 'beauty is skin deep,' it's really all in one's perception. Still, it has found its way into our pop culture.

This positive quote is of unknown origin and has been around since at least the mid-20th century. Glen Campbell had a song titled *When You Cry, You Cry Alone* in 1963 on his *Too Late to Worry, Too Blue to Cry* album. Stanley Gordon West used the phrase in *Growing an Inch,* in 1988. *Smile and the World Smiles with You* is the title of a 2003 album by the post-rock band, Sonna. At least two Internet blogs use this theme.

Another cute saying of unknown origin is 'keep smiling, it makes people wonder what you've been up to.'

Smoke screen

In a literal sense, a smoke screen is a mass of dense artificial smoke used by the military to conceal overt operations by troops, tanks or ships from the enemy. This idea was first proposed by Sir Thomas Cochrane for use by the British navy in 1812, but was not actually developed and activated until the American Civil War when it was used by the Confederate ship, R.E.Lee in running blockades against the USS Iriquois in 1859. It was also utilized in naval battles in both World Wars.

Metaphorically speaking, it is applied to any actions or statements used to conceal one's true intentions. Actually, it was being printed figuratively even before it was a reality in the military. This very early citation is from the English translation of *Dio lo vuole* by Charles Victor Prévôt, 1849, where it appears in quotes:

"This servant of the largest Protestant denomination in the U.S. calls the mightiest and most fanatical world onslaught against Christianity in 1,000 years a '**smoke screen.**'"

Smoking gun

The 'smoking gun' as a cliché meaning 'unmistakable evidence of a crime' originated in a Sherlock Holmes story, *The Adventure of the Gloria Scott* (a ship), in 1893. In that tale, Doyle wrote about a ghastly murder committed by a supposed chaplain on a prison ship. The reference goes like this:

"We rushed into the captain's cabin...there he lay with his brains smeared over the chart of the Atlantic...while the chaplain stood with a **smoking pistol** in his hand at his elbow."

Here, Sir Arthur chose to use the word 'pistol' rather than gun...a bit more precise, but the word 'gun' inevitably replaced it. The phrase appeared in occasional usage over the next eighty years as such, and bolted into our everyday figurative jargon when this came out in *The New York Times* on July 14, 1974, in an article by Roger Wilkins regarding the Watergate scandal which was the first of many such references:

"The big question asked over the last few weeks in and around the House Judiciary Committee's hearing room by committee members who were uncertain about how they felt about impeachment was 'Where's the **smoking gun**?'"

Smooth sailing

If one has smooth sailing on a project it means that he or she encounters no severe problems in accomplishing the desired result. In England, the phrase used is 'plain sailing.' The literal usage of this expression dates to the 14th century, meaning nautical navigation that is easy and uncomplicated.

The figurative use of the British cliché was known by around the turn of the 18th century, for in 1707, Edward Ward used it in this way in *The Wooden World Dissected*:

"Tho' he guide others to Heaven by the **plain-sailing** Rules of the Gospel."

The comic animated TV family, 'Simpsons' in 1999 used an alternative of clear sailing in *The Simpsons Bible Stories*:

Milhouse: Well, Lisa, we're out of Egypt. So, what's next for the Israelites? Land of milk and honey?

Lisa: [consulting a scroll] Hmm, well, actually it looks like we're in for forty years of wandering the desert.

*Milhouse: Forty years! But after that, it's **clear sailing** for the Jews, right?*

Lisa: [nervously] Uh-huh-hum, more or less.

Snag a red-eye***

A red-eye flight is one leaving late at night and arriving early the next morning. The term, now common in North America, was derived from the fatigue of having red eyes which can be caused from late night travel. Snagging a red-eye is catching such a flight, and only became used in the early twenty-first century. From 1819 the term red eye was used to describe a raw, inferior whisky. As applied to the condition of the eyes, it was first used about 1968. As applied to flights, it came much later. The earliest known example of the term **red-eye flight** was in *Obligations of the Bone* by Dick Cluster, 1992, page 78:

"Alex sipped while he called airlines in search of a **red-eye** flight."

The earliest available example of **snag a red-eye** is from chapter 8 of Betty Hechtman's novel, *A Stitch in Crime*, 2010:

"Mason disappeared in the fog and I went to the gift shop, hoping to **snag a red-eye**."

snail's pace, A

This idiom, meaning moving ridiculously slow, dates back to Middle English in the early fifteenth century according to leading etymologists. Snails are said to be the epitome of slow. Sometimes this is used sarcastically to describe some process that is seen as inefficient. The lightening-fast electronic world of email today has made the future of the Postal Service seem dismal. Traditional mail is now often referred to as 'snail mail.'

Snake in the grass

The imagery of this metaphoric cliché goes back to many ancient sources and folklore. The earliest is likely the biblical book of *Genesis*, or beginnings. In *Genesis 3*, the story is told of how the serpent, or snake, used as a type of the devil, through subtlety, slithered its way into Eve's intellect and convinced her to take a bite of the 'forbidden fruit.'

The origin of the word 'snake' began in the Indo-European root word meaning 'to creep.' This meaning crept down to the Old High German word 'snahhan,' (to crawl), then the Old Norse 'snakr,' and the Old English word, 'snaca.' By Middle English it was already snake.

An ancient Chinese proverb states, "He who is bitten by the snake avoids tall grass."

The snake's craftiness and subtlety coupled with its slithering through the grass to attack its prey has been long used in both literal and figurative senses.

A 'snake in the grass' has come to be an unmistakable image of an untrustworthy, deceitful person.

Snake oil

True snake oil originated in China, and is from the Chinese Water Snake. It was used as a cure for rheumatoid arthritis and joint pain. Snake oil also played a role in ancient Egyptian medicine, and was blended with the fats of other animals such as lions, hippopotamuses, crocodiles, etc. It was believed by the masses that it could grow hair on bald men.

Chinese laborers working in America on the trans-continental railroad lines introduced snake oil to Europeans to cure joint pain. There were no regulations in North America in the 19th century regarding drugs, so when charlatans got hold of it, all sorts of fake oils were created. These were hawked by the traveling salesmen who went about the country with their medicine shows selling 'a cure for what ails you' in a bottle to anyone who was gullible enough to fall for their lines. It was claimed that they often had some who would be paid to testify to the healing properties of their potion. As a result, the term 'snake oil' became used metaphorically for any product with exaggerated marketing but questionable benefits.

Snap judgement

This expression means making a decision without weighing out the consequences or having all the pertinent facts. The earliest known reference in print is in quotes, and found in an ad for a fishing lure in *Scientific American*, 8 July 1882:

> "The fish catch themselves by '**Snap Judgement**.' It's real fun to watch how it gathers them in."

snowball's chance in hell, A

Even to a greater degree than the old expression 'a ghost of a chance,' this idiom means that something has *less than* no chance of success. Both are used in negative connotations. Though a number of online sources claim that it dates back to 1931, likely originally from the *Online Etymology Dictionary*, the oldest actual reference available is from 2 September 1938, in the *Evening Independent News* in St. Petersburg—Florida, not Russia. It was in a political article about Roosevelt's reluctance to back Senator Pope, who had been defeated, as an Independent candidate in the Idaho primary. In this early citation, 'in hell' was not used.

> "Jim Farley was given a fill in on the intrigue when he passed through the state (of Idaho) on his return trip from Alaska. It convinced him that Mr. Pope, running as an independent, wouldn't have **a *snowball's chance*** to beat the machine. So he phoned Hyde Park by long distance, begging F.D.R. to make no commitments until he had learned the facts."

Then eighteen years later, on 20 August 1956, the *Victoria Advocate*—Texas, not British Columbia, ran a story in the *Matter of Fact* column by Joseph and Stewart Alsop concerning the impression left at the Democratic convention. Note that this is also political in scope. Here 'in hell' *was* used.

> "As for the outcome, well, they really did not think Stevenson had **a *snowball's chance in Hell*** of carrying their particular states if Eisenhower's health held up. Of course, you had to remember the big Democratic gains in 1954. But if you were really honest about it, the President's health was the one real factor to watch."

So angry I could bite nails

This cliché has been stated a number of ways: both mad and angry; chew nails, spit nails, and bite nails or rivets. It is derived from back talk of carpenters many years ago. Nails were often placed in the carpenters' mouths, especially when on a ladder, and then removed as needed to be hammered into the wall or roof. This process saved having to reach into a pocket or apron to find the proper size nail. When a nail bent or the carpenter hit his finger with a hammer he became so angry he could either bite through the nails or spit them out.

Through the passage of time, the phrase became figurative of anyone angry enough to do something unspeakable. Similar phrases are 'stark raving mad' and 'mad enough to kick a cat.'

Soccer mom

This expression originated about 1982 as a mildly derogatory term for middle-class suburban mothers who spent a considerable amount of time transporting their children to soccer games and other sporting events. It became popular in 1996, through use by politicians, and has continued to gain ground.

So lazy he wouldn't hit a lick at a snake

Someone who wouldn't attempt to kill a snake which was apt to bite would exemplify the height of lethargy. The earliest known reference to this expression is from the *American Magazine*, Volume 124, 1937:

"He's so lazy he **wouldn't hit a lick at a snake**. There's nothing sorrier in this world than a sorry white man."

Something is rotten in Denmark

William Shakespeare gets credit for this, because it is from *Hamlet*. The officer Marcellus, having just seen the ghost of Hamlet's father, the late King of Denmark, blurts out. "**Something is rotten in the state of Denmark!**" This has come to mean, 'something is definitely wrong here.'

Something's gotta give

This saying means that a situation has got to change eventually, and can't go on forever in its present state. It was inspired by a 1955 song written by Johnny Mercer in 1954. It was first performed by Fred Astaire in his 1955 musical film, *Daddy Long Legs*, then recorded, among others, by the McGuire Sisters as the flip side of 'Rhythm and Blues,' ironically itself reaching number 5 on Billboard's 'Hot 100' chart.

SOS

Many people believe that SOS means 'save our ships,' or possibly 'save, oh, save.' Another popular teaching is that it was originally 'save our souls.' All are wrong.

Here is the real 'scoop.' SOS, the international distress signal for ships, was chosen because of the significance of dashes and dots made for these particular letters in Morse code, and is known as a 'prosign,' from 'procedural signal.' All prosigns are transmitted without interletter gaps noted with an 'overbar.' S is three dots, and O is three dashes. Thus, since no gaps are noted, three dots, three dashes and three dots could actually represent other letter combinations in Morse code.

In reality, three of anything, according to expert Fred Bland, is a signal of distress. The signal used before SOS was CQD according to Mark Brader. The regular calling signal was CQ, plus D, representing distress. According to Brader, in 1912 when the Titanic was sinking, the signal sent out was CQD. According to Thomas Hamilton White, the current signal evolved from SOE, but since the last letter was a single dot, it was 'modified to be more distinctive and symmetrical.'

Sour grapes

This term has two related meanings: First, it can refer to bad feelings expressed about a situation which does not turn out the way a person feels that it should. Secondly, it can mean pretending not to be concerned about something a person desires but is not able to obtain. The earliest mention could have been from the *Bible*, in *Ezekiel 18:2*, written in Hebrew between 593 and 565 BC:

> "The fathers have eaten **sour grapes**, and the children's teeth are set on edge."

The above is from the *KJV*, 1611. The first English translation was in the *Cloverdale Bible* in 1535.

It was also in one of Aesop's fables, also deemed to have been written in the sixth century BC, between 620 and 560, *The Fox and the Grapes*. From Harrison Weir's English translation in 1884:

> "A famished Fox saw some clusters of ripe black grapes hanging from a trellised vine. She resorted to all her tricks to get at them, but wearied herself in vain, for she could not reach them. At last she turned away, beguiling herself of her disappointment, and saying: 'The **Grapes are sour**, and not ripe as I thought.'"

Due to closeness of dates it is uncertain which came first, both in original writing and in first translation to English. Both seem to give similar figurative definition to the phrase.

Sow wild oats

This is another of those phrases used today which most people would not suspect was passed down to us by a Protestant preacher, and what's even more surprising, it is from the 16th century. The phrase appears in one of Thomas Beccon's tracts from 1542, and a similar expression is credited to the Roman, Plateus.

Wild oats are inferior to the cultivated variety, and are difficult to rid from a field once they are present. Sowing one's wild oats has come to symbolize the youthful tendency toward promiscuity and unprofitable activities. It is often said that young men 'have to sew their wild oats,' much like saying, 'boys will be boys' (see) of younger males. It can be taken as an excuse for misbehaving and a lack of parental guidance for them to overcome the desires to rebel against authority.

Spare the rod and spoil the child

This is a rephrasing of the biblical admonision found in *Proverbs 13:24*:

> "He who spareth **the rod** hateth his son: but he that loveth him correcteth him betimes." (*KJV*)

It is used to justify corporal punishment, which has come under fire in modern times.

Speak of the devil

In America this phrase is used in a very light hearted jesting fashion to say 'we were just talking about you, and here you are.' Certainly it is not an attempt to demonize anyone.

In England, however, when this phrase was first coined as 'talk of the devil,' something else entirely was implied. It is found in a number of English as well as Latin texts from as early as the sixteenth and seventeenth centuries. Italian writer Giovanni Torriano first recorded this version in contemporary English, in his book of proverbs, *Piazza Universale*, in 1666:

"The English say, **Talk of the Devil**, and he's presently at your elbow."

Also, the following is from *Cataplus, or, Aeneas, his descent to hell: a mock poem in imitation of the sixth book of Virgil's Aeneis*, 1672, reprinted in W.C. Hazlitt's *English Proverbs and Proverbial Phrases* in 1882:

"**Talk of the Devil**, and see his horns."

Popular superstition of that era taught that it was dangerous to talk of the devil, and that doing so would cause him to actually appear. Shakespeare made mention of this often in *The Comedy of Errors*, and used this well-known phrase in reference to his appearance with men:

"Marry, he must have a long spoon that must eat with the devil."

This belief that reference to the devil was to be avoided even carried to the clergy, for Richard Chenevix Trench, Dean of Westminster from 1856 to 1863 wrote:

"'**Talk of the devil** and he is bound to appear' contains a very needful warning against curiosity about evil."

This teaching did not begin to lose its punch until the 19th century.

In 1982, Ozzy Osbourne released a live double album with the British title *Talk of the Devil;* in America, *Speak of the Devil*.

Spend a penny

This is a British and Australian idiom for 'use a public restroom,' particularly verbalized by women, due to the former coin operated facilities in those countries, primarily the U.K. The first such toilets were set up outside the Royal Exchange in London in 1850. Other countries in the British Commonwealth eventually followed suit, including not only Australia, but even the British Virgin Islands. The first use of the figurative phrase, however, came much later, in Hilda Winifred Lewis's *Strange Story*, 1945:

> "'Us girls,' she said, 'are going to **spend a penny!**'"

Use of the idiom has almost faded away, but it remains in the minds of those who vividly recall the pay toilets.

Spick and span

To understand the origin of this phrase, one must look at the etymology of the two strange words that are plastered together to form it. Spick, now archaic on its own, in its day had many meanings. It could either be a side of bacon, a floret of lavender, a nail or spike, or even a thatching spar.

Span also had more than one definition. It could be the distance from the tip of the thumb to the tip of the little finger, a measure of butter, a fetter or chain, or a chip of wood (as the Norse word spann-nyr).

Considering this, one could come up with a number of possible combinations for this cliché. But considering the true meaning, it is unclear which of these were used. The phrase, however, is very old and originally was 'spick and span-new,' or the equivalent in the spelling of the sixteenth century.

This early version was used in Sir Thomas North's translation of Plutarch's *Lives of the noble Grecians and Romanes*, from 1579:

> "They were all in goodly gilt armours, and brave purple cassocks apon them, **spicke, and spanne** newe."

This sounds as if these words were referring to cleanness and freshness. It has been suggested that the 'spick' alluded to a spike, or nail, which was shiny and new. Nails of the era were made of iron and were subject to tarnishing. But when new, they were shiny and sharp. This is reminiscent of 'neat as a new pin,' a phrase used in the U.K. where this all started. The *O.E.D.* suggests that the

506

Dutch word *spikspeldernieuw* referring to newly made ships is the origin of spick in this phrase. It's possible, but seems unlikely, since none of the early references are nautical in nature.

As for the origin of 'span,' fresh chips of wood also have a clean quality about them.

Another suggestion is that a spoon was originally made of wood and spelled 'spon.' One other idea is that the American terms for a fork and spoon were a spike and spon; and this related to keeping eating utensils clean. This seems unlikely as well, based on the other facts at hand.

Spicke, and spanne newe later evolved into simply *spick and span* which is first found in Samuel Pepys' *Diary*, in 1665.

> "My Lady Batten walking through the dirty lane with new **spicke and span** white shoes."

There is no way to be certain of the exact origin.

Spill the beans

In ancient Greece, voting was held by dropping beans into a container. A white bean meant you were for the candidate, a black or dark bean was a 'no' vote. Only the polling officials could empty the beans and determine the winner.

Occasionally a clumsy voter would knock over the container, spilling the beans, and reveal the results prematurely.

Today spilling the beans means revealing any secret before its time.

Spinning one's wheels

This means expending a great deal of effort without making any progress. It is derived from automobile wheels which are stuck spinning in mud or snow and are unable to move the car. While it may have been in use a while longer, the earliest verifiable source available is in *Billboard*, April 23, 1966:

> "While the industry may be said to be **spinning its wheels** in obtaining relief from punitive and archaic legislation at every government level, operators continue to face shrinking markets and increasing licensing overhead."

Spit it out!

This common idiom means, 'hurry up and say what you mean!' Spitting something out comes from discharging saliva or mucus which is bothering someone and indicates getting rid of it quickly. When stated in this manner it is meant as an order to quit stalling on saying something important. The term has been used in a literal sense in English since at least the early seventeenth century, but the earliest figurative citation known is in Harry Hazleton's *The Prisioner of the Mill, or, Captain Hayward's Body-guard,* 1864, chapter 2, p. 7:

"Now, look a here, you unconscionable dark; if you have got any thing to say, **spit it out**. Don't make a darn skunk of yourself."

Spittin' image

A most popular belief is that this was derived from 'spirit and image'—the idea that the person embodied the spirit and appeared as the very image of their father or mother. Early examples of the phrase in print, however, don't back this theory.

George Farquhar used this variation in his comedy play, *Love and a bottle,* in 1689:

"Poor child! He's as like his own dadda as if he were spit out of his mouth."

Then in Andrew Knapp and W. Baldwin's *The Newgate Calendar,* in 1824–1826 they wrote:

"A daughter, ... the very spit of the old captain."

The fact to note is that neither of these has our current wording and neither refers to spirit, but to spit. Even references from other languages in that time frame use similar wording in regard to this thought. The earliest example of anything close to spittin' image is 'spit and image' in 1895 when a writer known as 'E. Castle' published *Lt. of Searthey,* including this line:

"She's like the poor lady that's dead and gone, the **spit an' image** she is.'"

Only six years later we see the first known use of 'spittin' image.' Alice Caldwell Hegan (later Rice) in her best-selling novel, *Mrs. Wiggs of the Cabbage Patch,* in 1901 wrote:

"He's jes' like his pa - the very **spittin' image** of him!"

This version won out. Now it seems quite clear that this phrase derived not from 'spirit' or even 'splitting,' as others have also claimed, but that 'spit' referred to the saliva as the quintessential element of a person's DNA makeup.

Square meals

In medieval times, a dinner plate was a square piece of wood, called a trencher, or square. People always took their 'square' with them when they went traveling, in hopes of getting a square meal.

Square peg in a round hole

Putting a square peg in a round hole has been used as a metophor for a person being forced into a position for which he or she is unsuited since the early 19th century. It was coined by Sydney Smith (1771-1845), a great advocate of religious liberty, who was one of three who launched the *Edinburgh Review* in 1802, to which he contributed for 25 years. In 1804, Smith, in his speech, *Moral Philosophy,* said:

> "You choose to represent the various parts in life by holes upon a table. ... We shall generally find that the triangular person has got into the square hole, the oblong into the triangular hole and **the round person has squeezed himself into the square hole**."

This citation in *Aldershot, and all about it, with Gossip, Literary, Military, and Pictorial* by Marianne Young, 1857 points back toward the coining of the phrase, using it in the precise way it is today:

> "A friend of ours, an originally-minded and consequently entertaining old maiden lady, was wont to call one of those circumstances, which Sydney Smith illustrates by the figure of a **square peg in a round hole**, as an 'awkquiddity.'

Squaring the circle

As an idiom, this is used when someone is attempting to do something impossible. It is based on a problem proposed by ancient geometers as early as 1800 BC to construct a square with the same area as a given circle by using only a finite number of steps with a compass and straightedge. Even Plato believed it could be done. Robert Greene, in *The Principles of the Philosophy of Expansive and Contractive Forces*, 1727, stated:

> "...the Circumference of a Circle is not a Polygone of an Infinate Number of Sides and that the Infintesama of ab is not a Right Line; upon which, notwithstanding, all the Methods hitherto receiv'd of **Squareing the Circle**, by finding the Proportion betwixt the Diameter and Circumference do depend, and which Methods, we shall readily Join with this Lemma, in Refusing and Condemning."

In 1882, the task was proven by German mathematition Carl Louis Ferdinand von Lindemann (April 12, 1852 – March 6, 1939) to be impossible. Even before this—by 1871 it was used to represent an impossible task, as in *A Terrible Temptation* a comedy by Charles Reade:

> "He earnestly desired to solve for him a problem, which is **as impossible as squaring the circle**, viz., how to transmit our experience to our children."

squeaky wheel gets the grease, The

The ones who complain the loudest are granted the most attention. The current version of this proverbial metaphor is ascribed to American humorist Josh Billings (1818-1885) in a poem thought by most to have been written by him circa 1870, titled, *The Kicker*:

> "I hate to be a kicker,
> I always long for peace,
> But **the wheel that does the squeaking**
> **Is the one that gets the grease**."

However, the basic thought behind this saying is considerably older, and contrasts with philosophies of Eastern origin.

Stab someone in the back

This indicates an act of treachery or betrayal. It is commonly thought that the idiom has its origin in a right-wing legend that Germany did not actually lose WWI, but was 'stabbed in the back' or betrayed by civilians on the home front.

The idea of betrayal and literal backstabbing, however, has been a prevailing trend in history. The most famous betrayer is likely Judas Iscariot who betrayed Jesus for thirty pieces of silver in the 1st century. The most notorious backstabber is likely Marcus Junius Brutus, who betrayed Emperor Gais Julias Caesar, literally plunging a knife into the back of his friend. In Shakespeare's play, Caesar cried, 'Et tu Brute?' (And you, Brutus?)

Stand on one's own two feet

This figurative idiom means to be financially and physically independent; to be able to provide all of one's own needs without dependence on others. The earliest known citation is from *Britz, of Headquarters*, by Marcin Barber, 1910:

> "But there lurked beneath his departmental sense of duty the independence of a man who felt he could always **stand on his own two feet**, and that he could work alone, if need be, to accomplish the most difficult task."

Stand the tests of time

This proverbial expression indicates being useful, well-regarded and revered by many over a number of years. It has been in use since the 1830s, and an early example is from *The Last Days of Pompeii*, Volume II, Book III, chapter 10 by Baron Edward Lytton, 1834:

> "And that which has so long **stood the test of time** rarely succumbs to the lust of novelty."

Start from scratch

Starting from scratch is beginning a task without any preparation or advantage. But the origin of this oft-used phrase has nothing to do with preparing tasty pastries, and doesn't mean 'made from scratch' or basic ingredients.

'Starting from scratch' means starting 'from square one' when everything else has failed.

This saying began being used in the late 19th century, but the word 'scratch' has been in use since the 18th century when applied to the line drawn on the ground for the starting point of sporting events. The first such scratch had to do with cricket in England, as the boundary line for the batsman. In John Nylon's *Young Cricketer's Tutor*, 1833, he mentions this line from a 1778 work of Cotton:

> "Ye strikers... Stand firm to your **scratch**, let your bat be upright."

'Scratch,' 'mark' and 'line' became used later as the starting point for races and other athletic events (see 'toe the line').

The Fort Wayne Gazette, in April of 1887, contains what may be the first printed reference to "Starting from scratch," in relation to a cycling race.

"It was no handicap. Every man was qualified to and did **start from scratch**."

State of the art

This term was in use in a different vein as early as the mid-to-late 1700s. It now refers to the highest level of development in any given field at any current time, sometimes now called 'the cutting edge.' This early citation is found in *The Origin of Laws, Arts and Sciences*, 1761, by Antoine-Yves Goguet and Alexander Fugere published in Edinburgh, Scotland:

"After this general view of the **state of the art**-military amongst the Greeks in the ages which now employ us, we must say a word or two upon the discipline paculuar to Lacedaemonians and the Athenians."

In *The Edinburgh Practice of Phycic, Surgery and Midwifery*, by William Cullen, 1803, this application appears:

"…but as authors, even in the present improved **state of the art**, differ in opinion on these important points of practice, it is to be hoped that every laudable endeavour to obviate the difficulties attendant on parturition will promote a free enquiry on the subject, and ultimately have a tendrncy to the general good of society."

It continued to be used in this sense over the following two and a half centuries. By the mid-20th century it had been accepted as an adjective phrase, as in the 1956 printing of the play *Peter Pan*, by James Matthew Barrie, we find this:

"Their services range from provision of the single compound systems as used in the original play to the **state of the art equipment** used in the recent Broadway revival."

Stay the course

This familiar term refers to persisting at one's goal until desired results are realized. The initial citation, however, had a somewhat different application. The earliest known reference in print is from 1588 when British playwright Christopher Marlowe used it in *The Tragical History of Dr. Faustus* in a countervailing sense as stopping the course of something, as an execution may be 'stayed.'

By the late 19th century it was adapted to describe the stamina of horses being able to remain in a race. One such citation is from *The Saturday Review*, London, 14 October 1871:

> "There was nothing in his breeding, and, of course, nothing in his performances, to justify the belief that he could **stay the course**, even supposing that he was able to gallop at all in good company…"

By World War I it was being used in a sense of military ability. This example is from *The Parliamentary History of Conscription in Great Britain,* 1917:

> "We will not likely **stay the course** until 1918 at our current rate of expenditure."

Steal someone's thunder

This idiom means to use someone elses ideas for your own benefit, thus taking credit for them. It was derived from thunder making devices which have been used in theater productions since at least the early 18th century. In 1704, when British playright John Dennis's play, *Appius and Virginia,* was produced at Drury Theater in London, he improved the previous 'mustard bowl' in use for producing the sound of thunder. In his method, metal balls were rolled around in a wooden bowl. After the play folded, Dennis' new idea was soon used in a production of *MacBeth*. Dennis was infuriated. Literary critic Joseph Spence wrote about the experience. In 1893 Dennis was quoted in W. S. Walsh's *Literary Curiosities,* wording it thusly:

> "Damn them! They will not let my play run, but they **steal my thunder**."

Though the original words were considerably different, the phrase caught on.

Stick one's neck out (See: Risk one's neck)

Stick one's nose into someone's business

If one word were to be chosen to describe this undesirable practice it would be intrusiveness. The idea in this idiom is the source of nosey or nosy and has been around for hundreds of years. In the mid-1800s the expression 'Nosey Parker' is said to have appeared in England, and is claimed by some to have been used to describe the inquisitive park keepers hired to control the crowds in Hyde Park during the Great Exhibition in 1851 which is discussed at length in a book titled *Quaker to Catholic: Mary Howitt, Lost Author of the 19th Century* by British author Joy Dunicliff published in London by St. Clair Publications in 2010. The term does not actually seem to be found in print, however, until 1907 on a comic rugby postcard series. The use of the word nosey to describe someone 'sticking their nose in where it isn't wanted' dates back to at least the 1880s.

Another theory, propitiated by the *O.E.D.*, for 'Nosey Parker' is that it was originally 'nose-poker,' agreeing with the theme of this idiom.

Sticks and stones can break my bones, but words can never hurt me

Bullying has become a worse threat to our youth in the 21st century than ever before. Emotional upset can lead to poor self image, and unfortunately, even to suicide, one of the major causes of death among teens. This misleading taunt first appeared in *Folk Phrases of Four Counties* by G.G. Northall published in 1894.

Sticks / Stands out like a sore thumb

This expression, which emphasizes the fact that a sore thumb is usually bandaged and held apart from the rest of one's digits to protect it from further injury, means that someone or something is drastically different from other persons or things around, causing people to notice that fact. It is applied in several languages. It may have been around longer, but the earliest verifiable reference is from *The History of the Hen Fever* by George P. Burnham, 1855:

> "But, if ever there was an individual whose pure-bred dis-interestedness, whose incomparable generosity, whose astonishing sacrifice of self, **stuck out like a sore thumb**, these attributes have now been evinced, beyond the shadow of a shade of question, on thiss exhilarating occasion, through the astounding liberality of a gentleman, the initials of whose name are Finnyous Tee Barman!"

It began from this point to be used liberally by writers. In the original Perry Mason series, Earl Stanley Gardner used this idiom at least twice. The first was in *The Sleepwalker's Niece*, 1936:

> "'No,' he said, 'that's the one thing in the case that **sticks out like a sore thumb**, now that I stop to think of it.'"

Stick to one's guns

This idiomatic expression means to stand by one's convictions or beliefs. A form of it first appeared in print in James Boswell's *Life of Samuel Johnson*, 1769.

> "Mrs. Thrale **stood to her gun** with great courage in defense of amorous ditties."

By 1826, the phrase was used in its current form in a fairly literal sense in a story titled *Saints at Sea* from the *Naval Sketch-book* reprinted in several British publications including *The Portfolio*, 11 February of that year:

> "Then, as for coming to box, I'm sartain one half of 'em would have thought it a sin to have **stuck to their guns**."

A more figurative use of 'stick to your guns' per se was in use by the end of the 19th century as seen in this citation from page 115 of *Law Notes*, 1897:

> "You can work down here all right, in a way—in a country way, that is— and, as we have told you before, we believe you did the right thing, and, at all events, you must **stick to your guns**. Chopping and changing is never any good; in London now you would be like a square peg in a round hole."

Stick to one's ribs

This metaphoric expression refers to food which is satisfying and gives nourishment long after it is eaten. The first version of it dates to 1603, when it was coined in *The Bachelor's Banquet* Thomas Wilson's English translation of Erasmus's *Encomium* and other anonymous Rennaissance prose.

> "Someone…that offred her such Kindnes as **sticks by her ribs** a good while after."

Still waters run deep

This proverb is ancient and of Bactrian origin from a tiny area of ancient Persia now a part of Afghanistan. It means that when someone appears peaceful to the casual observer, there is often a lot more brewing inside his or her mind and emotions. The earliest mention of it in English was around 1400. In circa 1490, the Italian writer Laurentius Abstemius expanded it to a fable in Latin called *De rustico amnem transituro* in a work titled *Hecatomythium* later included in a European version of Aesop's Fables which was subsequently assembled by

Roger L'Estrange in a fable titled *A Country-man and a River* in 1692, leaving the indication that silent folks are dangerous.

> "A Country-man that was to pass a River, sounded it up and down to try where it was most fordable: and upon Trial he made this Observation on't: Where the **Water** ran **Smooth**, he found it **Deepest**; and on the contrary, Shallowest where it made most Noise. *There's More Danger in a Reserv'd and Silent, than in a Noisy, Babbling Enemy.*"

Stink to high heavens

This common phrase is likely, like 'Something is rotten in Denmark,' to have originated with the similar saying in *Hamlet*. The aforementioned uncle, the King of Denmark, uttered:

> "O, my offense is rank, **it smells to heaven**; It hath the primal eldest curse upon it, A brother's murder."

It is of note that this did not refer to an odor, but to a deed. In recent times the phrase is applied in its current form to actual foul odors.

Stir up a hornet's nest

Hornets are not classified as bees, but they are the largest type of eusocial wasp. Hornets in America are usually white-faced, and black-and-white-striped. They make huge grey pear-shaped paperlike nests where they lay their eggs and hatch their young. European hornets are dark brown and yellow (You may see these other places as well). There is a hole in the bottom through which they enter and exit their nest. Hornets, like skunks and some snakes, won't bother you unless you rile them.

When someone intentionally hits one of their nests or dashes toward them, watch out! That person is likely to get severely stung.

Stirring up a hornet's nest has been a metaphoric idiom for tempting trouble, like 'playing with fire,' since the early 18th century. The use of 'hornet's nest' as a source of causing trouble first appeared in Samuel Richardson's *Pamela* in 1739.

stitch in time saves nine, A

This means that by making a small effort soon enough, a larger amount of work may be avoided. The origin of this proverb is simply what the wording suggests and nothing more overt, as some have suggested. The phrase is of old Anglo-

Saxon origin and spoke of sewing up a hole in fabric before it became larger. This principle was first recorded in Thomas Fuller's *Gnomologia, Adages, Proverbs, Wise Sentences and Witty Sayings, Ancient, Modern, Foreign and British,* 1732.

"A stitch in Time May save nine."

stone's throw away, A

This idiom means very close. It is applied largely when speaking about the figurative distance of one physical location from another.

It is unclear who started this saying, but it has been in popular usage since at least 1830, when it appeared in *Three Courses and a Desert* by William Clarke and George Cruikshank on page 273:

"If you lived but **a stone's throw away**, I'd be wrong if I'd let you stir: though they say you were the first that arrested Pierce Veogh, it matters but little to me."

It is likely that the roots are biblical, as many references are made in the *Bible* to throwing stones. A method of execution in ancient Israel was stoning, and in order to make sure that the executioners got the job done, they needed to be close to the condemned individual. Jesus, when denouncing the prejudicial attitudes of the religious leaders of his day in relation to a woman caught in the act of adultery, a capital offense, said, "He who is without sin among you, let him first cast a stone at her." (*John 8:7, KJV*)

David, when going out to fight the giant, Goliath, as a young shepherd boy, took only a sling and five smooth stones from a stream (*I Samuel 17:1-58*). He ran to 'within a stone's throw,' as we would say, slung a stone and killed the great giant.

In our Judeo-Christian society in the U.K. and the U.S., we have been told these stories from our youth, so it is only logical that this would be the root source of such a common phrase, and that it would mean what it does today.

Stones thrown from slings were a common weapon in the ancient world. In Rome, slingers were known to have hurled their projectiles as far as 440 yards. Many of these were the size of golf balls. With this in mind, it would be easy to understand why we would refer to a house ¼ mile distant as 'only a stone's throw away.'

Stop and smell the roses

Used as a gentle reminder that a friend or family member needs to take time away from a whirlwind work schedule to relax and enjoy the simple pleasures of life, the origin of the saying is a bit cloudy.

It is believed by some to have its beginning in the United States, perhaps a hundred years or so ago. A tale is told of a lady who was an avid rose gardener, so engrossed in her work that she took no time for herself. A dear concerned friend told her that she should take time to stop long enough to enjoy the fruit of her labor by 'smelling the roses.'

In the early 1980s, former Beatle, Ringo Starr, recorded an album with this cliché as its title.

Stop on a dime

A dime is the smallest of American coins, and saying that something could stop on one simply meant that it could come to a halt very quickly or in a short distance. The origin, though, may be somewhat different. Resident Associate University of Tennessee professor Jonathan E. Lighter, in his *Random House Historical Dictionary of American Slang*, has an interesting theory about early taxi dancers in Harlem who worked for a dime. This scenario was made famous by Lorenzo Hart's lyrics in the 1930 song, *Ten Cents a Dance*. Their bosses pushed them to keep moving to earn more money. Stopping on a dime would mean taking a new customer. The song inspired a movie by the same name in 1931 starring Barbara Stanwyck.

Within the next quarter century the idiom was in full usage, and in 1954 a driver's training movie was released, titled *You Can't Stop on a Dime*.

Straddle the fence

This idiom indicates being undecided or uncommitted on an issue, often appearing to favor both sides. The earliest known citation is found in *The Columbian Union*, by Simon Williard, June 1814:

> "...to which they are members, because they condemn that party, fifty times worse, than they do the British party; that is to say, they act directly against their own vote and government, and for the enemies; so they don't **straddle the fence**, but are tories..."

Straight from the horse's mouth

This is a saying when a person wants to know the real story, not hearsay. This started because a horse's age can be determined by examining its teeth. It was said that a horse dealer may lie to you but you can always find out the truth 'from the horse's mouth.' The earliest known citation is from *The Bishop's Purse* by Cleveland Moffett and Oliver Herford, 1913, in chapter 17, page 185:

> "Lionel hesitated, then went on quickly. 'I got a tip yesterday, and if it wasn't **straight from the horse's mouth** it was jolly well the next thing to it.'"

Straight laced

Ladies of centuries gone by wore corsets, or a forerunner of a girdle, which would lace up in the front. A proper and dignified woman wore a tightly tied lace. Thus such a woman, who is likely straight faced as well, is now called 'straight laced.'

Straight shooter

Derived from being an excellent marksman with a gun, this idiom is often applied in business and politics, and refers to being honest in dealings with others. It has been in use since it appeared in *The Searchlight on Congress*, 30 June 1922, in an article about Iowa Senator Smith W. Brookhart, *What about Brookhart* by Walter Durand, pp 17, 18:

> "Brookhart has steady nerves and keen vision; he is 'a **straight shooter.**' He cannot be intimidated."

straw that broke the camel's back, The

There is no doubt as to the definition of this idiom. 'The last straw' and other such sayings are related, and mean that one problem after another has been piling up, and finally the entire weight of the situations was simply too much to bear. This phrase comes from an old Arabic proverb about a camel which is loaded to such a capacity that is no longer able to stand under the burden.

Charles Dickens receives credit for one of the earliest printed figurative reference to this in English in *Dombey and Son* published serially from 1846-1848.

"As the last **straw breaks the** laden **camel's back...**"

The phrase is used in many other languages including Spanish, French, Italian, Dutch and Swedish.

Strike while the iron is hot

This metaphoric expression means to take advantage of opportunities which arise quickly before it is too late. It is derived from a blacksmith which must strike a heated metal while it is white-hot in order to shape it properly before it cools. It is taken from *Damon and Pithias* a comedy by Richard Edwards, circa 1566:

> "I haue plied the harvuest, and **stroke when the yron was hotte.**"

Strong as an ox

This idiomatic expression is centuries old and goes back to Old French, Old Greek and Old Latin. Its thoughts were passed down in folklore through the tale of Paul Bunyan, who was said to utilize a blue ox named Babe. Oxen have been used by many civilizations as a beast of burden because of their great size and strength. It would make sense to describe someone who was exceedingly stout as 'like an ox.'

The earliest printed reference known is from *The Scripture Chronology Demonstrated by Astronomical Calculations*, by Arthur Bedford, 1730, Book II, chapter XI, page 268:

> "Some think, that by the Ox and Hawk, they only meant the sun, who is **strong as an Ox**, or as *(q)* David saith, *as a giant to run his course.*

Stubborn as a mule

Mules, which have been utilized by workers as beasts of burden for centuries and served well, are often noted for being unyielding creatures, and thus were chosen as the ensample for this simile. It depicts such a person as being diametrically opposed to change and unwilling to listen to a voice of reason. The earliest known reference in print is from a Scottish tale titled *The Expedition of Humphrey Clinker*, 1785, printed in *The Novelist's Magazine, Vol XIX*:

> "The captain, when left to himself, will not fail to turn his ludicrous side to the company; but if any man attempts to force him into that attitvde, he becomes **stubborn as a mule**, and unmanageable as an elephant..."

Stuck in one's craw

Meaning annoyed by something unpleasant but forced to accept it, this saying comes from food which is collected in a fowl's preliminary stomach, called a craw, where it is predigested through use of grit and stones swallowed before going on into the gizzard to finally desolve into either usable form or be separated into waste.

The earliest known citation is from *Old Times in Tennessee* by Josephus Conn Guilt, 1878, page 114:

"This remark **stuck in my craw**, and I meditated how I should be revenged."

Strut one's stuff

This is to dress, behave and perform ostentatiously in order to impress others. It is derived from the looks of a rooster or peacock which parades about to show off to the hens. The earliest known reference in print is from *Welcome to Harlem* by Claude McKay, 1928, chapter 18, page 264:

"Harlem n****r **strutting his stuff**..."

Stumble onto something

This expression refers to making an unexpected discovery without trying, or in some cases, being aware of what is found. It can be used in relation to new truth, archealogical discoveries, interesting information, etc. The expression came into usage in the late 19th century. A good example of an early citation is in *The Johnson Murder* by Annis Burk, 1885, in chapter XII, page 126:

"The officers at once came to the conclusion that they had accidentally **stumbled onto** a good clue."

Suck it up!

One claim is that this saying originated with World War II pilots who wore oxygen masks. If they happened to vomit into their mask they were forced to 'suck it up' or die from breathing acidic fumes.

In military contexts, however, this has never been proven. As far back as 1907, George Madden Martin used the phrase in a literal sense as sucking in ones stomach. In an article titled *Letitia, Nursery Corps, U.S.A.*, in *The American Magazine,* he wrote:

> "Throw up your head, drag in your chin, **suck up** your stomach, wipe that smile off your face!"

Figuratively it now means to endure difficult circumstances.

Sweep someone off his or her feet

Sweeping is obviously derived from a broom which whisks away anything in its path. Usually used to describe a romantic fixation, the idiom refers to a complete carrying away by someone or something overwhelming. The phrase goes back to at least 1913 when Florence L. Barclay used it in chapter fourteen of her Christian novel, *The Broken Halo*:

> "I remember being **swept** completely **off my feet** when I first met Jim."

Then in 1937 William Ralph Inge had reference to it in *A Rustic Moralist*, speaking of Nazism in the statement:

> "I only want to understand a movement which has **swept** a great nation **off its feet**."

Here it didn't apply to romance at all, but still related to being completely overwhelmed. Since then a number of writers carried the idiom on to use by the masses.

Sweep (something) under the rug

Sweeping something under the rug means that someone attempts to hide an unpleasant event from others. The rug symbolizes a 'cover up.' Some sources date the origin at mid-1900s, along with the disrespectful slang term 'rug rats' for children. The earliest actual citation available is from July 6, 1962, in *Congressman's Report* by Morris K. "Mo" Udall. The heading reads, "THE FARM PROBLEM – **SWEPT UNDER THE RUG** AGAIN". He was lamenting the House debate on the 1962 Farm Bill. Nothing was resolved

T

Tail between one's legs

This is used when someone has been humiliated, had their feelings hurt and pride damaged because of a clash with another party. It is derived from a dog which sticks its tail between its legs after it is scolded or hit.

This dates back to 1649 when it was used in *The Workes of that Famous Chirurgion Ambrose Parey* by Ambroise Paré and Adriaan van den Spiegel translated by Thomas Johnson, printed in London by Richard Cotes:

> "And knowing hee had given him his death's blow, took again his long cassack, and went away **with his tail between his legs** and hid himself, seeing that the little man came not again to himself, either for wine, vineger, or anie other thing that was presented unto him; I drew near him, and felt his pulse which did not beat at all…"

Take a back seat

This expression, meaning having to take a subordinate position to others, originated in the early 19th century in America, and came from the fact that seats in the back of a coach or toward the rear of a theater were considered inferior to those in the front.

The earliest known printed figurative reference is from the journal, *The International Steam Engineer*, January 1818:

> "On inquiry we find it is the 'carelessness and indifference,' 'the jealousy and apathy,' and 'knocking and fault-finding' that exists in the ranks of Labor itself, and so after standing the gaff as long as he could he is compelled to acknowledge that he is weary and sick at heart of the work and is ready to resign his 'thankless job' and **take a 'back seat**.'"

Here it is in quotation marks indicating a recently coined expression. *The Daily Wisconsin Patriot*, Madison, Wisconsin, in May 1859 carried the following clear citation:

> "The dispised foreign born slave—the much hated and often cursed 'Irish,' 'Dutch' and 'Norwegians,' must **take a back seat** in the exercise of all the foregoing announced privileges [voting, jury duty, etc.]—no man of foreign birth can vote until two years after he shall have received his full papers."

523

Take all you want, eat all you take

This was a food conservation slogan used in the United States during World War II which was printed on military mess hall posters. Following the end of the war in 1945, it began appearing on menus and posters in restaurants throughout the U.S. This was not its origin, however. On 22 November 1939 in his column in Madison's *Wisconson State Journal*, page 4, column 5, Walter Winchell wrote:

> "One of the strictest rules at Alcatraz is the rule about food. The food is served cafeteria style, and there's plenty of it. The rule, however, is, '**Take all you want—BUT eat all you take!**'"

In Bejing, China, it is a long-standing unwritten rule in buffet style restaurants that one must eat all that is placed on their plates or pay a hefty fine.

Take a load off

This is an idiom for 'sit down' or 'make yourself comfortable.' It was originally 'take a load off your feet' and came into usage in the 1930s. The earliest reference in print known is from *The Books of Charles E. Vor Loan, Old Man Curry, Stories of the Race Track*, 1929, page 178:

> "'Set down, Frank, and **take a load off your feet**,' said he hospitably."

A group called 'The Band' recorded a single on Capitol in 1968 titled *The Weight* in which the lyric included 'Take the load off Annie' (often used as fannie), credited to Robbie Robertson which became their signature song. Miss Annie Lee of the lyric, was actually Anna Lee Amsden, the longtime friend of one of the song's cowriters, Levon Helm.

Take a long walk off a short pier (or plank)

This Americanism is one of many ways of telling someone in a less-than-pleasant manner to go away and leave someone alone. It originated in the mid-20th century. The earliest available citation is from the Detroit poetry publication, *Work*, edited by John Sinclair and Ron Caplan, 1965, in *Spring and Autom Annals* by Diana DiPrima:

> "The freedom of walking the plank
> or of your leap
> '**go take a long walk on a short pier**'"

Take a rain check

This phrase and the practice of giving and taking of rain checks began with baseball. When a game was cancelled because of rain, ticketholders were given a 'rain check' for a future game. To prevent having to give rain checks the practice was started of covering the field with a tarp when rain occurred or was predicted before a game. *The St. Louis Post and Dispatch* included the following on 26 May 1884:

> "The heavy rain yesterday threw a damper over local operations. At each of the parks the audience had to be content with three innings and **rain checks**."

By the 1970s the phrase was being used metaphorically, and had spread outside the U.S.

Take a slow boat to China

This cliché means 'go away on a long trip and don't worry about when you come back.' It was popularized by a popular song titled *I'd Like to get you on a Slow Boat to China* written by famed Broadway composer, Frank Loesser in 1945, published in 1947. But Frank didn't actually originate the phrase. His daughter Susan, in her 1993 biography about her father, *A Most Remarkable Fella*, wrote:

> "'I'd like to get you on a slow boat to China' was a well-known phrase among poker players, referring to a person who lost steadily and handsomely. My father turned it into a romantic song, placing the title in the mainstream of catch-phrases in 1947."

The lyrics included:

> *I'd love to get you*
> *On **a slow boat to China**,*
> *All to myself alone.*
> *Get you to keep you in my arms evermore,*
> *Leave all your lovers*
> *Weeping on the faraway shore.*

The song was on the charts 19 weeks for Kay Kyser in 1948 and later recorded by Bing Crosby, Frank Sinatra, Jimmy Buffett and others.

Take it with a grain of salt

This common phrase means that one should consider the source of some new 'truth' before swallowing it 'hook line and sinker' (see).

This has been around since the seventeenth century, and comes from the fact that food is more easily swallowed if taken with a small amount of salt. Pliny the Elder (actually Gaius Plinius Secundus, 23 AD to 25 August 79 AD) translated an ancient antidote for poison with the words 'to be **taken** fasting, plus **a grain of salt**.'

Take no prisoners

Actually, this modern cliché is not as benign as it may seem on the surface. It represents a philosophy of taking an overly aggressive, merciless stance on some particular matter, often in politics or athletics. It originated from the now archaic military command meaning that all of the enemy should be annihilated in combat.

An early figurative use was in the 1985 Peabo Bryson hit song *Take No Prisoners* (In the Game of Love).

Take someone down a peg or two

When it is said that someone is taken down a peg or two it indicates that the person's exalted opinion of himself or herself has been notably diminished.

This cynical metaphor was in use from the late sixteenth century, where the first known citation comes from a play by John Lyly, *Pappe with an Hatchet*, in September of 1589.

> "Now haue at you all my gaffers of the rayling religion, tis I that must **take you a peg** lower."

Then in Joseph Mead's *Letters,* in 1625, he wrote:

> "A-talking of the brave times that would be shortly... when... the Bishop of Chester, that bore himself so high, should be hoisted **a peg higher** to his little ease."

This, though stated somewhat differently, conveys the thought behind the saying.

The narrative poem *Hudibras*, by the ever-popular Samuel Butler in 1664 said:

> "We still have worsted all your holy Tricks,
> … And took your Grandees **down a peg**."

The intriguing trend in these early printings is the fact that all of them have religious overtones. Some have suggested that the 'pegs' which inspired the cliché were those in a barrel which controlled the level of amount of drink removed from it. This seems unlikely due to the context in these examples. Another a bit more plausible suggestion is that the pegs were the series of indentations and knobs used to lower and raise the 'colors' or flags of a ship. Still there is no real proof of this either. The 'or two' was added later.

Take something by storm

To 'take something by storm' is a metaphor inspired in the wars of the past century. It is based on a military maneuver meaning to attack a target directly and completely overwhelm the enemy. Operation Desert Storm was the codename for a military action by the United States during the Persian Gulf War in January and February 1991, combating Iraq's invasion and occupation of Kuwait.

This metaphor may be applied to anyone or anything that unexpectedly overwhelms anyone or anything. A good figurative example would be when a city or country is 'taken by storm' by a new musical group or a play.

Take the bull by the horns

This idiom means to take charge of a difficult situation and bring it under submission and control. It has been speculated that it originated in Spain or America, and possibly derived from either bullrunning or Spanish bullfights in which the banderilleros aim darts into the necks of the bulls, then wave red cloaks and grab them by the horns to hold their heads down. The practice of grasping bulls by the horns continued in the early American West, and subsequently in rodeos and is known as 'bulldogging.'

However, in spite of another major reference work dating the first citation of this expression in English to 1873, it was in use seventy years earlier at the dawn of the 19th century, when we find a definition and explanation of the expression in *Arciologia of Miscellaneous Tracts Relating to Antiquity,* Society of Antiquaries of London, 1803:

"A proverb in use at the present day is grounded upon this ancient practice of signifying conquest by the capture of the horns. 'To **take the bull by the horns,**' is an equivalent phrase for '*to conquer.*' When Demetrius Phalereus was endeavouring to persuade Philip, the father of Perseus, king of Macedon, to make himself master of the cities of Ithome and Acrocorinthus, as a necessary step to the conquest of Peloponnosus, he is reported to have used the following expression, 'Having caught hold of *both horns*, you will possess the *ox itself.*'"

The reference given was an ancient Greek manuscript *Strabo*, Lib. VIII, page 361. Strabo (Στράβων *Strabōn*; 64/63 BC – ca. 24 AD) was a Greek philosopher and historian, and this refers to book 8 of his famed seventeen-volume *Geographcia*. Demetrius Phalereus, (Greek: Δημήτριος Φαληρεύς; c. 350 BC – c. 280 BC), to whom the original phrase was ascribed, was an Athenian orator.

Take the high road*

This common cliché refers to taking the rational and proper approach to solving a problem rather than the emotional or easy one. In modern days it gained popularity during the 1948 U.S. presidential race when it was said that Republican candidate Thomas E. Dewey chose "the high road" and allowed voters draw their own conclusions as to the route President Truman was traveling. It comes from the idea that a high road or highway is the easy way. In London, England, the main traffic arteries are called "high streets".

The old Highland Scottish ballad, *The Bonnie, Bonnie Banks o' Loch Lomand* (Donald MacDonald, 1746) goes. "Oh ye'll **take the high road** and I'll take the low road and I'll be in Scotland afore ye," seeming to indicate that the main thoroughfare is not necessarily the quickest route all the time. Some folklorists, however, state that the low road meant here was death. There was an ancient Highland belief that the soul of anyone dying away from his native homeland will travel back to its home.

The phrase was used figuratively in a political sense, though, as early as 1770 in *The Political Register and Impartial Review* by John Almon, page 269:

"Were I disposed to facrisice my opinions to views of ambition or interest, I have lived long enough in the world to know the nearest way to honour and preserment: I would **take the high road** of opposition…"

Take the reins

Somewhat like 'take the bull by the horns' infers taking charge of a situation; this has to do with assuming control of an organization or a government. Here, the obvious derivation is the correct one. When traveling by horsedrawn carriages was the primary means of transportation, the driver had to maintain a tight grip on the reins which were attached to the bridles in order to control the horses.

The earliest known citation of figurative use of this term is found in James Tyrrell's *The General History of England, both Ecclesiastical and Civil: Containing the Reign of Richard II*, 1703:

> "...so that as his Government was much disturbed by popular Insurrections, and rendered unsuccessful, by the jarring Councils and ill Management of his Governors, during his Minority; so, when he came to **take the Reins** of the Government..."

Take the wind out of someone's sails (See: **Knock the wind out of someone's sails**)

Talk shop

This expression refers to talking about business at nonbusiness functions or at times and/or in places in which business is not normally the topic of conversation. It originated in the mid-19th century. The earliest known citation is in *The Eton School Magazine*, No. V, London, 1842, in an article headed 'Pedants and Pedantry' which clearly shows it to be fairly new:

> "...the conversation of one who deals neither in classical allusions nor in *Echos de Paris* may be padantic in the extreme, though the words and expressions which it makes use of may all be drawn from the pure well of English undefiled. Nor do we include in this category those who **talk 'shop,'** as the phrase is; it must be something far worse than pedantry, it must be downright vulgarity, which leads a medical student to shock the ears, and spoil the appetites of ladies, with the revolting details of the dissecting-room."

Talk to the hand (because the ear's not listening)

This phrase started in the 1990s in America and was popularized by actor / comedian Martin Lawrence in his 1992 sitcom, *Martin*. Then in 1995, a magazine in Indianapolis finally recognized it as a cliché. When someone is using the phrase to tell another person to stop his or her unwanted chatter, an arm shoots out and a hand is jabbed into the face of the speaker.

In 2006, bestselling author Lynne Truss used the sarcastic phrase in the title of a book, *Talk to the Hand: the Utter Rudeness of the World Today*.

The phrase took off and has been used in a variety of motion pictures and television shows over the past several years.

Talk turkey

Though there are a variety of opinions by researchers on the origin of this American phrase meaning 'talk frankly and get down to business,' the one which seems to make the most sense is that it began in Colonial America in dealings between the natives and the colonists. There were plenty of wild turkeys about and the natives were well-equipped and trained to hunt them. There is one complex tale which says that a colonist and a native went hunting and agreed to share their spoils equally. The spoils supposedly consisted of four crows and four turkeys. The colonist is said to have given a crow for the native then a turkey for himself all the way through. The native's response was that the colonist only talked crow for him and talked turkey for himself. A brilliantly written book, *The Etymologicon*, by Mark Forsyth, tells the tale a little differently as one turkey and one buzzard, stating that it was a joke, but seemingly indicating that it spawned this cliché as well as 'cold turkey.'

Tanning someone's hide

This figurative phrase, meaning to spank someone, comes from tanning animal hides to make them into leather. It has been in use metaphorically since at least the early 19th century and quite possibly much longer. The earliest verifiable reference in the *Minutes of the Proceedings of the Naval Court Martial of Jenkin Rutford* held aboard His Majesty's Ship, Belleiste, in Halifax Harbor, Nova Scotia on 26 August 1807. It was printed in several publications including *The Naval Chronicle*, Volume 18, 1807:

> "Hill said, if it had been Mr. M'Cory in the boat, instead of me, he would have **tanned his hide**, and thrown him overboard."

Taste of one's own medicine

This idiom means a sample of the unpleasantness that one has been giving to others. It is derived from bad tasting medicines which were commonplace in the past. The earliest known citation is from *The Index*, a paper devoted to free religion, Thursday, 6 August 1874 in a letter to the editor:

> "...in case of uproarious persistence on their part to inculcate their dangerous 'views,' should lock up their meeting-houses, and send the preachers to jail; that would be giving the Doctor a **taste of his own medicine**..."

Test the waters

This metaphoric expression refers to approaching something new cautiously before deciding its merits and implementing it. The earliest known reference in print to the figurative use is from *The Washington Newspaper,* University of Washington Department of Journalism, July, 1922, in 'Ready for Press Convention' by Chapin D. Foster, President of the Washington Press Association at the time:

> "The Washington State Press Association seems to be embarking upon an uncharted sea in planning an all-newspaper program for its thirty-fifth annual convention at Pullman, July 14-15-16. But editors are anxious to **test the waters**."

Thank God it's Friday!

After the formation of the five-day work week in the U.S., the anticipation of the upcoming weekend at the close of the day on Friday sent a frenzy of happy feelings down the spines of American workers, particularly. Like a wave, when this saying came into being, in the 1960s people utilized it. It soon became shortened to TGIF.

The saying almost immediately spawned the name of a bar and grill called TGI Fridays, which first opened in Manhattan's Upper East Side in 1965. This rapidly became a meeting place for professionals and students in the area, and spread across the country, making the saying TGIF blossom even more in pop culture.

In 1978, a disco movie (first released in the Netherlands) called *Thank God it's Friday*, starring Donna Summer, took the saying to 'fever pitch.' Then in the '90s, ABC TV called their Friday night comedy line up 'TGIF,' in an effort to help families catch the fever.

That (or It) comes with the territory

This means that something is to be expected as a part of a particular job or under the given circumstances. This saying was coined by Arthur Miller in his classic play, *Death of a Salesman*, 1949:

"A salesman has got to dream, boys; **it comes with the territory**."

That dog won't hunt

This means that a belief, theory or practice is not valid or practical. The earliest citation is from 1933 in Thames Williamson's *Woods Colt,* a novel about the Ozarks:

"That feller is jest naturally a fool for the lack of sense, a-tryin' to mix whiskey an' lyin'. He ort t' of knowed **that dog won't hunt!**"

That don't make me no never mind

This means, 'It doesn't make any difference to me,' and is poor English at best. It's a U.S. Deep-South mountain expression. But in the South, from the Ozarks to the Appalachians, it has been used for many years. So much so that it has made its way into pop culture in movies and TV shows. It likely started about the 1970's, but has been prevalent over the past three decades in these areas among younger people. Where the idea came from is hard to trace.

That gives me the willies

Most etymologists state that 'the willies,' meaning 'nervous apprehension,' is of 'unknown origin.' There are, however, some plausible theories. One is that the term comes from 'willow tree' since 'willy' at one time was a word for the tree. The willow is said to have represented sadness. The saying 'she is in her willows' was used of a woman who had lost her lover or husband. That idea seems to tie in with the most logical theory.

In the ballet, *Giselle (ou les Wilis)*, by Jules-Henri Vernoy de Saint-Georges and Théophile Gautier, which premiered in Paris on 28 June 1841, the girl Giselle is possessed by 'Wilis.' The willies herein take their name from the Serbo-Croatian word 'vila' (in English, 'wili'), a wood nymph or fairy, believed to be the spirit of a betrothed girl who died after being jilted by her lover.

Some apply 'the willies' to the slang expression 'willie-boy,' meaning 'sissy'—presumed to be the sort who would be prone to 'the willies.'

That'll cost you an arm and a leg

In early America, there were no cameras. One's image was either sculpted or painted. Some paintings of George Washington, for example, showed him standing behind a desk with one arm behind his back, while others showed both of his legs and both arms. Prices charged by painters of the day were not based on how many people were to be included, but by how many limbs were to be painted. Arms and legs are 'limbs,' therefore painting them would cost the buyer more. Hence the expression, "Okay, but it'll cost you an arm and a leg."

This was because hands and arms are more difficult to paint.

That pales in comparison

This means that something is so much better (or different) than other similar items or examples that it is difficult to compare them. The earliest available reference in print to a form of it is from *The Plaindealer*, Saturday, 30 June 1837:

> "Shakspeare's blackest shadows are like those of Rembrandt; so intense, that the gloom which broodeil over Egypt in her day of wrath was **pale in comparison** — yet so transparent that we seem to see the light of heaven through their depth."

That's all she wrote

The true origin of this saying has been largely debated. It is thought to have originated from one particular incident involving something written by a woman to a man, though it seems impossible to pin down. It is equated with other popular phrases like, 'that's all there is to it,' and 'that's the end of it.'

There is a popular belief that this saying referred to the 'Dear John letters' written by the girlfriends of servicemen during World War II, which informed them that they had found someone else, and would not still be there with open arms upon their return. This certainly seems feasible. It is said that when the soldiers were asked what else their sweetheart said in the letter, they replied sadly, "That's all she wrote."

The phrase has come to mean anything that is over, and undeniably unrevivable.

That's cool!

'Cool,' used as a general positive epithet or interjection has been part and parcel of English slang since World War II, but may have been around a while longer. Originally in African American dialect, it meant 'excellent.'

It came into wider popularity in the late 1950s, as seen in this snippet from *The Long Dream* by Richard Wright, 1958:

> "'What?' Sam answered.
> 'I ought to shoot you,' Fishbelly said, giggling.
> Tony lifted a soft baritone:
>
> *"'When your spirit rises up stiff*
> *Looking for angel's hair*
> *Git down on your knees for a gift*
> *And work your back in prayer...'*
>
> *"'*Man, **that's cool** and crazy!'"

This citation is from *An Overpraised Season*: *A Play of Ideas in One Act* the two years later presented by Little Theater, Grossmont High, Grossmont, CA:

> "BETTY: What?
> LARRY: I said Bob's a nice guy. He's—**he's cool**!
> BETTY: Yes, **cool**."

Other languages, such as French and German have even adapted it into their slang.

That's rich

This expression generally means that someone has just criticized or reprimanded the speaker for something for which he or she is just as guilty, or that something someone just said seems rediculous. It is usually spoken in a jovial tone, and has been in use in this respect since the mid-19th century. The earliest known example is from *The Life and Adventures of Valentine Vox the Ventriloquist* by Henry Cockton, 1841: Carey and Hart Philidelphia

> "'I feared,' said Valentine, 'that he had entered into some unsuccessful speculation, and had become involved.'

"'Speculation!' cried Horace, 'Well come, **that's rich!** Why did you ever suppose that a regular old know-nothing out-and-out cove of his kidney and half enough pluck to-----'"

A good example of the usual jolly use is found in *Aldyth, or, Let the End Try the Man* by Jessie Fothergill, fifty years later in 1891:

"Lifton burst out laughing, for I had been speaking with intense earnestness. **'That's rich,'** said he. 'You two ancient critics discussing poetry, as if you could be laureates whenever you choose.'"

Recently, in urban settings, it has also come to mean the same as 'that's cool.'

That's so last year

This phrase is used to describe a practice which has fallen into disuse, and is often spoken regarding catchphrases like many in this volume. This serves to demonstrate the sweeping changes which are constantly occurring in our language. It only came into usage around the turn of the millennium.

That's the ticket!

This idiom dates back at least to the early 19th century, and means "That's just what is needed." The phrase hasn't changed since it first appeared in print in 1838 in *The clockmaker, or, the sayings and doings of Samuel Slick of Slickville* by Thomas Haliburton:

"They ought to be hanged, sir, (**that's the ticket**, and he'd whop the leader)."

However, it was brought to life in *NBCs Saturday Night Live*, by Jon Lovitz' character, Tommy Flanagan, in the 1980s. But the use of the word 'ticket' to mean 'the right thing' also spawned the saying 'Just the ticket,' also dating back to the 1800s.

One theory is that it is a corruption of the French phrase, *"c'est l'étiquette,"* meaning 'that's the proper thing or course of action.'

Another meaning of 'ticket' popular since the seventeenth century is 'a guarantee of some good thing' prompting other phrases like 'You can write your own ticket.'

That's the way the ball bounces

This idiom means 'that is how things happen; there is nothing one can do to change it. In December, 1955, Terry Fell released a song on RCA Victor label entitled *'That's the Way the Big Ball Bounces.'* About this time, the expression took off as a cliché.

Similar phrases include 'that's the way the cookie crumbles' and *'c'est la vie'* (see).

There ain't no such animal

This humorous double-negative figurative saying has been in use since the early 20th century. Its origin seems to have been two similar widely published stories from as early as 1901, which *may* have been about the same incident with an elderly farmer. One was about a 'dromedary' the other a giraffe. This complete version is from *The Gateway, a Magazine of the Times*, Detroit, November, 1907:

> "An aged Jersey farmer, visiting a circus for the first time, stood before the dromedary's cage, eyes popping and mouth agape at the strange beast within. The circus proper began and the crowds left for the main show, but still the old man stood before the cage in stunned silence, appraising every detail of the misshapen legs, the cloven hoofs, the pendulous upper lip, and the curiously mounted back of the sleepy-eyed beast. Fifteen minutes passed. The farmer turned away, and spat disgustedly.

> "'Hell, **there ain't no such animal!**'"

A year later, this earliest known figurative example is from the *Official Report of the Proceedings of the Pennsylvania Arbitration and Peace Conference*, Philadelphia, May, 1908, page 213:

> "That rustic shifted his quid of tobacco, spat, turned around, and said: 'Shucks, **there ain't no such animal**.' I say, there is no such thing as the possibility of universal peace unless the people have faith in it."

It can apply to anything thought highly improbable.

There ain't no such thing as a free lunch

This phrase arose from the fact that everything has to be paid for by someone. The term 'free lunch' came into use in the U.S. and to a lesser extent in Britain from the mid-19th century onward. The main use was to relate to food handouts to poor and hungry people who were in drastic need, but also applied to food given by saloon keepers to attract customers for alcoholic beverages. This, for example, is an advertisement for a Milwaukee saloon, in *The Commercial Advertiser*, June 1850:

"At The Crescent...
Can be found the choicest of Segars, Wines and Liquors...
N. B. - **A free lunch** every day at 11 o'clock will be served up."

Temperance lobbyists fought this practice and later others followed suit, introducing the *TANSTAAFL* (Acronym for the phrase) idea of economic thinking, hence, the phrase we have here. The thought was that the saloon customers always ended up paying for the food in the inflated cost of drinks. As a result, some saloon keepers were prosecuted for false advertising of free lunches, because customers couldn't partake in the food without a type of 'cover charge.'

Economist Milton Freeman has often been credited with coining this phrase, but that is not the case, though he was a believer in this principle, and published a book with that title in 1975.

The first actual printing of the phrase seems to be in an editorial *in The Long Beach Independent,* October 1943, referring to libertarian Vice President Henry A. Wallace, a strong opponent of the ideal:

"Some people say **there is no such thing as a free lunch**, but you listen to a fireside chat from Washington, and the voice will tell you all about it, and how you can make something for nothing."

The controversy over this issue raged in political arenas, and in 1949, Pierre Dos Utt published a book describing an oligarchic political system (in which power rests with a small number of people) based on his conclusions of the TANSTAAFL philosophy.

There are none so blind as those who will not see

This old proverb is often thought to be from the *Bible*. Though it is not, it may have been inspired by *Jeremiah 5:21*:

"Hear now this, O foolish people, and without understanding; which have eyes, and see not..." *(KJV)*

It was first recorded by John Heywood in his 1546 book of proverbs.

There are none so deaf as those who will not hear

This proverb is attributed to English Presbyterian minister, Mathew Henry in his *Complete Commentary* on the Bible (1708-1710). It is a truism.

There are no such things as problems, only opportunities

This proverb was popularized by author and motivational speaker, John Kehoe, who developed a program called 'Mind Power' in 1978, after spending three years in the forest in British Columbia, Canada. The saying, however, is anonymous and has been around much longer.

Two other quotes in this vein of great note are:

"A pessimist sees the difficulty in every opportunity; an optimist sees the opportunity in every difficulty."
—Sir Winston Churchill

"Opportunity often comes in disguised in the form of misfortune, or temporary defeat."
—Napoleon Hill

There, but for the grace of God, go I

This saying, used in modern day vernacular by believers and unbelievers in Christianity, has been in common usage since at least the mid-20th century. It means that should circumstances have taken a different course, anyone could have ended up in a horrible situation. Any of us could have been a criminal, homeless or terminally ill.

The coinage of the phrase is uncertain, with early tribute going to sixteenth-century evangelist John Bradford, who was, himself, later burned at the stake in 1555. This credit was propagated by claims that an early edition of *The Oxford Dictionary of Quotations* carried it. If this was true, it had removed the reference by the mid-19th century. The saying is nowhere found in the exhaustive writings of Bradford which remain.

There is nothing in a caterpillar that tells you it's going to be a butterfly

This means that sometimes looking at something or someone on the surface does not tell us the whole story. It is a quote from American systems theorist, architect, inventor and author, Richard Buckminster 'Bucky' Fuller (July 12, 1895 – July 1, 1983).

There's a fool born every minute

The first recorded use of this expression in print is in 1806 in *The European Magazine: and London Review* published by Philological Society of Great Britain. It says: "It was the observation of one of the tribe of Levi, [i.e. a Jew] to whom some person had expressed his astonishment at his being able to sell his damaged and worthless commodities, 'That there vash von fool born every minute'. "

There's a sucker born every minute

This is another often misrepresented quote, attributed to Circus giant, P.T. Barnum (1810–1891). His actual motto was something like 'There's a customer born every minute.'

Some believe that this saying came from conman Joseph Bessimer, nicknamed 'Paper Collar Joe,' while many insist that it was actually from David Hannum in reference to Barnum's part in what was called the *Cardiff Giant Hoax*, a proported ten-foot-tall petrified man said to have been uncovered by workers digging a well behind a barn in Cardiff, New York. The actual 'giant' was the creation of George Hull, an atheist who had it carved from gypsum wood by a German stone cutter after an argument at a Methodist revival about a scripture passage in Genesis about giants on earth before the flood. The carving, darkened to appear aged, was hauled to the farm of Hull's cousin, William Newell. Nearly a year later he hired men to dig it up, perpetrating the hoax.

Newell set up a tent and charged people to see it. Hull had sold his part for $23,000 to a syndicate headed by Hannum which moved it to Syracuse. Though it had been declared a fake by Archaeological scholars, it drew such crowds that Barnum offered $50,000 for it to display in his circus. When he was turned down, Barnum hired a man to secretly model the giant's shape in wax and create a plaster replica. He put his copy on display in New York, claiming that the original giant was a fake and his was the real one.

This saying may not have come from Hannum either, originally, for in December, 1883 *The New York Times* ran a story that contained the line, "'**There's a sucker born every minute**,' as the gamblers say."

There's gold in them thar hills!

This cliché is famously misquoted as being from Dahlonega, Georgia mint assayer, Dr. M.F. Stephenson, who in 1849, when Lumpkin County was the site of the first major goldrush in the U.S., stood on the courthouse steps and tried to persuade people to stay there rather than join in the California gold rush. His actual words were, "There's millions in it." Nevertheless, Stephenson's speech may have given rise to this saying. Some claim it was a result of the retelling of the story to Mark Twain who coined the phrase as spoken by his character, Col.'Mulberry' Sellars; but it is not in Twain's novel, *The American Claimant*, 1892.

The first actual reference known in print to a form of it is on 30 August 1897, *Omaha World-Herald*, Nebraska, in 'Incident of the Fight,' page 2:

"I wonder if **there is gold in them thar mountains**. By G--, I've got to find out, for I can't get back without some."

Then in *The Story of "Scotty" (Walter Scott), King of the Desert Mine* by Charles A. Taylor, 1906, page 23:

"'**There's gold in them hills**, Slim,' he muttered."

But the earliest known citation of the actual phrase is in the *Syracuse Herald* (New York) on 5 September 1922 in 'Outlines of a Day's History' by 'All's Well,' page 1, column 2:

"TWO old-time lines come out of memory cells and declare themselves immortal. One is 'Back to the mines!' and the other, '**There's gold in them thar hills**,' the gold meaning coal as the man who pays soon shall learn."

The use of the term 'old lines' leads us to feel that the phrase had long been popular.

There's method in my madness

There's no mystery to the origin of this saying. It's another from Shakespeare. It comes from *Hamlet*.

"Though this be **madness**, yet **there is method in it**."

It means that there is a reason behind the actions of the person, no matter how senseless it may seem.

There's more than one way to skin a cat

When brooding over not being able to accomplish a task the way one wants to it's always good to remember that there are other ways to arrive at the desired result. The earliest known citation for this proverb is in *The Gold Diggers,* by humorist Seba Smith in 1840.

> "'**There are more ways than one to skin a cat**,' so are there more ways than one of digging for money."

Note that the phrase was in quotes in the book, so it is obvious that it was already in use. Other forms were also in use during the 19th century like, 'more ways of killing a cat...' but this one stuck with us and has stood the test of time.

There's no fool like an old fool

This old adage means that as a person grows older he or she is more likely to do things carelessly, simply because he or she no longer cares about how others feel toward their antics. It was already in use in the mid-sixteenth century when it was passed down by John Heywood in his first book of proverbs in 1546:

> "But **there is no foole to the olde foole**, folke saie."

There's no place like home

This saying comes from a folk ballad entitled *Home! Sweet Home!* adapted from American author and dramatist John Howard Payne's opera *Clari, Maid of Milan*, with music by Englishman Sir Henry Bishop, composed in 1823. The tune begins:

> "Mid pleasures and palaces though we may roam,
> Be it ever so humble, **there's no place like home**..."

It was further popularized in the 1939 classic film, *The Wizard of Oz*, when Dorothy clicked the heels of her 'ruby slippers' together at the bidding of the Wizard and chanted: "**There's no place like home, there's no place like home**," and magically awoke in Kansas.

There's no time like the present

This idiom is an admonition to procede immediately rather than procrastinate. It dates to at least 1609, when it appeared in *The Theosophist Volume XXX* a magazine published in Madras India of 'Brotherhood, Oriental Philosophy, Art, Literature and Occultism' edited by Annie Basant, P.T.S., page 232:

> "...even as it is said, what was the Present has become Past, and bears a relation to another point in Future Time to the negation of the Present. Yet **there is no time like the Present**. The whole gist of life to the Occultist is merged in it."

There's plenty more fish in the sea

This figurative idiom is used following a breakup with a spouse or significant other, and infers that the lost love is not irreplaceable because there are a lot more persons seeking a relationship.

This was preceded by a more literal proverb, 'more fish in the sea than ever came out of it,' though in use much earlier, noted in the late 19th century, as in this example from *Domesticated Trout: How to Breed and Grow Them* by Livingston Stone, 1872:

> "The idea of a slowly but surely diminishing supply of fish is no doubt alarming, for the public have hitherto believed so devoutly in the frequently quoted proverb of **'more fish in the sea** than ever came out of it,' that it has never, except by a discerning few, been thought possible to overfish..."

In 1903, the following appeared in *Lean's Collectania*, Volume 2; Part 2 by Vincent Stuckey Lean and Julia Lucy Woodward in a selection of proverbs, giving credit to Scottish writers, Sir Walter Scott in *The Pirate*, one of his 1893 *Waverly Novels*, and Robert Burns classic 1834 poem, *The Carles of Dysart*, and showing that the current meaning was already in place:

> "'There's as guid a **fish i' the sea** as e're came out o't.—Ramsey; Scott, *Pirate*, iv.

> "Generally applied to a disappointed lover's consolation.

> "Hey ca' thro', ca' thro', damsels didna doubt it;
> There's better **fish i' the sea** than ever yet cam out o't."
> *The Carles of Dysart* (additional to Burns)

> "**Plenty more fish in the sea** is another reading."

542

Thick as thieves

This simile is American in origin and refers to the clannish closeness found among persons in a gang of outlaws as they existed in the 19th century. Each member knew not to tell anything about their operations or plans because it would tend to incriminate the rest. This also gives rise to 'honor among thieves.' The first known reference in print to this particular phrase is in *The Parson's Daughter* in 1833 by Theodore Edward Hook.

"She and my wife are **thick as thieves**, as the proverb goes."

There seems to be no proof that a proverb of this thought ever existed. A versatile North Carolina based band founded in 2003 took the name, Thick as Thieves.

Things went south

This has to do with an entity or field of endeavor taking a bad direction, as the stock market souring or a business going under. In ancient religious belief, hell is always pictured as being under the surface of the earth. The underworld in ancient Egyptian thought was the abode of the dead. If someone died, particularly when the person's life was lived poorly, descending was seen as the direction of the soul's flight. On a map, south is always depicted as downward. An early American phrase was 'Gone to Texas, absconded.' *Taalstudie*, 1888 a Dutch reference work containing French and English terms contains the following definition in Americanisms:

"G. T. T. = **Gone to Texas**. This is a kind of P. P. C. that absconding debtors leave for their creditors. Nouns become verbs, and verbs become nouns with very little difficulty in America."

This saying, per se, became popular in the late 20th century. The July 8th, 1991 issue of *InfoWorld* contained the following on page 106:

"There were no lathes or drill presses, no million-dollar chip-making machines to repossess if **things went south**."

Thinking outside the box

This metaphoric phrase means to reason from a new prospective rather than the generally accepted method. This has been widely used in recent times in business environments, especially with management consultants. A related expression is 'putting someone in a box,' or expecting them to conform to the statis quo. The 'box' now represents the confines of accepted thought, pattern or organization. The *idea* was originated in the U.K. by Edward De Bono as 'Lateral Thinking' in 1967.

The original reference to the 'box,' however, was to a specific box—a two-dimentional square. *Sam Loyd's Cyclopedia of 5000 Puzzles, Tricks and Conundrums (With Answers),* published in 1914, had in it the 'Nine Dots Puzzle' which was to be worked by following these directions: 'Draw a continuous line through the center of all the eggs so as to mark them in the fewest number of strokes.' Though not specifically stating so, the lines should have been straight. In the late 1960s and early '70s, the American management gurus who introduced the phrase resurrected Loyd's Nine Dots Puzzle.

Third time's the charm / Third time lucky

These two clichés are intrinsically tied together—one in the U.S., the other in the U.K.—the latter being first with the kudos on coining them both.

The whole idea of third time luck goes back to the numerology of past civilizations and the fact that certain numbers were thought to bring good fortune. Even in the *Bible*, the Israelites felt that certain numbers held privilege with God—the number three being one of them.

The first mention known in the English language, and the forebear of the British cliché, 'third time lucky' is from Shakespeare in *The Merry Wives of Windsor, Act V, Scene i* (1602):

> "Pr'thee, no more prattling:—go. I'll hold: this is **the third time**; I hope good **luck** lies in odd numbers. Away, they say there is divinity in odd numbers, either in nativity, chance or death.—Away."

And though the 'charm' version seems only in use in America, in *The Cabinet Album,* by Lewis B. Wayne, 1830, from England, we find:

> "Jack," says he, striving to make himself speak pleasant to him, "you've got two difficult tasks over you; but you know **the third time's the charm**—take care of the next."

Then, but three years later, in *The Port Admiral,* by William Johnstoun Neal, 1833:

> "Once more they struck it, and splinters of the oak fell among them; but it yielded not. '**Third time's lucky**, now again."—but no, it remained firm."

Both gentlemen likely had read the line from Shakespeare.

544

Thirty-nine and holding

This catchphrase for those wishing to remain young in the minds of others was inspired by American icon and comedian, Jack Benny (1894-1974). Benny was well-known for his straightfaced claim that he was only thirty-nine, as that is the age at which he had stopped counting birthdays.

In 1981 *Thirty-nine and Holding* was the title of a song on the Elecrta label by early rock star, Jerry Lee Lewis, his last major hit.

This too shall pass

This proverb means that no matter how devastating a situation seems at the moment, it is only temporary, and will eventually come to an end. It is from an ancient Persian legend dating to circa 1200 BC. The story is told in the writings of various Sufi poets of a great king who called his sages together and asked them for one saying which would remain a constant in all times and situations. After much deliberation they told him: "**This too shall pass**." According to many, the king was so impressed that he ordered that it be inscribed on a ring.

This saying was popular with early 19th century poet Edward Fitzgerald, and was later brought out in the 1859 address of Abraham Lincoln, before his election as the 16th American President, to the Wisconsin Agricultural Society, in which he summed up its impact by saying:

> "How much it expresses! How chastening in the hour of pride! How consoling in the depths of affliction."

thorn in one's flesh / side, A

This metaphoric cliché relates to something or someone who is continuously causing problems for someone; a chronic infirmity or annoyance. It is derived from the *Bible, II Corinthians 12:7*. Herein the Apostle Paul tells of a 'thorn in the flesh' which gives him much trouble:

> "And lest I should be exalted above measure through the abundance of the revelations, there was given to me **a thorn in the flesh**, the messenger of Satan to buffet me, lest I should be exalted above measure." (*KJV*)

The actual source of St. Paul's 'thorn' is much debated among theologians. A song recorded in 1986 by British pop duo, Eurythmics, and written by members of the band, Anne Lennox and David Stewart, **Thorn in My Side** was based on this cliché.

In 2009, Bon Jovi released a hard rock song by the same name on their album, *The Circle*. Island label Henson Studios, CA

Those who cannot remember the past are condemned to repeat it (See: **History repeats itself**)

Three may keep a secret, but two of them are dead

This is from Ben Franklin's *Poor Richard's Almanac*. If we would all think about the results of divulging information secrets would not get into the hands of the enemy (see: Loose lips sink ships). Even what we say in emails and on the phone is not guaranteed to stop there any more.

Three sheets to the wind

This old cliché refers to someone who is drunk and disorderly. It derives from 18th and 19th century English Naval terminology. The original phrase was 'three Sheets *in* the wind' and referred to the erratic behavior of a ship that has lost control of all of its sails.

In nautical terminology sheets were the ropes that adjusted the position of the sails with respect to wind velocity. The speed and direction of a sailing ship is controlled by the number of sails raised on each mast, the angle of the sails to the wind, called 'trim,' and the position of the rudder. If the sheets used to control the sails break or have been released, the sheet is said to be 'in the wind.'

If a sail were to be thrashing wildly in a strong wind with its sheet, or control rope, blowing about, it would be very difficult to regain control of the sail.

Prior to the early 19th century it was common for ships to have three masts. If the sheets on all three masts were 'in the wind,' the ship would lose all steering control. The ship's lack of control is compared to that of a drunken person whose actions are out of control.

Through thick and thin

This old adage has survived the tests of time. It means making it regardless of any obstacles which are placed in one's or something's path, and was derived from traversing on foot through the mixed heather and woodlands of England.

The earliest known citation is from Richard Baxter's religious text *A Saint or a Brute: The Certain Necessity and Excellency of Holiness*, published in 1662:

"Men do fancy a necessity [of holiness] where there is none, yet that will carry them **through thick and thin**."

Throw a curve ball

Obviously derived from baseball, this idiom refers to misleading someone by placing unexpected problems in his or her path. It can also apply to asking a question for which the person is not prepared. When a 'curve ball' is thrown by a pitcher, the batter is not aware of the problem until the ball approaches him or her. The phrase started appearing figuratively in the latter part of the 20th century. An example is found in *It Only Takes a Minute to Change Your Life* by Willie Jolly, 1997:

"...you've dreamed big dreams, you've done everything all the self-help books advised you to do, then life **throws** you **a curve ball!**"

Throw a monkey wrench into the works (or **machinery**)

This figurative phrase means to do something to divert someone's plans. It was derived from early union workers sabatoging a factory whose management failed to meet demands by pitching wrenches into the cogs of machines. In spite of other major dictionaries reporting the earliest figurative usage in print as being from the Manchester, U.K. tabloid newspaper, *The Daily Express,* in 1931, it actually had appeared much earlier in *Report of Proceedings of the 33rd Annual Convention of the American Federation of Labor,* 1913, page 385:

"Yesterday a telegram was sent to the president of the American Federation of Labor, and I find it embodied in the proceedings this morning, from our friend, Mr. Dolan. He has told the American Federation of Labor that Comerford went to New York and **threw a monkey wrench into the machinery** of amalgamation."

Throw cold water on

This common idiom means to discourage the advancement of something, particularly a cause about which other people seem enthused.

Plateus first used 'pour cold water on' in 200 BC, meaning to slander. In the way we use it today, throwing cold water on something has been around in English since the 19th century.

An early example is in George Eliot's Silas Marner, 1861, chapter eight.

"It was to be hoped that Mr. Godfrey would not go to Tarley and **throw cold water on** what Mr. Snell said there, and so prevent the justice from drawing up a warrant."

Throw enough mud against the wall, some of it will stick

This used figuratively may have either of two meanings. Either 'do enough of the same things and one will eventually be successful' or 'voice enough accusations against someone or some cause, and the reputation of the person or organization will ultimately suffer.'

It is likely derived from the technique of construction of walls by tossing of daub (mud mixed with straw) at a wattle (tree branches and twigs woven together). The phrase came into usage in the late 20th century, and was often used by sales managers to encourage their teams to continue trying to write sales even when they were getting poor quality credit risks. An early citation, this one regarding songs, is from *Billboard*, December 13, 1980:

"...you **throw enough mud against the wall some of it will stick**, I would have thought that one hit out of every 10 singles releases was a good average."

Later it began to be applied in the other manner, particularly in political senarios.

Throw good money after bad

This idiom refers to wasting money on a losing proposition. This began being popular in the mid-20th century. An early example is from the play *After the Fall* by Arthur Miller, 1964, page 16:

"You mean you saw everything going down and you **throw good money after bad**? Are you some kind of a moron?"

Throw in the towel

This is a boxing expression going way back to the early days of professional prizefighting. Many times the boxer couldn't get to his feet when the bell rang signaling the next round was beginning. If the manager knew the boxer was too weak to continue, he would throw in the towel that was used to wipe up blood, signifying surrender.

This adage now has the same connotation as the towel in days of old—quit while you still can, before the end result is worse.

Throw one's hat in (or into) the ring

When someone throws his or her hat into the ring it means that they have made a decision to join an effort or take up a challenge. In America we hear this phrase most often when a political candidate is announcing a bid for office.

The origin, though, was a quite different ring; a boxing ring. At one time these were actually circular spaces surrounded by an excited throng of observers, rather than the square, roped-off arenas that they became; thus the term, 'ring.' Any young man who thought he had 'a ghost of a chance' at winning a fight would literally throw his hat into the ring as a symbol of his willingness to take on the next opponent.

The expression goes back to the early 19th century, and an early printed reference is from *The Sporting Magazine* in 1805:

"Belcher appeared confident of success [in a boxing match], and **threw his hat into the ring**, as an act of defiance to his antagonist."

Five years later, this citation from *The Mirror of Taste*, in Philadelphia more specifically makes reference to challenge:

"A young fellow **threw his hat into the ring** and followed, when the lame umpire called out 'a challenge,' and proceeded to equip the challenger for the game."

Throw someone for a loop

This metaphoric phrase means to astonish someone; to take them utterly by surprise. It was in use by 1929, when it appeared in the U.S. Marine Corp publication, *The Leatherneck*, Volume 12:

"He just couldn't keep from displaying his prowess, and even a good horse gets horsey once in a while, and 'Sergeant' **threw him for a loop** and a vacation in Woodland's Sanitarium."

Throw someone under the bus

The expression, 'putting something or someone under the bus' actually wasn't coined until the last quarter of the 20th century. It means to treat someone very badly who is not deserving of such treatment. Firing a well-loved individual is one prime example. An article in *The Washington Post* in 1984 by David Remnick said:

> "In the rock 'n' roll business, you are either **on the bus or under it**. Playing 'Feelings' with Eddie and the Condos in a buffet bar in Butte is **under the bus**."

In the late 1980s it began being used frequently on a Boston radio station, then WROR, later WBMX, by station manager Joseph Kelly who stated his consideration of ending a network affiliation. In early 1988 he made the statement:

> "I'm thinking about **putting The Source under the bus**."

Afterward other station employees picked the phrase up and began to use it about political intrigue at the station. The station was then offered for sale as a result of an F.C.C. decision that RKO General, the owner, was 'unfit to hold broadcast licenses.' Use of the phrase then became more frequent on the new FM station after the new owners acquired a sports talk station, WEEI. The use was then picked up by print journalists who appeared on station broadcasts.

By the time of the 2008 political primary campaigns the term had gained great momentum, and described candidates distancing themselves from controversial figures. It was dubbed by David Segal of *The Washington Post*, 'the cliché of the 2008 campaign.'

Thumb one's nose

As an idiom, this means to scorn or ridicule someone. This is a phrase which evolved from an older one, and is based on a childish gesture made by spreading out the fingers of one hand upward, usually the right one for right handed children, and placing the tip of the thumb against the nose and wiggling the other fingers, often making taunting noises at the same time. The original name for this process was 'cocking a snook,' a phrase which dates to the late 18th century and first appeared in *The Wynne Diaries*, 1791:

> "They cock snooks at one on every occasion."

'Cock' was likely taken from a rooster, and possibly the appearance of the comb made by the upraised fingers. 'Snook' may have been a version of 'snout,' often used for 'nose.'

The expression 'turn up (his) nose' also showed up in print by the early 18th century, though in a slightly different perspective, in *The Connoisseur, or, Every man in his folly: A Comedy* by Mr. Connelly, 1736.

"L. *Const*, But, should some Fellow without Sense of Embriodery happen, by Affection of Wit, to discover his Want of it, you may see his Lordship **turn up his Nose**, and squint Surprize at any Man's daring to assume the Title of Fool, who wanted that of Lord."

'Thumb his nose,' in spite of reports putting it in the early 1900s, appeared first in 1879 in *In the Schillingscourt* by Eugenie Marlitt:

"Or he would stand in the gateway and lash at passing children with his long whip, and vary the amusement by stepping on ladies' trains, and give their wraps a sudden jerk, and **thumb his nose** at them."

Tickled pink

This expression is somewhat related to 'in the pink' and indicates making someone so well pleased that their countenance glows. It has been used in this respect since the early 18th century. The first known citation placing tickling in this vein of use has to do with tickling the ears, and is from Samuel Hieron's *Works*, 1617:

"Well might they haue their eares **ticled** with some pleasing noise."

Being 'tickled pink, however, didn't originate until the early 20th century, and first appeared in 1910, in the Decatur Illinois newspaper, *The Daily Review*, in a piece titled 'Lauder Tickled at Change.'

"Grover Laudermilk was **tickled pink** over Kinsella's move in buying him from St. Louis."

tide turning, The

This idiom refers to an altering of a previously stable course of events. In the realistic realm, 'the tide turning' has to do with the change from incoming to outgoing tide or the reverse. In a figurative sense, it was first introduced in Shakespeare's *Henry V* in 1598:

"Hostess:
"Nay, sure, he's not in hell: he's in Arthur's bosom, if ever man went to Arthur's bosom. A' made a finer end and went away an it had been any christom child; a' parted even just between twelve and one, even at **the turning o' the tide**: for after I saw him fumble with the sheets and play with flowers and smile upon his fingers' ends, I knew there was but one way; for his nose was as sharp as a pen, and a' babbled of green fields."

Tight as a drum

This simile means very taut or close-fitting, and is derived from the skin on a drumhead which is tightly stretched. Later it refered to drum shaped containers which had to be watertight in which products, such as oil, were stored. *The Weekly Inspector*, New York, Saturday, March 28, 1807, included the following citation in a poem which it stated was in a *Letter to the Printer of the Middletown Gazzette* 'Printed in a Gazette of the date February 6th, 1790':

> "'*With*' smooth '*plausibility's sign*' far '*extended*',
> And as **tight as a drum** with a calf skin new mended."

Tighten your belt

This metaphoric expression means to economize; to make ends meet on less money than previously. It is derived from a man's belt being tightened on his waist as the buckle is placed into another hole as he loses weight. It gained popularity during the depression of the 1930s. The phrase was used figurative as early as the late 19th century. An early example is in *The Optimist* by Charles Fredric Goss, 1897, page 215:

> "**Tighten your belt** and go on. You will find a date-tree to satisfy your hunger, a fountain to slake your thirst, a river to float your burden, an herb to heal your wound. All men are born to three things — labor, sorrow, and joy."

Tighter than Dick's hatband

This simile has to do with being frugle to the extreme. Dispite various attempts at identifying the origin of this simile, it originally refered to Richard Cromwell, the son of seventeen-century British quasi-king, Oliver Cromwell. Richard was 'Lord Protector' of England for a few months, September, 1658 to May, 1659, and felt that he had the right to succeed his father to the throne, but was quickly deposed by the military. 'Dick's hatband' refers to the crown which was deemed 'too tight' for him to wear safely.

Till the cows come home

Cows will take their time ambling back to the barn—unless they are dairy cows needing to be milked. But cattle in general were the premise of this saying, which has been with us since at least the early 19th century. The place of origin could have been Scotland. It first appeared in print in January, 1829 in *The Times*.

"If the Duke (of Wellington) will but do what he unquestionably can do, and propose a Catholic Bill with securities, he may be Minister, as they say in Scotland '**until the cows come home.**'"

In the 1933 film, *Duck Soup*, Groucho Marx, in his normal dry, straightfaced humor, made the statement:

"I could dance with you **till the cows come home**. Better still, I'll dance with the cows and you come home."

The saying seems no less popular today, and means for an undetermined, likely *lengthy* period of time.

Time and the tide wait for no man

This phrase emphasizes the truism that no human has the ability to halt the passage of time. The first reference to a form of it is in Middle English from *St. Marher*, 1225:

"And **te tide and te time** þat tu iboren were, schal beon iblescet"

Time flies

Proverbially time rushes along as if it had wings. Another such saying is 'time and the tide wait for no man.' The first reference of this proverb in English is from Chaucer's *Prologue to the Clerk's Tale*, from *Canterbury Tales*, in 1386.

"When we dowdle, our lives pass swiftly."

But the idea is *much* older and was expressed by Virgil (70-19 B.C.), who wrote in Latin in his epic poem, *Aeneid*:

"Fugit inreparabile tempus" (Time is flying never to return).

Time heals all wounds

This proverb poses the thought that with the passage of time, all hurts will eventually be forgotten. Though this may or may not be true, the earliest form of it comes from Greek comedy and drama playright, Menander (342BC- 291BC):

"**Time is the healer** of all necessary evils."

This was originally written in Greek. The earliest English form was from Chaucer, in *Troilus & Criseyde* (1374-1385) in Middle English:

"As tyme hem hurt, a **tyme doth hem cure.**"

Time to make the doughnuts

Started by a commercial for a doughnut company in the 1990s, this became a cliché for getting back to work.

Tip of the iceberg**

Only a small portion of an iceberg is visible to those who approach them on ships; the entirety of it may be many times larger, and likely poses a greater threat than it seems. The expression 'just the tip of the iceberg' is applied when a problem or scandal is much larger than it appears on the surface. The earliest verifiable printed reference to a form of this metaphor is found in the Quaker publication, *The Friend's Intelligencer*, September 28. 1912, under 'Book Notes' on 'The Case of Ralph', by James Oppenheim, printed in *Harper's Bazaar*, and seems to indicate that the expression was already well known:

"But what actually happens is that what you have 'in your mind' at any given moment is really in your mind; in other words, to use the well-known symbol, the conscious part of the mind is like the **tip of the iceberg** that shows above the water-line..."

Tit for tat

This curious expression relates to receiving a 'blow for a blow' retaliation for a wrong done. The earliest form of this was recorded circa 1466 in a book of poems penned by Charles, Duke of Orleans while a prisoner in England following the Battle of Agincourt.

"As strokis grete not **tippe, nor tapp**, do way The rewdisshe child so best lo shall he wynne."

In modern English this reads: 'As strokes great, not **tip, nor tap**, do the best for the uncouth child, lo he shall win.'

The first known citation 'tit for tat,' per se, is from John Heywood, in the parable *The Spider and the Flie*, 1556:

"That is **tit for tat** in this altricacion [*altercation*]."

Toast of the town

This antiquated metaphoric expression was applied to someone in a place in which he or she was revered highly. The term was already in use by the early-18th century, because the following appears in Pickering and Chatto's *Catalogue of Old and Rare Books* from circa 1806 in a description of a book published on 19 October 1737, *A Monument for Tom K_____g*:

> "BROADSIDE ENGRAVING (15 in. x win), representing a tomb, at each side a cask of Arrack and Brandy, standing upon some are figures of The Batter'd Rake, The **Toast of the town**, across the back is a semicircular scroll lettered Coffee, Tea..."

In its current use it was experiencing a heyday in the early nineteenth century. One example is from *The Scotts Magazine*, Edinburgh, March, 1805, in an article titled *An Old Maid's Dream*:

> "This, with a tolerable share of personal and mental accomplishments, soon brought a crowd of admirers about me, and at the age of eighteen I was the **toast of the town**."

To beat the band

The origin of this old idiom, meaning something done to excess, has a variety of attempts by reference works to explain its origin. One is that it came from 'to beat the banshee;' another, from a major phrase origin dictionary, links it to an older Irish expression, from 1830, said to have been 'to beat 'Banagher,' from a town in County Offalay, Ireland, which sent two representatives to Parliament to sew up an election. This reportedly spawned the saying, 'Well that beats Banagher.'

But there remains no concrete evidence of either of these. The most logical origin is the evident one. 'To beat the band' originated from music—someone singing loudly. The figurative usage first appeared in print in November, 1894 in *The United Service, a Monthly Review of Military and Naval Affairs*:

> "I was running from the provost one night, about two years ago, and I tried to give 'em the slip by dodging through the cart-path on the old road. But they knew the place and got after me **to beat the band**."

Two years later, in July, 1896, it showed up in *The American Angler* in an article titled, *Another Week on the Nantahala*, in quotes, indicating that it was now somewhat known as an idiom:

> "The faithful fishing we did was worthy of fuller creels than we brought in, and had the conditions been more favorable we would have taken trout '**to beat the band**.'"

To boot

Getting something 'to boot' means you get it in addition to the product or service bargained for. The term is a corruption of the Old English word *bot*, which meant profit or advantage.

To catch a bird, just put salt on his tail

This old saying has been around in varying forms since at least 1764, and may date, according to some, as far back as 1685.

The origin is from the old children's nursery rhyme, *Simple Simon*. Often a modified version is given which leaves out this fifth verse containing the thought of this phrase:

> *He went to **catch a** dicky **bird**,*
> *And thought he could not fail,*
> *Because he had **a little salt**,*
> *To put upon its tail*.

Simon was doomed to fail at everything because his reasoning was flawed. The point, as one might suspect, is that if someone can get close enough to sprinkle salt on a bird's tail, he or she is surely close enough to pick it up.

To err is human; to forgive, divine

This is neither the *Bible* nor Shakespeare; it's a quote from Alexander Pope. Pope was an English poet and satirist (1688-1704) and gave us several nice pleasantries which we use today, like 'A little learning is a dangerous thing' which is often misquoted using 'knowledge' for learning (see). Both were from *An Essay on Criticism*.

This phrase has been often used to remind us of the difficulty we humans have with forgiveness, a virtue which we would all do well to attain.

Toe the line

'Toeing the line' is conforming to an established standard. Demanding that one do so is a requirement for some agendas, both occupationally and politically.

This originated from placing one's toes in a strategically important position at or behind a line, scratch or mark for the beginning of a race, toe-to-toe prizefight or any other athletic competition. This practice was common in the 19th century in Britain, Scotland and Ireland, and for those immigrants who came over the Atlantic to America who had been accustomed to the practice in their native homeland. Thus, it may have been stated, "toe the mark," or whatever was being toed. When applied to the boxing matches, anyone capable of competing was said to be 'up to scratch.' This is also the origin of the saying 'start from scratch' (see).

In *The Diverting History of John Bull and brother Jonathan*, 1813, by 'Hector Bull-us,' a pen name used by James Paulding, the earliest known reference in print, 'mark' is the word used.

> "He began to think it was high time to **toe the mark**."

Obviously, the connotation here is figurative already, at this early date, rather than literal.

**To handle yourself, use your head,
to handle others, use your heart**

This proverbial quote is attributed to former American first lady, Eleanor Roosevelt (October 11, 1884 – November 7, 1962). It reminds us that in order to win others over to our way of thinking we must appeal to the mind, will and emotions of others.

To kingdom come

Often used as 'blow it to kingdom come' or 'from here to kingdom come' this refers to heaven as taken from the Lord's Prayer in *Matthew 6,* in the *King James Version* of the *Bible* in 1611. Though there were uses of 'going to kingdom come' in reference to the next life years earlier, an early reference to being 'blown' there is from *Chamber's Journal*, 3 October 1857:

> "Shall I never again feel the sweet serenity of soul which attended upon the consciousness of knowing that the fellows I blew **to kingdom come** were natural enemies…"

Tomorrow never comes

This proverbial truism serves to remind us that every day stands as a new day, and that that moment is 'today.' When we procrastinate until 'tomorrow,' we never get anything accomplished. The earliest known reference in print is found in *Traditions and Recollections, Domestic and Literary by Richard Polewhele*, 1826, page 186-187:

> "Tomorrow is the answer that every idle fellow gives to his own mind whenever the propriety of writing occurs. But **tomorrow never comes**."

Tongue in cheek

This phrase is a figure of speech used to indicate that a statement is spoken lightly or humorously and should not be taken at face value. A similar metaphoric expression is 'take it with a grain of salt' (see).

This evolved from the initial usage of the phrase to imply contempt, by 'thrusting' the tongue in the cheek, but which is now archaic. This was the case, however in *The Adventures of Roderick Ramdom* by Tobias George Smollett published in 1748:

> "He looked black and pronounced with a faultering voice, 'O! 'tis very well — damn my blood! I shall find a time.' I signified my contempt of him by thrusting my **tongue in my cheek**, which humbled him so much, that he scarce swore another oath aloud during the whole journey."

And from *The Fair Maid of Perth* by Sir Walter Scott, 1828:

> "The fellow who gave this all-hail thrust **his tongue in his cheek** to some scapegraces like himself."

By the late 1830s it was used as we see it today as illustrated in *Thomas Wright's Political Songs of England*, 1839:

> "It is a frontal attack, although perhaps a little **tongue in cheek**, against the operation of the criminal law."

Too big for one's britches*

This idiomatic expression refers to being conceited and arrogant; having too high an opinion of one's self. It was first used in print by noted American frontiersman and Congressman, David "Davy" Crockett, in *An Account of Colonel Crockett's Tour to the North and Down East: in the Year of Our Lord One Thousand Eight Hundred and Thirty-four,* published in 1835, on page 152.

> "I myself was one of the first to fire a gun under Andrew Jackson. I helped to give him all his glory. But I liked him well once: but when a man gets **too big for his breeches**, I say Good bye."

From there it spread and evolved into other similar sayings, such as "too big for his boots."

Too close for comfort

This cliché refers to a threat, disaster or other misfortunate event which is dangerously close. The earliest known reference in print is from *American Turf Register and Sporting Magazine*, March 1833 in a letter to the editor dated January 27, 1833:

> "The heat had been **too close for comfort**, and the gelding was known to be good for tough and in fine fix."

Too good to be true (See: **If it sounds too good to be true, it probably is**)

Too many chiefs and not enough Indians

This idiom has been around since the mid-20th century, and is totally American in origin and scope. It began when large numbers of Americans began realizing the need of higher education and there became more applicants than needed who were qualified for management and upper white-collar positions.

The television shows in the 1950s and '60s, as well as the motion picture industry, were overtaken by a large influx of 'cowboy and Indian' type westerns. The Native Americans were pictured as savages in too many cases, each with a chief who controlled the actions of their tribe.

When the situation arose in which college graduates were scrambling for positions within corporate America, the analogy of 'chiefs and Indians' was a natural metaphor to fit the situation of that era. Today it is not nearly as common to hear this phrase, but with the tragic economical condition existing, not only in America, but in Europe to an even greater degree, the thought behind it seems more apropos than ever.

Too many cooks spoil the broth**

This proverb means that when too many people are attempting to be in charge of the same project, they most often get in each other's way, and the end results are likely to be inferior. It has been in use in this sense since at least the early-to-mid-sixteenth century, according to the following 1539 quote from *The Period of the Reformation (1517-1648)* by Ludwig Häusser and edited by Wilhelm Oncken, published in 1648, page 198:

> "As early as 1539 he had said to Bucer, 'In the campaign in Wurtemberg all were led by him, but now several wanted to lead. **Too many cooks spoil the broth**. The Protestant League must not be made an idol of. The, Christian ranks did not always hold Christian sentiments — a great deal that was worldly was mixed up with them...'"

In 1662 it was passed down by Sir Balthazar Gerbier in *Three Chief Principles of Magnificent Building:*

> "When an undertaking hath been committed to many, it caused but confusion, and therefore it is a saying, **Too many Cooks spoils the Broth**."

Too many irons in the fire

Having too many irons in the fire alludes to having more to do that one can accomplish in the allotted time.

It started back in the days when blacksmiths were plentiful, had no thermometers, and used iron bars heated in flames in their shops. Trying to handle too many at once could be distracting and make them lose track of what they were trying to accomplish. Also, the color of heated iron changes with the temperature. As it goes from black to blue-purple, then red-orange-yellow, it tops out at white and can get up to over 2000 degrees Fahrenheit before burning up, according to Journeyman Blacksmith and Engineer Ms. B. MacNichol, who now lives in the Blue Ridge Mountains of North Georgia. It was absolutely not a job suited to much multi-tasking, and the smith had to be extremely cautious to only have what he (or she) could handle, and know what to do when. This is also where 'strike while the iron is hot' comes from.

Too rich for one's blood

This somewhat outdated expression refers to not being worth the price asked. It was used in various circumstances, like when a price on merchandise was considered exhorbitant, or when someone was in a game of poker and not able to meet the bet, and had decided to fold. The earliest available citation is from The University of Michigan's *Michigan Argonaut*, 13 January 1882 in an Operetta titled *Rosalie*:

> "**Ros.** May Heaven reward you.
> **W. W.** Oh, I shall go mad with ectasy. This is **too rich for my blood** — I mean — too late; all is lost."

Top drawer

In the magical Victorian age of the late nineteenth and very early twentieth centuries the top drawer of the bedroom chest of drawers is where the bourgeois stored their most prized personal possessions: their jewelry, their best clothes and the like.

Because of this, in this era, the term 'top drawer' came to portray in a figurative manner persons of high social standing based on the family background and holdings. They either were, or weren't TOP DRAWER.

British novelist, Horace Vachell, in *The hill, a romance of friendship*, published in 1905, had what may be the first citation of this phrase:

> *"You'll find plenty of fellows abusing Harrow,"* he said quietly; *"but take it from me, that the fault lies not in Harrow, but in them. Such boys, as a rule, do not come out of the **top drawer**."*

To the moon, Alice, to the moon!

This 'empty threat,' frequently used by Ralph Kramden, the Jackie Gleason character on the popular 1951-1955 American CBS TV sitcom, *The Honeymooners*, later became a catchphrase for getting someone back for a perceived wrong done to the speaker. When saying it, Kramden would make a fist and thrust it upward.

To the victor belong the spoils

This is a famous quote by New York Senator William Learned Marcy (1786-1857), which was recited in the U.S. Senate, 25 January 1832. Afterward, 'the spoils system,' by which loyal supporters of the newly elected officeholder are rewarded with appointive public offices, became popularly used.

Touch base / touch all the bases

These are sports related idioms derived from players touching all of the bases while making a run for home plate. 'Touch' base means make contact, while 'touch all the bases' indicates making certain that all points are covered in a discussion, sermon, lesson or conference. The earliest available printed figurative reference to 'touch base' is from an ad on page 42 on *Life* Magazine, June 16, 1947:

"**Touch base** with your Texaco Dealer today."

The earliest citation to 'touch all bases' is in quotes ten years later an article in *Popular Science*, January 1957 on page 98:

"Bombers must follow this 3,100-mile course — and '**touch all bases**.'"

Tough nut to crack

This metaphor means a difficult task or a person who is hard to deal with. The most complete explanation available of its origin comes from a website on 'Russian Idioms and History' and attributes it to Peter the Great in 1702, during the Great Northern War. The Russians had just fought for thirteen hours to win back the Fortress of Noteburg which had been taken over by the King of Sweden, freeing access to St. Petersburg and the Baltic trade routes. The infamous leader, in assessing this difficult victory said, "**Крепкий орешек!**" (*Hard nut to crack!*)

tough row to hoe, A, vs. Long row to hoe

The first phrase in the U.K. is 'a hard row to hoe.' It means the same as tough. This cliché evolved from the literal meaning and began to be in use from the first half of the 19th century. A tough row to hoe is applied to any difficult task which causes an almost unbearable burden on the person assigned to it.

The idiom 'long row to hoe' is a corruption of a nautical term, a long rode to ho. A rode is a length of chain and rope that is put out from one ship to another. A long rode is required in windy or stormy weather. To put a rope on a ship is to 'ho.' This is where the term 'heave ho' comes from. On the command 'heave' the group advances the rope; they release it on the command 'ho.' In times of storms the long rode to ho is difficult and takes much longer to accomplish.

Train wreck, Slow motion train wreck*

This metaphor is used to mean total confusion, utter disaster, ruin or disarray. It may be said of a situation, an entity or a person. One version of this, 'slow motion train wreck', is what it known as a mixed metaphor, combining two ideas into one figurative expression. Slow motion adds the intensity of scenes on television or motion pictures portraying exciting sequences being slowed down for effect.

This metaphor, however, did not start showing up in print until about 1990. The earliest known citation is from *Business Week*, found in archives of issues 3132 and 3133, page 161, in the article, 'May Never Shine Again', herein as a simile:

"For Lone Star Industries Inc. shareholders, following the company's fortunes has been akin to watching a **slow-motion train wreck**. In two years, share prices have plummeted..."

An early printing of the basic expression attributes it to emergency room physicians. It is from *Closer to Light* by Melvin Morse, M.S., with Paul Perry, page 2, 1991:

"In the blunt jargon of emergency room physicians, she was a **train wreck**."

Tried and true

This is originally a woodworking term. A try plane is used to create a flat surface on a piece of wood being leveled. When the surface has reached the desired state of perfection, it is said to be 'true.'

Tried and true as an idiom means that something has been proven to be the right way of doing or thinking 'beyond the shadow of a doubt' (see). Usually, this refers to methods of accomplishing a desired result which culminate in success.

Trump card

A 'trump' is any playing card of a suit that for the time outranks the other suits, such as a card being able to take any card of another suit. The word trump in this literal sense has been around since Middle English, 1250-1300, and comes from Old French and Old High German, *trumpa*, and was a variant of *trumba* the word from which trumpet comes. A trumpet makes a loud noise and 'trumps' the other instruments. In 1529, trump became an alternative of trumph. The word meaning 'surpass or beat' is attested from 1586. It was a corruption of Triumph, which was at the time a card game.

Another old related expression 'turned up trump,' which seems to trump 'trump card,' was in use from at least 1621, when it was in Robert Burton's *The anatomy of melancholy*.

"They turned up trumpe, before the Cards were shuffled."

Shortly earlier, an illusion is made by Shakespeare which seemed to be the harbinger of the figurative usage of 'trump.' He depicted card playing imagery in this allusion from *Anthony and Cleopatra* in 1606:

"…the queen, [Cleopatra] whose heart I thought I had"..."now lost, she has pack'd cards with Caesar and false-play'd my glory unto an enemy's triumph."

At least by the 18th century 'turn up trumps' had begun to be used in a figurative sense, with seemingly no reference to playing cards in Francis Grose's *Classical Dictionary of the Vulgar Tongue*, 1785:

"Something may **turn up trumps**, something lucky may happen."

Through the years, 'trump card' began to be used as a metaphoric expression for anything which suddenly appeared to outrank the ideas and practices of an opponent in any field.

Truth is stranger than fiction

This proverbial truism is attributed to George Gordon Byron, Lord Byron (22 January 1788 – 19 April 1824), in his satirical poem, *Don Juan*, published in 1823. The first four lines are:

"'Tis strange - but true; for **truth is** always strange;
Stranger than fiction; if it could be told,

564

How much would novels gain by the exchange!
How differently the world would men behold!"

Truth will set you free, The

This proverbial saying is from the words of Jesus in biblical text in *St. John 8:32*:

"Then you will know the truth, and **the truth will set you free**." (*NIV*)

It has often been used to extol the importance of finding the facts in any given situation before passing judgment.

Tuck one's tail and run

Often also, 'tucking one's tail between his legs' this is derived from dogs which, when frightened, put their tails between their legs and scurry away from trouble. It is used to accuse someone of cowardice. The earliest known figurative rerference to tucking one's tail is found in *The Meerut Universal Magazine*, Volume 1, on page 32, in verse IX of an admittedly unauthorized publication of the historic ballad, *The Devil Dutchman,* Agra, India, 1835:

"'Ha! ha!' said he, 'I'll take a tour to see the county's riches;
So he packed up his traps in half an hour
And **tucked his tail** in his breeches:
He went to Patna and to Oude,
A tiger he shot at Jounpore,
He put on an old green coat and vowed
He'd have a review at Cawnpore.
Tol de rol rol."

Turn a blind eye

This idiom means to consciously ignore something you know is happening. The saying is arttributed to British Admiral Lord Horatio Nelson (1758-1805) when he was said to have willfully decided to ignore a flag signal to withdraw while leading the attack against the joint Danish and Norwegian forces during the Battle of Copenhagen being commanded by Sir Hyde Parker in 1801. Though tales like this are sometimes exaggerated or false, this one has good evidence of being factual, as it was included in the biography *The Life of Admiral Lord Nelson, K.B. from His Lordship's Manuscripts* by James Stanier Clarke and John M'Arthur published in 1810.

Turnabout is fair play

This proverb means that whenever one has done something, even if it hurts or embarrasses someone else, they deserve the same treatment. Though the idea was already around a bit earlier, James Fenimore Cooper used the saying on page 13 of *Afloat and Ashore; or, The Adventures of Miles Wallingford* in 1844:

"...and he brought his son up a parson; now, **turnabout is fair play**, and the parson ought to give a son back to a man-of-war. I've been reading the lives of naval men, and it's surprising how many clergymen's sons in England go into the navy..."

Turn a deaf ear

This idiom refers to refusing to listen to a sincere request or need. The origin is uncertain, but it was in use by at least 1670, when it appeared in *Aerius Redivivus, or, The History of the Presbyterians* by Peter Heylyn, page 330:

"Which seeming to the King to serve then rather for a colour to excuse their Factiousness, than to lay any just restraint upon it, He **turned a deaf Ear** to their Petitions, as well concerning his proceeding with the Popish Lords..."

Matthew Henry (18 October 1662 – 22 June 1714) used this expression several times in his third volume of *An Exposition of All the the Books of the Old and New Testaments*, written circa 1708-1710:

"As they had **turned a deaf ear to** God's word, so God **turned a deaf ear to** their prayers, v. 13. As he cried to them in their prosperity, to leave their sins, and they would not hear, but persisted in their iniquities..."

Turn over a new leaf

This expression has to do with beginning anew, making a fresh start. It comes from turning over a new page, formerly known as leaves, in 'the book of life.' Though it was obviously in use before this, the earliest known citation is from *Saducismus Triumphatus: Or, Full and Plain Evidence Concerning Witches and Apparitions* by Joseph Glanvil, 1581, page 223:

"...I am now come to tell you, *That there is a God and a very just and terrible one, and if you do not **turn over a new leaf*** (the very expression as is by the Doctor punctually remembered) *you will find it so* (the Captain proceeded)..."

Turn over in one's grave*

This bit of hyperbolae is used to express such a great shock or surprise that if a deceased person would be made aware of it that the very idea would be so foreign to their way of thinking that it would figuratively send shockwaves through the person's body. The earliest printed version of this expression was used in *Cobbett's Weekly Political Record*, London, 20 August 1825:

"Poor Oracle! Your rattling must, surely make him **turn in his grave**."

The earliest known mention in print of 'turning **over**' in one's grave is found in *Dred, a Tale of the Great Dismal Swamp, by Harriett Beecher Stowe*, Volume 1, 1856, on page 254:

"Hang it all! she isn't going to marry a d—d Yankee! Why, brother **would turn over in his grave!**"

Turn the other cheek

This saying is a quote from Jesus in his famous 'Sermon on the Mount,' and is found in both *Matthew 5:39* and the parallel scripture in *Luke 6:29*. In the *King James Version*, 1611, the Matthew reference reads like this:

"But I say unto you, That ye resist not evil: but whosoever shall smite thee on thy right **cheek, turn** to him **the other** also."

Jesus' teaching was so contrary to that of 'an eye for an eye and a tooth for a tooth' in the Torah (*Exodus 21:24*) taught by the Jewish leaders of the day that he was hated by them, which ultimately led to his crucifixion.

This saying has become a cliché which is frequently used on television and in movies, and has become a part of our general jargon. Often it is used in the negative sense, such as 'I'm not very good at turning the other cheek.'

Turn the tables

This old expression has been in figurative use since at least 1634, when it appeared in Bishop Robert Sanderson's *XII Sermons*:

"Whosoever thou art that dost another wrong, do but **turn the tables**: imagine thy neighbour were now playing thy game, and thou his."

Note here the application to a game. It is applied to the switching of the advantage between two opponents in any endeavor. Some examples are a playing field, a business competition, a political election or a battle in time of war. It means that the stronger player suddenly takes the upper hand.

Turn up one's nose at

This means to reject something; to look at with disdain or contempt. In spite of a major idiom dictionary placing the earliest reference to this figurative phrase at 1779, it had appeared in a number of prior publications beginning in 1752. The following citation is from *Amelia* by Henry Fielding published in London that year:

> "Another answered, *I don't know, Madam, what she may do with her Head, but I am convinced she will never more **turn up her Nose at** her Betters.*"

Turn up trumps (See: **Trump card**)

Turn your face toward the sun and the shadows fall behind you

This bit of wisdom is a Maori Proverb from the aboriginal natives of New Zealand. Canadian politician Charlotte Whitton made it popular, thus many have attributed it to her.

The sun is the primary source of light, and represents positive energy. It means that when someone is looking at the light, metaphorically speaking, negativity falls away from him or her.

Twiddling one's thumbs

This activity, in the literal extent has been practiced for several hundred years. It involves the locking of the fingers of both hands and the twirling of the thumbs around one another. Twiddle, as a verb meaning trifling, is from the mid-sixteenth century. The earliest reference to the practice of twiddling the fingers available is in *Harrison's British Classiks: The Idler, Fitzosbourne's Letters*, 1787, page 90 in *Epigram on the Feuds between Mendel and Bonicini*:

> "*Tweedle dum and Tweedle dee*, I am persuaded the poet gave it *tweedle drum* and *tweedle key*. To tweedle signifies to make a certain ridiculous motion with the fingers…"

The earliest reference to 'thumbs,' per se, is from *Frederick de Montford*, a novel, Volume 1, by Edward Goulburn, 1811, page 176:

> "Why does not he do it now — instead of standing like a fool, **twiddling his thumbs** and saying nothing?"

The first notable figurative use, meaning 'having nothing to do' is found in 1843 in *The Yankee among the Mermaids* by William Evans Burton, on page 139:

> "So leave off **twiddling your thumbs**, and stretch away for Epsy's house, and fall in love directly. I've telegraphed her of your intention: she expects your arrival; go and report yourself…"

Two bricks short of load

This is one of a number of sarcastic, cutting clichés used to insult the intelligence of a person. The number of 'bricks' may vary. The earliest known printed reference was in *Herefordshire Speech; the Southwest Midland Dialect as Spoken in Herfordshire*, by Winifred Leeds, 1974, where it is listed in a cache of such expressions on page 15 as found here.

'A few (or two) fries short of a happy meal,' which refers to a children's meal at McDonald's Restaurants, claimed by Yvonne Lehman of Tennessee, came into usage about 2005.

Two edged sword

This has been used as a metaphor for anything that figuratively cuts deeply in every direction. The first mention of it is in the *Bible*, in *Psalms 149:5*:

> "*Let* the high *praises* of God *be* in their mouth, and a **twoedged sword** in their hand;" (*KJV*, 1611)

In *Hebrews 4:12*, it is used as a type of 'the word of God':

> "For the word of God is quick, and powerful, and sharper than any **two edged sword**…" (*KJV*)

Other writers picked up on this as soon as the early seventeenth century. Then, in 1648 it was used of the tongue in *Relations and Observations Historical and Political upon the the Parliament begun Anno Dom. 1604*, by Clement Walker:

> "…both Houses of Parliament, but received their answer, (as the Jews their Law) in thunder and lightening, a **two-edged sword** the tongue, and the report of Muskets the voice, which spake nothing but wounds and death."

The phrase was popularized in modern days relating to freedom in a book by social libertarian, occultist and Cal Tech rocket science researcher John 'Jack' W. Parsons (born Marvel Whiteside Parsons; October 2, 1914 – June 17, 1952), titled *Freedom is a Two-edged Sword*. It was written about 1950, and first published posthumously in 1996.

But he was not the first to use this analogy. The earliest known use of it in this respect, which was subsequently picked up by numerous writers, was about 100 years earlier in the *The Saturday Review of Politics, Literature, Science, Art and Finance*, 20 February 1853:

"The great principle of religious freedom is vindicated in the abolition of Church Rates; but religious **freedom is a two-edged sword**, and it remains to be seen if Dissent is to be as liberal to the Church as the Church is, whether on compulsion or not, liberal to Dissenters."

Two heads are better than one

Though not specifically saying 'heads,' the root of this clever proverb goes all the way back to the *Bible*. Its first appearance in English was in the *Miles Cloverdale Bible* published in 1535, *Ecclesiastes 34:9:*

"Therfore **two are better then one**, for they maye well enioye the profit of their laboure."

In John Heywood's *Dialogue conteinyng the momber in effect of all the prouerbes in the English tongue*, 1546, we find the first English notation of a close form of the proverb in this entry:

"Some heades haue taken **two heades better then one**:
But ten heades without wit, I wene as good none."

In this reference, head means 'mind.' The meaning of the saying is that when two thinkers combine their ideas, often the result is more profound than those of one alone.

Two's company and three's a crowd

Some sources list John Heywood's 1546 book of proverbs as the origin of this. However, the following is the only reference which comes close:

"Of things which in no wise might be bewrayd.
We twayne are one to many, (quoth I), for men say,
Three may keepe counsayle, if **two** be away."

It's possible that this is actually the root of this saying. But this phrase means that when two people want to be alone, the third is an unwanted 'spoke' in the wheel.

This exact phrase didn't come into everyday usage until the late 19th century, however. In 1876, Elzey Hay used the exact maxim in *A Family Secret* on page 91:

"That would spoil the tête-à-tête, you know; **two's company, three's a crowd**,— ha! ha! ha! and, besides, I could not leave Mrs. Norgood alone ; but, if you don't like the trouble of driving…"

A television show which ran from March 15th, 1977 to September 18th, 1984, and much longer in reruns, was a comedy take off on this principle called *Three's Company.* The program was based on the British sitcom, *Man about the House*, and featured two young ladies and a young man who lived in an apartment together in a totally platonic relationship. It starred John Ritter, Joyce DeWitt and Susanne Somers, launching their careers. The show spawned two spinoffs, *The Ropers* and *Three's a Crowd.*

Two shakes of a lamb's tail

This idiomatic expression for 'with lightening speed' is derived from how quickly sheep twitch their tales. The earliest reference in print is found in *Ingoldsby Legends* by Richard Barham, 1840. But it wasn't until a bit later when it became popular in magazines and novels. In *Hunt's Yachting Magazine*, 1 February, 1868, we find:

"…we had no time to spare, as the tide was falling fast, and out we tumbled, and in '**two shakes of a lamb's tail**,' we were under way and got outside with but six inches of water under our keel."

The quotes indicate that the phrase was in use, but was likely still unfamiliar to many readers.

Two ships passing in the night

This figurative phrase is used to mean the brief, often intense, meeting of two people who may never see one another again. Ships at sea often pass quickly. It comes from Henry Wadsworth Longfellow's epic poem *The Theologian's Tale; Elizabeth, iv,* published in *Tales of a Wayside Inn*, 1873.

"**Ships that pass in the night**, and speak each other in passing, only a signal shown, and a distant voice in the darkness; So on the ocean of life, we pass and speak one another, only a look and a voice, then darkness again and a silence."

Two steps forward and one step back

This catchphrase is based on an old antedote about a frog attempting climbing out of a well. Everytime he takes two steps toward freedom, he slides back a step, thus making his progress arduous and seemingly never ending. It was being used metaphorically of other things, as early as April, 1899, when this appeared in New York's *The Charities Review*:

"They are like convalescence from chronic diseases of long standing — '**two steps forward and one step back**.'"

In 1904, a revolutionary pamphlet by Vladamere Lenin was entitled, *One Step Forward, Two Steps Back* (see), intentionally rearranging the term.

Two wrongs don't make a right

This obvious truism has been around for centuries and is a variation of the original proverb published in James Kelly's *Complete Collection of Scottish Proverbs* in 1721:

"**Two** blacks **don't make a** white."

This had nothing to do with racism. It referred to wrongs and rights, and was later changed to what we know now, and the first known reference to something similar to 'two wrongs don't make a right' is in a poem by C. Acres published in 1734 in *The London magazine or Gentleman's monthly intelligencer*, Volume 3.

An orient star led thro' his blind-
Side, to a prize his eye of mind:
The lightning said, its he; in spite
*Of fate **two wrongs infer one right**.*
let fly; well shot thanks to my sparks;
A blind boy once has cleft the mark.

The implication of this proverb is that when people retaliate in regard to wrongs done against them it doesn't make things appropriate. Millions around the world saw the video posted on the Internet by a father in North Carolina in February, 2012 who shot his daughter's laptop in revenge for insults posted on her facebook account about him. Thousands praised the father gone rogue. But 'two wrongs really don't make a right;' proper parenting should begin by finding the cause of a child's anger and determining a way to change the circumstances.

A pleading 'bluesy-styled ballad' written by Smokey Robinson and Berry Gordy was released by Mary Wells on Motown label in 1963 with the title, *Two Wrongs Don't Make a Right* on the 'B side' of her popular hit, *Laughing Boy*.

Tying the knot (wedlock) (See: **All tied up in knots, tie the knot**)

U

Ugly duckling

Someone who blossoms from a less-than-handsome youngster into a near-perfect specimen of humanity as he or she matures is often dubbed an 'ugly duckling.' It is taken from Danish storyteller Hans Christian Anderson's (1805 – 1875) most popular fairy tale by this curious title. The beloved tale, which Anderson devoted a year in development, was first published 11 November 1843, and has been translated into more languages than any of his other stories, and has been adapted to a musical and film. It centers around one of the younglings hatched in a nest by a mother duck which was much different from its mates, and considerd gangly and unattractive, thus receiving much verbal battering. After leaving the barnyard and finding a new home, then heading out on his own, the ugly duckling sees a flock of migrating wild swans and wants to join them. Being too young to swim, he takes up residence with a farmer for the winter. When spring blossoms the swans once again arrive and light on a pond near him. Now fully grown, he decides to join them, even though they may reject him and kill him because he is so ugly. The swans, however, welcome him into their flock, because he looks just like them. After all, he was really a swan all along. Anderson later admitted that the story was an analogy on his own life.

Umpteenth (time, etc.)

This comical slang expression for an excessive undetermined number of times likely derived from a shortening of 'some-teen+th.' In spite of another popular dictionary stating is that 'ump(ty)' is slang for the dash in Morse code, and this plus -teenth formed the word, 'umpteenth' has been used since the early- 19th century. The first known citation is from *New Medical and Physical Journal, or, Annals of Medicine, Natural History and Chemistry* by William Shearman, 1815, Volume 9, page 474:

"The carotid and left subclavian arteries have been found obliterated by the pressure of aortic aneurism. Case **umpteenth**, demonstrative of this fact, peonliarly interesting..."

In 1838, this reference, making the term a bit more clear, appeared in *A General Biological Dictionary,* Volume 2 by John Gorton:

"He had scarcely attained his **umpteenth** year on his first arrival in England..."

The problem with the major dictionary's theory, which is widely published and accepted, is that 'umpteenth' was in print many years before Morse code, which Samuel F. B. Morse did not begin developing until 1836, and was not minor use until the early 1840s, and extensive use until the 1890s. Also, the most popular symbol for the dash is 'dah,' not *ump*.

Later, this gave way to 'umpty,' often 'umptyninth,' which could refer to larger indeterminate numbers.

Under the gun

This phrase is one in which the origin was quite literal. It came from the bygone days in which fortresses and castles armed with artillery were besieged by enemies. When the siege took place, the final step was to throw infantry against the broken walls and into the artillery battery on the solid walls remaining.

The attacking artillery was therefore 'under the gun' to complete the attack in a prompt manner.

Today anyone who is put 'between a rock and a hard place' (see) and forced to act quickly is said to be 'under the gun.'

Under the microscope

Something 'under the microscope' is being given close scrutiny, and subject to criticism. In a figurative sense, this began being used in the late 20th century. An early example is from page 174 of *Is Your Child Drinking* by Nancy Hyden Woodword, 1981:

"In effect, most felt that they were **under the microscope**, although how much of what they saw they wished to share was their decision."

Under the radar (See: **Fly under the radar**)

Under the weather

This is an age-old expression which derived from the days when all travel outside the boundaries of land was done on passenger ships. On cross-oceanic voyages, sea sickness was common. In the midst of a harsh storm, passengers would go below deck to be 'under the weather.' Another application was the nautical term, 'under the weather bow,' which is below the sharp end of the ship, and takes the brunt of the storm. Those passengers traveling there would tend to get even sicker.

Today the term is used to indicate any type of sickness or discomfort.

United we stand, divided we fall

There are a number of references to the saying, and its earliest exact quotation comes from *The Four Oxen and the Lion*, one of *Aesop's Fables* in the sixth century B.C. The following English translation is from the *Harvard Classics*, 1909-1914:

> *A LION used to prowl about a field in which Four Oxen used to dwell. Many a time he tried to attack them; but whenever he came near they turned their tails to one another, so that whichever way he approached them he was met by the horns of one of them. At last, however, they fell a-quarrelling among themselves, and each went off to pasture alone in a separate corner of the field. Then the Lion attacked them one by one and soon made an end of all four.*
>
> *"UNITED WE STAND, DIVIDED WE FALL."*

An indirect reference was also made in another of Aesop's Fables, *The Bundle of Sticks*, "Union gives strength."

Jesus made statements very akin to this. First, when he was accused by a Pharisee of exorcizing demons by the power of Beelzebub, 'the prince of devils,' in *Matthew 12:24-25*, to which he calmly replied, "Any kingdom divided against itself is laid waste; and any city or house divided against itself shall not stand. And if Satan casts out Satan, he is divided against himself; how then shall his kingdom stand?" (ESV) And in *Mark 9:38-40*, when his disciples complained that others were 'casting out devils' in his name who were not of his group of known followers, Jesus said, "He who is not against us is for us." (*v 40, NIV*)

575

The phrase in modern times became the motto of the Commonwealth of Kentucky, and is included in the third verse of the *Liberty Song*, composed by Isaac Shelby, Kentucky's first governor.

"Then join hand in hand
Brave Americans all,
By **uniting we stand**,
By **dividing we fall**;
In so righteous a cause
Let us hope to succeed,
For Heaven approves of
Each generous deed."

Until blue in the face

This idiom means until the point of exasperation; livid with effort. In spite of a major dictionary placing the first known printed figurative reference in 1864, it appeared in *Owain Goch* by William Bennett, Volume 1, page 4, 1827:

"Och, woman, talk **till** you're **blue in the face**, but say no more about Paddy."

Up and at 'em

This idiom means 'get the move on,' or get yourself up and get ready to do what is expected of you.

Adam Ant (defender of right), was a Hannah Barbera TV series in the 1960s with the oft-used saying '**Up and at 'em** Adam Ant.'

In spite of a quote by the Duke of Wellington in regard to Waterloo, offered in another cliché book, this was not the phrase's true origin. There are suggestions that it originated as a World War I battle cry, in other words, 'get out of the trenches and ready for battle.' This may have merit.

This saying became popular in the mid-20th century and was used to awaken children and get them ready for school, and to encourage workers to get busy at their jobs.

Uphill battle

This idiom refers to fighting against very unfavorable circumstances and great odds against success. It derived from use in field warfare, such as in the

576

American Revolution, when troops were facing opposing forces decending upon them from hillsides. The earliest known citation in a figurative setting is from *Corbitt's Political Register*, Volume XXI, 1812:

"I have said before, that they were colonies of Spain. Therefore, Mr. Foster, our Minister now in America, had scarcely taken time to eat his first dish of ham and fried eggs, when he began to complain of these invasions. He had an **uphill battle** to fight about the Orders in Council..."

Up in arms

This figurative expression means very upset; roused enough to desire to take action against someone. It originally was literal, and meant having the necessary weaponary to attack enemies. Shakespeare was likely the coiner of the phrase, as it appeared in three of his plays. An example is in *King Richard III*, circa 1591:

"March on, march on, since we are **up in arms**..."

Upper hand

This refers to being in charge of a situation. The saying, as we interpret it, was thought to come from the practice of holding on to a baseball bat at the bottom and the captains of the teams grasping just above the first until finally one has 'the upper hand' and the privilege of selecting the first member of his or her team.

However, this expression was already in figurative use long before the game of baseball was invented. In Queen Margaret's Monologue in Shakespeare's *King Richard III*, 1591 is found:

"Give mine the benefit of seniory And let my griefs frown on **the upper hand**. If sorrow can admit society."

Ups and downs

Ups and downs represent a mix of good and bad experiences in life, something to which every human can relate. As an idiom, this phrase has been used in America for at least the past one hundred years.

The first known mention was the title of a 1915 movie featuring Oliver Hardy.

The term can also apply to moodiness. A person with what is now known as 'bipolar disorder' experiences an inordinate amount of mood swings, or 'ups and downs' in their behavior patterns.

Other films and television shows have also used the name.

The mood of our modern age has brought a lot of attention to the thought of 'ups and downs.'

At least six current music artists have recorded songs or albums with this theme.

Upset the applecart

In the late 19th century, 'applecart' was wrestling slang for 'body.' To upset one's applecart was to throw them down.

Through the years it has come to mean that someone's plans have been foiled.

Up the creek without a paddle

This is the clean rendition of a World War II saying meaning to be in a dire prediciment. There is an earlier version, however, which goes back as far as 1884, to the political campaign song, "The Year of Eighty-four," which is included in *Blaine and Logan Songbook: A Collection of Republican Campaign Songs, National Songgs, War Songs, Rally Songs, &c. adapted to the popular melodies of the day*. It contains the following lines:

"With the years that come and go;
And soon we'll send it **up salt River**..."

A 'salt creek' or river leads through a salt marsh, or marshland to the ocean.

The earliest citation available of the actual expression, though obviously already known, is from *Heaven, Hell or Hoboken* by Ray Neil Johnson, 1919 on page 168:

"We were **up the creek without a paddle**."

Up to here

Usually using a hand motion as if cutting the throat, this metaphoric idiom means full or completely, and has been around since about the fourteenth century. A book by John W. Urban was published in 1984 called *I've had it—Up to Here;* a frequent way the phrase is used.

Up to snuff

In the early 19th century, when this phrase was first coined, it meant 'sharp and knowledgeable about what was trending.' Today it has evolved into something a bit different: 'up to the required standard.'

A parody of Shakespeare's *Hamlet* was written in 1811 by John Poole, titled *Hamlet Travestie.* Therein were likely the first two citations of this phrase.

"He knows well enough The game we're after: Zooks, he's **up to snuff**."

"He is **up to snuff**, i.e. he is the knowing one."

That being said, a little later reference in *Grose's Dictionary,* 1823 edition, links it to the powdered tobacco product, which had become fashionable for society folks to inhale in the late seventeenth century. In that day the cost was high and decorative boxes were the rage. The term is listed:

"**Up to snuff** and a pinch above it."

This was defined as 'flash.'

V

Vandalism

Here we must look at etymology. The Vandals were members of a German warrior-race which was present in the area south of the Baltic prominent during the fifth and early-sixth centuries. In 409 AD they invaded the Iberian Peninsula, crossing to Africa in 429. Under the leadership of King Genseric they sacked Rome in 455, mutilating public monuments. As a result, the term 'vandalism' was coined to mean destruction of works of art by revolutionary fanatics. Through the passing of time, it came to describe any useless destruction of property.

Variety is the spice of life

This proverbial expression was preceeded by one in the Ancient Greek play, *Orestes* by Euripides, 408 BC, 234:

"μεταβολή ράντων γλυκύ" (a change is always nice.)

The earliest reference in English to the saying is found in *The Task* Volume II, page 76, by William Cowper, 1785:

"Variety's the very spice of life, That gives it all its flavour."

Vanish into thin air

It was William Shakespeare who gave us the roots of this popular cliché. He came within a hair's breadth in *Othello* in 1604.

"Then put up your pipes in your bag, for I'll fly away; Go, **vanish into air**; away!"

Then, in 1610, a line from *The Tempest* was almost 'on the money.'

"These our actors, as I foretold you, were all spirits and melted into air, **into thin air**."

The term, 'thin air,' coined by Shakespeare, was later used by other authors, such as John Milton and William Blake.

Finally, in April of 1822, *The Edinburgh Advertiser* put it all together in an article about the situation looming between Russia and Turkey.

"The latest communications make these visions '**vanish into thin air**.'"

Va-va-voom!

This exclamation possibly dates back to the 1950s. It was the title for a piece of music by jazz composer Gil Evans used in a movie in 1985 called *Absolute Beginnings* based on a 1959 novel.

It was made famous by French football star Thierry Henry, and then utilized by Renault, a French auto maker, in an ad campaign in the U.K. It is now included in T*he Oxford Dictionary of the English Language*.

They define the phrase without reservation to mean just what it has come to be in modern late 20th and early 21st century slang—'the quality of being exciting, vigorous and attractive.' It has gone far past merely being applied to Renault, or any other automobile with good looks and fast acceleration. The phrase is used particularly by men to express the attractiveness and sex appeal of women.

Veritable smorgasbord

Smorgasbord is a Swedish term used from the early 20th century adapted worldwide which applies to a variety of food and has for the most part been replaced by the French term, 'buffet.' Veritable smorgasbord is metaphoric and means a vast, plentiful array of anything, and came into usage in the mid-20th century. An early example is from *Kiplinger's Personal Finance* Magazine, April 1959, page 19:

> "Wherever you live, whatever your interests, there's a **veritable smorgasbord** of adult education offerings available to you."

Vice versa

Like 'quid pro quo,' this is not something you may expect to find in this sort of reference book, but it is an ancient term, and the origins are of interest to many, I dare say. Of the many brief expressions in English used to describe things being the other way around, such as topsy-turvy, inside out, etc., the oldest is 'arsy-versy,' now archaic. This predecessor of the phrase being presented is first found in Richard Taverner's *Prouerbes or adagies with newe addicions, gathered out of the Chiliades of Erasmus*, published in 1539, and also contains the 'cart before the horse.' From the context, it was already in use, and from the source, it was attributed to Erasamus.

> "Ye set the cart before the horse - cleane contrarily and arsy versy as they say."

Fifty-two years later we find vice versa in Anthony Copley's *An answere to a letter of a Jesuited gentleman by his cousin* (1601).

> "They are like to bee put to such a penance and the Arch-Priests **vice-versa** to be suspended and attained as Schismaticall."

Vicious circle

Also known now as a 'vicious cycle,' this term was used by logicians in the 18th century to describe fallacious proof in this form:

> A depends on B

> B depends on C

> C depends on A

It was mentioned in the *3ʳᵈ Edition* of the *Encyclopedia Britannica* in 1792.

"He runs into what is termed by logicians a **vicious circle**."

A wider usage of the phrase was taken by the medical profession in the 19th century to describe conditions in which one system affects another and the health of the patient steadily deteriorates.

The broader use of this phrase in our day as an idiom can be any situation which seems to follow a continuous downward spiral, never improving.

W

Waiting for the other shoe to drop

This figurative phrase often means that someone has had an unfortunate incident happen which would likely lead to another event which could potentially be even more disasterous. It can also apply to any event which automatically follows the first happening. Etymologists most commonly believe that it was derived from an old story about a weary traveler who took a room in an inn. The innkeeper informed him that he would be staying in the room adjacent to a very light sleeper. When the traveler removed his shoes that night, and his first shoe hit the floor, he awakened the light sleeper, who then knew it would only be a brief moment before the other shoe would drop. The earliest printed reference to the phrase known is from The University of Michigan's *Michigan Alumnus*, October 1918, page 32:

"In spite of my best efforts I would await the next shell due each time just fifteen minutes later, and become rather disgusted and disgruntled if it did not burst exactly on time. The state of the nervous man **waiting for the other shoe to fall** was mild in comparison with my anguish of mind."

Waiting in the wings

As long as theaters have existed, actors who were awaiting their cue to enter from 'stage left' or 'stage right' have waited in the wings. This phrase has become a metaphor for all who wait patiently for opportunity to knock for them to play their parts in the drama of life. An early literal example of the phrase, however, is in quotes in *The Canadian Spectator, Montreal*, Saturday, January 5, 1878, on page 44:

"Personages are introduced to us, go on the stage, and then are left '**waiting in the wings**,' as it were, till we wonder how they can all come together in the main action at all."

The first known use as a metaphor is found on page 31 of *History of the Spanish American War* by Henry Watterson, 1898:

"When the volunteers were summoned by the President they walked on the scene as if they had been **waiting in the wings**. They were subjected to a physical examination as searching as that of a life insurance company."

Diana Ross had a hit recording titled *Waiting in the Wings*, written by Peter Sinfield and Andy Hill, and released by Motown in 1992. Its chorus rang out:

"When your heart is weary
When you want a love with no strings
I will be here waiting
Waiting in the wings."

Waiting on hand and foot

This figurative expression refers to taking care of all of someone's personal needs. This is a very old term, and began with handmaids and footsmen. Handmaids were women who took care of the personal needs of the rich, while footsmen did the 'footwork' of carrying messages. The earliest available printed reference to the expression appears in *Paul Preston's Voyages, Travels and Remarkable Adventures as Related by Himself*, 1847:

"He **waited on him hand and foot**, and was as attentive to him during the rest of the voyage as if he had been his own father."

Wake up call

In speaking of Flickers, the *Bulletin of the California Academy of Sciences* printed the following on 5 January 1887:

"In addition to the familiar scythe-whetting notes they have the peculiar '**wake–up' call** and its rapid prelude of monosyllables."

Even before the common use by hotels of a literal phone call requested to awaken someone at a particular time, this was used figuratively as a warning to take some action on a need which has been neglected but could be of primary importance. The earliest known citation is in the *Iowa City Press Citizen*, in 1922:

> "When tea or coffee stimulates the nerves at mealtime it seems pleasant, but then it gives the **wake-up call** at midnight and leaves nerves for sleep at mid-afternoon, the pleasure is gone and serious harm is on the way."

Walk a fine line

This is likely derived from walking a tightrope over a gaping cavern. It means to make difficult and risky choices between varying policies in an attempt to properly navigate a successful result. The earliest verifiable reference to the phrase is from a play *The Hidden River* by Ruth and Agustus Goetz first copyrighted in 1956 from a 1954 novel by Margaret Storm Jameson.

Walk and chew gum at the same time*

More often than not, this phrase is used to metaphorically illustrate someone's incompetence. It refers to the ability to multitask, or do more than one relatively simple thing at a time. The saying came into usage in the 1960s, and virtually every early citation includes a reference to being uncoordinated. One example is from *The New York Vegetable Grower's News*, Cornell University, Volume 19, page 419, 1962:

> "Are you kidding? My wife is so uncoordinated, she can't even **walk and chew gum at the same time!**"

Walking on eggshells

The exact origin of this phrase is unknown, but most agree that it is from an earlier expression, 'walking on eggs.' It means that one is having to be extremely cautious not to upset another person or persons in reference to a particular topic or matter due to the person's sensitivity about it. Other such expressions are 'walking on thin ice' and 'walking on broken glass.'

Walk softly and carry a big stick

Like so many other notable quotes, this one is a 'misquote' of 26th U.S. President Theodore "Teddy" Roosevelt (October 27, 1858 – January 6, 1919). He had actually referred to the saying earlier, but used it first in a speech at the

Minnesota State Fair on 2 September 1901. He actually said: "Speak softly and carry a big stick," referring to his foreign policy. But he said he was not the originator of this saying; that it was a West African proverb—a calim which itself has been disputed. As a political philosophy it was certainly older, resembling Machiavellian ideology. Rumor had it that his claim concerning the West African proverb was meant to be metaphoric.

The phrase has since been applied figuratively to all situations in which people needed to watch their step with those perceived as enemies.

Walk the plank

As an idiom, this now refers to someone being forced to resign from a position. It derived from pirate lore, and was actually used as an impromptu form of execution in the 17th and 18th centuries. The earliest documented reference, however, to the practice, which by this time was thought to be an alternative to death, is in Grose's *A Dictionary of the Vulgar Tongue*, 1788 edition:

> "**WALKING THE PLANK**. A mode of destroying devoted persons or officers in a mutiny on ship-board, by blindfolding them, and obliging them to walk on a plank laid ever the ship's side; by this means, as the mutineers suppose, avoiding the penalty of murder."

According to the British *Sailors' and Soldiers' Magazine*, July 1861 in the article 'Penzance Storm—Grace and Strength Prevailing':

> "To '**walk the plank**' therefore, became a common expression for temporary punishment; but when G. G. S. mentioned this in the Town Hall about Mr. Dark, the Mayor very naturally called upon him to demand of the words, and G. C. S. replied, 'He would have got a dipping in the sea.'"

A 20th-century example showing how the phrase is now used is found in *Popular Mechanics,* February, 1922 under the heading, '50,000 People Are After the Routine Jobs—*Break Away From This Competition*, Command Big Pay!'

> "Observe that when a business trims its crew, it is almost never the big-pay men who **walk the plank**."

Walk the straight and narrow

The 'straight and narrow' path refers to a very specific way to do something, which, when varying from it, may have disasterous results. The original idea comes from biblical theology, based on *Matthew 7:13-14*:

"Enter ye in at the strait gate: for wide is the gate, and broad is the way, that leadeth to destruction, and many there be which go in thereat:
Because **strait** is the gate, **and narrow** is the **way**, which leadeth unto life, and few there be that find it." (*KJV*)

This reference is obviously the basis for the following citation from *A Vindication of the Government in Scotland: During the Reign of King Charles II*, 1712:

"**Strait and narrow is the way** that leadeth unto life."

'Straight' has replaced the antiquated 'strait' in this regard.

Warts and all

This phrase, more often used in the U.K., means accepting something or someone 'at face value,' including their faults.

This is said to have derived from a statement made by Oliver Cromwell (seventeenth century) when instructing his portrait painter, Peter Lely, to portray a true likeness of him, including '...roughness, pimples, warts and everything...'

Wash one's mouth out with soap

Beginning in the 19th century, this was a physical punishment for using profanity. Even prior, in the *Legal Examiner* in Britain in 1832, is the earliest example of anyone forcing another to ingest soap as a punishment. A man returned home to find his wife intoxicated. According to the article, he found a piece of kitchen soap on the ground and crammed it into her mouth, saying: "She has had plenty of water to wash with, she ought now to have a little soap."

In 1872, the first mention of washing out the mouth of a child with soap heard swearing was recorded. *The Chinese Recorder and Missionary Journal* printed the following:

"A friend of the writer in America called into the bath room a little son who was heard for the first time to swear, and **scrubbed his mouth out with soap** and a nail brush."

The article went on to recommend that the same be practiced in China. As late as the mid-20th century the threat of washing a child's mouth out with soap was still cliché in America, though rarely put into practice.

Waste not, want not

The earliest reference to this proverb in print is found in the *Welsley Letters*, 1772, and it was listed as a title of a work available in the *Weslyan-Methodist Magazine* under 'Shilling Illustrated Large-type books specially suited for working people,' on page 6 of the Religious Tract Society's *List for the Season*, December 1882.

It is a truism which reminds people that being thrifty enables one to have needs met in difficult times.

watched pot never boils, A

When we get 'bent out of shape' (see) over any situation that it seems will never get to a conclusion, the time seems to crawl at 'a snail's pace' (see).

A pot will eventually boil, of course, no matter who looks on. The phrase was first coined by British novelist, Elizabeth Gaskell, in her first novel, *Mary Barton* published in 1848—in its exact current phrasing.

Water under the bridge (or **over the dam**)

The original expression was British, and is 'water under the bridge;' the Americanism 'water over the dam' is another variant. It means that what happened in the past needs to remain in the past, and there's no use in worrying about it now.

Early examples of the original form of the idiom are actually from American authors. *Since Yesterday* by Fredrick Lewis Allen, was published in 1939, and contained the following:

> "How much **water had gone under the bridge** since 1932, when Roosevelt had first been a candidate for the House!"

Then from another American book, the 1946 Perry Mason novel *The Case of the Borrowed Brunette* by Erle Stanley Gardner:

> *"That's all right,"* Mason said. *"That's all **water under the bridge** now."*

In more recent years the variant with 'over the dam' has been coined.

Water, water everywhere, but not a drop to drink

This is another slight misquote. It is from *The Rime of the Ancient Mariner*, by English poet, literary critic and philosopher, Samuel Taylor Coleridge (October 21, 1772 – July 25, 1834). In the poem, the Mariner shot the Albatross and thus was cursed. The drinking water all gone, only sea water surrounds the ship, no fresh water is to be found. The verse actually reads as follows:

> "Water, water everywhere,
> And all the boards did shrink
> **Water, water everywhere**
> **Nor any drop to drink**."

Way out in left field*

This idiom means out of touch, odd, or in some cases, misguided. It was derived from the left field of a baseball diamond. There is, however, some disagreement concerning its origin.

Some writers infer that it comes from the remoteness of left field to the entirety of the park. This seems unlikely because only in very asymmetrical ballparks is left field more distant than right field. Other researchers suggest that it alludes to the 'wrongness' of left as opposed to the 'rightness' of right (See getting up on the wrong side of the bed).

Perhaps the most acceptable theory being presented is that the saying originally alluded to inmates of the Neuropsychiatric Institute, a mental hospital, which was located behind left field in Chicago's old West Side Park. Thus being told you are 'out in left field' would mean you seemed as peculiar as a mental patient. It is certain that this term has been used figuratively for various kinds of eccentricity and the state of being misguided since the first half of the 20th century. By 1947 it was frequently used in writing. One example is from *Collier's Weekly*, Volume 120, page 104: "'Denham is **way out in left field** on this ruling,' said Vermont's Senator George D. Aiken...'"

Ways to Sunday

This means any conceivable way that something can be done. Used in print in almost any multiple including three ways, four ways, five ways, six ways, seven ways, eight ways, nine ways, ten ways, twelve ways, fifteen ways, seventeen ways, twenty ways, forty ways, sixty ways, a hundred ways, a thousand ways, a million ways and even 'all ways,' to Sunday; 'both ways to Sunday' seems to have come first, and dates back to at least 1837. It appeared in *Bentley's Miscellany, Volume 2* in a story named *Portrait Gallery--No. IV; Cannon Family, Journey to Boulogne*, from the time of Alexander the Great.

> "Lucy, who had rather a cast in each eye, which had induced the wits of Muckford to christen her Miss Wednesday (as they pretended that she looked **both ways to Sunday**,) Miss Lucy those pernicious sponsors called the swivel; Kitty, a stout, short, beautiful creature, in whose form graceful undulations made up for length, they nicknamed the Carronade."

Sunday represents the end of one week and the beginning of the next. It seems logical that 'both ways' being the first usage, it initially meant looking at an issue from both sides. As time went on, writers started recognizing that a large variety of perspectives existed and began extending the number of possibilities.

Sir Humphrey Davy used 'forty ways to Sunday' in an article published in *Motor Age Magazine* on 2 January 1919 entitled, *Tea Wagons for Repair Shops.*

> "There are a lot of us who don't care much for afternoon teas, but they've got some of our repair shops beat **forty ways to Sunday**."

The most popular number in modern age seems to be six. This could be because there are only six other days in a week.

way to a man's heart is through his stomach, The

The first known version of this proverb is from second American President, John Adams [October 30, 1735 (O.S. October 19, 1735) – July 4, 1826], who stated in a letter:

> "The shortest **road to men's stomachs is down their throats**."

In 1841, the *Literary Gazette and Journal of the Belles Lettres* called this a 'maxim' on page 577:

> "'**The way to** an Englishman's **heart is through his stomach**,' saith the maxim..."

In March 1848 *The Dublin Review*, published in London, called it 'an old saying':

> "That '**the way to a man's heart is through his stomach**,' is an old saying, more strictly true than most would, perhaps, be inclined to admit."

A phrase origin dictionary published in New York, attributes the 'including of all men' in the saying it to 'Fanny Fern in *Willis Parton*,' and puts its date at circa 1872. Actually, Willis Parton was a psudenym for Fern, and the quote was years earlier, as evidenced in *The Western Review*, Vol. 1. Page 108, February 1869:

"Fanny Fern says **the way to a man's heart is through his stomach**."

Weak as water

Numerous similes have been prevalent in our language for hundreds of years, and in 1870, a unique volume was compiled which listed a section of similes. Similes, by their nature, are self explanatory. This was one that was included. It was titled *Dictionary of Phrase and Fable*, and it was by Reverend Ebenezer Cobham Brewer in England. Many editions have been reprinted, and subsequently revised. It also dealt with history, the arts, science, religion and mythology. Water, in its unadulterated form, has no strong properties as alcohol, or even coffee, thus the analogy. This expression is applied to persons who have lost their physical strength, if even temporarily.

Wear one's heart on his or her sleeve

This means to show one's emotions openly. In the Middle Ages in Britain, knights reportedly wore the colors of the young ladies whom they were courting on their sleeves. But wearing one's heart on his or her sleeve was not an expression of the days of knights and high-spirited steeds. It was first recorded in Shakespeare's 1604 play, *Othello*. Iago's scheming plan was to pretend to be open and vulnerable so as to appear to be faithful.

"IAGO:
It is sure as you are Roderigo,
Were I the Moor, I would not be Iago:
In following him, I follow but myself;
Heaven is my judge, not I for love and duty,
But seeming so, for my peculiar end:
For when my outward action doth demonstrate
The native act and figure of my heart
In compliment extern, 'tis not long after
But I will **wear my heart upon my sleeve**
For daws to peck at: I am not what I am."

Weasel out of

This colloquialism originated in the early-to-mid 20th century, and is based on the slender weasel and the sneaky way one is able to slink into and out of small holes. This snippet from *History of the Commune* of 1871, by Lissagaray, 1898 is a forrunner to the saying:

> "The ambitious young man had slunk like a **weasel out of** this civil war into which he had heedlessly thrown himself."

Though it was obviously already in use as an idiom, the earliest known citation in print is from chapter 10 of *Wolf in Man's Clothing* by Mignon Good Eberhart, 1942:

> "Instead of lying, you—you evade, you **weasel out of** making a direct statement, you— oh, it's fantastic, really."

'Weaseling out of' a duty or job assigned or expected of someone means 'find a way to avoid doing it.'

Weather the storm*

An idiom meaning 'survive difficulties;' it has been around since the mid-1600s. The earliest known printed reference is on page 247 of *Abstracts on Money, Prices and Agriculture in the United Kingdom*, 1655:

> "Pessimism is an unworthy feeling, and there is little doubt but that agriculture will **weather the storm**, and survive as it has done in previous crises, but the laissez-faire attitude with which many view the present state of affairs is to be deplored."

Welcome as flowers in May

Sometimes now 'welcome as the flowers in springtime,' this was originally printed in *A Hand-book of Proverbs*, by John Ray first published in London, England in 1670.

It is used freely to tell people in a pleasant way that they are appreciated and that what is done for them is done freely—not because something is expected in return.

Well-heeled

This one, in a literal sense, dates back to the early 1800s when the heels of the shoes would run down and only the rich could afford to get them repaired by cobblers. Many people in the United States even went without shoes in the spring and summer, and some were able to only wear them on special occasions. It now means well-to-do.

Well, I'll swanny!

Spelled either simply swan, swany, swanny, swanee or swaney, this is a euphemism for 'I'll swear.' According to the *OED*, it was likely a derivative of Northern England dialectal 'Is wan,' or 'I s'wan ye,' a short form contraction meaning 'I shall warrant (you)' or 'I'll be bound.' The first time it appeared in the dictionary was in 1823, though 'swan' was recorded from the late 18th century. In the 19th century Christians were taught that using the word 'swear' was improper.

We're not in Kansas anymore!

Of course this phrase came from the 1939 classic film, *The Wizard of Oz.* When Dorothy and her little dog, Toto, were transported to the mystical Land of Oz by the tornado which swept them away from 'Auntie Em's' Kansas farm, Dorothy realized that they were indeed not in Kansas anymore.

The phrase caught on quickly and came to be used to mean that someone is in unfamiliar territory, either literally or figuratively.

Were you born in a barn?

This is a question that hundreds of mothers asked their children through the past 200 years when they came in the house and left the door open in the winter in the U.S. They literally meant a *barn*, which is drafty and cold whether the doors are open or closed.

There is a similar phrase, 'Were you born in Bardney?' which apparently preceded this expression, and referred to leaving a door open in England.

Bardney in Lincolnshire was the site of an important monastery called Tupholme Abbey. When King Oswald, was killed in 642 AD, they tried to bring his bones into the abbey but the monks kept the doors shut. The British phrase likely had influence on the coining of the American one.

Wet behind the ears

This phrase had its origin in the United States in the early 20th century. All farmers were accustomed to the helplessness of baby animals, which are naturally wet at birth. When the little one begins to dry, the areas behind the ears are usually last to do so, causing the saying, 'it's still wet behind the ears.'

As per usual, this saying soon came to represent the helplessness and naiveté of beginners when trying to develop new skills. Someone who is 'still wet behind the ears' is either just learning, or this may be applied to a young boy, who seems to know nothing of life's complexities. At any rate, the person so evaluated has a lot to learn.

The earliest known printed reference is in the *Portsmouth Daily Times* (Ohio) in October 1941.

"There is not much in the matter so far as the organ [the courthouse record] is concerned except it is so new that it is **wet behind the ears** yet."

What am I, chopped liver?

This sarcastic question is a familiar line used by American comedian Rodney Dangerfield (born Jacob Cohn, November 22, 1921 – October 5, 2004), in the late 1970s to early '80s, which, accompanied by a slight shrug, is a cliché for 'Don't ignore me! Am I not as important as others?' But he is not the originator of the saying, though he did popularize it. It is a Jewish American English expression in use by the burlesque era. The proper enunciation was "So? Vat am I? Chopped livah?"

Chopped liver, most often chicken liver, has traditionally been served as a side dish, particularly by Jewish families, and may not be appreciated by most people, thus is often overlooked.

What else is new?

This expression, used after someone tells something which just occurred, means, 'well, this has happened before; what can we expect?' The earliest verifiable citation is in *Tales Tersely Told* by Paul Victor Loth, 1899, on page 187:

"I first heard it in Chicago, I believe, on my American trip. **What else is new?**"

What goes around comes around

There is a printed reference to this phrase in the U.S. in Eddie Stone's book, *Donald Writes No More,* 1974, but the roots are much older. It became popular in America around that time.

There is a much older version, being used in Virginia, possibly in the 19th century, was 'what goes around a horse's back comes around a horse's belly.' This was likely the basis of the current saying. Some British folk say that it started there, and has been passed down from generation to generation.

Its meaning is something like 'you get what you give' and getting 'a dose of our own medicine'—that whatever we dish out will be dished back.

What goes up must come down

This old saying, commonly attributed to Isaac Newton regarding the law of gravity, is not one of his, as he disproved this with evidence of 'hyperbolic orbit' for an object sent up at sufficient force to escape gravitational pull. The earliest available reference in print is in *Hints to my Countrymen* by Theodore Sedgewick, 1826:

> "When one boy among a dozen throws a stone into the air, crying out, that **'what goes up must come down**,' it is very likely so to happen."

What happens in Vegas stays in Vegas

This originated as the slogan used by Las Vegas Convention and Visitors Authority and their ad agency, R & R Partners, who purchased the copyright for 'what happens here stays here' for $1.00 in 2004. The resultant ad campaign brought record business to the Las Vegas strip.

The saying has become synonymous for secrets being kept in the area in which events take place. The intent, however, was expressed as early as the 1940s when the U.S. Government placed a billboard in Oak Ridge, Tennessee to remind the workers on the secret Manhattan Project which developed the atomic bomb for use in World War II. The sign, which depicted the three wise monkeys, read:

> "WHAT YOU SEE HERE
> WHAT YOU DO HERE
> WHAT YOU HEAR HERE
> WHEN YOU LEAVE HERE
> LET IT STAY HERE"

What rock did you crawl out from under?

This figurative, insulting question or any reference to someone 'living under a rock' indicates the speaker's dislike and lack of trust for the other person. Lizards, worms and snakes which normally are found under rocks are not something which most people like to pick up or embrace. The earliest available citation is found in *New York Magazine*, August 1st, 1988, on page 29, in the article, *Last Judgment* by Jeanie Kasindorf:

"At the next break, Mary Koster said to Fink, 'You slime, **what rock did you crawl out from under**?'"

What's a nice girl like you doing in a place like this?

What's a Nice Girl Like You Doing in a Place Like This? is the title of a short film produced in 1963 by Martin Scorsese produced while he was a student at Tisch School of the Arts at New York University. It became a comical ice-breaker for a man to ask a lady, and various versions have been used in comedy skits.

What's sauce for the goose is sauce for the gander

Also used with 'good,' rather than sauce, in the U.S. this saying commonly means 'what is good for a woman, a man should be willing to do.'

The saying in this form goes back to at least 1704, when it was recorded in *Brown's New Maxims*. An earlier form not using the word 'sauce' was reportedly in use from 1579.

What's that got to do with the price of eggs in China?

This version, which is American in origin, was first merely '...the price of eggs.' This was in use as early as the 1920s. By the '40s some had changed it to 'the price of tea in China.' Supposedly because the tea in China is about as unimportant to most conversations in the U.S. as one could imagine. This may have come from the simple idiom, 'All the tea in China.' When *eggs in China* were brought into the equation is unclear. In the U.K. the equivalent is 'What's that got to do with the price of fish.' In Scotland the saying is often, 'What's that got to do with the price of cheese,' and in Northern Ireland, 'the price of a sausage.' Some even say 'the price of rice in china,' or 'beans in Albuquerque.' There is even 'the price of peas in China.' It merely relates to something entirely irrelevent.

What's your name? Puddin' Tain, ask me again and I'll tell you the same

This rhyme has been spelled a number of ways through the centuries. The 'Táin' anciently referred to an Irish High King. The 'Puddin' Táin' is claimed by some researchers to have been someone who was not actually royal but a pretender who was derided as the High King of the 'Puddings.' There seems to be no real evidence of this.

The earliest available version of this phrase, however, is a rendering of *The History of the Jesuits in England* (1580-1773). In the modern English version it reads in part:

> "The names of the devils said to possess the sufferers were: Fraretto, Fliberdigibet, Hoberdicat, Cocobatto, **Pudding of Thame**, Hobberdidance..."

This being in England it would tend to make more sense, because Thame (the 'h' is silent) is the name of a town in Oxfordshire. It seems that 'Pudding of Thame' in this reference, however, was a devil—not something with which most would want to be identified.

But there are still other versions. The following appeared in the Journal of the Royal Asiatic Society of Great Britain and Ireland, *Dialect Notes,* in 1895. A version from Sussex published in 1861 as being from 1825 is:

> **"What's your naum?**
> **Pudding and taum.**"

Kansas newspaper editor William Allen White wrote a short story called *The King of Boyville* published in his book titled, *The Real Issue* in 1896. Perhaps the above 1895 version influenced his citation of the rhyme. Here is a quote from the story:

> "When a new boy, who didn't belong to the school, came up at recess to play, Piggy shuffled over to him and asked him gruffly: **'What's your name?'**
>
> **'Puddin' 'n' tame, ast me agin an' I'll tell you the same**,' said the new boy, and then there was a fight."

Originally, many say, this was a children's rhyme of Scotch-Irish origin. The entire rhyme, according to a child of the 1940s at that time was:

> ***What's your name?***
> ***Puddin' Tame.***
> *Where do you live?*
> *Down the lane.*
> *What do you eat?*
> *Pigs' feet.*
> *What's your number?*
> *Cucumber.*

It was adapted by African-Americans, and widely popularized after it was turned into a hit song by the Alley Cats in 1962 called *Puddin' N' Tain (Ask Me Again,*

I'll Tell You the Same). In the mid-20th century it was used to mean 'none of your business.'

What the dickens!

This old exclamation did not come from Charles Dickens, as some may have thought, but from an ancient name for the devil. This is merely another way of saying 'what the devil.' In fact, Shakespeare used it in *The Merry Wives of Windsor* published in 1602.

"I cannot tell **what the dickens** his name is my husband had him of."

'Like the dickens' is also in common usage.

What you don't know can't hurt you

"Oh what a tangled web we weave, when we first we practice to deceive." That's a quote from Sir Walter Scott in *Marmion Canto VI, Stanza 17.* But it could well apply to this old cliché. What one doesn't know could hurt worse than the person can imagine. The plot to murder Julius Caesar on the Ides of March in 44 BC was not known to him, but because of it, he lost his life. President Kennedy did not know what awaited him that fateful afternoon of November 22nd, 1963 in Dallas Texas, but his short life on earth was snuffed out that day.

The oldest version of this dubious proverb comes from *A Petite Palace of Pettie His Pleasure* by George Pettie written in 1576.

"So long as I **know it not**, it **hurteth mee not**."

This is also untrue in relationships.

What we've got here is a failure to communicate

This is a line from the 1967 film, *Cool Hand Luke,* spoken at different points during the movie; first by a prison warden played by Strother Martin, then by Luke, the prisoner played by Paul Newman. It has been used in songs and a variety of later films and television shows. It has become cliché and is understood to be a statement of fact.

Wheel and deal

This is an idiom for operating shrewdly, often unscrupulously, for one's own benefit. It was derived from the ancient use of a wheel to control the flow of water downstream. Wheeling and dealing suggests gaining control over the situation of trade, which is almost as vital as water. The saying came into common use in the mid-1950s and was not necessarily seen as a bad thing. The earliest known citation is from an ad on page 81 of *Billboard Magazine*, June 2, 1956:

> "DISTRIBUTORS - We are overstocked on NEW and USED POOL TABLES! We will **wheel and deal!**"

When all is said and done

Originally 'After all is said and done.' A major dictionary of Idioms stated that this idiom was first published in 1560. It actually goes back a lot further, to Aesop (circa 620 – 564 BC), the preeminent teller of fanciful fables. It's the moral of *The Tortoise and the Hare*:

> "After **all is said and done,** more is said than done. "

This wonderful saying has now become a bit worn, and is being replaced by 'At the end of the day' (see). It indicates that when all is considered, this is the conclusion. The sad deduction of the great King Solomon after trying everything which man has envisioned to achieve peace of mind is stated in *Ecclesiastes 1:14*:

> "I observed everything going on under the sun, and really, it is all meaningless—like chasing the wind." *(NLT)*

When hell freezes over

This is a way to strongly assert that something will never happen. The earliest known citation is from *Captain Roger Jones of London and Virginia*, by Lewis Hampton Jones, 1891, page 412:

> "As near as I can recall the language, they received this answer from the boy they wrote to: 'As to taking the oath, I will agree to take it when Frank Jones does, and Frank has just been consulted and says he will take it **when hell freezes over...**'"

A similar expression is 'when pigs fly' (see).

When in Rome, do as the Romans do

This is not from the *Bible* as many have believed, but the timing is not far off. In 387 AD when St. Augustine arrived in Milan, he observed the fact that the Church there didn't fast on Saturday as did the Church in Rome. He consulted the bishop of Milan, St. Ambrose.

The bishop's answer was: "When I am at Rome, I fast on a Saturday; when I am at Milan, I do not. Follow the custom of the Church where you are." The statement was changed to "When they are at Rome, they do there as they see done" by Robert Burton in *The Anatomy of Melancholy* (1621). Eventually it was altered again to "When in Rome, do as the Romans do."

When it rains it pours

This saying, per se, was started as a slogan for Morton Salt Company in 1911, and was created by A. W. Ayer and Son, an ad agency hired by Morton to come up with a catchy slogan for their new and improved salt. After rejecting a couple of slogans, this one caught Mr. Morton just right, and it has become a catch-phrase for actual rain showers as well as calamities and unexpected and unwanted surprises which may befall us—when one problem comes, they seem to come in bunches.

But this was not the origin of the thought, which is actually unknown but dates prior to 1726 in the U.K., when it was used as the title of a work about a white bear by John Arbuthnot.

"It cannot **rain** but **it pours**; or London strow'd with rarities."

When my ship comes in

The origin of this metaphoric phrase is the obvious. In centuries past, in coastal towns a major source of the income of locals was interest in trading companies. When the ship in which they had invested took to sea with cargo, they lived in anticipation of the profit they would be paid when it returned. At that time, all shareholders would be paid their share. This was like a farmer running credit based on the harvest. They would pay their debts 'when their ship came in.'

Through the years this phrase came to mean when anyone 'struck it rich' they would fulfill their life's dreams, or purchase something they had long desired.

More often than not, however, there was no real source for their hope, and it was like an item on a wish list which would always remain 'pie in the sky' (see).

When one door closes another door opens

This is from a quote by Alexander Graham Bell (1847-1922), the Scottish-born inventor of the telephone. The total quote is:

> **"When one door closes another door opens**; but we often look so long and so regretfully upon the closed door, that we do not see the ones which open for us."

When pigs fly

When this phrase is used, the speaker has no hope that the matter being discussed will ever reach fruition. This current version was not the first. The original saying was recorded in John Withals' Latin American dictionary, *A Short Dictionarie for Younge Begynners* in the section on proverbs, page 593, 1616 Edition only.

> "**Pigs fly** in the ayre with their tayles forward."

This expressed sarcasm and the thought that some folks were exceedingly gullible.

Thomas Fuller, in *Gnomologia,* in 1732, got a bit closer to our present meaning.

> "That is as likely as to see **an Hog fly**."

Then in 1835, in *The Autobiography of Jack Ketch*, by Charles Whitehead, we find:

> "Yes, **pigs** may **fly**, but they're very unlikely birds."

Like so many others, it has evolved to what it is today.

When push comes to shove

This idiom means 'as a last resort when something has to be done regardless of the circumstances.' In spite of a major phrase dictionary placing the earliest citation at 1958, it was used as early as 1936 in Anna Wendell Bontemps' *Black*

Thunder, in two places. One, on page 58, said 'Let **push come to shove**.' The other, on page 248 reads:

> "Thing you need to do is see how fast a good general can run **when push come to shove**."

Then in 1947, it appeared precisely in current form in the English version of Jacque Romain's Haitian text, *Masters of the Dew*, translated by Langston Hughes (a friend of Bontemps) and Mercer Cook:

> "You're still alive! Bite your tongue, swallow your cries! You're a man! **When push comes to shove** you've got what it takes."

When the cat's away, the mice will play

This gnomic idiom means that when the person in authority is absent, the subordinates are apt to take advantage of their freedom by breaking rules because some workers lack self-discipline. Though earlier versions existed in both Latin, *Dum felis dormit, mus gaudet et exsi litantro* (When the cat falls asleep, the mouse rejoices and leaps from the hole) and early fourteenth century French, *Ou chat na rat regne* (Where there is no cat, the rat is king), the first English usage was in Middle English, circa 1470 in *Harley MS 3362*, as listed in *Restrospective Review*, 1854:

> "The mows lordchypythe [rules] ther a cat ys nawt"

A version of it was then used by Shakespeare in *Henry V*, I, ii, 1599:

> "To her unguarded nest the weasel Scot Comes sneaking, and so sucks her princely eggs, **Playing the mouse in absence of the cat**."

Among other citations, it was listed in John Ray's *A Hand-book of English Proverbs*, 1670:

> **"When the cat is away, the mice play**."

When the dust settles*

This idiom means when matters have calmed down. Here 'dust refers to turmoil or confusion. The expression has been in use figuratively since the mid-20th century. An early example is from *A Short Story*, Chapter XVI, The Contemporary Short Story, 1947 (author unknown), page 76:

> **"When the dust settles** we may think differently."

When the going gets tough, the tough get going

Usually meaning that when it is difficult to accomplish a task, those who want to badly enough will find a way to do it, this could be a variant of 'where there's a will there's a way' (see).

Sometimes this is attributed to a quote from Joseph P. Kennedy, patriarch of the Kennedy political family, one son of which was President John F. Kennedy. Others say it came from Norwegian-born football player and coach, Knute Rockne. Oddly enough, both of these famous men were born in 1888, though Rockne died much earlier, in 1933, while Kennedy outlived his famous son by almost six years, passing away on November 18th, 1969. Regardless of the original coiner of the phrase, it became popularized in the song by Billy Ocean by that name from the soundtrack of *The Jewel of the Nile*, the sequel to *Romancing the Stone*, both starring Michael Douglas and Kathleen Turner.

It became a common slogan for sales organizations during the 1980s and '90s.

Where there's a will there's a way

This proverb is meant to keep people from giving up under difficult circumstances. The earliest reference to a version of it is in *Jacula Prudentum, or Outlandish Proverbs and Sentences* by George Herbert in 1640; it is number 730:

> "To him that **will, wais are not wanting**.

William C. Hazlitt used our modern version in *New Monthly Magazine* published in London in February 1822:

> "**Where there's a will, there's a way**.—I said so to myself, as I walked down Chancery-lane...to inquire...where the fight the next day was to be."

In the 20th century there are plenty of examples including this citation in *Good Night Little Spy* by German-born Canadian author Eric Koch in 1979:

> "I've no idea how it can be done. But **where there's a will, there's a way**."

Where (or **while**) there's life there's hope

This proverb means 'as long as someone is still alive there is reason to believe in an improvement in a troublesome situation.' The saying persists in Christian texts through the centuries. The earliest known reference is from John Preston's

Life eternall, or, a treatise of the knowledge of the divine Essence and Atribvtes, 1634, in the sermon, 'A Heavenly Treatise of Divine Love,' page 435:

> "...I cannot deny it, but that the time of this life is the time of grace, & offering of reconciliation, and that so long as **there is life, there is hope."**

Where there's smoke there's fire

This means 'when something appears amiss, it likely is.' This idiomatic proverb is American in origin. It is often used to indicate that where rumors are flying enough, people suspect foul play, or legends exist in cultures, there is likely some truth to the tales. It has been in popular usage since at least the 1920s and a related saying in the U.K. is 'No smoke without fire.' American artist, Russell Paterson (1893-1977) did a striking full-length illustration of a fashionably-dressed 'flapper' holding a cigarette with a stream of smoke curving upward, then downward and around. This phrase is its title. It was done in the 'roaring '20s' as evidenced by its content. Other early references, if existent, are illusive, but recent papers are filled with the saying, especially in relation to the death of the 'King of Pop,' Michael Jackson, in 2010. The use of the phrase derived from the simple truism that if smoke is wafting through the air, it didn't get there without a flame or ember producing it.

Where the rubber meets the road

This idiom means at the point of decision; the moment of truth when it really counts. It came from a television jingle frequently used at sporting events in the 1960s and 70s by Firestone Tire and Rubber Company:

> "Wherever wheels are rolling,
> No matter what the load,
> The name that's known is *Firestone*
> **Where the rubber meets the road."**

Whet your appetite

This idiom refers to the stimulation of an interest in anything. The earliest known citation is in Thomas Dekker's Elizabethan play, *If it be not good, the diuel is in it* (*If This Be Not a Good Play, the Devil is in It*), 1611:

> "[He] seekes new wayes to **whet dull appetite**."

Which came first—the chicken or the egg?

This quandary, about which the debate still rages today between creationists and evolutionists, is as ancient as Aristotle (384-322 BC) who wrote the following:

"If there has been a first man he must have been born without father or mother – which is repugnant to nature. For there could not have been a first egg to give a beginning to birds, or there should have been a first bird which gave a beginning to eggs; for a bird comes from an egg."

From: François Fénelon: *Abrégé des vies des anciens philosophes*, Paris 1726, page 314 French, Translation: *Lives of the ancient philosophers*, London, 1825, page 202 English.

Whistle britches*

Though not that common in general speech, this old folklore expression has had various negative connotations depending upon the time and location, and has been largely used in rural America. The 1969 *Kentucky Folklore Record* lists it as a synonym for 'ragamuffin' (a dirty, ill dressed child). According to other etymologists it refers to flatulence, or a person who passes gas often. In Texas, it is reported, it means someone who is an egotistical liar.

A 1930 Pennsylvania folklore publication, *Thirteen hundred old time words of British, Continental or aboriginal origins, still or recently in use among the Pennsylvania mountain people*, Issue 12, page 65, has the following somewhat different definition:

"**WHISTLE BRITCHES**—Trousers worn so tight that they squeak when the person takes a step."

In *Paul Green's Wordbook: an Alphabet of Reminiscence* (a North Carolina Folklore masterpiece by the famous Dramatist Laureate) first published in 1990, the expression is defined similarly: 'Corduroy pants which make a scrubbing noise as they rub together.' Then, in Jack Campbell's 2008 novel, *Guantanamo Remembered,* we find the phrase also referring to wearing apparel:

"I pictured him as a long-legged kid running around base in Navy khaki shorts the airmen called '**whistle britches**.'"

Whistle while you work

This common saying is the title of a song with music written by Frank Churchill and lyrics by Larry Morey for the 1937 Disney animated film, *Snow White and the Seven Dwarfs*. But its origins are considerably older, from slave days, when kitchens were separate from the rest of the house because of the fire hazard which they posed. The slaves working in the kitchen were required to whistle while the food was being carried from the kitchen to the house for family and guests in an effort to keep them from eating it.

whistling woman and a crowing hen always come to no good end, A

This comical old folk saying has been phrased many ways over the past 160 plus years—it is likely much more ancient. The earliest known reference in print is from *Notes and Queries: A Medium of Inter Communication for Literary Men, Artists, Antiquaries, Genealogists, Etc.* (Edinburgh, Scotland, 1851), page 164, and is from the printing of the paper on August 10, 1850:

> **"A whistling woman and a crowing hen,**
> Is neither fit for God nor men."

It is herein called, 'an old proverb often quoted in this district.' Since then versions include a bragging woman and various endings, but the one in the above quote seems likely to be the original, as it appears in a number of older citations. One 1871 source (*The Yorkshire Magazine, Volume 1*) states that the crowing of a hen was taken as a sign of evil or a token of death in a family. Several sources mention a similar French proverb.

White elephant

This is something that is costly to obtain or maintain and provides little benefit or value. The idea comes from the Burmese belief that albino elephants are sacred. In Burma they can't be used for work and they must be cared for with great diligence.

Giving a white elephant as a gift, however, would be done only to someone considered an enemy. The idea behind this is that your enemy's wealth would eventually be erased with the funds required to provide for the sacred elephant.

Whittle away at something

This is an idiom for working slowly and deliberately toward a goal. It is derived from whittling on wood to form a desired product; a term which has been in

English since the sixteenth century. The earliest known figurative citation is in *Mary Barton and Other Tales* by Elizabeth C. Gaskell, 1895, on page 443 in *Bessy's Troubles at Home*, and refers to a school lesson:

> "But I can't go to bed. I don't know my lesson!" Mary looked happier, though the tears were in her eyes.

> "I know mine," Bill said triumphantly.

> "Come here," said Jem. "There, I've enough time to **whittle away at** this before mother comes back. Now let's see this difficult lesson."

Who are you, and what did you do with........*

This saying is used when a surprising change occurs in someone's behavior. In spite of a number of sources who claim this originally came from old movies, the phrase goes back to at least September, 1878 when a form of it was cited in the London magazine, *Temple Bar,* in a serialized story titled *"Limmers"; or, Twenty Years Ago*, Chapter VI by George Livingstone:

> "'No, you horrible creature you, **who are you? and what have you done with** my gentleman?'"

Another printed citation occurred in 1912. In the above example, the person speaking is doing so in a jovial manner, but it's not quite the parody used in today's jargon. The earliest available example of the modern usage is in a 27 November 1988 Garfield cartoon:

> "Dinner's on, Garfield. Oh, nothing for me, thanks. I'm not hungry. - - **WHO ARE YOU, AND WHAT DID YOU DO WITH** GARFIELD?! That was a joke. Garfield."

In more recent years use of this expression has become very popular on television and in print.

Who died and made you God (boss, Elvis, president, king, queen, etc.)*

Forms of this expression, all meaning "Who put you in charge?" have been in use since at least 1940 when the following appeared on page 42 of *Father and Son* by James Thomas Farrell:

"'Say, you, **who died and made you boss?'** Liz cried out."

From the late 1970s to the mid 1980s, many variations appeared in print. The 'God' version was printed in 1982 in *Southern Discomfort* by Rita Mae Brown, on page 44.

"**'Who died and made you God?'** Blue Rhonda, ever hostile to authority, got her back up."

Other versions continued to evolve after that.

Whole ball of wax

There are a number of similar phrases, such as 'the whole shebang,' and 'the whole enchilada.' This one, however, has been in use longer than most.

Until recently, researchers assumed it was from the 1950s. But it goes much further back. The earliest known reference is from the *Atlanta Constitution* on 25 April 1882:

"We notice that John Sherman & Co. have opened a real estate office in Washington. Believing in his heart of hearts that he owns this country, we will be greatly surprised if Mr. Sherman does not attempt to sell out the **whole ball of wax** under the hammer."

Around that time period there are other printed references in American newspapers to 'the whole ball of wax,' so it would be reasonable to assume that it was already well-known in the late 19th century.

However, another, only a few months later, found in the *Indiana Democrat* (Pennsylvania), just prior to the election, has the idiom in quotation marks, apparently indicating that it was known, but had been recently coined.

"The Democrats can beat the **'whole ball of wax'** this season."

No one seems to be sure why a ball of wax was used, however there is an old belief that it is a humorous modification of *whole bailiwick,* a word which dates to the 15th century, and can mean 'a special domain.'

Whole hog or none

To go whole hog is derived from Southern pork barbeque, where the entire hog is cooked. Whole hog or none means that something to be done should be done properly and not halfway. One of the earliest figurative citations of the phrase is in 1849 in *Report of the Debates and Proceedings of the Convention for the Revision of the Constitution of the State of Kentucky,* page 376:

> "Do, at least, let us be consistent. To use a homely phrase, 'I want to go the **whole hog, or none.**' Let the people have the whole power of electing whom they wish."

whole nine yards, The

This expression, like many others, applies to the entirety of a thing.

The origin and first coining of this phrase is fraught with contention, some claiming it to have been coined as early as medieval days. No reference in print appears *anywhere*, however, until the early 1960s. Nothing even in World War II (the length of a belt of ammo for a machine gun) as some have also claimed. The very first actual citation appears in a short story by Robert Wegner titled, *Man on the Thresh-hold* printed in an issue of a quarterly literary journal, *Michigan's Voices,* in 1962. Here is the extensive sentence, word for word:

> "Marjorie's fault, and if all this howling and yelling up and down through the furnace pipes didn't stop soon they'd have the kids awake and then we can all take positions at one of the vents and bellow at each other—great sport, real civilized living in the modern urban home—then the dog would catch on and go ki-yi-yi-ing from one to the other of the shouting pyjama clad participants mad, mad, mad, the consequences of the house, home, kids, respectability, status as a college professor and **the whole nine yards**, as a brush salesman who came by the house was fond of saying, **the whole** damn **nine yards** and Marjorie with her credulous countenance which allowed him to tell her with a perfectly straight face—and she would believe him, not knowing the difference, not seeing the point, not recog-nizing the irony and it was this dimensional lack that hurt, her inability to see more than two converging or conflicting planes at a time—tell her it was a left-handed screw driver he needed."

After this, the phrase gained popularity and came to mean what we know today. Some say this refers to nine cubic yards, the capacity of concrete trucks (or coal trucks or garbage trucks). Some say it is the nine yards of material that tailors use to make a top quality suit or a kilt or kimono. Others have claimed that the yards are the spars of sailing ships, saying that ships can continue to change direction as long as new sails are unfurled, culminating with the final ninth sail. It is also believed by some to be of a mystical significance relating to the number nine. Still others have said that it refers to the amount of dirt in a rich man's burial plot or the yards in football; none of which 'hold any water.' There are a number of other totally speculative claims, but you get the point.

Whatever the hidden meaning, a movie with this phrase as its title was released in 2000, starring Bruce Willis and Matthew Perry, about 'a hit man with a heart.'

Why buy a cow when you can get the milk for free?

This phrase most often means 'why get married when you can have sex without that commitment,' but can be adapted to other examples. The origin is uncertain, but forms of it have been in use since at least the late 19th century, as observed by this reference found in Benjamin Orange Flower's *The Arena*, Volume 2, 1892, on page 362, in a novelette, '*The Shadow of the Noose*' by Ferdinand C. Valentine:

> "My mother did not hesitate to openly declare that Aunt Helen had been deserted by numerous lovers because (to quote my mother) '**why should they buy a cow when milk** was so cheap?'"

Thirteen years later it appeared in current form, using 'free' on 16 October 1905, in the large Georgia newspaper, the *Atlanta Constitution*, page 7, column 4:

> "Some claim that Hoke Smith does not control The Journal, and has no personal organ. He would be a fool to **buy a cow when milk is free**. Why should he want an interest in a paper that seems to place him on a pedestal of virtue unequaled since St. Paul?"

Note that this reference had nothing to do with marriage.

Wide berth

This expression is most commonly used as 'keep a wide berth of' or 'give a wide berth to.' Often it has been misspelled as 'wide birth.' It originally was, like others found in this volume, a nautical term, taken in the seventeenth century from the berth of a ship, the place where a ship is moored. It was a derivation of berth as a word meaning 'bearing off' indicating making room for something, i.e., a ship. An early citation of a form of it comes from Captain John Smith in *Accidental Young Seamen*, 1626:

> "Watch bee vigilant to **keepe your berth to windward**."

The phrase as it is more often used today came in 1829 from Sir Walter Scott's *Letters on demonology and witchcraft*:

"Giving the apparent phantom what seamen call **a wide berth**."

Wild goose chase

A wild goose chase is a hopeless quest, which those pursuing would much rather have been spared. This saying is one from William Shakespeare, who brought us so many of these clichés. It comes from *Romeo and Juliet*, 1592:

"Romeo: Switch and spurs, switch and spurs; or I'll cry a match.

"Mercutio: Nay, if thy wits run the **wild-goose chase**, I have done, or thou hast more of the **wild-goose** in one of thy wits than, I am sure, I have in my whole five."

The basic feeling here is that chasing a goose will likely end in frustration, since wild ones can rise to flight 'before you can say Jack Robinson' (see). In Shakespeare's day, however, this related to a race in which a number of horses followed a lead horse and mimicked wild geese in flight.

By 1811, *Grose's Dictionary of the Vulgar Tongue* defined the term in the sense we know it today.

"A tedious uncertain pursuit, like the **following** a flock of **wild geese**, who are remarkably shy."

In 1978 a British film starring Richard Burton, Roger Moore, Hardy Kruger and Richard Harris named *The Wild Geese* was released about Irish Mercenaries who embarked on a near-impossible mission, leaving Ireland to serve in various armies in Europe.

Wild horses couldn't keep (or drag) me away***

This expression, "Wild horses couldn't drag me away" is found in an original Rolling Stones song called "Wild Horses" written by Mick Jagger and Keith Richards, released on their "Sticky Fingers" album in 1971. But in spite of many reporting this as its origin, the term, derived from the fact that wild horses are strong and dangerous, and can pull with great strength and resolve, was in use a full century earlier. The first citation of a form of the expression is from *The London Journal*, October 7, 1871, in a serial titled 'Lady Thornhurst's Daughter' by Mrs. Harriot Lewis, Chapter 18:

> "I would die for you, my lady, as you know, and **wild horses couldn't** draw from me a secret of your ladyship's."

Then, in 1883, in Edward King's *The Gentle Savage*, on page 54 we find:

> **"Wild horses couldn't drag him away** from that piano."

Willy-nilly

This curious expression was originally used to refer to an act done whether someone else wants it done or not, but currently more likely to mean something carried out in a haphazard manner. The earliest known citation of a version of it was in Old English, circa 1000 in Aelfrick's *Lives of Saints*:

> "Forean the we synd synfulle and and sceolan beon eadmode, **wille we, nelle we.**"

Shakespeare used versions of it in two plays. *The Taming of the Shrew*, 1596:

> Petruchio: [To Katharina] "Thus in plain terms: your father hath consented that you shall be my wife; your dowry 'greed on; 'And, **Will you, nill you**, I will marry you.' [*I.e. I will marry you, whether you like it or not.*]"

Then in *Hamlet*, 1602: "First Clown: Give me leave. Here lies the water; good: here stands the man; good; if the man go to this water, and drown himself, it is, **will he, nill he**, he goes. [I.e. *If a man chooses to drown he enters the water, if he chooses not, he leaves.*]"

It is actually derived from a shortening of will ye, nill ye (whether it is your will or not).

In 1898, Sir Walter Besant uses the term in the current form in *The Orange Girl*:

> "Let us have no more shilly shally, **willy nilly** talk."

Wind blowing in the right direction

This has been used figuratively since the early 20th century to mean that conditions are right to take action on a matter. The earliest citation available is found in *Parlimentary Debates* of 1907, published in 1908, which used obvious metaphors:

"Mr. PENDERGAST said that he objected to the Worker's Accident Compensation Bill being struck out. It was one of the kites put up to see how the wind was blowing, but it was pulled down before the wind commenced to blow.

"Mr. BENT said the **wind was blowing in the right direction**, but he did not mind leaving it on the paper, and he would not kill it to-night."

Window of opportunity

This metaphoric expression refers to a brief period of time during which advantage of something must be taken before the ability to do so is forever lost. It has been in use in English since the dawn of the 20th century. An early example of a form of it comes from *The Punch, or the London Charivari*, 25 November 1908 in 'Quick Hand Mementoes of an Auto Exhibition':

"I asked, thinking to open a bow-**window of opportunity** for him to do himself a bit of good."

Wing and a prayer

This saying is used to express hopeful doubts of success in an endeavor. In World War I, when a flyer returned despite a badly damaged wing, he reported that he had been praying that he would make it back safely. Afterward it was said that he made it on a wing (the one good one) and a prayer.

Win hands down

This means to win easily and without doubt. One would likely think that this is derived from card games where the hands of cards are placed on the table 'face down.' Or it seems that it could be from boxing, when a champ goes into the ring with his hands at his side, and the opponent is almost ready to concede without swinging the first punch. Both are incorrect. But it is from a sport— horse racing.

In order to make certain that a horse will run properly, jockeys need to retain a tight rein, and keep their hands on the horse's neck. In order to slacken his grip and drop his reins, a jockey must be so far ahead that he is certain to place first. This is called 'winning hands down.' As far back as the 19th century, this was referenced in *Lyrics & Lays*, published by a British company in Calcutta in 1867.

> "There were good horses in those days, as he can well recall, But Barker upon Elepoo, **hands down**, shot by them all."

Early in the 1900s it began to be used in a figurative sense to denote winning at anything with little or no effort.

Winners never quit and quitters never win

Now quite the cliché, this is a quote attributed to legendary Green Bay Packers' coach, Vincent T. 'Vince' Lombardi, who in his tenure there (1959-1967) won five league championships. It is used as a reminder that in order to succeed, persistence is paramount. Lombardi, however, did not originate the slogan, which was used by boys' clubs as early as the 1920s, and verifiable citations exist by February 1936 when it appeared on page 47 of *Boys' Life Magazine* as the motto of the Beaver Patrol in London, Ontatio, Canada:

> "'**Winners never quit — Quitters never win**.' And by the way, how is your Patrol Motto? Is it worthy of being considered for our thought of the month?"

Winner, winner, chicken dinner

This old expression is used in fun when someone has won something. Legend has it that it originated as a result of the fact that many years ago every casino in Las Vegas had a three piece chicken dinner with a potato and another side for $1.79. A standard bet back in those days, goes the legend, was $2, hence when you won a bet you had enough for a chicken dinner. So, the victory cry became "Winner, winner, chicken dinner!" This entire tale is difficult to prove.

The crude 2008 movie, *21*, and ESPN color analyst, Randy Petersson, actually popularized the phrase in modern days. In the film it was said to have originated at Binion's Horseshoe Casino in Las Vegas, now a Harrah's property. The narration by an unseen male while cards fly across the screen in the opening scene is:

> "'**Winner, winner, chicken dinner**.' Those words had been dancing around my head all night. I mean, it's Vegas lore, that phrase. Just ask any of the

old-time pit bosses, they'll know. It was a Chinese dealer at Binion's who was first credited with the line. He would shout it every time he dealt blackjack. That was over 40 years ago, and the words still catch. '**Winner, winner, chicken dinner**.' There it is! '**Winner, winner, chicken dinner**.'"

Binion's actually did serve a 10 ounce New York strip steak for $2.00, however, according to *The St. Louis* (MO) *Herald*, 27 March 1994, in the article "No such thing as free lunch—says who?" by Carolyn Olson, Travel, page 2T:

"A 10-ounce New York strip steak with salad and baked potato for $2 at Binion's Horseshoe from 10 p.m. to 5:45 a.m."

But the Chinese blackjack dealer likely picked the phrase up from an earlier source. David Guzman, co-author of *A Guide to Craps Lingo from Snake Eyes to Muleteeth*, revealed in an email:

"'**Winner Winner Chicken Dinner**' came from alley craps back in the Depression. They used to play craps in alleys and didn't always use $$$, but if they did it use $$$ and they were winning, it meant they could afford chicken for dinner that night."

Guzman feels that the saying may have had its roots in Cockney rhyming slang.

Another story is that in the late 1960s and early '70s at trap league 'meat shoots' in Waseca, Minnesota, teams of sportsmen would compete by shooting at flying clay pigeons. The winners would take home a frozen chicken. The announcer would call out, "Winner, winner, chicken dinner!" Again, the earlier origin could have caused them to use this line.

Win on Sunday, sell on Monday

It was NHRA innovator, auto industry legend and Ford dealer, Bob Tasca, Sr., who coined the phrase in the 1960s. It was originally applied to auto racing, and caught the attention of manufacturers and promoters of other products. It became an adage for marketing in all fields. It means that in order to be a hot-selling product something has to do well in comparison to competitors in its field.

Win-win situation

This means that there is virtually no way to lose in a venture—even in the worst case scenario. The expression was coined by Stephen R. Covey in his runaway best-selling book, *The 7 Habits of Highly Effective People* in 1989.

Witch hunt

This phrase derived from literal searches for evidence of witchcraft practice which resulted in mass hysteria and often lynching or burning at the stake of those suspected of this 'craft.' The classical period of witch hunts in both Europe and North America was the Early Modern era from circa 1480 and 1750.

Since it later became apparent that countless innocents were brutally murdered as a result of this pandemonium, the term came to be used figuratively by the second half of the 20th century for a frantic search for evidence against others for groundless charges. Allen Weinstein's *Freedom and Crisis*, 1974, showed that it was likely in use by the early 1950s:

> "In 1951 Senator Joseph McCarthy, whose crusade against communism became a **witch hunt**, lashed out at Marshall. He published a speech attacking Marshall's wartime strategy, his mission to China, and his actions as Secretary of State..."

With bells on

Though actual derivation of this phrase is unclear, with theories ranging from the bells on court jesters' costumes to Navy bell bottom trousers (both of which are unlikely). When someone says that he or she will be at a social event 'with bells on' it means that the person will attend eagerly and ready to participate in the activities. It is more likely that the saying came about due to the decorative and festive nature of bells such as the 'jingle bells' in the familiar Christmas tune, and the fact that they were used on sleighs and horses' attire associated with gaiety at the time when the expression came into being in the late 19th century to early twentieth. The first known citation is found in the quarterly fraternity publication, *The Eleusis of Chi Omega*, August 1910:

> "Sigma will be there, **'with bells on**.' Even now, enthusiasm is at highest pitch over the prospect of again being with those so closely joined in the bonds of love and service. What with our reunion and Sister Letty Mae McRoberts' house party..."

Note the quotations indicating a relatively new expression.

With flying colors

In olden days, if a country's fleet won a decisive victory over an enemy, the ships would sail back to their home port with their colors proudly flying from their masts. Now this is used to mean an easy win or passing grade.

With friends like you, who needs enemies?

Versions of this saying have been around for hundreds of years—even before it was known in the English tongue. The original Latin phrase from which it is derived was: *Dai nemici mi guardo io, dagli amici mi guardi Iddio!* The literal translation is: 'I (can) protect myself from my enemies; may God protect me from my friends!'

Another old version, which some believe to be the original, is: 'He who has a Hungarian for a friend needs no enemy.' Other nationalities also have such derogatory phrases.

It is used in good-natured jest among friends—usually of the same racial background, and not as a true put down.

With one hand tied behind my back

This expression is used to mean that the speaker can accomplish a given feat with little or no effort. The earliest known citation is from *Blackwood's Edinburgh Magazine* in a letter of apology from Samuel Sure for not having written an article for that edition, June 1822:

> "Why I offer to swim him **with one hand tied behind my back**! There's for you. But somewhat too much of this — As I am a Christian and a Contributor, what a shew of Trouts!"

Without a hitch*

In this idiom, a hitch refers to a difficulty or obstacle. Something which goes off without a hitch is a plan which is executed with no problems whatsoever. It has been used this way since the late nineteen century. The earliest verifiable figurative citation is from a correspondence to the editor from Havana in *The Louisiana Planter and Sugar Manufacturer*, 13 May 1899:

616

"...although it was very heavy work breaking the hard pan at the bottom of the ordinary horse cultivation, the engines ran very smoothly and **without a hitch**, which speaks well for the workmanship and general arrangement of the parts."

W.C. Stubbs, PhD, main editor, New Orleans, LA, U.S.A.

Without batting an eye

This metaphoric saying relates to something which is or can be done, showing no emotion and without giving any previous thought to it. The term 'to bat' came from a bird batting or fluttering its wings used in the sport of falconry, and was adapted to blinking of eyelashes as early as the 19th century. The earliest verifiable citation of 'without batting an eye,' which is in quotes, is from *The Cannoner* by Augustus Buell, an American Civil War documentation, first published in 1890:

"This Terry Gorman was a fat, jolly Irish boy, with just a bit of brogue, and he could tell his whoppers with a perfectly straight face and '**without batting an eye**.'"

Woe is me!

This phrase, which has been used as a cliché for a person's declaration of failure and depression, is from the *Bible, Isaiah 6:5, King James Version*, 1611:

"Then said I, **Woe is me!** for I am undone; because I am a man of unclean lips, and I dwell in the midst of a people of unclean lips: for mine eyes have seen the King, the LORD of hosts."

wolf in sheep's clothing, A

This descriptive metaphor for a person who appears to be a friend, but is in truth a foe, is a biblical expression and comes from *Matthew 7:15 (NIV)*:

"Beware of false prophets which come to you in **sheep's clothing**, but inwardly they are ravening **wolves**."

Shakespeare used a form of it in *Henry VI Part I (I,3,53-55):*

"Winchester goose! I cry, a rope! A rope!—
Now beat them hence; why do you let them stay?—
Thee I'll chase hence, thou **wolf in sheep's array!**"

Women—you can't live with 'em and you can't live without 'em

This saying, one of a number of similar ones coined by comedians and writers, using both women and men, has been termed a phrase which only placates the problem that a person seems to have. Kermit the Frog is famous for using this catchphrase in speaking to Bert and Ernie on PBS's *Sesame Street*, but the idea was in use as early as July 1921, when a form of it appeared in the American Telephone and Telegraph publication, *Long Lines*:

> **"You can't live with them and you can't live without them**."

In the latter 20th century the saying as we know it was used in numerous publications including the tabloid, *Weekly World News*, May 30, 1989, page 33 in the article 'Judge insults gal victim at her trial':

> *"Somebody once said to me, '**Women — you can't live with them and you can't live without them**,'" Judge Allen said. Later, he added another comment even more upsetting to Miss Thacker. "There isn't anyone worth the trouble you've caused..."*

Won't take no for an answer

The meaning is literal. When someone tries to tell someone that they are not going to do something, they refuse to accept it. Versions of it have been in our vernacular since 1866, when Wilkie Collins wrote this in *Armadale*:

> "Mr. Pedgift the elder had risen in the law; and Mr. Pedgift the elder now **declined to take No for an answer.**"

Then in 1912, the exact phrase was used by Alice Brown in her novel, *Robin Hood's Barn*:

> "That's the next step with people like you who **won't take no for an answer.**"

word to the wise is sufficient, A

This old proverb is used when wanting to issue a nameless warning about impending danger which could occur and about which his audience should be aware. To use the phrase indicates a faith that the person or persons being addressed will heed it and not need another warning. The earliest known citation is from *A supplement to Kennedy's Ophthalmographia, or Treatise of the eye* by Peter Kennedy, London, 1739, in 'Book of Operations of Surgery,' page 153:

> "And thus we observe (in such Café) *that the less tampering is the best,* and so we would *use dry Lint;* yet we find it sometimes *beneficial* to tamper a little as yet, with our dear *Bascilicon, & c.* but **a Word to the Wise is sufficient,** *and the best way therefore is to be guided by the Patient what Medicines to continue."*

"A word to the wise is enough" is even older (See: **Forewarned is forearmed**).

Works for me

This now common catchphrase indicates that another person and the speaker have reached an agreement as to how something is to be done, often when there was a difference of opinion. It was the producers' hook used in the 1984-1991 television police drama, *Hunter,* by the laid-back title character, Sgt. Rick Hunter, played by Fred Dryer, who popularized it.

Previously 'it works for me' was often used to express some method which had proven to be successful to an individual. As early as March, 1955, it was used as a stand alone expression in *Boy's Life:*

> "It **works for me**. You may get more hits with a lighter or heavier model."

Worth its weight in gold

This popular idiom means that something has extreme value. At various points in history several commodities have actually been worth their weight in gold at that given time including salt, aluminum and even black pepper. The idea of comparing values and virtues to precious gems and metals dates at least to the 10th century BC when Israel's King Solomon penned the *Proverbs.* In personifying Wisdom he wrote in *3:15*:

> "She is more precious than rubies: and all the things thou canst desire are not to be compared unto her." *(KJV)*

Since at least 1660 it has been used figuratively to explain the value of art and intangibles. The following citation appeared that year in *The Learned Man Defended and Reform'd* by Daniello Bartoli and translated into English by Thomas Salusberry, on page 392, regarding a famous piece of art:

"A wonderfol work it was, and how much the lesse rich for the matter, so much the more precious for Art; by which the rust, which is a fault in the Iron, became a virtue to the Brasse, and made it **worth its weight in Gold**."

Worst case scenario

A scenario is a basic outline of events as they may develop in any given situation. A 'worst case' scenario is the most negative possible projected example of what could potentially come to pass. The expression began to be used in the early 1970s, as evidenced by this citation in quotes from *New York Magazine*, November 25, 1974 in 'The City Politic' by Michael Kramer on page 13:

"And now, Nelson Rockefeller's **'worst case' scenario** has come true — the man who survives to haunt him is the one man above all he had hoped would now be politically dead."

Wouldn't be caught dead

Usually accompanied by in a certain place, wearing a certain piece of clothing, etc., this idiom means that the person using it is very adamate about his or her feeling on the matter. The earliest available citation is from the comedy play, *Popping by Proxy; A Farce in One Act* by O.E.Young, 1899:

"I can't bear to git out, so I s'pose I must do the other thing; but I **wouldn't be caught dead** poppin' the question myself. My heart would tumble into the pit o' my stummick and my upper lip fly round like a button on a barn door if I undertook it…"

Wrap someone around one's little finger

This figurative phrase means that one person has another in a position in which they can manipulate and control him or her. It is most often used of a dominate female and a subordinate male relationship. The earliest known citation is from the 1911 play, *The Woman's Mascarade (a comedy in one act)* by Nora Del Smith:

"If she didn't feel she had him **wrapped around her little finger**, she'd stop her craziness."

Write one's own ticket

This means to be able to control one's destiny and chose whatever job or financial arrangement is most desired. It was derived from someone at an election poll or horse race writing out their own ticket. The earliest known figurative citation, which is a slight reflection of the original usage, is from *The New York Times*, 3 November 1925, page 2, in an article titled "Offers of 15 to 1 on Walker Go Begging."

> "Mr. DeChadenedes said that any one wishing to back the Republican candidate could **write his own ticket** and name his own price."

X

Xerxes tears

This expression relates to a military leader's deep concern for those under his command. It was derived from the legendary story of Xerxes I (519 BC - 465 BC), the great Persian king, who, when preparing to invade Greece in 480 BC is said to have been greatly troubled over the impending loss of life which was about to take place, and tearfully stated:

> "Of all this multitude who knows how many will return?"

X out

This means, when used literally, to cross something written or printed out, usually an error, by using an x. The term has been around since at least the late fifteenth to early sixteenth century, in Middle English. An early citation is from *The Boke of Justyces of Peas: The Charge of all the Processe of Cessyons, Warrantes, Supersedias & All that Longeth to Ony Justyce to Make Endytementes of Haute Treason, Petyt Treason, Felonyes, Appeles, Trespas Vpon Statutes, Trespas Contra Regis Pacem, Nocumentis, with Dyuers Thynges More as it Appereth in the Kalender of the Same Boke*, 1506 by Sir Anthony Fitzherbert:

> "...**x out** it be en tyme of wacte en the defence of the tealmee and the statute gyueth power..."

By 1710 the meaning seemed quite clear as instructions in *Complete Works of Mr. Thomas Brown*:

"X Out oft be same, Epist. 20. Lib. 2."

Figuratively Xing someone out refers to getting rid of him or her. One example is in *Misty Row*, a 2005 novel by B.K. Shropshire:

> "She smiled wickedly to herself, as she eyed the old butler, thinking of a way to **X him out** of the picture."

X marks the spot

This is the identification of the location of some particularly important discovery or event. It was originally used on 'treasure maps' to mark the spot at which the prize was supposedly buried. By 1912 it was being printed as 'The X marks the spot,' as on page 10 of *A Cowboy Detective* by Charles A. Siringo:

> "The **X Marks the Spot** Where the Author Stood When the Soldiers Arrived 501 Orchard and Guards."

Then in June 1917 this citation without the initial 'the' appeared in the new monthly fraternal publication *Roycroft*, in the article 'Dore's Sad Art':

> "William Randolph Hurst in his palmiest days never faked a photograph, *X marks the spot where the murderer stood,* to equal the artistic realizations of certain of Gustov Dore's visions of Hell and its suburbs."

It was used in the early days of newspaper photography for the scene of a crime.

Y

Yada, yada*

It may strike some as odd to learn that the word yada, correctly pronounced 'yaw-dah,' is Hebrew meaning to know or to perceive. This led some to feel that this saying came from Yiddish slang.

This modern Americanism, however, is one of exasperated disparity used to indicate that something just said was predictable, repetitive or tedious. It is the now-more-common equivalent of the twentieth-century phrase, blah, blah, blah. Forms of this saying emerged following World War II, first as 'yatata, yatata and yaddaga, yaddaga. The expressions most likely come from words used for unnecessary jabber such as the Scottish, '*yatter,*' or the Norwegian, '*jada, jada,*

jada,' meaning 'yeah, yeah, yeah.' The earliest American form was printed in an ad in an August 1948 edition of *The Long Beach* (CA) *Independent*:

"Yatata ... yatata ... the talk is all about Chatterbox, Knox's own little Tomboy Cap with the young, young come-on look!"

Yada, yada, per se, came into usage in the early 1970s. On American songwriter and poet Dory Previn's *Mythical Kings and Iguanas*, released in May, 1971, the number two cut was the song, *Yada Yada La Scala*, in which the expression was defined:

"**Yada yada** La Scala
yada yada yada yada yada
Let's stop talking talking talking
wasting precious time
Just a lot of empty noise
that isn't worth a dime
Words of wonder
words of whether
should we shouldn't we
be together
Yada yada yada yada yada"

Yellow-bellied

For hundreds of years the color yellow has been associated with cowardice and treachery. In ancient France, the doors of traitors' houses were daubed with yellow dye. The medieval 'yellow star' which was later utilized by the Nazis, branded Jews as having 'betrayed Jesus.' In medieval paintings, Judas Iscariot, the ultimate symbol of treason to Christians, was portrayed wearing yellow garments. In Spain, victims of the Inquisition wore yellow clothing to imply that they were guilty of heresy and treason. In the old American West, during the early 19th century, anybody thought to be worthless was called a 'yellow-dog.'

The combination of yellow, symbolizing cowardice and treachery, with the belly or 'guts,' representing stamina, grit and heroism, speaks clearly the reason for this catchphrase. A person with guts is a person with courage. The oxymoron 'yellow-bellied' was thus an obvious way of saying the person had no courage.

'Yellow-belly' began to be used in England as a 'mildly derogatory' nickname in the late 18th century. Grose's, *A provencial glossary; with a collection of proverbs, etc.,* 1787, lists this term.

> "**Yellow bellies**. This is an appellation given to persons born in the Fens, who, it is jocularly said, have yellow bellies, like their eels."

A General Dictionary of Provincialisms, by William Holloway, 1839, also lists this phrase in the same light.

> "**Yellow-belly**, A person born in the Fens of Lincolnshire (From the yellow, sickly complexion of persons residing in marshy situations)."

The usage of this phrase to describe a coward, per se, first appeared around 1925 in the U.S.

Yeoman's service

Also used as 'yeoman's duty' or 'yeoman's work,' this idiom refers to good, useful, committed, workman-like service. The name 'yeoman' was first applied to high-ranking servants of royal households as early as circa 1300. Later it was the name given to a tenant farmer, above a laborer but below a landowner. Both earned a reputation for their honest and faithful service. Today yeomen are petty officers in the U.S. Navy. The phrase is the best known, of course, because of the Shakespearean reference in *Hamlet, V.ii, 1602*:

> "I once did hold it, as our statists [statesmen] do,/A baseness to write fair, and labored much/How to forget that learning, but, sir, now/It did me **yeoman's service**."

Yes sir-ee bob, no sir-ee bob, no sir-ee bobtail Johnson

This is another example of a phrase changing and evolving over time. The earliest printed citation of 'yes sir-ee' is found in Philadelphia's *Dollar Newspaper,* in early July 1846:

> "'Will you take this man to be your lawful husband?' said the Justice; to which she responded with breathless haste, '**Yes, sir-ee**'."

In the 1950s 'No siree Bob' was used on the popular *Howdy Doody* NBC TV show, as 'Buffalo Bob' Smith was the name of the puppeteer.

The first printed addition of 'bob' with 'yes siree' occurred in Billie Holiday's autobiography, *Lady Sings the Blues,* 1973, chapter 24, on page 203:

"**Yes siree bob**, life is just a bowl of cherries."

Over the next few years American Southerners began changing it to 'bobtail & bobtail Johnson.'

You are what you eat

A phrase which has become increasingly popular in the late twentieth and early-twenty-first centuries, the thought of this came from another time and another culture. It was originally written in French in *Physiologie du Gout, ou Meditations de Gastronomie Transcendante,* by Anthelme Brillat-Savarin in 1826:

"Dis-moi ce que tu manges, je te dirai ce que tu es." (Tell me **what you eat** and I will tell you **what you are**.)

It is to stress the fact that in order to be healthy, one must ingest a healthy diet.

You buy them books, send them to school, and all they do is eat the covers

Like many old humorous sayings, this one has been worded a number of ways, including with buy you books twice instead of send them to school, and with I and we at the start and you as the subject. It has been in use since the 1960s, and is worded to fit the situation. It means that people with no common sense don't know how to appreciate being taught the important lessons of life. It doesn't seem to have been picked up by authors, but has certainly made the rounds in pop culture.

You can bet your bottom dollar

This American phrase means that one can be very certain of something. On 7 February 1855 'bottom dollar' was used with quotes in the New Orleans paper, *Daily Picayune* in an article titled 'From Mississippi,' page 1, column 3:

"There is not a man among their friends who would not go his '**bottom dollar**' on them, as will be seen by their sticking to them if they resume, which it is presumed they will."

The first printed reference to this precise phrase was in the historic Wisconsin newspaper, *La Crosse Independent Republican*, as well as the *Galveston News* in Texas in an article, 'One of the Polk Men,' page 1, column 7, on 16 September 1856:

> "I'm goin' to vote for you (James Polk—ed.)— **you can bet your bottom dollar** on that!"

No explanation as to why the reference to James Polk. Ex-President Polk was not running again for President and it *was* an election year. Buchanan was elected.

You can catch more flies with honey than with vinegar

Meaning 'kindness is a better way to win friends than anger,' this first appeared in *Piazza universale di proverbi Italiani (A common place of Italian Proverbs and Proverbial Phrases),* by Giovanni Torriano, F & TW London, 1666. It was recorded in America in 1774 by Benjamin Franklin in *Poor Richard's Almanac*.

You can choose your friends but you can't choose your family

This axiom, implying that you should stick by your family no matter what happens, is from Harper Lee's immortal, *To Kill a Mockingbird,* 1960, '62.

> *"Aunty,"* Jem spoke up, *"Atticus says **You can choose your friends but you sho' can't choose your family**, an' they're still kin to you no matter whether you acknowledge 'em or not, and it makes you look right silly when you don't."*

Coining a new proverb:

You can feed a pig white truffles but that doesn't make it a connoisseur

This is a new proverbial phrase herein coined. European white truffles, which are fungi, are the most expensive food in the world, often selling for as much as $3600 a pound. In fact, one two-pound truffle sold for $300,000 according to a January 8, 2012 *CBS News Special Report*. Pigs are very fond of truffels and where present root to try to unearth them. This new version of this proverb means much the same as earlier sayings (See: **You can put lipstick on a pig but it is still a pig**). You can dress up a lousy product, place it in the most desirable locations, etc.; but unless there has been a genuine transformation the attempt is wasted. This can also apply to a sloppy, noncaring person.

You can fool all of the people some of the time,
you can fool some of the people all of the time,
but you cannot fool all of the people all of the time

This is a well-known quotation most often attributed to 16th American President, Abraham Lincoln, yet questioned by some. This was claimed as early 1888 in *An Open Letter to Hon. Henry Cabot Lodge* by William Newton Osgood, who said, on page 9, that it was used in one of his debates with Douglas (Illinois Senatorial Campaign, 1858):

> "You will readily recall the saying of Lincoln, in his famous debate with Douglas, '**You can fool all of the people some of the time, you can fool some of the people all of the time, but you cannot fool all of the people all of the time**.'"

The problem is that this does not appear in the text of the LD Debates. A flurry of books and magazines carried the claim in the late nineteenth and early twentieth centuries. Some quoted it in reverse, but with the same meaning, as in the New York society monthly, *Munsey's Magazine,* May 1897 by Mr. Frank Munsey himself in 'The Publisher's Desk':

> "While thinking over the problem my mind reverted to the saying of the immortal Lincoln: '**You can fool some of the people all of the time, and you can fool all of the people some of the time, but you cannot fool all of the people all of the time**.'"

Alexander McClure reiterated the saying as Abe's in his 1901 book, *Lincoln's Own Yarns and Stories.* McClure was a close friend of Lincoln, who appointed him Assistant Adjutant General, so it is very possible that it really was stated by him at some point. Others to whom the saying is attributed include P.T. Barnum and Mark Twain, but here there is no hard evidence either.

A variant uses 'please' rather than 'fool.'

You can lead a horse to water but you can't make it drink

This is a very old proverb in the English language, and is still in popular use after all of these centuries. It was recorded as early as 1175 in *Old English Homilies.*

> "Hwa is thet mei thet **hors** wettrien the him self nule **drink**en? (Who can give water to the horse that will not drink of its own accord?)"

Its implied meaning goes for people—they will only do what they have a mind to do.

You can put lipstick on a pig but it is still a pig

This variant of the 'can't change a pig' cliché was only coined in the late 20th century. It means that attempts to alter a faulty product are futile. The premier offering was 'None can make goodly silke of a gotes fleece.' It was coined by Alexander Barclay in *Certayne Eglogues* in 1515. This was quickly altered in 1579 by Stephen Gosson in *The Ephemerides of Phialo* who wrote of 'seekinge too make a silke purse of a Sowes eare' from which evolved the yet-popular 'You can't make a silk purse from a sow's ear.' Then Thomas Fuller, a British physician, noted the phrase 'A hog in armour is still a hog' in 1732 in *Gnomologia, Adagies and Proverbs*, but it was already in print in Captain John Stevens' *A New Dictionary of Spanish and English and English and Spanish* in 1726:

"An **hog** in armour is **still** but **an hog**."

Francis Grose's *Classical Dictionary of the Vulgar Tongue* in 1796 stated that a 'hog in armour' alludes to 'an awkward or mean looking man or woman finely dressed.' Evangelist Charles Spurgeon, in his *The Salt-Sellers*, 1887, recorded a variation:

"A **hog** in a silk waistcoat is **still a hog**."

You can take that to the bank

This Americanism implies that something has real value and is worth protecting. Figuratively it is applied to information, facts, or beliefs which are strong and true. It was derived from depositing funds in a bank to keep them safe. It came into common usage in the latter part of the 20th century. An early example is found in the Cesar Romero play, *Welcome Home: A Comedy*, by Marty Davis, 1978, presented in Drury Lane Theater, Evan Park, Illinois in 1981:

"DANIEL. *(Sipping the hot coffee)* I don't know why my daughter is so good to me. . .

"JOHN. Because she's a doll, that's why! And **you can take that to the bank!**"

628

You can take the boy out of the country but you can't take the country out of the boy

This humorous American saying has taken a lot of shapes. The earliest citation seems to be from a caricature of famed actor, James 'Jimmy' Stewart in 1938. Cartoonist Henry Major worked with Arthur 'Bugs' Baer, who did the footnotes on *Hollywood with Bugs Baer and Henry Major*. The phrase was verbatim to the above with the sole difference being 'a boy' rather than 'the boy.'

Other similar phrases included 'You can take the girl out of the chorus line but you can't take the chorus line out of the girl,' and 'You can take Björk out of Iceland but you can't take Iceland out of Björk.'

You can't con a con

This means that someone who is adept at deceiving others is difficult to deceive. It came into usage sometime in the mid-to-late 20th century, and by November, 1983 was called an 'old saying' in the article, 'Laying it on the Line: Bo Lozoff and the Prison Ashram Project' in *Yoga Journal*:

> "The old saying is true, '**You can't con a con.**'"

You can't fight city hall

This means it is very difficult to overcome bureaucratic regulations.

Fighting city Hall was mentioned as early as 15 February 1912 when this appeared on page 49 of *CIE*, the official journal of the Bartrenders' International League of America:

> "'**Fight City Hall**' is the one suggestion which meets complainers at 12 St. Mark's Place, especially when they file a kick..."

Note the quotation marks around the phrase. It was used in several publications over the first part of the 20th century.

A song, *Poor Little February*, by Lester Lee, Danny Shapiro, and Jerry Seelen is mentioned in a *New York Post* article on 19 May 1941 as a being 'new.' The lyrics read:

> "Poor little Feb, go **fight city hall**!"

Then a book first copyrighted in 1946 and published in 1949, *Go **Fight City Hall*** by Ethel Rosenberg popularized the saying.

The April 11, 1955 edition of *Life Magazine* carried the following in an article *Slum Fighter Levi Tells What to Do* on page 134:

"The saying **'you can't fight city hall'** expresses the mood of many American citizens who are convinced that urban conditions really cannot be corrected."

You can't get blood out of a turnip

Though it has been suggested that this humorous term, often associated with the 'Deep South' of the U.S., came from the biblical story in *Genesis* in which God refused Cain's offering from his crop in favor of Abel's blood offering from an animal.

The phrase is first found in print in 1836. It is from Captain Frederick Marryat in *Japhet, In Search of a Father*.

"There's no getting blood out of a turnip."

Its meaning now as an idiom is that debtors cannot get money from someone who is indigent. Another less-known phrase is 'you can't get blood out of a stone.'

You can't go home again

This famous saying is the title of a novel by Thomas Wolfe published posthumously in 1940, and was a part of his large yet unpublished manuscript entitled *Vanity Fair*. As a saying it means that once you leave your childhood home you develop a new lifestyle based on changes in your life. In the meantime, the evolving landscape and constantly changing atmosphere of your native hometown is so different when you return years later that it is no longer 'home.'

You can't have your cake and eat it too

This implies that a person has to choose between two alternatives, rather than 'straddling the fence' (see).

This is another one passed down by John Heywood in his 1546 publication, *A dialogue Conteinyng the Nomber in Effect of All the Prouerbes in the Englishe Tongue*.

"wolde you bothe **eate your cake, and have your cake**?"

A French equivalent expression is *vouloir le beurre et l'argent du beurre,* literally meaning 'to want the butter and the money for the butter.' But the French have a way of sweetening it up by adding, *et le sourire de la crémière* (and the smile of the *female* butter maker). Other languages have alternatives, all humorous.

You can't keep a good man down

This proverbial saying means that a person with a strong character and a desire to succeed will not be deterred by hardships and stumbling blocks which inevitably occur. The earliest citation known is from Opie Perceval Read's novel, *Emmett Bonlore*, 1891, page 356:

"As Solomon said when he took his place on the woolsack, **you can't keep a good man down**."

But Read was obviously not the originator, for in January 1899 in the *Locomotive Fireman's Magazine* the following appeared on page 97:

"The old saying, '**you can't keep a good man down**,' will be exemplified in the experience of Locomotive Engineering…"

You can't make a silk purse out of a sow's ear (See: You can put lipstick on a pig and it is still a pig)

You can't pick cherries with your back toward the tree

This quote from American banker/financier J.P. (John Pierpont) Morgan (1837-1913) is used to mean that winners don't turn their backs on responsibility. A person has to focus on what is important if they expect to reach their desired result.

You can't soar with eagles if you hang out with turkeys

The idea of people 'soaring like eagles' comes from the *Bible*.

"'They will **soar** on wings like **eagles**; they will run and not grow weary, they will walk and not be faint.' *(Isaiah 40:31, KJV).*

631

The actual origin of this saying, however, is unclear. It has some slight variations, but the meaning is the same. A person can not be successful if he or she chooses to associate with unsuccessful people. The earliest known version is found in chapter four of *How to Solve the Mismanagement Crisis* by Ishak Adizes, 1979:

"Here is a typical (E) expression: 'It is difficult to **soar** like an **eagle** when **you** are surrounded by **turkeys**.'"

Then two years later we find the earliest known verifiable mention in print of a close version of this actual proverb in *Mother Jones' Magazine*, November, 1982 in a Tee Shirt Ad on page 52:

"IT'S HARD TO **SOAR** LIKE AN **EAGLE WHEN** YOU'RE SURROUNDED BY **TURKEYS**"

The current version has been prevalent since the turn of the millennium.

You can't teach an old dog new tricks

The actual meaning of this today is supposed to be that younger people learn more easily, and that is usually true. This saying, like most animal idioms and proverbs, has been with us for hundreds of years, and has become personified because the similarities between animal and human behavior patterns.

But a lot of retired people have learned new skills and crafts.

The idea behind this saying has been around since at least the mid-sixteenth century. It was brought down to us by a good friend of proverbs, John Heywood, in his 1546 book. The earliest reference to the idea from which this sprang, however, is from John Fitzherbert in *The boke of husbandry* in 1536.

"...and he [a shepherd] muste teche his dogge to barke whan he wolde haue hym, to ronne whan he wold haue hym, and to leue ronning whan he wolde haue hym; or els he is not a cunninge shepeherd. The dogge must lerne it, whan he is a whelpe, or els it will not be: for it is harde to make **an olde dogge** to stoupe."

'Stoupe' here meant 'put its nose to the ground and find a scent.'

You can't trust him (or **her**) **as far as you can throw him** (or **her**)

This witty saying is derived from the fact that even a grown man can seldom throw another one farther than at his feet. Thus, one impossibility becomes the basis of another. It means that it is impossible to trust the person. Though it had to be in use earlier, the earliest known citation of a version of this phrase is on page 85 of William Tegg's *Proverbs from Far and Near: Wise Sayings &c*, 1875:

> **"Trust him no further than you can throw him."**

You can wish in one hand and crap in the other and see which one get's filled first

Burgess Merideth's character, Max Goodman, in the 1993 comedy film *Grumpy Old Men* spoke these words to his son. It is used to mean that wishing without putting some effort into making a wish come true does no good. In spite of a slang dictionary's claim that it originated in the 1920s, various forms of it were in use since the late 18th century. The earliest known reference is from *Porcupine's Works; Containing Various Writings and* Selections by William Corbett, Volume 9, published in May 1801, in a 'Gazette Selection' from September 1798:

> **"You may wish in one hand** and spew in the other, and see which will be **full first**; but you will never wish the Kingdom of Ireland into a Republic."

You don't have to be a rocket scientist to figure that out (See: **It's not rocket science**)

You don't know jack

In ages past, a jack was a common guy, and about every occupation had a jack; hence, 'jack of all trades.' 'Jack and Jill' in the famed Nursery Rhyme were average young children. 'All work and no play made Jack a dull boy' (a quote from James Howell's *Proverbs* (1659).

'You don't know jack' has been used for at least the last three decades to mean that this person doesn't know very much.

The phrase, which originally ended in an expletive, has spawned: a 1995 computer game series, with a 2011 latest entry; a television game show based on the video games; a 2010 film about 'Dr. Death,' Jack Kevorkian, and a song by country music artist Luke Bryan.

You get out of life (or **'something'**) **what you put into it**

This proverbial truism means that in life a person is dealt equally back only in accordance with the effort exerted. No one should expect to receive something for nothing. It was obviously in use earlier, but the first actual printed version available is from *The Women's Magazine*, January 1914, on page 8, where it is referred to as an 'old saying' in the article 'Why Some Men Succeed':

> "Thrift is good, but the old saying that **you get out of life what you put into it** is undoubtedly true in regard to kindness and friendship."

You get the picture

This figurative expression means 'you understand based on what has been stated.' It has been in use since at least the early 20th century, and the first known reference in print is from *The Rotarian*, February 1927, in 'Points of Friction' by Miles H. Krubine, page 28:

> "If you look on civilized Charleston as the tortoise, and on roughneck Kansas as the elephant engaged in holding up the civilized cosmos, **you get the picture** I am trying to symbolize."

You go, girl!

This modern enthusiastic expression is used, usually by other women, when encouraging another woman of any age to accomplish something challenging or ground breaking. In 1990 a Tennessee Walking Horse was named 'Hattie Go Girl.' Then in 1992, when Whitney Houston starred in the box office smash, *The Bodyguard*, with Kevin Costner, the expression 'You go, girl!' popped up regarding her unusually brave performance, and by 1993-'94 it exploded on the scene, first among African American women then spreading to all females.

You have to break a few eggs to make an omelet

This old proverb is most usually used ironically. It has a number of variations, and means that in order to accomplish something worthwhile it is necessary to make sacrifices involving casualties; in other words, 'the end justifies the means' (see). It was supposedly spoken by Lenin to justify killing thousands of Russians during his effort to develop a 'better' communist state, and French Revolutionist Maximillian de Robespierrie (6 May 1758 – 28 July 1794) in 1790 who said *"On ne saurait faire une omelette sans casser des oeufs"* in justification of earlier executions, before his 1793 'Reign of Terror,' after which he met the same fate which he had so freely administered, at the guillotine.

You know the drill*

This cliché is used often to mean that the one to whom it is being said is very familiar with a certain procedure because he or she has either done it or seen it done numerous times. It has been in use since the mid-20th century. Though not the original citation, an early verifiable figurative reference is in *Negro Digest*, June 1969, page 89 in an excerpt from the unpublished novel, *The D.C. Blues*, by African American writer, Sam Greenlee, who was soon famous for *The Spook that Sat by the Door*:

> "All right, let's go now. We stand outside the office until the Boy Scouts come out; then we go right in. **You know the drill.**"

You made your bed, now sleep in it

Many a parent has used this phrase with an adult child who has attempted to come home after a rocky relationship. Figuratively, it means that the person being addressed put himself or herself in the predicament from which escape is being sought, and will have to face the consequences with no help from others. Actually, this was originally a French proverb in the fifteenth century, *'Comme on faict son lict, on le treuve'* (As one makes one's bed, so one finds it).

Variations of it in English date from as early as circa 1590, according to G. Harvey *Marginalia* (1913). This one was:

> "Lett them…go to there bed, as themselues shall make it."

It was listed in *Kelly's Scottish Proverbs* in 1721 as:

> "**As you make your bed, so you lye down**. According to your Conditions you have your Bargain."

This fairly well sums up the current meaning. Several variations have been around through the years.

You need (that, him, her, etc.**) like a hole in the head** (or **like a dog needs side pockets**)

These and other similar facitious analogies began popping up in American slang in the early-1960s. They obviously meant, 'you have no need of _____ whatsoever.' An early example is from the final act of Sidney Kingsley's three-

635

act play, *Night Life*, first presented at New York's Brooks Atkinson Theater October 23, 1962:

"IGGY. Come on. **You need him like a hole in the head**."

You missed your calling*

This usually sarcastic remark means that one has a hidden or unused talent which could have taken their life in a different direction.

A person's calling was anciently proclaimed to be by divine design. In Rev. W.D. Mahon's 1884 English translation of the *Archaeological Writings of the Sanhedrin and the Talmuds of the Jews* taken from the ancient parchments and scrolls of Constantinople and the Vatican being 'the record made by the enemies of Jesus of Nazareth in his day' (first century AD), on page 143 we find the following in remarks attributed to Herod, allegedly spoken to the Magi who had, as a result of a dream, followed a star to find and worship Jesus as a child:

"If you have a dream as the basis of your confidence, I am thinking that **you have missed** the mark, **and mistaken your calling**."

In the 1892 version of Aldémah's *The Queens: being passages from the lives of Elizabeth, queen of England, and Mary Queen of Scotland,* the following application of the expression appears on page 49 in Scene III, Act i, and is the Queen speaking to the Duke of Norfolk:

"Your Grace, **you have** indeed **missed your calling**."

The saying was being used jovially by the early 1900s. One excellent example is in *Recreation* magazine, April, 1903 in a possible allegory, 'THEY ROAST THE REVEREND BRISTEBACK,' in a facetious letter from a reader (A.W. Davis) regarding a minister supposedly jailed for hunting violations:

"You have **missed your calling**; your place is in a slaughter house."

You never miss the water till the well runs dry

This idiomatic proverb is attributed to a number of old ones. The earliest known is Scottish and recorded in 1628:

636

"Manie wats [know] not quhairof [whereof] the wel sauris [tastes] quhill [until] it fall drie." (J. Carmichaell *Proverbs in Scots* no. 1140)

This is the next reference known from Thomas Howell's brother, James, in his 1659 book (mentioned above), *Proverbs*:

"Of the **Well we see no want, till either dry**, or Water skant."

An R&B song titled *You Don't Miss Your Water (Till the Well Runs Dry)* was written by David Craig and recorded by American singer William Bell on Stax Records in Memphis, Tennessee in 1961. It became Bell's signature song. The soulful chorus was:

"But when you left me
And said bye-bye
I missed my water
***My well ran dry.*"**

It was covered by Otis Redding on his critically acclaimed album, *Otis Blue*, and later recorded by The Byrds on *Sweetheart of the Rodeo*. Then an extended version was released as a single by The Triffids in 1985.

A very similar song by Little Esther Phillips and Al Drowning is titled *You Never Miss Your Water (Till the Well Runs Dry),* and another with the same title was released by Whisper.

Young whippersnappers

Originally, this had to do with cowboys and roping steers in the old American West. The seasoned ropers had to train the young ones in the important skills of snapping the rope and lassoing the steers. They called the trainees 'young whippersnappers.' Thus a novice came to be known colloquially as a 'young whippersnapper.'

You only live once

This saying means that one should enjoy life to the fullest because there is only one chance to do so. The earliest known citation is found in *The Poor Relations, Second Episode, Cousin Pons* by Honoré de Balzac, 1896, translated, 1898 by William Walton, page 74:

"'**You only live once**,' said Madame Cibot. Born during the revolution, she was ignorant, as you see, of the catechism.

Your eyes are bigger than your stomach

This figurative expression is used to chastise someone who seems to be taking more food than he or she can eat. Also, it may be used as an afterthought, even as an excuse, when one has taken food and left it on his or her plate when exiting the table. It is also used in other cultures and languages in which leaving food on the plate is viewed negatively. It has been around for about 200 years in English. The earliest available citation is from *The New Sporting Magazine*, July 1833 in 'A Trip to Paris with Mr. Jorrocks':

"Oh **your eyes are bigger than your stomach**, Mr. J...."

Your goose is cooked

This phrase means that a person has done something that he or she will sorely regret. All hope is gone, and that person is now in deep trouble.

One theory of the very early origin of this saying is that in the denizens of a besieged city in the 16th century hung out a goose to show their attackers that they were not starving. This so enraged the enemy that they burned the town and cooked the goose.

Another belief is that it referred to the 'goose that laid the golden eggs,' which the farmer killed to get the gold inside. Hence, the saying, 'don't kill the goose that lays the golden eggs' (see), meaning do not destroy the one thing that will continue to provide for your needs.

There were references to 'gone goose' as early as 1830, meaning a person beyond hope. One such example that year was in a newspaper called *The Massachusetts Spy*, which printed the phrase, 'You are a gone goose, friend.'

It seemed that the idea of 'cooking someone's goose' was floating around by 1845. In a South Carolina newspaper, *The Southern Patriot*, on 22 February of that year, the following humorous article appeared:

"HOW TO COOK YOUR NEIGHBOR'S GOOSE.—Collar him, take a moderate sized stick, hickory will do, stir him up; apply offensive epithets; when he boils over with rage, continue dressing, baste sufficiently, and when he's properly served out, **his goose is cooked**."

Printed reference to this phrase in the sense we know it dates to England in a ballad published in London in 1851 bemoaning the Pope's appointment of Cardinal Wiseman as Archbishop of Westminster.

"If they come here we'll **cook their goose**, the Pope and Cardinal Wiseman."

Your name is mud (or **Mudd**)

This is one not to be taken for granted. After Abraham Lincoln was assassinated at Ford Theater in Washington, DC, on 'Good Friday' evening, 14th April 1865, his killer, actor John Wilkes Booth, who was in great pain from an injury he sustained in a fall from the stage, and a friend, rode on horseback to the plantation home of Dr. Samuel Mudd. Their arrival was at about 4:00 A.M. Dr. Mudd treated Booth. At daybreak Mudd had a neighbor make Booth a set of crutches.

Mudd later denied knowing Booth, but was taken to trial, where testimony was given that they did indeed know each other. Mudd was convicted of treason and sentenced to life in prison. He later confessed to lying to protect his family. He became so nationally hated that someone who is harshly disliked is sometimes told, "Your name is Mudd!"

But, this was not the *true* origin of the popular slang saying, no matter what we think in the U.S., for it was in circulation long before there was even a President Lincoln, as it was listed by 'J. Bee' a pseudonym for John Badcock, in *A Dictionary of the Turf, etc.,* in England in 1823!

"**Mud** - a stupid twaddling fellow. 'And **his name is mud**!' ejaculated upon the conclusion of a silly oration, or of a leader in the Courier."

Since it was originally 'mud,' not Mudd, that is not its origin. The composition of mud is dirt and water. Actually, it began to be used figuratively as early as the sixteenth century—the 1500s—to refer to things which were worthless. It later was applied to people as early as 1703 in the account of London's low-life, *Hell upon Earth*.

"**Mud**, a Fool or thick skull Fellow."

Then, in the 19th century there were many printed examples of 'as fat as mud,' 'as rich as mud,' as sick as mud,' etc. These comparisons, meaning decaying and worthless, were enough to use it with someone's name as an insult. Other sayings such as 'dragged through the mud,' and 'mud in your eye' came along as well as 'your name is mud.'

Your neck of the woods

This expression was first coined in colonial America to relate to the particular area of the country in which a colonist lived. 'Neck' had been used in the English language since the mid-sixteenth century to refer to a narrow strip of land, usually surrounded on three sides by water, because it seemed to resemble the neck of an animal. The early Americans used the word to refer to a narrow stand of timber, or expressly to a settlement formed in a particular section of the woods. Since the countryside was covered with forests, 'your neck of the woods' was your neighborhood. Even NBC's *Today Show* weatherman, Al Roker, still uses this common Americanism in talking of the weather in the viewers' particular region.

Yours truly, yours aye

This informal conventional phrase, sometimes used at the end of a letter, also often spoken to avoid the use of a personal pronoun, simply means 'I,' 'me' or myself.' It has been in use for hundreds of years. 'Yours' has been in English since 1526. The earliest verifiable citations are found in *Letters of the Late Mr. Laurence Sterne to his Most Intimant Friends*, published in London in 1775 in which three of the letters are signed, '**Yours truly**, L. Sterne'.

The Scottish equivalent is 'Yours aye,' and more accurately means 'Yours always.' The earliest known example of this is from a letter dated March 1801 from Lord Nelson to Lady Hamilton in which he used this ending:

"Recollect I am forever **yours, aye**, forever and while life remains. Yours, yours faithfully,

"Nelson and Bronte

"I charge my only friend to stay well and think of her Nelson's glory."

It was printed in *Love Letters of Eminent Persons* edited by Charles Martel published in London in 1860.

A fully Scottish example appeared in *The Humour of the Scot 'neath NorthernLights and Southern Cross*, James Inglis, 1894, page 105:

"Said the Free Kirk champion: 'D'ye ken, Davie, what yon deavin', ding-dong, great muckle bell o' **yours aye** minds meo'?"

You scratch my back, I'll scratch yours

This is a type of 'quid pro quo' (see); if you do someone a favor, they will do one for you. It is of nautical derivation, like a good many of these expressions.

Back in the seventeenth century when this saying was first coined the punishments in the British Navy for being AWOL, drunk or disobeying the orders of one's superior were very severe. One method was to tie the disobedient sailor to a mast and require another sailor to flog him with a cat-of-nine-tails. Crew members would make deals between them to only strike the other lightly (merely scratching the other's back), to insure that they would receive the same treatment should the process be reversed.

You've got another think coming

This snappy saying came into usage in the very early 20th century, and is meant to convey the belief that the person to whom it is said has a gross misunderstanding of something. The earliest known citation is from an article titled *A Frankenstein of "the Fancy"* by Kennett Harris published in *Everybody's Magazine* in April 1906:

> "If you think it's easy to grab off a ten every day in the week, **you've got another think coming**. Are you skeered?"

You would have to be living under a rock

This idiom is used of an ignorant or obtuse person. It simply means that the person has obviously been living in isolation from the events going on in the world and has little or no knowledge of reality. It is used sarcastically when speaking to someone fitting into this scenario. The earliest available citation to this usage is from the September 5, 1960 issue of *Life*, page 17 in a letter to the editor:

> "Whoever wrote the editorial about 'Votes for Women' (LIFE, August 15) must have been **living under a rock**. Starry-eyed is starry-eyed, male or female. Forty years of women's suffrage may have modified their dream, as you say."

641

Z

Zero tolerance

This term came into common usage in the United States in the 1970s as a way of enforcing laws against certain crimes for which the federal or state government, company or group involved wanted constituents to know that it would not be tolerated under any circumstances. To enforce the law, extra law enforcement officials would be assigned to high crime areas in which the problem existed. The first known printed reference to the phrase with this connotation is in the *New York Times* in December of 1972.

"Federal officials say the calculations were based on 'assuming **zero tolerance**' from now on for ineligibility and overpayments."

The phrase was in limited use in engineering circles as early as the 1950s. It likely evolved from the name of a precision tool which came into use in the early 1940s called a 'Zero Tol.'

Zigged when he should have zagged

This cliché means that one goes in the wrong direction when charting a specific course. The earliest known reference for this is a popular musical operetta presented in 1926 called *The Desert Song*. In Act I, the final four lines are:

Susan: Bennie, why didn't you zigzag and avoid the bullets?

Benjamin: I did zigzag,

Susan: Then how were you shot?

*Benjamin: I must have **zigged when I should have zagged**.*

Zonked out

This is an Americanism which came into use in the late 1950s and meant to become unconscious as a result of alcohol or narcotic drugs.

It has come, as an idiom, to mean any form of unconsciousness or exhaustion from any source, including becoming so tired from work or exercise that a person or even an animal falls asleep.

642

Bibliography

Reference books

A Collection of Scots Proverbs; Allan Ramsay; J & M. Robertson, Glasgow, Scotland, 1785

A Compleat Collection of English Proverbs; John Ray; W. Otridge, S. Bladon, London, England, 1678

A complete collection of genteel and ingenious conversation; Jonathan Swift; London, U.K., 1738

A Complete Collection of Scottish Proverbs; James Kelly; London, U.K., 1721

A dialogue conteinyng the number in effect of all the prouerbes in the Englishe tongue; John Heywood; London, England, 1546

A Dialogue Conteynyng Prouerbes and Epigrammes; John Heywood; London, England, 1592

A dialoge of comforte against tribulation; Henry More London; England, 1529

Adagia; Erasmus, (third volume of his Latin proverbs), Venice, Italy, 1508

A Dictionary of Catch-phrases: British and American, from the Sixteenth Century to the Present Day; Paul Beale, Eric Partridge; Dorsett Press, New York, NY; U.K., 1988

A Dictionary of Similes; Jenners Wilstach; Little, Brown & Co., Boston, MA, U.S.A., 1917

A Dictionary of the French and English Tongues, Randle Cotgrave, printed by Adam Islip, London, England, 1611

A Dictionary of the Turf; J. Bee, pseudonym for John Badcock; page 98, London, England, U.K., 1823

A General Dictionary of Provincialisms; William Holloway; London, England, U.K., 1839

A Glossary of Words and Phrases Usually Regarded as Particular to the United States, Second Edition; John Russell Bartlett; Little, Brown and Co., Boston, MA, U.S.A., 1859

A Hand-book of Proverbs; John Ray; London, England, 1670

A Handbook of Proverbs, English, Scottish, Irish, American, Shakespearean and Scriptural, James Allan Meir, George Routledge and Sons, London and New York, NY, U.S.A., 1871

An American Dictionary of the English Language; Noah Webster; revised and enlarged by Chauncey Allen Goodrich, page 909, Harper Brothers, New York, NY, U.S.A., 1845

An apology against—A modest confutation of the animadversions upon the remonstrant against Smectymnuus; John Milton, London, England, April, 1642

A New Dictionary of Spanish and English and English and Spanish; Captain John Stevens; J. Darby, London, England, 1726

A New Dictionary of the Terms Ancient and Modern of the Canting Crew; B.E., Gent; London, England, 1698

A New Universal Dictionary of the Marine; ref. to 'wake' on page 616, William Burney; London, U.K., 1830

An universal dictionary of the marine; William Falconer; T. Cadwell, London, U.K., 1769

A Pig in a Poke; small references, Grange Books; Hoo NR Rochester, Kent, U.K., 2003

A provencial glossary; with a collection of proverbs, etc.; Francis Grose; London, England, U.K., 1787

Arbothnot; Lewis Baboon; London, England, 1712

A Short Dictionarie for Younge Begynners; John Withals; Latin American dictionary, Section on Proverbs, page 583, England, 1616 Edition

A TAD Lexicon; T. A. Drugan; Leonard Zwilling, New York, NY, U.S.A., 1927

At the Grass Roots; Jay Elmer House; Crane and Co. Topeka, KS, U.S.A., 1905

B.E.'s New Dictionary of the Terms Ancient and Modern of the Canting Crew; London, England, circa 1698

Body, Boots, and Britches; H. W. Thompson, J.B. Lippincott, Philadelphia, PA, U.S.A., 1939/ 1940

Calendar of the Royal College of Surgeons of England, London, UK, 1874

Cassell Dictionary of Slang; Jonathon Green; Wingfield and Nicholson, London, U.K., 2000

Certayne Eglogues; Alexander Barclay; London, England, 1515

Classical Dictionary of the Vulgar Tongue; Francis Grose; London, U.K., 1785, 1788, 1796, 1811,

Collection of Proverbs in Scots, James Carmichaell; ed. M. L. Anderson; Edinburgh, Scotland, U.K., 1957

Dialect Notes; American Dialect Society; Tuttle, Morehouse and Taylor, New Haven, CT, U.S.A., 1900, 1920

Dialect Notes; The Journal of the Asiatic Society of Great Britain and Ireland; London, U.K., 1985

Dictionarium Bratannicum, Nathan Baily, London, England, 1730

Dictionary of Americanisms: A Glossary of Words and Phrases; John Russell Bartlett; Bartlett and Welford, New York, NY, U.S.A., 1848

Dictionary of Clichés; James Rogers, small reference, Ballantine Books, New York, NY, USA, 1985, 1986

Dictionary of Phrase and Fable; Rev. Ebenezer Cobham Brewer; Cambridge, U.K., 1870, 1894

Douce MS; Franciscan manuscript, William of Wykeham; Rome, Italy, 1350

Elegies; Sextus Propertius; Ancient Rome, date unknown

Encyclopedia Britannica, Volume II; Society of Gentlemen in Scotland; A. Bell and Colin Macfarquhar, Edinburg, Scotland, 1771

Encyclopedia Britannica, 3rd Edition; Edinburgh, Scotland, 1792

English Proverbs; W.C. Hazlitt; London, U.K., 1882

Exposition of the Old and New Testament, Volume 2; Matthew Henry; written early 18th century, Joseph Ogle Robinson, London, U.K., 1828

Facts on File Dictionary of Clichés; Second Edition; edited by Christine Ammer; Checkmate Books, New York, NY, USA, 2006

Glossary of North Country Words; J. T. Brockett; London, U.K., 1825

Gnomologia, Adages, Proverbs Wise Sentences and Witty Sayings, Ancient, Modern, Foreign and British; Thomas Fuller, MD, London, England, 1732

Glossographia; Thomas Blount, London England, 1656

Herefordshire Speech; the Southwest Midland Dialect as Spoken in Herfordshire; Winifred Leeds, Herfordshire, England, U.K., 1974

Hoyle's Games Improved; Edmond Hoyle; Revised and Corrected by Charles Jones, London, England, 1779

Jacula Prudentum; or Outlandish Proverbs and Sentences &c (no. 49); George Herbert, London, England, 1651

John Cotgrave's English treasury of wit and language and the Elizabethan Drama; Sir John Cotgrave, Gent; Gerald Eades Bentley, London, England, 1655

John Ryland's Library; XIV.92; London, U.K., 1930

Lean's Collectania; Volume 2; Part 2; Vincent Stuckey Lean and Julia Lucy; Woodward, London, 1903

Library of Congress Catalogue of Copyright Entries; Washington, DC, U.S.A., 1939, 1945, 1955

London Review of English and Foreign Literature; W. Kenrick; London, England, 1767

Morris Dictionary of Word and Phrase Origins; William and Mary Morris; Harper-Collins, New York, New York, 1962, 1971, 1977, 1988

MS, S. Harward; Trinity College, Cambridge, England, 1609

New Language of Politics; An Anecdotal Dictionary of Catchwords, Slogans and Political Usage, First Edition; William Safire; Random House, New York, NY, USA, 1968

New Maxims; Thomas Brown; England, c.1704

New Song on New Similes; John Gay, England, 1732

Notes and Queries: A Medium of Enter-communication for Literary Men, General Readers, etc., Fourth Series, Volume Nin;, London, U.K., 1872

Old English Homilies, 1175; reproduced by Early English Text Society, London, U.K., 12-3-1998

Paroemiologia Anglo-Latina; John Clarke; London, England, 1639

Paramoigraphy; a book of proverbs, James Howell; London, England, 1659

Piazza universale di proverbi Italiani (A common place of Italian Proverbs and Proverbial Phrases); Giovanni Torrianno; F & TW, London, U.K., 1666

Proverbs from Far and Near: Wise Sayings &c; William Tegg; London, U.K., 1875

Prouerbes or adagies with newe addicions, gathered out of the Chiliades of Erasmus; Richard Taverner; London, England, 1539

Random House Historical Dictionary of American Slang; Jonathan E. Lighter; Random House, New York, NY, U.S.A., 1987

Richard Taverner's Interpretation of Erasmus' Proverbs; Richard Taverner; London, England, 1545

Scottish Proverbs; David Fergusson; Cantici Canticorum, Edinburgh, Scotland, 1678

Slang and its Analogues Past and Present, Volume 2; John Stephen Farmer and William Ernest Henley; London, U.K., 1891

Slang and its analogies past and present, Volume 3; John Stephen Farmer, William Ernest Henley; London, U.K., 1893

Slang and its analogies past and present' Volume 5; John Stephen Farmer, William Ernest Henley; London, U.K., 1902

S.W. Cushing's Wild Oats Sowings; or the Autobiography of an Adventurer, Daniel Panshaw, New York, NY. 1857

Taalstudie; a Dutch reference work, Americanisms; Bloom and Oliversie; TE Kuilenberg, Bij, Netherlands, 1888

The American Heritage Dictionary of Idioms; Christine Ammer; Houghton Mifflin Harcourt, Boston, MA, USA, 1997

The Australian Language; reference book by Sidney John Baker; Australia, 1945

The Cambridge Dictionary of American Idioms; Paul Heacock; Cambridge University Press, Cambridge, UK, 2003

The Canting Academy; Richard Head; glossary containing phrases formerly used by thieves and vagabonds, London, England, 1673

The Concise Oxford Dictionary of Proverbs; John Simpson and Jennifer Speake; Oxford University Press, Oxford and New York, Third Edition, 1998

The Dictionary and Cyclopedia, New Volumes, Volume XII. page 964 The Century Co. New York, NY, U.S.A., 190

The Dictionary of American Slang, Originally published in 1960; Collins Reference, 3 Sub Edition; New York, NY, USA, 1998

The Encyclopedia of Word and Phrase Origins; Printed by members of the Norman Society, London, England, UK, 1906

The Etymologicon; Mark Forsyth; Icon Books, Ltd., London, U.K., 2011

The Facts on File Encyclopedia of Word and Phrase Origins; Robert Hendrickson, Revised Updated Edition; Checkmark Books, New York, NY, U.S.A., 2000

The first tome or volume of the Paraphrase of Erasmus vpon the newe testament; Nicholas Udall's First English translation; Whitchurch, Edward, London, England, 1548

The flowers of wit, or a chance collection of bon mots; Henry Kett; Lackington Allen, and Co., London, England, U.K., 1814

The Home Book of Proverbs, Maxims and Familiar Phrases; Burton Egbert Stevenson; McMillan, New York, NY, U.S.A., 1956

The Oxford Dictionary of Proverbs; Oxford University Press, New York, NY, U.S.A., 1998

The Oxford English Dictionary (OED), Second Edition, Version 4.0; Oxford University Press, New York, NY, U.S.A., 2009

The Pocket Magazine of Classics and Polite Literature; John Arliss; London, England, U.K., 1832

The Poetick Miscellenies of Mr. John Rawlett; England, 1687

The Progressive Dictionary of the English Language; Samuel Fallows; Philadelphia, PA, U.S.A., 1835

The Pronunciation of English Words derived from the Latin (S.P.E. Tract No. IV.); John Sargeaunt; Clarendon Press, Oxford, U.K., 1940

The Random House Dictionary of Popular Proverbs and Sayings; Gregory Y. Titelman; Random House, New York, NY, USA, 1996

The Rutledge Book of World Proverbs; Jon R. Stone; Rutledge, Taylor and Francis Group, New York, NY, U.S.A., 2006

The Soldier's War Slang Dictionary; T. Warner Laurce; Category Books, London, U.K., 1939

The Underworld Speaks; Albin J. Pollock's directory of slang; Prevent Crime Bureau, San Francisco, CA, USA, 1935

The World's Work: A History of Our Time, Volume 8, Walter Hinds Page, Arthur Wilson Page, Doubleday, New York. NY, U.S.A., August, 1904

The Yale Book of Quotations; Fred R. Shapiro; Yale University Press, New Haven, CT, U.S.A., 2006

2107 Curious Word Origins, Sayings & Expressions from White Elephants to a Song and Dance; Charles Earle Funk; minor reference, Galahad Books, New York, NY, U.S.A., 1993

Vocabulum, or The Rogue's Lexicon; George W. Matsell; The Lawbook Exchange, Ltd., London, U.K., 2005

Vulgaria; William Horman, headmaster of Winchester and Eton; England, 1519

Vulgaria quedam abs Terencio in Anglica[m] linguam traducta; Terence; Theodoric Rood and Thomas Hunte, Oxford, England, 1483

Why You Say It; Garrison Webb; Rutledge Hill Press, Nashville, TN, U.S.A., 1992

Wise-Crack Dictionary by George H. Maines and Bruce Grant, New York, NY, U.S.A., 1926

Wise Words and Wives' Tales: The Origins, Meanings and Time-Honored Wisdom of Proverbs and Folk Sayings Olde and New; Stuart Flexner and Doris Flexner; Avon Books, New York, NY, U.S.A., 1993

Woorkes. A dialogue conteynyng prouerbes and epigrammes; John Heywood's second book of proverbs; London, England, 1562

Wordsworth Book of Euphemism; Neaman, Judith S. and Silver; Carole G. Wordsworth Editions, Hertfordshire, UK, 1995

Other Books

Abrégé des vies des anciens philosophes; François Fénelon; Paris 1726, page 314 French, Translation: *Lives of the ancient philosophers;* page 202, English; London, 1825

Abridgment of the Debates of Congress, from 1789 to 1856; United States Congress by Thomas Hart Benton; published by D. Appleton, Washington, DC, U.S.A., 1857, 1858

Absolute Beginnings; Colin MacInnes, novel; MacGibbon & Kee, London, U.K., 1959

Abstracts on Money, Prices and Agriculture in the United Kingdom, page 247 Richard Wodnothe, London, U.K., 1655

A Bundle of Burnt Cork Comedy by Harry Lee Newton, pp 96, 197; T.S. Dennison and Co., Minneapolis, MN, USA, 1905

A Call to Account, , page 223; Chris Hajek; Dundurn Press; Canada, 2003

A Christmas Carol; Charles Dickens; London, U.K., 1843

A Companion to the Temple; Thomas Comber; England, 1676

A Complete Collection of State Trials and Proceedings for High Treason; Volume 32, William Clobett; London, U.K., 1824

A Cook's Tale; Geoffrey Chaucer, from *The Canterbury Tales;* Geoffrey Chaucer, England, 1395

A Country-man and a River (in a version of Aesop's Fables); Roger L'Estrange; London, England, 1692

A Cowboy Detective; Charles A. Siringo; W.B. Conkey Co., Chicago, IL, U.S.A., 1912

Accidental Young Seamen; Captain John Smith; London, England, 1626

A Chronicle of Secession; William Mumford Baker; page 194, New York, NY, U.S.A., 1866

A Circuit Rider: A Tale of the Heroic Age; Edward Eggleston; J.B. Ford and Co., New York, NY, U.S.A., 1874

A Companion to the Temple; Thomas Comber; London, U.K., 1676

A Compleat Collection of Genteel and Ingenious Conversation, According to the Most Polite Mode and Method; Jonathan Swift; London, U.K., 1738

A Complete Collection of State Trials and Proceedings for High Treason, Volume 2; page 68, London, England, 1730

A Connecticut Yankee in King Arthur's Court; Mark Twain; page 307, S.L. Clemmons, Harper and Brothers, New York, NY, U.S.A., 1889

A Conspectus of American Biography; page 739, New York, NY, U.S.A., 1906

A Damsel in Distress; novel, P.G. Wodehouse; George H. Duran, New York, NY, U.S.A., 1919

A Defence of Poetry; Percy Basshe Shelly; London, U.K.; written, 1821, published, 1840

A Defense of the Ancient Historians; Francis Hutchinson; Powell, Dublin, Ireland, 1734

Adventures of Gil Blas of Santillane; Translator Tobias Smollatt,—translated from the original *L'Histoire de Gil Blas de Santillane* by Alain-Rene Le Sage; Scotland; published anonymously, England, 1750

Aesop's Fables: The Four Oxen and the Lion, and *The Bundle of Sticks, Mercury and the Woodcutter, The Fox and the Lion; other fables, The Boy Who Cried Wolf, The Snake and the Crab, The Tortoise and the Hare; The Fox and the Grapes;* Aesop, Greece, sixth century B.C.

Aesop's Fables; William Claxton's English translation, London, England, 1484

A Family Secret, a novel; Elzey Hay; page 91, J.P. Lippencott and Co., Philladelphia, PA, U.S.A., 1867

Afsluttende uvidenskabelig Efterskrift; Søren Kierkegaard; Copenhagen, Denmark, 1846

Afloat and Ashore; or, The Adventures of Miles Wallingford; James Fenimore Cooper; page 13, Baudry's European Library, Paris, France, 1844

A Girl Named Mary; Juliette Wilbor Tompkins; Bobbs-Merrill Co., Indianapolis, IN, U.S.A., 1918

A Guide to Craps Lingo from Snake Eyes to Muleteeth; David Guzman, Chris Feagan; Snake Eyes, U.S.A., 1999

Aldershot, and all about it, with Gossip, Literary, Military, and Pictorial; Marianne Young; G. Routledge and Co., London, U.K., 1857

Alice in Wonderland; Lewis Carroll, Macmillan and Co., London, U.K., 1865

Alaska 1955 U.S. Congress House Committee hearings before the Subcommittee on Territorial and Insular Affairs; U.S. Government print office, Washington, DC, U.S.A., 1956

Aldyth, or, Let the End Try the Man; Jessie Fothergill; London, U.K., 1891

All round the Wrekin; Walter White; Chapman and Hall, London, England, U.K., 1860

All Trees were Green; Michael Harrison; England, U.K., 1936

Amelia; Henry Fielding; A. Millar, London, U.K., 1752

A Memorial of the Great Rebellion; Francis Henry Buffum; Franklin Press: Rand, Avery, & Co., Boston, MA, U.S.A., 1882

A Merchant Seaman Talks: My Name is Frank, by Frank Laskier, page 41; George Allen and Unwin, Ltd., London, 1941

American Nabob: novel, Holmes Moses Alexander; Harper and Brothers, New York, NY, U.S.A., 1939

American Writers: *A Collection of Literary Biographies, Volume One;* Mary Weigel; edited by A. Walton Litz and Leonard Unger; Scribner, New York, NY, U.S.A., 1974

A mirrour or glasse to know thyselfe; John Frith; London, England, 1532

A Most Remarkable Fella; Susan Loesser; Donald I. Fine, New York, NY, U.S.A., 1993

An Account of Colonel Crocket's Tour to the North and Down East; Davy Crocket; published by Cary and Hart, Philadelphia, PA, U.S.A., 1835

An answere to a letter of a Jesuited gentleman by his cousin; Anthony Copley; London, England, 1601

An Apology for the Life of George Anne Bellamy, George Anne Bellamy, London, UK, 1785

Ancient Law-Merchant; Gerald De Malynes; The Netherlands, 1622

Ancren Riwle; Anonymous monastic prose book; England, 1225

Andrew Carnegie; Joseph Frazier Wall; page 197, University of Pittsburg Press, Pittsburg, PA, U.S.A., 1989

A New Home, Who'll Follow, Or Glimpses of Western Life; Mrs. Mary Cleavers (Caroline Kirkland); Kessinger Publishing, London, England, UK, 1872

An Exposition on the Lord's Prayer by Ezekiel Hopkins, Lord Bishop of London-Derry, page 133, London, England, 1692

Anne of Green Gables; Lucy Maud Montgomery; L.C. Page and Co., Boston, MA, U.S.A., 1908

Anne on the Island; Lucy Maud Montgomery; McClelland, Goodchild and Stewart, Canada, 1915

Anne's House of Dreams; Lucy Maud Montgomery; McClelland, Goodchild and Stewart, Canada, 1917

An Old Fashioned Girl; Louisa May Alcott; New York, NY, U.S.A., 1902

An Open Letter to Hon. Henry Cabot Lodge; William Newton Osgood; page 9, Mass. Tarriff Reform League, Boston, MA, U.S.A., 1888

An Open Letter to the Christian Nobility of the German Nation Concerning the Reform of the Christian Estate, 1520, Charles Michael Jacobs, page 65, Lutheran Theological Seminary, Mt. Airy, Pennsylvania, 1915

A Petite Palace of Pettie His Pleasure; George Pettie; London England, 1576

A Pisgah-Sight of Palistine and the Confines Thereof; British theologian and historian, Thomas Fuller; London, England, 1650

A Place for Every Thing; and Every Thing in Its Place; Alice Bradley; Haven, D. Appleton and Co., New York, NY, U.S.A., 1857

A Poet's Proverbs; Arthur Guiterman; E.P. Dutton and Co., New York, NY, U.S.A., 1924

A Practical Treatise Concerning Humility; John Norris; London, U.K., 1707

Archaeological Writings of the Sanhedrin and the Talmuds of the Jews taken from the ancient parchments and scrolls of Constantinople and the Vatican being the record made by the enemies of Jesus of Nazareth in his day; page 14; translated by Rev. W.D. Mahon; Perrin & Smith, St. Louis, MO, U.S.A., 1884

Arciologia of Miscellaneous Tracts Relating to Antiquity; Society of Antiquitaries of London; London, U.K., 1803

Are You Decent? Willaim Smith; G. P. Putnam and Sons, New York, NY, U.S.A., 1927

Armadale; Wilkie Collins; Smith Elder & Co., London, U.K., 1866

Arte of Rhetorique; Thomas Wilson; London, England, 1560

A Rustic Moralist; William Ralph Inge; G.P. Putnam's Sons, London, U.K., 1937

A Short Story, Chapter XVI, The Contemporary Short Story, (author unknown), page 76, London, U.K., 1947

A Step from the New World to the old and Back Again; Henry Tappan; Appleton and Co., New York, N.Y., USA, 1852

A Stitch in Crime; Betty Hechtman, chapter 8; Penguin Group, NY, U.S.A., 2010

A supplement to Kennedy's Ophthalmographia, or Treatise of the eye; Peter Kennedy; 'Book of Operations of Surgery;' page 153, London, U.K., 1739

A Tangled Chain; Jane Ellen Panton; Ward and Downey, London, U.K., 1887

A Tenderfoot in All the Topics; Mack Cretcher; Crane and Company, Topeka, KS, U.S.A., 1918

A Terrible Temptation; Charles Reade; Estes, London, U.K., 1871

A Treasury of Sermon Illustrations; Charles Langworthy Wallace; Abingdon-Cokesbury Press, Nashville, TN, U.S.A., 1950

A treatise containing the practical part of fortification; John Muller; London, U.K., 1755

A Treatise of Military Discipline; Humphrey Bland; London, England, U.K., 1743

At the End of the Day: How Will You Be Remembered? James W. Moore; Abingdon Press, Nashville, TN, U.S.A., 2002

Autobiographical Sketches 1790-1803; Thomas De Quincy; page 453, London, U.K., 1863

A View of the Times, Their Principles and Practices: Volume I, The Rehersal; page 78; Charles Leslie's translation of alchemist Philalethes' seventeenth-century Latin writings, W. Bowen; London, U.K., 1750

A Vindication of the Government in Scotland: During the Reign of King Charles II; London, England, 1712

A Warning for Faire Women; Anonymous; George Sanders, London, England, 1599

A Wife for a Month; John Fletcher; London, England, 1624

A work on liberty; Thomas Hobbes; Wiltshire England, 1656

Ayenbite of Inwyt; Dan Michel; Kent, England, 1340

A Young Maid's Fortunes; published that year by Mrs. S. Hall (Anna Maria Felding); Dublin, Ireland, 1840

Back in the Day: Oral History, Folklore, and Outhouse Tales (or, Tales from the Three-holer) from Kennebec County, Maine, Volume 4; Messalonskee High School; Oakland, Maine, 2001

Back-in-your-face Guide to Pick-up Basketball; Chuck Wielgus and Alex Wolff; Everest House, New York, NY, U.S.A., 1986

Barnaby Rudge: A Tale of the Riots of 'Eighty; Charles; London, U.K., 1841

Battlefield Earth; Ron Hubbard; St. Martin's Press, New York, NY, U.S.A., 2011

Beat 'em or Join 'em by Clemett Garibaldi Lanni, Rochester Alliance Press in, Rochester, NY, U.S.A., 1931

Bentley's Miscellany, Volume 2; Portrait Gallery--No. IV; Cannon Family, Journey to Boulogne; Charles Bentley; London, U.K., 1837

Bentley's Miscellany Volume XLI, A Fisherman's Third Letter to His Chum in India; Charles Bentley; London, U.K., 1857

Best 143 Business Schools; page 20, Nedda Gilbert; Princeton Review Publishing, Random House, New York, NY, U.S.A., 2004

Bible

Genesis 2:7, 17, 3, 4:9, 5:21-27, 8:11 (NKJV), 22:12 (KJV), 47:27(ERV)

Exodus 3:8, 3:17, 5-12, 21:24, 33:3

Leviticus 11

Deuteronomy 8:3

I Samuel 17:1-58

II Samuel 31:4-5(Cloverdale Bible, 1535)

Ezra 6:9

Job 15:7, 19:20 Geneva Bible, 1560, 33:21(TLB, 1984)

Psalms 8:2 (KJV), 17:8, 23:1, 91:5, (Miles Cloverdale Bible, 1535), 100:3, 149:5 (KJV)

Proverbs3:15(KJV) 13:24(KJV), 16:18 (KJV), 17:22 (New KJV), 22:8, 23:7a (KJV), 26:17(KJV), 27:10, New American Standard Version

Ecclesiastes 1:14 (NLT), 4:6 (NIV), 9:4, 10:1(KJV), 10:20, 34:9 (Miles Cloverdale Bible, 1535)

Isaiah 6:5, (KJV, 28:23, (Miles Coverdale Bible, 1535), 40:15(KJV), 40:31, 40:31(KJV), 48:22and 57:20, 21 KJV, Miles Cloverdale Bible 53:7(ESV), 60:1 (KJV), 65:5, KJV, 1611

Jeremiah 5:21, 13:23a, 23:23-24 (NLT)

Ezekiel 18:2 (KJV, Miles Cloverdale Bible)

Daniel 5:1-4

Hosea 4:8 (KJV)

Matthew 3:11, 5:18, 5:37(ESV), 5:38, 39 (RSV); 45(KJV), 6:14, 6:22-23(ASV), 6:24(KJV), 6:34, 7:6,13-14(KJV), 7:12, (Miles Coverdale Bible, 1535), 8:25, 13, 12:24, (KJV), 12:24,25(ESB), 13:12(KJV), 14:8(NIV), 15:14, 16:8b (KJV), 19:20 (Wycliffe, 1382), 20:11-16, 24-32(ESV), 23:24(KJV), 26:52(KJV)

Mark 9:38-40, 15:37 (KJV)

Luke 3:26 (KJV), 4:23(KJV), 6:9, 15:1-6, 27(KJV) 19:46, 21:9; 22:44 (KJV, NIV)

John 8:7(KJV), 8:32(NIV), 11:44, 18, 19:17

Acts 8:32, 20:35

I Corinthians 13:8 (NIV), 15:52,(KJV)

II Corinthians 12:7 (KJV)

Galatians 5:4 (KJV); 5:22, 23(WYC), 6:7

I Timothy 4:7, 5:8 (KJV), 6:10, (KJV, NIV, ASV, NLT, D-R B)

II Timothy 4:1 Wycliffe, 1385, *(KJV)*, 1611, *4:7 (NIV)*

Titus 1:15 (NIV)

Hebrews 4:12(KJV), 8:12

Revelation 8:1 (Miles Cloverdale Bible), 21:9(KJV)

Bealby: A Holiday; H.G. Wells; London, U.K., 1915

Bill Nunn's Column Book, Bill Nunn, Westphalia Press, Loose Creek, MO, U.S.A., 1984

Blackbirding in the South Pacific, or, The first white man on the beach; William B. Churchward; S. Sonnenschein & Co., London, U.K., 1888

Black Thunder; Anna Wendell Bontemps; page 58, page 248, McMillian, New York, NY, U.S.A., 1936

Blaine and Logan Songbook: A Collection of Republican Campaign Songs, National Songgs, War Songs, Rally Songs, &c. adapted to the popular melodies of the day; S. Brainard and Sons, Cleveland, OH, U.S.A., 1884

Bond and Free, A Tale of the South; Ellen M. Ingram; New York, NY, U.S.A., 1882

Bonfire of the Vanities, Tom Wolfe, Farrar, Straus, Giroux, New York, NY, U.S.A., 1987

Booth and the Spirit of Lincoln: A Story of a Living Dead Man; J.B. Lippincott Company, New York, NY, U.S.A., 1925

Boscobel; Emma Mersereau Newton; W.B. Smith and Co., New York, NY, U.S.A., 1881

Britz, of Headquarters; Marcin BarberMoffat; Yard and Co., NY, U.S.A., 1910

Brother Jonathan or the New Englanders, John Neal, London, U.K., 1925

Build a Better Mousetrap; Ruth Kassinger; p. 1, John Waley & Sons, Hoboken, NJ, U.S.A., 2002

Bullets for the Bridegroom; David Dodge; McMillan Co., New York, NY, U.S.A., 1944

Burton Dane; Alfred E. Chirm; Alice Harriman, page 249, New York, NY, U.S.A., 1912, 1913

Business Directory and History of Jackson County (Kansas); Elizabeth N. Barr; Topeka, KS, U.S.A., 1907

Cases of Conscience; Bishop Joseph Hall; London, England, 1649

Candide; Voltaire; France, 1759

Canterbury Tales, Book IV; Geofrey Chaucer; London, England, 1386

Can't Wait to Get to Heaven; Fanny Flag; Ballantine Books division of Random House, New York, NY, U.S.A., 2007

Cap and Gown, the yearbook of the University of the South p 72; Sewanee, Tennessee, U.S.A., 1918

Caps for Sale (A Tale of a Peddler; Some Monkeys and Their Monkey Business); Esphyr Slobod-kina; Harper Collins, New York, NY, USA, 1987

Captain Roger Jones of London and Virginia; Lewis Hampton Jones; page 412: Joel Munsell's Sons, Albany, NY, U.S.A., 1891

Carlito's Way; Edwin Torres; New York, NY. U.S.A., 1975

Cases in Parliament: resolved and adjudged, upon petitions and writs of error; Bartholomew Shower; House of Lords, London, Great Britian, 1698

Catalogue of Copyright Entries, Third Series; 1968 Cuna Supply Cooperative application to the U.S. Copyright Office, Washington DC, U.S.A., 1971

Catalogue of Old and Rare Books; Pickering and Chatto, London, England, circa 1806

Catriona or *David Balfour;* Robert Louis Stevenson; London, U.K., 1893

Certain Tractates; Ninian Winget; William Blackwood and Sons, Edinburgh, Scotland and London, England, 1562

Champagne before Breakfast; Hy Gardner, H. Holt and Company, New York, NY, U.S.A., 1954

Charles and Julia; W. William Averell; printed for Edward White, London, England, 1581

Chesterfield Letter 9 Oct. 1746, III. 783; (First published 1932) Echo Library, Teddington, Middlesex, U.K., 2007

Chronicles of St. Mary's; S.D.N., Joseph Masters; London, U.K., 1868

Chums; Harleigh Severne, Griffith and Farran, London, U.K., 1878

Civil-Military Relations: An Annotated Bibliography; 1940-1952, Columbia University Press, New York, NY, U.S.A., 1954

Clarissa, or the History of a Young Lady; Samuel Richardson; London, England, 1748

Closer to Light; Melvin Morse, M.D. with Paul Perry, page 2, Random House, New York, NY, U.S.A., 1991

Closing of the American Mind; Allan Bloom; Simon and Schuster, New York, NY, U.S.A., 1987

Complete Works of Mr. Thomas Brown; Thomas Brown; S. Briscoe, London, England, 1710

Conclusion, from *Walden;* Henry David Thoreau; Ticknor and Fields, Boston, MA, USA, 1854

Congressional Record of the United States, the First Session of the 22nd Congress, in the *Diary of Alphonso Wetmore* from 1828 used by the Secretary of War, Hon. Lewis Cass; Washington, DC, USA, 7 December 1831

Consumer Health, Products and Services; Jessie Helen Haag; Lea & Febiger, New York, NY, U.S.A., 1976

Contemplative Man; Herbert Lawrence; Printed for J. Whitson, London, England, 1771

Cops and Constables, American and British Fictional Policemen; Earl F. Bargainnier and George N. Dove; Bowling Green State University Press, Bowling Green, OH, U.S.A., 1986

Corbitt's Political Register: Volume XXI; London, U.K., 1812

Country of the Pointed Firs; S. O. Jewett; Haughton Mifflin, Boston, MA, U.S.A., 1896

Crazy Like a Fox; Sidney J. Perelman; first published 1944, Garden City Publishing Company, New York, NY, U.S.A., 1945

Critical Teaching and Everyday Life; Ira Shor; originally published in Canada, 1945, renewed 1980

Curiosities of Litterature; Isaac Disraeli; Volume 1, page 370, Lilly, Wait, Coleman and Holden, Boston, MA, U.S.A., 1833

Damascus and Palmyra: A Journey to the East; Volume 1, George Greenstreet Addison, (pages 165-166), Richard Bentley, London, U.K, 1838

David Brown, D.D., LL.D.: professor and principal of the Free Church College, Aberdeen: a memoir; William Garden Blaikie; Hodder and Straughton, London, U.K., 1898

David Copperfield; Charles Dickens; Hablot, Knight, Browne, London, U.K., 1850

Dead to the World, or, Sin and Atonement by Klara Bauer, Rockwell and Churchill, Boston, MA, U.S.A., 1874

Death of a Peer; 'Dame Edith' Ngaio Marsh; New Zealand, London, U.K., 1940

Death Warmed Over; Mary Collins; Charles Scribner and Sons, New York, NY, U.S.A., 1947

Defence of the Government of the Church of England; Dr. John Bridges; M. Marprelate, Gent; London, England; written 1587, printed 1588

Design with Type; Carl Dair; University of Toronto Press, Toronto, ON, Canada, 1967

Desperate Characters; Paula Fox; W.W. Norton, New York, NY, U.S.A., 1970

Diary; C. Davis; U.S., 1865

Diary; Samuel Pepys; London, England, 1665

Diary; The First Earl of Shaftsbury; London, England, 1646

Diary and Letters of Madam d'Arblay; letter penned by Fanny Burney on 16 October 1786 published by Charlotte Barrett; Henry Colburn, London, U.K., 1842

D*ifferent Strokes for Different Folks: An Analysis of the Urban Lower Class Negro's Personality and Culture as Revealed in His Music, Rhythm and Blues;* thesis by Michael William Jacobs, published by Jane Addams Graduate School of Social Work; University of Illinois at Chicago, IL, U.S.A., 1969

D*o lo vuole;* Charles Victor Prévôt, (English Translation) Largo Montecalvario, Naples, Italy, 1849

Discours in Spain; Rousseau; originally published 1750, translated by J.R. Spell, Hispanic Review, Volume 2, No. 4 (Oct., 1934); pp. 334-344 published by University of Pennsylvania Press, Philadelphia, PA, U.S.A., 1934

Dombey and Son; Charles Dickens; London, U.K., published serially from 1846-1848

Domesticated Trout: How to Breed and Grow Them; Livingston Stone; Office of the Fishing Gazette, London, U.K. 1872

Donald Writes No More; Eddie Stone; Holloway House, Los Angeles, CA, U.S.A., 1974

Don Quixote; Miguel de Cervantes, Juan de la Cuesta; Spain, 1605, 1615; English translation, 1612, 1620

Down and Out: Studies in the Problem of Vagrancy; Mary Kingsland Higgs; published in the Student Christian Movement, New York, NY, U.S.A., 1924

Dracula; Bram Stoker; Archibald Constable and Company, U.K. & Republic of Ireland, 1897

Dramatic Works, John Dryden (1631-1700) about 1672, published London, U.K., 1935

Dred, a Tale of the Great Dismal Swamp, by Harriett Beecher Stowe, Volume 1, page 254; Brenhart Tauchnitz, Leipzig, Germany, 1856

Ecclesia Restaurata; Peter Heylyn; London, England, 1661

Edwin Alden & Brothers American Newspaper Catalogue; Cincinnati, OH, U.S.A., 1874

Effective Living, an Interdisciplinary Approach; Lois Smith Murray; Harper, New York, NY, U.S.A., 1960

Eight Cousins, Louisa May Alcott, New York, NY, U.S.A., 1875

El Ingenioso hidalgo don Quixote de la Mancha; Miguel de Cervantes; Spain, first published in Spanish also in the early seventeenth century, (1605, 1615) and translated into English shortly thereafter (1612, 1620).

Emmett Bonlore; Opie Percival Read; 2 references, F.J. Schulte and Co., Chicago, IL, U.S.A., 1891

Emmett Lawler, Jim Tully; Harcourt, Brace and Co., New York, NY, U.S.A., 1922

Emperor and Mystic: The Life of Alexander I of Russia; Francis Henry Gribble; E.P. Dutton & Co., Boston, MA, U.S.A., 1931

Enchiridion Militis Christiani (*Handbook of a Christian Knight*); (first written in Latin 1503-1504), Switzerland, Desiderus Erasmus; English Translation, London, England, 1533

Engineering and Mining Journal, McGraw Hill, New York, NY, U.S.A., 1930

England in the Reign of King Henry the Eighth, the Life and Letters of Thomas Starkey, London, England, circa 1538

English Works; John Wyclif; Oxford, England, circa 1380

Epistle to Cobham, Alexander Pope; pp 149-50, London, U.K., 1734

Essayes and characters of a prison and prisoners; Geffray Marshall; England, 1612

Essay on Liberalism; Andre Vieusseux; page 130, Pewtress, Low, and Pewtress, London, U.K., 1823

Essays of Elia; Charles Lamb; London, U.K., 1823

Essays on the Intellectual Powers of Man; Thomas Reid; L. White, Dublin, Ireland, 1786

Euphues and His England, John Lyly; London, England, 1580

Euphues: The Anatomy of Wit; John Lyly; London, England, 1578

Europae Speculum; Sir Edward Sandys; Paris, France, 1599

Evelina, or the History of a Young Lady's Entrance into the World; Fanny Burney; Thomas Lowndes, England, 1778

Examen poeticum; John Dryden; London, England, 1706

Executive Decisions; Rossall James Johnson; Southwestern Publishing Co., Cincinnati, OH, U.S.A., 1976

Experiment Perilous; Margaret S. Carpenter; Little Brow & Co., Boston, MA, U.S.A., 1943

Facts and Evidences on the Subject of Baptism; Charles Taylor; London, U.K., 1816

Failure is Not an Option; Gene Kranz; Berkley Publishing, New York, NY, U.S.A., 2000

Fake It Till You Make It; Inside Amway; Phil Kerns; Victory Press, Mooresville, NC, U.S.A., 1982

Fantastic Fables; Ambrose Bierce; Putnam, New York, NY, U.S.A., 1899

Father and Son; James Thomas Farrell, Edition 3 Vanguard Press, New Youk, NY, U.S.A., 1940

Fathers and Sons; Ivan Turgenev, *The Russian Messenger*, St. Petersburg, Russia, 1862

Father's Rights: Hard Hitting and Fair advice for Every Father; Jeffrey Leving and Kenneth Dachman; page 125, Basic Books, New York, NY, U.S.A., 1998

Favorite Poems from the Best Authors; Amy Nealy; Easy Street, poem by E.N. Stevens, 1894

Festial; (EETS) I. 230; John Mirk; Shropshire, England, circa 1389

Festivals; Arthur Day; (a book of sermons) London, England, 1615

Fifteen Decisive Events in California History, by Rockwell Dennis Hunt, page 50, Historical Society of Southern California, University of California, Berkley, 1959

Flow: The Psychology of Optimal Experience; Mihaly Csikszentmihalyi; Harper and Rowe, New York, NY, U.S.A., 1990

Folk Phrases of Four Counties; G.G. Northall; London, U.K., 1894

Fools Rush in Where Angels Fear to Tread; E.M. Forster; William Blackwood and Sons, London, U.K., 1905

Footprints Under the Window, Franklin W. Dixon, Simon and Shuster, New York, NY, U.S.A., 1933
Forty Liars and Other Lies, Bill Nye; page 119, Belford, Clarke and Co., Chicago, IL, U.S.A., 1883

Foure Sonnes of Aymon; William Caxton translator; Octavia Richardson, editor; London, England, 1489

Foxes Book of Martyrs; John Fox; London, England, 1570

Frederick de Montford; a novel, Volume 1; Edward Goulburn; page 176, John Ebers, London, U.K., 1811,

Freedom and Crisis; Allen Weinstein; Random House, New York, NY, U.S.A., 1974

Freedom is a Two-edged Sword; John W. Parsons; written about 1950, first published posthumously New Falcon Publications, Las Vegas, NE, 1996

From a Colonial Governor's Note-book; a history of the Caribbean and West Indies, Sir Reginald St. Johnson; Hutchison and Co., Ltd. London, U.K., 1936

From Pillar to Post; anonymous; London, U.K., 1864

Gammer Gurton's Garland, or, the Nursery Parnassus; Joseph Ritson; printed for R. Christopher, London, U.K, 1783

Garden of Pleasure; James Sanford; London, England, 1573

Garrick's vagary, or, England run mad; with particulars of the Strafford Jubilee; S. Bladon, London, England, 1769, (David Garrick's writings about Shakespeare)

Geographica, Lib. VIII; page 361, Stabo (Στράβων *Strabōn);* Greece, 64/63 B.C. – circa 24 A.D.

Geographical, Historical, Political, Philosophical and Mechanical Essays; Lewis Evans; B. Franklin and D. Hall, Philadelphia, page 29, 1855

Glory for Me; MacKinlay Kanto;, Coward-McCann Inc., New York, NY, U.S.A., 1945

God's Statesman, The Life and Work of John Owen; Peter Toon; page 52, Paternoster Press, Milton Keynes, U.K., 1972

Go Fight City Hall, Ethel Rosenberg; New York, NY, U.S.A., 1949,

Golden Girl; Nancy Tilly; Dell Publishing Co., New York, NY, U.S.A., 1988

Gone with the Wind; Civil War epic, Margaret Mitchell, McMillan, New York, NY, U.S.A., 1936

Good Night Little Spy; Eric Koch; Virgo Press, Toronto, ONT, Canada, 1979

Growing an Inch; Stanley Gordon West; Lexington-Marshall Publishing Co., Bozeman, MT, U.S.A., 1988

Guantanamo Remembered, Jack Campbell, page 160, Author House, Bloomington. IL, U.S.A., 2008

Gulliver's Travels; Jonathan Swift; London, U.K., 1727

Hall's Chronicles of Richard III, (A Source for Shakespeare's play) Oxford, England, 1548

Hans Beer-Pot; Dabridgcourt Belchier; London, England, 1618

Hard Times; Charles Dickens; Hablot, Knight, Browne, London, U.K., 1854

Harley MS 3362, circa 1470 listed in *Restrospective Review,* British Library, 1854

Harrison's British Classiks: The Idler, Fitzosbourne's Letters, page 90 in *Epigram on the Feuds between Mendel and Bonicini;* Harrison and Co., London, U.K., 1787

Hawk Eyes; Robert J. Burdette; G.W. Carleton and Co., New York, NY, U.S.A., 1879

Heads of the People: or, Portraits of the English; essay titled *Tavern Heads,* Charles Whitehead; Robert Tyas, London, U.K., 1811

Heaven, Hell or Hoboken; Ray Neil Johnson, page 168; E. S. Hubbard Printing, Cleveland, OH, U.S.A., 1919

Hecatomythium; Laurentius Abstemius; fable in Latin called *De rustico amnem transituro,* Italy, 1490

Hell upon Earth; anonymous; London, England, 1703

Henry Fielding; Tom Jones, London, England, 1749

Henry VI's Triumphal Entry into London; John Lydgate; London, England, circa 1435

Hereward the Wake; Charles Kingsley; T. Nelson & Sons, London, England, circa 1035-1072

Hidden workes of darkenes brought to publike light; William Prynne, page 47; Thomas Brudenell, London, England, 1645

Highways and Byways of the South; Clifton Johnson; MacMillan and Co., New York, NY, U.S.A., 1904

Hints to my Countrymen; Theodore Sedgewick; J. Seymour, New York, NY. U.S.A., 1826

His Friend Miss McFarlane; Kate Langley Bosher; chapter 20; Harper & Brothers, New York, NY, U.S.A., 1919

History of New Netherland or, New York Under the Dutch; Edmund Bailey O'Callaghan; page 168: Bartlett and Welford, New York, NY, U.S.A., 1848

History of the Commune of 1871; Lissagaray, Ballentine Press, Edinburgh, Scotland, U.K., 1898

History of the Spanish American War; Henry Waterson; page 31, The Werner Co., New York, NY, U.S.A., 1898

His True Arte of Defense; Giacomo di Grassi;   London, England, 1570

H. Murray: Life & Real Adventures; Hamilton Murray; J. Burr, London, England, 1759

Hoi Toide on the Outer Banks: The Story of the Ocracoke Brogue; Walt Wolfram and Natalie Schilling-Estes; page 40, University of North Carloina Press, Raleigh, NC, U.S.A., 1997

Hollywood Girl, novel, Patrick McEvoy; Simon & Schuster, New York, NY, USA, 1929

Hollywood with Bugs Baer and Henry Major; Arthur 'Bugs' Baer and Henry Major; Daniel Murphy and Co., Inc., New York, NY, U.S.A., 1938

Homer Travestie (A Burlesque Translation of Homer); Thomas Brydges; G.G. & J. Robinson, London, England, U.K., 1797

How to Solve the Mismanagement Crisis; Ishak Adizes; Dow Jones-Irwin, New York, NY, U.S.A., 1979

Icebergs; Rebecca Johns; Bloomsbury Publishing, London, U.K., 2007

I Couldn't Care Less; Anthony Phelps; Harborough Publishing, London, England, UK, 1946

If I were King; Justin Huntley McCarthy; Grossett and Dunlap, New York, NY, U.S.A., 1901

Indiscretions of Archie; P.T. Wodehouse; Herbert Jenkins, London, England, U.K., 1921

Ingoldsby Legends; Richard Barham; London, U.K., 1840

In Pastures New; George Ade; McClure, Phillips and Co., New York, NY, U.S.A., 1906

Intermarriage, Interfaith, Interracial, Interethnic; Albert Isaac Gordon; Beacon Press, Boston, MA, U.S.A., 1964

In the Schillingscourt; Eugenie Marlitt; A.L. Burt, New York, NY, U.S.A., 1879

Introduction to the Young Ladies Elocutionary Reader; William and Ana U. Russell; James Munroe and Company, Boston, MA, USA, 1845

Is it Possible to Make the Best of Both Worlds? Thomas Binney; James Nisbet and Co., London, U.K., 1925

Island in the Sun; Alec Waugh; Farrar, Straus and Giraux, New York, NY, U.S.A., 1955

Is Your Child Drinking; Nancy Hyden Woodword, Putmam, Ne York, NY, U.S.A., 1981

It All happened in Renfro Valley, Pete Stamper, University Press of Kentucky, Lexington, KY, U.S.A., 1999

It Hit Me Like a Ton of Bricks; Catherine Lloyd Burns; North Point Press, Division of Farrar, Straus and Giroux, New York, NY, U.S.A., 2006

It is Never Too Late to Mend; Charles Reade; London, U.K., 1856

It Only Takes a Minute to Change Your Life; Willie Jolly; McMillan, New York, NY, U.S.A., 1997

It's a Jungle out There; Susan Collins; Harper Collins, New York, NY, U.S.A., 1924

Ivanhoe; Sir Walter Scott; A. Constable, London, England, UK, 1820

I've had it—Up to Here; John W. Urban; Adams Press, Chicago, IL, U.S.A., 1984

Jacob's well: an English treatise on the cleansing of man's conscience; Anonymous; originally published circa 1450, Ed. Arthur Brandeis, EETS o.s. 115. Kegan Paul, Trench, Trübner & Co., London, U.K., 1900

Japhet, In Search of a Father; Captain Frederick Marryat; England, U.K., 1836

Jesuit Relations; Reuben Gold Thwaites; Burrows Brothers Co., Cleveland, OH, U.S.A., 1644

Jesus, the Son of Man; Kahil Gabrin; Alfred A. Knopf, New York, NY, U.S.A., 1928

Jonah's Gourd Vine; Zora Neale Hurston; Harper Collins, New York, NY, U.S.A., 1934

Journal of the Senate of the United States of America, 1804, in an article titled *William Duane & Son* on page v, Michael Glazier, Wilmington, DE, U.S.A., 1804

Journal to Stella; Jonathan Swift; London, U.K., 1710-1713

Klosterheim; or The Masque; Thomas De Quincy; Whittemore, Niles and Hall, Boston, MA, U.S.A., 1855

Lady Sings the Blues; Billie Holiday; chapter 24, page 203, Barrie and Jenkins, London, U.K., 1973

Lady Windermere's Fan; Oscar Wilde; London, U.K., 1892

Law Notes; page 115, London, U.K., 1897

Lawrie Todd; John Galt; page 247, Henry Colburn and Richard Bentley, London, U.K., 1830

Legal Examiner, Volume 1; page 508, Great Britain Courts, London, U.K., 1832

Legends of a Log Cabin; Chandler Robbins Gilman, page 198, George Dearborn, New York, NY, U.S.A., 1835

Leisure Thoughts in Prose and Verse; Thomas Palmer Moses; Samuel Badger Portsmouth, NH, U.S.A., 1849

Letters of Harriett, Countess Granville, 1810-1845, Volume II; edited by her son, Edward Frederick Leveson-Gower; Longmans, Green and Co., London, U.K., 1894

Letters of Perigrine Pickle; George Putnam Upton; Western News Co., Chicago, IL, U.S.A., 1869

Letters of the Late Mr. Laurence Sterne to his Most Intimant Friends; Laurence Stone; T. Becket, London, U.K., 1775

Letters on demonology and witchcraft; Sir Walter Scott; London, England, 1829

Life Begins at Forty; W.B. Patkin; Columbia University, New York, NY, U.S.A., 1932

Life eternall, or, a treatise Of the knowledge of the divine Essence and Atribvtes; John Preston; Sermon, 'A Heavenly Treatise of Divine Love,' page 435, London, England, 1634

Life in a Putty Knife Factory; H. Allen Smith, Doubleday, Doran and Co., New York, NY., U.S.A., 1943

Life in Sing Sing; by "Number 1500;" Bobbs-Merrill and Company, Indianapolis, IN, U.S.A., 1904

Life in the Ranks of the British Army in India and on Board a Troopship; J. Brunlees Patterson, John and Robert Maxwell; Milton House, London, U.K., 1885

Life of Henry W. Grady; Joel Chandler Harris; Atlanta, GA, U.S.A., 1890

Life of Samuel Johnson; James Boswell, London, U.K., 1769

Life without Drudgery; (1854-1863) *The Writings of Henry David Thoreau;* vol. 4, p. 458, Henry David Thoreau; Houghton Mifflin, Boston, MA, U.S.A., 1894

Light in August; William Faulkner; original copyright, 1932, Vintage books, Random House, New York, NY, U.S.A., 1985

Littell's Living Age, Volume 1; Eliakim Littell, Robert S. Littell; page 206, Littell and Co., Boston, MA, U.S.A., 1844

Lincoln's Own Yarns and Stories; Alexander McClure; John C. Winston Co., Chicago, IL, U.S.A., 1901

Literary Gazette and Journal of the Belles Lettres; London, U.K., 1841

Littell's Living Age, Fifth Series Volume LX; Robert S. Littell; Littell and Co., Boston, MA, U.S.A., 1887

Little Ten Minutes, or A Pastor's Talks with Children; talk, *Love's Scales, Why the Baby Wasn't Heavy;* Frank Tappan Bayley, D.D.; published in London, Edinburgh, New York, Chicago and Toronto, CA, 1909

Little Women; Louisa May Alcott; London, U.K., 1868

Lives of the noble Grecians and Romanes; Plutarch; Sir Thomas North's translation; London, England, 1579

London and Its Environs Described; set of books published by R. and J. (Robert and James) Dodsley, London, U.K., 1761

Louisa May Alcott's Life, Letters and Journals, letter dated in New York, Dec. 4, 1875 Library of Alexandria, Baltimore, MD, U.S.A., 1924

Love for Love: a Comedy; William Congreve; page 108, T. Johnson, London, England, 1720

Love Letters of Eminent Persons; edited by Charles Martel; letter, March, 1801 from Lord Nelson to Lady Hamilton, published by Ward, Lock and Tyler, London, U.K., 1860

Lt. of Searthey; E. Castle; London, U.K., 1895

Luther's Commentarie upon the fiftene psalms; Martin Luther; Henry Bull's English translation, London, England, 1577

Lyrics & Lays; Pips, Wyman Brothers, Hare St. Calcutta, India, 1867

Maggie: a Girl of the Streets, Stephen Crane, page 120, D. Appleton and Co., New York, NY, U.S.A., 1896

Major Jones' Courtship; William T. Thompson; Augusta, GA, USA, 1842

Manual of British Rural Sports: Fourth Edition; "Stonehenge;" page 161, Routledge, Warnes and Routledge, London, U.K., 1859

Marriage: How to Keep a Thing Growing; John W. Drakeford; Impact Books, Atascadero, CA, U.S.A., 1979

Mary Barton; Elizabeth Gaskell; (published anonymously) London, U.K., 1848

Mary Barton and Other Tales; Elizabeth C. Gaskell; page 443 in *Bessy's Troubles at Home,* Smith, Elder and Co, London, U.K., 1895

Masonic Odes and Poems; Robert Morris; Knight and Leonard, Chicago, IL, U.S.A., 1880

Masters of the Dew; English version of Jacque Romain's Haitian text; translated by Langston Hughes and Mercer Cook; Reynal & Hitchcock, New York, NY, U.S.A., 1947

Matthew Henry's Complete Bible Commentary; Matthew Henry; England, 1708-1710

Memoirs; John Quincy Adams; first published J. B. Lipincott and Co., Philadelphia, PA, U.S.A., 1874

Memoirs; William Hickey (1749-1830) Alfred Spencer, Hurst & Bkackett, Lomdon, U.K., 1913

Memoir of the Life of Leiutenant General Daniel Burr; W. Bulmer and W. Nicol, London, U.K., 1821

Memoirs of the Life of Mrs. Elizabeth Carter; Montagu Pennington; F.C. & J. Rivington, London, U.K., 1807

Memory and the Executive Mind; Arthur Raymond Robinson; M.A. Donohue and Co., Chicago, IL, U.S.A., 1912

Men are from Mars, Women are from Venus; John Gray; Harper-Collins, New York, NY, U.S.A., 1992

Metamorphosis; Ovid, English translation by Arthur Golding; London, England, 1565

Millionaire 101; Emanual Sarmiento, Jr.; title for Lesson 8 on page 4: Brickell Int., LaVergne, TN, 2004

Misty Row; B.K. Shropshire; i Universe, Lincoln, NE, U.S.A., 2005

Molly Bawn; Margaret Wolfe Hungerford, pseudonym, 'The Duchess'; Hurst and Co., New York, NY, U.S.A., 1878

Moralia; Plutarch; Chaeronea, Greece, circa 95AD

Most Interesting Voyages and Travels in All Parts of the World Volume 8; John Pinkerton; Longman, Hurst, Rees, Orme and Brown, London, U.K., 1811

Murder Day By Day; Irvin Shrewsbury Cobb, Bobbs-Merrill New York, NY, USA, 1933

Museum of Foreign Literature, Science and Art; Volume 44, *Jack Hinton, the Guardsman;* Charles Lever; page 419, E. Littell and Co., Philadelphia, PA, U.S.A., 1842

Mystery of godliness considered in LXI sermons wherein the diety of Christ is prov'd upon no evidence than the Word of God and no other View than for the Salvation of Men; Thomas Bradbury; Tho. Cox, London, U.K., 1726

Naaman the Syrian, his Disease and Cure; Daniel Rogers; London, England, 1642

Narcotics and Narcotic Addiction; David W. Maurer and Victor H. Vogel; 3rd Edition, Charles C. Thomas, Springfield, IL, U.S.A., 1967

Narrative of the life of David Crockett; David Crockett; E.L. Cary and E. Hart, New York, NY, USA, 1834

Narrenbeschwörung (Appeal to Fools); Thomas Murner; Germany, 1512

New Campus Writings; Judson Jerome and Nolan Miller; Second Edition, Tillie Olsen's 'Hey Sailor, What Ship;' Bantam Books, New York, NY, 1957

New Medical and Physical Journal, or, Annals of Medicine, Natural History and Chemistry; William Shearman; Volume 9, page 474; Royal College of Physicians, London, U.K., 1815

New Sonnets and Pretty Pamphlets; Thomas Howell; London, England, 1570

Nightmares and Dreamscapes; Stephen King; Signet, New York, NY, U.S.A., 1994

Ninety-three; English translation of Victor Hugo's French novel; London, U.K., 1874

Northern Memoirs, calculated for the meridian of Scotlan'; Richard Franck; London, England, 1648

Notes and Queries: A Medium of Inter Communication for Literary Men, Artists, Antiquaries, Genealogists, Etc.; page 164, Edinburgh, Scotland, 1851

Notes and Queries: A Medium of Ente-communication for Literary Men, General Readers, etc., Fourth Series, Volume Nine; by Oxford Journals; published in London, U.K., 1872

Number Seventeen; Henry Kingsley; London, U.K., 1875

Nuttie's Father; Charlotte Mary Yonge (1823-1901); MacMillan, London, England, U.K., 1885

Obedience of Christian Man; William Tyndale; London, England, 1528

Obligations of the Bone; Dick Cluster, page 78; St. Martin's Press, New York, NY, U.S.A., 1992

Observations by Mr. Dooley; Finley Peter Dunn, page 149-150; Harper and Brothers. New York, NY, U.S.A., 1906

Odyssey; Homer, Greece

Official Gazette of the United States Patent Office; Washington, DC, U.S.A., 1924

Of Human Bondage; W. Somerset Maugham; Geroge H. Duran Co., London, U.K., 1915

Of Mice and Men; John Steinbeck, Covici Friede, New York, NY, U.S.A., 1937

Of Prelates; John Wycliffe, London, U.K., 1382

Ogeechee Cross-firings; Richard Malcolm Johnston, page 9; Harper and Brothers, New York, NY, U.S.A., 1889

Old Times in Tennessee; Josephus Conn Guilt; page 114: Tavel, Eastman and Howell, Nashville, TN, U.S.A., 1878

Oliver Twist; Charles Dickens; (Chapter 43), London, U.K., 1839

One Day in the Life of Ivan Denisovich by Aleksandr Isaevich Solzhenitsyn, Farrar Straus Giroux, NY, (1971 English Translation) original copyright by Soviet Literary Magazine *Novy Mir*, 1962

One in Twelfth U.S. Infantry, 1798—1919; Knickerbocker Press, New York, NY, U.S.A., 1919

One Trick Pony; Daniella Brodsky; Random House, New York, NY, U.S.A., 2008

On Nature's Trail: A wonder book in the wild; F. St. Mars; Hodder and Stoughton, New York, NY, USA, 1912

On The Origin of the Species by Means of Natural Selection; Charles Darwin; John

Murray, London, England, UK, 1859

Orbital System of the Universe; Anthony Welsch; 1875, page 122, Allen and Bowers, Clinton, IA, 1875

Ornithological Rambles in Sussex; Arthur Edward Knox, page 227; John Van Voorst, London, UK, 1849

Our Boys and Our Girls; Oliver Optic; New York, NY, U.S.A., 1871

Our Cruise of New Guinea; Arthur Louis Keyser; W. Ridgway, London, U.K., 1845

Outlandish Proverbs; (no. 343), George Herbert; London, England, 1640

Outlaws of America: The Underground Press and its Content, Roger Lewis; Penguin Press, New York, NY, U.S.A., 1972

Over the Wire and on TV: CBS and UPI Campaign '80; compiled by Michael J. Robinson and Margaret A. Sheehan CBS, UPI, Russell Sage Foundation, New York, NY, U.S.A., 1983

Owain Goch; William Bennett; (solicitor),Volume 1, page 4, Longman, Rees, Orme, Brown, and Green, London, U.K., 1827

Pamela; Samuel Richardson; London, U.K., 1739

Paris Sketch Book; William Makepeace Thackeray; London, U.K., 1840

Parlimentary Debates of 1907; London, U.K., published in 1908

Paroemiologia Anglo-Latino; John Clarke; London, England, 1639

Paul Green's Wordbook: An Alphabet of Reminiscence, Appalachian Consortium Press, Boone, NC, U.S.A., 1990

Paul Preston's Voyages, Travels and Remarkable Advantures as Related by Himself; Paul Preston; Monroe and Francis, Boston, MA, U.S.A., 1847

Peck's Red-headed Boy; George Wilber Peck, page 42; Hurst and Co., New York, NY, U.S.A., 1901

Perspectives of American English; Joey Lee Dillard; citing the *Jewish Digest* and the *New York Times;* Mouton Publishing Co., The Hague, Netherlands, printed Great Britain, 1980

Peter, A novel of which he is not the hero; F. Hopkinson Smith; page 265, Charles Scribner's Sons, New York, NY, U.S.A., 1908

Pharmacomastix: Or, the Office, Use, and Abuse of Apothecaries Explained; Charles

Lucas; London, England, 1785

Phillip Brooks, the Man, the Preacher and the Author; Newell Dunbar; John K. Hastings, Boston, MA, U.S.A., 1893.

Philosophical Transactions; England's Royal Society, London, U.K., 1736

Pick-Me-Up; poem *If Wishes Were Aught;* London, U.K., 27 August 1892

Piers Plainnes Seaven Yeres Prentiship; Henry Chettle; London, England, 1595

Piers Plowman; B text, William Langland, ed. W. W. Skeat; Early English Text Society, 1869, original, London, England, circa 1377

Pigs to Market; George Agnew Chamberlain; Bobbs-Merrill Co., Indianapolis, IN, U.S.A., 1920

Pilgrimage; Samuel Purchas; England, 1613

Pinocchio; Carlo Collodi; Florence, Italy, 1883

Platform and Pulpit; George Bernard Shaw; London, U.K., 1932

Plinius Naturalias Historia XXXI; Pliny the Elder, Gaius Plinius Secundus (23 AD – August 25, 79 AD); Rome, 1ST Century AD, English translation, John Bostock and H.T. Riley; London, England, UK, 1855

Plutarch's Lives of the noble Grecians and Romanes; late first century, Plutarch; originally in Greek, Sir Thomas North; English translation, London, England, 1579

Poems on several occasions Together with the song of the three children; Mary, Lady Chudleigh; Printed by W. B. for Bernard Lintott, London, England, 1703

Poems Public and Private; Edited by John Conlee; Originally Published in *William Dunbar: The Complete Works;* Medieval Institute Publications, Kalamazoo, Michigan, U.S.A., 2004

Political Ballads; Milton Oswin Percival; London, England, 1731

Popular Tales from the Norse; Christian Asbjorbnsen, George Webber Dasent; story *Buttercup* Translations from the Norske Folkceventyr into English R.& R. Clark, London, U.K. for Edmonston and Douglas, Edinburgh, Scotland, U.K., 1859

Porcupine's Works; Containing Various Writings and Selections by William Corbett, Volume 9; Corbett and Morgan, London, U.K.; published in May, 1801, in a 'Gazette Selection' from September, 1798

Principles of Psychology; William James; New York, NY, U.S.A., 1890

Private Sea Journals; Admiral Sir Thomas Pasley, bart., 1778-1782; published by J.M.

Dent and Sons, London, U.K., 1931

Proceedings of the Annual Meeting of the State Association of Young Men's Christian Associations (YMCA); New York, NY, U.S.A., February 17-20, 1887

Prosopopoia, or, Mother Hubberd's Tale; Edmund Spenser; London, England, 1591

Psmith Journalist; P.G. Wodehouse; Adam & Charles Black, London, U.K., 1915

Public Papers of the Presidents of the United States; Harry S. Truman; Washington, DC, U.S.A., 1940

Pudd'nhead Wilson's Calendar; Mark Twain; New York, NY, U.S.A., 1894

Quaker to Catholic: Mary Howitt, Lost Author of the 19th Century; Joy Dunicliff; St. Clair Publications, McMinnville, TN, U.S.A., London, U.K., 2010

Quevedo's Comical Works; John Stevens' English translation; London, England, 1707

Quintessence of Ibsenism; George Bernard Shaw; Brentano's, New York, NY, U.S.A., 1913

Racing Maxims and Methods of Pittsburgh Phil; George E. Smith; Casino Press, E.W. Cole, New York, NY, USA, 1908

Rainbow Round my Shoulder: The Blue Trail of Black Ulysses; Howard Washington; Odum, Indiana, University Press, Blumington, IN, U.S.A., 1928

Ranier of the Last Frontier; John Marvin Dean; Thomas Y. Crowell, New York, NY, U.S.A., 1911

Readings in Guidance; Lester D. and Alice Crow; David McKay Co., New York, NY, U.S.A., 1962

Readings in Marketing; Phillip R. Cateora; Meredith Publishing, New York, NY, U.S.A., 1967

Reason and Religion, or the Certain Rule of Faith; Edward Worsley; page 332: Michael Cnobbaert, Antwirp, Belgium, 1672

Real Life in London, Pierce Egan, London, U.K., 1821

Recollections of a New York Police Chief; George Washington Walling; Caxton Book Concern, New York, NY, U.S.A., 1887

Reflections on a Flower Garden; James Hervey; J. & J. Rivington, London, England, 1746

Reflections on Life; Stanley J. St. Clair, St. Clair Publications, McMinnville, TN, U.S.A., 2010

Reflections on the Love of God; Lorenzo Dow; J. Borne, Bemersley, England, UK, 1836

Reflections on several of Mr. Dryden's plays; Elkanah Settle; Printed for William Whitwood, London, England, 1687

Relations and Observations Historical and Political upon the the Parliament begun Anno Dom. 1604; Clement Walker; London, England, 1648

Riligio Medici, Sir Thomas Browne, London, England, 1642, 1643

Religious Meditations, Of Heresies; Sir Francis Bacon; London, England, 1597

Remaines of a Greater Worke Concerning Britaine; William Camden; London, England, 1614

Remember the Golden Rule; Brant Parker and Johnny Hart; New York, NY, U.S.A., 1971

Reminiscences; Henry Angelo; Paris, France, 1830

Report of Proceedings of the 33rd Annual Convention of the American Federation of Labor; held in Seatle, Washington, page 385, The Law Reporter Printing Co., Washington, DC, U.S.A., 1913

Report of the Debates and Proceedings of the Convention for the Revision of the Constitution of the State of Kentucky; R. Sutton; page 376, A.G. Hodges and Co., Frankfort, KY, U.S.A., 1849

Report of the Forest Divorce Case; Catherine Norton Sinclair Forest; New York State Superior Court, Dewitt and Davenport, New York, NY, U.S.A., 1852

Reports and Cases Argued and Determined in the Supreme Court of Judicator; Skilding and Haight v Warren, May, 1818; William Johnson; New York Supreme Court, Ney York, NY, U.S.A., 1819

Reports of Cases Argued and Determined in the Circuit Court of the United States for the First Circuit; In a case in Massachusetts in October, 1819, compiled by attorney William P. Mason; Wells and Lily, Boston, MA, U.S.A., 1824

Rhubarb; Harry Allen Smith; Doubleday, New York, NY, U.S.A., 1946

Robin Hood's Barn; Alice Brown; The McMillan Company, New York, NY, U.S.A., 1912

Rochester Sketchbook; Arch Merrill; Aquarian Books, Chicago, IL, U.S.A., 1946

Roots; Alex Haley; Doubleday, New York, NY, U.S.A., 1976

Rory O'More; Samuel Lover; London, U.K., Richard Bentley, 1837

Roughing It; Mark Twain; American Publishing Company, Chicago, IL, U.S.A., 1872

Royal Commission on the Press; minutes of Great Britain's Parliament, G.E. Eyre and W. Spottiswoode; London, U.K., 1812

Russian Prohibition; Ernest Baron Gordon; American Issue Publishing Co., Waterville, OH, U.S.A., 1916

Russia on our Minds: Reflections on another World; Delilah and Ferdinand Kuhn; Doubleday, New York, NY, U.S.A., 1970

Rustic Speech and Folk-lore; Elizabeth Wright; New York, NY, U.S.A., 1913

Sacred Poems or Brief Meditions Of the day in generall and all the days in the weeke; Edward Browne; poem titled 'Of the Night,' page 14, London, England, 1641

Saducismus Triumphatus: Or, Full and Plain Evidence Concerning Witches and Apparitions; Joseph Glanvil; page 223, J. Collins, London, England, 1581

St. Marher, writings; Britain, 1225

St. Ronan's Well; Sir Walter Scott; Archibald, Constable and Co., Edinburgh, Scotland, 1834

Sam Loyd's Cyclopedia of 5000 Puzzles, Tricks and Conundrums (With Answers); Sam Loyd; Lamb Publishing, New York, NY, U.S.A., 1914

Saratoga: an Indian Tale of Frontier Life; Daniel Shepherd; page 64, T.B. Peterson and Brothers, Philadelphia, PA, U.S.A., 1787

Sartor Resartus; Thomas Carlyle; London, U.K., 1831

School for Scandal; Richard B. Sheridan; London, England, 1777

Science: Sense and Nonsense; John Lighten Singe; Ayer Publishing, Manchester, NH, U.S.A., 1951

Second Fruits; John Florio; London, England, 1591

Seed-Time and Harvest, Fritz Rueter, English translation London, U.K.,1878

Select Beauties of English Poetry, Volume 2; Henry Headley; *Lesbia on her Sparrow;* W. Cartwright, London, U.K., 1787

Selected English Works; John Wyclif; London, England, circa 1380

Martialis Epigrammata selecta: *(Select Epigrams of Martial), Book XII;* Ep. LXIV, translated into English by Gulielmus Hay, U.K., 1755

Sense and Sensibility; Jane Austen, Thomas Egerton; Military Library, Whitehall, London, U.K., 1811

Sermons; John Foxe; London, U.K., 1570

Sermons on Various Subjects; Christmas Evans, translated from the Welsh by J. Davis; London, U.K., 1837

Several Sermons on the Fifth of St. Matthew; The Reverend Dr.Anthony Horneck; Sermon XI, Second Edition, London, England, 1706

Shipwreck: the Strange Adventures of Renny Mitchum, messboy of the trading schooner "Samarang;" Howard Pease; Doubleday, New York, NY, U.S.A., 1957

Silas Marner; George Eliot; chapters 8, 11 and 14, London, U.K., 1861

Since Yesterday; Fredrick Lewis Allen; New York 1939, later, Harper Collins, New York, NY, U.S.A., 1975

Skating on Thin Ice; Nicholas Walker; Blackie Children's Books, Blackie & Son, London, U.K., 1988

Sketches from Cambridge by a Don; Sir Leslie Stephen; Kessinger Publishing, LLC, London, England, UK, 1865

Slight Reminiscences of the Rhine, Switzerland and a Corner of Italy; Mary Baddington; Volume 2, page 125, Carrey, Lee and Blanchard, Philadelphia, PA, U.S.A., 1835

Social Theory and Social Structure, Robert K. Merton, Free Press, New York, NY, U.S.A., 1949, 1857, 1968

Society and Solitude: twelve chapters; Ralph Waldo Emerson; James R. Osgood, Boston, MA, U.S.A., copyright 1870, 1876

Some Fruits of Solitude; William Penn; Philadelphia, PA, U.S.A., 1693 and (ed. 5), 1699

Songes and Sonettes, aka *Tottel's Miscellany;* Richard Tottel's poetical anthology; London, England, 1557

used it in *Sonnets of a Suffragette;* Burton Braley, p 188; Brown and Howell Co., Chicago, IL, U.S.A., 1913

Southern Discomfort; Rita Mae Brown, page 44; Harper and Row, New York, NY, 1982

Speeches, Poems and Miscellaneous Writings; Charles Jewett, M.D.; page 146, Boston, MA, U.S.A., 1849

Stars on the Sea; Frances van Wyck Mason; J.B. Lippincott Company, Philadelphia, PA, U.S.A., 1940

Stiff Upper Lip, Jeeves; P.G. Wodehouse; London, UK, 1935

Strange Story; Hilda Winifred Lewis; Random House, New York, NY, U.S.A., 1945, 1947

Strength for Service to God and Country; Norman Eugene Nygaard; Abingdon-Cokesbury Press, Nashville, TN, U.S.A., 1942

Summary of Proceedings of the National Convention of the American Legion; August 26 to September 1, 1949, page 35, Indianapolis, IN, U.S.A., 1949

Superstition and Education; Fletcher Bascom Dresslar; University of California Publications, Berkley, CA, U.S.A., 1907

Table Talk: Being the Discourses of John Selden, Esq. Relating Especially to Religion and State; John Seldon; Oxford, England, 1654, published 1689

Tale of Melibee; Geofrey Chaucer; London, England, 1386

Tales of Life and Death, Hon. Grantley F. Berkley, page 71, Chapman and Hall, London, U.K., 1870,

Tales of My Landlord; Sir Walter Scott; Waverly Novels; London, U.K., 1816

Tales Tersely Told; Paul Victor Loth; page 187, Moniter Co., Chicago, IL, U.S.A., 1899

Talk to the Hand: the Utter Rudeness of the World Today; Lynne Truss; Profile Books, London, U.K., 2006

TANSTAAFL A Plan for a New Economic World Order; Pierre Dos Utt; Cairo Publications, 1949

Tarlton's Jests and News Out of Purgatory; James O. Halliwell; Printer to HRH Prince Albert, London, U.K., 1844

Tarzan of the Apes; Edgar Rice Burroughs; A.C. McClurg, Great Britain, printed by A.L. Burt Co., New York, NY, U.S.A., 1914

Teacher's Manual; Thomas H. Palmer; Marsh, Capen, Lyon and Webb, Boston, MA, U.S.A., 1840

The Adventurer; Samuel Johnson and others; page 309, Harrison and Company, London, England, 1793

The Adventures of a Kidnapped Orphan; various authors; London, U.K., 1747

The Adventures of Huckleberry Finn; Mark Twain (Samuel Langhorne Clemmons); Chatto & Windus, London, England, UK, 1884

The Adventures of Mr. Verdant Green, pseudonym, Cuthbert Bede (Edward Bradley); James Blackwood, London, U.K., 1854

The Adventure of the Gloria Scott, *The Memoirs of Sherlock Holmes;* Sir Arthur Conan Doyle; London, England, 1893

The Adventures of Roderick Ramdom; Dr. Tobias George Smollett; London, U.K., 1748

The Adventures of Tom Sawyer; Mark Twain; American Publishing Company, Chicago, IL, U.S.A., 1876

The African Abroad; William Henry Ferris, page 396, The Tuttle, Morehouse and Taylor Press, New Haven, CT, U.S.A., 1913

The Amazing Theater; James Agate, Benjamin Brom; Bronx, NY, U.S.A., 1939, 1969

The American Review: A Whig Jouranal, *Volume 5;* George H. Colton; New York, NY, 1847

The Americans, in their Moral, Social and Political Relations, Volume One; Francis Joseph Grund; March, Capon and Lyon, Boston, MA, U.S.A., 1837:

The Anatomy of Melancholy; Robert Burton; (2 references) London, England, 1621

The Arena; Volume 2; Benjamin Orange Flowers; page 362, novelette, 'The Shadow of the Noose' by Ferdinand C. Valentine; Arena Publishing, Boston, MA, U.S.A., 1892

The Art of War; Sun Tzu; China, sixth century B.C.

The Author's Earnest Cry and Prayer; Robert Burns; Kilmarnock, Scotland, 1786

The Autobiography of Jack Ketch; Charles Whitehead; Carey, Lee and Blanchard, London, England, UK, 1835

The Autobiography of Leigh Hunt; J.E. Morpurgo, Leigh Hunt; Cresset Press, London, U.K., 1949

The bachelor's banquet; 1603, Thomas Dekker; Vizzetelly & Company, London, England, UK, 1887

678

The Ballad of the Flim-flam Man; Guy Owens; page 66, MacMillan, New York, NY, U.S.A., 1965

The Banks of the Ohio; James Kirk Paulding; A.K. Newman and Co., London, U.K., 1833

The Best of Both Worlds; Thomas Binney; Edward Knight, London, U.K., 1898

The Bishop's Purse; Cleveland Moffett and Oliver Herford; D. Appleton and Co., New York, NY, U.S.A., 1913

The Betrothed; Sir Walter Scott; London, U.K., 1825

The boke of husbandry; John Fitzherbert; London, England, 1534

The Boke of Justyces of Peas: The Charge of all the Processe of Cessyons, Warrantes, Supersedias & All that Longeth to Ony Justyce to Make Endytementes of Haute Treason, Petyt Treason, Felonyes, Appeles, Trespas Vpon Statutes, Trespas Contra Regis Pacem, Nocumentis, with Dyuers Thynges More as it Appereth in the Kalender of the Same Boke; Sir Anthony Fitzherbert; London, England, 1506

The Book of Household Management; Isabella Mary Beeton; S.O.Beeton Publishing Co., London, U.K., 1861

The Book of Margery Kempe; Jonathan Cape; London, England, circa 1438, published 1932

The Books of Charles E. Vor Loan, Old Man Curry, Stories of the Race Track; Charles E. Van Loan, page 178, Geo. H. Duran Co., New York, NY, U.S.A., 1929

The Boot on the Other Leg: or Loyalty above Party; Mathew Carey; New York, NY, U.S.A., 1863

The Broken Halo; Florence L. Barclay; chapter 14, G.P. Putman's Sons, London, U.K., 1913

The Bugbears; Francis Kinwelmersh; London, England, 1580

The Cabinet Album; Lewis Bingley Wayne; Hunt, Chance and Co., London, England, UK, 1830

The Calcutta Review; Vol. 2; Vol. 33; page 365, University of Calcutta, Calcutta, India, 1856

The Canterbury Tales: Prologue; Geoffrey Chaucer; England, 1386

The Canterbury Tales; The Reeve's Tale; Geoffrey Chaucer; England, circa 1395

The Canterbury Tales; Prologue to The Summonour's Tale; Geoffrey Chaucer; England, circa 1389-1395

The Case of Christopher Atkinson, Esq.; Christopher Atkinson, London, U.K., 1785

The Case of the Borrowed Brunette; Earl Stanley Gardner; William Morrow & Co., New York, NY, U.S.A., 1946

The Cases of Polygamy, Concubinage, Adultery and Divorce; 'the most eminent hands,' London, England, 1732

The Child in America, Behavior Problems and Programs, W.I. Thomas, p. 572, Alfred A Kompf, NY, U.S.A.,1928

The Children's Pew; J. Reid Howatt; London, U.K., 1893

The Chirsten State of Matrymonye; Myles Coverdale; London, England, 1541

The Clockmaker, or the Sayings and Goings of Saamuel Slick of Slickville; Thomas Halliburton; Nova Scotia, Canada, 1838; Richard Bentley, London, England, UK, 1839

The Columbian Union; Simon Williard, Jun. of Massachusetts; Hudson, NY, U.S.A., 1814:

The Comic Latin Grammar; Second Edition, Chris Stray; Charles Tilt, London, U.K., 1840

The Commentaries on the Laws of England Volume 2; William Blackstone; Clarendon Press, Oxford, England, U.K., 1768

The Complete English Copyholder; A guide to lords of manors, Volume 1, page 155, R. & N. Nutt, London, U.K., 1735

The Compleat Fencing-master; a manual for aspiring swordsmen, Sir William Hope; London, England, 1692

The Compleynte until Pite; Geofrey Chaucer; London, England, 1368

The Congressionat Globe for the Second Session; Thirty-third Congress; page 244, Washington, DC, U.S.A., 1855

The Cosmographical Glass; William Cunningham; London, England, 1559

The Court and Character of King James I; Sir Anthony Weldon; Swanscombe, Kent, Eng-land, 1650

The Decline and Fall of the Roman Empire; Edward Gibbon; Strahan & Cadell, London, U.K., 1781

680

The Diverting History of John Bull and brother Jonathan; 'Hector Bull-Us'; Inskeep and Bradford, New York, NY, U.S.A, 1813

The Dividend; Joseph Knox Stone; page 33, Dorrance, Pittsburg, PA, 1927

The Doctors' Book of Home Remedies II; Sid Kirchheimer; Bantam Books, New York, NY, U.S.A., 1995

The Draft in Baldwinsville; Artemus Ward (Charles Farrar Brown); Harper and Brothers, New York, NY, U.S.A., and London, England, U.K., 1862

The Edinburgh Practice of Phycic, Surgery and Midwifery; William Cullen; Edinburgh, Scotland, U.K., 1803

The Electric Kool-Aid Acid Test; Tom Wolf; Farrar, Strauss and Giroux, New York, NY, U.S.A., 1967

The Ephemerides of Phialo; Stephen Gosson; London, England, 1579

The Exhibition Speaker; P.A. Fitzgerald; D.M. Dewey; New York, NY, U.S.A., 1856 one-act romantic comedy play, *Hob and Nob* by Madison Morton

The Exposition of Humphry Clinker; Dr. Tobias G. Smollett; Harrison and Co., London, U.K., first published 1771, Edition of 1785

The Fables of LaFontaine, Jean de LaFontaine, P.27, translated by Elizur Wright, William Smith, London, UK, 1842

The Fair Maid of Perth; Sir Walter Scott; London, U.K., 1828

The Fall of the British Tyranny, or, American Liberty Triumphant; John Leacock; page 48, Styner & Cist, Philidelphia, PA, U.S.A., 1776

The Fearie Queene; Edmund Spenser; London, England, 1590

The First Book of the Preservation of Henry VII; John Payne Collier, page 25; R.B., London, England, 1599

The First Two Decades of Life; Ralph Vickers Merry and Frieda Kiefer Merry; Harper and Brothers, New York, NY, U.S.A., 1950

The Flint Heart, a Fairy Story; Eden Phillpotts; E.P. Dutton and Co., New York, NY, U.S.A., 1910

The Folklore Historian, Volume 24; Edited by Nancy C. McEntire; published by Indiana State University, Terre Haute, IN, U.S.A., 2007

The Four Last Things; Sir Thomas More; England, 1522

The French Revolution; Thomas Carlyle; London, U.K., 1837

The Friend, a Religious and Literary Journal; Philadelphia, PA, U.S.A., March 10, 1910

The Friend of Peace; Philo Pacifious; Joseph T.Buckingham, Boston, MA, U.S.A., 1816

The Games and Diversions of Argyleshire; Robert Craig Maclagan; The Folk-Lore Society, David Nutt, London, U.K., 1901

The General History of England, both Ecclesiastical and Civil: Containing the Reign of Richard II; James Tyrrell; W. Rogers, London, England, 1703

The Gentle Craft; Thomas Deloney; Mayer and Muller, Berlin, Germany, 1903

The Gentle Savage, Edward King, page 54, Kegan Paul, Trench and Co., London, U.K., 1883

The Gnoors Come from the Voodvork Out; Reginald Bretnor; 1950

The Gold Diggers; Seba Smith, New York, NY, U.S.A., 1840

The Great Harmonia; Being A Philosophical Revolation of the Natural, Spiritual and Celestial Universe; Volume 1; page 118, Andrew Jackson Davis; Benjamin B. Mossey and Co., Boston, MA, U.S.A., 1850

The Gulistan, or Rose Garden; Persian poet, Sa'di; written in 1259, translated into English by James Dumoulin; Calcutta, India, 1807

The Gypsy Queen's Vow; May Agnes Fleming; page 308: Beadle & Adams, Hurst and Co., New York, NY, U.S.A., 1875

The Haunted House; Charles Dickens, Elizabeth Gaskell, others; Chapman and Hall, Ltd., London, U.K., 1859

The Headless Horseman, or a Strange Tale of Texas; Thomas Mayne Reid; Oxford University Press, London, U.K., 1866

The Heart's Ease; Simon Patrick; London, England, 1699

The Higher Powers of Body, Mind and Spirit; Ralph Waldo Trine; London, U.K, 1918

The hill, a romance of friendship; Horace Vachell; London, U.K., 1905

The Historie of Foure-footed Beastes; Edward Topsell; London, England, 1607

The History and Life and Death of His Most Serine Highness; Samuel Carrington; London, England, 1659

The History of British Work and Labour Relations in the Royal Dockyards; Routledge, London, England, UK, 1999

The History of Corpus Christi College; Thomas Fowler; London, England, 1599

The history of King Philip's war; Increase Mather; London, England, 1676

The History of Little Goody Two-Shoes; anonymous; London, England, 1765

The History of the Hen Fever; George P. Burnham; James French and Co., Boston, MA, U.S.A., 1855

The History of the Worthies of England; Thomas Fuller; London, England, circa 1661

The Humour of the Scot 'neath NorthernLights and Southern Cross; James Inglis; page 105, David Bouglas, Edinburgh, Scotland, U.K., 1894

The Idiot; published in English, Fedor Dostoieffsky; London, U.K., 1887

The Iliad; Homer; Greece, circa 700-800 B.C.

The Iliad; Book XXII; Homer; Greece, (circa eighth century B.C. as translated by Pope between 1715 and 1720), also translated by William Cullen Bryant; Fields, Osgood and Co., Boston, 1870

The Improvisatore, or, Life in Italy; Hans Christian Anderson as translated by Mary Howitt; first published 1835, Richard Bentley and Son, London, U.K., 1845

The Indicator, Volume III, Number 7; Aaron Burr; Amherst College, Amherst, MA, USA, February 1851

The Job; Sinclair Lewis; Chapter 13, Harper and Brothers, New York, NY, U.S.A., 1917

The Johnson Murder; Annis Burk; chapter XII, page 126, V.O. Severanob, Indianapolis, IN, U.S.A., 1885

The Last Days of Pompeii; Volume II, Book III, chapter 10, Baron Edward Lytton; Harper and Brothers, New York, NY, U.S.A., 1834

The Learned Man Defended and Reform'd; Daniello Bartoli; translated into English by Thomas Salusberry, page 392, R&W Leyborne, London, U.K., 1660

The Life of P.T. Barnum; autobiography of Phineas T. Barnum; 1855; reprinted by the University of Illinois Press, Chicago, IL, USA, 2000

The Life of Reason, Volume 1; George Santayana; Charles Scribner's Sons, New York, NY, U.S.A., 1905

The Lady of the Barge; short story, *The Monkey's Paw;* W.W. Jacobs; 1902, sixth edition, Harper of Brothers, New York, NY, U.S.A., 1906

The Legend of St. Katherine; anonymous; England, circa 1225

The Life and Adventures of Martin Chuzzlewit; Charles Dickens; Chapman and Hall, London, U.K., 1844

The Life and Adventures of Valentine Vox the Ventriloquist; Henry Cockton; Carey and Hart, Philidelphia, PA, U.S.A., 1841

The Life and Opinions of Tristam Shandy, Gentleman; Lawrence Sterne; Harrison and Co., London, U.K., 1787

The life and strange sdventures of Robinson Crusoe; Daniel Defoe; London, England, 1719

The life and writings of Major Jack Downing; Seba Smith; Lilly, Wait, Colman and Holden, Boston, MA, U.S.A., 1833

The Life of Admiral Lord Nelson, K.B. from His Lordship's Manuscripts; James Stanier Clarke and John M'Arthur; T. Bensley, C. Cadell and W. Davies, London, U.K., 1810

The Life of Alexander Pope Esq.; by Owen Ruffhead, Esq.; London, U.K., 1769

The Life of Guzman d'Alfarache or the Spanish Rogue by Mateo Aleman, English translation, page 99, London, England, 1708

The Light That Failed; Rudyard Kipling, first published in *Lippincott's Monthly Magazine*, London, U.K., 1890

The Long Dream; Richard Wright; Versa Press, Inc. East Peoria, IL, U.S.A., 1958

The Lovers; or, The Memoirs of Lady Sarah B___ and the Countess P___ by Pierre Henri Treyssac de Vergy; page 60, J. Roson, London, U.K., 1769

The Man in Lower Ten; Mary Roberts Rinehart; Grosset and Dunlap, New York, NY, U.S.A., 1909

The Man Next Door; Emerson Hough; D. Appleton, New York, NY, U.S.A., 1918

The Mechanics of Surgery; Charles Trux; Hammond Press, Chicago, Il, U.S.A., 1899

The Midshipmen's Trip to Jerusalem and Cruise in Syria; Augustus Adolphus Lynne, page 162; Spottiswoode and Co., London, U.K., 1872

The Milkmaid and Her Pail; Aesop's fable from 570 BC

The Mill on the Floss; George Eliot; William Blackwood & Sons, Edinburgh, Scotland, U.K., 1860

The Mistress of Shenstone, Florence Luisa Barclay, page 181, Grosset and Dunlap, New York, NY, U.S.A., 1910

The Modern Part of an Universal History from the Earliest Accounts to the Present Time; The History of Leon and Castile; various authors; London, U.K., 1782

The Naughty Girl Won; Religious Tract Society, London, U.K., 1799

The Naval Chronicle; Volume 18; Court Marial of Jenkin Rutford; London, U.K., 1807

The Naval Sketch-book; William Glascock; Henry Colburn, London, U.K., 1825, 1826

The Nazi Years - A Documentary History; J. Remak (ed.); article, 'David Lloyd George's impression after a meeting with Hitler on 4 September 1936;' pp. 80-82, Prentice-Hall, New York, NY, U.S.A. 1969

The Negro and His Songs; Howard Washington Odom and Guy Benton Johnson; University of North Carolina Press, Chapel Hill, NC, U.S.A., 1925

The Newcomes; memoirs of a most respectable family; William Makepeace Thackeray; Harper and Brothers, New York, NY, USA, 1857

The Notebooks of Lazarus Long; Robert Heinlein; Able Books, New York, NY, U.S.A., 1978

The Old China Hands; Charles Grandison Finney; Doubleday & Co., New York, NY, U.S.A., 1961

The Old World and Its Ways; William Jennings Bryan; Thompson Publishing Co., St. Louis, MO, U.S.A., 1907

The Optimisty; Charles Fredric Goss; page 215, The Robert Clarke Co., Cincinnati, OH, U.S.A., 1897

The Orange Girl; Sir Walter Besant; Dodd and Mead, New York, NY, 1898, 1901

The Origin of Laws, Arts and Sciences; Antoine-Yves Goguet and Alexandre Conrad Fugère; Edinburgh, Scotland, 1761

The Oxbow Incident; Walter Van Tilburg Clark; Penguin Group, New York, NY, U.S.A., 1943

The Parliamentary History of Conscription in Great Britain; London, U.K., 1917

The Pastor's Fire-side; Jane Porter; Colbern and Bentley, London, U.K., 1832

The Penny Pulpit: A Collection of Accurately Reported Sermons by the Most Eminent Ministers of Various Denominations; Sermon by Charles H. Spurgeon, 'A Free Salvation;' James Paul, London, U.K., 1859

The People, Yes; Carl Sandburg; Harcourt, Brace and Company, Orlando, FL, U.S.A., 1936

The Period of the Reformation (1517-1648); Ludwig Häusser, edited by Wilhelm Oncken, Translated by Mrs. G. Sturge; page 198, American Tract Society, New York, NY, U.S.A., 1648

The personal history of David Copperfield; Charles Dickens; London, U.K., 1850

The Pickwick Papers; Charles Dickens; chapter 49, London, U.K., 1837

The Pilgrimage of Perfection; William Bonde; London, England, 1526

The Pirate; Waverly Novels, Sir Walter Scott; London, U.K., 1893

The Pit, Volume 2; Frank Norris, Leipzig; Bernhard Tauchnitz, Nice, France, 1903

The Poetical Works of Alexander Pope Vol. 4; The Dunciad, Book 1, page 109; J. Bell, London, U.K., 1788

The Poetical Works of William Summerville, Volume II, 'The Night-Walker Reclaimed', line 264: G. Cawthorn, London, U.K., 1797

The Political History of England; Volume 1 (of 12), Thomas Hodgkin; London, UK, 1808

The Political History of the Devil; Daniel Defoe; London, England, 1726

The Political Register and Impartial Review; John Almon, page 269, Henry Beevor; London, U.K., 1770

The Poor Relations, Second Episode, Cousin Pons; Honoré de Balzac; 1896, Translated, by William Walton; page 74: Geo. Barrie & Sons, Philadelphia, PA, U.S.A., 1898

The Port Admiral; William Johnstoun Neale; Cochrane & McCrone, London, England, UK, 1833

The Posthumous Papers of the Pickwick Club; Charles Dickens; Wm. H. Colyer, New York, NY, U.S.A., 1838

The Practical Works of Richard Baxter; Volume III, George Virtue; London, U.K., 1838

The Principles of the Philosophy of Expansive and Contractive Forces; Robert Greene; University Press, Cambridge, U.K., 1727

The Prisoner of Azkaban; J.K. Rowling; the Harry Potter series, book 3; Bloomsbury, London, England, UK, 1999

The Prisoner of the Mill, or, Captain Hayward's Body-guard; Harry Hazleton; chapter 2, page 7, The American News Co., New York, NY, U.S.A., 1864

The Rat; Mottram Andrews Hewitt; Adam & Charles Black, London, 1904

There Ain't No Such Thing as a Free Lunch; Milton Freeman; New York, NY, U.S.A., 1975

The Real Issue; William Allen White, short story, *The King of Boyville;* Way and Williams, Chicago, IL, U.S.A., 1896, 1897

The Real Life and Adventures of Hamilton Murray; London, U.K., 1759

The regal rambler; or, eccentrical adventures of the devil in London; Thomas Hastings; London, U.K., 1793

The Register of Debates in Congress; Washington, DC, U.S.A., 1833

The Rehearsal, George Villiers, London, U.K., 1671

The Rescuing of Romish Fox; Wyllyam Turner; Basyl, London, England, 1545

The Rights of Man, Edition 2; Thomas Paine; London, U.K., 1792

The Scarlet Letter; Nathaniel Hawthorne; Tickson, Reed and Fields, Boston, MA, U.S.A., 1850

The Scripture Chronology Demonstrated by Astronomical Calculations; Arthur Bedford; Book II, chapter XI, page 268, London, England, 1730

The 7 Habits of Highly Effective People; Dr. Stephen R. Covey; Free Press, New York, NY, U.S.A., 1989

The Story of Gadsby; Rudyard Kipling, A.H. Wheeler, London, U.K., 1889

The Task; Volume II, William Cowper; page 76, 1785

The Testimony of William Erbery, William Elbery; Oxford, England, 1658

The Theater of Bernard Shaw, Ten Plays Chosen and Discussed; Volume 1, Dodd, Mead, New York, NY, U.S.A., 1961

The Treatyse of the Buryall of the Masse; William Barlow; Essex, England, 1528

The Ugly Duckling; Hans Christain Anderson; Denmark, 1843

The United States Congress record of the Quality Stabilization Hearings; Washington, DC, U.S.A., April and May, 1962

The University Review; University of Missouri at Kansas City, MO, U.S.A., 1938

The vanity of dogmatizing, or confidence in opinions etc.; Joseph Glanvill; London, England, 1661

The Washington Merry-go-round; Horace Liveright; New York, NY, U.S.A, 1931

The Way of Lao-tzu; Lao-tzu; Chinese philosopher (604 BC - 531 BC)

The Whitby Glossary; London, U.K., 1855

The Wife of Bath's Tale (and Prologue); Geofrey Chaucer; London, England, c. 1387 - 1395

The Winds of Chance; Rex Beach; page 35, Harper and Brothers, New York, NY, U.S.A., 1918

The woful history of the unfortunate Eudoxia; Carl Theodor von Unlanski's biography; published in England, U.K., 1816

The Wooden World Dissected; Edward Ward; J. Graham, London, England, 1707

The Woods Colt; Thames Williamson; Harcourt, Brace and Company, New York, NY, U.S.A., 1933

The Words of Martin Luther King, Jr.; Coretta Scott King; New Market Press, New York, NY, U.S.A., 2008

The Workes of that Famous Chirurgion Ambrose Parey; Ambroise Paré, Adriaan van den Spiegel; translated by Thomas Johnson; Richard Cotes, London, England, 1649

The Works and Remains of the Reverend Robert Hall (an English Baptist Minister 1734-1831) compiled by Olinthus Gregory, "Politics and the Pulpit," p. 46 from the *Journal of Commerce*, 1 June 1830; printed by Henry G, Bohn, London, 1846

The Works of the Rev. Phillip Skelton; page 405, Phillip Skelton; Dublin, Ireland, 1770

The Works of Benjamin Franklin; Philadelphia, PA, U.S.A., 1817

The Works of Jeremy Bentham, Volume IV; page 225, Jeremy Bentham; Edited, John Browning; London, England, UK, 1843

The Yankee amongthe Mermaids; William Evans Burton; page 139, T.B. Peterson and Bro., Philadelphia, PA, U.S.A., 1843

The Young Duke; Benjamin Disraeli; J. & J. Harper, New York, NY, USA, 1831

The Wynne Diaruies; Elizabeth Wynne; U.K., 1791

Thomas Wright's Political Songs of England; Thomas Wright; Camden Society, London, U.K., 1839

Three Chief Principles of Magnificent Building; Sir Balthazar Gerbier; London, England, 1662

Three Courses and a Desert; William Clarke and George Cruikshank; page 273, Vizetelly, Branston and Co., London, U.K., 1830

Three Rousing Cheers for the Rollo Boys; Corey Ford; George H. Doran Co., New York, NY, U.S.A., 1925,

Thrilling Adventures of the Prisoner of the Border; P. Hamilton Myers; Derby and Jackson, New York, NY, U.S.A., 1857

Through Some Eventful Years; Susan Bradford Epps diary; J.W. Burke, Macon, GA, U.S.A., 1926

To Kill a Mockingbird; Harper Lee; J.P. Lippincott and Co., Philadelphia, PA, USA, 1960

Tom Brown at Oxford; Thomas Hughes; Harper and Rowe, New York, NY, U.S.A., 1861

Tom Sawyer, Detective; chapter 3, Mark Twain, New York, NY, U.S.A., 1896

Torpedo Junction; Robert Joseph Casey; Bobbs-Merrill Co., Indianapolis, IN, U.S.A., 1942

Tout vient à qui sait attendre; Violet Fane (Mary Montgomerie Lamb, Baroness Currie) (1843-1905); London, England, UK, circa 1889

Toxophilus, the School of Shooting; Roger Ascham; London, England, 1545

Travels in the Confederation; Johann Davis Schöepf's 1788 German book; Alfred J. Morrison's English translation; Wm J. Campbell, Philadelphia, OA, U.S.A., 1911

Treasure Island; Robert Louis Stevenson, Cassell and Co., London, U.K., 1883

Tristram Shandy; Laurence Sterne; London, U.K., 1761

Troilus and Criseyde; Geoffrey Chaucer; general references, also book V, st. 112, London, England, 1374-1385

Twelve Years a Slave: Narrative of Simon Winthrop: A Citizen of New York; Simon Winthrop, David Watson; page 179, Auburn: Miller, Orton and Mulligan, New York, NY, U.S.A., 1855

Twisting the Rope; Rebecca A MacAvoy; page 14, e-reads, R.A. MacAlvoy, New York, NY, U.S.A., 1986

Two Books of Mr. Sydrich Simpson; Minister of Cambridge, *Faith or, believing, is Receiving Christ;* page 154, Peter Cole, London, England, 1658

Uncle John; George John Whyte Melville; Volume II, page 90, Leipzig; Bernhard Tauchnitz, Paris, France, 1874

Uncle Tom's Cabin; Harriet Beecher Stowe; New Era, New York, NY, U.S.A., 1852

Ut Mine Stromtid, or *An Old Story of My Farming Days,* German publication, 1862, translated into English, London, U.K., 1878

Very Good, Jeeves! P. G. Wodehouse; London, U.K., 1930

Walden; Henry David Thoreau; Ticknor & Fields, Boston, MA, U.S.A., 1854

Waverly Novels; Introduction to *The Abbot;* Sir Walter Scott; Parker Edition, Boston, MA, U.S.A., 1831

Waverly Novels, Kenilworth the Pirate; Sir Walter Raleigh, Edinburgh, Scotland, U.K., first published 1821

Western Clearings; Caroline Matilda Kirkland; Wiley and Putnam, New York, NY, U.S.A., 1846

Westward! Dana Fuller Ross; Random House, New York, NY, U.S.A., 1992

Westward Ho! A Tale; James Kirke Paulding; New York, NY, U.S.A., 1832

What is the Fletcher Music Method; Mrs. Evelyn Ashton Fletcher Copp, page 52; Brookline, Massachusetts, 1915

What Price Football: A Player's Defense of the Game; William Barry Wood; Houghton Mifflin, New York, NY, U.S.A.,

Whistle Stop; Maritta Wolff; Random House, New York, NY, U.S.A., 1941

White Monkey; John Galsworthy; C. Scribner's Sons, London, England, U.K., 1924

Wolfert's Roost and Other Papers; Washington Irving; G.P. Putnam Co., New York, NY, U.S.A., 1855

Wolf in Man's Clothing; Mignon Good Eberhart; chapter 10, Random House, New York, NY, U.S.A., 1942

Won't You Come Home, Billy Bob Bailey? Louis Grizzard; Peachtree Publishers, Atlanta, GA, U.S.A., 1980

Word Myths: Debunking Linguistic Urban Legends; David Wilton; pp. 66-67, Oxford University Press, New York, NY, U.S.A., 2004

Works; Thomas Becon; London, England, 1560

Works; Thomas More; London, England, 1530

Writers of Today: Models of Journalistic Prose; selected and discussed by John William Cunliffe; Columbia University, The Century Co., New York, NY, U.S.A., 1922

Wyandotte; James Fenimore Cooper; chapter 3, New York, NY, U.S.A., 1843

XII Sermons; Robert Sanderson, Bishop of Lincoln; London, England, 1634

Yet Again; Max Beerbohm; London, U.K., 1909

You Can Be a Hoot: To the Man Over 50, Over 60, Over 70, Harold Stanley French, page 246, New Century Publishing Co.; Indianapolis, IN, U.S.A., 1999

You Can't Go Home Again; Thomas C. Wolfe, Harper Brothers, New York, NY, U.S.A., 1940

Young Cricketer's Tutor; John Nylon; London, England, UK, 1833

Poems, Songs, Albums

Advice; poem published in *The Balance and Columbian Repository;* Hudson, NY, U.S.A., 29 May 1805

Aeneid; Latin epic poem, Virgil (70-19 B.C.)

Against All Odds; soundtrack song from movie by Phil Collins; Columbia Records, Hollywood, CA, U.S.A., 1984

A Good Fellow; paper called *The Minor Drama*, published by William Taylor and Company, New York, NY, U.S.A., 1850

An Essay on Criticism; Alexander Pope; London, U.K., 1711

Another Day, Another Dollar; composed and sung by Wynn Stewart; Jackpot Records, Las Vegas, NE, U.S.A., 1962

Another Day, Another Dollar; Gang of Four; Warner Brothers Records, London, U.K., Los Angeles, CA, U.S.A., 1962

Another Day, Another Dollar; Alison Krauss and Union Station; album *Every Time You Say Goodbye;* Rounder Records, Cambridge, MA, U.S.A., 1992

A Sadder but Wiser Girl for Me from *Music Man;* Rogers and Hammerstein; Hollywood, CA, U.S.A., 1962

A Select Second Husband; poem by John Daves; England, 1616

Ask Me No Questions, I'll Tell You No Lies; Jo Stafford; 1950

Ask Me No Questions and I'll Tell You No Lies; The Bangles; V2 Records, U.K., 2000

Ask Me No Questions; Johnny Thunder; Mercury Records, 1974

A Spending Hand; Thomas Wyatt; England, 1530s

A Tale of Paraguay; Robert Southey, Esq., L.L.D.; lengthy narrative poem, London, U.K., 1825

A Wife; poem by Thomas Overbury; England, 1613

Baby Get It On; Ike and Tina Turner in their album, *Acid Queen,* United Artists; Los Angeles, CA, 1975

Beowulf; Chapter XXIV, Anglo-Saxon, anonymous; 8th—11th century

Between the Devil and the Deep Blue Sea; written by Ted Koehler and Harold Arlen; recorded by Cab Calloway; Classics Record Label, New York, NY, U.S.A., 1931

Cataplus, or, AEneas, his descent to hell: a mock poem in imitation of the sixth book of Virgil's AEneis; printed for Maurice Atkins, London, England, 1672

Catch a Falling Star; Paul Vance, Lee Pockriss, Perry Como; RCA International, New York, NY, U.S.A., 1957

Comus: A Mask Presented at Ludlow Castle; John Milton; first presented at Michaelmas, Ludlow Castle, Shropshire, England, 1634

Confessio Amantus; (The Lover's Confession) John Gower; narrative poem, England, 1390

Dance Around the Truth; album*: I Just Wanna Do My Thing;* Jamie Lee Thurston; Snakebite Records, Richmond, VA, U.S.A., 2009

Diamonds are a girl's best friend; song by Julie Styne first introduced by Carol Channing; Broadway production of *Gentlemen Prefer Blondes;* New York, NY, U.S.A., 1949

Divina Commedia (The Divine Comedy); epic poem, Dante Alighieri; Italy, 1308-1321

Don Juan; George Gordon Byron, Lord Byron, satirical poem, London, U.K., 1823

Don't Try This at Home; Billy Bragg album; Elektra Label, Atlantic Records, New York, NY, U.S.A., 1991

Easy Come, Easy Go; Elvis Presley, Sid Wayne, Ben Wiseman; title song from movie; Paramount, Hollywood, CA, U.S.A., 1967

Easy Come, Easy Go; album and title song (Aaron Baker, Dean Dillon); MCA Records, George Straight; Produced by Tony Brown, Nashville, TN, U.S.A., 1993

Easy Come, Easy Go; (Diane Hildebrand and Jack Keller) Bobby Sherman; Metromedia, Records, Hollywood, CA, U.S.A., 1970

Easy Street; poem by E.N. Stevens; New York, NY, U.S.A., 1894

Emotional Rollercoaster; Vivian Green, album; A Love Story; Columbia Records, New York, NY, U.S.A., 2002

Epistle to Ramsay; William Hamilton; U.K., 1719

Everything's Coming up Roses; lyrics by Stephen Sondheim, music by Jule Styne; used in the Broadway musical and film *Gypsy;* New York, NY, Hollywood, CA, U.S.A., 1959, 1962, respectively

Finnigin to Flannigan; Strickland Gillilan; 1910

Five Hundreth Poinrtes of Good Husbandrie; instructional poem, Thomas Tusser; London, England, 1573

Fools Rush in (Where Angels Fear to Tread); Rube Bloom and Johnny Mercer, recorder by Brook Benton, Elvis Presley and many others; first released 1940

Fresh as a Daisy; pop song by Emitt Rhodes; Dunhill Records, Los Angeles, CA, U.S.A., 1969-'70

Generydes, a Romance in Seven Fine Stanzas; anonymous medieval poem; Trinity College Library, Cambridge, England, circa 1440

Get up and Bar the Door; traditional Scottish folk song published Scotland, 1776

Gunaikeion; (a poetic history of women), page 286, 1624

Heads are Gonna Roll; The Hippos; Interscope Records, Santa Monica, CA, U.S.A. 1999

He Ain't Heavy, He's My Brother; by Bobby Scott and Bob Russell; Kelly Gordon, Abby Road Studios, London, U.K., 1969

Heroides; poem by Ovid, Greece, circa 10 B.C.

Home! Sweet Home! Words by John Howard Payne, melody by British composer, Sir Henry Bishop; first performed in London, U.K., 1823

Hudibras; satirical narrative poem by Samuel Butler; London, England, 1664

I Can Feel it in My Bones; album, *The Need of Love;* Earth Wind and Fire; Warner Brothers Records Burbank CA, U.S.A., 1971

I'd Like to get you on a Slow Boat to China; Frank Loesser; New York, NY, written 1945, published, 1947

I Heard it Through the Grapevine; Norman Whitfield and Barrett Strong; first released by Smokey Robinson and the Miracles; Motown Records, Detroit, Michigan, U.S.A., 1967

I'm Hot to Trot; recorded by Terry Fell, by Gene Tabor; X Records, Bloomington, IN, U.S.A., 1955

In the Closet; Michael Jackson; Epic Records, New York, NY, U.S.A., 1991

It's Alright Ma (I'm Only Bleeding); Bob Dylan; Columbia Records, New York, NY, U.S.A., 1965

It's a Man's, Man's, Man's World; sung by James Brown, co-written by Brown and Betty Jean Newsome; King Label, New York, NY, U.S.A, released 1966

Keep the Faith; Michael Jackson song, Dangerous album; Epic Records, New York, NY, U.S.A., 1991

Keep the Faith; Bon Jovi album; Mercury Records, Nashville, TN, U.S.A, London, U.K., 1992

Keep those Cards and Letters Coming In; Ernest Tubb and Loretta Lynn album titled *Mr. and Mrs. Used to Be;* Decca Records, Nashville, TN, U.S.A., January 1, 1965

Laughing Boy; Mary Wells; Motown Records, Detroit, MI, U.S.A., 1963

Leap of Faith; Kenny Loggins; Sony Records, New York, NY, U.S.A., 1991

Leap of Faith; Michelle Branch; Album, *Broken Bracelet;* Twin Dragon Records, Tucson, AR, U.S.A., 2000

Liberty Song; composed by Isaac Shelby; Kentucky, U.S.A.

Life Begins at Forty; written by Jack Yellen and Ted Shapiro sung by Sophie Tucker; New York, NY, U.S.A., 1937

Love Makes the World Go 'Round; lyrics by Clyde Fitch and melody by William Furst; New York, NY, 1896

Marmion Canto VI; Stanza 17; Sir Walter Scott, London, U.K., 1808

Milk and Honey; John Lennon, Yoko Ono; Polydor Records, London, U.K., 1984

Moral Song; William Edward Hickson; London, U.K., 1857

Mother Goose Melody; John Newberry; England, circa 1760

694

My Melancholy Baby; Words & Music by George A. Norton & Ernie Burnett, performed by Tommy Lyman; New York, NY, U.S.A., 1927

My name is Kelly; song by Howard Pease; 1919

Mythical Kings and Iguanas; Dory Previn, United Artists, Beverly Hills, CA, U.S.A., May, 1971

Not a Dry Eye in the House; song written by Diane Warren, CD recorded by Meat Loaf; Virgin Records, Ltd., London, U.K., 1995

Ode; Alfred O'Shaughnessy, *Appleton's Journal;* Appleton and Co., New York, NY, U.S.A. 1873

Ode on a Distant Prospect of Eaton College; Thomas Gray; London, U.K., 1742

One for my Baby (and One More for the Road); (Musical, *The Sky's the Limit*); Harold Arien and Johnny Mercer, sung by Fred Astaire; Hollywood, CA, U.S.A., 1943

Overbury's Wife; Thomas Overbury; England, 1613; published, 1614

Poem; Oliver Goldsmith; Ireland, 1700s

Poem (unknown title); by C. Acres; published in 1734, London, England

Poor Little February; Lester Lee, Danny Shapiro, and Jerry Seelen; New York, NY, U.S.A., 1941

Primrose Path; poem by Ogden Nash; 1936

Puddin' N' Tain; Alley Cats on Philles label; Phillidelphia, PA, U.S.A., 1962

Rocky Mountain High; John Denver; R.C.A. Records, New York, NY, U.S.A., 1972

Signed, Sealed and Delivered; country LP, Lefty Frizzell, song by Cowboy Copas and Lois Mann; AllMusic label, Nashville, TN, U.S.A., 1968

Signed, Sealed, Delivered, I'm Yours; Stevie Wonder; Motown's Talma label, Detroit, MI, U.S.A., 1970

Smile and the World Smiles with You; album by the post-rock band, Sonna; Temporary Residence, Ltd. Brooklyn, NY, U.S.A., 2003

Sticky Fingers, album, song, 'Wild Horses', The Rolling Stones, London, U.K., 1971

Stop and Smell the Roses; Record album produced by Paul McCartney, George Harrison Harry Nilsson, Ronnie Wood, Stephen Stills, Ringo Starr, sung by Ringo Starr; RCA, London, U.K., 1980

Street Ballad, London Labour; H. Meyhew; London, U.K., 1851

Take No Prisoners (In the Game of Love); Peabo Bryson; Polygram, New York, NY, U.S.A., 1985

Talk of the Devil / Speak of the Devil; Ozzy Osbourne; live double album (heavy metal), Castle Communications, London, England, 1982

Ten Cents a Dance; song from *Simple Simon;* lyrics by Lorenzo Hart; music by Richard Rogers, Hollywood, CA, U.S.A., 1930

The Babes in the Woods; narrative poem by Rev. Richard H. Barham in *The Ingoldsby Legends;* Thomas Ingoldsby; published London, U.K., 1856

The Best Is Yet to Come; composed by Cy Coleman with lyrics by Carolyn Lee, 1959, version sung by Frank Sinatra; Reprise Records, Division of Warner Brothers, Inc., New York, NY, U.S.A., 1964

The Bonnie, Bonnie Banks o' Loch Lomand; Highland Scottish ballad, Donald MacDonald, Scotland, 1746

The Firm of Grin and Barrett, Sam Walter Foss (1858-1911)

The Freaks Come Out at Night; Whodini's dance hit; Zomba Recording, LLC, London, U.K., 1984

The Iliad; Homer, Greece, c. 700-800 BC

The Lay of St. Odille; narrative poem by Rev. Richard H. Barham in *The Ingoldsby Legends;* Thomas Ingoldsby; published London, U.K., 1856

The Lost Heir (long narrative poem); Thomas Hood; England, U.K., 1845

The Meditation XVII; John Donne, London, England, (1572-1631)

To a Mouse on Turning up in her Nest with the Plough; Kilmamock Volume; Robert Burns; London, U.K., 1785

The Preacher and the Slave; folk song by labor activist Joe Hill; U.S.A., 1911

The Romance of the Rose (le roman de la rose); Guillaume (de Lorris), Jean (de Meun); poem (Translated by Charles Dahlberg); France, 1400

The Theologian's Tale; Elizabeth, iv; Wadsworth Longfellow; published in *Tales of a Wayside Inn,* 1873

The Trial by Existence; Robert Frost; New York, NY, U.S.A., 1915

Thorn in My Side; Bon Jovi, hard rock song album, *The Circle,* Island label; Henson Studios, CA, U.S.A., 2009

Thorn in My Side; British pop duo, Eurythmics, written by band members Anne Lennox and David Stewart; RCA, London Studios, U.K., 1986

Tippecanoe and Tyler Too; theme song of William Henry Harrison's political campaign; U.S.A., 1840

Troylus and Crisedye; French narrative poem, Geoffrey Chaucer; England, 1374

Two Wrongs Don't Make a Right; Berry Gordy, Smokey Robinson, sung by Mary Wells; released by Motown Records, Detroit, MI, U.S.A., 1963

Va-va-voom! Gil Evans and his Orchestra; Virgin Records, Ltd., London, U.K., 1986

Waiting In the Wings; written by Peter Sinfield and Andy Hill, Diana Ross; Motown Records, Detroit, MI, U.S.A., 1992

When I was a Lad; Gilbert and Sullivan, parody sung by Allan Sherman and Lou Busch; ASCAP, Burning Bush Music, WB Music Corp, Los Angeles, CA, U.S.A., 1963

When Lide Married Him; poem by James Whitcolm Riley; Indianapolis, Indiana, U.S.A., 1894

When the Going Gets Tough the Tough Get Going; Wayne Anton Braithwaite, Barry James Eastmond, Mutt Lange, Billy Ocean, sung by Billy Ocean; soundtrack for *The Jewel of the Nile;* 20th Century Fox, Hollywood, CA, U.S.A.,1985

When You Cry, You Cry Alone; *Too Late to Worry, Too Blue to Cry* album; Glen Campbell; Capitol Records, Nashville, TN, U.S.A., 1963

Why am I always the Bridesmaid? Leigh, Collins, & Morris, (song) sung by Lily Morris; New York, NY, U.S.A., 1917

Why Come ye not to Courte; John Skelton; Line 198, London, England, published c. 1550

Work; poem by George Gascoigne; England, 1572

You Don't Know Jack; song by country Music artist, Luke Bryan; Capitol Records, Nashville, TN, U.S.A., 2011

Plays, musicals, operas, ballets

A Christmas Carol; Charles Dickens; Chapman & Hall, London, England, U.K., 1843

After the Fall; Arthur Miller; page 16, New York, NY, U.S.A., 1964

All American; Mel Brooks, musical play; Dramatic Publishing Co., Woodstock, IL, U.S.A., 1962

All's Well that Ends Well; William Shakespeare; England, 1601

A Man's World; written by Rachel Crothers; Richard G. Badger; Boston, MA, U.S.A., 1915

American Abroad; R. B. Peake, two-act comedy; London, England, U.K., 1824

A Midsummer Night's Dream; William Shakespeare; England, 1596-1598

An Overpraised Season: *A Play of Ideas in One Act;* presented by Little theater, Grossmont High, Grossmont, CA, Samuel French, Inc.1960

Anthony and Cleopatra; William Shakespeare; England, circa 1623

Antigone; Sophocles; Greece, 442 B.C.

Appius and Virginia; John Dennis; Drury Theater, London, England, 1704

As You Like It; Act V Scene IV; William Shakespeare; epilogue, spoken by Rosalind; England, written in late 1599, published, first folio, 1623

Big Bucks; Pat Cook; Dramatic Publishing Co., Woodstock, IL, U.S.A., 1982

Cat on a Hot Tin Roof; Tennessee Williams; first presented Morosco Theater, Broadway, New York, NY, U.S.A., March 24, 1955

Clari, Maid of Milan, opera, John Howard Payne, Sir Henry Rowley Bishop; First performed at Theatre Royal, Covent Garden, London, U.K., 8 May 1823

Cradle Snatchers; starring Kitty Ladd, Susan Martin and Ethyl Drake, written by Russell Medcraft and Norman Mitchell; Broadway, New York, NY, U.S.A., 1925

Damon and Pithias; Richard Edwards' comedy play; London, England, 1566

Death of a Salesman; Arthur Miller; Eliza Kazan, Morosco Theater, New York, NY, U.S.A., February 10, 1949

Down an Alley Filled with Cats; Warwick Moss, page 15 in Act 1, New South Wales, Australia, Samuel French, Inc., New York, NY, USA, 1987 1987

Electra; Sophocles, Rome, circa 409 B.C.

Englishmen for my Money or A Woman Will Have Her Will; play by William Haughton; London, England, 1598

Every Man in His Humour, Ben Johnson, London, England, 1598

Flying Scud; Dion Boucicault; Holborn Theatre Royal, London, U.K., October 6, 1866

Foole upon Foole; Robert Armin; London, England, 1605

Giselle (ou les Wilis); Ballet by Jules-Henri Vernoy de Saint-Georges and Théophile Gautier; Premier Paris, France, 28 June 1841

Gentlemen Prefer Blondes; Broadway play, New York, NY, U.S.A., 1949

Gorboduc; Thomas Norton and Thomas Sackville; first performed before Queen Elizabeth London, England, 18 January 1562:

Gypsy: A Musical Fable; Broadway production based on a book by Arthur Laurents about Gypsy Rose Lee; New York, NY, U.S.A., 1959

Hamlet; 2 general references, *Hamlet; Act 3, Scene 2, Act 4, Scene 2, Act V, scene 2,* The *Second Quatto,* William Shakespeare, England, 1602, 1604

Henry IV; Part 1; William Shakespeare; England, 1597

Henry IV; Part 2; William Shakespeare; England, 1598

Henry V; I, ii; general reference, *Henry V;* William Shakespeare; England, 1598- 1599

Henry VI; William Shakespeare; England, 1591-1604

Hob and Nob; one-act romantic comedy play, Madison Morton; published in *The Exhibition Speaker;* P.A. Fitzgerald; D.M. Dewey, New York, NY, U.S.A., 1856

If it be not good, the diuel is in it (If This Be Not a Good Play, the Devil is in It); Thomas Dekker; London, England, 1611

It's a small world after all; Richard M. Sherman and Robert B. Sherman; U.S.A., 1964

Julius Caesar; William Shakespeare; England, 1599

Kensington Gardens; a comedy, John Leigh, England, 1720

King John; William Shakespeare; England, 1595

King Lear; William Shakespeare; England, written between 1603 and 1606, published in 1608

King Richard III; General reference; *Act 5, Scene 3, Line 117; Queen Margaret's Monologue,* William Shakespeare; England, c. 1591

Lady Windemere's Fan; Oscar Wilde, Elkin Mathews and John Lane; first produced on at the St. James's Theatre in London, U.K., 22 February 1892

Love and a bottle; George Farquhar; comedy play, London, England, 1689

Love's Labours Lost; William Shakespeare, England, 1588

MacBeth (general ref.); *MacBeth, Act 4, Scene 3;* William Shakespeare, England, 1605

Make New Friends, but Keep the Old or *New Friends and Old Friends;* Dr. Joseph Parry (5-21-1841--2-17-1903); Danville, PA, U.S.A., late 1800s

Make New Friends; Girl Scout song, anonymous; date unknown

Marmion, Canto VI, Stanza 7; Walter Scott; London, U.K., 1808

Milk and Honey; Broadway Musical by Jerry Herman and Don Appell; New York, NY, U.S.A., 1961

Mr. Roberts, play by Thomas Heggen and Joshua Logan, act 3, scene 3, Fitelsson, Lusky, Aslan and Couture, New York, NY, U.S.A., 1948

Much Ado about Nothing, William Shakespeare, London, England, 1598-1599

Night Life; Sidney Kingsley; three-act play, first presented at Brooks Atkinson Theater, New York, NY, U.S.A., October 23, 1962

Orestes; Euripides; 234, Greece, 408 B.C.

Othello; William Shakespeare; England, 1604

Pappe with an Hatchet; John Lyly; London, England, September, 1589

Peter Pan; James Matthew Barrie; Samuel French, Inc., New York, NY, U.S.A., 1956

Piers Plowman; William Langland, London, England, 1377

Popping by Proxy; A Farce in One Act; O.E.Young; Walter H. Baker & Co. Boston, MA, U.S.A., 1899

Prophetess; John Fletcher, Philip Massinger; England, 1622

Promos & Cassandra; B3, George Whetstone comedy; England, 1578

Richelieu or the Conspiracy; Edward Bulwer-Lyton; Act II, Scene ii, London, U.K., 1839

Romeo and Juliet; William Shakespeare; England, between 1591 and 1595

She Stoops to Conquer; Oliver Goldsmith; London, U.K., 1773

She Would and She Would Not; Scene IV, Colley Cibber; England, 1702

Shooting Fish in a Barrel: the Child Ballad in America; Donald K. Wilgus; UCLA, CA, U.S.A., 1953

Soddered Citizen; play by Maramion Redux performed by the King's men at Blackfriar's Theater, circa 1630

Some Heads are Gonna Roll; Judas Priest; Columbia Records, New York, NY, U.S.A., 1984

Something's Gotta Give; Johnny Mercer; 1954, recorded by McGuire Sisters; Coral Records, New York, NY, U.S.A., 1955

Sylla, a tragedy; translated from the French of Etienne de Jouy by Victor Joseph; scene VIII, page 111, Ibtson and Palmer, London, U.K., 1829

Tancred and Sigismunda; Thomson; Act IV, Scene 1, published in *The British Drama*, London, U.K., 1804

Tenth Eclouge, line 69, Virgil, Rome, 70 BC

That's the Way the Big Ball Bounces; Terry Fell; RCA Victor label, New York, NY, December, 1955

The Best of Both Worlds; three-act play by Monica Ewer; London, U.K., 1925

The Connoisseur, or, Every man in his folly: A Comedy; by Mr. Connelly; London, England, 1736.

The Critic; Richard Brinsley Sheridan, John Douglas; New York, NY, U.S.A., 1848

The Death of Wallenstein; Frederich Schiller's tradgic German five-act play, translated into English by Samuel Taylor Colerage: G. Woodfall; London, U.K., 1800

The Desert Song; operetta, music, Sigmond Romberg, lyrics, Oscar Hammerstein II, Otto Harbach, Frank Mandel; Broadway, New York, NY, U.S.A., 1926

The East Indian: A Comedy; August von Kotzebue, German play, A. Thompson's English translation; T. N. Longman & O. Rees, London, U.K., 1799

The Hidden River; Ruth and Agustus Goetz; Curtis Publishing Co., New York, NY, U.S.A., 1956

The Hind and the Panther, John Dryden, London, U.K., 1687
The Hind and the Panther Travers'd to the story of the Country-Mouse and the City-Mouse, Matthew Prior and Charles Montagu, London, U.K., 1687

The Kicker; possibly by Josh Billings (Henry Wheeler Shaw, 1818-1885); Poughkeepsie, NY, U.S.A., 1870

The Life and Death of King John; Scene vii, William Shakespeare; England, 1598

The Massacre at Paris; Elizabethan play by Christopher Marlowe; London, England, 1593

The Merchant of Venice; William Shakespeare; England, 1586

The Merry Wives of Windsor; Act V, Scene I; William Shakespeare; England, 1602

The Mourning Bride; William Congreve; London, England, 1697

The Old Batchelour; William Congreve; a comedy of manners, produced in London, England, 1693

The Queens: being passages from the lives of Elizabeth, queen of England, and Mary Queen of Scotland, Scene III, Act I, page 49, Aldémah, Francis J. Schulte, Chicago, IL, U.S.A., 1892

The Rage; Frederick Reynolds; Theater-Royal Covent-Garden in London, U.K., 1795

The Rivals, Epilogue; Irish playright Richard Brinsley Sheridan; London, U.K., 1776

The Taming of the Shrew; William Shakespeare; England, 1596

The Tempest; William Shakespeare; England, 1610

The Winter's Tale; William Shakespeare; England, 1611

The Woman's Mascarade (a comedy in one act) by Nora Del Smith; Broadway Publishing, New York, WY, U.S.A., 1911

Thomas à Becket; George Darley, Edward Moxon; London, U.K., 1840

Troylus and Crisedye; tragedy, William Shakespeare; (2) England, circa 1602

Twelfth Night; II, iii; William Shakespeare; England, 1601

Us; Regina Spektor; Transgressive / WEA, London, U.K., 2006

Venus and Adonis; William Shakespeare; England, 1593

Walpole, or, Every Man Has His Price; Baron Edward Bulwer Lytton; first performed in London, U.K., 1869

Welcome Home: A Comedy; starring Cesar Romero, Marty Davis; 1978, presented in Drury Lane Theater, Evan Park, Illinois, 1981

Wit Without Money, Comedy, John Fletcher, London, England, 1625

Newspapers, Journals, Magazines and other such Publications

Ada Evening News; quote from Don Meredith, page seven, column one; Oklahoma, December 17th, 1970

Albany Medical Annals (NY); Volume 17, Albany, NY, U.S.A., 1896

All the Year Round, A Weekly Journal; story titled *A Hard Road to Travel;* Charles Dickens; August 15, 1868; *Volume 5;* page 271, 1871; Volume XV; Charles Dickens; London, U.K., April 17, 1887

Almanac of the Federal Judiciary; page 149, Aspen Law and Business, Aspen, CO, U.S.A., 1988

American Agriculturist, Vol. 3, No. 7, New York, NY, U.S.A., July, 1844

American Bar Association Journal, Volume 1; Number 3, American Bar Assoc., Salt Lake City, UT, U.S.A., July, 1915

American Business; Volume 19; Dartnell Corporation, New York, NY, 1949

American Flint; The American Flint Glass Workers' Union publication, Volume 39, page 58, Toledo, OH, U.S.A., 1950

American Horticulturist; Volume 25, article about Barn Weevles; Orange and Judd, New York, NY, U.S.A., 1866

American Magazine; story by Victor Speer titled *Vision in Baxter Bay;* Frank Leslie, December, 1893; Volume 124, 1937; Volume 150, page 140; Crowell Collier, Springfield, OH, U.S.A, 1950, January, 1952

American Speech; Journal of Duke University, Durham, NC, U.S.A., December, 1927, 1928

American Speech; Folk Sayings from Indiana, Paul Brewster, Duke University Press, Durham, NC, U.S.A., December, 1939

American Speech; Volume 12; University of Alabama Press, Tuscaloosa, AL, U.S.A., 1937

American Turf Register and Sporting Magazine; letter to the editor dated January 27, 1833; John Stuart Skinner; Baltimore, MS, U.S.A., March, 1833

Anthologia Hibernica, Richard Edward Mercier and Co., Dublin Ireland, January, 1794

Appleton's Journal; Appleton and Co., New York, NY, U.S. A. 1873

Atlantic Monthly; J.E.B. Stewart; Gamaliel Bradford, Jr.; 1913

Atlantic Monthly; Volume 21; Making of America Project, April, 1860, page 27, article 'Pittsburg' Tichner and Fields, Boston, MA, U.S.A., January, 1868 ; April, 1918, February, 1932

Ballou's dollar monthly magazine; Volume 5; New York, NY, U.S.A., January, 1857

Baseball Digest; article about San Francisco Giant's Willie McCovey;, April, 1961; page 81, article about Manager James Joseph Dykes; Highland Park, IL, U.S.A., July, 1967

Billboard Magazine; New York, NY, U.S.A.; March 28, 1942 page 10, page 13; article *"March of Time" Pays Visit to Music Row—Sees Everything, Tells Almost Nothing,* page 15, January 8, 1944; article 'Kyser Going Back to Hill,' page 5, November 5, 1945; July 6, 1946; August, 1946; 'Dressing Room Gossip,' November 4. 1950; March 17, 1951; September 22, 1951; ad on page 81 June 2, 1956; October 20, 1958; April 23, 1966

Black Belt Magazine; page 40, story by Dan Ivan, 'Honor among Thieves;' El Segundo, CA, U.S.A., February, 1975

Blackwood's Edinburgh Magazine; William Blackwood, Edinburgh, Scotland, U.K., August, 1827; April, 1831, chapter 14 of a serial titled *Tom Cringle's Log* by Michael Scott later published in 1834 as a novel, October, 1832 ; August, 1839; *The Green Hand, a "Short" Yarn, Part VI,* Edinburgh, Scotland, U.K., December, 1849

Boys' Life; article, 'Through the Fire' by James Ames; Boy Scouts of America; article,'Meet Don Strong in March' January, 1919; article, 'Courage,' Earl Reed Silvers, October, 1920; ad, July, 1930; story titled 'Arm of Guilt' by William Hayliger; page 6,May, 1936; sports article, *Winning Streak,* by B.J. Chute; page 8, February, 1938; article, 'Danger in the Air' by Richards Bennett; October, 1944; reference to phrase in article; Boy Scouts of America, New York, NY, U.S.A., March, 1955

BPC Banker's Magazine, Ltd.; Volume 221, London, U.K., 1977

Brick and Clay Record; Chicago, IL, U.S.A., 1 February 1912

Bulletin for Atomic Scientists; page 6, address by Robert J. Oppenheimer delivered to the Awards banquet of the Science Talent Institute in Washington, D.C., March 6, 1950; Educational Foundation for Nuclear Science, Inc., Chicago, IL, U.S.A., January, 1951

Bulletin of the Atomic Scientists; article titled *Scientists Have a Duty to Society* by Murray S. Levine, Chicago, IL, U.S.A., December, 1951

Bulletin of the California Academy of Sciences; San Francisco, CA, U.S.A., 5 January 1887

Business Week; archives, issues 3132 and 3133, page 161, article, 'May Never Shine Again', Zachery Schiller, Cleveland, OH, U.S.A., McGraw Hill, New York, NY, U.S.A., 1990

Capitol Hill News; Oklahoma City, OK, U.S.A., 1911

Changing Times; Kiplinger, New York, NY, U.S.A., April, 1976

Chemical News Journal of Physical Science; Sir William Crookes; article on the Society of Public Analysts about the Sale of Food and Drug Act that year in Britain; London, U.K., February 26, 1875

Crawford County Courier; Prairie du Chien; Wisconsin, U.S.A., 1852

Chambers Journal; William and Robert Chambers, London, U.K., 1883

Chamber's Journal; William and Robert Chambers, London, U.K., 3 October 1857

Changing Times; Kiplinger, Washington, DC, U.S.A., August, 1950, February, 1952

Chicago Sun-Times; Chicago, IL, U.S.A., December, 1999

Chips Ahoy; Magazine interview with Rear Admiral Grace Hopper; U.S. Navy, Washington, DC, U.S.A., July, 1986

Church Missionary Record; detailing the proceedings of the Church Missionary Society, London, U.K., February, 1833

CIE; official journal of the Bartrenders International League of America, page 49, Cincinnati, OH, U.S.A., 15 February 1912

Cincinnati Magazine; Cincinnati, OH, U.S.A., July, 1977

Cobbett's Weekly Political Record, London, 20 August 1825

Collier's Illustrated Weekly; Volume 101, Berwyn, PA, U.S.A., 1938

Collier's Illustrated Weekly, Volume 120, page 104, Berwyn, PA, U.S.A., 1947

Collier's Magazine; Volume 74, P.F. Collier, Berwyn, PA, U.S.A., 1924

Cosmopolitan Magazine; article titled *The Curious Tribe of McFee* by Peter B. Kyne; New York, NY, U.S.A., September, 1922

Catalogue of Copyright Entries, Third Series; Volume 8; U.S. Copyright Office, Library of Congress, Washington, DC, U.S.A., January to June, 1954

Computerworld, article, page 58, Farmington, MA, U.S.A., May 12, 1986

Corks and Curls, Volume 18; The University of Virginia, 1905

Current Opinion, Travel, Adventure and Sport; Current Literature Publishing Co., New York, NY, U.S.A., June, 1892

Daily Advertiser; Boston, Massachusetts, 'From the Connecticut Courant,' page one, 17 July 1819

Daily Courier: ad, page 18, column 8, placed by Holmes Motor Company; Waterloo, Iowa, U.S.A., June 6th, 1950

Daily Evening Picayune; San Francisco, CA, U.S.A., Dec. 3, 1851

Daily Express; Derek Marks, Editor; London, U.K., March 17, 1969

Daily Kennebec Journal; Augusta, Maine, U.S.A., May, 1914

Daily Picayune; article 'From Mississippi;' page 1, column 37, New Orleans, LA, U.S.A., February, 1855

Debates: Official Report, Volume 2; Canadian Parliament House of Commons, Canada, 1889

Decatur Republican; Decatur, IL, U.S.A., 1869

Direct Marketing; Volume 37; Hoke Communications publication, Garden City, NY, U.S.A., 1974

Dollar Newspaper; Philadelphia, PA, U.S.A., early July, 1846

Druggists' Circular; Volume LI; New York, NY, U.S.A., 1907

Dry Goods Reporter; article, *Full Steam Ahead for 1915;* Chicago, IL, U.S.A., January 2nd, 1915:

Ebony Magazine, Navy ad, page 43, Midtown West, New York, NY, U.S.A., May, 1977

Economic Journal; published on behalf of the Royal Economic Society, London, U.K., 1952

Electrical Review; Chicago, IL, U.S.A., Saturday, 19 January 1918

Electrical Worker; a magazine published by The International Brotherhood of Electrical Workers, Springfield, Ill, U.S.A., May, 1914

Engineering and Mining News; published by McGraw Hill Co., New York, NY, U.S.A., 1919

Europe: Revue littéraire mensuelle; Les Éditions Denoël, Volume 24, Paris, France, 1946

Evening Independent News; St. Petersburg, FL, U.S.A., September 2, 1938

Evening State Journal; Lincoln, Nebraska, USA, 1937

Everybody's Magazine; The Ridgeway Co., New York, NY, A Frankenstein of 'the Fancy' by Kennett Harris, April, 1906; The Game of Light by Richard Washburn Child on page 49, July, 1914; reference, December, 1924

Field and Stream Magazine; Bonnier Corp., New York, NY, U.S.A., July, 1979

Field and Stream; Boulder, CO, U.S.A., October, 1988

Folk-say; Volume IV; Oklahoma Folk-Lore Society, Tulsa, OK, U.S.A., 1932

Forum; Forum Publishing Co., New York, NY, U.S.A., Volume 29, 1900; Volume 77, 1927

Forest and Stream; magazine; Charles Hallock, New York, NY, U.S.A., 11 February 1892

Fort Wayne Gazette, article, Ft. Wayne, IN, U.S.A., September of 1895

Fur News and Outdoor World; article, *The Little Big Horn or Why Custer Lost;* Summerville, NJ, U.S.A., October, 1920

Galveston News; Galveston, Texas, USA, 15 August 1954, page 22; article, 'One of the Polk Men,' page 1, column 7, 16 September, 1856

Game Breeder and Sportsman; Volumes 35- 36, page 240; Game Conservation Society, Inc., U.S.A., 1931

Gleanings in Bee Culture; Volume 17; 'A.I. Root,' story entitled 'Our Homes,' Medina OH, U.S.A., 1889

Golden Hours; a magazine for boys and girls; Hitchcock and Walden, Cincinnati, OH, U.S.A., January, 1877

Graham's Magazine; 'Meena Dimity,' N.P. Willis; Philidelphia, PA, U.S.A., September, 1843

Great Hours; a magzine for boys and girls; poem, 'Making it Skip,' Hitchcock and Walden, Cincinnati, OH, U.S.A., June, 1879

Hamilton Intelligencer; article, 'No Time to Swap Horses,' Hamilton, Butler Co., OH, U.S.A., September 10, 1846

Harper's Bazaar; Harper & Brothers, New York, NY, U.S.A., 21 December 1889

Harper's Magazine, article; 1888; *Volume 97;* Harper & Brothers, New York, NY, U.S.A., 1898

Harper's New Monthly Magazine; Loss and Gain; a Tale of Lynn; December, 1854; *Captain Tom: A Resurrection;* April, 1860; *Volume 32, Issue 191;* Harper & Brothers, New York, NY, U.S.A., April, 1866

Hartford Courant, Hartford, Connecticut, 2 December, 1956

Hawke's Bay Herald; Volume XXXII, Issue 10610, Page 5, 15, Australia, May, 1897

Humble Pie; William D. Emerson; Dramatic Publishing Co., Chicago, IL, U.S.A., 1910

Hunt's Merchants' Magazine and Commercial Review; Freeman Hunt, Thomas Prentice Kettell, Isaac Smith Homans; New York, NY, U.S.A., 1855

Hunt's Yachting Magazine; Hunt and Co., London, U.K., 1 February 1868

Huron Reflector; Norwalk, OH, USA, 1830

Hearst's International Combined with Cosmopolitan; Volume 188, International Magazine Co, New York, NY, U.S.A., 1945

InfoWorld; page 106: Mervo Park, CA, U.S.A., July 8, 1991

International Journal of Nonprofit and Voluntary Sector Marketing; volume 4, issue 2; article "Nonprofit community increasing nervousness about Year 2000," by Gary M. Grobman; 1999

Iowa Citizen; Iowa City, IA, U.S.A, October 9, 1891

Iowa City Press Citizen; Iowa City, IA, U.S.A., 1922

Jet Magazine; Chicago, IL, U.S.A., April 16, 1968

Judge's Library; New York, NY, U.S.A., December, 1900

Kentucky Folklore Record, Vol. 15-19, page 73, listing 81, Kentucky Folklore Society, Louisville, KY, U.S.A., 1969

Kiplinger's Personal Finance Magazine; page 19, New York, NY, U.S.A., April 1959

Kiwanis Magazine; Roe Fulkerson, article, *He Ain't Heavy, He's My Brother;* Detroit, MI, U.S.A., 1924

Knickerboker, or New York Monthly Magazine; Washington Irving's *The Creole Village;* November, 1836; Editor's Table; New York, NY, U.S.A., October, 1851, June, 1855

Kynoch Journal; Kynock Works, Witton, Birmingham, U.K., 1905

La Belle Assemblée, or *Bell's Court and Fashionable Magazine;* London, U.K., June, 1812

Labor Markets: Theories and Practices in the United States during the 1970s; discussion paper by Gordon L. Clark and Meric S. Gertler; John F. Kennedy School of Government, Cambridge, MA, U.S.A., 1981

La Crosse Independent Republican; La Crosse, WI, U.S.A., 16 September, 1856

Ladies' Home Journal; Volume 43, Part 1; LHJ Publishing, Lawrence, KS, U.S.A, April, 1926

Lawrence Daily Journal; Lawrence, KS, U.S.A., September 25, 1894

Les Réalités; issue 50, political bulletin; Paris, France, 1927

Life Magazine; page 39, an article *A. F. of L. Ditches a Racketeer but Cannot Ditch its Critics;* Time, Inc., Chicago, IL, U.S.A., October 27, 1941; ad, page 42, quip on photo, page 6, October 25, 1943; June 16, 1947; article *Slum Fighter Levi Tells What to Do;* page 134, April 11, 1955; page 17, letter to the editor, September 5, 1960; page 88, article, *You Can't Fool an Old Bag Like Me* about author Hedda Hooper, April 12, 1963; 'The Story of the Accused Killer of Dr. King', page 27, May 3, 1968

Lincoln Daily News; Lincoln, Nebraska, U.S.A., 15 August, 1914

Literary Curiosities; W.S.Walsh, London, U.K, 1893

Littell's Living Age, Volume 45, *Annie Orme;* Rachel Sinclair (first published in *Sharpe's London Magazine*) London, U.K., 20 November 1852

Locomotive Fireman's Magazine; page 97: Brotherhood of Locomotive Firemen and Engineers, Peoria, IL, U.S.A., January, 1899

London Charivari; Volume 265; Punch Publications, London, U.K., 1973

Long Lines; American Telephone and Telegraph publication; New York, NY, U.S.A., July, 1921

Los Angeles Times; Los Angeles, CA, U.S.A., March, 1951

Machinist's Monthly Journal; Int. Assoc. of Machinists, Washington, DC, U.S.A., January, 1920

Magazine of Fantasy and Science Fiction; Winter-Spring, New York. NY, U.S.A., 1950

Marketing Keys to Profits in the 1960s; American Marketing Association, New York, NY, U.S.A., 1960

McClure's Magazine; 'A Red Haired Cupid' by Henry Wallace Phillips; S.S. McClure Co., New York, NY, U.S.A., August, 1901

McMillian's Magazine; London, U.K., September, 1893

Medical Advance; H.C. Allen, M.D., James E. Forrester; Volume 45, Chicago, IL, U.S.A., January, 1907

Michigan Alumnus; page 32, University of Michigan, Ann Arbour, MI, U.S.A., October, 1918

Michigan Argonaut; Operetta titled *Rosalie;* The University of Michigan, Ann Arbor, MI, U.S.A., 13 January 1882

Milk Plant Monthly; Volume 46; Chicago, IL, U.S.A., 1957

Milwaukee Daily Sentinel and Gazette; Milwaukee, WI, U.S.A., October, 1839

Milwaukee Daily Sentinel; Milwaukee, WI, U.S.A., August, 1853

Moody's Monthly Magazine; article, *Mortgage Indebtedness Increasing;* Moody Corporation, New York, NY, U.S.A., May, 1907

Moody's Magazine; article titled 'An American System of Economics' by C.A. Bowsher; Moody Corporation, New York, NY, U.S.A., May, 1912

Mother Jones' Magazine; Tee shirt ad on page 52; Marion, OH, U.S.A., November, 1982

Motor Age Magazine; Tea Wagons for Repair Shops; Sir Humphrey Davy; Chicago, IL, U.S.A., 2 January 1919

Mountaineer; Salt Lake City, UT, U.S.A., 1860

Muncey's Magazine; Frank A. Muncey and Co., New York, NY, U.S.A., 'The Publisher's Desk,' May, 1897; Vol. 83, January, 1925

Negro Digest; Johnson Publishing Co., Chicago, IL, U.S.A., two references, June, 1969

New Hampshire Statesman and State Journal; Concord, NH, U.S.A., August, 1834

New Monthly Magazine; William Hazlitt; London, England, February, 1822; 1826

News-Democrat; poem, *Howdy;* Uhrichsville, Ohio, May 13, 1902

New Sporting Magazine; painting, R. Ackerman; London, England, UK, July, 1837

New York Daily News, article, page 3, Interview, Judge Solomon Wachtler New York, NY, U.S.A., January 31, 1985

New Yorker Magazine; Peter Arno cartoon illustration; New York, NY, U.S.A., March 1, 1941

New York Magazine; New York, NY, U.S.A.; 'The Smart Set,' May, 1912, page 58, November 15, 1971;*Volume 4*, page 99, 1971; article 'The City Politic,' page 13, November 25, 1974; page 24, February 2, 1987, article, 'A Wolf in the Kitchen;' article, 'Last Judgement' by Jeanie Kasindorf, page 29, August 1st, 1988

New York Post; article on 19, New York, NY, U.S.A., May 1941

New York Times Magazine; article by William Safire re article by David Bird in *The New York Times* regarding homeless men in 1981; New York, NY, U.S.A., December 26, 1988

Niles' National Register; in *Mr. Barney's Letter;* William Ogden Niles; Washington, DC, U.S.A., 12 May 1838

Niles Weekly Register; Baltimore, MD, U.S.A., 5 February 1820

Oakland Tribune; Oakland, CA, U.S.A., February, 1921, October, 1941

Once a Week; edited by Eneas Sweetland Dallas, story titled 'The Walking Posters;' Bradbury, Evans and Co., London, U.K., 22 June 1867

Orchard and Garden; magazine published by J.T. Lovett in Little Silver, NJ, U.S.A., July, 1888

Oxnard Press Currier; Oxnard, CA, U.S.A., August, 1946

Parisian Magazine; short story, A Bundle of Letters, Henry James; France, December 18, 1879

Philidelphia Scrapbook and Gallery of Comicalities; Philadelphia, PA, U.S.A., Saturday, 17 May 1834

Photoplay Magazine, Johnny Weissmueller quote, Macfadden Publications, Chicago, IL, U.S.A., June, 1932

Picayune; newspaper, New Orleans, LA, U.S.A., September, 1844

Poetry: A Magazine of Verse Volume XIX, Courage; by Karl Wilson Baker, page 16; edited by Harriet Monroe; October – March, 1921-1922

Poor Richard's Almanac; Benjamin Franklin; Philadelphia, PA, U.S.A., various editions, 1732-1758

Popular Aviation and Aeronautics; magazine, article about Lt. James Dyer; Beck Dist., New York, NY, U.S.A., February, 1929

Popular Aviation; magazine, article, 'Aftermath' page 106; Ziff-Davis Publishing Co., Chicago IL, U.S.A., July, 1939

Popular Boating Magazine; New York, NY, U.S.A., February, 1965

Popular Mechanics; '50,000 People Are After the Routine Jobs—*Break Away From This Competition*, Command Big Pay!' February, 1922; Yamaha ad, page 227; Chicago, IL, U.S.A., April, 1968

Popular Photography; Zif Davis Publishing, Chicago, IL, U.S.A., March 1947

Popular Science; New York, NY, U.S.A., October, 1873; April, 1883, article The Legal Status of Servant-Girls, January 1926; article on page 98, January, 1957,

Portsmouth Daily Times; Portsmouth, OH, U.S.A., October, 1941

Princeton Alumni Review; letter to the editor, page 4; Princeton, NJ, U.S.A., May 11, 1951

Princeton Alumni Weekly; May 19, 1939; page 21; February 11, 1955; On the Campus' by Calvin Fentress III , Princeton University Princeton, NJ, February, 1960

Printer's Ink; advertising trade journal, Fred R. Bernard's ad title; New York, NY, U.S.A., December 3, 1931

Proceedings of Annual Convention; The Minnesota Dairymen's Association, Volume 18, page 118; Harrison & Smith Printers, Minneapolis, MN, U.S.A., 1896

Public Utilities Fortnightly, Volume 27, page 528, Henry Clifford Spur; Public Utilities Reports, U.S.A., 1941

Publication of the American Dialect Society; J.P. Lippincott, Philadelphia, PA, U.S.A., 1948

Publisher's Weekly; article Communications, page 17, F. Leypold, Publisher's Board of Trade, New York, NY, U.S.A., January 6, 1877

Puck; Volume 10, Issue 103, Keppler and Schwarzman, New York, NY, U.S.A., 1882; January 6, 1909

Quarterly Journal of the Geographical Society of London; Volume 33; London, U.K., 1877

Radio Times; B.B.C., London, U.K., January, 2007

Railroad Magazine; Volume 46, article, 'In the Days of the Old Eighty-Five' by J.W. Hinds; Popular Publications, Chicago, IL, U.S.A., July, 1948

Reader's Digest; 1940s; Volume 106, page 2, article by DeWitt Wallace and Lela Acheson Wallace, Reader's Digest Assoc., Chappaqua, NY, 1975

Recreation, 'THEY ROAST THE REVEREND BRISTEBACK,' letter from a reader (A.W.Davis), G.O. Shields, New York, NY, U.S.A., April, 1903

Right On! Dorchester Publishing, New York, NY, U.S.A., 1971-2011

Rowing and Track Athletics; Crowther and Ruhl; McMillan and Co., New York, NY, U.S.A., 1905

Roycroft; Bert Hubbard, editor, article 'Dore's Sad Art;' East Aurora, NY, U.S.A., June, 1917

Rural Areas Development at Work; page 15; U.S. Department of Agriculture report; 1964

Sailors' and Soldiers' Magazine; Soldiers' and Steamers' Friends Society, London, U.K., July, 1861

St. Nicholas; an illustrated magazine for boys and girls, *Volume 45, Part 2* by Mary Maples Dodge, *Daddy Pat's Letters from the Front;* The Century Co., New York, NY, U.S.A., 1919

Santa Cruz Sentinel, page 32, Santa Cruz, CA, U.S.A.; Friday, 17 May 1974

Science News; article, 'Stomach Butterflies Scramble EGGs,' Joanne Silberner; Society for Science and the Public, Washington, D.C., U.S.A., February 22, 1986

Scientific American; ad for fishing lure; Munn and Co., New York, NY, U.S.A., 8 July 1882

Shell Aviation News; quote from an issue; London, U.K., 1948

Southern Literary Messenger; story titled 'The German's Daughter,' Thomas White; Richmond, VA, U.S.A., November, 1840

Southern Patriot; page 1; Charleston, SC, U.S.A., February 22nd, 1845,

Spirit of the English Magazines; article titled *Maurice and Berghetta;* Munroe and Francis, Boston, MA, U.S.A., January 1, 1820

Stars and Stripes; Washington, DC, U.S.A., October 18th 1918

Syracuse Herald, Syracuse, NY, U.S.A., March, 1919

Syracuse Sunday Standard; Syracuse, NY, U.S.A., November, 1884

Temple Magazine, "Limmers"; or, Twenty Years Ago, Chapter VI by George Livingstone Richard Bentley and Son, London, UK, September, 1878

Terre Haute Express; editorial by John Babsone; Lane Soule, Terre Haute, IN, U.S.A., 1851

The Adams Sentinel; Gettysburg, PA, U.S.A., March, 1834

The American Angler; article t, *Another Week on the Nantahala;* New York, NY, U.S.A., July, 1896

The American Economist; American Tariff League, New York, NY, U.S.A., February 10, 1911

The American Homoeopathist; New York, NY, U.S.A., June 1, 1893

The American Kennel Gazette; Volume 52; Raleigh, NC, U.S.A., 1935

713

The American Magazine; article titled *Letitia, Nursery Corps, U.S.A.*; George Madden Martin; Phillips Publishing Co., Springfield, OH, U.S.A., 1907

The American Magazine; Volume 105; Crowell-Collier, Berwyn, PA, U.S.A., 1928

The American Masonic Register and Literary Companion; U.S.A., April 4, 1840

The American Museum Journal; Volume 3; American Museum of Natural History, New York, NY, U.S.A., 1788

The American Stone Trade; Chicago, IL, August, 1921

The Antique Automobile; Antique Automobile Club of America, Hershey, PA, U.S.A., November, 1955

The Argosy; Griffith Gaunt, Charles Reade, Chapter 41, serialized; Strahan and Co. Magazine Publishers, London, UK, November, 1866

The Atheneaum; Murray's 'Journal of the English Agricultural Society,' Volume 1, Part 1; London, U.K., April 13, 1839

The Athens Messenger; Athens, OH, U.S.A., June, 1870

The Atlanta Constitution; Atlanta, Georgia, U.S.A., April 25, 1882; July, 1882; 16 October 1905, page 7, column 4; November, 1901; 20 March 1903

The Atlantic Monthly; Volume 199; Boston, MA, U.S.A., 1957

The Australian Journal; 'Thoughts on Threats;' Clarson, Massina and Co., Melbourne, Australia, June 30, 1866

The Automobile; article, *How to Make My Car Pay for Itself;* Automotive Industries, New York, NY, U.S.A., December 30, 1909

The Balance and Columbian Repository; Ezra Sampson, George Chittenden; Harry Croswell, Hudson, New York; 29 May, 1805; 22 October 1805

The Baltimore Sun; article, "No Matter How Thin You Slice It: Gab Of Collegiate Papas And Self-Starting Flappers Is Always Bolognie Anyhow And In Sort Of Code," Katherine Scarborough, page MS1; Baltimore, MD, U.S.A., May 9, 1926

The Bedford Gazette; Bedford, PA, U.S.A., September, 1951

The Bee; newspaper story; Danville, Virginia, August 27, 1941

The Bee-hive: A Musical Farce; John Gideon Milligan; The Theater Royal, Lyceum, W.H. Wyatt, London, England, U.K., 1811

The Berkshire Evening Eagle; Pittsfield, Berkshire, MA, USA, February, 1947

The Big Spring Herald; Big Spring, TX, U.S.A., December, 1976

The Bismarck Tribune; Bismarck, ND, U.S.A., December, 1921

The Black Diamond; a magazine published by Lehigh Coal and Navigation Company; Pittsburg, PA, U.S.A., March 7, 1908

The Boston Globe; Boston, MA, U.S.A., 1980

The Boston, Lincoln, Louth & Spalding Herald; Boston, Lincolnshire, U.K., January, 1833

The Boston Morning Post; Boston, MA, U.S.A., 23 March, 1839

The Bridgemen's Magazine; page 33 in 'The Wanderings of Two Backerups;' New York, NY, U.S.A., in September, 1903

The Bridgeport Telegram; Bridgeport, CT, U.S.A., Private Samuel S. Polley; 1918

The British Magazine and Review, Harrison and Co., London, UK, August, 1783

The Canadian Spectator; page 44; Montreal, ON, Canada, Saturday, January 5, 1878

The Capitol; Annapolis, MD, U.S.A., January, 1973

The Capitol Times; car ad, newspaper; Madison, Wisconsin, June, 1971

The Captain Magazine; serial by P.G. Wodehouse; London, U.K., 1910

The Carles of Dysart; Robert Burns; London, U.K., 1834

The Casket, Flowers of Literature, Wit and Sentiment; Atkinson, Philadelphia, PA, U.S.A, March, 1830

The Century Magazine, The Century Co., New York, NY, U.S.A., April, 1884

The Century Magazine; 'Pride' by Julian Rothery; New York, NY, U.S.A., 1916,

The Century illustrated monthly magazine; Volume 48; The Century Co., NY, U.S.A., October, 1894

The Charities Review; New York, NY, U.S.A., April, 1899

The Charleston Daily Mail; Charleston, WV, U.S.A., May, 1954

The Chautauquan; Volume 5; number 1, published by the Chautauqua Institution Literary and Scientific Circle, 'Editor's Outlook' on page 51; Chautauqua Press, Meadville, PA, U.S.A., October 1884

The Chemical News and Journal of Physical Science; William Crookes, page 285, in Proceedings of Society; London, U.K., June 26, 1794

The Chinese Recorder and Missionary Journal; Shanghai, China, Volume 39, page 452; 1832; December, 1908

The Christian Register; Unitarian Conference, Boston, MA, U.S.A., 1 September 1921

The Clearfield Progress; newspaper, Cartoon, *'Our Boarding House with Major Hopple;'* Clearfield, PA, U.S.A., 1938

The College Courant; Yale's weekly journal, New Haven, CT, 25 June 1870

The Columbia Reporter; Columbia, WI, U.S.A., November, 1845

The Commercial Advertiser; Milwaukee, WI, U.S.A., June 1850:

The Coshocton Tribune; Coshocton, OH, U.S.A., February, 1934

The Daily Colonist; Victoria, B.C., Canada, October, 1921

The Daily Intelligencer; Doylestown, PA, U.S.A., December, 1985

The Daily Nevada State Journal; Reno, NE, U.S.A., February, 1876

The Daily News; Newport, RI, U.S.A., April 15, 1954

The Daily Review; 'Lauder Tickled at Change;' Decatur IL, U.S.A., 1910

The Daily Telegraph; caption to a picture; London, U.K., June 2, 1981

The Daily Wisconsin Patriot; Madison, WI, U.S.A., May, 1859

The Democratic Review; (magazine); New York, NY, U.S.A., 1851

The Dental Register, Cincinnati, Ohio, USA, June, 1892

The Deseret Weekly; article 'The Indian Scare'; Latter Day Saints, Salt Lake City, UT, U.S.A.; Saturday, 22 November, 1800

The Dial; edited by M.D. Conway, lecture by Sir William Hamilton; Cincinnati, OH, U.S.A., November, 1860

The diary of Sarah Knight in *The Journals of Madam Knight and the Reverend Mister Buckingham;* written in 1704 and 1710, and published in *American Speech;* American Dialect Society, Duke University Press, Durham, NC, U.S.A., 1940

The Dog Fancier; Volume 21, Number 1; Battle Cr eek, MI, U.S.A., January, 1912

The Dothan Eagle; Dothan, AL, U.S.A., September, 1944

The Dublin Review; Thos. Richardson and Son, London, U.K., March, 1848

The Dublin University Magazine; Volume 16; Number 92, Dublin, Ireland, January, 1840

The Dublin University Magazine; novel by F.W. Currey printed as a serial; London, U.K., 1875 -1876

The Dunkirk Observer-Journal; Dunkirk, NY, U.S.A., September, 1888

The Edinburgh Advertiser; Edinburgh, Scotland, U.K., April, 1822

The Edinburgh Magazine; Edinburgh, Scotland, U.K., 1787

The Edinburgh Review; Edinburgh, Scotland, U.K., 1833, 1839

The Electric Magazine of Foreign Literature, Science and Art; Leavitt, Trow and Co., New York, NY, U.S.A., 1845

The Electric Review; monthly periodical, article by William Hendry Stowell; London, England, U.K., 1816

The Electrical Review; 'The Work of Scudamore' by Rollo Appleyard; H. Alabaster and Gatehouse, London, 23 June 1906

The Eleusis of Chi Omega; Chi Omega Fraternity, George E. Howard, printer, Washington, DC, U.S.A., August, 1910

The Eton Bureau; from the Eton School, London, page 191, 1842

The European Magazine and London Review; Philosophical Society, London, U.K., November, 1801, 1806

The Evangelical Magazine and Missionary Chronicle; page 5, Westley and Davis, London, U.K., January, 1834

The Evening Democrat; newspaper; Warren, PA, U.S.A., October, 1900

The Evening News; article, *The King of All Liars;* North Tonawanda, New York, NY, U.S.A., 23 April, 1895

The Examiner; New York, NY, U.S.A., Saturday, 25 December 1813

The Examiner; letter; London, U.K., Sunday, 7 March 1819

The Farmer's Magazine; Maryland State Agricultural Society, Boston, MA, U.S.A., Friday 31 August 1821

The Fireside, Annual; Rev. Charles Bullock; Hand and Heart Publishing, London, U.K., 1877

The Fort Wayne Gazette; Fort Wayne, IN, U.S.A., April, 1887

The Friend, a Religious and Literary Journal; Philadelphia, PA, U.S.A., March 10, 1910

The Friend's Intelligencer, 'Book Notes' on 'The Case of Ralph', by James Oppenheim, printed in *Harper's Bazaar* Philadelphia, PA, September 28, 1912

The Frontier Times Magazine; J. Marvin Hunter; Volume 25, Number 08; Ft. Worth, TX, U.S.A., May, 1948

The Galaxy; page 93; Aheldon and Co., New York, NY, U.S.A., January, 1874

The Galveston Daily News; Galveston TX, U.S.A., June 1881, December, 1889:

The Gateway, University of Alberta, "The Wildside of Greed Shown in Wall Street. article on page 7; Alberta, Canada, January 5, 1988

The Gentlemen's Magazine; F. Jefferies, 1770, March. 1771; Sylvanus Urban, Gent, William Pickering; John Bower Nichols and Son; January, 1839; *Will He Escape?* Evans, & Co., London, U.K., September, 1869

The Globe; Kansas City, KS, U.S.A., May, 1881

The Grey River Angus; Grey River, NZ, article, May 23, 1874

The Guthrian; Guthrie Center, IA, U.S.A., 26 January 1970

The Hartford Courant; Hartford, CT, U.S.A., October 14, 1938

The Harvard Advocate; 'Kentucky Bell' page 89; Harvard University, Cambridge, MA, U.S.A., March 7, 1901

The Harvester World; Volume 20; International Harvester Company, Chicago, IL, U.S.A., 1929

The Helena Independent; Helena MT, U.S.A., January 1928

The Illinois Chemist; footnote, page 57; University of Illinois, Urbana, IL, U.S.A., November, 1915

The Illuminating Engineer; ad for Cooper Hewitt Lamps, E Leavenworth Elliott; Illuminating Engineering Publishing Co., New York, NY, U.S.A., November, 1911

The Index; letter to the editor; Boston, MA, U.S.A., Thursday 6 August, 1874

The Indiana Democrat; Indiana, PA, USA, fall, 1882

The Inlander; (University of Michigan student magazine), Willard C. Gore, 'Student Slang', December, 1895

The International Steam Engineer; Chicago, IL, U.S.A., January 1818

The Iowa Homestead; Des Moines, IA, U.S.A., November 1921

The Judge; Leslie-Judge Co., 225 Fifth Ave., New York, 29 June 1912

The Judges Library; New York, NY, U.S.A., 1903

The Journal of geography; Volume 8; National Council for Geographic Education, National Council of Geography Teachers (U.S.), American Geographical Society of New York, NY, U.S.A., 1909

The Kansas City Star; 'History of sliced bread little known on 75th anniversary;' Kansas City, MO, U.S.A., 07-29-2003; archived from the original on 08-12-2003

The Kenosha Times, Kenosha, Wisconsin, July, 1857

The Kenyon Review; Kenyon College, Volume 31; Edited by John Crowe Ransom; Gambier, OH, U.S.A., 1969

The Ladies' Repository; article, Caroline Soule, 'A Soldier of the Republic'; Methodist Episcopal Church, Cincinnati, OH, U.S.A., May, 1864

The Lady's Magazine; Louis A. Godey; London, U.K., 1830

The Lancaster Journal; Lancaster, Pennsylvania, 1818

The LatterDay Saints Millinnial Star; Salt Lake City, UT, U.S.A., Thursday, 10 August 1905

The Leavenworth Medical Herald; Volume 4, page 26; Leavenworth, KS, U.S.A., June, 1870

The Liberal and the New Dispensation; Volume 12; article titled *'Borrowing Trouble;'* 1803

The Listener; Volume 18; British Broadcasting Corp., London, U.K., 1937

The London Journal, in an serial titled 'Lady Thornhurst's Daughter' by Mrs. Harriot Lewis, Chapter 18, October 7, 1871

The London magazine or Gentleman's monthly intelligencer; London, England; Volume 3, 1734; May, 1780; article titled 'Janus Weatherbound,' January, 1823

The Long Beach Independent; editorial; Long Beach, CA, U.S.A., October, 1943, August, 1971

The Maine Farmer's Almanac; various issues; World Almanac Books, New York, NY, U.S.A., 1819-to date

The Mansfield News; Mansfield, OH, U.S.A., May, 1920

The Medical Times; London, U.K., Saturday May 2nd, 1846

The Murfreesboro Post, article, *Should it be Cold Hands—Cold Heart?* Kestner, Mark, D.O.; Murfreesboro, TN, U.S.A January 20, 2015

The Museum Studies Journal; Volume 1, Issue 4; John F. Kennedy University, San Francisco, CA, U.S.A., 1984

The Leatherneck; U.S. Marine Corp publication, Volume 12; Washington, DC, U.S.A., 1929

The Lima News; Lima, OH, U.S.A., November, 1949; January 1973

The London Review of Literture; Germanicus, A Tragedy; by 'A Gentleman of the University of Oxford;' London, U.K., 1775

The Louisiana Planter and Sugar Manufacturer, W.C. Stubbs, PhD, main editor, New Orleans, LA, U.S.A., 13 May 1899:

The Lumber Trade Journal; John W. Long, Arthur R. Carr, New York, NY, U.S.A., 15 January 1922

The Massachusetts Spy; article, Isaiah Thomas; Worchester, MA, USA, June 14, 1815, 1939

The Meerut Universal Magazine; Volume 1, page 32; verse IX of an unauthorized publication of the historic ballad, *The Devil Dutchman;* Agra Press, Agra, India, 1835

The Middlesex Currier; Middlesex, England, UK, February, 1832

The Milwaukee Sentinel; Milwaukee, WI, U.S.A., article published in July, 1928

The Mirror of Taste; Bradford and Inskeep, Boston, *MS*, published in Philadelphia, PA, U.S.A., 1810

The monthly miscellany; or Gentleman and Lady's Complete Magazine; Vol. II; London, England, U.K., 1774

The Monthly Review, or Literary Journal; Ralph Griffiths, George E. Griffiths, London, U.K., September 1785

The National Provisioner; American Meat Packer's Association's New York and Chicago weekly trade publication, Chicago Section, April 8, 1911

The Nation; Volume 44, number 1146; (a weekly journal); The Evening Post Publishing Co., New York, NY, U.S.A., June 16, 1887

The Newark Daily Advocate; Newark, OH, U.S.A., October, 1900

The New Catholic World; Volume 180; Paulist Fathers, New York, NY, U.S.A., 1954

The Newport Mercury; (newspaper); Newport, RI, U.S.A., June, 1887

The News; Frederick, MD, USA, May, 1942

The New Sporting Magazine; A Trip to Paris with Mr. Jorrocks; London, U.K., July, 1833

The New York Farmer and American Gardner Magazine; D. K. Minor, New York, NY, U.S.A., May 1835

The New York Gazette and weekly Mercury; New York, NY, U.S.A., May 17, 1773

The New York Globe; Keeping Up with the Jonses; Arthur 'Pop' Momand; New York, NY, U.S.A., 1913-1939

The New York Literary Journal; Volume 4; New York, NY, U.S.A., 1821

The New York Magazine; New York, NY, U.S.A., 1904, February 15, 1971

The New York Sun; New York, NY, U.S.A., April, 1896

The New York Teacher, and the American Educational Monthly; Volume 8; New York, NY, 1871

The New York Times; article; New York, NY, USA, August, 1862; ad, 23 October 1862, 30 May 1861; December 1883; page 7, statement by Captain Jack Abernathy; New York, NY, 9 June 1910; March, 1920; January 21, 1922; 3 November 1925; article "Topic of the Times," page 33, 29 November 1933 page 2, in an article titled 'Offers of 15 to 1 on Walker Go Begging;' article, December, 1972, July 14, 1974; article titled, *Dance Around the Truth*, story about Tanaquil Le Clercq, February 15, 2012

The New York Tribune; New York, NY, U.S.A., 22 September 1918; unspecified date, early 1900s

The New York Vegetable Grower's News, New York Vegetable Grower's Assoc., Cornell University, New York, NY, U.S.A., Volume 19, page 419, 1962

The Novelist's Magazine; Vol XIX: The Expedition of Humphrey Clinker; Harrison and Co., London, U.K., 1785,

The Olean Evening Times; article by Allene Sumner Olean; New York, NY, U.S.A., March, 1926

The Opal: A Monthly Periodical of the State Lunatic Asylum; Utica, NY, U.S.A., 1852

The Oshkosh Daily Northwestern; Oshkosh, WI, U.S.A., November, 1969

The Outlook, Magazine; Volume 76; New York, NY, U.S.A., January, 1904

The Philadelphia Aurora; article; Philadelphia, PA, U.S.A., 1798

The Philosophical Magazine and Journal; Alexander Tilloch, article 'Return of the Discovery Ships'; Richard and Arthur Taylor, London, U.K., November, 1820

The Photographic Journal of North America; Edward L. Wilson Co., Philadelphia, PA, U.S.A., May, 1918

The Pittsburg Bulletin; How to Succeed at Life; Andrew Carnegie, 19 December 1903

The Port Arthur News; Port Arthur, Texas newspaper; March 20, 1936, February, 1946

The Portsmouth Times; Portsmouth, OH, USA, April, 1898

The Portfolio; John Duncombe; London, U.K., 11 February, 1826

The Post Standard; (newspaper); Syracuse, New York, NY, U.S.A., September 4, 1906

The Plaindeale; New York, NY, Saturday, 30 June 1837

The Practical Druggist; article by W.H. Cousins of Wichita Falls, Texas, titled *'Substitution;'* Denver Chemical Manufacturing Co., New York, NY, U.S.A., August, 1914

The Present State of Europe; Volume 12; London, England, January, 1701

The Prison World; Volume 11, page 18; American Prison Association; Bruce Publishing Co., Milwaukee, WI, U.S.A., 1949

The Punch, or the London Charivari; London, UK, 25 November 1908

The Puritan, an illustrated magazine for free churchmen; Volume I and II, p 36; February to December, 1899

The Railroad Telegrapher, Volume 30, Part 1, St. Louis, MO, U.S.A., 1913

The Railwayan Magazine; Kansas City Public Service Company, Kansas City, MO, U.S.A. June, 1920

The Record Chronicle, Denton, Texas section 2, page 2, column 4; 24 December 1956

The Religious Intelligencer; Nathan Whiting; New-Haven, CN, U.S.A., 9 November 1833

The Reno Daily Gazette; story; Reno, NV, U.S.A., 1876

The Rotarian Magazine; official publication of Rotary International, Evanston, IL, U.S.A.; February, 1927; 'Points of Friction' by Miles H. Krubine, page 28; excerpts from: May, 1927; January, 1938; April, 1944; August, 1945 and February 1975

The Sailor's Magazine and Naval Journal; American Seaman's Friend Society, New York, NY, U.S.A., October, 1849

The St. Louis Globe-Democrat; St. Louis, MO, U.S.A., August 1886

The St. Louis Herald; article 'No such thing as free lunch—says who?' by Carolyn Olson, Travel, page 2T; St. Louis, MO, U.S.A., March 27, 1994

The St. Louis Post and Dispatch; 26 May 1884; St. Louis, MO, U.S.A., January 10, 1989

The Saturday Evening Post; The Black Cat; short story, Edgar Allen Poe; August 19, 1843; 3 September 1903, 22 April 1905; article, 'Who's Who and Why'; November 6, 1909; page 12, story titled 'On Main Street'; July 10, 1912; story by Harry Leon Wilson entitled 'Ruggles of Red Gap'; January 2, 1915; March 20, 1915; Volume 187, Issue 7, in an article titled 'Hit the Line Hard,' on page 93; April 5, 1915; story titled 'The Golden Idol' by Christine Jope Slade; April 16, 1921; *Volume 201;* 1929; *Volume 219;* page 137; Philadelphia, PA, U.S.A., 1947

The Saturday Review of Politics, Literature, Science, Art and Finance; London, U.K., 20 February 1853

The Scots Magazine; 'The History of John and His Household;' Edinburgh Literary Miscellany, August, 1823

The Searchlight on Congress; article about Iowa Senator Smith W. Brookhart, *What about Brookhart,* Walter Durand, pp 17, 18; Washington, DC, U.S.A., 30 June 1922

The Sheboygan Press; Sheboygan, WI, U.S.A., December, 1929

The Smart Set Magazine; John Adams Thayer Corp., New York, NY, U.S.A., May, 1912

The Soda Springs Sun; Soda Springs, ID, U.S.A., July, 1942

The Southern Literary Messenger; Edgar Alan Poe; T. W. White, Richmond, VA, U.S.A., January 1835

The Southwestern Reporter; Volume 177, West Publishing Company, Eagan, MO, U.S.A., 1915

The Spectator, reprinted in a volume in 1729 by J. Tonson; London, U.K., Wednesday, 30 July 1712

The Spectator; Chilton Company, Philadelphia, PA, U.S.A. June, 1890; unknown volume number, 1944

The Sporting Magazine; John Wheble, Editor; London, U.K., 1805

The Station Agent, railroad magazine, Cleveland, OH, U.S.A., September, 1890

The Stevens Point Daily Journal; Stephens Point, WI, U.S.A., May, 1909

The Strand Magazine; syndicated series *An African Millionaire* by Grant Allen; London, U.K., 1896-1897

The Syracuse Herald; article, *'Great Life, Writes Soldier at Camp;'* Private Walter J. Kennedy; Syracuse, NY, U.S.A., June 29, 1918

The Teacher, Volume II, Number 24, New York, NY, U.S.A., April, 1890

The Teacher's Visitor; Volume 5, edited by William Carus Wilson; London, U.K., July-December, 1846

The Texas Outlook; Volume 44; Texas Teachers' Association, Austin, TX, U.S.A., 1960

The Texas Railway Journal, Fort Worth, TX, U.S.A., November, 1913

The Theosophist Volume XXX; a magazine of 'Brotherhood, Oriental Philosophy, Art, Literature and Occultism;' edited by Annie Basant, P.T.S., page 232; Madras India, 1609

The Threshereman's Review; editorial review, page 24; St. Joseph, MO, U.S.A., January, 1904

The Times; London, U.K., 1788; January, 1829; March, 1939

The Times Literary Supplement; London News International, London, U.K., 1908

The Tuapeka Times; Lawrence, New Zealand, August, 1889

The United Service, a Monthly Review of Military and Naval Affairs; A.R. Hamersly, Philladelphia, PA, U.S.A., November, 1894

The United States Literary Gazette poem titled 'To Fancy' by 'Lonnol,' Cummings, Hilliard and Co., Boston, MA, U.S.A., 1 August 1825

The United States Medical Investigator, Volume XVII; page 225, Duncan Bros., Chicago, IL, U.S.A., 1883

The U.S. Forestry Bureau Bulletin; Washington, DC, U.S.A, 1905

The Victoria Advocate; Victoria, TX, U.S.A., August 20, 1956

The Washington Newspaper; University of Washington Department of Journalism, 'Ready for Press Convention,' Chapin D. Foster; Seatle, WA, U.S.A., July, 1922

The Washington Post; 8 July 1912, 17 May 1924; article, January, 1983; article by David Remnick; article, 'Smokey Bear Caught on Like Wildfire; Icon's Popularity Kept Artist Busy During His Decades at the U.S. Forest Service;' Washington, DC, U.S.A., December 1, 1995

The Weekly Inspector; poem from: *Letter to the Printer of the Middletown Gazzette;* 'Printed in a Gazette of the date February 6th, 1790; New York, NY, U.S.A., Saturday, March 28, 1807

The Western Review; Volume 1, page 108, February; Reed, Browne and Co. Chicago, IL, U.S.A., 1869

The West Virginia Bar; West Virginia Bar Association, Morgantown, WV, February, 1896

The Wilkes-Barre Gleaner; article, *'Who'll turn Grindstones, from essays from the desk of Poor Richard and the Scribe;'* Charles Miner, Wilkes-Barre, PA, U.S.A., 1811

The Windsor Magazine; article, June, 1896; article, *The Desert Air* by Dornford Yates; Ward, Lock and Bowden, Ltd., London, U.K., August, 1919

The Winnipeg Free Press; article on cinematic drama; Winnipeg, Manitoba, Canada, March, 1944

The Women's Magazine; page 8, article, 'Why Some Men Succeed;' New Idea Publishing Co., New York, NY, U.S.A., January, 1914

The XIX Century, Volume 2, "Early Literary Progress in South Carolina," January 1870

The Yorkshire Magazine; Volume 1; Yorkshire Literary Union, Yorkshire, U.K., 1881

Thirteen hundred old time words of British, Continental or aboriginal origins, still or recently in use among the Pennsylvania mountain people, Henry W. Shoemaker, Issue 12, page 65, Times Tribune Press, Pennsylvania Folklore Society, Pittsburg, PA, U.S.A., 1930

Time Magazine; New York, NY, U.S.A., 1936; April 28, 1952; July 31, 1973

Transactions of the Commonwealth Club of California; San Francisco, CA, U.S.A., February, 1922

Transactions to the State Medical Society of Wisconsin; Volume 33; Tracy, Gibbs and Co., Madison, WI, 1899

Tri Weekly Newspaper; Galveston, Texas, January, 1863

Typographical Journal; International Typographical Union, Mergenthaler Linotype Co., New York, NY, February, 1915, September, 1917

Vanity Fair; New York, NY, U.S.A., November, 1927

Verbatim; quarterly language publication; Chicago, IL, U.S.A., Chearsley, Aylesbury, Bucks, U.K., winter 1979-'80

Volpore, Ben Jonson, 1605, produced 1606, first printed in quarto, George Eld for Thomas Thorpe, London, England, 1607

Wall Street Journal, news story, New York, NY, U.S.A., 1923

Watchman and Wesleyan Advertiser; newspaper, London, U.K., unkown month and day, 1859.

Waterloo Daily Courier; Waterloo, IA, U.S.A., September 3, 1946

Weekly World News; Horoscope section, page 42, Lantana, FL, U.S.A., March 7, 1989

What We Found behind the Scenes in European Research; from *The First Annual Reunion Dinner of the National Research Council, European Labratory Tour;* The Waldorf-Astoria, New York, NY, U.S.A., Friday October 29, 1937

Whistle While You Work; song with music written by Frank Churchill and lyrics by Larry Morey for the animated film, *Snow White and the Seven Dwarfs,* Walt Disney Productions, Hollywood, CA, U.S.A., 1937

William & Mary College Quarterly; Williamsburg, VA, published Richmond, VA, U.S.A., 1710

Wisconsin Herald and Grant County Advertiser; Lancaster, WI, U.S.A., 1845

Wisconson State Journal; page 4, column 5, *On Broadway with Walter Winchell;* Madison, WI, U.S.A., 22 November 1939

Work; John Sinclair and Ron Caplan, *Spring and Autumn Annals* by Diana DiPrima; Artist's Workshop, Detroit, MI, U.S.A., Summer, 1965

Weekly World News; article 'Judge insults gal victim at her tiral,' page 33; London, U.K., May 30, 1989

Yachting; (Vol. XV, No. 2); the New York, NY, U.S.A., February, 1914; ad for 1998 Corvette, page 1, July 1998

Yoga Journal; article, 'Laying it on the Line: Bo Lozoff and the Prison Ashram Project;' Berkley, CA, U.S.A., November 1883

Motion Pictures, TV and Radio

Absolute Beginnings; Directed by Julien Temple; Palace Productions, Buckinghamshire, UK, 1985

Adam Ant; Hannah Barbera TV series; Hollywood, CA, U.S.A., 1960s

A Damsel in Distress; from the novel and screenplay by P.G. Wodehouse, starring Fred Astaire, Joan Fontaine, George Burns and Gracie Allen, Ira Gershwin musical directed by George Stevens; R.K.O. Pictures, Hollywood, CA, U.S.A., 1937

A Fish Called Wanda; starring John Cleese and Jamie Lee Curtis; MGM, London, U.K. and Hollywood, CA, U.S.A., 1988

Against All Odds; starring Jeff Bridges and Rachael Ward; Columbia Pictures, Hollywood, CA, U.S.A., 1984

American Idol; quote from Stephen Tyler; FOX TV, Hollywood, CA, U.S.A., May 8, 2012

Apollo 13; Ed Harris quote; Hollywood, CA, U.S.A., 1995

A Summer Place; romantic drama starring Richard Eagan, Dorothy McGuire, Troy Donahue and Sandra Dee; Warner Brothers Pictures, Hollywood, CA, U.S.A., 1959

Atta Boy; silent movie starring Monte Banks and Virginia Bradford, Ernie Wood, Directed by Edward H. Griffith; Monte Banks Enterprises, distributed by Pathé Enterprises, Hollywood, CA, U.S.A., 1926

Atta Boy's Last Race; silent movie starring Dorothy Gish and Keith Armour; Dir. by George Siegmann; released by Hamilton Film Corp.; Los Angeles, CA, U.S.A., 1916

Bad Blood; starring Jack Thompson; New Zealand; U.K.; Southern Pictures, released Australia, 1982

Bad Blood; starring Staine and Michael Yebba; Hollywood, CA, U.S.A., 2011

Beverly Hills 90210, Fair Dinkum Productions, Spelling TV, Fox TV, CBS, Hollywood, CA, 1992-1999

Big Sky; Howard Hawks Western film; R.K.O. Radio Pictures, Hollywood, CA, USA, 1952

Blazing Saddles; starring Mel Brooks, Slim Pickens; Warner Brothers, Hollywood, CA, USA, 1974

Boys Will be Boys; comedy film; William Beaudine; London, UK, 1935

Brady Bunch, TV show Episode 73, season 4, Paramount Pictures, ABC TV, Hollywood, CA, U.S.A., September 22, 1972

Brave Heart; epic motion picture starring Mel Gibson; Marquis Film, Ladd Company, The Icon Productions, and Paramount Studios; filmed on location in Scotland, U.K. and Ireland; released Hollywood, CA, U.S.A., 1995

Bright Eyes; starring Shirley Temple, James Dunn, Fox Film, Hollywood, CA, U.S.A., December 28, 1934

Bucket List; starring Jack Nicholson and Morgan Freeman; Warner Brothers Pictures, Hollywood, CA, U.S.A., 2007

Casablanca; starring Humphrey Bogart, Ingrid Bergman; produced by Hal Wallis; Warner Brothers, Hollywood, CA, U.S.A., 1942

Chinatown; Robert Evans; Paramount Pictures, Hollywood, CA, USA, 1974

Daddy Long Legs; musical film, directed by Jean Negulesco, starring Fred Astaire, Leslie Caron, 20th Century Fox, Hollywood, CA, 1955

Diamonds are Forever; Ian Fleming, starring Sean Connery; United Artists, London, U.K., 1971

Different Strokes; NBC; Hollywood, CA, U.S.A., November 3, 1978 to May 4, 1985, ABC; Sept. 1985 to March 1986

Dr. Strangelove; Stanley Kubrick; Columbia Pictures, Hollywood, CA, USA, 1954

Down to Earth; by Homer Croy with screenplay by Edward Burke; Paramount Publix Corp, New York, NY, Hollywood, CA, U.S.A., 1932

Duck Soup; directed by Leo McCarrey, starring Groucho Marx; Paramount Pictures, Hollywood, CA, USA, 1933

Easy Come, Easy Go; film based on a play by Owen Davis; Directed by Frank Tuttle; Paramount Famous Lasky Corporation, Hollywood, CA, USA, 1928

Easy Come, Easy Go; Hal Wallis; Elvis Presley; Paramount Pictures, Hollywood, CA, USA, 1967

Even Stevens; Disney Channel TV show; Brookwell McNamara Entertainment, Hollywood, CA, U.S.A., June 17, 2000 to June 13, 2003

Field of Dreams; starring Kevin Costner, Amy Madigan, Ray Liotta, Timothy Busfield, James Earl Jones; directed by Phil Alden Robinson, Lou Puopolo; produced by Lawrence Gordon, Charles Gordon, Lloyd Levin, Brian Frankish; Universal Pictures, Hollywood, CA, U.S.A., 1989

Forrest Gump; starring Tom Hanks, Robin Wright, Sally Field, Gary Sinese; directed by Robert Zemeckis; Paramount Pictures, Hollywood, CA, U.S.A., 1994

Gentlemen Prefer Blondes; starring Marilyn Monroe; Hollywood, CA, 1953

728

Go for Broke! Starring Van Johnson, directed by Robert Pirosh; MGM, Hollywood, CA, U.S.A., 1951

Good Will Hunting; written by Ben Affleck, Matt Damon; directed by Gus Van Sant; produced by Lawrence Bender; Miramax Films, Hollywood, CA, USA, 1997

Grumpy Old Men; starring Jack Lommon, Burgess Merideth, Walter Matthau, Ann-Margaret, Daryl Hannah; Warner Brothers, Hollywood, CA, U.S.A., 1993

Gypsy; musical film, starring Rosalind Russell, Natalie Wood, Karl Malden; Warner Brothers, Hollywood, CA, U.S.A., 1962

He Said, She Said; TV game show hosted by Joe Garagiola; NBC, Hollywood, CA, U.S.A., September 15, 1969—August 21, 1970

Horse Feathers; Groucho Marx, Harpo Marx, Chico Marx, Zeppo Marx, Thelma Todd; Paramount Pictures, Hollywood, CA, U.S.A., 1932

Howdy Doody; TV show, Bob Smith; NBC, Hollywood, CA, U.S.A., 1947-1960

Hunter; TV Police drama, starring Fred Dryer and Stefanie Kramer; created by Frank Lupo; Producers, Stephen J. Cannell, Roy Huggins; Columbia Pictures, Warner Brothers, Hollywood, CA, U.S.A., 1984-1991

Inherit the Wind; starring Spencer Tracy, Frederick March and Gene Kelley; Universal Studios, Hollywood, CA, USA, 1960

Jaws; directed by Steven Spielberg, starring Roy Scheider and Richard Dreyfuss, Universal Pictures, Hollywood, CA, U.S.A., 1975

Keeping up with the Joneses; short b/w silent film on Women's style; Gaumont, Hollywood, CA, USA, 1928

Keeping up with the Kardashians; Reality TV series; Kim Kardashian, Eliot Goldberg, Jeff Jenkins; E! Calabasas, CA, USA, 2007-

Leap of Faith; Steve Martin, Debra Winger, Paramount Pictures; Hollywood, CA, U.S.A., 1992

Let's Pitch Woo; starring Charles Boyer and Danielle Darrieux; Paris, France, 1938

Lifeboat; from the novel by John Steinbeck; produced by Alfred Hichcock; directed by Kenneth Macgowan; distributed by 20th Century Fox, Hollywood, CA, U.S.A., 1944

Love Me, Love My Mouse; Tom and Jerry Cartoon film; MGM, Hollywood, CA, U.S.A., 1966

Mad About You, TV Sit Com, Paul Reiser, NBC, Hollywood, CA, U.S.A., 1992-1999

Martin; sitcom, Martin Lawrence; HBO Productions, Hollywood, CA, U.S.A., 1992

Mary Tyler Moore Show; Season 4, Episode 13, *I Gave at the Office;* MTM Productions, Hollywood, CA, U.S.A., 8 December1973

Mauvia's Song aka *Bad Blood;* starring Juliette Bionche; AAA Classics, France, 1986

Meet the People; Arthur Freed, E.Y. Harburg; M.G.M., Hollywood, CA, U.S.A., 1944

Melrose Place, Darren Star Productions Spelling TV, Fox TV, Hollywood, CA, 1992-1999

Music Man; Rogers and Hammerstein; Hollywood, CA, U.S.A., 1962

One in a Million; Maylasian TV series running from 2006 to 2009

Rachel, Rachel; starring Joanne Woodward and James Olson; Warner Brothers, Hollywood, CA, U.S.A., 1968

Rio Bravo; Howard Hawks Western; Warner Brothers, Hollywood, CA, USA, 1959

Romancing the Stone; starring Michael Douglas, Kathleen Turner; 20th Century Fox, Hollywood, CA, U.S.A., 1984

Roots; Alex Haley; starring Olivia Cole, Ben Vereen, LaVar Burton, John Amos, Lesilie Uggams, many others; TV Miniseries; A.B.C., Hollywood, CA, U.S.A., 1977

Saturday Night Live; NBC, Hollywood, CA, U.S.A., 1975 - 1976, 1980s episodes

Second Chance / Boys Will be Boys; American TV sitcom; David W. Duclon and Gary Menteer; Fox, Hollywood, CA, U.S.A., 1987-1988

Seseme Street; PBS, New York, NY, U.S.A., episode, unknown date

Showgirl in Hollywood; directed by Mervyn McElroy; produced by Robert North; Staring Alice White; First National Pictures, WB, Hollywood, CA, U.S.A., 1930

Sleeping With the Enemy; directed by Joseph Ruben; starring Julia Roberts, Patrick Bergin; 20th century Fox, Hollywood, CA, U.S.A., 1991

Stepford Wives; directed by Bryan Forbes; starring Katherine Ross and Paula Printess; Palomar Pictures, Hollywood, CA, U.S.A., 1975

Sweet Dreams; starring Jessica Lange and Ed Harris; directed by Karel Reisz; HBO, Hollywood, CA, U.S.A., 1985

Take It or Leave It; CBS radio quiz show which ran from April 21, 1940, to July 27, 1947, and from 1947-1950 on NBC, which changed its title to *The $64 Question* on September 10, 1950 and ran till 1947; Hollywood, CA, U.S.A.

Ten Cents a Dance; film starring Barbara Stanwyck; MGM, Hollywood, CA, U.S.A., 1931

730

TGIF; Friday night 2 hour comedy show; ABCTV, Hollywood, CA, U.S.A., 1988-2005

Thank God it's Friday; disco movie; directed by Robert Klane; starring Donna Summer; Casablanca Filmworks, Motown Productions, Hollywood, CA, U.S.A.; Released Netherlands, 1978

The Cat's Pajamas; starring Betty Bronson, Sally Winton, Ricardo Cartez and Arlette Marchal; Hollywood, CA, U.S.A., 1926

The Daily Show, Jon Stewart, Comedy Central, Hollywood, CA, U.S.A., 1996 to date

The Dean Martin Comedy Hour; Dean Martin, Golddiggers; NBC, Hollywood, CA, U.S.A., 1968

The Goodies; British comedy TV series; The Brooke Taylor Graeme Garden, Bill Oddie; London, U.K., 1970s and early '80s, episode 1975

The Godfather Part II; starring Al Picino, Robert Duvall, Diane Keaton; directed by Francis Ford Coppola; Paramount Pictures, Hollywood, CA, U.S.A., 1974

The Honeymooners; (1951-'55) starring Jackie Gleason and Audrey Meadows, Art Carney, Joyce Randolph; Jackie Gleason Enterprises, C.B.S. Films, Hollywood, CA, U.S.A., 'to the moon' and *A Woman's Work is Never Done* episode, 1955

The Jewel of the Nile; starring Michael Douglas, Kathleen Turner; 20th Century Fox, Hollywood, CA, U.S.A., 1985

The Lone Ranger; Radio and TV Show; Hollywood, CA, U.S.A., 1933- 1950s

The Man Who Knew Too Much; starring Leslie Banks, Edna Best, Peter Lorre; directed by Alfred Hitchcock; Gaumont British Dist., Ltd., London, U.K., 1934

The New Adventures of Sherlock Holmes; radio series broadcast on Blue Network/ Mutual Broadcasting System, U.S.A., 1939 – 1947

The Real McCoys; ABC TV comedy series starring Walter Brennan, Richard Crenna and Kathleen Nolan; produced by Danny Thomas in Desilu Studios, Hollywood, CA, U.S.A.,1957 - 1962

The Simpsons; TV episodes; Hollywood, CA, U.S.A., 1991, 1999

The $64,000 Question; TV show; 1955 - 1958 / spin-off show, *The $64,000 Challenge;* 1956 - 1958, Hollywood, CA, U.S.A.

The Sky's the Limit; musical motion picture starring Fred Aistare; RKO Pictures, Hollywood, CA, U.S.A., 1943

The Today Show; Al Roker, meteorologist; NBC TV, New York, NY, U.S.A.

The Whole Nine Yards; starring Bruce Willis and Matthew Perry; directed by Jonathan Lynn; Warner Brothers, Hollywood, CA, U.S.A., 2000

The Wild Geese; starring Richard Burton, Roger Moore, Richard Harris, and Hardy Kruger; directed by Andrew V. McLaglen; Richmond Productions, London, U.K., 1978

The Wizard of Oz; Screenplay, Noel Langdon; produced by Mervyn LeRoy; MGM, Hollywood, CA, U.S.A., 1939

Top Gun; starring Tom Cruise, Kelly McGillis, directed by Tony Scott; Paramount Pictures, Hollywood, CA, U.S.A., 1986

Twelve Angry Men; directed by Sidney Lurnet; produced by Henry Fonda, Reginald Rose; starring Henry Fonda, Lee J. Cobb, E. G. Marshall; United Artists, Hollywood, CA, U.S.A., 1957

21; starring Jum Sturgess, Kate Bosworth, Kevin Spacey, Lawrence Fishbone; directed by Robert Luketic; Sony Pictures, Hollywood, CA, U.S.A., 2008

Under-Cover Man; starring George Raft and Nancy Carroll; directed by James Flood; Paramount Pictures, Hollywood, CA, U.S.A., 1932

You Can't Stop on a Dime; Sid Davis Productions, Hollywood, CA, U.S.A., 1954

You Don't Know Jack; TV game show; Paul Rubens; directed by Keith Truesdale; Casey-Werner Mandabach; A.B.C. TV, New York, NY, U.S.A., 2001

Miscellaneous

Ad Campaign, Mutual of Omaha Insurance Company 'Hang Ten Campaign,' Omaha, NE, U.S.A., 1980s

Ad Campaign, Hang Ten, Los Angeles, CA, U.S.A., 1962

An act for preventing tumults and riotous assemblies, and for the more speedy and effectual punishing the rioters; England, July, 1715

Ancient Persian legend; dating to circa 1200 B.C.

A pistle to the christen reader; essay; John Frith; London, England, 1529

Band, One in a Million; Scottish Psychedelic rock; Glasgow, Scotland, 1967

Bank veto; U.S. President, Andrew Jackson; Washington, DC, U.S.A., 1832

British one pound banknote; (notation from)

Campaign Slogan; R & R Partners, Las Vegas, NE. U.S.A., 2004

Cartoon; William Morgan "Billy" De Beck, 1923

Comic rugby postcard series; 'The Adventures of Nosey Parker;' London, England, 1907

Congressional Record; prayer, Dr. Ogilvie, Congressional Record, page 22493; Washington, DC, U.S.A., September 28, 1998

Congressman's Report; Democratic Arizona Congressman Morris King 'Mo' Udall; July 6, Washington, DC, U.S.A., 1962

Fable of the Bald Man and the Fly; Phaedrus; Rome, 15 B.C.—50 A.D.

Fall from Grace; painting, Michelangelo; Rome, 1508-1512

Festo Sancti Michaelis; Sermon 1, sect. 3; translation from Richard Chevenix Trench, Archbishop of Dublin page 148; *On the Lessons in Proverbs;* Dublin, Ireland,[1853] 1856

FIFA football World Cup; Monterrey, Mexico, 1986

Garfield Comic Strip, John Davis; Universal Press Syndicate, Kansas, City, MO, USA; 27 November 1988

Handwritten diary of William Richardson; 1815

Illusion; (pulling a rabbit out of a hat) popularized by French magician, Herman the Great, 19th century

It's a small world; Disneyland ride built for the New York World's Fair, 1964; opened in California, 1966

Lateral Thinking; Edward De Bono; U.K., 1967

Letter from social philosopher Jeremy Bentham to George Wilson; London, U.K., 1781

Letters; Joseph Mead; London, England, 1625

Letter; Thomas Lechford; New England, 1640,

Letter to Jean-Baptiste Leroy; Benjamin Franklin; PA, U.S.A., written in 1789

Letter to Major-General Robert Howe; George Washington; VA, U.S.A., 17 August 1779

Letter to my Friend A.B.; Ben Franklin; PA, U.S.A., 1748

Letter to the Editor of the *Portland Currier;* (Maine) written by American humorist Seba Smith (1792–1868) as coming from fictional Major, Jack Downing; U.S.A., September 14, 1833

Letter written by first lady Abigail Adams; Massachusetts, U.S.A., dated 13 November, 1800

Little Orphan Annie comic strip; No rest for the Wicked, Harold Gray; USA, 1933

Man on the Thresh-hold; short story by Robert Wegner printed in an issue of a quarterly literary journal, *Michigan's Voices;* U.S.A., 1962

National Basketball Association (NBA) Playoffs; Son Cook; U.S.A., April, 1978

Nation's Business; Newsletter of the U.S. Chamber of Commerce; Washington, DC, U.S.A., May, 1977

Notes on the poems of Dryden; Martin Clifford; England, circa 1677

Occasional Discourse on the Negro Question; Thomas Carlyle, essay; Published in *Frazier's Magazine for Town and Country*); London, England, U.K., 1849

Of Cunning; Francis Bacon essay; London, England, 1612

On Lord Clive; Lord Thomas Babington Macaulay essay; England,   U.K., 1840

Operation Desert Storm; U.S. military maneuver combating Iraq's invasion and occupation of Kuwait; January and February 1991

Painting: Onmia vicit amor; Italian artist Agostino Carracci, Italy, 1599

Peanuts; cartoon strip by Charles Schultz

Proceedings of the American Medico-Psychological Association; American Pyscological Association, Philadelphia, PA, May 15-18 1894

Program; Mind Power; John Kehoe; 1978

Prologue to the Clerk's Tale; from *Canterbury Tales;* Chaucer, London, England, 1386

Quote; Abraham Lincoln; Wisconsin, U.S.A., 1859

Quote; Cicero; (106-43 B.C.)

Quote; David Segal of *The Washington Post;* 2008

Quote; Dean Martin; 1968

Quote; Doug Armstrong (NHL)

Quote; Edward Young

Quote; Eric Beheim

Quote; Forest E. Witcraft

Quote; George Buchanan; Scotland, (1506-1582)

Qoute; Henry David Thoreau

Quote; Henry Ford

Quote; J.P. Morgan

Quote; John Adams

Quote; John Emerich Edward Dalberg-Acton, 1st Baron Acton

Quote; Joseph Kelly, radio station manager, WROR; Boston, MA, U.S.A., 1988

Quote; Leon Trotsky

Quote; Les Brown, speaker and author

Quote; Malcolm Forbes

Quote; Napoleon Bonepart, France

Quote; Napolean Hill

Quote; Oliver Cromwell; England, 1599-1658

Quote; Richard Buckminster Fuller

Quote; Ronald Reagan

Quote; Saint Ambrose, Bishop of Milan; 387 A.D.

Quote; Saint Bernard of Clairvaux; Clairvaux, France (1091-1153)

Quote; Samuel Johnson

Quote; Sydney Smith; speech, *Moral Philosophy;* 1804

Quote; Sir Baron Robert Walpole; London, U.K., 1800s

Quote; Sir Winston Churchill; London, U.K.

Quote; Sonny Liston, 1958

Quote; Terry Bradshaw

Quote; Theodore Roosevelt; 1901

Quote; Thomas E. Dewey, Republican presidential candidate, U.S.A., 1948

Quote; Thomas Jefferson; U.S.A., early 1800s

Quote; Thomas Hutchinson; 1765

Quote; William Learned Marcy; New York Senator; 1832

Quote; William Pitt the Elder, Earl of Chatham

Quote; Will Rogers, humorist; U.S.A.

Rear Platform Remarks in Montana; President Harry S. Truman; September 30, 1952, later published in *Public Papers of the Presidents of the United States, Harry S. Truman* page 637, Washington, DC, U.S.A., 1953

Resignation; Peter, Lord Carrington; London, U.K., 5 April 1982

Richard H. Adams, Jr. papers; (MS#0358) U.S. Civil War Records, Alabama, U.S.A., 1862

Saying; Jack Benny, comedian; U.S.A.

Scientific conclusion; Carl Louis Ferdinand von Lindemann, 1882

Search Quotes; J. Cole lyrics, unidentified song; U.S.A.

Sermons; Bishop Robert Sanderson; London, England, 1621

Sermon; Ephriam Udall; London, England, 1548

Speech; British statesman, Richard Cobden; England, U.K., 1841

Speech; Abraham Lincoln; U.S.A., June 9th, 1864

Speech; Richard M. Nixon, U.S. ex-President, 1975

Speech; William Henry Harrison, U.S.A., October 1, 1840

Stan Freberg Presents the United States of America: The Early Years; Stan Freberg's comedy album; Capitol W/SW-1573, New York, NY, U.S.A., 1961

Study; Max Planck Institute; Germany, 2009

Sumner County, Tennessee court records; U.S.A., 1790

Telephone call from Yovone Lehman of McMinnville, TN, 8-26-2015

Television Jingle; Firestone Tire and Rubber Co., U.S.A., 1960s and '70s

The Code of Hammurabi; Middle East, 1780 B.C.

The Market for Lemons: Quality Uncertainty and the Market Mechanism; paper, George Akerloff; 1970

The Mothers of Invention; Frank Zappa's American 1960s to 70s classical jazz-rock band; CA, U.S.A.

The Newgate Calendar; Andrew Knapp and W. Baldwin; London, U.K., 1824–1826

The Pied Piper of Hamelin (Legend); (Germany), sixteenth century, supposedly happening in 1284

The Proceedings of the National Conventionof the Industrial Union of Marine and Shipbuilders of America; Baltimore, MD, U.S.A., 1943

The Ruined Man Who Became Rich Again Through a Dream, story from medieval Arabic literature, 14th century A.D.

The Selected Letters of Theodore Roosevelt; 1890s first published 1951, edited by H.W. Brands; Rowman & Littlefield Publishers, Lanham, MD, USA, 2007

The Ten Commandments; Palestine, circa 1450 B.C.

The Three Little Pigs, childreen's story; unknown author and date

The Tragedies of the last Age consider'd and examin'd by the Practice of the Ancients, and by the Common Sense of all Ages; in a Letter to Fleetwood Shepheard, Esq. by Thomas Rymer, Grays-Inn, Esquire; England, 1678

The Wizard of Id; cartoon strip, Brant Parker, Johnny Hart, syndicated; U.S.A., 1967

Toshogo shrine of the Shinto religion in Nikko, Japan; seventeenth-century carving of three wise monkeys

Tract by Thomas Beccon; England, 1542

Trial of Impeachment of Judge Levi Hubble; Senate of the state of Wisconsin; June, 1853

Truffles, the Most Expensive Food in the World; CBS News Special Report; January 8, 2012

U.S. Command on Public Information; bulletin issued for Major General M.W. Ireland; March, 1919

U.S. Military humorous story; World War II

U.S. Military posters; mess halls; World War II

Volkswagen, Think Small Ad Campaign; Julian Koenig, 1950s *Volkswagen ad;* 1974 ; *Volkswagen Jetta TV ad* using Wynn Stewart's *Another Day, Another Dollar;* Deutsch L.A. Ad Agency, Los Angeles, CA, USA, 2010

Where there's Smoke there's Fire; mural color illustration artist, Russell Patterson (1893-1977); New York, NY, U.S.A., 1920s

Which, Right or Left; political article; USA, 1855

You Don't Know Jack; PlayStation computer game series; Jellyvision and Berkley Systems, 1995-2011

ACKNOWLEDGEMENTS

Special thanks to the following persons who assisted in various ways in the development and/or completion of this book:

S. John St. Clair, son; editor, contibutor

Rhonda Prater St. Clair, dedicated spouse, business associate; proofer

D. Kent Hesselbein, friend, business associate, graphic designer; cover design

Niven J. Sinclair, Esq., friend, British entrepreneur; major contributor

Michele Doucette, friend, Canadian educator, associate, editor, author; review

Eric J. Abalos, grandson; back cover photo, original version

Scott A. St. Clair, son; contributor

Nate Wolf, friend, insurance executive; contributor

Steve St. Clair, friend, associate, distant cousin, back cover photo

Paul Bernhardt, friend, retired engineer; contributor

Carol Ghattas, librarian; contributor

Melanie Brock, friend, aerobics instructor; contributor

Elizabeth Lane, friend, Keeper of the Westford Knight; contributer

Ron Cunningham, friend, veteran law enforcement Captain; contributor

Kelly Marlow, friend, radio announcer; contributor

Tammy Cornett Ballew, friend; contributor

Yvonne Lehman, contributor

Made in the USA
Las Vegas, NV
04 April 2021

20768386R20427